Carol Ozment Green, Retired Educator.

One would never know the McCord family was not native to our wonderful little town of Lindale. Having moved from Alabama in 1975, they immediately became active in the community. Randall bought his father's local pulpwood company while wife Joyce Anne began teaching in Pepperell schools where sons Scott and Jamie were students. Randall has spent countless hours researching the history of Lindale, interviewing lifelong locals, and dedicating himself to an enormous task of recording the history of a town that means so much to so many! It was done with great love and loyalty. Accordingly, it gives me great pleasure to endorse this book, Lindale, Lint and Leather. Happy reading and may this work bring back many wonderful memories to those who were fortunate to be a part of this community and enlighten others to the significance of a special cotton mill town.

Carol Elaine Green is a 1974 honor graduate of Pepperell High School who also holds a 1978 BS in Education from Shorter College Summa Cum Laude (with highest distinction) and a 1982 master's degree in Primary/Middle School from Berry College. Professionally, she first taught ten years at her alma mater and then combined twenty plus years as part/full time mentoring Main Primary students. Along the way she became the wife of Byron Green PHS class of 1968; they have a thirty-four-year-old son Andrew and two grandchildren Ford and Wilder. Carol is the daughter of Joe Tom and Frances Loveless Ozment both of whom were born in the second decade of twentieth century in state line farming community of Farill, Alabama. During depression year of 1933 the two eloped and left country life for a steady paycheck at Pepperell Cotton Mill and Lindale Village A Street where they birthed three boys and a daughter with Carol being youngest. The attractive Lindale lady retired from public school in 2012 after more than thirty-four years. However, the past ten years have been productive with homeschooling local youths. Cogreen1005@yahoo.com.

Anne Williamson Shumaker, Educator, Columnist and College Trustee.

Randall McCord's book needed to be written—and it needs to be read by every youth and adult! The very captivating tome salutes the history and people of Lindale Mill and Village. McCord's book definitely encourages appreciation of the workers' sacrifices, work ethic and contributions of time and talent which promoted the success of the mill and its valuable role in the economy of the area—before, during and after the great depression.

Anne Shumaker is a native of Jasper, Alabama and a resident of Centre since post college days; retired educator; newspaper columnist; 30-year trustee Judson College est. 1838 in Marion, Al.; Cherokee County Historical Museum board officer; AB Judson College; MS Jacksonville State University and additional studies in aerospace science; a state alternate in the Teacher in Space program. She is married to Centre attorney Albert Shumaker.

LINDALE, LINT, AND LEATHER

1825–2001
Lindale, Georgia—The Rise and Fall of a Southern Cotton Mill

Randall McCord

Copyright © 2023 Randall McCord
All rights reserved
First Edition

PAGE PUBLISHING
Conneaut Lake, PA

First originally published by Page Publishing 2023

ISBN 979-8-88960-301-6 (hc)
ISBN 979-8-88960-282-8 (digital)

Printed in the United States of America

CONTENTS

Foreword vii
Prologue ix
Acknowledgments xiii
Introduction xix

Larkin Barnett (1802–1862) 1
Cotton, Looms, Samuel Slater, and Eli Whitney 9
Henry Woodfin Grady (1850–1889) and the New South 13
John Paul Cooper (1858–1927) and a Georgia Giant in the Revival of Cotton in the
Early 1900s 16
Henry Parish Meikleham (1872–1937) 25
The Village 33
Edward Russell "Slick" Moulton in Lindale 41
The Great Depression (1930–1939) and Robert Donald Harvey Sr. (1899–1963) 47
Northwest Georgia Textile League 51
Lindale Goes to War 56
Wartime Baseball 86
Northwest Georgia Textile League Postwar 88
Ernest Olin "Shorty" Hall (September 1, 1911–February 5, 1993) 93
Willard Lee Nixon (1928–2000)—The Yankee Killer 96
Jack Bowdoin Gaston (1911–1994) 105
Nathaniel McClinic (1924–2004) 113
Lindale Schools (1896–1926) and Pepperell Schools (1926–Present) 118
Sara Hightower (1911–1991)—Library Pioneer in the State of Georgia 120
Edward Russell "Slick" Moulton (1900–1979)—Lindale's Indiana Jones 122
John William "J. W." Sutton Jr. (1919–1975) 127
Otis Forrest Gilbreath (1924–1993) 131
Interscholastic Competition—Football 137
"Coach Hanging Up His Whistle" by Jim O'Hara (December 12, 2006, *Rome News-Tribune*) 272
Interscholastic Competition—Basketball 275
Interscholastic Competition—Baseball 388
Richard William Wolfe (1925–2008) 470
The Demise of Lindale Mill 476
The Last Generation 482

Notes 489

FOREWORD

Writing the foreword to a book about a place that, in some respect, no longer exists is a daunting task. Writing it from a remove of almost 50 years and 1,400 miles makes it more challenging, but my memories of the time and place are vivid. While I wish words could describe the Lindale of my childhood and youth, they cannot, nor can an artist's brush paint it. It isn't my task to describe those memories. Randall McCord uses his decades of living and working in the area to do that. Within these pages is a sweeping look at all that Lindale was: the history, the culture, the people, the community, the businesses, and—of course—Textile League baseball and Pepperell Dragons sports. Mr. McCord interviewed me in the early stages of his project and impressed me with his detailed and nuanced knowledge of Lindale. My family was never Lindale blue blood, so I was surprised and honored when he invited me to write this foreword. Our story is like that of most Lindaleans; except for Dad's father, all my family was generally hourly workers.

Census records show that most of Dad's side of the family lived west of Atlanta in the late 1800s. The Mill opened in 1896, and census records show that the young man who would become my grandfather lived with his family on D Street in early Lindale 1910. They had followed the call of good, steady work. Even though most of them were adolescents, my grandfather (an only son) and most of his sisters were already working in the Mill as operatives as they were called in those days—later to be known as mill workers, mill hands, or the pejorative lintheads. This was the era before child labor laws and occupational safety and, thus, the era of photos of barefoot children in tattered clothing working in the mills. Most of my mother's family followed the same call, though they mostly came from counties adjoining eastern Floyd. I went to work in the Mill on my sixteenth birthday and worked there on summer and holiday school breaks, weekends, right up through the last weekend before finishing college and entering the Navy in 1978. That experience is essential to who I am. My Lindale blood isn't blue, but cut me and I bleed indigo. I wear denim more often than not and will for the rest of my life.

The Mill paid on Thursday, so Fridays were usually shopping and market days for Mill families. The Lindale core at that time had a grocery store that operated under various names over the years, Knight's Department Store (previously Brittain Brothers), several barbershops, and almost all goods, services, and community institutions anyone would ever need. Friday afternoons often meant a trip to downtown Lindale for an occasional visit with Company nurse Ms. Douglas, RN, at the clinic. Our working Dad would sometimes give us a well-timed peek and wave from a mill door as Mom and I walked to my inoculation time or perhaps a later treat from the soda fountain in the adjacent drugstore, and probably a haircut from Peanut Covington.

I still hear the low rumbling hum the Mill produced, so omnipresent that the village seemed eerily quiet when the Mill shut down for vacation every summer. The toasty fragrance of cloth moving through the Finishing Department wafts through my mind; the green lights (no red, please!) on the safety status board outside number three gate still flows. In my mind's eye, the forklifts still fascinate me as they scoot around the shipping department's loading docks. To say that those of us of a certain age (the last generation) have seen Lindale change a great deal is an understatement. We now usually look back through rose-colored, soft-focus lenses. Most of my memories of Lindale are of warm sunny days, though I know it cannot be so, and in honesty, I do recall cold rainy days. But the truth is, Lindale was a great small town in an era when small towns were the heart and soul of our Nation. This is the fact, not mere nostalgia.

With *Lindale, Lint, and Leather*, Randall McCord offers us a glimpse—the best possible glimpse—of Lindale as she was. And a wonderfully fond glimpse it is.

Keith Baker
Commander, United States Navy (Retired)
Lindale Mill (June 13, 1972–June 24, 1978)
Pepperell High School Class of 1974
Buena Vista, Colorado. Kbaker6474@me.com
January 2023

PROLOGUE

I have a story to tell... My story concerns the transformation of an almost remote farmland area into a thriving textile town, its growth and development. Some of the individuals, great and small and their investments are into my tale.
—The opening paragraph of *A History of Lindale* (1997), Mrs. Polly Johnston Gammon

Virginia Anne "Polly" Johnston Gammon

When the mill finally shut its doors on September 24, 2001, the end of an era ended also. But thanks to Virginia Anne "Polly" Gammon, we are able to look back at the history of her hometown. Older Lindaleans recognize daily articles in the *Rome News-Tribune* entitled "Lindale and Vicinity" written by her husband, Lang Gammon, and in later years coauthored by Polly. As a lifelong citizen of the Village, she operated the main switchboard at West Point Pepperell/Greenwood for many years before retiring in 1989; afterward, she became the driving force in community projects including tedious compilation of documents that led to the Old Brick Mill being placed on National Register of Historic Places. This quest encompassed four years and was submitted in January 1991 with the approval listing in September 9, 1993. However, it was her *A History of Lindale: The Research of Polly Gammon* that dwarfs other accomplishments and established her as Lindale's First Lady of Letters. The 152-page gift to the people of Park Street was published posthumously in 1997 and tells the story in words reinforced by priceless black-and-white prints that give the readers an insight into a Southern textile community. There are maps, letters, and deeds in addition to collected stories, handwritten notes with accompanied newspaper articles. For several months before she passed away in May of 1996, Polly would bring reams of research to Mr. James Gibbon's office where he would edit and type up the findings prior to approval on next visit. The finished work was published by the Art Department of Rome with first printing on October 1997.

Editor's note: The original manuscript, photographs, and all related notes used in the book have been donated by the Gammon Estate to the Special Collections Department of Sara Hightower Library. These materials are available for on-site viewing and research during regular hours. Although photocopies are allowed with permission, no material is allowed to leave the collection.

Regarding Mr. Gibbons, the following letter was written in 1997 by Mrs. Mildred Lee Sutton to him in appreciation of his tremendous help finalizing Polly Gammon's work. Although the exact date of the missive is uncertain, it is cited in an email from Johnny Sutton sent to Randall McCord on May 16, 2020. The opening paragraph is reproduced here:

> Mr. Gibbons,
> As a Lindalean and friend of Polly, I want to thank you for your excellent work in helping her to fulfill a dream of writing the *History of Lindale*; I'm sure Polly would be pleased and happy that her goal was achieved. My husband, J. W. Sutton, and I became friends with Polly and Lang Gammon when they asked Sutt to write the "Lindale News" during their summer vacations—then later, when they married, the couple became our neighbors on Central Avenue.

Polly first came upon her lifework quite innocently; the local post office passed along a letter from a "faraway university" student who was researching how various towns got their name. Although the thesis student picked Lindale randomly, Ms. Gammon decided to help; it was while she hunted for an answer that she realized "the rich history passing through her fingertips." Polly said later, "I became totally enrapt in the project." As research engulfed her, there came about an understanding that history must be shared for all to gain insight into the present and future. She found pleasure in thinking of "the Cherokee Indians hunting, fishing, raising their maize, and having campfires on the same ground I have walked over so many times." Polly envisioned the two communities we know as Silver Creek and Lindale as one cohabited by the Cherokees and white settlers. Roman Calder Willingham spoke of this in his novel *Eternal Fire*: "In this peaceful land, pretty birds sing and the woodbine twines. Violets and forget-me-nots bloom in the meadow. The wind is soft as a baby's smile, and as warm and gentle as mother love."

Early on, the inquisitive lady became fascinated with pioneer Larkin Barnett who arrived in the middle 1820s and established a plantation around the creek. Her interest then moved to Massachusetts Mill and their choosing our land for a new textile investment with capable

Captain H. P. Meikleham as the first permanent superintendent. But I have strayed from telling the reader about Polly Gammon.[1]

Virginia Anne "Polly" Johnston was born to Samuel and Laura Johnson, who married a Johnston, in Lindale on October 22, 1924; the birth address was 1 Silver Street but always referred to in the family as down on the corner. The couple married circa 1890 and birthed four girls and three boys with Bonnie (Bon) being the first in 1907 and Polly the youngest in 1924. According to one source, Polly is an English variant of Molly or Mary. Another reference expanded the name to mean "a caring, loving, and beautiful girl, always impresses a man no matter what, can trust mostly everyone; she has funny and kind friends, but the best features are her eyes and personality." When the new baby girl was born in 1924, oldest sister, Bonnie, was seventeen years old; Bon came to see her newborn sibling and asked for the name. When told it had not been decided, she said, "Whatever you do, don't name her Polly. I can't stand that." Well, Virginia Anne is her legal given name, but Polly is on the tombstone.

Amazingly, father Samuel Johnston was born during the Civil War in January 1862 and lived until late 1941. Mother Laura Johnson began life on May 11, 1884 and lived until spring of 1927, dying of influenza when their youngest (Polly) was just three years old, leaving a sixty-five-year-old husband with seven young'uns. Both parents are interred in Wax Cemetery in the Silver Creek community. Virginia Anne spent elementary and middle grades at Pepperell.[2] After finishing junior high, a move to Rome's Cooper Hall ensued. The girls' high school senior yearbook (BAJEMP) stated she entered in 1937, was class treasurer in 1939, senior class vice president in 1940, assistant editor of the 1941 annual, and salutatorian of her senior class. Polly was also on the swim team, played volleyball, and was a member of Wig 'n Pen. The Sara Hightower special collections department has possession of most of the surviving BAJEMPs. The name was derived from the first graduating class members' initials which were Betty, Ann, Johnnie, Evelyn, Myra, and Polly (Featherston). They present an enduring look at Polly's high school years as well as prewar life in Rome.

The pretty petite senior graduated in May 1941 as class salutatorian and immediately enrolled in West Georgia College; at the end of first year in Carrollton, she discontinued her studies and returned to Lindale probably because of the death of father, Samuel, the previous fall and prospects for good employment at the Mill that was now on a wartime footing.[3] For the rest of the war decade, work at the Mill took up much of her time. However, on June 16, 1950, and after a long courtship, she married Langdon Bowie Gammon, fourteen years her senior. Lang began working at Lindale in 1928 and eventually became editor of the "Lindale News," a daily feature of the *Rome News-Tribune* in 1935 that lasted until Sunday, January 14, 1968. Lang died seventeen months after discontinuance at age fifty-eight. Polly lived another twenty-seven years after her husband's demise; she passed away in May 1996 at age seventy-one (they are interred together at Myrtle Hill Cemetery in the OR section, lot 337, grave 1).

The years following Lang's death were productive. While working as the Mill switchboard receptionist, she enjoyed the people and history of her hometown. True to her name, she was vivacious, funny, and caring. Polly had a unique one-word way of approving a letter, email, or an ample helping of friend Hattie McClung's fried chicken: "supercalifragilisticexpialidocious!" On a planned vacation flight to New York, her host expressed concern of how to recognize a traveler from Atlanta in the maze of a big-city airport. The friend soon received a package in the mail with a note saying, "Wear these Mickey Mouse ears in the terminal as we deplane; I will have a matching cap."[4] Now, without Lang, she spent much of her personal time at Silver Creek Presbyterian or visiting, caregiving, and entertaining friends of her village; being childless, she doted on youngsters around the community, especially during holidays. A last will and testament in 1996 reflected this when Polly gave chosen cousins all belongings inside designated rooms of her home; to make this time special, each chamber was lit with an individual candle. After she retired from the Mill in 1989, most of her professional energy was spent on *A History of Lindale*, which was completed and published posthumously in 1997. Without this invaluable work, I would not have attempted to write *Lindale, Lint, and Leather*.

ACKNOWLEDGMENTS

Robert "Bob" Baker was the driving force behind this history of Lindale. Had he not noticed a similar work in Sara Hightower Library while working security, it probably would not have happened. Bob was able to lead me along the factual trail of his hometown, providing pages of written documents, pictures, videos, and first-person witnesses to many events. He provided scores of names and phone numbers that built the framework to this extensive manuscript. The octogenarian knows everyone or at least how to get in touch with everybody in Lindale. We used Polly Gammon's 1997 *A History of Lindale* as a guide for these following 455 pages. With Polly no doubt watching over us, the writing consumed five years. In defense of the extended time from start to publish, the reader must understand writing is a hobby, not a full-time vocation of the author. The "Leather" part of the book alone contains approximately 2,750 high school game write-ups beginning in 1951 and ending in 2001. Additional events such as Class D League baseball predate the enormously popular Textile League of 1930–1950. My critic Joyce Anne McCord is concerned this reporting overwhelms the other sections; however, each contest identifies individual or family names which are what the story is about. Contained in *Lindale, Lint, and Leather* are dozens of biographies that are supported by scores of interviews; however, due to the passage of time, many are second-person variety. "The Village" ("Lindale") section is marked as a section of its own but is pervasive throughout. It contains some of the most poignant stories of all as poor hardscrabble farmers made their way to a steady paycheck at the Mill. Of the three, "Lint" became the most difficult to explain because of its technical nature. Fortunately, textile engineer and former mill manager Rip Johnston retired to the area; he has helped reduce the workings inside the redbrick walls to my level.

About Mr. Baker

Robert William Baker was born on November 22, 1932, to William Clarence and Vera Roberta West Baker at 207 Grove Street in Old Town Lindale, Georgia. In that year, the family consisted of two sisters, Ellen Juanita (1927) and Julia Carolyn (1929), who were birthed not far away on Hillside Street. Both locations were West Point Pepperell Company houses reserved for people employed by the mill. Prior to the beginning construction of Massachusetts Mills of Georgia in 1895, the maternal side of the family lived in the farming community of Gore fifteen miles north of Rome. Grandfather Robert Marvin West and two brothers hitchhiked to the start-up site seeking general labor. All three proved such good workers, the plant hired them as soon as it began making cloth. Directly Robert Marvin relocated his family, which included Bob's mother, Vera Roberta, to Lindale; he stayed on in the cloth room, rising to second hand before retiring with forty-five years' service. He passed away in 1945. Paternal grandfather William Clarence Baker was raised in the Doyle Road area on the opposite side of the county. His family also farmed before moving to millwork. By the early 1930s, Vera Roberta was expecting a third child. However, for an unspecified reason, the father separated from his family six months before Bob was born in November. It would be a decade before the youngster ever saw his father. The three siblings attended Pepperell schools through freshman year with the only son moving to McHenry High for the tenth and eleventh years before graduation in 1949. At the time, Georgia taught their children through eleven grades only.

It was at Pepperell that Bob met his future wife, Margaret Ann Marion; she finished one year ahead of him before transferring to Rome Girls High. Several months following graduation, the former junior high classmates married on February 11, 1951. While Bob worked at the mill which made them eligible for Company housing on E Street, Margaret worked as a business secretary in town before accepting a better-paying job with Borden Ice Cream Company on Dean Street, Rome. On February 9, 1953, the couple welcomed son Phillip "Phil" Marion Baker on E Street. Around 1974, Margaret moved up to Floyd Junior College where she was secretary to the director of nursing. Bob had remained at West Point Pepperell for ten years before moving to Liberty National Insurance Company for fifteen years; in 1974, he began working for the Georgia Department of Labor. Meanwhile in 1983, Ms. Baker became secretary to the Floyd County school superintendents, which have included Dr. Nevin Jones, Terry Jenkins, and Jackie Collins. In 1996, Bob and Margaret retired on the same day. The couple spent the following years nurturing their son, daughter-in-law, and grandchildren. Margaret passed away on April 18, 2012. Bob is still active and resides in the Rome area.[5]

Scott Reese "Rip" Johnston Jr.

The Johnston family is a part of the fabric of Lindale. Although twentieth-century Aunt Polly was perhaps the most famous member, the Scotch-Irish family came out of the Carolinas in the late 1700s just in time for the Civil War. The patriarch of the Lindale-era family was Samuel Johnston who was born during the War Between the States on January 19, 1862, and died at the beginning of World War II on October 16, 1941. In 2001, Nora Jane Gaskin Esthimer wrote in a biography of her grandfather that "the Johnstons, the Mill and Lindale are inseparable." She speculates he was there at construction; however, although his economic welfare depended on Massachusetts Mill, the entrepreneur was never employed by the Mill *per se*. He contracted to maintain all the grounds at the Mill and Village while also owning and operating the Dray Line. This was a four-wheeled flatbed wagon pulled by horses that brought cotton bales from the nearby depot to the Mill dock and then brought back finished weave products to the outbound rail. He more than earned his keep, after a while, by convincing company-hired carpenters that high-sloping expensive snow roofs were unnecessary in Georgia. When Sam married Laura Johnson in 1906, he was forty-four or twenty-two years older than his bride. They birthed seven children between 1907 and 1924 with Scott Reese Johnston Sr. (1920) and Polly being last in line.

Scott Reese "Rip" Johnston Jr.'s contribution to *Lindale, Lint, and Leather* should not be underestimated as he was the perfect associate for a researcher—a locally born and raised lad who rose to plant manager of the Mill. First and foremost, he loves this community. Secondly, he has a great memory supported by a vast library pertaining to Lindale; he also has a vast knowledge of the inside of the Mill and the technical changes that happened before and during his professional life. Hopefully I have been an engineer-in-training on this project.

Rip's fraternal family were most all reared at "down on the corner" house before moving to "the house on the hill," which are locations best described by Rip himself. There was early schooling at Pepperell Elementary and carefree summers spent at the swimming hole near the Old Brick Mill. In interviews, I was amazed by his knowledge of the goings-on inside the red-brick walls. Textiles are more complicated than most folks know. I learned this lesson listening to Rip and his cousin Sam talk shop during countless meetings. For me, they were able to separate the term *cotton mill* from *textile industry*. Many of my friends and relatives across the state line worked graveyard shift at Lindale cotton mill. It did not sound very glamorous or complicated. However, there is not enough space here to detail how smart these workers were in keeping marketable cloth rolling off the looms.

Scott Reese Johnston Jr. was born on July 3, 1951, at McCall Hospital; he was schooled through fifth grade at Pepperell before transferring to Darlington where he graduated in 1969. He entered Georgia Institute of Technology in the fall and graduated with a BS degree in textiles 1974. He served eight years in the US Army Corps of Engineers reserve before being discharged in 1982. After two years in Texas as a field engineer for Associated Dallas Laboratories in Dallas, Texas, the twenty-six-year-old worked for West Point Pepperell and Greenwood Mills for the next nineteen years, rising to Lindale plant manager. In 1996, he moved to Liberty's South Carolina plant as general manager; three years later, he relocated to Synthetic Industries in Chickamauga, Georgia. In 2003, Rip signed on with Shaw Industries and managed four of their facilities in Northwest Georgia before retiring to the Lindale area in 2016. Rip is married to the former Margaret Williams of Decatur, Alabama; they have two daughters, Elizabeth and Mary.[6]

Rene Fountain

Various dictionaries explain the term *benefactor*, Latin to English, as "one who does good deeds; a friendly patron who expects nothing in return." In early fall of 1975, Rene Fountain and wife, Martha, were one of the first Lindaleans met by the McCords who were searching for housing prior to relocating from Weiss Lake. The visitors from Alabama soon discovered the Lakeview couple were avid Crimson Tide fans also. Although we ultimately bought and moved to a home in Silver Creek, a bond was formed which remains today. As the years passed, we met for Dragon games and followed Bama from New Orleans to Honolulu. At a customary lunch meeting with Rene in the early August of 2018, I mentioned Mr. Bob Baker had approached me about writing a blue-collar history of Lindale. Bob was working security at Sara Hightower when he noticed a library copy of *The Cotton Picking Centre Warriors*, published in 2015. This book contained 739 pages about 100 years of Cherokee County High School football and cotton. He thought I, the coauthor, who frequented 205 Riverside Parkway often, was a good fit for the story. Yet as early classes began at PHS in 2018, I was still soul-searching the proposal; it was a broad subject which, I knew, covered almost two centuries. With an estimated four years of research and writing, age seventy-nine was a concern.

Rene was raised in the Village by his mother and stepfather Coffia. Both he and wife, Martha, attended and graduated from Pepperell schools in 1968; their three sons, Keith and twins Kelley and Kevin, passed through Dragon hallways in 1986 and 1991, respectively. As a young man, he entered the fast-food business and advanced to ownership of several successful Bojangles restaurants. By nature, Franklin Rene Fountain is a quiet, reserved fellow who, over the years, has supported many community projects. Consequently, at another luncheon in late August, the Lindale history resurfaced. As Rene spoke about growing up in the Village with Pee Wee, Otis, Tate, and Park Street, it was obvious he was proud of his roots. Before dessert arrived that day, he looked over the table at Earl and me and said modestly, "Randall, if you'll write it, I will pay for it."

Editor's note: During Navy service on Oahu in the early 1960s, I discovered Hawaiians have a special phrase used for appreciation—"Mahalo nui loa." In this almost five-year journey to publication, several people have earned a "thank you very much." From Sara Hightower Library, Danielle Colby and Brian French are exemplary aides to researchers. Access to the special collections and microfilm rooms were always made available as was interlibrary loan services. In Floyd County's amazing archives located off Riverside Parkway, director Greg Helms (PHS 1976) provided reams of documents pertaining to local schools. He deserves a "Mahalo nui loa" also. The beauty of hand-painted color portraits resides throughout this work; Pat and Charlie Gilbreath (PHS 1969 and 1968) provided these murals of Lindale from their personal collection. They tell the story of our town without words. Whenever private copies of Dragon yearbooks were missing, our principal Mr. Jason Kouns and media specialist Stephanie Cox gave me free access to their entire inventory, thereby saving hours of foraging—again, "Mahalo nui loa." In late 2022, Pepperell High School made available all annuals online at dragonyearbookPublisherPublisher-Issuu.

INTRODUCTION

There was a land of pioneers and cotton fields called the Old South; here in this pretty world weaving took its last bow...here was the last ever to be seen of doffers and second hands...Look for it only in books, for it is no more than a dream remembered—a village gone with the wind.
—Paraphrased introduction of David O. Selznick's 1939 film *Gone with the Wind*[1]

For several months, Lindale, Georgia, native/historian Bob Baker searched for someone to record a comprehensive story of his hometown, which was a small prosperous textile hamlet established at the end of the nineteenth century. In early August of 2018, Mr. Baker, who was working security at the Sara Hightower Library in Rome, happened upon a recently published volume of local Southern history. The coauthor of the book was an acquaintance who frequently visited the Riverside Parkway site. When asked to consider writing about Lindale, I was at first hesitant yet agreed to begin tentative research and look into a general outline. Three weeks later with some trepidation, I began work on a quest that lasted more than five years and ultimately covered parts of two centuries. With Bob as mentor, the two acknowledged that under no circumstances was the endeavor an attempt to supplant Mrs. Lang Gammon's 1997 work. However, more than three decades has passed since Polly penned her research papers. As a matter of time and technology, much information has come to light since then; hopefully, I can compile and add to her story.

One of the first principles of writing is never choose a broad subject. That edict was broached quickly; secondly, select an area the writer knows—again, a transgression for I was born and raised several miles away in Alabama, leaving knowledge of the topic secondary at best. More likely a native of residential Old Town, New Town, or Jamestown could certainly have written a more personalized account. Yet there was one advantage. In 2015, former Cherokee County varsity players Tommy Moon and I coauthored a 739-page narrative, which included 3,067 footnotes, of their high school football team entitled *The Cotton Picking Centre Warriors*. The well-received book encompassed 101 years (1908–2009) of not only pigskin but also cotton and local history.

I discovered in preliminary research into Lindale Mills that start-up workers were all born in the nineteenth century. As this group passed away, their place was taken by another line of descent, one that was hardened by the Great Depression and World War II. At present, few of this group survives, but they passed along the pride and love of community to postwar offspring usually referred to as baby boomers. The fourth and final generation, great-grandchildren of first mill hands, witnessed or oversaw the dismantling of the cotton mill in 2001. These last weavers and loom fixers have, for the most part, helped preserve the history of the mother Massachusetts Mills of Georgia. Fortunately, there is a wealth of materials pertaining to the Village including partial histories printed by the company and individuals. For more than fifty years, a daily feature in the *Rome News-Tribune* reported on the happenings in Lindale. Judge C. W. Bramlett began as first reporter during the early years of the twentieth century. Charles J. Ogles then wrote news beginning with the second decade; Langdon B. Gammon joined the mill in 1928 and became editor of "Lindale News" in 1935. On January 14, 1968, the articles were ended as local independent write-ups. These day-by-day reports provided a unique journal detailing life in a textile community.

With that said, I continued to struggle for a plausible theme. A year-by-year chronology covering the village, the mill, and athletics (*Lindale, Lint, and Leather*) was not practical, for it would read like chloroform in print, i.e., presenting only numerical facts and events can be impersonal as well as boring. Finally in late January of 2019, my wife, Joyce Anne, suggested telling the story through the people, common or otherwise, of the cotton-mill era. It was a most exciting and practical suggestion, for it allowed us to be selective in a broad sort of way. Obviously plantations, bricks, railroad tracks, cotton, spindles, cloth, millhouses, baseball diamonds, Dragons, and creeks are important to this tale, but it is people living and deceased who give these objects life. We discovered two interwoven units as a basis of research—millwork and textile work. The former manned looms while the latter offered vocational support beyond the hum and scent of huge redbrick buildings; some mastered both trades. From these weavers, nurses, overseers, coaches, carpenters, agents, teachers, investors, and athletes, the saga of Lindale is revealed. A note of caution should be inserted at this point. Contained herein are various assumptions, educated guesses, and commonsense deductions based on scores of personal interviews, scrapbooks, old sixteen-millimeter film, county archives, and a vast amount of published and unpublished collections. Where there is a conflict, writer's privileges can be defended or merely left to the reader's discretion.

We soon established a baker's dozen of outstanding individuals from the Village; documentation of their accomplishments set them atop the historical hierarchy, thereby relieving me of arbitrarily slighting any person or family. Accordingly, *Lindale, Lint, and Leather* is told primarily through Larkin Barnett, John Paul Cooper, Captain Henry Parish Meikleham, Edward Russell Moulton, R. Donald Harvey, Garland Howard Smith, Willard Nixon, Nathaniel McClinic, J. W. Sutton, Otis Forrest Gilbreath, Polly Johnston Gammon, Richard Wolfe, and Lynn Hunnicutt. Beginning with pioneer Larkin Barnett circa 1825, I placed each biography into the history of Park Street thoroughfare. As the months passed, it was surprising to discover none stood above the other. Upon finishing a particular profile, I confidently thought nothing could surpass this personage, yet in their own way, the next in line equaled the preceding one. This is very unusual. True, each had varying professional strengths and boundaries, but the totals were equal. There is not enough time or pages to document all the astounding accomplishments emanating from the mill village of Lindale. But we can explain these phenomena "a proud blue collar work-ethic mixed with a loving community."

LINDALE, LINT, AND LEATHER

The mill's four generations have all experienced the triumvirate book title. Six hundred families lived in attractive and well-constructed single-home or duplex houses built by the company. Thanks to the first permanent agent, who came on board in 1901, the streets and grounds became secure, clean, and well-kept. Children played in the streets of this happy place. The mill itself was a living, breathing part of four generations, many of whom escaped the poverty of hardscrabble farming for a regular paycheck. Lint, which accumulated in the hair and clothes of workers, was a badge of their economic survival and work ethic. It was the membership symbol passed down from 1896. Recorded history shows that while most Southerners endured terrible times during the 1930s, our local community lived in high cotton and suffered hardly at all. Current Floyd County manager and Pepperell graduate (1987) Jamie A. McCord said recently, "Employment at Lindale Mill during the depression was like winning the lottery." As evidence, there are two black-and-white sixteen-millimeter silent films (DVDs) available in Sara Hightower Library, one showing employees honoring Captain H. P. Meikleham on his sixty-fifth birthday. The June 5, 1937, picnic-like celebration features healthy, smiling, well-fed/dressed people cheering their beloved Textile baseball team's 2–0 victory over Atco. It should be noted here that traces of Rome/Floyd County leather baseballs appeared as far back as post-Reconstruction times. Class D League teams performed professionally in Lindale/Floyd for years, but it was not until 1931 that the Textile Association came into being. It dominated sports for the next quarter century.

The Section "Lindale Goes to War" encompasses twenty-seven pages taken mostly from the *Rome News-Tribune* and West Point Pepperell publications *Home Front News* and *Lindale Goes to War*. They are quite comprehensive and detail the traumas of war on the home front as well as lines of battle. Lindale supplied more support and servicemen/women per capita than any other textile company. The reader should be amazed at the sheer number of participants in the ETO, CBI, and the vast Island War. The War Department condolences sent to loved ones KIA and MIA are very touching seven decades later. Official high school interscholastic play for Pepperell did not begin until the fall season of 1951 when the football team recorded a 7–3 slate against established programs of Trion, Bremen, Carrollton, and Model. Better still the spring of 1952 saw the Class B state baseball trophy awarded to first-year participant PHS. The post–World War II era began the transition from dominant adult-centered athletics which featured 35-year-old men competing to more youth-focused activities. Now 12- and 17-year-old girls and boys ran the bases and shot the baskets while parents and grandparents cheered them on. This section of the book required many hours of research into the 3 major sports and provided over 2,500 writeups. A casual reader of this long narrative may ponder if we sacrificed our goal by highlighting a mother lode of games, yet beyond the star characters featured herein, in each contest, there is a name, a face, or a family who played their role in this story of Lindale. Research reveals that both adult and youth arenas enjoyed immense support of local mill agents as well as the parent company in Massachusetts; sports was a glue that held the mill village together. Although this policy waned in the 1980s, it is acknowledged here and should never be underestimated. The demise of the mill in 2001 suggests free trade and friendly takeovers caused the closing. The years since postwar accelerated change within an industry that was anchored in the late nineteenth century; it failed to adjust or bow to the inevitable economics of a new textile world.

LARKIN BARNETT (1802–1862)

*He was a small, sinewy man, weighting about 130 lb., as active
as a cat, as quick in movement as he was active.*
—Georgia historian George Gillman Smith

On page 3, part I of her research papers, recognized Lindale historian Polly Gammon (1924–1996) once made an observation about the naming of her hometown: "If I were called upon today to re-name this community, it would be an easy task. I would name it in honor of Larkin Barnett, for to me, he was the spark that kindled, and then fueled Lindale—providing both property and people." When Scotland-born pioneer Barnett migrated from Fayette County into Indian-owned land near Silver Creek (south Floyd County) in the middle 1820s, he found a rich valley inhabited by Cherokee Indians with walled villages and fields already stumped and dwellings in place with a large spring-fed creek coursing between the north/south ridges. Maize, beans, squash, sunflowers, and gourds grew around each village in abundance. It was here in this fertile valley that he built his cabin and "planted his orchard." Later census records of 1850 and 1860 show the Scot as a farmer; more than likely, he initially acquired land from the Cherokees at the going rate of $1 per acre or less to establish a corn and wheat farm. Being a natural Scot, he desired more open land.[8] The Highlander countryman had been recruited to colonial America in the mid-1730s to act as a buffer against Spanish Florida. They were willing because of changing economic conditions in the homeland. Georgia governor James Oglethorpe wanted settlers who were accustomed to "hardship, militant in nature, and willing to become frontier farmer-soldiers." Oglethorpe got that and more. Once security was achieved, Highlanders turned their energy toward farming, cattle, timber mercantilism, and trade with local Indian tribes.[9]

Barnett's lineage was middle-class conservative being thoroughly independent and self-reliant. Though generally not cultured, they believed in farming, schools, and Presbyterian churches. Their creed was short and simple: the Bible, as they understood it, was the final arbiter on all questions.[10] His group became yeoman farmers who engaged in subsistence agriculture on 50 to 200 acres as opposed to large middle Georgia planters. Larkin was a member of the Floyd County Whig party which stood for all the above; he was elected state delegate for the August 1852 convention in Macon.[11] On page 316 of *The Story of Georgia*, Emory College historian George Gillman Smith (1836–1910) passes to his readers a graphic description of what could be Larkin Barnett: "He was a small, sinewy man, weighting about 130 lbs., as active as a cat, as quick in movement as he was active, and always presenting a bright, cheerful face. He had an amiable disposition, a generous heart, and was as brave a man as nature makes."

In 1829, a North Georgia gold rush in Lumpkin County (Dahlonega) festered tensions between white settlers and Native Americans, prompting President Jackson to sign the 1930 Indian Removal Act, trading land east of the Mississippi River for the same in Oklahoma Territory. Consequently, a land lottery system was established to fairly distribute vacated Georgia land. Barnett entered into the last Cherokee land lottery, along with 85,000 other eligible Georgians in 1832. Records in the Floyd County deed room show this as "plot 51 Larkin Barnett, Gitten's, Fayette." More than likely he bought the draw from a person named Gitten in his native county. The numbered parcels were placed in one drum and the entrants name in another; an official then drew and matched the two together. A grant fee of $18 paid per land lot closed the deal. All told, the system distributed plots for 7¢ per acre to 20,000 fortunates of which Larkin won plot number 51 for 160 acres in the Silver Creek water shed; the deed was recorded in 1833. A final drawing occurred later in the year that dealt out forty-acre lots thought to contain gold deposits. This system actually served 2 purposes. First, it increased the state population. Secondly, the sweepstakes spread political power from the aristocratic planters to smaller farmers.

In 1806, Thomas Jefferson gave advice to pioneers. The third president said, "You will find your next want to be mills to grind your corn, which by relieving your women from the loss of time in beating it into meal, will enable them to spin and weave more." After claiming his 160-acre homestead in 1832, our frontiersman possessed everything needed to process corn and wheat for personal and commercial use. Therefore, common sense tells us that Larkin built or had access to a grist mill on the spot; other settlers along the creeks coursing through the valley (Chambers a.k.a. Rounsaville and Porters) also utilized the swift water to establish working sites. According to Floyd County "Deed Book C," page 383, dated October 6, 1837, Barnett added 320 adjoining acres from one Moses Bradbury; the asking price was $3,500 paid in hand to seller and conveyed to said Larkin Barnett his "heirs and assigns" all of land lot number 68 and two-thirds of number 69 and one-third of number 76. The first mention of mills on the site occurred in the same year of 1837 when he bought the 54 acres of lot number 76 that included "one half the mills now on said property." The following year (1838), he purchased the remaining two-thirds (107 acres) of the same land lot and the remaining half interests in the mills ("Deed Book C," page 442). The three purchased lots, 68, 69, and 76, added to his original lottery property on Silver Creek, which now totaled 640 acres. (According to the index of conveyances of real estate in Floyd County, the Barnett family at one time owned approximately 1.5 square miles in the Silver Creek area.)

Interestingly, the kinds of mills on lot number 76 appear in "Deed Book J," page 603; it states that there is "a place where the old carding machine stood, the grist and saw mill sites as well as a miller's house." The meaning of carding machine is possibly a rudimentary cotton gin as this was well after Eli Whitney patented his cotton gin in 1794.[12]

Lindale's Old Brick Mill was built circa 1845. So states Mr. Donald Gregory Jeane on page 50 of his fascinating 142-page doctoral dissertation submitted in 1974 to the graduate faculty of the Louisiana State University and Agricultural and Mechanical College; in it, Mr. Jeane gives us a unique look at the historical site. On page 47 of *The Culture History of Grist Milling in Northwest Georgia*, he states that our mill was the "oldest and most substantial" in Floyd County. Obviously there had existed several wooden mills at the end of the water race before Barnett constructed the existing brick structure as it stands today. Mr. Jeane's research states that our structure stands alone, for no other kind existed in Northwest Georgia. He compared architectural styles with other buildings of known origin and determined a construction date as 1845. Over the years, several other dates have been given as the year of origin; however, most undoubtedly refer to wooden structures over the creek. However, the site of the milling has not changed, only the structures that sat over Silver Creek. The building that stands today is constructed with handmade brick fired locally from nearby clay. According to the bronze National Register of Historic Places plaque attached to the west wall by Polly Gammon in 1993, much of the work was done by slave labor.

The building itself is a thirty-six-foot square two-story structure with one room on each level accompanied by arched windows and doors. There is a loft and a semibasement that floods in extreme tides; this under room still houses the first (west side) paddle wheel bushing made of terra-cotta; this tubelike opening supported the long main axle. A large overshot wheel (twelve-foot diameter), which was at first wooden and then converted to iron, was turned by water to operate the corn and wheat stones. The millrace tapped the creek well over a half mile upstream. A ditch, dug along the contour of the mountain, carried the water by gravity flow to "an elevated wooden mill race" that spanned a lower part of the creek for a distance of several hundred feet. The original west-facing wheel was shifted at some later date to the south side. In all likelihood, it had two runs of stones for grinding both wheat and corn. The architecture was similar to that of New England. This was unusual at the time for the South, which was usually built with cheap available pine.

Whether by chance or plan, the highly successful Silver Creek Mill business soon became an important gathering place for news-hungry farmers and entrepreneurs. Typically, a mill area contained a sawmill upstream, cotton and grist mills downstream, a blacksmith shop, general store and post office, miller's house, and a hostelry. Many of these facilities were not on a road or trail necessitating paperwork clearly indicating right of way to and from the complex. The above information from pages 47–50 of Mr. Jeane's 1974 dissertation is a fine description of early Lindale.[13]

Legend has it that some products achieved fame when a fifty-pound sack of ground flour was shipped to the 1840 Paris World's Fair where it won the premier prize. Yet according to a 1982 written correspondence between Polly Gammon and a world's fair official Monsieur Grouens of Paris, records reveal Napoleon forbade these events the first half of the nineteenth century. M. Grouens did add that small local fairs existed under the title "world." Nevertheless, the village we know today as Lindale was seeded from this venture. During the Civil War, Union troops pillaged the area and "severely damaged" the huge wheel. Postwar, Captain Jacob Henry Hoss rebuilt and restarted the operations, and it soon became known as Hoss Mill. Later, the family often held reunions at the site; Tennessee-born Captain Hoss is buried a few feet north of the entrance to Silver Creek Methodist Church. Today, the brick structure stands in the third decade of the twenty-first century as a tribute to the era's masonry skills.[14]

On December 17, 1860, and probably because of failing health, Larkin Barnett sold the property (now known as Silver Creek Mill) for $5,300 to William Cabe of Marengo County, Alabama, located 140 miles north of Mobile on the Tombigbee River (the legible quill pen document shows a recording date of October 1, 1863). The conveyance included land lots number 76 and number 69 plus 2 acres where the grist and saw mills are located in addition to the millwright's house. This deed is written in quill pen and ink as are many of this time by various recorders which make them difficult to decipher.[15]

In 1868, Rome's William Hemphill Jones bought the property back and lent his name to the site for twenty-eight years (1867–1895). Mr. Jones was the son of pioneer settlers whose Hemphill uncles were considered two of the early "founders" of Rome. Other than Barnett, he was the most significant owner of the site. Upon his death in 1883, sisters Mary Jane and Sarah Elizabeth inherited the property. In March of 1895, representatives of Massachusetts Mills bought the two-acre property for $5,000; consequently, the business and community name of Jones Mill Community faded into history. In 1880, a detailed account by the Manufacturing Census for Floyd County explained the importance of grinding grain. It shows the above subject mill operators "had on hand $6,000; they employed three hands and operated 12 hours a day during May-November. Wages were .75 cents a day or $100.00 for the year around; the mill had three runs of stone, did custom work half the time, and market work the other half. The water fall was 16' and it had one overshot wheel which processed 31,000 bushels of wheat and 62,000 bushels of other grains far outpacing it competitors."[16]

Prior to this "building of industry" in the early 1830s, Larkin married Elizabeth Olive Davis, and as children began to arrive (they had nine), he began construction of a one-level expansive brick home on the western slope of the settlement and south of the creek. This has been determined to be what is now called the Jamestown part of Lindale. Twelve chimneys built with fired or air-dried blocks protruded from the roof, indicating like number of rooms which housed children as well as long-staying visitors. It was not unusual for guests to remain around for a year or even two. A spring-fed freshwater system with hydraulic ram filled a large water tank located in the yard. Gravity spigots supplied "creature comforts to the extent of having water in the house," which was situated "westerly and close to beautiful springs with a pond." Regrettably, on New Year's Day of 1847, Ms. Barnett-Davis passed away; survivors included her husband and children (it is believed some of the nine offsprings did not reach adulthood).

Continuing on page 6 of her research papers, Polly Gammon explained that widower Larkin Barnett remarried in 1848 to Emaline M. Knowles (1825–1897). She subsequently birthed eight children and presided over the large household in Jamestown. Later in life, chronic joint pain, a form of rheumatism, made walking very difficult. Since rolling chairs were not available, the lady improvised by using a straight-backed chair system to bounce along the sturdy pine floors of the house. In 1862, Larkin passed away at sixty years of age. He bequeathed the first house and all lands south of the creek to his heirs and second wife, Emaline. Following his stepmother Emaline's death on July 4, 1897, firstborn son, Daniel Webster Barnett, tore down the original home and recycled old brick for the foundation of a second two-level family dwelling on the hill. This structure was equipped with all the amenities of the original home but added innovative acetylene gas lighting in the chandeliers and an outside concrete building that housed necessary tools and equipment. This two-story home was referred to as Lakeview. It was valued at $12,000 and considered one of the finest homes in Northwest Georgia. However, when this second two-story home burned around Christmas in 1910, owner Daniel Barnett had been a widower for several years. Along with his two grown children, Daniel Jr. and Mary, the father rebuilt a third more "modest" structure at the same homeplace. As the years passed, a section of this site became burial grounds. When much of the surrounding land began to change hands, the Barnetts were disinterred and moved to Rome's antebellum twenty-five-acre Myrtle Hill Cemetery. Today, there are seventeen members of the family now resting in section OR. Rumor has it that several original unmarked mounds of plantation slaves remain "under a grove of trees in a bend of the creek on the northeast side of what is now Jamestown."

The modest third house burned around the time eighty-five-year-old Daniel Webster Barnett passed away in March of 1936. Following this fire, Pepperell Mills bought the hillside land; they rebuilt a fourth structure and leased the dwelling. For historical purposes, we list these succeeding occupiers: Homer Smiths, the Craddock family, the R. M. Gibbons family, the E. C. Mulls, and lastly the Henry Holcomb family. When the Company sold its residential property to renters and others in the middle 1950s, the Holcombs bought their lodgings and named it Mockingbird Hill because of like birds nesting there. In 1964, the widow Holcomb sold to the Doyal Jacksons. However, this fifth structure was also ill-fated, being destroyed by fire in December of 1975; consequently, the Jacksons rebuilt on the same ground. This home still stands and marks a total of *six homes* built on the same plot.[17]

Referring back to the early 1830s, "Larkin the builder" had constructed a place to live and a place to work; finally, he looked for a place to worship. More than likely at the bidding of his first wife, Olive, who was of the first comers Primitive Baptist, a serene wooded spot in the bend of Silver Creek was chosen. It lay a quarter mile upstream from the grist wheel, and it was here he constructed a church. Polly Gammon states on pages 26 and 8 of her research papers that "there is no official date of the erection of the building...Family tradition has it constructed in the 1830s on property donated by Barnett."[18]

Church history says for years it served as the only house of worship in the area. Gammon says, "Early religious life in Lindale was somewhat overlapping, denominational-wise. Larkin's building and grounds were used by everyone with Evangelical revival meeting held in the woodshed near the railroad tracks."[19] During this time, the building operated solely under Primitive Baptist (called disparagingly Hard Shells) until part of the congregation split away into Missionary sub-denomination; the former held simple meetings with preaching, praying, and singing a cappella.[20] Larkin and Elizabeth Olive preferred this simplistic conservatism and encouraged the disassociation.[21]

In January of 1862, Larkin Barnett passed away. One year afterward, the Barnett family deeded the property away as shown in the Floyd deed room "Index of Conveyances Real Estate": "Larkin to grantee 'Primitive Baptist Church' parts of lot #76, a deed and gift on July 20, 1863 by administrator."[22] In 1932, historian M. L. Jackson stated that the congregation disbanded seven years later in 1870. Sometime later (August 1885), Jackson says evangelist of Cherokee Presbytery Reverend J. D. Burkhead visited Silver Creek and preached a revival for several days. As a result, on the thirty-first day of August 1875, he welcomed and organized fourteen members into a Presbyterian church.[23] Four months later, C. P. Whitehead with wife, Georgia Ann, bought the property from the Primitive folks, and in a deed dated December 30, 1875, they deeded/donated the building to Messrs. E. R. Lumpkin and R. H. Porter, who were ordained elders of the now named Silver Creek. This date is recognized as the beginning of present-day church. According to records, four of the founding members of said church were Lumpkins. Although the original structure stands today intact, there is one difference. Before 1950, the building faced south toward the railroad. Before the tracks were laid, an east-west Indian trail probably existed. Later as roadways developed on the other side of the creek, the church foundation was twisted a quarter turn toward the rising sun.[24]

COTTON, LOOMS, SAMUEL SLATER, AND ELI WHITNEY

They live in cotton houses, ride in cotton carriages, they buy cotton, sell cotton, think cotton, eat cotton...and dream cotton.
—English visitor to antebellum Mobile

Only the good Lord knows the birth of the first cotton seed; nevertheless, there are traces of the fiber dating back thousands of years ago. In Job 7:6, the Bible says, "My days are swifter than a weaver's shuttle." Archeologists exploring caves in the Tehuacan Valley of Mexico found bits of bolls and pieces of cloth dated to 5,000 BC. Two thousand years later in Pakistan, cotton was "being grown, spun and woven into cloth." When Alexander the Great invaded India in 326 BC, his soldiers moved from woolen clothes to the more comfortable cotton garments. Several millennia later, Columbus found the plant growing in the Bahamas Islands. English colonists founded Jamestown in 1607, and a decade later, they were growing cotton along the river bottoms.[25]

The Southern states of the United States were ideal for growing the white fiber. On the front page of its May 18, 1902, edition, the *Rome Tribune* quoted Alabama senator John T. Morgan who explained (paraphrased here) that no part of the world can ever hope to compete with the Southern states in cotton growing. This is owing to climate conditions. The Gulf Stream and trade winds bring warm rains just at the time needed. Consequently, the area James River, Virginia, to Abilene, Texas, with its frost-free days is given a month's start on any section of the world in cotton planting. The senator cited the hot, relatively dry weather in July and August which makes the plant grow, and then the almost rainless autumn season which is perfect for gathering. Although the area hosts a third of the good farmland in the United States, the soil is not primary for growing white gold, for it will grow on the poorest sandy land or the thinnest red land if properly fertilized; furthermore, it can be cultivated on hillside or in valley.[26]

By the early 1830s, the South produced the majority of the world's cotton. In addition, King Cotton exceeded the value (55 percent) of all other US exports combined while creating the wealthiest men in the nation. Prior to the Civil War, Alabama, Georgia, Louisiana, and Mississippi were producing more than half of the world's cotton. In 1858, a British visitor to antebellum Mobile once observed: "Mobile is a pleasant cotton city of some 30,000; they live in cotton houses, ride in cotton carriages, they buy cotton, sell cotton, think cotton, eat cotton, drink cotton, and dream cotton."[27]

Reconstruction brought about the disassembly of the Old South plantation system. This arrangement had shut out the average man from economic participation. However, the shift from slavery to tenant and sharecropping farms brought more, not less, cultivation of the plant. As a result, the market bloomed, even surpassing prewar production. In 1873, 6 steamboats brought in 30,000 bundles. Daily announcements in the local gazettes noted the *Sidney P. Smith* left Sunday for Cedar Bluff and returned yesterday with 200 bales. Because of its highly developed transportation lines, Rome (the first chartered railroad was 1839) quickly became the ginning and cotton-selling center in Northwest Georgia and Northeast Alabama. During peak periods, the *Tribune* noted 1,500 to 2,000 bales a day of our annual 80,000 units of the fleecy staple railroaded from Hill City. They ended up in Canada, the UK at Manchester and Liverpool, in addition to Antwerp and Genoa. Other than paddle wheelers, there were usually little or no freight charges on local bales; many farmers hauled their own loose cotton to the gin and then to town. Floyd County historian Mike Ragland (1945–2019) wrote, "Presses were built near the railroad depots, most with side tracks to ease the shipping of thousands of bales on railroad cars during the busy season." Then he added, "Cotton was to Rome what gold was to California and oil to Texas. It was the life-blood of trade and industry." By 1873, the white fiber was a major industry which gave birth to the City's famous *Cotton Block*.[28]

Colonial America grew in two major directions—westward and inward. The frontier formed our national character and gave us the ever restless pioneer moving toward the setting sun. The inward movement or Industrial Revolution began in the New England states and spread southward. Leading the way was textiles, specifically cotton-woven fabric or cloth. Four-fifths of the people on earth wear cotton clothing exclusively. It possesses durability, wearability, and longevity. It is most comfortable with a unique trait of absorbing and releasing moisture easily.[29]

Weaving of cloth is one of the longest existing skills in the world. Thousands of years ago, humans learned to twist and stretch plant material into small fiber. The next natural process consisted of interlocking, or weaving, the horizontal and vertical threads together. In the early days of the Republic, yarn and cloth making were the duty of the household. Pictures of a woman sitting at her spinning wheel are part of our American heritage.[30] The twentieth century gave us visuals of Mohandas K. Gandhi draped in plain loincloth, working at his spinning wheel. There is a deeper meaning to spinning at home. It is a statement of self-sufficiency and independence—the American colonies and the Indian Raj (rule) from England. Large amounts of fabric first entered the world markets through India and the Far East where millions of nimble fingers were available to make it. The invention of the flying shuttle mechanization could beat the nimble fingers every time and increase profits through lower labor prices. England denied other nations access to her technology until the late 1870s. The eighteenth century weaving industry in the British Isles was well advanced and highly protected; consequently, all manufactured cloth in the colonies was imported.[31]

As George Washington (1732–1799) was being inaugurated in New York City, there were two ongoing attempts at textile manufacturing in America—a Beverly, Massachusetts, small cloth mill and a Charleston yarn shop run by the widow Frances Ramage. Both were simple mills powered with a horse tethered to a harness while moving around a rotating pedestal. Washington's new government openly encouraged business enterprise; on a visit to the New England site in 1789, he praised its owner and commodities which actually became the first to produce domestic cloth by machinery. Although both operations were short-lived, the Massachusetts legislature voted funds to help promote textiles (the word is from Latin *texere*, meaning "to weave"). The recipient of the £200 (equivalent to $30,000 currently) grant was Colonel Hugh Orr of Bridgewater, who was the owner of an arms company. Orr, with the help of two Scottish immigrants, quickly constructed a small commercial mill. A legislative committee examined his operation and quickly approved funds to be given to the engineers supplemented by six tickets in the state's land lottery. Drafted plans of this state unit were distributed to others.[32]

However, it took two engineers/inventors born three years apart on two continents to bring the necessary technology to America's rudimentary machines, thus fanning its Industrial Revolution—Samuel Slater (1768–1835) and Eli Whitney (1765–1925). The former was born into a prosperous agrarian family in England's Derbyshire County. The young Slater received a good education with high marks in math and mechanical aptitude. The youngster began learning his trade as a ten-year-old cotton mill laborer working from daylight to dark seven days a week. Ten years later, he grew into an ambitious young man with unique mechanical skills and a burning desire to own his own business. However, no financial backers were willing to chance a twenty-one-year-old in the already crowded field.

England was the first advanced nation to manufacture cotton cloth on greater quantities using machinery driven by single system. Businessmen in the colonies felt the desirability of making the goods which previously they had imported; consequently, they were eagerly searching for someone with expert knowledge of mill workings and were prepared to pay. By chance, Slater's hometown newspaper printed an ad that promised £100 to any experienced man willing to bring his secrets to America. Current British laws forbade citizens with knowledge of textiles to leave the country. These statutes were not just a threat; they were fervently enforced, i.e., fines, twelve months in prison, or possible death sentences. Undaunted, Samuel "memorized every aspect of how the machines worked, sewed his credentials into a coat layer, disguised himself as a farm hand and, without telling even his family, sailed to America arriving in autumn of 1789." Forever afterward, in his hometown, he was known as Slater the Traitor.[33]

Upon arrival, Slater received word that Moses Brown of Pawtucket was experiencing mechanical difficulties adapting the state drafts to spinning jenny. A letter soon summoned him. By 1791, using a waterwheel as power source, Slater set up a British design that provided for continuous spinning; soon, the mill was able to card and spin cotton into thread. Impressed with the young Englander, Brown quickly proposed he run the factory. However, the guest bartered knowledge into partnership with a newly formed textile company and meshed the firm into a perfect Yankee–Red Coat economic system. Twelve months later, the enterprise produced its first cloth. The looms then wove eight thousand yards so quickly that sales agents could not keep up with demand.[34]

Initially, the fledgling businessman hired children to work and make repairs inside the narrow spaces of the machines; however, American parents, as opposed to British, refused to relinquish authority over their children. He countered by employing entire families with mothers weaving and husbands building new mills or additions. He also made arrangements for factory worker housing and schools, thereby establishing the mill village system. In actuality, textile manufacturing was the first industry to arise out of a merchant and government system to maximize exports, giving rise to the factory system with its tight-knit units that had a common touch. When "Slater the Promoter" died in 1835, the United States realized $47 million ($1.3 billion today) in cotton trade annually. Utilizing the immigrant traits of ambition, risk-taking, and flexibility in business, he had amassed a net worth of $1.2 million (equivalent to $34,000,000 today).[35]

By 1812, cotton mill development spread throughout New England; Massachusetts (the hub of the universe) and Rhode Island led the way. Two years later, Harvard-educated businessman Francis Cabot Lowell formed the Boston Manufacturing Company; this model corporation featured a mill building with unified control of all aspects of production and distribution of finished goods. Scot Smith of the *Investor's Business Daily* wrote in 2015 that "the Industrial Revolution quickly spread to pretty much every thing else."[36]

However, without Eli Whitney's gin (short for engine), the cotton industry in the South would have been delayed for decades. As a youth, Whitney (1765–1825) enjoyed a comfortable farm life in Worchester County, Massachusetts; he graduated Phi Beta Kappa from Yale (New Haven, Connecticut) in 1792 and prepared to enter law school; however, the 27-year-old possessed an affinity for the applied arts or mechanical engineering. Lacking funds for jurisprudence studies, he accepted a teaching offer in South Carolina.[37] En route aboard ship, he met Catherine Greene, owner of Savannah's 2,200-acre Mulberry Grove Plantation. At the time, silk was the preferred cloth for Europe, and mulberries were the preferred food for silkworms. The widow of Revolutionary War hero General Nathanael Greene offered him a position reading the law (apprenticeship) and tutoring in Chatham County.[38] The overseer of her estate saw the mechanical aptitude of the young Whitney and quickly presented him with a challenge. Long-staple cotton growing along the coastal areas was relatively easy to separate fiber from seed whereas predominate upland short-staple took one hand all day to extract a pound of lint.[39] Legend has it that Eli observed a hungry cat "raking goose down" through coop wire rather than picking out whole morsels. He devised a hand-cranked rotating drum with a series of hooks that acted like a strainer or sieve. In a day his single machine could clean 50 pounds of lint from cotton seed.[40] He patented the cotton gin in 1794; 10 years later, bale exports reached 93 million pounds and doubled each decade until the beginning of the Civil War. In New England, agriculture on rocky hillsides and narrow valleys was not as profitable as below the Mason-Dixon Line. Sadly the expanding production of upland farms and plantations rejuvenated slavery in the American South. Nonetheless, cotton, the loom, and gin were forever linked in Lindale history.[41]

HENRY WOODFIN GRADY (1850–1889) AND THE NEW SOUTH

The region's dependence on the wares of the North would have dire consequences.

Henry Grady

If Slater and Whitney were the fathers of the American Industrial Revolution, Henry Grady was its voice. He was born in 1850 Athens and, as a teenager, witnessed fierce Civil War fighting in his home state of Georgia. Father William was killed by a Union soldier, forcing the mother to raise him alone. At the university, he received a classical bachelor of arts degree in Anglo-Saxon languages, history, and literature, graduating in 1868 as an eighteen-year-old.[42] A series of brief journalistic jobs followed, the most important being a "free lance" position for the newly established (1868) Atlanta Constitution. A year later, he accompanied the state's leading editors on a press train excursion into Northwest Georgia. In a way, it was a coming-home junket for Grady, for as a youth he regularly visited the other branch of the family, specifically Uncle Henry A. Gartrells who resided in Floyd Springs. As the train moved to Cartersville, Chattanooga, and finally to Rome, Henry used his "loquacious pen" to shoot readable articles back to the home newspaper via telegraph tolls. He described and promoted the area's unsurpassed resources, saying, "All that was wanting was for someone to make a start, and induce men of means…to aid in developing the same." The Atlanta proprietors were not impressed and responded with, "We are compelled by pressure upon our space to abbreviate and condense the report of your Press Excursion proceedings." Arriving in Rome on Friday, September 3, at the "unearthly hour" of 1:30 a.m., he found *Weekly Courier* Captain Melville Dwinell still at his desk; Grady presented his New South yarns to the Hill City editor who "ate his contributions with a relish." What followed was astonishing; for several weeks, the four-page paper ran three long columns or more spiced with youth, enthusiasm, and hard labor. The remarkable narratives woke up Rome's citizens and warranted Henry W. Grady a job as associate editor.[43]

A year later, he tendered a resignation to become editor and business manager of the *Daily Commercial*, Rome's first everyday newspaper. A three-year residency in the City of Seven Hills brought about a new bride. In the fall of 1871, Athens sweetheart Julia C. King and Henry were married. They moved to the old Wood home at Broad and Sixth Avenue where he did best journalistic work enhanced by a budding oratory career. On page 250 of his *History of Rome and Floyd County*, George Magruder Battey Jr. wrote, "A free-hearted fellow was Henry Grady…traversed many an untraveled thoroughfare to obtain a glimpse of types which the average man of his sphere seldom sees in their element."[44]

By 1880, he had divested himself of the *Commercial* and bought one-quarter interest of the Atlanta *Constitution*. As a thirty-year old managing editor, Grady used the state's most influential newspaper to promote Northern investment and Southern industrial growth to his 120,000 readers.[45] He preached unity and trust between the two former warring regions, adding the southland is a "perfect democracy…a social system compact and closely knitted, less splendid on the surface, but stronger at the core; a hundred farms for every plantation, fifty homes for every palace; and a diversified industry that meets the complex needs of this complex age." Along the way, he successfully lobbied for the establishment of Georgia Institute of Technology with primary goals toward vocational and industrial education.[46]

Henry Woodfin Grady's crowning achievement occurred in Lower Manhattan at the famous Delmonico's restaurant on December 22, 1886. He opened a talk before the charitable New England Society of New York with, "There was a South of slavery and secession—that South is dead." The large group of businessmen, including J. P. Morgan and H. M. Flagler, then received a wonderful speech entitled "The New South." To the politicians and capitalists present, he preached the unification of the regions into a single union and bolstering industries below the Mason-Dixon. Consequently, Northern investors would reap rewards both monetary and moral. By the same token, Southerners, who were two generations behind the North because of the blight of slavery, would regain their financial and economical independence following the "rough-fingered hold of the Reconstruction."[47] On a postwar fact-finding trip, Oscar Crosby, former assistant treasurer for the United States, stated, "Conditions in Europe are not as bad as those that faced the South after the Civil War…none of these nations are bankrupt…which a far different condition of affairs."[48] Henry Grady was preaching to the choir, for most of the New England manufacturing investors seated in the audience were eager to escape unions, long winters, high-priced labor and freight from cotton fields to mill.[49]

Three years later in an 1889 lecture before the Bay State Club of Boston, the Georgian upbraided his Southern kinsmen for their economic shortcomings. He promised that "the region's dependence on the wares of the North would have dire consequences." Making his point, the young Georgian told a heartfelt story:

> I attended a funeral once in Pickens County in my State. This funeral was peculiarly sad. It was a poor *"one gallus"* fellow, whose breeches struck him under the armpits and hit him at the other end about the knee—he didn't believe in décolleté (bare neck) clothes. They buried him in the midst of a marble quarry: they cut through solid marble to make his grave, yet a little tombstone they put above him was from *Vermont*. They buried him in the heart of a pine forest, and yet the pine coffin was imported from *Cincinnati*. They buried him within touch of an iron mine, and yet the nails in his coffin and the iron in the shovel that dug his grave were imported from *Pittsburg*. They buried him by the side of the best sheep-grazing country on the earth, and yet the wool in the coffin bands and the coffin bands themselves were brought from the *North*. The *South* didn't furnish a thing on earth for that funeral but the corpse and the hole in the ground. There they put him away and the clods rattled down on his coffin, and they buried him in a *New York* coat and a *Boston* pair of shoes and a pair of breeches from *Chicago* and a shirt from *Cincinnati*, leaving him nothing to carry into the next world with him to remind him of the country in which he lived, and for which he fought for four years, but the chill of blood in his veins and the marrow in his bones.[50]

Much of the ensuing capital-lured South was spent to erect cotton textile mills especially during the last quarter of the nineteenth century; however, Northwest Georgia's earliest known manufacturing was established in 1846 by three businessmen on the banks of the Chattooga River appropriately called Trion. The plant, located on Indian lottery land, began with forty employees that later wove course woolens for the Confederate Army. Afterward, the company evolved into a benevolent employer leading other area towns and cities to seek the industry. Daniel Scott Wilson (PHS 1995) is a fourth-generation textile mill worker; the Shorter College and West Georgia graduate chaired the social studies department at his alma mater in Lindale before recently moving to assistant principal at Cedartown High. His expertise includes Southern textile history. In August of 2007, Wilson cited historian Wilbur J. Cash's claim that pioneer folks mindset of hard work was refined by the ensuing plantation system. Postwar and Reconstruction supposedly brought the physical South to an end; however, the move into brick-and-mortar mills engendered a continuation of this hardworking heritage sans borders. A by-product of work inside redbrick walls was the release of homebound women from manual "spin and loom chores of family clothing." Now, with full male approval, she entered the work force permanently.[51]

After Trion's success, it became a matter of civic pride to have a cotton mill in your community; consequently, by 1890, there were four hundred such operations throughout the region—add one more—for in 1894, a group of Yankee stockholders organized a corporation sited in south Floyd County, which they named the Massachusetts Mills in Georgia.[52]

JOHN PAUL COOPER (1858–1927) AND A GEORGIA GIANT IN THE REVIVAL OF COTTON IN THE EARLY 1900S

John Paul Cooper had a good idea—to bring the prosperous northern cotton mills to the place where the cotton was grown.

Contrary to popular beliefs, the seeds of Lindale Mill began not in Boston but Floyd County with the son of a Civil War veteran. John Frederick Cooper was an attorney living in Rome with wife, Harriet Smith Cooper, when commissioned into the CSA; he died from wounds received in the first battle of Manassas. Firstborn son John Paul Cooper (1858–1927) grew up and attended secondary school in Rome up to a point when he was forced to work full-time supplementing his widowed mother's teaching salary. Two younger brothers also added to the young man's trusts. Although university studies were impractical, the preeminence of education and business acumen followed him the rest of his life. The former came from his mother, Harriet, who honed her talents as a history teacher and published author in the postwar at Cherokee Baptist Female College which she founded; this school was a forerunner of Shorter College.[53] The business skills came from JPC's paternal grandfather, Major Mark Anthony Cooper, who accumulated an antebellum fortune, which was all lost to Confederate bonds.[54] As a young man in the 1880s, JPC married Alice Lawson Allgood and became a broker through his relationship with cotton magnate Mr. Theodore Frelinghuyen Howel (1845–1895), whose warehouse took up nearly a block on Rome's East First Street between First and Second Avenue. Mr. Howel, who died suddenly at fifty, was born in nearby Cherokee County Alabama, was self-educated, and served three years in Jeb Stuart's Confederate division. At the end of the war decade, he entered the brokerage world in Rome which said about him, "He was just a country boy, but he knew cotton."[55]

Surprisingly the South raised more cotton after the war than before. In 2018, Mike Ragland's research reported in the *New York Sun* held that during the last 15 years of slavery, the area grew 46,675,591 bales whereas the four years afterward it rose to 56,438,335. From Howel, Cooper learned to locate, buy, and ship the white fiber north for a profit. The true cotton factor was a versatile man of business in an agrarian society. He gave advice concerning the condition of the market or the advisability of selling or withholding his crop; he bought for his client a large proportion of the farm supplies. During the busy season, August to February, the local *Tribune* reported as many as 2,000 bales a day shipped north from Broad Street by rail—an average 80,000 bags annually of high-quality staple. The city's rivers, which were navigable 200 miles downstream into Alabama and 100 miles upriver, brought a steady inflow of the fleecy bolls to port. No other product of the day had such a real value.[56]

With the unexpected death of Howel from a stroke in March of 1895, young Cooper took part ownership in the company. Prior to this, his boss had sent him to New England to "break into the cotton market." He was one of the first Romans to make regular business trips to industrial and financial districts of Lowell and Boston, which were located thirty miles apart. Since the 1820s, the former was the leading industrial city in the northeast. It should be noted here that in 1846, JPC's grandfather Mark Anthony Cooper traveled to the Lowell area observing the local cotton mills. He kept a personal notebook and "surely shared it with his grandson." This is the first known contact between Rome and Lowell. As time passed, the Cooper family began to spend half the year in Boston. Eventually a close personal trust developed between the honest Southerner and the treasurer of the Massachusetts Mills, Charles L. Lovering (1833–1908). The *Business History Review* noted in September 1952 that "the treasurer is usually the chief executive officer. It is he who makes the managerial decisions, and it is he who is responsible only to the board of directors." Lovering understood his company could not continue to make coarse cloth in Lowell and export it at a profit. It was through this relationship that the two businessmen formed a good idea: *bring the prosperous New England mills to the place where cotton was grown*.[57]

Although Lovering saw this advantage, his company's stockholders were reluctant to "gamble" on area dirt farmers projected as mill hands. Conversely, New England operatives had been spindle-trained for years (unfortunately they had also been trained in union strikes). The national panic of 1893–1898 added to their distrust of the plan as was the thousand miles between New England and Northwest Georgia. However, the treasurer understood Cooper had a trusting interest with growers, pickers, and shippers in the area. A cotton factor was versatile in the business of agrarianism; he was able to navigate alongside the farmers who promised, "I'll pay you back in the fall." Just as important was the real character of potential operatives, i.e., they were the rank and file of country mountain people as opposed to the dregs of folks around large cities. Mr. Cooper saw what Henry Grady believed fifteen years earlier, "a social system compact and closely knitted, less splendid on the surface, but stronger at the core." However, with persistence and the help of some faithful backers, courage, and foresight, Charles Lovering formed a new state-chartered company (Massachusetts Mills in Georgia), a branch of his established cotton mill.[58] On November 27, 1894, the new company directors put their faith and trust in the honest Southerner and unanimously voted to build a mill somewhere in the state with a $600,000 line of credit (twenty-six years later, the mother company happily bought Lovering's successful venture).[59]

At this time, an unusual business arrangement occurred. In the last decade of the nineteenth century, the powers that be resided in Rome, and they, led by John Paul Cooper, preferred the mill located in Floyd County. Consequently, on March 3, 1895, a group of local entrepreneurs (referred to as syndicate) consisting of Reuben G. Clark, Theodore F. Howel, Arthur R. Sullivan, Arthur W. Tedcastle, William Leander McKee, Daniel W. Barnett, and John Paul Cooper formed an independent corporation named the Lindale Company, state of Georgia, Floyd County. Its stated purpose was "pecuniary gain to the stockholders." The amount of cash raised amounted to $25,000 divided into shares with par value of $100 each. Through their investments in local cotton, mercantile, and farming, the group would benefit from the establishment of a mill nearby. Being located 1,000 miles away, Lovering certainly needed a mediator he could trust, and common sense was Floyd Countians knew the grounds better than Yankees. Although Cooper's corporation was entitled the Lindale Company, he agreed to perform as a search engine for the best local sites with 1,000 acres or more; lying within would be 250 acres for a cotton mill. Control of all surrounding mercantile and tenant leases would be retained as would arable land use for stockholders. As the reader will see, JPC worked diligently on several parcels; nevertheless, there was obvious partially toward South Floyd. The purpose of the Lindale Company was profit whether with Massachusetts Mills or another customer.[60]

This was not an easy task. On January 25, 1896, the *Rome Tribune* reported, "No less than 500 land agents have gone from the southern states to the north for the purpose of presenting the advantages of different localities." In 2018, local historian Barry Wright III compiled and published a wonderful 411-page portrait of his grandfather based on family records. The book, *John Paul Cooper 1858–1927: A Georgia Giant in the Revival of Cotton in the Early 1900s,* reveals how Pepperell came to the lands originally owned by pioneer Larkin Barnett. Two entire chapters covering 35 pages of the work show what has been missing until now—that Mr. Cooper investigated several different sites (other than Lindale) for Massachusetts Mills of Georgia; this has been substantiated with private letters and papers in Mr. Wright's collection. Consequently, JPC promoted skillfully and without bias 3 major sites and several minor ones. Ultimately, treasurer Charles Lovering and his engineer Arthur Hunking narrowed the search to 1 of the 7 parcels. Had he not chosen Silver Creek as the prime manufacturing site, it is entirely likely the old community grist mill named Jones Mill (circa 1880s–1890s) would have, in time, spread through the farmland where Lindale now resides.

Using weekly correspondence posted to the treasurer in Boston, JPC presented a picture of available lands on the seven parcels. These missives reveal how Massachusetts Mills of Georgia came to South Floyd.

The First Site, Lavender Mountain Station

This location still shows on current Floyd County maps. It is an intriguing place even today and was near the top of the list for the company intermediary who reported on it on April 11, 1893 (paraphrased here). This land lies ten miles (it is closer to twelve plus miles on today's routes) to the northwest of Rome, a bit south of Huffaker Road and Simms Mountain. On a scouting trip Thursday, October 6, 2022, Rip Johnston and I used the former's Army training and map skills to pinpoint this prospective site. A north turn at Huffaker Road off Georgia 20 in Coosa at Evans Service Station will lead to Big Texas Valley Road. At this intersection lies Lavender Mountain Station with Cabin Creek flowing steadily nearby. Mr. Cooper noted a permanent steadily "spring-fed living stream" from the mountainside that never goes dry. And most importantly, a more than ample supply of good cotton exists about the Cabin Creek Valley which covers most of the three thousand acres available. The Central and East Tennessee Railroads run through the property which has a few families living nearby and a stop called Lavender Station. One hundred and twenty-nine years later, the area is wooded and still sparsely settled but with fine homes. JPC thought the railroad availability certainly critical to any cotton mill; both RR companies would offer Rome freight rates. In addition, the former would supply a spur track into the grounds as well as the spinning area. The East Tennessee would probably reciprocate. The County Board of Commissioners for Roads would certainly use chain gangs to build and macadamize the access. Much of the $6-per-acre land is cultivatable; Cooper wondered in writing if three thousand acres may be more ground than Massachusetts Mills can use. He added that a small settlement at the rail station is optioned at a higher price. Also the people at Lavender were willing to make another tender of their land when they were ready.[61]

The Second Site, Early's Creek

April 16, 1895. Another tract also shows on current Floyd maps. JPC termed this site as countrified. It lies fourteen miles west of Rome just below Lavender and beyond Coosaville (sic). The land is snug against the Alabama State Line and lies well south of Old River Road bounded by the river and Southern Railroad which would guarantee Rome freight rates and agrees to a spur. The Coosa would permanently protect them against all comers later. The water supply is "ample." More importantly, the greatest advantage there is a free supply of the best character of cotton this section affords. Howel Cotton Co. can give them a good fiber supply easily without raising the current price while competitor Cartersville must raise them an eighth to a quarter cents in order to attract sufficiently, or else they must ship it. At Early's, they may command the

Rome market, for they can boat it there at about 15¢ per bale. A three-mile road would likely come their way in the future. This land is reasonable in price.[62]

The Third Site

A subplot to this communications was proposed land purchases in other parts, the *Flat Woods* located south of Early's Creek. This area ranges west along Brushy Branch and Melson Road tracking to the Alabama state line. It was priced cheaper but was dismissed primarily because of the lack of a vibrant stream for boiler use.[63]

The Fourth Site, Johnson Tract

A letter Cooper to Lovering on April 26, 1893, described this land as a thousand acres seven miles east of Rome, embracing a fine creek flowing from springs. It possesses a worksite and cornmill. The land touches the river, and the Rome Railroad Independent Line, which runs from the city to Kingston, has agreed to make the same freight arrangements as offered by the Central. Mr. Johnson's property is listed for sale at $15,000. The lot and fraction of lot marked "Reynolds" (Reynolds Bend, apparently) adjoining him on the railroad can possibly be bought also.[64]

The Fifth Site, Mitchell Farm

On May 20, 1893, Cooper wrote to Lovering that this site is 1,400 acres 4 miles from Rome; it is scheduled to be sold by administrators in September. Part of the 18-mile track of Rome-Kingston Railroad as well as the Etowah River run through it. An agreed bid of $20,000 would purchase. These lands are called the finest in this section. Overflow covers the bottoms and constantly enriches it but does not wash. A sufficient portion is not subject to overflow.[65]

The Sixth Site, Rounsaville Brothers Tract

Messrs. Rounsaville's part of the proposed site is somewhat vague. They apparently owned multiple lands at Chambers Mill on the upper side of Silver Creek. However, the brothers agreed to accept the requirements outlined by Cooper for protection against other mills building close by on their parcels; guaranteed water privileges are included. He added, "These are vital points as concerns the Silver Creek site, I believe." The brothers have indicated a lower purchase price than before, perhaps $1,000 to $2,000; a shrewd agent could possibly save several thousand on any of the potential sites.[66]

The Seventh Site Silver Creek

JPC's letter to Lovering on January 28, 1895, clearly indicates the former preferred the Silver Creek Property (Jones land). He wrote, "Have seen Rounsaville and stated a sale was hopeless, and asked him for a site of 200 acres your choice. He won't do this, says he can sell elsewhere." He understands that he was to get the Jones Flour Mill (Silver Creek) place in order and report to Lovering. With this said, John Paul Cooper should merit a historical marker or bronze bust somewhere near the heart of Lindale.

With Cooper's work done, Lovering appointed a professional engineer, Arthur W. Hunking, to confirm the Lindale Company's findings. The Civil War veteran investigated several sites (his notes may be viewed on page VI of Polly Gammon's *A History of Lindale*) below the Mason-Dixon line before settling on our peaceful valley with its centerpiece Old Brick Mill. Essentially, he found that the character of the mill site is "excellent." Coursing through the established water race is a creek fed by ten springs; the source begins to collect ten miles away in a wet weather gulley near Polk County at Reeseburg Road/Relay. Along its way north, underground water overflows to the surface at what years later was called Congo Springs. On June 29, 2019, present owner of the property, Ronnie Kilgo, explained the naming of the area:

> The mill bought the land for water right; however, it was also used as a Boy Scout camp for many years. Part of the Scout training was a hike along the railroad tracks south from the Old Grist Mill to the springs. As the foliage thickened out in the countryside, the boys begin to refer to it as "like the Congo jungle" in central Africa portrayed in popular Tarzan movies of the era.

Lindale native Johnny Sutton added, "That the tracks were a thoroughfare...quickest way to the woods. Just walk a mile down the tracks and you're in no man's land."

At this point, the creek forms a "bold and beautiful" stream with water as clear as crystal before emptying into the Etowah River in downtown Rome. The source has a capacity of five million gallons daily. Although there is a trace of carbonate lime, termed somewhat hard by Hunking, it is "the purest cold water that ever passed between lips." The north-south valley supplies ample cheap land along with raw cotton grown throughout the area that is part of the eighty thousand bales annually at Rome; geographically, it is five miles south of Rome, Georgia, which showed a somewhat inflated population of fifteen thousand in a county of forty thousand.

There are more than enough lands for a cotton mill. Furthermore, two rail lines, Central of Georgia and Southern, run parallel near the creek. These tracks move an increasing amount of freight and passengers between Chattanooga and Atlanta. Side spurs to the manufacturing area are accepted. Price of coal for boilers is $1.15 to $1.25 per ton; production freight to New York is 60¢ per hundred pounds. This "scouting report" by Mr. Hunking was dated February 4, 1895.[67]

Historical records show the arrival of antebellum railroads at mid century brought about increased trade activity to the as yet unnamed site. This forced human and animal traffic along the south, heading to cross the tracks in order to reach the grist mill; therefore, it soon became known as Holder's Crossing, named so after the current caretaker of the grain and lumber businesses. A north-facing photograph taken in 1895 confirms only four houses and a small store.

Mr. Cooper had options on 1,000 acres at the Silver Creek site. At first, his company offered to sell a select tract of 250 acres to the Mill; however, on second thought, he wrote to Lovering, "I have been thinking the cost of any land would be a drawback and I think it well to say that if we can show a location which suits you, and we surely can, *some of us would be glad to buy the tract and deed it free of charge to Massachusetts Mills in Georgia* thereby creating a wholly-owned mill property and village. The site is available for all you wish to build, providing you do not liquidate it or sell rum or allow it to be used for mercantile purposes or permit a tax levying corporation on the property."

The seven owners of the Lindale Company would get a return from the trade and commerce and leasing the cultivatable land or perhaps farming the land themselves. *Mr. Lovering liked the idea so well that it became the basis for his decision to build Massachusetts Mills of Georgia at Silver Creek.* All the above history would have been lost forever had it not been for JPC, who was the final corporate secretary, and his grandson Barry Wright who discovered a little unnoticed ledger in family files with a crumbling spine that said, "The Lindale Company."

On April 27, 1895, the *Atlanta Journal* told its front-page readers that the contracts were in place and construction work on the big Massachusetts cotton mill, located a few miles from Rome, would commence on Wednesday, the first day of May. A large force of workmen would be employed, and in a short time the brick structures would begin to rise. The *Journal* also stated that the coming of this industry to Rome would materially develop the whole of this section and would be the means of bringing more capital to Georgia. Although Henry Woodfin Grady died prematurely in December of 1889, he no doubt was smiling down on Lindale.[68]

The *Rome Tribune* posted on page 1 of its December 10, 1895, edition that the Silver Creek Valley is one of the finest sites for manufacturing enterprises in North Georgia. It continued eloquently, "In a few years smoke from the tall chimneys [later the two smokestacks were affectionately called Bread and Butter] will float above the peaceful valley and the hum of busy machinery will be borne on the mountain breezes that sweep this lovely land."

In early 1895, plans for the first mill were drawn up by the Massachusetts engineering firm Lockwood, Green, and Company. Immediately, orders were placed to Lowell Machine Shops for equipment. This company was established in 1824 and was known for producing high-quality cotton machinery. The total cost for land acquisition, building construction, and inside mechanization of the enterprise budgeted $573,500; this was over and above what local contractors were paid. Shortly after, engineer Arthur Hunking was named first agent of the mill. He was now directly responsible for getting the mill up and running. On Wednesday May 1, 1895, work began on the big Massachusetts Mills in Georgia.

It was announced in April that contract for the erection of the buildings went to V. J. Headden & Sons of New York. However, Messrs. Lovering and Hunking used local resources as much as possible. An agreement with Rome Brick Company was soon struck, and production of five million bricks began to come off the assembly line. They promised eighty thousand per day via rail. The company was located near trackside adjacent to what is now Darlington School campus. Eventually five hundred railcar loads of brick would be delivered. The first load arrived in Lindale on Friday, May 3. The Southern locomotive backed them into the center of the construction site using the half-mile spur built by local hands. Awaiting the arrival were workers of Gallivan Construction Company who contracted to lay bricks on-site. Although some of the bricks were embossed with "Trammell," all blocks were supplied by Rome Brick Company, and most carried its emblem. In June of 1902, the *Rome Tribune* printed a commercial ad touting the Morrison & Trammell Brick Company, perhaps suggesting a subcontractor. However, Gammon clearly states that the Trammell family actually owned Rome Brick with J. A. Rounsaville acting as president and operating officer. She also reports this gentleman was one of Rome's "most prominent and enterprising citizens." Today, a street off Old Lindale Road is named for him.

At this time, a caution went out to laborers who were coming in numbers to apply for building construction: "Labor will not be needed for at least a month; save your self some walking time to the site." On page 1, January 6, 1896, the *Tribune* noted that Superintendent Captain Crawf Moore, "the king of road builders," will take convicts to Lindale for 2 days of roadway work before returning to Broad Street elevation project. The article also noted that plans for a mill bridge are forthcoming with construction, which would soon be in place. Mill number one began operations in 1896, with a second mill following in 1898. A third began operations on May 1, 1903, pushing the number of spindles to 70,000 in 1902. Polly Gammon marveled that land could be purchased, buildings erected, and looms installed in such a short period, adding that it was mind-boggling especially with the rudimentary tools available. At the same time, three coal-powered Cahall boilers were in place with the creek supplying water; the factory operated on self-generated steam totally until 1921 when Georgia Power built a substation near the Silver Creek Presbyterian Church. All three mill buildings served to manufacture cotton ducking (linen canvas), cotton drills (khaki), osnaburg cloth (grain sacks, upholstery), and cotton sheeting (bed linens). By 1903, the mill employed 1,393 workers, 374 of which were under the age of 16; in addition, an old photograph of one weave room shows 71 workers, 58 of which are women. Apparently, females made the best weavers.

In 1896, a group of Northern capitalists passed through Floyd County inspecting future manufacturing sites; their spokesman told Agent Arthur Hunking, "In Lindale, you have the finest location and cotton mill plant I ever saw." The reason for their visit was northern mills were "turning out goods in access of the demand while southern mills continue to find a ready market." They also commented a very favorable impression upon the people of Rome, for their "readiness to welcome and encourage all who come in name of progress."

Sometime in the last decade of the nineteenth century, our community acquired its name. Polly Gammon researched federal records and determined that the first post office designated "Lindale" occurred in 1883; this dispels the rumor that it was named for Lynn, Massachusetts, for it was eleven years before New England textile investors came searching for land. Furthermore, a plat dated November 17, 1895, confirms existence of the community name and location. Supportive of this, an old villager once told Polly, "It was Lindale when there was nothing but the Old Brick Mill and a post office alongside the railroad track." A word-of-mouth folk tale alleges that railroad man George Seaborn Black chose the name from a novel he had read. At the time, policy stated that a train could not stop for mail or passenger service unless a community was identified. Black, who later worked in and about the mill, apparently took it upon himself to legitimately stop the locomotives at Holder's Crossing (the area was also loosely called Boozville, taken from a local family name), which he renamed Lindale. When faced with multiple options, award-winning Hollywood director John Ford believed that "when the legend becomes fact, print the legend."[69]

HENRY PARISH MEIKLEHAM (1872–1937)

Wow! Nearly everyone stood and bowed in his presence.
—Hattie McClung

By 1902, the seven-year life of the Lindale Company had run its course. Mr. Cooper was extremely active in his cotton enterprises as well as board membership with Shorter and Berry Colleges; furthermore, the corporate investment money could be of use elsewhere. The remaining stockholders met on March 15, 1902, and motioned to sell all property to the Massachusetts Mills in Georgia for $28,500. Barry Wright states that "perhaps the most important act behind the sale of the Company was Lovering's hiring of Harry P. Meikleham as General Manager."[70]

Substantial evidence tells us the small Georgia locale had three founders who could have lent their name to the Village. Neither *Larkinville*, *Meikleham Town*, nor *Cooperton* would be incorrect. This we do know, the Lindale we know and love did not exist prior to Captain Henry Meikleham's ("Meek-l'am") arrival on Tuesday, January 1, 1901. The former varsity crew (row-ing) member stood 6 feet, 3 inches tall and weighed 240 pounds. The stellar athlete was a "Republican and Episcopalian whose genuine booming laughter brought cordiality and neighborliness to his greeting." He was born to Septimia Anne Randolph and David Scott Meikleham on May 28, 1872. Their home was in Riverdale, Westchester County, which was a turn-of-the-century upper-class neighborhood in the northwest portion of the Bronx. His mother was the granddaughter of Thomas Jefferson. This union produced twin great-great-grandsons, Frank Sidney, who died in less than three months, and Henry Parish Meikleham, who lived sixty-five years.

Young Henry withdrew from New York City's Columbia University early and started as an apprentice at the famous Boston Manufacturing Company founded by Francis Cabot Lowell. He quickly rose to overseer of the combing room, moved to Starks Mills in Manchester, New Hampshire, as carding supervisor; superintendent of Aiken Manufacturing Company in Bath, South Carolina, came next, followed by agent of Massachusetts Cotton Mills, Lindale, Georgia, in 1901.

Although the start-up company constructed and operated a profitable operation almost to a fault, there were built-in problems in the mill and village when the twenty-nine-year-old Northerner arrived. Many of his workers were from failed farms, migrants from other mills, or widows with as many as seven children; the promise of steady work and pay beckoned. There was a hard-living, restless element that made it unsafe for women to venture outside her home, especially at night; occasionally, "there was shooting down the straight streets." In five years, Lindale had become a dirty industrial village with bare unfinished grounds; little grass, flowers, or shrubbery; and hardly a tree. The houses were overcrowded with poor families living two to a room; livestock roamed the area freely; and drinking water, which was not tested, came from the reservoir built on an eastern ridge. Typhoid fever and smallpox were accepted as inevitable; no doctor lived closer than two miles. There were no school buildings; amusements were drinking moonshine alcohol and playing cards or dice on the banks of Silver Creek. Worse, youngsters must entertain themselves. The cause of some unsavory conditions must lie at the feet of Reconstruction, which was less than two decades past. Clashes occurred between the unskilled Southern operatives and their Yankee supervisors. In addition, wages were low, which brought the least capable people. Gammon says on page 8 that a week's pay for six eleven-hour shifts brought a loom fixer $9.00; card grinders received $5.28; sweepers, $1.32; fly frame hands, $5.41; warp spinners, $2.15; and filling spinners, $1.32. In his *Images of America*, writer Bobby McElwee cited on page 83 that average wages in 1898 were 5.3¢ per hour. Mundane and mindless repetition at the jobsite fostered frustration among the hands. However, the most harmful effect on Lindale mills was the lack of a permanent agent. In the span from 1895 to 1901, three plant managers, Hunking, Beach, and Southworth all served temporarily on their way to other plants. Fortunately, Henry Meikleham arrived primed and ready for the task ahead, accompanied with the body of an athlete and a practical, rather than a theoretical, mind. It was not always a peaceful quest, but he never backed down from what he thought right for the people. In a 1983 research paper submitted to the social science department at Georgia Tech, Glenn Hopkins wrote, "He arraigned the gunslingers in his office and told them, 'There'll be no more shooting in Lindale. If you want to dispute that you'll have to whip me; otherwise I'll whip you. But if you do whip me, you can shoot the damn things in my office.'" *There was no more shooting.* The Company would later institute a rule against discharging a firearm of any type on land owned by Massachusetts Mills.[71]

Prior to his arrival, Meikleham married the former Virginia Grafton on June 9, 1897. They occupied a huge multiroom two-level house on Grove Street built in the same year. The cultured easterner, who was four years his junior, was a talented rider who tended and cared well-bred horses. Lindaleans remember her riding the area gracefully while wearing the unheard-of divided skirt attire which enabled her to ride astride the animal instead of the ladylike accepted sidesaddle. Yet despite her lithesome gaits about the valley, the mill folks struggled to understand. Once on a jaunt through town, she stopped to talk and ask directions from a family sitting on the front porch. The following day, gossipers said, "Can you believe she stopped here with that skirt on, and Pa and Nobe were sitting right on the porch in front of her?"

Virginia brought high society to the Village. On December 14, 1902, the *Rome Tribune* posted at the top of page 10 that "Elegant Reception Given by Mrs. Meikleham Thursday." The article written by feature writer Beulah S. Moseley stated that "one could not enter a more delightful home than the Meiklehams…luxuries adorn including steam heat and electric light…throughout prevails the artistic atmosphere so requisite to the ideal home." Mrs. Meikleham glided around the rooms wearing a clinging gown of pink veiling. The gala event was attended by numerous ladies of Rome as well as honorees Mrs. Junkin and two misses—all cousins of the bride. The mother and two daughters made themselves "charming and agreeable" to the social gathering. The guests lingered in the pleasing surroundings not bidding adieux until well after sunset. The lights of the great Lindale factory "flamed like beacon stars" above those departing.

Henry and Virginia's childless marriage lasted fifteen years, ending in 1912, more than likely because the captain was wedded to his job. He waited fourteen years before remarrying on January 16, 1926, to Juliet Howell Graves, a widow from Rome. Juliet outlived her husband almost two decades, dying in 1955. Thirty-six-year-old divorcee Virginia Grafton Meikleham later married an Army officer and faded from local history.

Polly Gammon wrote that for almost forty years, Henry Meikleham reigned over Lindale like a "20th Century Moses." The hearts of Park Street warmed to his genuine good nature and friendliness. Local author Hattie McClung added, "Wow! Nearly everyone stood and bowed in his presence." Yet he demanded discipline of his flock and was always quick to tell his people to "do as I say, not as I do." He had human faults, but selfishness or uncaring was not part of them; the goal was always the betterment of the people of Lindale.[72]

In many ways, his heart was too big for his own good. Polly Gammon related this story:

> A mill hand was driving Meikleham to Rome but before they drove off an old man came up and said, "Cap'n, my boy is in jail." The Agent replied, "It's a good thing, I told you to run him away. He is not good. I'll help keep him in jail." The father replied, "Well, if you won't help me, I don't know who will." When they arrived in town the Captain said, "If you don't mind, drive me by the jail; I've got to get that old fellow's boy out for him."

The Captain loved the common man. In a February 27, 2020, interview, longtime Lindale resident Earl Robinson related a story passed along to him from dad Herman. Mill warehouses were three floors high served by elevators. In later years, hands operated them individually. In the Meikleham era, an operator was stationed on the first floor to manually open the large slatted gate; more importantly, he was in place for security. All operatives were required to wear metal badges with picture (Bob Baker has preserved one of the badges for posterity); also department authorization lists were in place. When in town, the Captain did walk-throughs daily. One morning, he appeared at the main elevator without credentials and asked the attendant, Skunk Pilcher, to open the gate. Seeing no identification, and not recognizing his boss, Skunk refused, saying, "I can't let you go up." The mill manager said, "Do you know who I am?" The young man replied, "I don't give a damn who you are—you ain't gettin' on this elevator." Realizing the moment, a smiling Captain said, "Son, you know your job. I want you to go to Brittain Brothers and buy yourself a new set of clothes—and tell them to put it on my bill." Skunk obviously became a favorite. Seeking company on a motor trip to Rome, the manager recognized Skunk standing at the Car Line Stand. He stopped and called out to him. "I'll go, but you got to circle around to pick me up. I don't want to get run over crossing that road!" A bemused Captain did as he was told.

Meikleham's philanthropy was not pretentious. For years, he sent Pepperell graduates (at the time, Lindale schools did not have grades 9 to 12) to the nearby Darlington School at his own expense. He was a keen judge of human nature and chose these young men carefully. Later, he expected the protégés to perform at a high level as they moved on to college.

Years after his death, an old-timer was asked to name the best man ever in Lindale. He replied, "It was Cap'n Meikleham—sober." When queried as to who was second best, he quickly replied, "It was Cap'n Meikleham—drunk."[73]

There were pushbacks to some of the Captain's policies. Although Georgia did not have a child labor law, its practice was being discussed locally as well as nationwide. In 1903, Lindale employed 1,393 operatives—374 were under the age of 16. Numerous pictures survive of mill hands that confirm underage workers. Children in the South traditionally worked at the forge, the plow, and the loom. Farm parents were accustomed to little children working in the fields and felt no qualms about them laboring inside. Furthermore, Meikleham had a mill to run. Every day he was in town, the Captain made an inspection tour of the plant. The stress of competition as well as families needing their children to work took precedent. A competing mill superintendent stated the dilemma:

> Sometimes, when a father comes to me and says that he needs Jennie's help now, I put him off and try to keep Jennie in school. But in a few weeks the father will be at me again, and say that he has the offer to work somewhere else. "Any better pay than here?" I will ask. "Oh, no," he will answer. "But they have work for Jennie too. That's the way it goes," he continued. We simply have to put the little tots at work, or we will lose our hands to somebody else.

Captain Meikleham defended his child labor policy by providing certificates from Ordinary Court about youngsters who were primary sources of income for the family. Epps Turner, Willie Bannister (both over thirteen), and Luther Wilderson (fourteen) were supporting widowed mothers while James Hall (fourteen) had a disabled father whose wife deserted. The agent volunteered to produce birth records for all young hands (a letter dated December 16, 1913, is available in Gammon research files that expands the above statements). In the village, early marriages naturally resulted in newborns. The superintendent ordered a community clubhouse built near the main gate with a shedlike structure adjoining it. This dual-purpose building was used for eating lunches brought from home and as a "titty house." Before a woman was hired on, mothers with nursing children must agree to arrange that the baby be brought to the rustic shelter for breastfeeding during her lunch break. Meikleham's underlying motives were to survive the family and provide a regular paycheck. "He never could resist the appeal of another human being in trouble."[74]

In the first year of the twentieth century, Columbia University economics PhD Charles Spahr wrote a series of articles about "America's Working People." The first cotton town he visited below the Mason-Dixon line was Lindale. The author's mindset was that demand for better economic conditions and social change would be festering in the workplace and village; he found quite the opposite. Shift workers told of recession wages lowered somewhat but not drastic cuts like local farmers or northern textiles were experiencing. On the contrary, there was a feeling of cheerfulness pervasive among the workforce; this continued to departments manned by children as young as nine and ten years old in which Spahr assumed the system was robbing them of childhood. Surprisingly, "they went about their work with so much spring, and seemed to have so much spirit...that I was completely nonplussed [dismayed]." He interviewed three of the youngest only to find them proud of their work and wages—not "conscious slavery" as expected.[75]

Superintendent Meikleham loved gatherings for his flock. The first occurred six months into his reign and was featured on page 1 of *Rome Tribune's* July 4, 1901, edition: "Big Barbecue Given by Big Cotton Mill." The paper noted, "It was probably the largest and most successful celebration in the history of Floyd County." The Cedartown Brass Band and Lindale musicians first serenaded everyone with "My Country 'Tis of Thee" and "Stars and Stripes Forever." This was followed by a stirring vocal rendition of "Dixie" from the children. A commanding recital of the Declaration of Independence by Thomas Jefferson's great-great-grandson the Honorable H. P. Meikleham continued the day's patriotic theme. Most likely it was the first occasion many in the audience heard "the greatest document of human history."

The local gazette reported 3,000 attendees enjoyed a 1-hour keynote speech by Congressman Judge John W. Maddox who paid homage to presidents Washington and Jefferson as well as Patrick Henry and Robert E. Lee. The historical review concluded that the South has as much a right to celebrate the nation's birthday as any part of the country. Afterward, the hungry Southerners paid tribute to the event by consuming 35 carcasses (sheep, hogs, and goats); 1,200 loaves of bread; half a barrel of pickles, and 5 boxes of lemons. Ms. Laura Griffits, along with 25 factory girls, was in charge of food service. Mrs. Virginia Grafton Meikleham and her guest Countess Sachendorff of Germany enjoyed the gala while the former's husband was heartily congratulated on the success of the day. The Massachusetts Mill of Georgia funded the festivities.[76]

Early on, alcohol was a problem for some men workers. In the autumn of 1901, a dispensary bill in state legislature was proposed and supported by many in Rome and Floyd County. *Dispensary* was a term used to denote a locally controlled liquor store. Section I of the bill stated that "a dispensary for the keeping and sale of spirituous, malt, vinous and other intoxicating drinks." On Friday, January 24, 1902, the *Rome Tribune* noted on page 8, "There will be a rousing anti-dispensary rally and speaking at Lindale Monday evening." The Honorable H. P. Meikleham and others would talk against the fallacies of such measures. They would be backed by church people and honest men. Following a bitter cold night, the front page of the *Tribune* noted the next day in bold that "Large Crowd Hears…Dispensary Advocates Torn to Tatters." Yet supporters of the bill held that it was a financial rather than moral issue. Of course, the lawmakers in Atlanta supported both sides of the issue, saying the liquor question should be kept out of politics while supporting the endorsement of a local option.[77]

The agent did not forget his primary business—profit. The new mill number three came on line at the end of 1902, giving the huge complex 1,165,000 square feet manufacturing floor space. Its 50 new looms brought the total to 1,800; in addition, 51,000 new spindles resulted in a 250 percent increase. During the busy season, the Company was shipping from 12 to 20 railcar loads daily. Two years later, 55 million yards of goods were made in Lindale, which was 15 percent of Georgia's annual production; this increased the payroll to $5,000 per week.

Cheap energy and raw materials combined with low competition for its cloth next to the absence of organized labor earned stockholders significant gains. Bituminous coal fueled the plant's boilers at $1.50 per ton whereas northern factories used the more expensive ($5.00) and less efficient anthracite to make steam. A high percentage of white fiber was bought direct from large farms or as "spot" (street) cotton on the banks of Rome's rivers. This eliminated

30¢ a bale commission as well as $2.00 per bag in freight to brokers; much of the raw material was purchased at the low end of the market and stored for later use. Consequently, dividends increased several thousands of dollars a year to a mill already making high-profit coarse cloth with nonunion wages.

On Friday, June 3, 1902, the *Rome Tribune* noted on page 1 that local-made cotton goods clothe the "Heathen Chinese [a term used in the day for those not Christian, Jew, or Muslim], furnishes shelter for the Klondike miner, penetrates the forest of the Amazon, were on the firing line in the South Africa [Boer] War, crosses the Andes on backs of Llamas, and like the British drum beat, follows the sun around the world in sails of many ships." Rome's *Hustler* newspaper prophesies six years prior was coming true "that bringing the U.S. cotton spindle and loom to the cotton field has doomed the Old World establishments."[78]

The naysayers would later be envious reading the *Rome Tribune* on January 22, 1896, which said, "Southern cotton mills are all doing well, are working to their utmost capacity, and find ready markets for their outputs." As Meikleham's yearly mill wages grew to $260,000, Hill City civic leaders (the combined city/county payrolls were nearing $2,000,000 annually) began lobbying for better access to the Lindale market. At the time, the mill paid their hands in denominations of 50, 20, 10, and 5 in folding money; anything below was issued in silver dollars fondly called wagon wheels. To the Rome merchants, pure silver in the cash drawer traced back to Massachusetts Mill.

Rome boasted a thriving retail center in want of customers, yet only dirt road wagon trails, which frequently turned muddy, existed on the five miles between suburb and city. "Lindale and Vicinity" feature writer Charles Ogles once described, "The pike road [usually meaning toll road] between Rome and Lindale was about the muddiest thing ever seen yesterday and day before, during the rains."

The local paper repeated a rumor on Saturday, May 3, 1902, that City Electric Railway Company might extend their line from Mobley Park to Lindale. It should be noted here that the park now encompasses the Darlington School campus. Looking back to 1832, planter Major Philip Walker Hemphill bought five hundred acres of land and built an antebellum columned home called Alhambra (a fortified palace on a hill). By 1877, the property passed to Samuel G. Mobley and along the way became known primarily as Mobley Park. In the 1890s, City Electric purchased and developed the original land into a genuine entertainment site where Romans caught the rails from downtown to enjoy swimming, fishing, picnicking, weddings, and political speeches. There were also horse races, stage shows, and professionally organized baseball games. The famous Seventh Calvary occasionally camped summers here at the turn of the century. Mike Ragland speculated the first county fair (later Coosa Valley Fair) occurred here. In 1912, cotton merchant John Paul Cooper acquired the property then referred to as DeSoto Park; on July 7, 1922, he deeded six land lots to Darlington for the school's new campus.[79]

On October 15, 1902, City Electric corporate president Seymour Cunningham visited to discuss the project with his local stockholders. It was determined weekend passengers from the village in addition to a large number of families living along the proposed route would more than justify the investment. By early December, most financial arrangements were settled with Romans encouraged to purchase $25,000 in bonds; the necessary rights and privileges were acquired followed by orders for twenty of the most up-to-date vestibule streetcars each holding twenty-eight souls. On Sunday, February 1, 1903, the *Tribune* told its readers, "ON TO LINDALE!" Fourteen months later, the three miles of rails were completed, giving Lindaleans access to Sunday afternoons in Mobley Park as well as the primary terminus in Rome. April 3, 1904, marked the first trolley arrival in Lindale. Captain Meikleham met the carload of civic leaders and entrepreneurs at the turnaround point of B Street south end where a lively prepared celebration ensued. On the first day, an astounding twenty-five carloads holding seven hundred paying (5¢ one-way fare) customers enjoyed the forty-five-minute trip to Broad Street.

A landmark Car Line Stand stood on-site for many years complete with waiting rooms and available snacks. Although the building was owned by Daniel Barnett, it was operated by Tan Knowles. Later, a new building which still stands just north of the tracks was erected with more amenities. The original roadbed is still visible at several points along the route, one being at the dead end of Alexander Street just off Old Lindale Road. The twenty-eight-year-old line was discontinued in 1932 due to competition from gas-powered buses and automobiles which cut the travel time to town in half; however, City Electric and successors surely recouped their investment in almost three decades of operation.[80]

THE VILLAGE

I think Heaven will be a lot like Lindale.

—Nancy Smith Hunter

Rome News-Tribune feature writer Charles Ogles posted in May of 1929 that "in 1894, Lindale did not exist except as a spot on the earth which was then being used for a cotton field." Jim Rumley reflected in the *Mill Whistle* newsletter of January 2006 that at this time "pioneer families set forth to the South's last frontier—the mill towns." Eventually, 95 percent of cotton mill families lived in company housing. By 1895, Massachusetts Mills of Georgia began building its industry on Silver Creek. As the brick walls went up, so did 58 some odd wooden duplex-designed homes for workers (many of these 2-story structures stand today). Company dwellings were a necessity in pre–automobile, trolley, and bus era. By the mid-1930s, the Mill controlled 638 units totaling 2,307 rooms; at the same time, applications on file (some 2 years old) for housing reached 110 families or 200 potential employees. Renting director Charles H. Edmondson stated on December 13, 1932, that "if we had space available the list would double…50 new houses at present would be a great help."[81]

When the whistle blew, scores of people walked from duplexes to jobs. Each side was designed to handle five or six persons, yet it was not unusual for some to house mothers, fathers, children, relatives, and friends. The *News-Tribune* reported in February of 1929 that a husband and wife lived with ten children in one side of a unit. They confirmed this with a list of the offspring's names with ages: "Patrick is 21; Emanuel is 19, Grace 16, Nellie 13, Donny 11 John D. 8, J. B. 6, Mary Lou 5, Annie Fahy 4 and Inez is 2." Still country folks did not complain, for they were used to such.[82]

The first of three residential sections was built south of the creek and east of the mill and was called Old Town because a succeeding subdivision was built on the Rome side (north) of the tracks and named New Town by the locals. Polly Gammon described the third neighborhood on page 79 of her research papers. This area was first called West Side Addition and then Jamestown after James W. Houseal. In 1920, the Polk County native and Georgia Tech 1905 honor graduate oversaw the project. He engineered twenty-six four- and five-room single-family houses erected at the edge of a cornfield and built mostly for second hands or foremen. In the next twenty years, approximately two dozen more units were constructed with the last two being for Dr. Joe Stegall Sr. in 1933 and Dr. O. W. Jenkins in 1940. Mr. Houseal was captain of the 1904 Georgia Tech football team; he passed away at a Cedartown hospital in October 1957 at age seventy-five.[83]

Beginning with Old Town, contractors first built each unit with a backyard "wood house or shed." The carpenters used these for working storage; at the same time, a small pathway/back alley was cut between abutting backyards that later functioned as a delivery road for firewood, coal, and ice. Many of these narrow alleyways still remain in Lindale proper. High slanting roofs à la New England were prevalent among these first units; later, local carpenters convinced their Yankee planners that steep-slope snow roofs were unnecessary in the South. This freed up much project time and money. All told, the company spent $100 per room on construction costs.

Workers flooded into the newly finished community which housed 1,393 employees by 1903. Statistics reveal by the turn of the century, 95 percent of Southern textile families lived in factory housing. On Friday, September 9, 1902, the *Tribune* posted on page 8, "Great Demand for Houses...impossible to get nice cottages with nearly every house in Rome occupied." The US Bureau of Labor reported in 1910 that "all the affairs of the village and the conditions of living of all the people seemed to be regulated by the mill company. Practically speaking the company owns everything and controls everything." Within the village, mill hands created a new way of life by weaving together their rural heritage and the experiences of factory labor. They were not necessarily looking to do *well* but to do *better.* Lindale historian M. L. Jackson wrote, "It has always been the desire of Mr. Meikleham to have the citizens feel that they were just a 'Big Family' and that anything good for Lindale is good for them all." He added that the Captain acted a father to every employee and inhabitant, and his reward is the unfailing love of every one of them. Case in point was his complete frankness and honesty as foreman of a jury trying several young blacks accused of crap shooting. He told the judge, "I refuse to indict them unless you indict the members of my poker playing club."[84]

Just prior to his passing in March of 2019, Lindale/Floyd County's favorite homespun writer/historian Mike Ragland wrote a poignant story about his grandparents in the Sunday, July 1, 2018, *Rome News-Tribune*. At the turn of the century, one grandfather lost his small Chattooga County farm to the boll weevil; he trekked to Lindale and found work to support the family. The other grandparent was "follerin' a mule's ass down a thousand rows of skimpy cotton" in Ball Ground when the animal fell dead in the furrow. A cousin helped him bury the beast where it lay; he then gave his wife every penny the family possessed, bagged up a passel of biscuits, and hiked west sixty miles from Cherokee County to Lindale. After three months of millwork, he rented a house and earned enough money to go back to the country and bring the wife and three baby girls to their new dwelling. "Upon seeing the home the mother began to pray, for to her, it was sent from Jesus."[85]

In 2009, Pulitzer Prize writer Rick Bragg wrote 156 pages about these souls in *The Most They Ever Had*, which was a touching story about the Jacksonville, Alabama, cotton mill. Northern roving reporter Charles Spahr said of these Georgians in 1900, "It was not doing *well* that makes people happy, but doing *better.*" In 1947, Mr. Ted Forbes, vice president of the Cotton Manufactures Association of Georgia, said the greatest source of pride should be in the people who work in our mills. "They are a homogeneous group of almost pure Anglo-Saxon ancestry, being largely descended from the pioneers who settled and developed the Coastal Piedmont sections of the Southeast. They are intelligent, industrious and learn new skills quickly and easily. They are loyal, independent, are jealous of their inalienable rights and individual liberties." Mr. Spahr countered this statement with some interesting comments about Lindale. He believed employers in the South and North hired whites or blacks from economic rather than moral considerations. In Lindale, the former were employed for all the "inside" work and the latter for the "outside." In the "yard," the monopoly of blacks was as complete as the monopoly of the whites in the weave room. There seemed less animosity in South Floyd because all were in it together; it was not rich against poor. Spahr noted no "peril" in the village as idle men were replaced by African Americans who served as teamsters or other outside work. (the 1948 Company yearbook pictures 178 African Americans). Yet with the absence of trade unions, most mills paid lower wages. Wives and daughters were usually domestics in the village. Housing, if available, was on the edge of town. Rick Bragg said that it may not have been the ideal job, but unlike farming, there was a check every Friday. During the Great Depression years, everyone inside or outside at Lindale practically won the lottery.

However, most expected to return home to the country after making enough money to pay off the farm mortgage and buy needed stock and implements. The Mill managers made life easier for these farmers-at-heart folks by permitting them truck patches and farm animals to offset low wages and amenities not available in other villages.[86]

Upon being named superintendent in 1901, Mr. Meikleham found his surroundings in disarray; it was a cluttered place with animals roaming the streets, unkempt yards, and a lack of pride within the people. He quickly posted a set of rules for renters that began with this: "As a tenant you are encouraged to practice the Golden Rule with your neighbors and fellow-workers." Children should not be loud and boisterous, the premises are to be kept clean and sanitary at all times, and the planting of privet hedge was encouraged and admired. He then removed the cows, chickens, and pigs to adjoining company land and directed the messy residents to "clean up or move out." Tenants were expected to vacate millhouses immediately after termination of their employment. In the Thursday, February 27, 1930, edition of the *News-Tribune*, Charles Ogles reported the superintendent's removal of undesirable families. "Four families were given orders by the mill management to vacate their houses and move out of the town." Two weeks prior, several families were also given eviction notices. Captain Meikleham told his overseers that because help was plentiful, the time was nigh to weed out the undesirables.

He controlled the mischievous local youngsters by calling in their parents and asking, "Do you like your house? Do you like your job?" After the Christmas holidays of 1929, H. P. Meikleham told the *News-Tribune*, "I think that was simply wonderful!" He had just been informed there was not a single man, visitor, or passerby seen drunk in Lindale or a single arrest for disorder of any kind had occurred for the five days of holiday season. Everybody had a happy and quiet Christmas, and all were back at their jobs. Although fireworks were banned during the season because of cotton stored outside warehouses, it was the happiest yuletide since the mill was erected nearly thirty-five years ago. This decree was softened by the announcement from auditorium manager H. W. Neal that following the approval of its patrons, the Village would soon have talking movies. Charles Ogles reported on November 14, 1929, that the Company has purchased the most expensive equipment available today for "the handsome and commodious" auditorium, which opened in May of 1921; however, prices would go up. But still the cost of a new flick was cheap. Retired mill boiler man Tallmadge Pitts saved a movie ticket from his youth. It shows the price being 12¢ cents with 2¢ being for tax. Part of those 12¢ cents surely came from silver dollars as the Mill did not pay employees in paper money below $5 bills; every Friday, the payroll train would arrive, and a chest of silver dollars called wagon wheels would be unloaded and taken to the Mill for disbursement (several excellent photos exist of this interaction). Consequently, as the coins circulated across the county, each merchant understood the importance of its source. Pepperell discontinued the tradition in the mid-1940s. Conversely, some local mills paid employees in scrip or coins minted with the company name; these coins were redeemable only in company stores which often had inflated prices.[87]

As time passed, Village amenities grew proportionally. Polly Gammon quoted a young man recently hired by the Captain, "The casual visitor to Lindale often pauses to wonder at the immaculate cleanliness and orderliness of the thriving mill village of 5,000 people. Every house is painted white, every house has more than three rooms, every house has electric lights and running water, every house is surrounded by neat, sanitary premises." Polly Gammon noted on page 11 that streetlights were installed in 1921. The Village houses now had electricity free to the residents; a single forty-watt bulb was provided along with a twenty-five-watt for each additional room. In time, families were charged $1 per month for service. Charles Ogles's article in "Lindale and Vicinity" said, "There is hardly a week goes by but that some visit is not made to Lindale by men and women interested in either the establishment of a new mill village in some part of the country or in bettering one that they may now have. Lindale is looked upon with great respect as a model of how a mill town should be organized and run."

John Paul Cooper wrote to the corporate treasury in 1908, "I found Lindale looking very natural, and extremely well, the whole village seems neat and smart. The trees are in bloom in their first leaves, and the little flower yards just beginning the coming into commission. Meikleham seems happy and says things are getting along comfortably and smoothly, in the village and in the mill…I find signs everywhere of considerable business…and merchants are prosperous and cheerful…The winter has been mild with an abundance of rain…there has not been a fire in my house since I arrived.[88]

With spring approaching, the superintendent encouraged families to reregister for garden plot numbers assigned to them by the mill last year. As the weather warmed, the Company posted this in the *News-Tribune*. The main road down on Railroad Street had been blocked off to automobile traffic and diverted to the back driveways to allow children the main street for play. Auto drivers were advised not to go in at the lower end of that street. Special Lindale officer J. R. Baron was given instructions to arrest and fine speeders who violated state laws.

In early fall of 1926, Hattie McClung's father, along with five other adult family members, traveled a hundred miles from Blue Ridge, Georgia, looking for work in Lindale. Two months later, he got off work and went after his wife and children. Hattie's remembrances are quoted and paraphrased in the following. "I had never been in a town and never seen such big houses with stairs. I must have run up and down those stairs at least a dozen times." The elder McClung bought new furniture, a new woodstove, and a "great big dresser" that Hattie could see all of herself. Although the new cookstove pleased Mom the most, the children rejoiced when new cotton bedding replaced the old-time mountain mattresses which were stuffed with straw and feathers. Doing better meant a duplex with a living room and kitchen downstairs and bedrooms upstairs, and no one locked their doors night or day. There was unheard-of running water from a shared faucet. Washtubs or pans were used for body bathing. Kerosene lamps provided lighting as in the hills, but soon Company electricity brought wonderment to the family. All floors were wood, which were scrubbed periodically with Red Devil Lye. There were no indoor bathrooms. In her book *Eighty Years of Memories*, she described the toilet facilities as located in a woodshed built on the delivery lane between rows of houses. "The seat was just a plank with two holes in it; the other opening was boxed off to give some privacy. Underneath was a wooden tub to catch the waste. They came by two to three times a week to empty this into an iron tank wagon pulled by a team of mules. If the help spilled any they threw lime over it." Heat for the duplex was provided by fireplaces with coal or wood stored in the same shed as the toilet. This was provided by the Mill at cost. The lure of jobs and amenities soon brought flocks of friends and relatives from the Ridges. Yet the duplexes were not all bliss. When a widow with seven kids moved in on the other side, there was chaos. "The kids would steal everything that would come loose—even our old hen and chickens...Oh, what a mess!" Still it was a lot safer in Lindale than in the mountains. Hattie remembers Blue Ridge being quite isolated where "we never saw anyone." Now she lived in a village with kids from everywhere. People flooded in from Alabama, Georgia, and other places searching for jobs. They talked and dressed differently unlike people in North Georgia.

By the time all the McClungs "got settled in," it was thought too late to enroll in school. In September, she fibbed a bit and enrolled in second grade rather than fourth because more playmates were in the lower class. She wrote later, "My folks thought that was all right as long as you were in school learning something...the school building was huge—two stories high with a basement; we saluted the flag and sang the 'Star Spangled Banner' and said the Lord's Prayer every morning. We had big blackboards and real chalkboard erasers. I had a new box of crayons. The boy in front of me stole my orange crayon and chewed it up."[89]

On February 12, 1988, Mrs. Vera Baker (Bob Baker's mother) of 207 Grove Street was interviewed by her first cousin Samuel Spence of Columbus State University. It is paraphrased in the following. Mrs. Baker had been living in the same house since 1911. She said, "That'll be 77 years this coming November." Mrs. Baker reiterated Hattie McClung's description of Millhouses. "All structures were duplexes with two rooms upstairs; each had a small porch and yard. Toilets were in the woodhouse outside. One spigot with a sink serviced both sides; we bathed in "big old washtubs, kind of like primitive days." We had no laundry facilities at all. Bare wooden floors were scrubbed. A fireplace and a little woodstove were our only heat. Later, the other side had hardwood floors, a chandelier, marble fireplace, and plastered walls thanks to the master mechanic who resided there. In November of 1958, we bought our house from West Point Pepperell. I paid $8.11 per week. At the time of the interview, the Mill was working good time. Hands were working two twelve-hour shifts and being paid for forty. At one time, all her children were employed by Pepperell. Mrs. Baker retired after forty-three years total with thirty-seven logged in the weave shop. "I worked six weeks learning to weave without pay. They pay them now and the shop is air-conditioned now with not as much lint. Oooh-wee that blue Chambray was bad for lint. My husband Stude Baker worked in the boiler room—great big coal furnaces used to heat water to turn the steam electrical generating turbines. I'd go take the stroller and take them [children which included two small daughters] down there at night and sit with him and watch the gauges. Of course now they use natural gas instead of coal."[90]

Former retiree from the electrical department Don Milton told the *News-Tribune* in 2007, "Those days were pure happiness. It was safe back then, and everybody took care of everybody else." Local *News-Tribune* columnist Pam Walker added, "Mill workers took care of each other's children when parents had to work. When there was a death or illness, mill workers cleaned their neighbor's house and cooked their meals. They comforted the families of their bereaved neighbors. They celebrated holidays and birthdays together." Former Floyd County commissioner Jim Givens (1991–1994) went one step further by saying, "Lindale was a Utopia south of Rome." Keith Baker is a retired US Navy commander living in Colorado. In a November 2020 interview, the 1974 PHS graduate reminisced about his boyhood in the Village. The youngster would walk over to the main gate and wait on grandparents to finish their shift. When asked what he remembers most about those times, his thoughts were a bit more visceral or deep down. "I remember the feeling of a steady hum coming from within the redbrick walls—and the fragrance of cotton that misted the air as it turned into cloth." As a youngster, Jo Stegall Jr. lived with his parents in Jamestown at 20 Terrace Street. When questioned about life in Lindale, he remembered there was camaraderie in the streets as the kids played together with a feeling of equality where no one family or person thought themselves better than the other. In the prewar, Colonel George Patton's Fort Bennington cavalry bivouacked in the nearby grove at Terrace. Where else in the world could an eight-year-old mingle with troops in his backyard? However, there was disappointment when Mom forbade sleepovers under army canvas. Nevertheless, it must have been exciting watching the cavalry saddle up on its way to Chattanooga. In two interviews, January, 31, 2022, and October 4, 2022, now retired DMD Jo Stegall Jr. (his father was longtime Company dentist) revealed, "The most unique experience about life in Lindale was the Sunday afternoon band concerts on the Village green." He continued, "When Paul B. Nixon's home talent band began to warm up, I would leave the baseball game and head to the grassy lawn of the auditorium. *It was the happiest time of my life.*" Nancy Smith Hunter is a retired Pepperell elementary teacher whose father, Garland Howard Smith, managed the Mill after Mr.

Harvey retired. In a personal interview on August 30, 2019, she told of a time caring for a Village friend with terminal illness. One day as the two talked about life after death, the subject turned to the hereafter and what it would be like. Finally, the dying friend asked, "Nancy, what do you think Heaven will be like?" Her reply was, "I think heaven will be a lot like Lindale."[91]

The Lindale Band

In 1907, Mr. and Mrs. Edward S. Nixon, along with daughter, Lucia, and eighteen-year-old son, Paul, moved from Chattanooga to Rome. A year later at the request of Captain H. P. Meikleham, the father and son were asked to organize a Company band.[92] Gammon noted in her research papers in page 67 that the Captain believed in wholesome recreation; hence, one of the agent's "prize hobbies" turned out to be his band."[93] The Tennesseans immediately began to search for talented beginners and experienced musicians, rounding up a group that was so enthusiastic, they purchased their own instruments and helped pay the director from their own pockets. Meanwhile, the Nixons opened a music store on Broad Street, which supplied the city with inventory for many years. To help fund the program, the Captain used admission charges from a motion picture machine set up in a mill store. In 1910, young Nixon traveled to Germany for study under noted teacher Van Lier. In his absence, Mr. Carlton Merck directed the ensemble. In 1913, the student returned to Atlanta, playing engagements and continuing his studies in arrangements and compositions until America entered World War I. The young musician enlisted and shipped out with the Fifty-Sixth Infantry to France where he received the Distinguished Service Cross for bravery in action. In 1920, Meikleham called again to take charge; consequently, the band grew very rapidly as it began to perform Sunday afternoon concerts in the warm months on the grassy green of the auditorium.[94] Occasionally in the 1930s, the crowd assembled in the baseball park for more comfortable grandstand seating. People from forty miles around came to enjoy the afternoon. There was always a variety of tunes and vocal solos during the two-hour concert, including "Tip Toe Thru the Tulips," "La Traviata," "Hinky Dinky Parley-voo," "Dixie," "The Merry Widow," "America the Beautiful," and "The Star-Spangled Banner."[95]

Perhaps the seeds of Lindale music were brought by the former hardscrabble farmers who now manned the looms. In Charles Spahr's 1900 work entitled *America's Working People*, he describes a first fact-finding evening in Lindale. "After arriving by train at 6:00 p.m. the ticket agent recommended a boarding place owned by a foreman of the Mill. As the parents were not home from work yet, the oldest daughter acted as hostess in preparing supper which was served at 8:00 for family and four boarders. In conversation the father/foreman revealed an interest in theology, politics and music." As a matter of fact, Spahr said, "The whole town was interested in music if we could judge from the amount we heard for an hour after supper." Traditionally country people are known for "picking and fiddling" on their front porches late in the day. His host observed that "there is more bad playing in this town than in any other in the country." Mr. Spahr agreed halfway but qualified his observation with, "The musical ambition of the village was decidedly a pleasant one."[96]

For the next seventeen years, Nixon stayed "behind the baton" before suffering a heart attack in 1939; in World War II, the group transitioned under H. Floyd Greer as the Pepperell State Guard Band. When this group was dissolved postwar, Ralph Champion Jr. and B. W. Moak headed up musical energy in South Floyd as it moved into the Pepperell School program; however, Paul B. Nixon remained as director emeritus.[97]

As an outgrowth of the Lindale musicians, Nixon helped organize and lead the Rome Symphony Orchestra, which gave its first performance on May 11, 1922; his artistic genius merited a citizen's award from the local chamber of commerce.[98] Almost a half century later, his Park Street ensemble would play its final concert in January 1957. Its founder passed away on November 28, 1962; he is interred in Myrtle Hill Cemetery.[99]

EDWARD RUSSELL "SLICK" MOULTON IN LINDALE

Cap'n said: "I want you to manage our baseball team and become principal of the High School." The twenty-nine year old young man thought a minute and replied, "You don't have a high school." The Cap'n responded, "I want you to start one!"

Just how Captain Meikleham found Slick at Auburn is unclear; probably it was his prowess as a baseball player/manager (his minor league career spanned from 1924 to 1926 and from 1928 to 1930. Baseball was the mill agent's favorite pastime; he believed interest in the sport relieved some of the mundane parts of millwork and was the glue that held the town together. By the late 1920s, several of Auburn's players performed for the Company-owned Class D representative during the summer months in addition to working at the mill for extra money. Also the agent undoubtedly was attracted to the school's technical studies in textiles. When offering the job at Lindale, which was now Pepperell Manufacturing Company, to Moulton, the Captain said, "I want you to manage our baseball team and also become Athletic Director, Principal and Superintendent of the high school." The twenty-nine-year-old Alabamian thought a minute and replied, "You don't have a high school." The superintendent responded, "I want you to start one!" At the time, Lindale school was grades 1 to 7.[100]

Lindale Baseball Club 1929 from left to right: back row—Moulton, first base (MGR); Stoughtenborough, pitcher; Griffith, pitcher; Howard (Jack Smith), second base; Pugh, right field. Middle row—Baker, pitcher; McDonald, pitcher; Currie, third base; Walker, utility; Hardwick, pitcher. Front row sitting—Alexander, center field; Poindexter, catcher; Stevens, catcher; Dobbins, left field; Woods, pitcher; Smith, shortstop (not in picture).

The first public mention of the new man came on Thursday, March 28, 1929, in the *Rome News-Tribune*. Charles Ogles's almost daily feature, "Lindale and Vicinity," reported, "Capt. Harry P. Meikleham, president of the Lindale baseball club, this morning announced positively that E. Russell Moulton better known as 'Slick' of Auburn, Ala. would pilot the Lindale club through the Georgia-Alabama league during the coming season…the mill leader is to be recommended for his judgment and success in securing so valuable a man to manage…The Class D league will begin play May 10, 1929." A schedule of 101 games would feature the locals on eleven Saturdays and the Fourth of July. From that moment forward into the middle 1980s, all levels of Lindale baseball were feared. Legend has it that every male child born in the Village is thrown a baseball—if dropped, he was sent to live with his grandmother in another town. Captain Meikleham gave Moulton carte blanche for expenses; all squads received first-class equipment and uniforms. This tradition continued for decades. His philosophy was simple, "Get a good team, pay 'em well, feed 'em well, but kick 'em off when they start loafing." The roster included players from ten Southern colleges; ours was the only mill in the world which owned a professional ball club in a *bona fide* league subject to the jurisdiction of Judge Kennesaw Mountain Landis, czar of professional baseball. Although the team was the Captain's hobby, it belonged to the Lindale people. Polly Gammon wrote on page 69 of her research papers, "The Captain believed as long as laborers get fair pay, comfortable and clean living quarters, and are given time and opportunity to enjoy either directly or indirectly the pleasures of healthful recreation, that the germ of communism, of strikes and lock-outs, will not find a place in which to plant its insidious tentacles." The players enjoyed the best attendance, sincere friendliness, devotion to the sport, and a bighearted director who followed the team everywhere. The *Rome News-Tribune* "Past Times" edition of August 2007 reported on page 46, "He also gave his athletes good jobs in the mill and let them off on Fridays and Mondays so they wouldn't be tired out on weekends."[101]

Nineteen days before the first official pitch of 1929, the excitement in the village was palpable as the diamond was "completely refurbished with the catcher's territory, box and infielders' positions around the bases inset with black soil that not only added to the beauty of the field, but was pleasing to the eye; hand lawn mowers manicured the sodded infield and outfield areas; the fences and stands were sprayed with dark green paint." Supervisor Earl Donaldson oversaw the program while Mr. Moulton finished his duties as head baseball coach at Auburn, which was actually two days after the beginning of the Georgia-Alabama season. Before that, Donaldson welcomed twenty-five players in tryouts on Saturday, April 23. After two exhibition losses, the Lindale squad met their new manager on Saturday, May 5. Slick must not have liked what he saw, for two days later, the *News-Tribune* reported, "'SLICK' MOULTON WIELDS AX ON 12 PEPPERELLS." An opening-season loss at Carrollton did not dampen the excitement for the next day's home opener on Park Street. Charles Ogles's "Lindale and Vicinity" column featured this headline: "ALL SET FOR OPENING GAME OF GA.-ALA. LEAGUE HERE SATURDAY AFTERNOON AT 3 P.M. ALL STORES IN LINDALE TO CLOSE FOR GAME, LINDALE BAND TO PLAY AND LARGE CROWD EXPECTED." He continued, "The band will be on hand 30 minutes before the first pitch and will perform between half innings. Everything in Lindale will be closed tight from 2:30 o'clock Saturday afternoon until after the game, and customers of all business places are asked to be governed accordingly. Those agreeing to close their places of business for the game are: Brittain Bros. Co., the Lindale Cafe, the Lindale Market, the Lindale Shoe Shop, the Schram Barber Shop, H.A. Duckett, store stand and market, Watkins Barber Shop, the auditorium, all departments, and the Car Line stand and perhaps the Bramlett Grocery Store."

Furthermore, Captain Meikleham thought he best close the Mill at three thirty every weekday afternoon of a game (starting time was four o'clock). On non-game days, the Mill would close at the usual 5:30 p.m. To offset loss time, the mill would start at 6:00 a.m. during the season and close at 3:30 p.m. Weekend contests would begin at the normal 3:00 p.m. first pitch.

Ideal weather and 1,171 fans saw the locals defeated for the second time by Paul Fittery's visiting Carrollton nine. A road trip to Anniston saw Slick Moulton take control of the team; he took the mound himself for the first contest which ended in a 4–4 tie. The wins were not coming as expected, but Slick told Charles Ogles, "With a little more defense in the outfield, his club could be on a par with any other." This was a brash statement for a team that was destined to lose its first eight games. However, five weeks into the schedule, Mr. Ogles reported Pepperell was on a roll, "Lindale All Agog over Baseball, Now Team Tops League." On Saturday, June 15, the squad swept a doubleheader from Talledega, 16–5 and 6–2. On Sunday, the *News-Tribune* wrote, "It was one of the wildest afternoons ever experience here. Manager Camp of the Indians swapped punches with Umpire Vick in the sixth inning of the first game but no blood was shed." By the end of June, the Pepps held on to first place with a 20–14 slate.

Monday, July 1, found all Lindale enjoying a ten-day vacation period. Charles Ogles reported, "There are quite a few visitors in Lindale, former residents, or those with relatives here, and there are quite a good number off fishing, or visiting friends and relatives." It was the "week of all weeks" as seven games were scheduled for the park highlighted by a double bill with Cedartown starting at two fifteen next Saturday. However, it was the Independence Day crowd that broke the record for attendance—1,100 paying customers![102]

A month later on August 8, Mrs. Russell Moulton gave birth to a daughter in hometown Mobile where she resided prior to relocating to Lindale. The newborn was named Clara Ellen (thereafter called Cissy) after her mother. The proud father slammed two home runs on August 16 against Anniston as his team continued to perform well in leading the second half season with a 20–14 record. People in Lindale are beginning to realize why their manager was dubbed Slick. Charles Ogles reported on August 19 that "our ball team eased off to Talledega." The squad reached there for the evening meal and off to bed for a good night's rest prior to a pair of contests. Villagers were informed on game day that updates would be posted by innings on the scoreboard at Brittain Bros. They would be available for the postseason also. The Pepps quickly increased their lead to four full games as they moved to 23–14 atop the standings, eventually winning the second half of the split season by 31–17. Unfortunately, Carrollton swept the postseason playoffs to become league champions; however, Lindale won the postseason attendance count easily. On September 11, manager Moulton left for Mobile to see his wife and newborn daughter. Their newly constructed bungalow in Jamestown would soon be ready for the family.[103]

Captain Meikleham loved baseball, and Lindale (called Meiklehamites by opponents) loved the sport. Floyd County has a long tradition of baseball. In postwar 1868, organized play was already prevalent with teams such as Constellation Base Ball Club, which competed with other nines in the city of Rome. The sport expanded when industry moved to the New South in the late 1880s. The *Rome Tribune-Herald* noted in March of 1901 that "just now there is a wave of enthusiasm throughout the south that predicts a successful revival of interest in the game." Although the local newspapers reported the sport sporadically, an early page 1 article in the

Sunday, May 12, 1895, edition of the *Rome Tribune-Herald* indicated the summer sport would take the lead as the boys were "already practicing with spirit." It added that S. B. Albea, a catcher from Cave Spring, and pitcher Sam Graham would provide a very strong battery for Rome. The paper also reported City Electric Railway has spent liberally on the North Rome playing grounds. The diamond was in excellent shape for the first contest on Monday, May 20, against Piedmont, Alabama, or Silver Creek. Game-day streetcar connections would be available to all fans. Admission to these games was 25¢ cents with 10¢ extra in grandstand; ladies were usually admitted free. Prior to a game against Atlanta, the *Tribune-Herald* stated on September 26, 1902, that "the local team [Rome] is now one of the best independent nines ever gotten together in the south." A year later, it also praised the diamond at Hamilton Park (present-day location of Barron Stadium) as "one of the finest ball parks in the South...one that could bring a major league team here for spring practice." Local stockholders met on April 8, 1902, in Rome to formulate a plan for entering the professional Georgia State League. It added that other surrounding cities were now showing interest in semipro or independent squads.[104]

For the next three decades, the sport bounced from sandlots, barnstorming, and various legitimate leagues sponsored by stockholders—the Georgia State, Appalachian, and Georgia-Alabama Leagues being prominent. Rome and Lindale took the lead in forming competitive squads—the Rome Hillies and the Rome-Lindale Romans. Playing venues included Hamilton Park, renamed Barron Park in 1925, and another unnamed field mentioned in the *Tribune-Herald* on Sunday, May 12, 1895: "The City Electric Railway Company has been at work on the *grounds at North Rome* and they are in excellent shape. They have spent a great deal...and are doing all in their power in the interest of the sport. The street car accommodations will be excellent." In 1915, Rome won the Georgia-Alabama championship while playing some of their games at "the driving range." In addition, the *Tribune-Herald* reported in July 1919 that "in a loosely played contest on the *Fairbanks diamond* in West Rome between a scrub team made up of part of the regular team and a few youngster, and the Fairbanks aggregation, the latter one by a score of 7 to 5. The Fairbanks team is going strong, having played nine games and came out victorious in seven of them. The batteries for Fairbanks were Chester, Horn, and McClain, and for Rome, Burnes and Moss."

Before 1914, the community produced various sandlot and independent squads which struggled to make ends meet. In 1912, Ms. Lillian Duke, who was a social worker by trade, became the manager of a Lindale Baseball Club. The petite village nurse and civic leader not only led the squad on several out-of-state games, she argued with umpires with whom she disagreed. A black-and-white print published in the *Rome Tribune-Herald* shows the "kindly faced Lady in White" with her starting nine. Some familiar names were identified in the photo, i.e., Roy Cook, Vernon Greer, George Chafin, Frank Roberson, Will Baker, and Earl Donaldson. Each player displayed TDC (the Dooley Club) on the uniform front; these old English letters probably indicated a sponsor. Frequently local well-known businesses such as Coca-Cola and Battey Hospital supported these squads. Polly Gammon wrote that the team played "a kind of cow-pasture pick-up games with clubs from the surrounding area, including Berry and Armuchee."[105]

Professional baseball coached by a Mr. Webber occurred in 1913 under the Georgia-Alabama association. A year later on Sunday, April 12, 1914, the *Tribune-Herald* reported mill master mechanic R. W. Van Tassel was elected to replace Webber with the hope of better financial conditions than heretofore. No figures exist to determine the losses of the previous year; however, in 1912, Rome Baseball Association reported a $3,000 loss on attendance of 21,209 for 51 games which is "poor to say the least of it." To help out, Lindale played a benefit game with Piedmont with the proceeds over and above the expenses of the teams, going to the Rome Baseball Corporation. Much of the Van Tassel program expenses are to relocate and build a new baseball park. The *Tribune-Herald* explained this on Wednesday April 22, 1914, "The location of the new baseball park will be moved from the old location [it was not identified] which was too far out of town." The new site just north of number three mill had for some time been used for street carnivals and showgrounds. A covered grandstand with comfortable seats for both home and visitors is under construction along with bleacher seats on the ground. Cushions may be rented for 5¢. Strict admission is 25¢ for grandstand and 10¢ for bleachers. A surviving 1914 photograph shows the home squad posed in front of this new grandstand. This league operated from 1913 to 1917 before disbanding. After 2½ years without baseball, Captain H. P. Meikleham spearheaded a reorganization in January of 1920. It was revived for 2 years in 1928 to 1929. It returned for a final time in the late 1940s. The Captain's community seemed to revere the sport more than others as they retained many of the team pictures and history in company publications.[106]

THE GREAT DEPRESSION (1930–1939) AND ROBERT DONALD HARVEY SR. (1899–1963)

He closed by saying, "There is not enough money in the world to make me leave Lindale…I know if any of us get hungry we will all get hungry together."

R. D. Harvey, general manager

R. Donald Harvey was born on June 23, 1899, and lived until July 5, 1963. Donald joined Pepperell Manufacturing in Lindale, Georgia, in 1920 as a twenty-one-year-old after graduating from Georgia Institute of Technology. He became plant superintendent in 1937 following H. P. Meikleham's sudden death and remained so until retiring in 1955. Mr. Harvey's civic and community interests were many, varied, and accomplished. He was chairman of the Board of Education of the Lindale Schools, a trustee of Darlington School for Boys, the Georgia Tech Research Institute, which primary purpose is the development of industry in Georgia and the South. He was elected to membership in ANAK, the top Georgia Tech student and alumni honorary society. He was a member of the Board of Regents, University System appointed by two governors, and past chairman of the Textile Operating Executives of Georgia in addition to presidency of the Cotton Manufacturers Association of Georgia. He was elected to the board of directors of Pepperell as one of only two Southerners in recognition of outstanding ability and leadership. For many years, he was a member of the regional executive committee of the Boy Scouts of America; chairman of the Lindale American Red Cross Chapter and secretary to Lindale Hospital Services as well as president of Lindale Charities Association; a member of Lindale Methodist Church board of stewards with past presidency of Auditorium Bible Class; Lodge No. 455 Free and Accepted Masons; American Legion McClain-Sealock Post No. 136; Order of Eastern Star Lindale Chapter No. 265; Oostanaula Tribe No. 38; Improved Order of the Red Men; Chi Phi social fraternity; a member of the board of directors of the National City Bank; a director of the Citizens Federal Savings and Loan Association; a member of the Floyd County Democratic executive committee; and a member of the Coosa Country Club. Mr. Harvey was a true sportsman; his hobbies were hunting, fishing, boating, and horseback riding.

The above extended paragraph describes the life accomplishments of Robert Donald Harvey Sr.; however, let us now explore the human side of the man who came on board Pepperell Manufacturing Company in the second decade of the century and stayed thirty-five years before retiring in September of 1955 because of health issues.[107]

Mr. Harvey was the grandson of Judge R. D. Harvey (1826–1887) a lifelong Floyd County resident and member of the Georgia Bar; he practiced law, served as mayor of Rome in 1857 before being named to Superior Court bench from 1870 to 1873. The judge died from injuries sustained from a runaway horse on March 12, 1887. His son, Robert Harvey (1863–1944), was also a member of the Georgia Bar; Robert was also involved in farming and real estate. In 1888, he married Ms. Annie Johnson; at the time of his death in March of 1944, the family resided at 605 West First Street. The union produced two children, Edith and R. Donald.[108]

Our subject was the third generation of Harvey men born (June 25, 1899) in Rome, Georgia. He grew up on the city's West Eighth Street as well as the Johnson Farm on the Etowah River. Early education was in the local public schools while secondary studies occurred at Darlington School for Boys, graduating in 1916. It was here he acquired the lifelong nickname Crip due to a broken leg suffered in a school basketball game. Following prep school graduation, a family scrapbook shows young Donald in a US Navy uniform. This time frame coincides with the Mexican border wars and the beginnings of World War I. He received a degree in textile engineering from Georgia Institute of Technology in June of 1920; four years later on September 11, 1924, the twenty-five-year-old engineer married Lila Willingham, daughter of Mr. and Mrs. Wright Willingham of Rome. The couple raised three children—Mrs. Edgar Johnson, Donald Harvey Jr., and Tom Harvey. There are three grandchildren, Edgar, Harvey, and Lucy Johnson.[109]

Mr. Harvey was hired straight out of Georgia Tech by Captain Meikleham in 1920. During the first four years with Massachusetts Mills of Georgia, he worked in every part in the plant. Addressing his community many years later, he said, "I remember quite well the experiences of working in the departments...You taught me a large part of what I know about manufacturing...A lot of you probably remember that, on many occasions, I was not a very apt pupil but you have put up with me anyway." We suspect that Mr. Harvey was just self-deprecating, for his people knew him as warmhearted, affable, and friendly—the daily millwork just endeared the young engineer to the shift hands. In 1924, he moved to Polk County's Aragon Mills as assistant superintendent and six months later was made head of the plant. In October of 1926, Donald returned to Lindale to work for what was now Pepperell Manufacturing Company. On January 1, 1930, he was promoted to mill superintendent and three years later named assistant agent to Captain Meikleham.[110]

The aforementioned position is much like the executive officer of a naval ship; he is expected to run the everyday operation leaving the commander to deal with major planning and strategy. Blessedly, the thirty-eight-year-old Roman learned his lesson well, for the captain passed away unexpectedly of a heart attack in New York on Friday, July 23, 1937. At midnight, Mr. and Mrs. Harvey, Attorney Barry Wright, and Henry Autry flew out of Atlanta to accompany the body to Charlottesville, Virginia. At 3:00 p.m. on Sunday, services were held in Christ Church before internment at the Jefferson ancestral cemetery in Monticello. Forthwith, the chairman of Rome and Floyd County Commissions issued a proclamation: "With hearts heavy in the sorrow that has come to us in the death of our beloved Captain Harry P. Meikleham…we ask that every citizen of Floyd County stop wherever they may be and bow their heads in respectful tribute to him at three o'clock Sunday afternoon." At the same time, his flock assembled inside the village auditorium to pay tribute. The captain's favorite song was "My Faith Looks Up to Thee"; it was sung by the entire congregation. The Reverend Fred H. Ray, pastor of Lindale Methodist Church, made an appropriate short talk; the vast assemblage stood in silent prayer at the conclusion of the service. As Lindale mourned, *News-Tribune* reporter Lang Gammon posted on the Sabbath that many other Lindale, Rome, and Floyd County folks traveled north for the sad occasion, Charles H. Edmondson, R. M. Wyatt, Bob Simmons, *T. P. Hay Jr.*, Comer Turley, Dr. Jo H. Stegall Sr., Hal T. Gilbert Jr., E. Russell Moulton, Lee Borders, Mr. and Mrs. A. A. Chapman, Ms. Mae Young, Henry Neal, B. W. Moak, Johnny Troupe, R. M. Gibbons, Earl Donaldson, Mr. and Mrs. F. D. Hand, Mr. and Mrs. J.D. Walker, and others.[111]

Two days after the funeral, R. Donald Harvey was named agent of Pepperell Mill. The 1,700-plus employees and the company had long ago grown to trust him; they knew him as a "young southern executive with technical training and a deep fatherly affection for his people." On December 15, 1937, the new leader met with his workers in the auditorium to give a state of the union address. He explained the current three-day workweek might run for months because stock of goods in the warehouses was increasing; in the last three weeks, the mill weaved 3,100 bales of cloth and shipped about 700. He praised the 1,400-participating-employee Christmas saving fund which totaled $40,000, yet he cautioned all to spend frugally in the coming yuletide season. He railed against unfair taxes which take 30¢ out of every dollar earned, adding to operating losses. There may come a time when we sell below manufacturing costs to survive; a current tax law forces all corporations to pay out practically all profits to stockholders rather than securing reserve funds for periodic downturns in the economy. A large cotton crop has dropped the price to 9¢ a pound; this harms growers as well as mills. They both make money at 15¢. At present, Congress was considering a bill that would reduce acreage. Mr. Harvey was concerned this would grossly affect our export market, which brings more money to Southern farmers than all other crops combined. The legislature was urged to place a tariff on jute used in bale wrapping as well as packaging. Some mills in the Carolinas are lowering wages; hopefully they could keep their pay a little above others in the area. He issued a challenge to the hands: "If we all work together and make our cloth of better quality and at a lower price than our competitors, we will all prosper." The streets and homes in the village were in excellent condition. Few people had been charged with drunkenness and "raising hell in general." He added that alcohol consumption was a personal business; however, on the street it became his business. Thanks to the annual physicals given to operatives by Dr. Methvin in the expanded first aid room, there had been less sickness this fall. The mill premises had been inspected by their insurance company; the engineer found all was well and their "safety first" program working well. One of the worst needs in the community was a large modern school building, but the agent could not predict when it would happen. Hopefully, the Mill would be running full-time by the next meeting. In the meantime, Mr. Harvey reduced house rent in half. He reiterated that his door was always open to all.[112]

NORTHWEST GEORGIA TEXTILE LEAGUE

The marriage was a natural—Mills and Baseball. Both rose together and, in the end, both shared the same fate of becoming memories.
—The eloquent Jim O'Hara, *Rome News-Tribune* staff writer, August 2007

In the offseason of 1930, minor league baseball shut down. Hundreds of players were released from their contracts; to these unemployed young men, the amateur Northwest Georgia Textile League which formed was godsent. It played twenty seasons from 1931 to 1954 minus the war years and fielded sixteen different teams including the original group of Lindale, Cedartown, Atco, Anchor Duck, Rockmart, and Tubize. The new organization was financially supported by local cotton mills. The players were paid to work in the mill and for performing on the diamond. Jim O'Hara wrote in August of 2007, "It was a marriage made in heaven—mills and baseball... hard times were balanced by good times at a baseball diamond sacred ground where the daily grind of working to try and make ends meet was replaced by balls, strike, hits and runs."[113]

In 2010, Dalton State College historian Heather S. Shores produced a wonderful paper about the league entitled "Working to Play, Playing to Work: The Northwest Georgia Textile League." On page 2, she contends that the mill villages of the early 1900s were self-sustaining—a place to live, eat, and shop—that baseball was a way to prevent workers from being idle after hours. There was no major league close by, nor national radio broadcasts or television superstations to bring the sport into living rooms. On page 11, Heather describes how the outing was a dress-up affair with ladies in hats and gloves and men in ties; entire families could walk to the games and enjoy an afternoon in the sun visiting, gossiping, or arousing a romance. Ken Burns contends that mills believed this encouraged teamwork and a way to spend spare time that might otherwise be "devoted to labor agitation."[114]

In his 1994 film documentary about baseball, Burns explains America's love affair with the game with a quote by Walt Whitman, "Well—it's our game...America's game...it belongs as much to our institutions...as our Constitution's laws." In the same year using Pbs.org/KenBurns/baseball/about, Burns added, "Nothing in our daily life offers more of the comfort of continuity, the generational connection of belonging to a vast and complicated American family, the powerful sense of home, the freedom from time's constraints, and great gift of accumulated memory than does our National Pastime."

In reality, Lindale was late to the game. Burns reported that by 1914, nearly every industry had a league. Railroads, steel, coal, meat-packers, automotive, banks, and even yellow cab fielded teams. Thousands turned out to watch their squads. On September 20, 1914, in Cleveland's Brookside Stadium, a hundred thousand watched as the Strollers downed the Cleaners 8–3. Simultaneously, women performed in a league with the Goodyear Girls, Westinghouse Maids, and the Miller Rubber Maids being prominent.[115]

Teams could carry fifteen to twenty on their roster provided they were white men employed by the mill; three young participants were allowed if their parents were operatives. The age of the team ranged from eighteen to thirty-five years. Shift jobs paid them $12 to $14 per week with an extra $4 to $7 for baseball. This was good money; however, it gave the mill economic control. On game days, the entire team was given light or no duty prior to the Saturday and Sunday games, which were always called after working hours. By 1938, Tubize added lights to their park, which added night contests during the week.

College players were sought after because of athleticism; they in turn could hone their skills in the summer months, not to mention earning good money doing it. Auburn, Vanderbilt, and Oglethorpe provided many collegians to the local rosters. Many returned to the area after graduation and rose to positions of importance in the companies. Several Textile players showcased their skills which led to athletic scholarships; Lindale standout Willard Nixon starred at Auburn for two years before being drafted by Boston.[116]

Editor's note: In June of 2007, historian Tom Klenc of McDonough, Georgia, produced a wonderful research guide of the entire life of the Northwest Georgia Textile League. His expressed goal was "to provide the reader an indexed summary of the *Rome News-Tribune* articles covering the League, teams and players, from 1931 to 1954." There are over three thousand news articles on the Textiles appearing during this period in the local paper. Unless otherwise noted, most of this era's entire documentation comes from his work. Rome's Sara Hightower Regional Library has on file an accessible copy of Mr. Klenc's work. This is page 45 of Mr. Tom Klenc's work.

1931

Monday, March 30. The league was set with six teams: Anchor Duck, Atco, Cedartown, Lindale, Rockmart, and Tubize. Officials had scheduled thirty games. The season opened Saturday, April 11. Pepperell Mill hired third baseman Jack Smith, shortstop Earl Donaldson, and Slick Moulton. Page 7.

1932

The league opened play on April 2. Captain H. P. Meikleham of Lindale was president of the association. The new Tubize Park opened on April 9 with a fence all the way around the field and grandstands with grass added to the infield. All three local clubs, Shannon, Lindale, and Tubize lost their opening games last week. Page 19.

1933

Thursday, March 3. Atco hosted the Petrels from Oglethorpe University this Saturday in an exhibition game. All the teams had several players with professional and college experience.

The league expected to exhibit Class D or better caliber of baseball. Sunday, April 2. At Lindale, Bill Gaston relieved Lukor in the third inning and kept the Shannon hitters guessing. Lindale surprised the "dark horse" Shannon, 11–4. Page 31.

1934

Sunday, March 18. Club representatives met and adopted a fifty-game schedule. April 1. In exhibition play, Lindale defeated Tubize, 17–9, at Lindale Park. Rockmart and Lindale appeared to be two of the strongest teams in the league. Monday, April 9. Lindale's Lefty Baker struck out eight batsmen in a 10–7 victory. Baker is a former Georgia-Alabama player. Page 45.

1935

Sunday, March 3. C. J. Wyatt was named association secretary, succeeding Slick Moulton; umpires were paid an additional amount and called only away from their hometown. This year, the league operated with a split season. In exhibition action, Tubize downed Lindale 6–0. Gaston and Moulton pitched for the latter. Page 57.

1936

Friday, March 6. Tubize increased its seating capacity to 2,650; the Cincinnati Reds and the Washington Senators played there on April 3. Just prior to their arrival, the Floyd County had a flurry of snow and wintry temperatures. Sunday, March 15. Manager Russell Moulton assembled the Pepperells. Returning players included catchers Bo Sheppard and Ralph Free, Joe Gaston at first base, Macgregor at second base, shortstop Earl Donaldson, Johnny Teat at third base, with Jack Gaston, Asa Wall, and "Shorty" Hall in the outfield. The pitchers were Ed White, Slick Moulton, Bill Gaston, Alfred "Shoat" Crump, D. Meroney, Lefty Covington, and possibly Byron Erwin. Leonard Bolt recovered from a foot injury. Page 73.

1937

Sunday, March 14. A thirty-six-game schedule began on April 10, which gave squads four weeks' training; three days later, the Giants and Indians played an exhibition game at Tubize Park. Cedartown-raised Whitlow Wyatt pitched for the latter. The Giants started their full lineup. Gene Baggett from Chattanooga was the new shortstop for the Pepps; he paired with last year's leading hitter outfielder Jack Gaston. The association's managers agreed that this year could be its brightest. On Friday, April 16, the bearded, long-haired House of David baseball team from Benton Harbor, Michigan, lost 15–1 to Pepperell. Moulton was wild in the late innings but had the visitors "eating out of his hand with a tantalizing curve ball." Thursday, May 6. The Army's Sixth Cavalry from Fort.
Oglethorpe was camped in Jamestown's grove. They played an exhibition game against Lindale before moving on to summer maneuvers at Fort Benning. Page 89.

1938

Tuesday, March 8. Lindale manager Slick Moulton cited the previous year's RBI leaders as Bo Sheppard, 29; Jack Gaston, 27; and Shorty Hall, 18. Jack Gaston was recognized as the best Lindale ballplayer. He led the club in batting average, hitting left- and right-handed. Gaston played the outfield and "gets them all that come his way." Tubize planned night games on Tuesday and Thursday nights. Lindale defeated Anchor Duck by the score of 20–6 with Shorty Hall going 6-for-6 at the plate. Page 103.

1939

Thursday, March 23. The league had seven teams this year; Lefty Rogers arrived from Chattanooga to pitch for Pepperell. For the first time, the top four teams participated in a post-season playoff. Thursday, April 6. The defending Southern League champions Atlanta Crackers will visit Tubize tomorrow at 3:15 p.m. Page 123.

1940

Sunday, March 2. The league opened with seven teams. March 12. Slick Moulton had a roster of Bill Cordell, second base; Shorty Hall, shortstop; Johnny Teat, third base; Aggie Lumpkin, outfield; Jack Gaston, outfield; Gene Baggett, outfield. Pitchers were Shoat Crump, Ed White, and Lefty Rogers. Players from local high schools, colleges, semipro, teams and professional organizations were expected. Sunday, March 31. The Atlanta Crackers and Brooklyn Dodgers played an exhibition game at Tubize Park next Wednesday. Lindale won the title by defeating Rockmart; however, the squad had to come back with four straight wins in the playoffs to claim the trophy. Pitchers Lefty Rogers and Raymond Stowe were outstanding in the series. Stowe hurled the final game that gave the Pepps their first Textile banner with a 7–4 win. Page 141.

1941

March 12. League directors met in Hotel Forrest and approved seven teams.
The season schedule was shortened by six weeks to accommodate increased operations at the Goodyear plants. March 13. Slick Moulton called for pitchers and catchers to report; he added three Auburn pitchers Jimmy Jordan, Walter Milner, and Lloyd Cheatham. June 16. Lindale came in second in the first half with a 7–5 record well behind Tubize at 10–1. August 22. Tubize won the league with a 20–4 record followed by Lindale with 16–8. The former swept Lindale in the playoffs 4–0 to claim the championship. Thursday, August 28. According to league secretary C. J. Wyatt, hard-hitting Jack Gaston of Pepperell won the batting title with an average of .435; he hit safely thirty-seven times. Eight other teammates batted .300 or higher with first sacker John Stowe, tallying .406; Gene Baggett followed with .385. Page 161. Late in the season, there was a hint of another conflict in the *News-Tribune* when Lang Gammon posted that "Lindale Defense Outfit Steps with Power Unit." The men dressed in full uniform with shouldered rifles

were put through the manual of arms before falling out and going to Barron Park where they drilled with a Georgia Power unit. As the baseball season faded in Lindale, the local newspaper printed an ominous message: "Konoye Places Japan on Wartime Footing." The last open-air band concert of the season occurred on the last Sunday of August with a large part being patriotic songs, "Victory March," "The Liberty Bell," "Stout Hearted Men," "Onward Christian Soldiers," "God Bless America," "Dixie," and "The Star-Spangled Banner."[117]

School superintendent E. Russell Moulton announced the 1941 opening-day enrollment reached 958 students; 643 pupils signed up for grammar classes while 325 were junior high schoolers. The old building housed grades 1 to 5 while the new building opened to grades 6 to 9 students. Ms. Estelle Weathers was principal for the lower grades. Mr. Moulton named sixteen schoolboy patrolmen for the year. Serving were Tommy Yarbrough, Donald Burkhalter, Hugh Padgett, Earl McClung, Kelly Stansell, R. L. Tidwell, and Wayne Davis. The high school guards were stationed at the Jamestown and Duckett's store corner.

Monday, September 1. Before one of the largest crowds to witness a Tubize Park game, Lindale downed Rockmart 3–1 to earn a spot in the World Series of amateur baseball; Lindale would defend its title against Tubize Rayons at home on Saturday, September 6, 1941. The Pepps lost the series in four straight beginning with the home opener, 6–3, followed a 6–4 loss on the road, a 10–2 defeat back in the village before dropping a series-ending 6–1 game on opponent's field. In early December, Mr. Moulton received news that his younger brother Pat was elected president of the Southeastern Baseball League. He was presently sports editor of the Mobile *Press-Register*.

Monday, September 15. Mill manager R. D. Harvey praised the South Lindale Church of God congregation in dedication of their new building. He noted, "I am fully aware of the many sacrifices you people have made in contributing to this building fund…I have never known a group who worked together any better or any harder.[118]

The prewar Textile League champions were the following:

1931—Cedartown
1932—Atco
1933—Cedartown
1934—Lindale and Shannon (cochampions)
1935—Shannon
1936—Shannon
1937—Shannon
1938—Tubize
1939—Tubize
1940—Lindale
1941—Tubize

LINDALE GOES TO WAR

*Charles H. Abrams is on board the destroyer U. S. S. Dale berthed in
Pearl Harbor. No word has been received about him yet.*
—Lang Gammon in the *News-Tribune* on December 10, 1941

This large thirty-one-page piece on World War II is comprehensive and uses three main sources which include publications *Lindale Goes to War* and *Home Front News* along with *Rome News-Tribune*. In almost every instance, the sources are noted in the text.

On Monday, December 8, 1941, the *News-Tribune* front page blasted the Japanese attack on Pearl Harbor with an ominous but misnomered "**U.S. Wars on Japan**." The next day, Lang Gammon reported, "No Casualties Confirmed Regarding Lindale Men." He then listed **Hudon Mathis**, **Raleigh Gribble**, **Owen Kirkland** and Sergeant **Donald Peacock** as serving in the Hawaii area. Three months later, **Raleigh Gribble**'s mother received a reassuring letter from her son, which said, "Mama, I know you remember me in your prayers. The Good Lord is watching over me." Also mentioned as safe and well were **Sergeant and Mrs. D. T. Edge**; however, no word had been received from **Udell Graham** who was stationed in Honolulu. Wednesday, December 10, 1942—Mr. Lang Gammon wrote that **Charles H. Abrams**, son of R. F. Abrams, of South Lindale was aboard destroyer USS *Dale* in harbor last Sunday when the "Japs staged their knife in the back aggression." No word had been received about him as yet. Later, it was known Radioman Abrams actually turned the alarm on his ship when the attack began; he would eventually serve sixty-one months on *Dale*. The DD received fourteen battle stars in such noted battles as Guadalcanal, Aleutians, Marianas, Betio Atoll (Tarawa), and Philippine Sea. Sunday, December 14—The *News-Tribune* headline appeared to be whistling in the dark with its page 1 banner: "**Axis Dealt Severe Blow on Three Fronts**." A day later, Second Lieutenant **Robert McCamy** of Pepperell's Unit 194 announced that local state defense corps troops would not be called out of their home counties for military duty. The *News-Tribune* reported on Tuesday, January 13, 1942, that Sergeant **Donald Peacock** of Hawaii's Schofield Barracks was "O.K. and not to worry." This was courtesy of a letter sent to his mother.

When the United States declared war on Germany and Japan in 1941, things began to change for the mill as production goals focused on preparing war goods. The people of Lindale took pride in knowing that a fabric familiar to men in the American Army, olive drab herringbone twill, came from the looms of Pepperell Manufacturing. This cloth was used to make some of the general fatigue uniforms worn by soldiers when they went about their daily work. Chambray for the Navy was confirmed by former employee **Richard Holcombe** who said his uniform was made of cloth manufactured in Lindale. One-third of the looms made cotton flannel for gun patches, process gloves, and bandages. (Editor's note: Unless otherwise noted, the primary source for personal news from the war is found in the mill's publications entitled *Home Front News*.)

Mill hands were working hard in the war effort and being paid well. Bob Baker provided us with a pay stub dated July 1, 1945; it shows that Mr. R. M. West logged 48 hours and received $48 before deductions. On page 19 of its August 2008 special edition of "Past Times," the News Publishing Company explained how the Mill did its part to help operatives in other ways, "The plant purchased four 40-passenger buses to transport employees living in outlying districts to and from work. Named the Wheeler Transportation Company, the transport service helped offset the wartime shortages of gasoline, tires and automobiles while providing employees with reliable ways to work. The service is estimated to have eliminated the driving of 216 autos averaging about 3,000 miles per car."

Growing up in Lindale and learning to swim in Silver Creek saved former weaver **J. W. "Jud" Penley's** life. When his ship USS *Yorktown* was hit by Japanese torpedoes and aerial bomb during 1942's Battle of Midway, the captain ordered abandon ship. He went over the side without a life jacket or any belongings. Jud thought, *Just stay afloat, that's all you do*. Several hours of treading water passed before rescuers finally pulled him from the oil-soaked sea. He was now aboard the battleship *West Virginia* and used the $25 bonus check recently sent from the mill to servicemen for purchase of new uniforms. **Edward "Bud" Hendrix** also worked as a weaver in the Mill. He was one of the first boys from Lindale to leave when the threat of war first came up. He joined the Navy on January 17, 1941. In support of the Guadalcanal operation, **Bud's** carrier, USS *Wasp*, was struck by 3 torpedoes from I-19 on September 15, 1942. The explosions were so bad, he received flash burns. Unable to control the resulting fires, the captain ordered abandon ship. *Wasp* was scuttled later that evening, eventually losing 193 dead in addition to 366 wounded sailors. The petty officer second class spent 3 hours in the water before being rescued. **Bud** survived the war after serving 5 years, 11 months, and 12 days and earning 2 Purple Hearts. In June of 1942, **Earnest P. Jones** sent word from Australia that he had arrived and was "doing fine." In July, news from "somewhere" in England had former outstanding Textile League player **Jack Gaston** with the US Eighth Air Force. His mother, **Mrs. L. L. Gaston**, of 216 Grove Street, also had sons **Bill** and **Joe** serving in the Army. Lifelong Lindale resident **Max Walker** was aboard troop transport USS *Barnett* when the First Marine Division waded ashore on Guadalcanal at 0900 on August 7, 1942. It was the first time to hear hostile gunfire. "I was scared, I'll admit that," he said later. At midnight, the Japanese fleet caught them unaware; the ensuing battle off nearby Savo Island was a slaughter. Walker personally witnessed the sinking of battle cruisers *Astoria, Quincy, Vincennes, Canberra,* and the *North Hampton*. In a 1993 *News-Tribune* interview, he said, "The next day we picked up thousands of survivors." At 214 B Street, **Mr. and Mrs. Marshall Throneberry** bid farewell to their son **Roland** who would leave in September for Naval Pre-Flight School in Athens. **Sergeant J. D. Rickman and Dovie Ann Bolt** were married in Silver Creek on August 8 just before he reported to Keesler Field, Mississippi. On August 8, **Ms. Maxine Smith** wedded **Lieutenant Ivan E. Hirshburg** in the Lindale Methodist parsonage; he would now report to Turner Field in Albany to receive his wings. Lang Gammon notified his readers on Monday, October 2, that pioneer Lindalean **William R. Erskine** passed away. He came to Lindale forty years ago from Lowell, Massachusetts, to oversee the Carding Department. William was noted throughout the textile industry for his ingenious ability.

On Monday, October 5, 1942, the *News-Tribune* printed part of Gene Dowdy's letter home:

> Boy, this Navy life is great. I am sure glad I joined the Navy instead of the Army. I bet I have gained five pounds already. The only thing wrong with the Navy is that they feed you too much, and is it good! They have the nicest bunch of officers, and fellows I have ever met. We get up at 5:30 every morning and go to bed at ten. Well, so long, write soon and I will do same. Love, Gene.

Three days later, the same paper followed up with "Shorty" Knowles's note home:

> Well, how's everything in Lindale these fine days? I guess everybody is busy doing their Christmas shopping now. I sure wish I could be home this year, but I guess I'll spend my second Christmas here in Texas. Well, I finally made the grade and finished school last Thursday and leaving for basic flying school in the morning. We are going over to Goodfellow Field, over at San Angelo, Texas. We get our formation flying and our night flying in basic, and they are bigger ships and everything. We also study radio and more navigation and weather. When I first joined the Air Corps I thought all we had to do was fly, but now I've found out different. We study weather reports, and by looking at the clouds and everything we can tell if it's going to rain or not I finished my ground school with an average of 75.3 for the whole course; not so good, but it's good enough to get by. My average was along with the rest, most of them in the seventies. I got my Christmas box from the Pepperell employees today and it sure was nice. I want to thank all the people who are responsible for it. The pen sure writes good and the other things were just what I needed, too. I'll send you my new address when I get there and find it out. I wish all my friends a Merry Christmas—"Shorty" Knowles.

On December 16, 1942, **Ms. Charlotte Earwood** of Powder Springs was wedded to **Radioman Third Class Charles Abrams**—Judge Harry Johnson officiating. Feature writer Lang Gammon posted an article in the Wednesday edition of the *News-Tribune* dated December 23, 1942, entitled "**General MacArthur Thanks Pepperell Employees**." The general's message read, "We are dedicating this Christmas Day to the defeat of our enemies…until there is peace on earth and good will to men…we, the soldiers on the firing line, give thanks to you soldiers on the production line for the sinews of war that make our victory possible." One week before this proclamation, **J. F. Powell**, **seaman second class**, wrote from Norfolk to Mill employees, "Received your Christmas package, and was really proud that the Pepperell employees remembered me. The gift was more than nice and I assure you that I'll always remember your kindness."

Beginning in the first month of 1943, a plethora of young local females joined the military. On January 14, the *News-Tribune* reported that **Bobbie Garner** has enlisted in the Naval Reserve. She would soon travel to Iowa State Teachers College for training. **Bobbie** had worked for Pepperell the past six years. Four days later, the same gazette posted that **Mary Ruth** Camp would be sworn in tomorrow as a Navy WAVE. In a month, she would report to Officer Training School at Iowa State College. **Mary Ruth** attended Lindale and Cave Spring schools and was a talented vocalist. By the middle of April, Ms. Camp was on the job at the naval air station in Lakehurst, New Jersey. It was reported on March 4, 1943, that **Hazel Chafin** had enlisted in the SPARS. She was a Cave Spring graduate, worked at Brittain Brothers, and was a valued member of the mill Spinning Department. **Hazel** would report soon to Hunter College in New York City. On February 1, 1943, Mr. Gammon notified the readers of his feature "Lindale News" that **Ms. Ruth Sanders** has enlisted in the women's branch of the Coast Guard known as SPARS. The popular Lindalean was a valued member of Brittain Brothers Company. She possessed a beautiful voice that was often featured in the Lindale Methodist Choir. **Ruth**, who was educated in Lindale and Cave Spring, served almost three years honorably. It was announced on February 12 that another young lady has enlisted in the Navy. **Mrs. Natalie Craton** would soon report to Cedar Falls, Iowa, for training. She attended Pepperell Schools and was a dedicated member of Lindale Baptist Church; **Natalie** graduated from Cave Spring High School in 1935.

On January 6, it was reported by the local newspaper that a former Pepperell employee, **Lieutenant Harry M. Gibbons**, was the commanding officer of Company B 705th tank destroyer battalion in Camp Hood, Texas. He recently spent a week with his parents in Lindale. On January 19, 1943, Lang Gammon received a letter from two former Lindale *News-Tribune* carrier boys. **Horsie Henderson** and **Buck Jenkins** were serving with the First Marine Division on Guadalcanal and sent word back to the local youngsters that they "be very thankful that you are not old enough to join in this type of work." On February 18, "News of Lindale" reported that **Private John T. Leonard** was a prisoner of the Japanese in the Philippines. His mother, **Essie**, was a Pepperell employee and resided in the Hollywood Community. The *News-Tribune* posted on April 14 that **James "Johnny" William Mathis** was recently commissioned as gold bar second lieutenant at Fort Benning; the gazette noted the promotion was a tribute to his "fine spirit and keen intelligence." **Johnny** grew up at 14 Central Avenue and was a mainstay of the Pepperell baseball club; he also worked at the mill.

In the summer of 1943, **Mrs. Laura Sealock** of 2 West First Street received a personal letter from the South Pacific, informing her that son **Herman Edward "Cooter" Sealock**, seaman first class, was killed in action. A shipmate of **Cooter** wrote Mrs. Sealock, "It was June, 1943 at 5:24 p.m. that we met our fate. It was our second day of sailing out of Sydney when the torpedo hit; everything happened so quickly that **Herman** really never had a chance. I'm certain he did not suffer, as he was in the part of the ship where the explosion occurred." Later, the **seaman first class** was given a military funeral and interred on Marlsborough Road, Sydney, Australia. The Navy Department indicated plans were made to return the remains home after cessation of hostilities. The young man was educated in local schools before joining the Pepperell Spinning

Department; he would have been twenty-two years old on his next birthday. Four months after death, he was posthumously awarded the Purple Heart medal, which was established by **General George Washington** at Newburg, New York, August 7, 1782. Secretary of the Navy Frank Knox later wrote **Mrs. Sealock** that "I desire to offer to you my personal condolence in the tragic death of your son." Lang Gammon noted in the *News-Tribune* that "**Cooter** was a normal, healthy American boy who attended the local Baptist Church, was full of fire and spirit and established an enviable record in baseball and boxing." The mother also had a son serving in the Army, thought to be in Iceland.

The *News-Tribune* posted on Friday, June 4, 1943, that **Sergeant Glenn Baker** returned home for the first time in seven years. He had served in the Aleutians, prewar Japan, China, Hawaii, and the Philippines. **Glenn** was headed to Fort Benning for Officer Candidates School. On June 6, the same paper said **Seaman J. W. Jarrell** has been cited for meritorious conduct in keeping with the "highest traditions of the Navy" for action off Guadalcanal last fall. The award was signed by William F. Halsey, admiral, United States Navy. Also in June, **Second Lieutenant R. A. Duckett**, son of **Mr. and Mrs. H. A. Duckett**, 5 Terrace Avenue, Lindale, reported to Rogers Field in Oklahoma for duty as a pilot.

Another Lindale airman, **Ensign Isaac Lanier Smith**, recently graduated from Naval Air Corpus Christi; he spent a few days with his parents at 113 B Street before reporting to Jacksonville Naval Base for operational training. A few months later, now **Lieutenant Junior Grade Smith** flew in the South Pacific as a dive bomber pilot. In July of 1943, **Emmett Cabe** was a gunner's mate aboard *LST 370* heading for the invasion of Sicily. For days, the beaches at Gela had been pounded by Allied naval guns and aircraft. On Invasion Day, the *370* raced toward the landing area, dropped its ramp in the sand, and unloaded its cargo of soldiers. "Then the crew saw four humorous signs placed a few feet apart just out of the surf which read: *Kilroy was here, so now are we, we're going to Berlin, you wait and see.*" Thirteen months later, there was no levity for **Cabe** on the Normandy beach. As the *LST* dropped ramp, a German soldier lay dead nearby in the sand with an arm outstretched. Remembering that fateful day many years ago, he said, "I have seen the face of terror, I have felt the stinging cold of fear, I have lived the times most would say are best forgotten. But at least I can say I am proud of what I was, a sailor." In August, Lieutenant Ivan Hirshburg had been given the Army's Distinguished Flying Cross for duty in the China-Burma-India (CBI) Theater. His wife, **Maxine**, is the daughter of **Mr. and Mrs. Albert D. Smith** of 216 C Street; she would graduate from UGA in December. Also in August, the War Department confirmed that **Smiley B. "Fat" Cooper** of South Lindale has been wounded in the Southwest Pacific.

On September 24, 1943, Lang Gammon announced the attractive mill-published book *Lindale Goes to War* was printed and being distributed as fast as possible. All service people and employees would receive a free copy.

On November 3, 1943, the feature "News of Lindale" reported that **Seaman Clyde Howard Roberson** was killed in action exactly one year from his enlistment. **His parents, the G. L. Robersons** of South Lindale, were notified by Navy Department telegram. They had two other sons both on active duty with the Navy.

The bold front page of the Tuesday, December 7, 1943, *News-Tribune* said, "**Battey Army Hospital Dedicated to Mercy.**" The 160-acre, $3,000,000 Army installation had been a "cherished dream" of many North Georgians, none more so than Rome Chamber of Commerce member **J. L. Storey**. The hospital represented "the community's part in the home-front phase of World War II." As the war progressed, movies were shown in the Lindale auditorium for soldiers from Battey. They found it to be their favorite place to visit on weekends.

As second shift ended on the twenty-third, mill workers received a respite from chores with a short Christmas holiday; regular hours resumed on midnight Sunday. The *RNT* printed on page 12 of the Sunday, December 12, 1943, edition that the London area *Stars and Stripes* reported on Thanksgiving that a Lindale soldier has the distinction of being the first American to stand guard at Buckingham Palace. Military policeman **Sergeant Lewis Baker** was usually out patrolling the capital city, but on this eve, he was assigned guard duty for a special party for general officers numbering three hundred. The group was guests of the king and queen accompanied by the two princesses. The day after Christmas, word reached Lindale that **Harry M. Gibbons**, son of **Mr.** and **Mrs. R. M. Gibbons**, has been promoted to the rank of captain. The former Pepperell employee was a graduate of Infantry School Fort Benning and Tank Destroyer School, Camp Hood, Texas. On December 29, a report from England said Brigadier General Pleas B. Rogers presented the Good Conduct Medal to Lindalean **Sergeant Lewis E. Baker**. In explaining the award, the General complimented the **Sergeant's** hometown, "True fidelity and trustworthiness are qualities which in themselves serve as unquestionable evidence of good character, and the qualities of character so demonstrated are clearly the result of home and family influence." On the last day of 1943, the War Department sent word to **Mrs. Maxine Smith Hirshburg** of 216 C Street that her husband, Ivan, was seriously wounded on a December 10 flight over Burma; the captain sustained a fracture to the right jaw, gunshot wounds to the left hip and right shoulder—additional information forthcoming. As a flight commander, he was recently awarded the Air Medal and Distinguished Flying Cross with Oak Leaf Clusters for outstanding service. Also on the last day of 1943, the *News-Tribune* reported **Marine Private Fred Maynor** saw combat in the November 1943 Battle of Tarawa; he is the husband of **Mrs. Iva Lou Maynor** of Lindale Motor Corps. Seven months later (May 8, 1944), **Fred** was seen on the village auditorium screen in *With the Marines at Tarawa*. The stirring color film was taken by combat photographers of the Second Marine Division and shows horrific action on the Pacific atoll. He wrote his wife afterward, "Came through with a burned leg, a skinned knee, and one trouser leg missing." He added, "It was no picnic." Somewhere in New Guinea, **Sergeant Robert Van Tassel** was awakened at 2:00 a.m. by an awful noise. Too frightened to breathe for a minute or so, he grabbed a flashlight in one hand and gun in the other to kill the monster. His buddies awoke also and approached to give help only to find a small anteater wandering about. Now he was known as **Ant Eater Van**. Later in the war, he would be wounded in the Philippines. At the same time, his brother **Private First Class John M. Van Tassel** would serve in Okinawa with an infantry company.

As World War II began its third year, there was somber news in Lindale. On Wednesday, February 16, 1944, the *News-Tribune* announced that **Mr. and Mrs. Clayton H. Hendrix** of 6 South Second Street were notified of the death of their son **Private First Class William**

H. Hendrix. The message from Washington read, "**The Secretary of War Henry L. Stimson tenders his deep sympathy to you in the loss of your son...Little that we can do or say will console you for the death of your loved one.**" **Report received states that he died on February 3 in Kwajalein Atoll, Marshall Islands, as a result of a wound received in action**. The young soldier was a machine gunner attached to an amphibious infantry unit. He was born in Lindale, educated in local schools, worked in the Weaving Department, and would have been twenty-two years old in August. His parents had three other children in the armed forces. **Private Quincy Mitchell** joined the Army in 1940 and saw active duty for several months in the South Pacific. It was reported on February 8, he had come home to Lindale with an honorable discharge and planned to go back to work at the Mill making chambrays and herringbone twills for the armed forces.

On February 22, 1944, the *News-Tribune* reported that **Mrs. H. A. Cole** of the Wax Community received the order of the Purple Heart, bestowed **posthumously** upon her son **Private Thomas A. Cole** who was KIA on December 2, 1943. A while ago, the private had volunteered for overseas field artillery duty in the Mediterranean area. He was a former Pepperell employee and just turned twenty-one last October. His uncle was Bob Baker, carding second hand in number three mill. Three days later, Langdon Gammon notified the people of Lindale of the death of **Private First Class William Dean Carver**. He was KIA on January 26 in Italy. **William** is the husband of the former **Ms. Blanche Duckett** of 5 Terrace Avenue. Before joining the military in October of 1942, he was connected with the Dyeing Department and was a member of the Methodist Church. In addition to his wife and parents, there were seven sisters and two brothers surviving. On a happier note, "News of Lindale" reported the marriage of **Mary Frances Piper** to **Private Stephen Pajor**. The ceremony occurred on February 3, 1944, in Borough of Manhattan. **Mrs. Pajor** attended Lindale and Cave Spring schools and was now on the nursing staff of McCall Hospital. The groom was serving with the Army Air Forces at Hunter Field, Savannah, Georgia. Also on the third, **Sergeant Palmer J. Bashaw**, husband of the former **Ms. Clara Duncan** of Cedartown Road, was reported MIA over Italy. The sergeant was a radio operator on a heavy bomber first seeing action in Sicily. On March 7, **Chief Petty Officer Roy R. Proudfoot** was pictured in the *Central of Georgia Magazine*. Roy, who was in his twenty-second year with the Navy, had duty "somewhere" in the Pacific. Father **H. L. Proudfoot** was a section foreman with the railroad. In March of '44, HFN posted that **First Sergeant Henry A. Bruce** has been recommended for the Legion of Merit in the Army Air Forces "somewhere" in Italy. In recommending the Lindalean for the coveted award, **Lieutenant Colonel Charles A. Plamondon** drew up the following order: "**Henry A. Bruce**, 34261752, now First Sergeant...with minimum personnel he maintained efficient and adequate guard at all times...he found time to instruct the men of the unit in drill and instructed honor guards...in addition, he personally supervised the training of French recruits...through long hours devoted to duty. Having the above in mind, I request **Sgt. Bruce** to be considered as a recipient of the Legion of Merit."

Mrs. Frances Roberson Knowles of 204 Walnut Street was notified by the War Department that her husband, First Lieutenant **William H. "Shorty" Knowles**, has been reported MIA (missing in action) since April 1, 1944, in the ETO (European Theater of Operations) area. A further communiqué confirmed the lieutenant bailed out of his Liberator bomber and was wounded prior to his capture by the Germans. A few weeks later, the enemy reported he has fully recovered.

On April 4, **Mrs. Nora Atwood** of 110 C Street received a thank-you from White House **private secretary Grace G. Tully**, stating that **President Roosevelt** appreciates so much the crocheted service flag sent earlier in the year honoring his four servicemen sons, **James, Elliott, John, and Franklin Jr.** He also acknowledged the friendliness and goodwill evidenced in the accompanying letter. Later in April, **Mr. and Mrs. Roy Penley** of 109 B Street received a cablegram notifying them that their son **Sergeant David B. Penley** has been liberated from a Nazi stalag. His plane was shot down twenty-one months ago over Gelsenkirchen, Germany. In May, **Private First Class Edward L. Jackson** was awarded the Purple Heart for action on the Anzio Beachhead. **Ms. Verna Gaston** of Lindale Motor Corps was among the members of the latest nurse's aide class graduating at St. Peter's Episcopal Church, Rome. The group supplements the regular staff in civilian hospitals. Later in the war, the *Home Front News* (*HFN*) reported that Lindale's goal for a war loan drive was $80,000, but it went "way over the top" with $102,875! The newsletter then reported that in an eighteen-month period, forty-seven employees did not miss a day's work.

On Tuesday, June 6, 1944, Lang Gammon reported that Lindale Methodist has announced a special prayer be given tonight for the coming Allied invasion of France. A few days later, **Mr. and Mrs. W. B. Ellington** were notified that their son Staff Sergeant **Raymond W. Ellington** was injured in France on June 6, 1944, and has been awarded the Purple Heart. He was a member of the Eighty-Second Airborne Division. Sadly, Private **Dewey L. Williams**, son of the **Reverend and Mrs. Joe Williams** of Silver Creek, was killed in action on June 24, somewhere in France. He had volunteered for service in May of 1941. On Sunday, January 28, 1945, a memorial was held at Wax Missionary Baptist; three church speakers and the Wax Quartet and Choir led the service. On January 25, **Mrs. Iola Williams** of 25 Yarbrough Street was notified by the War Department that her husband, **Private First Class Grady Williams**, has been wounded in action in Belgium. A few hours before the telegram arrived, Grady called home. **Private Frank Connell** wrote that he is in Italy and sees **John Jennings** and **Raymond Corntassel** quite often. Lieutenant **James W. "John" Mathis** had been wounded in action in France. He is married to the former **Rebekah Sanders**. Also, **James "Trigger" Treglown** has been wounded in France; the communiqué stated the private accounted for four German snipers before he was injured in the right leg. On the lighter side, **Mrs. Joe Knight** was spending two weeks in California with her husband, Staff Sergeant **Joe V. Knight**, who was stationed in Van Nuys. In June of 1944, two former Pepperell employees, privates **Leroy C. Phelps** of the Weaving Department and **John C. Potts** of carding, were with the Eighty-Second Airborne Division which captured Saint Mere Eglise in Normandy on D-Day. The small town was a primary junction to feed German reinforcements to the coast; however, the Eighty-Second parachuted in behind the enemy lines three hours before the beachhead landing. The mayor of the small hamlet asked the *fourragere francaise* be awarded. In June of 1944, manager **Earl Donaldson** was in Lindale striving to field a decent sandlot baseball team. He commiserated with fans, "They're either too young or too old."

On July 4, 1944, Langdon Gammon posted that **Parks H. Durham Jr.** was KIA. He was the brother of **Mrs. Mark Groves**. The number 26 defined an unfortunate pattern in **Durham's** military career. He was wounded in action on September 26, 1943, rejoined his company on December 26, and was killed in action on January 26, 1944. Incidentally, former Lindalean **William Dean Carver** died on the same day with the same unit. **Mrs. Jim V. Groom**, of 312 Park Street, had been notified by the Army that her husband, **Sergeant Groom**, is missing in action in France. His wife was the former **Mildred James**. On July 9, the War Department notified **Mr. and Mrs. C. H. Edward** of 304 Park Street that **Army Private John H. Edwards** has been wounded in France; John worked in the Spinning Department prior to enlisting. **Mr. and Mrs. Bob Baker** of the Wax Community received word on July 24, 1944, that son Private **Clarence O. Baker** has been seriously wounded in action in France. He was now hospitalized in England. Three days before, another Lindalean was also injured in France and was now convalescing in England. **Army Private First Class Donald H. Greer's** parents who reside at 4 Terrace Avenue had been notified of the leg wound. **Donald** was a lifeguard at the auditorium swimming pool prior to military service. **Ervin Coolidge Green** wrote his parents the **L. E. Greens** of Lindale that he had met up with Lindaleans **Albert Roberts** and **Roland Ellington** in Italy.

Sergeant **Joe Paul Henderson**, formerly of the Spinning Department and now a member of the veteran 894th Tank Destroyer Battalion in Anzio, had been decorated by Corps Commander General Crittenberger. The Lindalean was wounded last spring near the beachhead. It was learned later there was more to Paul's story. In 1992, he told the *News-Tribune*, "I was mess Sergeant when I got hit. I had no business being on the front line, but I was just doing something a little extra for the men." He continued, "I'd go up one morning and cook hotcakes for one platoon and the next morning I'd go up and cook them for another platoon. I had to go under the tanks, which were dug in, and that was when I got hit." His unit, the 894th Tank Destroyers, 1st Armored Division, logged more than six hundred days' actual combat, which was an all-time combat record for Americans.

Henderson said, "We spent the entire time fighting." In appreciation, the French people awarded the unit *Croix de Guerre avec Etoile de Vermeil*. **Sergeant Oscar F. Kay** was also recognized by France. Oscar worked in the Spinning Department prior to the war while several of his families were now connected with the weave room. In October '44, Marine Private **Alvin D. Satterfield** was wounded by shrapnel on Guam, Marianas Islands. In other action, Major General V. E. Prichard cited Private **Martin Connell** of Lindale for "courage, devotion to duty, and disregard for his own life" in rescuing a wounded soldier to safety.

A casualty release from Washington announced the death of **Seaman Lonnie Paul Studdard** who went down with the destroyer *Warrington* on September 13, 1944. The loss was due to a great Atlantic hurricane near Bahamas; only 73 sailors of a crew of 321 were rescued. **Pharmacist's Mate First Class Chubby Garrett** would soon return home from the South Pacific after thirty months of action. His parents resided at 219 Grove Street. Private **Harry G. Lovell** of Silver Creek, Route 1 was reported MIA since September; however, the War Department just informed his parents, **the John D. Lovells**, that their son is well and returned to his outfit. In October of 1944, Corporal **Robert Mount**, US Army, who had spent a number of months in the Pacific theater, was on a thirty-day furlough at home with mother, **Mrs. R. B. Mount**. America had not lost its sense of humor however; in an Army hospital, one nurse warned another, "These are dangerous cases. They are almost well."

Corporal **George W. Melton** was on a short leave after being away for over four years serving in the China-Burma-India Theater. The War Department notified Mr. and Mrs. **L. R. "Jack" Burkhalter** that their son Private **Ralph H. Burkhalter** was killed in action in Italy on September 14, 1944. He was educated in schools here and was formerly connected with the Spinning Department. A month later, more bad news came to Lindale when Private **Clarence E. Burkhalter** Jr. of the Parachute Infantry was reported MIA in Holland.

The commanding officer of Sergeant **John L. McClinic**, whose father was groundskeeper at the Pepperell Baseball Park, had been given a citation for his "soldierly qualities, fine spirit, loyalty to duty and his leadership over men."

September 1944—If anyone on Park Street wondered if the war was almost over, the *HFN* dispelled the notion; the following men were called up by the draft:

- Willard Edward Bridges
- James Albert Bryan
- George Leslie Curry, Jr.
- Robert Harry Fritz
- Odell Debbs Hall
- Walter Alexander Moore
- Donald Lester Ray

The best of luck to each of you.

Mr. and Mrs. George M. Chafin recently welcomed their daughter **Hazel Ware** home for a week; **Hazel** was a member of the SPARS and was stationed in Washington, DC. **Trigger Treglown** was recovering in an English Army hospital from wounds suffered in the drive on Saint Lo, France. He was hit by German machine gunfire while wading across a swamp to make contact with another unit. After field medics came to his rescue, the private first class said, "They are great guys and they can't be beat." **Ms. Claudia Stepp** had been elected to succeed **Mrs. Harry Foss** as captain of the local Red Cross Motor Corps. Boatswain's **Mate James Abney** was on home leave after serving in the assault force for Sicily, Anzio, and Normandy invasions. **Mrs. Mary Bruce** of 103 Park Street had heard from twin sons, **Methvin**, who was in the invasion of Philippines, while eighteen-year-old **Seaman Melvin** was aboard USS *Biloxi* in the same area. In 2014, Rome native coach **Larry Bing** was going through a hope chest kept by his mother; inside was a nondescript book that Bing immediately identified as his deceased father's wartime journal aboard the light cruiser *Biloxi* (nicknamed *Busy Bee*). Aboard were **G. L. "Curly" Bing, Melvin Bruce**, and **Charles Bert Payne**; the three local boys were fast friends who saw many Pacific battles together including the Philippines, Iwo Jima, and Okinawa. Lindale **seaman Bruce** remembers the ship getting hit by a torpedo and Japanese planes dropping a bomb on them. **Curly Bing's** journal confirms this dated November 23, 1944: "We hit Luzon at 0600 and at 1215 we had our first surprise attack in a long time The Japs fired torpedoes and hit us with dive bombers at the same time. It was a surprise attack for our radar didn't pick up the planes."

Later, Bruce humorously recalled hanging out at bars on shore liberty and getting left behind by the *Busy Bee*. Marine Corps Commandant **General A. A. "Archie" Vandergrift** has awarded the Bronze Star and Purple Heart medals posthumously to Private **Martin James Camp** whose parents reside in Silver Creek.

When Navy Shipfitter **James C. Fincher** served aboard the repair ship USS *Regil* in the Philippine Islands, the crew would trade food supplies with the locals for parakeets, mongooses, and monkeys. One sailor always brought his male monkey to open-air deck movies to which his pet scampered about, stealing white hats before running up the mast. Pandemonium prevailed as the animal performed broken field running as swabbies tried to retrieve their covers. In the melee, the playful primate would rappel down a guide wire as the crew tried to grab him. A thick coat of grease applied to the escape route puzzled him for a while until the little animal countered by using his long tail for traction.

On August 4, 1944, Private First Class **William Roberson** was reported wounded somewhere in Italy. He was the son of **Mrs. C. I. Roberson** of South Lindale and was connected with the Weaving Department previously. Two days later, word was received that **Sergeant Jim V. Groom** is MIA in France; his wife is the former **Mildred James** of 312 Park Street. In the 1944 summer heat of Burma, Army Radioman **George Melton** had shed all but his shoes and shorts. He watched casually as two P-47 Pursuit planes glided down the runway; a miscalculation brought collision and high octane fire. One pilot escaped through his cockpit while the other struggled with his shoulder straps. The young man from Park Street watched as the fires grew, and the duty rescuer struggled with his asbestos suit. With explosion imminent, **Melton** quickly ran to the plane and used his hunting knife to free the pilot and drag him to safety; for this feat, our hometown hero won a Bronze Star. In the spring of 1944, Private **George Trotter** was undergoing basic training at Fort Knox, Kentucky, where he recently qualified as expert on the machine gun. In February of the same year, **Lieutenant Virginia Proudfoot** of the US Nurse Corps visited her parents in Jamestown. The *HFN* posted, "**Good Luck, Pvt. Trotter!**" The War Department notified Mr. and Mrs. **Clayton Hendrix** that their son Army **Private First Class William H. Hendrix** was killed on February 3 in the Pacific area. **William** was awarded the Purple Heart posthumously. In August of 1944, the **Reverend and Mrs. Joe Williams** of Silver Creek were informed of the death of their son **Private Dewey L. Williams**; he fell somewhere in France. Also in August, Private First Class Fred **Burkhalter** wrote from his foxhole in France that he had met cousin **John Burkhalter**. They enjoyed reading the *HFN* together. Also in August, **Ms. Mae Young** retired as village nurse after a quarter century of service. **Army Private Lloyd M. Robinson** had been overseas for sixteen months without seeing anyone from Lindale; then he "finally run across" three old buddies **Sergeant John Jennings Jr.**, **Corporal Raymond Corntassel**, and **Private Frank Martin Connell**. On August 10, 1944, Silver Creek Methodist Church recognized young men who have gone to war: **Norman Lee Burkhalter**, **Milburn H. Bruce Jr.**, **Sherman R. Baker**, **G. W. Trotter**, **Harry S. Farrer**, **James L. Farrer**, **Joel B. Roberts**, **William P. Roberts** and **Douglas Gresham**. Four days later, information was received that **Army Private First Class Hershel J. W. Wooten** has been wounded in France; he is the son of **Harvey N. Wootens** of Lindale and husband of **Maidred Adams Wooten**. Ten days later, Lindale could not catch a break, for it was announced that **Private Theodore Smith** was also wounded in France and was now hospitalized in England. He was married to the former **Grace Baker** and the son of the **H. R. Smiths** of 14 South Third Street. On August 23, Lindale native **Sergeant Robert T. Ford** took matters in his own hands in destroying a German half-track and personnel threatening his unit. He was awarded the Silver Star for gallantry in action against a numerically superior enemy. Robert made his home with uncle **Marvin H. Pendergrass** of 320 Park Street. On September 6, 1944, *News of Lindale* reported that nineteen-year-old **Marine Private Alvin Satterfield** has been wounded in the Pacific theater; **Alvin's** grandmother **Mrs. Ida Satterfield** had "a son, five grandsons and seven nephews serving overseas with the Armed forces." The next day, Lang Gammon's feature printed that **Army Private Alfred F. Moon** has been wounded in the leg; his parents, the **O. R. Moons**, of South Lindale were informed the injury occurred in Italy. **Alfred** was employed in the Spinning Department prior to induction in December of 1940. On October 10, 1944, **Mr. and Mrs. Raden Sullins** received notification that son Private **Jack Sullins** was MIA in Germany. **Private Sullins** survived and later told the *News-Tribune* in August of 1992 that he was "plain old walking infantry," carrying automatic weapons, flamethrowers, bazookas, and everything else. He tramped through Anzio, Naples, Rome, and southern France. In the latter action, he was captured and taken to Stalag 7A near Munich. After receiving no word for months, the **Sullins** family assumed **Jack** was KIA. His brother **Starling** helped liberate the same POW camp; however, his brother had been wounded in a camp bombardment and removed to a nearby Catholic hospital and later, after liberation, to a stateside medical treatment center. Unfortunately, none of his letters reached Lindale. On his return home, he said, "I thought they knew I was alive, but they didn't. I walked around the house…and there was Daddy sweeping the porch. He just dropped the broom…and called my youngest brother to get Mother from the Mill. I thought they would squeeze me in two before they turned me loose."

Sergeant **Frank C. Stone** recently wrote the *HFN* that his air group celebrated its two hundredth mission in early December. **Major Glenn Miller** and his orchestra performed at the event. A few days afterward, the noted band leader was MIA and later confirmed KIA over the English Channel. Lindale icon **Nath McClinic** was not supposed to be in combat; he was assigned to an amphibious Duck ferrying supplies to the Japanese island of Iwo Jima. Things changed when Navy Seabees ashore were all killed. **McClinic** was ordered to the beach where the Fourth Marine Division desperately needed supplies. He was under constant enemy fire for several hours. Days later during an air raid, he received severe burns to his arms and shipped out to a hospital in Hawaii. **James C. Fincher** was from Silver Creek; he was stationed in New Georgia (Solomon Islands) near a PT anchorage that berthed Lieutenant John F. Kennedy's famous PT-109. Fincher said Japanese planes came over nightly to bomb the small torpedo boats, but most times, the enemy bombardiers would miss their targets and pound them. Sometimes the Navy boys would cause them some grief as they came barreling into the docking after night patrols. Because their latrines were mounted over the surf, these small crafts would hang them as they roared by. Humorously, their crew would paint an outhouse on the bow as a trophy.

In January of 1944, **Ms. Virginia Fritz**, daughter of **Mr. and Mrs. Frank Fritz** of 123 C Street, had been voted the perfect pinup girl by a platoon of the Army Medical Corps in the combat zone of Germany's Siegfried Line. The soldiers discovered her picture in the Mill's publication of *Lindale Goes to War*. Their commanding officer was **Captain Field C. Leonard**, son of Pepperell president **Russell H. Leonard**. As teenagers, Corporal **Edward Henderson** of 207 Park Street and Private First Class **David C. Jenkins** of 311 Grove Street were compadres in Lindale, Georgia. With trust and friendship, they joined the Marines together and left for Parris Island, South Carolina, on December 29, 1941. For twenty-nine months, they fought the Japanese with the famed First Marine Division on Guadalcanal and Peleliu. Both were now at home on furlough; their first separation would occur soon when **Corporal Henderson** traveled to Florida and **Private First Class Jenkins** to New River, North Carolina.

By February of 1944, the *HFN* reported that Lindale has 758 boys in the armed services. In the last publication of the year, the readers got a worldwide sample of Lindale's servicemen and women:

England	Pvt. Lumas L. Gable Sgt. Frank C. Stone Pvt. Robert E. Johnson Pvt. Ernest Winters Pvt. James C. Moore	Pfc. William E. Cargle Pvt. Joseph Ray Keith Pfc. Jeremiah Brown Pfc. E. P. Steadham
Ireland	Cpl. Ernest F. Bruce	
France	Pfc. Fred Stokes Cpl. Fred Burkhalter Pvt. Ernest Winters Cpl. Lester D. Hughes Cpl. John Burkhalter Pvt. Leroy C. Phelps Sgt. Groover Gilbert Sgt. Herbert Dean Butler	T/5 Eugene Richardson Pfc. Grady Earl Bradshaw Cp. George H. Denson Pfc. Arthur Murphy Pvt. George J. Hudson Lt. Owen Kirkland Pfc. Robert Bruce Cp. Joseph R. Keith
Austria	Pfc. Clyde J. Sparks	
Belgium	T/4 Fred Burkhalter Pvt. R. R. Roberts	Pfc. James C. Moore
Holland	Pvt. Leroy Phelps	
Luxembourg	Pvt. O.A. Satterfield Sgt. Russell A. Covey Pvt. Melvin M. May	
Guadalcanal	Cpl. Paul S.H. Terrell	
South Pacific	S/Sgt. Robert L. Wade	

Aleutians	Pvt. Albert Bray	
India	Sgt. Ernest I. Bobo S/Sgt. Eddie McHenry Cpl. Robert B. Kyle	Pvt. James E. Hancock Pvt. V. D. Hollingsworth Cpl. Robert B. Kyle
Italy	Pvt. Arthur B. Kitchen Pvt. Lloyd M. Robinson Pfc. William E. Roberson Pvt. Frank M. Connell Pvt. Grady C. Lacey Pfc. Fred Stokes 1st/Sgt. Henry A. Bruce	Pvt. James Hall Cpl. Norman L. Burkhalter Sgt. George B. Hughes Pvt. James N. Moon Sgt. Samuel R. Eden Pfc. Harry Farrer
Corsica	Pvt. Harold L. Bolt Sgt. Carl R. Keener	
NEI	S/Sgt. Richard C. Stager	
Belgium	Pfc. James C. Moore Pvt. R.R. Roberts	
Hawaii	Cpl. Raleigh Gribble Capt. Harry M. Gibbons Pfc. Roscoe Bradshaw	
New Guinea	Pfc. Carl G. Wilson Pvt. Grady Dean Mathis Pfc. Methvin S. Bruce	T/Sgt. Clifford Smith Cpl. Earl Cabe
Saipan	Pvt. Henry C. Tolbert	
Germany	Pvt. Norman S. Baker Pfc. William H. Moon Pfc. Roy J. Treglown Cpl. Ben W. Blanslit S/Sgt. Ernest M. Calloway Sgt. Lindsey F. Brewer	Pfc. Tommy Sheffield Pfc. R. R. Roberts Pfc. Fred J. Hutchins F. Sgt. Charles Paul York Pvt. Moses Lewis Mathis Sgt. Carl R. Keener
Philippines	Pfc. Carl G. Wilson T/5 Ned R. Neal	Pfc. Methvin S. Bruce

Sardinia	S/Sgt. George L. Johnson
Marshall Islands	Pvt. Henry C. Tolbert
Czechoslovakia	Sgt. Hubert Carver

In February of '44, the Gammon newsletter reported Pepperell has manufactured 13,996,855 yards of herringbone twill for the Army and has weaved 36,719,998 yards of chambray, which would make 15,000,000 shirts for the Navy (the mill became the country's largest manufacturer of chambray). During cotton-picking season, Rear Admiral W. B. Young cabled Lindale that all sailors wear bluebell chambray shirts manufactured by Pepperell, for they were light, comfortable, and had prevented many combat flash burns. **Mill manager R. Donald Harvey** said the past year saw enough cloth produced to equip every serviceman with seven shirts apiece. The mill was currently producing 170,000 yards per week of tent twill for the Army. Later in the summer, "News of Lindale" reported in a Mill absenteeism checkup showed 47 employees have worked 18 straight months without missing a shift. In July of 1944, **manager R. D. Harvey** invited all employees to view *Cotton at War*. The movie "leaves no doubt as to the vital importance this material plays toward an Allied victory." It finishes with a stirring quote: "In the mills and factories at home, the cotton workers are fighting a war. Every man and woman who spins, weaves, cuts and sews—everyone whose hands touch cotton, is helping to contribute his part of the pattern of freedom." A year earlier at the Production Awards, **William C. "Bill" Duncan** was recognized as the Mill's oldest point of service employee. He came from Dalton in 1894 and helped install the first spinning room frames in his lifelong department.

On page 2 of the July 1944 *Home Front News*, the following were listed as home on furlough:

- Private C. L. Bagley, Camp Mackall, North Carolina
- Private First Class Randy Brewer, Colorado Springs, Colorado
- Private Claude M. Brown, Fort Eustice, Virginia
- Corporal Henry Johnson Jr., US Army
- Private First Class N. E. "Teck" Milton, New Mexico
- Ernest Ray Lucker, US Navy
- Ross Rogers, US Navy
- Specialist Second Class Natalia Craton, Glenco, Georgia
- Private Clarence E. Bryan, Everett, Washington
- Private First Class Charles F. Brown Jr., Fort Lewis, Washington
- Private First Class Clarence B. Bradshaw, Fort Dix, New Jersey
- Sergeant Johnnie Stroupe, Camp Gruber, Oklahoma
- Private Harold L. Bolt, Everett, Washington
- Sergeant Harry P. Helton, Cherry Point, North Carolina

- Sergeant George P. Barton, Cherry Point, North Carolina
- Machinist's Mate Second Class Edward "Buster" Bramlett, US Navy
- Private Paul Alton Walraven, Fort Jackson, South Carolina
- Aviation Ordnanceman Second Class William E. Dowda, US Navy
- Captain William E. May, US Army
- Seaman First Class Robert P. Hutchins, US Coast Guard
- Private First Class Mather M. Garrett, New Port News, Virginia
- Corporal Jack W. Holsomback, Fort Ord, California
- Houston C. Holbrooks, US Navy

On August 7, 1944, the family of **Private First Class Jesse Donald Brown** received the dreaded cablegram: "The Secretary of War desires me to express his deep regret that your son **Jesse**." The young man was Lindale and McHenry educated and belonged to the Baptist Church. His mother, Mrs. **W. R. Graham**, and wife, the former **Lorene Chafin**, survived. He was KIA in France.

On September 19, **Mrs. John Christian** of 16 West Second Street had been notified that her brother **Army Private Edgar Beauford** is MIA in the ETO; another brother, **Private Leon Beauford**, was wounded on June 6. On Thursday, October 5, 1944, the War Department notified **Mr. and Mrs. L. R. "Jack" Burkhalter** that their son **Private First Class Ralph H. Burkhalter** was KIA on September 14, 1944, while serving in the Italian campaign. He was educated in the Pepperell Schools and worked in the spinning room. Forty-seven days later, **Grady Howard** and family of 212 Walnut Street were notified that brother Army **Private Max Howard** was killed in action in France on September 12; another brother, Private **George V. Howard**, was KIA in Italy on October 18, 1943. On October 8, **Mrs. David Thompson** of 211 Garden Street had been informed that her brother **Second Lieutenant James C. Rogers** had been wounded in Italy; no other details were available. Three days later, **Mr. and Mrs. Bob Baker** of the Wax Community again received bad news from the War Department; their twenty-year-old son **Private First Class Clarence Baker** was seriously wounded in France. **Clarence** previously worked in the Spinning Department. Another son, **Robert M. Baker Jr.**, of the Medical Corps, died in February of 1942 when his B-29 Flying Fortress went down in Brazil, killing the entire crew. **Robert** was the first Lindale casualty on foreign soil. He was also employed in the Spinning Department and worked there for seven years before entering service. A third son, **Charlie M. Baker**, was now serving with a tank destroyer unit in the ETO. A day later, the War Department notified the **Melton family** that their son **Private James Wesley Melton** was seriously wounded in France last month. **James**, who was a carpenter by trade before the war, had a brother, **Clifford D.**, serving in the Navy. On a happier note, **Mrs. Joe Knight** recently spent two weeks with her husband who was stationed in Van Nuys, California. **Staff Sergeant Robert L. Wade** had been assigned to the Air Apaches unit, a hard-hitting bomber strafers in the Southwest Pacific. He was educated in Lindale and an employee in the Mill. His brother **Clarence** was in the Navy. On October 25, 1944, **Private First Class John Jenkins Jr.** was reported MIA in France; his parents reside at 311 Grove Street. **John** was connected with the Spinning Department previously; he has a brother, **Private First Class David C. "Buck" Jenkins**, who had spent twenty-nine months with the famous First Marine Division in the Southwest Pacific. On the same day, **Clarence E. Burkhalter Jr.** was reported MIA in Holland; he was with a parachute infantry unit which took part in the Normandy Invasion. His parents, the **C. E. Burkhalters**, lived on Cedartown Road. One day later, the local newspaper printed that **Seaman Second Class Henry Ford**, husband of **Mrs. Evelyn Kines Ford**, of 2 Central Avenue is serving aboard the USS *Texas*. The old thirty-year-old battlewagon was straddled by a German battery off Cherbourg during the invasion and was now being refitted in the Brooklyn Navy Yard. In late October, the *RNT* reported that **Private First Class Luther Salmon** was with the ETO's Eighth Air Force as an interior guard for heavy bombers; he was connected with the dyehouse of the Lindale plant. On Sunday, October 22, 1944, word reached Lindale of the wounding of **Sergeant H. F. Stansell Jr.** Born in the village, the **sergeant** worked in the Finishing Department before seeing action in Germany. In late October, word from "somewhere" in Italy said **Private First Class Hubert Sitten** has been wounded; the former mill employee was serving as an infantry automatic rifleman with the Fifth Army.

In November of '44, **Seaman First Class Marion H. Barnes** wrote the *HFN* from his duty station in England that he is going to be married to a girl from Wales, **Ondina "Babs" Richards**. The staff responded with, "Our very best wishes to you both." News from the cloth room was that music was now piped in for employee enjoyment; "Sunrise Serenade" and "Paper Doll" were the favorites. On November 15, "News of Lindale" reported the Bronze Star for meritorious service in France was presented to **Sergeant Lindsey Brewer**; he is married to the former **Frances Abrams** and the son of **Mrs. Cora Brewer** of 2 South Third Street. Lindale received bad news on November 30, 1944, via Lang Gammon's column; a casualty list from the War Department revealed two Lindaleans, **Army privates first class Alvin Hesler** and **Joseph W. Hinton**, who were wounded in ETO action. There was no information as to the severity of the injuries. **Alvin Hesler** was formerly connected with the Carding Department. Word was received on December 1 that **First Lieutenant R. A. Duckett** is now convalescing in Battey General Hospital; he was a veteran of thirty-eight missions on an attack bomber in New Guinea. The Lieutenant is the son of **Mr. and Mrs. H. A. Duckett** of 5 Terrace Avenue. *Home Front News* reported **Private Earl Shaw** as MIA in Italy; the War Department notified his mother, **Matilda Shaw**, in December of 1944. Earl is the brother of **Coy Shaw**, cloth room, and the nephew of **P. J. Youngblood**, second shift guard at number one mill gate. **Johnnie Eugene Stroupe** mailed his Purple Heart home from France. He was hurt on September 15 while fighting with Patton's Third Army. The *News-Tribune* printed on December 4, 1944, that **Corporal Henry M. Johnson** has been wounded in France. His parents lived on 12 South Second Street; Henry was educated in Lindale and Cave Spring schools. He was connected with the Mechanical Department of Pepperell. On the eleventh, Lang Gammon's "News of Lindale" reported that **Mrs. G. A. Baker** of Silver Creek was notified that her son **Private First Class Sherman R. Baker** was MIA in Germany; he was connected with the Spooling Department of Pepperell. A second son, **James M. Baker**, was with the Navy in Norfolk. On the twelfth, the War Department notified **Margaret Westmoreland** Ivy of 311 D Street that her husband, Infantry **Private First Class James F. Ivy**, was killed in action in France. **James** was an Alabama native who was educated in Huntsville and Auburn. On the same day, **Mrs. H. S. Fritz** of Silver Creek received a Purple Heart for her brother **Charles D. Helton**; the Army private was seriously wounded in France a month ago. Five days before

Christmas, **Private Johnnie Cochran** was KIA. **Johnnie** was the husband of **Minnie P. Cochran** of 312 D Street; he was employed in the number three picker room of the Carding Department. During December's Battle of the Bulge, **L. C. Stager's** Tenth Armored Division was trapped by the Germans in Bastogne, France. Although they were under constant fire from the enemy, his platoon found time to procure and cook turkeys. Just as it was ready to eat, the brass passed the word to move out. He said later, "We did, but we took our meat with us." Seven years earlier on May 23, 1937, Lang Gammon featured then high school senior **L. C.** in a *News-Tribune* article entitled, "Stager Displays Shining Example of Will to Win." It explained that the son of Mr. and Mrs. Dave Stager of the Barker community would receive his diploma tomorrow night at Cave Spring High School. Gammon wrote that "this in itself is not unusual for a number of students will do the same. However, this young man has been attending classes every day after working second shift (3:00 to 11:00) in the Carding Department. Just think it over, school during the first shift then to the Mill for the second shift—We salute him."

The January '45 issue of *Home Front News* reported, "The mill closed down for the Christmas holidays on Saturday, December 23, at 8 a.m., and the old familiar whistle blew again on Tuesday, December 26, at 8 a.m. We all had a very nice Christmas, but our thoughts were constantly of the boys and girls in the military."

Private First Class Trigger Trelown received a leg wound during the drive on Saint Lo; he spent time in England convalescing before being moved to the general hospital in Tuscaloosa. Rifleman **Private Harry G. Lovell** of Silver Creek, Route 1, was back with his outfit in Italy after being reported as MIA since September 28. On January 2, "News of Lindale" reported that **Corporal Nicholas "Nick" Powers Jr.** was fighting in eastern France with the 397th Infantry Regiment. His unit was "driving piston-like" against the middle of the German lines near the Rhine River. **Nick's** parents reside on Route 1, Lindale. Also in January of 1945, the Bronze Star for heroic and meritorious service was awarded posthumously to **Private First Class Martin James Camp**, USMC; the medal was presented in Silver Creek to James's father, **William M. Camp**, on behalf of **Lieutenant General A. A. Vandergriff**, Commandant of the Marine Corps. The Camps have two other sons serving in the military. The **Raden Sullins** family received word on January 7 that son **Private Will J.** is a prisoner of the Germans. He had been MIA since September of 1944. Two other sons were serving, **Louis Sullins** of the Navy and Army Private **Starling E. Sullins**. On January 10, 1945, **Mr. and Mrs. J. D. Stager** of Lindale Route 1 received a letter from their son **Loranza C. Stager** (affectionately called **Molly** by the family) who was with General Patton's Third Army, which was still engaged in the Battle of the Bulge (December 16, 1944–January 25, 1945). The private praised the Red Cross for doing a "swell job." He added, "They give us coffee and donuts daily. It helps plenty just to see an American girl who can speak to you in your own language. They wear G. I. clothes, boots and all. They wade the mud and live a very rugged life." The *News-Tribune* reported on January 12 that **Private First Class John Jenkins Jr.**, formerly of the Spinning Department, was no long MIA. His parents, **Mr. And Mrs. John S. Jenkins**, of 311 Grove Street, said their son was back with his unit in France after going missing on December 9, 1944. On January 21, the *News-Tribune* printed that **Private First Class Robert H. Duke** is serving with the Air Transport Wing "somewhere in France." The radio operator kept Douglas C-47s on destination throughout the UK and the continent ferrying high-priority passengers, mail, and cargo. He is the son of **Mr. and Mrs. Jesse Carl Duke** of Lindale Route 1 and was connected with the Spinning Department previously. One day later, two Lindale soldiers were reported wounded. The first, **Army Private First Class Donald H. Greer**, had been injured for a second time (the first was at La Haye de Puits on July 7 of last year) in France fifteen days ago. His mom, **Mrs. Vernon Greer**, lived at 4 Terrace Avenue. The other Lindalean, **Private First Class Leon Beauford**, had also been hit twice; the first occurred on invasion day last June, and the latter happened recently in Belgium. **Mrs. John Christian** of 208 D Street had been informed of her brother's misfortune. On January 23, "News of Lindale" reported **Sergeant David New** has been cited by **General H. S. Hansell Jr.** of the Pacific theater's Twentieth Bomber Command for "hard labor, ingenuity, and a kind of stubborn will that typifies the spirit of American pioneering; you also made with your own hands a place to live and a place to work, overcoming obstacles which were not foreseen." The officer was referring to the construction of a B-29 air base on Guam Island. **Sergeant New's** wife, **Mrs. Pauline Brown New**, and their son, **Norman**, resided at 304 B Street. Column three of the same publication brought sad news to Silver Creek. **Private First Class William Keith Holmes Jr.** was killed in action. The private, known affectionately as **Bill**, died on Christmas Day 1944; he was the only son of the late **W. K. Holmes Sr.** and a nephew of **Mrs. W. J. Pitts** of Route 1. On January 29, Lang Gammon reported that **First Lieutenant Hollis Smith** is returning to Lindale for a much deserved thirty-day furlough; the lieutenant had completed fifty-two missions over German-occupied territory as navigator on a B-17 Flying Fortress. His wife is the former **Lucille Barton** of Gather Park and a member of the McHenry faculty. **Hollis** was a 1943 graduate of Mount Berry College. The following day, "News of Lindale" printed that **Mrs. John Maloney** of 21 Betts Street had received a letter from son **Army Private John Thomas Leonard** who was a Nippon (Japanese) prisoner of war. **John** reported his health is good and sent best regards to friends in Lindale. In February of 1945, **Mrs. G. A. Baker** of Silver Creek was notified that her son Private **Sherman Robert Baker** was MIA in Germany. He was connected with the Spooling Department before joining the Army. His brother **Seaman Second Class James M. Baker** was stationed in Norfolk. Staff Sergeant **Robert "BW" Woodard** was serving in England providing antiaircraft protection for cargo and troop ships in the channel waters. January 11, 1945—**Army Corporal Buel Nelson "Dee" Meroney**, whose parents live at 107 C Street, was home on a twenty-one-day leave; he left for overseas on September 24, 1942, and had seen duty in New Zealand, New Caledonia, Guadalcanal, New Guinea, and the Russell Islands. He is married to the former **Sarah Blue** and worked in the Weaving Department. Lindale had a bit of excitement on February 17, 1945, when **Brittain Brothers** was robbed of $600 in silver. On February 21, **Max Gaston** stared at death through his gunsight on carrier USS *Saratoga*; six suicide planes (kamikazes) had gotten past the Iwo Jima picket destroyers, and one had a bead on the Lindale native. "I had him in my sights. I could see the pilot grinning as he dived toward me but there was no way to stop him." The enemy pilot missed by mere feet, crashing just above the young Marine, killing four shipmates. All told, the attack caused 315 casualties on the *Sara* but not **Max**. A month before, the War Department regrettably notified **Mrs. C. E. Schram** of 301 Grove Street that her son Private **First Class Charles Edward Schram** of the Army Air Corps was accidently killed in Karachi, India. The message stated, "Six of his closest buddies served as pallbearers." **Charles** was previously connected with the Weave Department of the mill; five sisters and three brothers survived. Army **Private First Class Aubrey W. Reynolds's** outfit ran into seven pitched battles with the Japanese on Leyte Island. The successful penetration was led by Filipino guerillas supporting **Aubrey's** Twenty-Fourth Infantry. Also in February of '45, **Fireman First Class Paul Alton Kilgo** spent thirty days' leave with his wife and son after overseas duty. He would soon report to amphibious training in Norfolk.

Staff Sergeant Robert "BW" Woodard was stationed on the south coast of England manning gun positions that protected the port and channel waters. Aerial Engineer Staff Sergeant **Clyde V. Roper** was in the China-Burma-India Theater flying the longest aerial route in the world—the notorious Hump of the Himalayan Mountains. Sergeants **Joe Paul Henderson** of 215 C Street and **Oscar F. Kay** of Wax Community were members of the 894th Tank Destroyer Battalion. Both have been awarded the *Croix de Guerre avec Etoile de Vermeil* given by French troops fighting in the Italian front. Private **John E. Brannon** of George Patton's Third Army after receiving the Combat Infantry Badge said, "It's just another pretty medal, but there's no doubt about it, the man that wears it has seen plenty of hell." Former Weaving Department employee **Walter E. Stroupe** was now a paratrooper fighting in the mountains of Leyte Island, Philippines. In the same theater Technical Sergeant **Robert L. Wade** was a radio gunner on a B-25 Mitchell bomber. The former plant employee had flown 48 missions and 276 combat hours with the 345th Bombardment Group in the Pacific theater. Marine Corps Private **Frank Penley** had been wounded in Iwo Jima Island. A bullet or shell fragment hit his breast and right arm, cutting a shirt wallet in half before clipping his dog tags. Sergeant **Ernest I. "Shorty" Bobo** was on a 21-day leave at the home of **Mr. and Mrs. J. G. Welch**. He had been overseas for 29 months and carried 2 battle stars. **Shorty** was affiliated with the cloth room. Private **Roy M. Nesbit** had shipped a German rifle to his brother C. D. of Wax Community. He is the husband of the former **Mabel Holcomb** of Silver Creek, Route 1, and worked in the Weaving Department before the war. Corporal **Richard Lee Gilmore** was attached to a tank destroyer battalion in the ETO. He wore four major medals on his chest and was connected with the weave room. **Lee Mathis** of the finishing room was watching a motion picture called *Fury in the Pacific* recently; suddenly he recognized his own son Army Private **Clyde C. Mathis** wading ashore on a Japanese-held island. **C. W. "Gabe" Bramlett** Jr., son of **Judge and Mrs. Bramlett**, had been granted an honorable discharge from the Navy. He and wife, **Hazel**, were guests on 127 D Street. The George Hutchins family announced their son Seaman First Class **Robert P. Hutchins** has been awarded an honorable discharge after 3 years' service in the US Coast Guard. After 36 months in the ETO, Staff **Sergeant Edward N. Jackson** had returned to Lindale. The former Paint Department associate brought with him 8 battle stars, the ETO ribbon, Presidential Unit Citation with oak-leaf cluster, the *Croix de Guerre avec Palme* (received from General de Gaulle), and the Good Conduct Medal. He is the son of **Mrs. J. F. Jackson**, 109 Park Street, and married to the former **Pauline King**. Private **Grady L. Lewis**, USMC, was in the Naval Hospital, Charleston; he was wounded in Okinawa with the 6th Marine Division. **Grady** wrote the *Home Front News* recently and told us how much he enjoyed it. **Edward H. Hendrix** of Lindale was a petty officer second class aboard the carrier *Essex* when the Japanese began kamikaze attacks. Off Okinawa, a suicide plane was hit and exploded just before it reached **Edward's** battle station. Falling shrapnel came down on him, bringing "a million dollar wound." He said later, "I still carry some in my back." In February of 1945, *HFN* reported **Fireman First Class Paul Alton Kilgo** was home from overseas on a thirty-day leave; he would spend the time with his wife before going to amphibious training in Norfolk. *HFN* also reported that **Mrs. John Maloney** of 21 Betts Street received a card from her son **Private John Thomas Leonard**, who was a prisoner of the Japanese. The note says his health is good and sends best regards to his friends. **Mrs. John Christian**, sister of **Private Leon Beauford**, told the February '45 newsletter that he has been wounded twice, once on June 6 in Normandy and again while fighting in Belgium; his mother, **Mrs. John Christian**, lives at 208 D Street. In the same month, **Winston D. Teat** of the Quartermaster Section in France had been promoted to corporal; **Winston** was a former Pepperell employee. Also in March, another Japanese prisoner of war, **Private Cecil W. Colley**, mailed this letter home from the Philippines: "Hello Mamma, Daddy and all. I am well and all right." **Private Colley** was captured early in the war by the Japanese. His family last heard from him on August 8, 1941, just before being shipped out for the PI. Also in March, Private First Class **Clarence O. "Bud" Landers Jr.** was awarded the Combat Infantryman Badge for action against the enemy "somewhere in Germany." A Lindale man had been awarded the Soldier's Medal for rescuing "three wounded Americans from a minefield." in Granville, France. **Private First Class Gilbert Steadham** performed the deed near Granville, France, last August. He is married to the former **Nellie Garrett**; his brother **Elbert Steadham** served with the Army also. **Private Joseph L. "Abie" Gaston** had been awarded the Purple Heart for action in Belgium; he was an ambulance driver with the 30th Division. Former Pepperell employee **Winston D. Teat** had been promoted to corporal with the Quartermaster Corps in France; he also participated in the Italian campaign. Everyone in Lindale was glad to see **Captain Hoyt Holcomb** last month; he has been in a convalescent hospital in Daytona Beach, Florida, after receiving wounds in the European theater. The Captain's awards were amazing: Presidential Unit Citation, Combat Infantryman Badge, Silver Star, Bronze Star, Purple Heart with four Oak-Leaf Clusters, Good Conduct Medal, Pre–Pearl Harbor Ribbon, and European Theater of Operations Ribbon, and three Combat Stars.

On March 17, 1945, Undersecretary of War Robert P. Patterson informed the plant, "I am pleased to inform you that you have won for the fourth time the Army-Navy Production Award for outstanding achievement in the war effort." It was not an easy task, for employee turnover was massive. Personnel manager W. E. Betts sometimes hired 200 to 300 people a day. The huge drain to the war effort and the nomadic existence of workers accounted for much of this. Also, "some simply found textile work not to their liking." And yet the quality of fabric improved due to dedicated hands that helped train new people continuously while putting in 6, 7, and 8 shifts a week (Mr. Harvey instituted a 48-hour week in February of 1943 with time and a half paid over 40 hours). Records for the month of January show that 3,223 hands worked a total of 680,828 accident-free hours. One longtime hand put it simply, "The more hours we work, the fewer hours our boys will have to suffer the hardships of war."

At three o'clock on Saturday afternoon, April 14, 1945, all machinery in the Pepperell plant was stilled in memory of **Franklin D. Roosevelt**. Manager R. D. Harvey proclaimed, "In deep respect for our late President, a great leader and outstanding American of our generation." By April of 1945, Private **Carl L. Green** had been in the Pacific theater for thirty-seven months with an antiaircraft artillery unit. The former Weaving Department hand was now spending a twenty-one--day leave at his parents' house on 110 F Street. Also in May, **Sergeant H. F. Stansell Jr.** had been wounded for a second time in the ETO. His parents resided at 315 D Street. The *HFN* reported in the same month that **Sergeant Lewis E. Baker** of the Army's 707th Military Police Battalion spent last summer patrolling the famed Red Ball supply route across Northern France. The **Throneberry boys, Fred and Roland**, were furloughing at their parents' house at 214 B Street. The brothers have not seen each other in four years. **Corporal Earl Cabe**, son of **Mr. and Mrs. J. W. Cabe** of 312 B Street, saw action in the dramatic retaking of Bataan and Corregidor, Philippine Islands; he was formerly with the Spinning Department. Radio operator **Private First Class Robert Harry Duke** and crew were forced to bail out of their plane while flying the Hump. Fortunately, the former Spinning Department employee had been found and returned to his unit. Air Force **Sergeant Robert L. Wade Jr.** was on a thirty-day furlough in Silver Creek. **Robert** had completed fifty missions in the Pacific theater. A casualty report from the Army listed Private **Wingrave P. White** as wounded in ETO combat.

During the war, movies continued to be shown in the auditorium; soldiers from Battey Army Hospital enjoyed weekend visits to watch Hollywood's latest flicks. Marine **Sergeant Paul W. Shiflett Jr.** spent a short furlough in Lindale with his grandmother **Mrs. A. D. Miller**. According to recent information published in April of 1945, Staff Sergeant **James V. Millican** of the Sixth Army Rangers helped liberate more than five hundred American prisoners near Cabanatuan, Luzon, Philippines. The **sarge** is an eighteen-year Army veteran. The mission occurred after trekking twenty-five miles behind Japanese lines. Also in April, **Staff Sergeant and Mrs. Robert Woodard** were to be congratulated upon the birth of their son **Robert Jr.** at Floyd Hospital. The sergeant was presently serving in Holland. Another blessed event occurred in the fourth month when **Marine Corps Corporal Willard Maxwell "Max" Gaston** and **Ms. Sara Emily Dooly** were united in marriage by **Reverend J. V. Jones** of Second Avenue Methodist Church. The sergeant had been serving in the Pacific theater for several months. Silver Creek's **James M. Baker** could be one of a kind. He served eleven months early in the war with the US Army but was discharged due to illness of his father; later, he joined the Navy and was now serving in New York. Also in May, Sergeant **H. F. Stansell Jr.**, whose parents lived at 315 D Street, had been wounded a second time in Germany; he was presently hospitalized in France. **Mr. and Mrs. Lee Cox** of Route 1, Silver Creek, had been notified that son **Harold L.** has been wounded and evacuated to an American hospital in Paris. **Private Frank Penley** was wounded in Iwo Jima while fighting with the Fourth Marine Division; he had evacuated to Pearl Harbor. **Seaman First Class Calvin Clifford Piper** had seen nineteen months of sea duty in the Pacific. He would soon be home for a short furlough.

There was jubilation in Lindale with the announcement of Germany's surrender on May 8, 1945, but concern for our troops in the Pacific area. **Mr. and Mrs. J. C. Duke** were relieved to hear their son **Robert Harry** was returned to friendly forces after being forced to bail out over the China-Burma-India supply route. Also in May, **Mr. and Mrs. M. C. Throneberry** of 214 B Street welcomed their Navy men sons **Fred** and **Roland** home on leave. First Lieutenant **William H. "Shorty" Knowles** had been freed from Prison Camp Stalag Luft I, near Barth, Germany. The first officer bailed out of his B-24 Liberator bomber on April 1, 1944. Shorty participated in a number of missions over enemy-occupied territory before being downed. He was the son of **L. R. Knowles Sr.** of 115 D Street; his wife, **Frances**, resided at 204 Walnut Street and was informed by the War Department on May 26, 1945. After an extended Lindale furlough, he was assigned to San Antonio for further duty.

These local boys were on furlough in June: **B. J. Pendergrass**, **US Navy; Private Leon Stager**, U**S Army; and Petty Officer Third Class Thomas Edward McCoy**. Private First Class **Donald H. "Bud" Greer** had recovered from wounds received January 7 at La Haye de Puits, France; he was the son of **Mrs. Vernon Greer** of 4 Terrace Avenue. **Donald's** unit spent 128 days in constant combat. He related later that German snipers "got the Lieutenant and scout through the head, one squad leader through the neck and my squad leader through the thigh. And, he would have parted my hair if I hadn't moved my head but the bullet hit my rifle, ricocheted and went through the side of my hand."

In June of '45, **Seaman Second Class Newton P. Wheeler Jr.** was returning to his base after spending a short leave with his parents at 309 Grove Street. He was earlier aboard a heavy cruiser during the Normandy Invasion. Manager Harvey announced that the mill would close at midnight, June 30, and start back up on July 8, 1945. The employees would enjoy a well-deserved rest for the first time since Pearl Harbor. Russian General Mihail A. Siazoff had presented Lindale's First Sergeant **Charles P. York** a decoration in appreciation for crossing the Elbe River and linking up with the Red Army. The Lindalean was attached to the 771st Tank Battalion of the Ninth Army. He is the son of **Mr. and Mrs. Wesley York** of Cedartown Road and sister of **Mrs. Zonnelle Brown** who worked in number one card room on second shift. Army **Private John E. Brannon**, whose parents **Mr. and Mrs. C. C. Brannon** reside at Lindale Route 1, had received the Combat Infantryman Badge; he was attached to the 76th Division of George Patton's Third Army. In a letter to friends in Lindale, he wrote, "**It's just another pretty medal, but there's no doubt about it, the man that wears it has seen plenty of hell**." In July of 1945, Boatswain's Mate First Class **William Mote** had spent twenty-six months overseas participating in landings on Salerno, Sicily, and Italy. During the former invasion, his ship fired on a Nazi tank which crawled over a small knoll overlooking the beach. The ship now carried a trophy-like tank painted on its side. Ship's Cook Third Class **Melvin Bruce** had been overseas for seventeen months in the Pacific; he was now on short leave at 103 Park Street. The young seaman was connected with the Henry Autry Funeral Home before enlisting. His brother **Melvin** wrote the *Home Front News* from New Guinea that he was on the baseball team there, but "he would much rather be in Lindale and on Earl Donaldson's team."

After returning to duty, **Staff Sergeant Raymond W. Ellington** was missing in action and reported captured by Germans on January 3, 1945. He was liberated in July of 1945. The young paratrooper is married to the former **Jewel Hawkins** of Summerville and prior to service was connected to the Weaving Department. As discharge points accumulated in July of 1945, several Lindaleans were mustered out of the service, including Corporal **Norman Lee "Skeet" Burkhalter** who spent twenty-eight months in the Mediterranean war zone. Private **John H. Edwards**, who was wounded in France, had endured thirty months of fighting in the ETO; **Robert Kennington** of the famous Fourth Infantry Division soldiered eighteen months in the European combat zone winning the Bronze Star, the ETO ribbon with five battle stars as well as the Good Conduct Metal. **David Richard Edge**, son of **First Sergeant and Mr. David Edge**, reported to Great Lakes Naval Training Center for boot camp. **Mrs. Lila Proudfoot Jordan** of 9 Terrace Avenue received notice that her husband, **Lieutenant James W. Jordan**, was injured on June 22 while seeing action on Borneo Island. He was the son of **Mr. and Mrs. C. W. Jordan** of Roanoke, Alabama. **Sergeant David R. Millican** of South Lindale had fought gallantly with the 507th Parachute Infantry during the Normandy landings and had been awarded the Presidential Unit Citation ribbon. When Army Private **Alfred Fayhue "Pee-Wee" Moon** returned home from Italy, he would bring ten commendations with him. Before induction in 1940, he was associated with the Spinning Department. In July 1945, Captain **William "Dick" Baker** was slightly wounded in the Philippines where he participated in the liberation of the islands. The same month, *HFN* received a letter from **Private First Class William E. Cargle** in Lytham, England, announcing his marriage to a British lady. Also in July, **Seabees Electrician's Mate First Class Grover Cleveland Day** had been given an honorable discharge for the second time! He had served in both world wars. **Pharmacist's Mate First Class Eddie C. Lemming** missed his April issue of *HFN*; the printers immediately mailed **Eddie** another copy. Boatswain's Mate Second Class **Glenn R. Morris** spent a short leave with his wife, the former **Faynell Givens**, and his parents, the **R. E. Morrises** of Silver Creek. He had participated in incredible eight amphibious invasions including North Africa, Sicily, Guadalcanal, Saipan, Guam, Tinian, Leyte, Luzon, and Iwo Jima. In September of 1945, Corporal **John R. Forrester** returned from the European theater to spend a short furlough in Lindale with his wife, the former **Marguerite Burkhalter**, and young daughter, **Ellen Ann**; his parents, the **T. P. Foresters**, lived at 112 F Street. **Private First Class Harold Cox** was spending a furlough with his parents at Route 1, Silver Creek. He was wounded while fighting near Cologne, Germany. Corporal **William M. Mathis Jr.** also returned from the ETO for a furlough at his mother and father's home on B Street. He was attached to the 20th Armored Division. A third soldier, **Clarence B. Bradshaw**, returned from Europe to spend a thirty-day leave with family in Silver Creek. He was attached to the 807th Tank Destroyer Battalion. Sergeant **Roy D. Pirkle** left Lindale on December 5, 1943, to serve with the 121st Infantry Division in Europe. He was currently enjoying a fifty-day furlough here. Also in September of '45, Army Private **James Hammontree** was home spending a thirty-day leave with his wife, the former **Doris Robinson**, of 107 Grove Street. **For the last 6 months, James** had duty in Trier, Germany. He would report to Camp Hood, Texas, shortly. Corporal **Ernest F. "Dink" Bruce** was wounded in combat when his unit crossed the Rhine River. He was resting in Lindale with a Purple Heart and five battle stars. **Mr. and Mrs. J. L. White** of 3 South Fourth Street had welcomed their son **John L.** home for a thirty-day leave; he was in the vanguard during the Normandy Invasion and received the *Croix de Guerre* medal. Another Lindalean closely involved during D-Day was Seaman First Class **Paul Beam Jr.**, whose ship, the *LST 508*, ferried wounded soldiers from Utah and Omaha beaches back to England. Sergeant **Groover L. Gilbert** had returned from the ETO and was enjoying a short leave with his wife, the former **Madeline Lewis**, of 128 C Street and his mother, **Mrs. R. L. Gilbert**, of 105 A Street. He received the Purple Heart while attached to the 26th Infantry Division. A former worker in the Weaving Department was **Master Sergeant Mark B. Melton**; he recently returned to the United States aboard *Queen Mary* after serving at the Army's 151st General Hospital in England. Army Private

John Paul Carver served forty-six months with the famed 9th Infantry Division in the ETO. He received a discharge at Camp Gordon, Georgia, and had returned to Lindale with numerous medals. **Another Carver** from Lindale, **Sergeant Hubert**, was in Czechoslovakia when the war ended, and he considered himself lucky. His company went ashore in the third wave on June 6, 1944, with two hundred men. When war in the ETO ended eleven months later, only twelve, counting **Hubert**, had escaped death, capture, or injury. Two veterans of war, **Melvin Mitchell May** and **K. C. Hopkins**, had returned to their jobs in the mill. **May** served in the ETO where he received the Purple Heart for action in the Luxembourg-German border. **Hopkins** took boot camp and training in the Hospital Corps School in San Diego. Former Army Corporal **Clifford F. "Curly" Robinson** had returned to the Weaving Department after three years in the European-African-Middle Eastern Theaters. Private **Albert T. Roberts** had received an honorable discharge after serving in the ETO with the 16th Engineers of the 1st Armored Division. Navy Chief Petty Officer **Clyde Hines** and wife were visiting **Mr. L. B. Hines** of 306 Grove Street; **Clyde** was retiring after twenty-four and a half years of duty.

On page 2 of its October 1945 issue, the *Home Front News* posted historically, "The rising sun has set [victory over Japan] behind the clouds of the Atomic Bomb—never to rise again and threaten the freedom of a peaceful nation. Complete Victory is a reality now—thanks to all of you for a job well done." Victory was announced by the old mill whistle at 6:00 p.m., Tuesday, August 14. All machinery stopped at once. After two days of rejoicing, **manager Mr. R. D. Harvey** paid everyone for the two victory holidays. On August 26, the Pepperell State Guard Band assembled on the auditorium lawn for a season-ending concert. Highlighting the program was the introduction of "The R. D. H. March" composed by **Mr. Paul Nixon** and dedicated to **Robert Donald Harvey**; a special cornet solo by Lieutenant **Broadus W. Moak** was enjoyed by the summer's largest crowd.

Three of the five **Mull** brothers were visiting their parents, **Mr. and Mrs. E. C. Mull**, of Lindale. **Private Gilbert** was home from Europe, **Navy Fireman Second Class J. C.** had come from the Atlantic, and **Private William** was a member of the Ninth Air Force in England. **Privates Marion and Elbert** were stationed at Camp Wheeler, Georgia, and Lille, France, respectively. Corporal **William F. Gribble** had transferred from England to South Dakota. Former Carding Department employee **Grady E. Bradshaw** was home in Silver Creek. He returned from serving two years in the ETO's 9th Air Force. Petty Officer Third Class **L. R. Lloyd** was visiting relatives in Silver Creek after spending twenty months in the Pacific. He participated in the invasions of Saipan, Leyte, Luzon, and Iwo Jima. In October of 1945, Technical Sergeant **Otis Forrest Gilbreath** returned from the ETO and spent a thirty-day furlough at home with his wife, the former **Pauline Timms**, of 404 Park Street. **Otis** had served twenty months with a Signal Heavy Construction Battalion of the 7th Army and would report later to Camp Gordon in Augusta. He was entitled to wear the ETO ribbon with six battle stars and Good Conduct Medal. Also in October, **Private First Class Joseph Darrell Milton** had earned an ETO battle star while serving with the 723rd Railway Operating Battalion in Muchen Gladback, Germany. Army veteran **Carl Lee Green** had returned to his job in the Weaving Department; he served four years in the Pacific theater including Society, New Hebrides, and Solomon Islands. Pharmacist's Mate First Class **Eddie C. Lemming** complained about missing the April 1945 issue of *HFN*; the newsletter promptly mailed a new copy. After eighteen months with the 9th Air Force, Private **James T. Jones** was enjoying a thirty-day furlough with his parents of the Lindale Subdivision. **James** saw action at Normandy, Belgium, Northern France, and Germany. **Willard W. Wright** of the 36th Infantry Division and 8th Air Force would report to Fort McPherson after visiting his parents in South Lindale. **Mr. and Mrs. H. F. Stansell** of 315 D Street welcomed their son **Sergeant Stansell** home for a thirty-day furlough. He saw action with the 9th Division in France, Belgium, and Germany and earned numerous combat citations. He would report to Finney General Hospital, Thomasville, Georgia. Sergeant **Otis Sitten** was severely wounded on April 9 while fighting in Germany. He was presently visiting his parents in Lindale before reporting back to Lawson General Hospital, Atlanta. Otis had received several medals for bravery. Staff Sergeant **James C. Millican** had served more than two years in the Pacific. He was currently visiting his parents, **Mr.** and **Mrs. M. S. Millican**. **James** would wear six battle stars on his chest when reporting to Fort McPherson for reassignment. In October '45 **Edward "Horsic" Henderson** returned to Lindale; he fought the Japanese with the 1st Marine Division at Guadalcanal, Cape Gloucester, and Peleliu. Edward had more medals than he could carry. Former **Sergeant Russell Andrew Covey** had returned to his job at Pepperell. He joined the Army in January '42 and served in Normandy and the Rhineland and held eight major medals. The October issue of *HFN* recognized **Private First Class Fred M. Howell Jr.**, **Corporal William A. Couey**, **Staff Sergeant L. D. Smith**, and **Sergeant Arthur L. "Bud" Treglown** serving with a trucking company in Assam, India.

The *Home Front News* of November 1945 wrote, "November finds Lindale slowly but surely returning to normal peacetime conditions. The familiar faces and friendly smiles of a good many of Lindale boys are appearing in greater numbers daily." To date, sixty boys had returned to their place as efficient workers at Pepperell. Private **Joseph L. "Abie" Gaston** had returned to his parents' home on 216 Grove Street following his discharge from the Army; **Joseph** was wounded in Germany on October 8, 1944. Navy man *William Harbin "Billy" Coker* has received his separation papers after more than three years of service in the Asiatic-Pacific area. He had assumed a position with Knight's Department Store. Staff Sergeant **Joe Knight**, husband of the former **Leota Brower** of 2 South Third Street, had been discharged in San Bernardino, California. He was the brother of **Jack Knight** of Lindale. **Robert Edd Martin** had been promoted to captain in the Army Air Force. He was the son of **Mr. and Mrs. M. T. Martin** of 305 Park Street; **Robert** is married to the former **Martha Guest**. After thirty-six months overseas with the 49th Station Hospital, Private **Paul Edward Groves**, son of **Mr. and Mrs. John Groves**, of South Lindale had returned home for a forty-five-day leave. He was inducted on April 8, 1942, and saw duty in Iceland before being sent to England for the remainder of the war. Corporal **Thomas G. Morton** was married to the former **Martha Jean Bramlett**; while attached to the 411th Infantry Regiment near Schlottenback, Germany, **Thomas** merited the Bronze Star for heroism in combat. The same medal was awarded to Private **Gilbert J. Mull** for action in Friesham, Germany, on March 3, 1945. Captain **Zula Adell Colquitt** was visiting with her mother, **Mrs. W. E. Colquitt Sr.**; she had spent twenty-five months overseas with the Army Nurse Corps (Emory Medical Unit) in Africa and the ETO. The captain was affiliated with the Lindale and Opelika divisions of Pepperell. **Mrs. A. B. Chandler** of Versailles, Kentucky, recently toured the plant escorted by **Donald Harvey**. She was the wife of Senator and High Commissioner of Major League Baseball **Happy Chandler**; son Ben was a student at Darlington School.

The *HFN* noted a letter received from Private First Class **Fred M. Howell Jr.**, **Corporal W. A. Couey**, and **Staff Sergeant L. D. Smith** thanking the newsletter for its work. The three were stationed in Assam, India. Two months after the war ended, **J. C. Ragsdale** reported from Guam that he was taking care of all the power plants and highways on the Island. **Private First Class Moses Lewis Mathis** had been overseas for fifteen months without seeing anyone he knew from home. In October, the former Pepperell cloth room employee happily reported meeting up with his brother **Jimmy A. Mathis**. The reunion took place in Jena, Germany. In the same month, it was reported that **Private Grady L. Lewis** was wounded on Okinawa while fighting with the Sixth Marine Division. The son of **Mrs. Nora Lewis** of 128 C Street was now in the Naval Hospital, Charleston. Electrician's Mate First Class **Grover Cleveland Day** was a veteran of World War I and II. The first duty was as a corporal in the Army, the latter as a Navy CB in the Pacific area. He had returned to 108 C Street with an honorable discharge. Seaman Second Class **Newton P. Wheeler Jr.** entered the Navy in January 1944; a short time after boot camp, he was aboard a heavy cruiser during the Normandy Invasion. A year later, the former Spinning Department worker was in training for mine warfare in Little Creek, Virginia, before duty on a new minesweeper. **J. C. Ragsdale** was stationed in Guam where his battalion was charged with maintaining the island's public works. Before joining the Army, **Moses Lewis Mathis** worked in the Pepperell cloth room. After going fifteen months without seeing anyone from Lindale, finally the private first class met up with his brother, **Private Jimmy A. Mathis**, in Jena, Germany. **Seaman Second Class Newton P. Wheeler Jr.** was still in the Navy and awaiting assignment to a new minesweeper in Little Creek, Virginia. In the eleventh month of 1945, **Army Sergeant Edward N. Jackson** had been granted an honorable discharge. In thirty-six months overseas, the sergeant had earned eight battle stars, the ETO ribbon, the Presidential Unit Citation with oak-leaf cluster as well as the Good Conduct Medal and *Croix de Guerre avec Palme*. The latter award was presented to him in Sardinia by General de Gaulle on September 19, 1944. Army **Private James N. "Red" Moon** was hit by a sniper's bullet while serving with the Sixth Army in Europe. He returned to battle in six days. James was now on furlough in Lindale where he worked in Pepperell's Slashing Department.

Before he joined the Army in September of 1942, Sergeant **John F. Burkhalter** worked in the Carding Department of the mill; after eighteen months in Europe, the sarge was enjoying a thirty-day leave at his parents' home. He had rated numerous medals.

In November of 1945, peace began to settle on the world. **Mr. and Mrs. R. C. Ford** of 219 Garden Street welcomed their son **Robert A. Ford** home for a thirty-day furlough. He spent the last eleven months in the Pacific area and was receiving treatment at the Army Hospital, Camp Butner, North Carolina. Private **James I. Hitchcock** of the occupation force wrote from Utsunomiya, Japan, that he hopes to be returning home next year. Also from Asia/Far East, Private **Virgil Hollingsworth** sent *Home Front News* a bit of Chinese money from Shanghai. After passing through China-Burma-India theater, **Virgil** said, "Lindale is still the best of all." Private **William S. Covington** in Corregidor, Philippines, wrote the *HFN* that he has met up with Lindalean **Hubert Stepp** in Manila. Marine Corps Corporal **Fred O. Maynor Jr.** was spending thirty days with his wife, the former **Iva Lou Head**; he participated in Tarawa, Saipan, Tinian, and Okinawa campaigns and would soon report to the Naval Hospital at Leandro, California. Before his return to duty, Boatswain Mate Second Class **Buford O. Treglown** was honored with a going-away dinner at his parents' home. Another farewell event occurred at the home of **Mr. and Mrs. Frank Sisson**; the honoree was Private **Jack R. Henderson** who would soon depart for overseas duty. The crew of USS *Nicholson*, which included Lindale Gunner's Mate Third Class **Elmer Dunehoo Chambers**, finished a long hard Pacific campaign as they sailed Nicholson into Tokyo Bay for occupation duty. **Theo Sartin** resumed his job in the Spinning Department soon after discharge on October 14 at Maxwell Field, Alabama. In the same month, *HFN* reported recently promoted **First Lieutenant John O. Camp** was married to the former **Dorothy Barton** of North Lindale; he was now stationed on Oahu serving with an ordinance unit. Staff Sergeant **Richard Stager** served with B Battery, 496th AAA Gun Battalion in New Guinea and the Philippines. To warn of incoming enemy aircraft, the unit had a high-pitched siren that chillingly reverberated through the jungles. The soldiers ran to their posts while looking for death to come out of the sky. A few days after the war, **Stager** was strolling downtown when a fire truck came up behind him with its siren screaming. The veteran experienced a flashback. He said later, "I think if there had been a manhole open, I would have jumped in!" In 1935, **Forrest McKelvey** of Silver Creek enlisted in the Georgia National Guard. On November 25, 1940, he entered active duty and remained with the military unit in some form until retiring as a colonel in 1970. There were duty stations in Georgia, California, and New England before being assigned to an antiaircraft unit in Europe. After eighteen months in the ETO, Forrest was discharged in October 1945. He promptly reenlisted in the guard and stayed twenty-five more years "until they kicked me out because of age."

In December of 1945, Lindale Methodist Church hosted Lieutenant **John W. Molton** as guest speaker. He said, "America must awaken and step forward as a unified force if a lasting peace is to become a reality." After serving thirty-three months with the Coast Guard's SPARS (*Semper Paratus*—Always Ready), **Ruth Sanders** had received an honorable discharge and returned to her hometown. On October 17, Private **Joseph Maxwell** of Silver Creek had received a point-system honorable discharge at Fort McPherson. Also receiving separation papers were two boatswain mates **Lester Alton Steadman** and **James M. Abney** as well as Gunner's Mate **Raiden M. Abney**. Private **Roy Hatch** of 201 Park Street had returned to the plant after twenty-three months in the Pacific. **Radioman First Class Charles Abrams** was home on leave after three years away from friends and relatives. Seaman **J. D. Bailey** was on leave after sailing aboard USS *Idaho* into Tokyo Bay for the signing of Japanese surrender documents. Gunner's Mate Third **Class Elmer Dunehoo Chambers** of the destroyer Nicholson survived almost all major Pacific battles; there was a sense of pride when the ship sailed into Tokyo Bay for occupation duty in August 1945. On page 48 of her history book, **Polly Gammon** noted Pepperell provided 690 "Lindale boys and girls fighting on battlefields." Seventeen of those were commissioned officers.

Fallen Heroes of Lindale, Georgia in World War II

Robert M. Baker	Sherman R. Baker	Jessie D. Brown
Ralph H. Burkhalter	Martin J. Camp	Belton R. Carver
William D. Carver	James R. Cox	Thomas A. Cole
Johnnie B. Cochran	William H. Hendrix	George V. Howard
Louis F. Jarrell	Owen E. Kirkland	Huel K. McCollum
Clyde H. Roberson	Charles E. Schram	Herman E. Sealock
Henry C. L. Smith	Edward A. Stone	Dewey L. Williams

On page 13 of its June 1945 edition, the *Home Front News* printed the reason why we fight for freedom:

> I can go to any church I please—
> I read, see and hear what I choose—
> I can express my opinions openly—
> My telephone is untapped—
> I join any political party I wish—
> I can vote for what and whom I please—
> I have a constitutional right by jury—
> I am protected against search and seizure—
> Neither my life nor my property can be forfeited without due process of law.—

On Thursday, November 29, a formal military ball sponsored by **Shanklin-Attaway and R. J. McClain Legion Posts** was held at the Coosa Country Club. Former active/inactive military were attired in full dress uniforms; Jack Kraynck's twelve-piece orchestra provided dance music until 2:30 a.m. Also in November, **Judge and Mrs. C. W. Bramlett** recently welcomed their son **Gabe** and wife, **Hazel**, home to 127 D Street; the electrician's mate first class was honorably discharged from the Navy. **Gunner's Mate Second Class Samuel Johnston Jr.** had been honorably discharged after participating in five invasions and several raids in the South Pacific and Aleutian Islands. He was with family in North Lindale. **Carpenter's Mate Third Class L. R. Lloyd** of Silver Creek rated battle stars from the ETO as well as Asiatic-Pacific Theater. He had been honorably discharged. **Coast Guard man Robert P. Hutchins** of 16 Terrace Avenue had been honorably discharged in Savannah. **Richard Holcombe** went to work in the mill in his teens; he later served in the Navy for nineteen months, returning to Lindale in 1945 where he earned 42¢ an hour in the machine shop. He said, "It was a good, hard work. Lindale was an exceptionally good place to live and work—it had everything."

The July '45 edition *Lindale Goes to War* printed on page 2 that after four years of unbroken work, plant manager Donald Harvey gave the employees a break from midnight, Saturday, June 30, until Sunday, midnight, July 8, 1945. It would be a "deserved rest" for the mill hands who have not had a vacation since Pearl Harbor. Upon returning, employees would start the push toward final victory in World War II. Two years earlier in the same publication, he cited **643 Lindale boys on the military Roll of Honor**. As a result, "we have replaced many of these men with women. At present all of our card hands are women. Due to shortage of men many girls are now weaving, doffing, sweeping and timekeeping; they are also brushers, laboratory and clerical employees. Not a single woman has refused an assignment that she has been offered and had it not been for their splendid cooperation our production would have suffered. Today we have 220 more women on our payroll than we had one year ago."

WARTIME BASEBALL

From 1942 to 1945, there were no official Textile teams. Following the attack on Pearl Harbor, the Northwest Georgia Textile League suspended play for the war years (1942–1945). However, on Sunday, March 29, 1942, a county association was formed with Tubize, Lindale, Anchor Duck, and the Orphans (Rome). These communities were short travel time from one another and conformed to mileage restrictions caused by the war. The latter smorgasbord squad consisted "for the most part" of players from Shannon and Rockmart; it was funded by local businessman C. J. Wyatt as opposed to the other three mill-sponsored teams. Mr. Wyatt's group was too young or too old for the draft or were "orphans" from the former suspended organization. He graciously divided the gate receipts among his players. In Lindale, Slick Moulton promised a competitive nine, predicting that attendance could surpass the NWGTL figures of the past eleven years. Since war materials were already being rationed, the squads debated playing with retreaded baseballs—used balls with new covers; however, since the old minor league rules were adopted, that idea was voted down. Playing times were at the discretion of the host. Admission was set at 10¢ and 25¢; servicemen were given free entry. Later, many of the Sunday gate receipts were donated to the Navy Relief Society. Presumably, the war caused a shortage of umpires, for Mr. Wyatt canvassed for qualified men.

The Floyd County League opened play on Saturday, May 2, 1942, with the idea of keeping baseball going until the old league resumes. But if fans thought the new pastime was just a game, the write-up of the Sunday, June 28, game changed their minds: "Protests and fights in the crowd broke out during the Tubize vs Anchor Duck contest." By August 31, the abbreviated season had ended with Anchor Duck winning (23–13 record) the only first-place trophy, but it was not before another fight occurred with Tubize. Baseball researcher Tom Klenc reported that "the fans expressed a relief that the season was finally over with all the fighting and arguments."[119]

The following year on Sunday, May 2, 1943, Lang Gammon posted in his "News of Lindale" column that "although no league has been formed, fans are gratified over the efforts of the mixed squads of youngsters and stars from the old Textile loop. The war-time brand of ball… has been given the spectator's stamp of approval." These independent squads were supported by the larger mills. But by this time, most of the best athletes were "consumed" by the Army and Navy, their place taken by mercenary sandlot baseball, i.e., Bill Cordell's Chattanooga's Dixie Spinners led by former Pepperell star Bill Cordell. As the war moved along, Lindale manager Earl Donaldson bemoaned the condition of his players, saying, "They're either too young or too old." In the June 1944 edition of *Home Front News*, manager Earl Donaldson said he had only one veteran from past diamond campaigns, Bo Sheppard. The old manager even "enlisted" a former player home on leave to pitch against Brighton. For example, Navy man Bud Lukor took the mound against the visitors and limited them to two hits.[120]

However, stable school squads took the forefront. Pepperell Junior High School was fielding a well-coached team headed by Earl Donaldson. The *News-Tribune* printed a starting lineup on Thursday April 15, 1943: Landers (second base), Mathis (left field), Kelley (first base), Sheppard Walker (third base), Garrett (right field), Leach (shortstop), Espy (center field), and Nixon (pitcher). Also, Lindale recreation director Ish Williams organized a three-league summer neighborhood program consisting of teams Jamestown, Old Town, New Town, West First and Second, Silver Creek, and South Lindale. The first group were youngsters from nine to eleven; the intermediate would be boys twelve to thirteen; the older players, fourteen years and older. In addition, Director Williams formed two amateur loops; the Junior League circuit for boys thirteen to fifteen. The other, named Midget League, was composed of those twelve and under. It was assumed that the better players would perform in the amateur league.[121]

NORTHWEST GEORGIA TEXTILE LEAGUE POSTWAR

Lee Mowry added that "Growth of youth baseball and the loss of friends and family to the war kept the league from reclaiming its special role in the area."

The 1946 postwar Textile League restarted with five of the original clubs. Immediately a war-weary populace flocked to the stadiums (1,500 to 3,000 fans) yearning for a simpler time and entertainment; consequently, the old organization expanded to 8 teams and changed its name to West Georgia Textile League. Rome radio station WLAQ broadcast the events with announcer Lee Mowry giving play-by-play. The league championship series rivaled the Dixie Series in the South and the World Series of the major league. But there were cracks in the system.[122]

1946

April 14. In the postwar as peace settled over the land, Ralph Primm was elected president of the association, which included Tubize, Lindale, Shannon, Cedartown, and the Atco Supertwisters. April 28. Seventeen-year-old Willard Nixon shut out Shannon 1–0 with fourteen strikeouts. The next day, Jack Gaston went eleven innings in a 7–4 victory over against the same squad. May 6. Willard Nixon blanked Cedartown 9–0 to begin three straight shutouts. Lindale completed a 25–7 schedule as champions. September 16. Top batters for the club were J. M. Culberson, .463; Jack Gaston, .428; and Willard Nixon, .379. Leading hurlers were Jack Gaston, 7–0, and Willard Nixon, 12–4. The championship roster included the following:

Donaldson	Manager	Gene Baggett	Outfield
Jack Gaston	Pitcher/outfield	Joe Gaston	First Base
Shorty Hall	Infield	Charles Hopkins	Outfield
Jim Jordan	Pitcher	L. R. Knowles	First Base
John Mathis	Outfield	Earl McClung	Catcher
Forrest McKelvey	Pitcher	Willard Nixon	Pitcher
Dudley Sheppard	Catcher	Melvin Stamey	Shortstop
Hubert Stepp	Third base	Johnny Stowe	Outfield
Johnny Teat	Second base	Lardy Walker	Infield/outfield

1947

February 26. Officials met in the Pepperell cafeteria for a business session. Awaiting the arrival of manager Clarence Dawson, Slick Moulton opened spring practice on March 20 for Lindale. Veteran players Jack Gaston, Melvin Stamey, Johnny Teat, Gene Baggett, John Stowe, John Mathis, Bo Sheppard, and Shorty Hall were expected. College players Willard Nixon, L. R. Knowles, Hubert Stepp, and Lardy Walker were expected at the end of the school year. May 25. Commissioner of Baseball A. B. "Happy" Chandler told a cheering crowd at Lindale Park that he was going to see that baseball was operated honestly and decently. Afterward, Lindale pitchers Gaston and Jordan teamed up to down Tubize 8–3 while Shorty Hall went 3-for-4 at the plate. The commissioner was in town to deliver the graduation address at Darlington where his two sons Ben and Dan were students. One of the highlights of the season occurred on June 16 when third baseman Shorty Hall set a record by hitting 4 round-trippers in 4 consecutive innings off 4 different pitchers in a 25–4 romp over Tubize. September 21. In the postseason, Pepperell downed Brighton 7–2 to go up 3–2 in the championship series behind Willard Nixon's 13 strikeouts. The following day before 2,135 fans, the Lindaleans won the league series, defeating Brighton 10–6. Pepperell's leading hitters were Knowles, .486; Nixon, .382; and Hall, .370.

1948

March 19. The league agreed to play a forty-game season beginning on April 17 and ending on August 29. February 16. College pitcher Willard Nixon continued as the top twirler at Auburn; a major league organization would most likely sign him soon. April 18. Lindale started the season with a 17–7 win over Dalton with slugger Jack Gaston hitting two home runs. In an early October night game at Pepperell Park, Brighton ace J. M. Culberson led his team to the championship when he pitched a five-hitter to claim the best-of-seven series over Lindale, 7–2. WLAQ Radio's most valuable players were Jack Gaston and Jimmy Jones of Brighton.

1949

April 3. The NWGTL consisted of teams Brighton, Pepperell, Atco, Aragon, and Trion and begin play on Saturday, April 23. Brighton won the first half standing with Lindale number two; the same scenario repeated in the second part of the schedule. September 25. However, the Pepperells defeated Brighton 3–2 in five games for the championship. Lindale second baseman Sam Talley won the *News-Tribune*/WLAQ outstanding player trophy. He won the first two games of the series with home runs. The squad members and their wives were feted to a postseason banquet at the American Legion Post in Lindale courtesy of Pepperell Manufacturing Company.

1950

March 8. League representatives met in Rome's Greystone Hotel. The six-team league began play on April 29. Twenty-one days later, Lindale manager Bo Sheppard opened workouts. August 21. In the postseason best-of-three semis, Lindale faced Tallapoosa-American Thread; unfortunately, the newcomers "dumped" the Pepperells 7–6 in the deciding game. September 14. Shannon swept the Threaders four games to none, claiming the championship. *News-Tribune*/WLAQ outstanding player award went to Brighton's J. M. Culberson who was the winning hurler in three of the games; he also batted .445.

1951

The league consisted of American Thread of Tallapoosa, Brighton, Pepperell, and Trion; the thirty-game schedule began on Friday, May 4, and play games on Friday nights and Saturday and Sunday afternoons. September 3. In the postseason championship series, Luke Nasworthy hit two home runs in the 5–0 sweep over second-place Lindale. Shannon claimed the championship with a 22–7 overall record. WLAQ most valuable player was Nasworthy; Ken Culberson batted .444 and was awarded a watch for the highest average.

1952

May 1. The league consisted of Tallapoosa American Thread, Aragon, Brighton of Shannon, and Pepperell of Lindale; they played a thirty-game schedule beginning Friday night, May 2. The first half standings showed Brighton as number one with the Pepps in third place; the second half was a repeat with Lindale missing the postseason playoffs. September 8. Brighton again won the championship, winning four of five games over Tallapoosa in addition to an 18–10 season record. However, the Threaders' first base/pitcher Harvey Sheffield was awarded the MVP by WLAQ.

1953

The Textile League opened on May 1 and finished August 16; it was comprised of Tallapoosa's American Thread, Anchor Rome, Aragon, Brighton, Chattooga County, and Pepperell. April 29. Opening ceremonies of Lindale-Brighton game included a dedication of Claude Satterfield Memorial Park. Claude was a player/manager killed in an auto accident during Christmas holidays 1950. June 16. Jim Yarbrough and Baltimore Smith reported to the Jacksonville Beach Seabirds of the Class D Florida State League; they played on the Pepperell High School squad that won the 1952 State Class B title. The Cincinnati Reds signed the youngsters out of high school. July 19. All Friday-night games were "washed out by heavy downpour." August 27. Pepperell lost a 3–0 thriller against Brighton, eliminating them from postseason. The Pepps' final record was 19–11. September 10. Twice defending champion Brighton defeated Anchor Rome 10–6 in the best-of-five series to win the league again in addition to a 22–8 season slate. September 10. Shannon outfielder Jerry Bell was named WLAQ most valuable player.

1954

The final season of the NWGTL included teams Brighton, Pepperell, Anchor Rome, and Chattooga County; thirty games were scheduled. April 29. Manager Jack Gaston announced his Lindale Textile squad would play the Pepperell Dragons' nine in two exhibition games this weekend. August 16. Pepperell won the league's second half with an 11–4 record but finished 17–13 and number two overall behind Anchor Rome's 18–11. The playoffs began with Anchor Rome nipping the Pepps 4–2 despite Troy Coffia's nine strikeout effort. Game 2 followed the same script with Anchor winning 2–0. August 25. The third contest played on the PHS high school field, and broadcast on WLAQ saw the visitors win again 7–5. Monday, August 30, 1954. Anchor Rome, in a four-game sweep, won the final NWGTL championship, downing their Lindale hosts 5–4. WLAQ named Claude Shoemake of the winning club MVP with a batting average of .530; the Pepps' Baltimore Smith was second with a .380. In a team photo, the last league champions were identified as V. R. Jefts, Lefty Hutchins, Claude Shoemake, Luke Gravely, Russ Lyons, Bob LeCroy, Frank Kerce, R. L. Ozment, James Coheley, Charlie Padgett, Cary Brooks, Al Brown, and Nevin Kerce.

The postwar league champions were the following:

1946	Lindale
1947	Lindale
1948	Brighton
1949	Lindale
1950	Brighton
1951	Brighton
1952	Brighton
1953	Brighton
1954	Anchor Rome

The union disbanded after the 1954 season due to decreasing attendance. The turnstile count peaked in 1947 at 480,000; however, by 1951, it had dropped to less than 175,000. The era of depression, war, and escapism had passed. A post–World War I ditty asked, "How ya gonna to keep 'em down on the farm after they've seen Paree?" Several decades later, Bob Dylan sang, "Come gather 'round people, wherever you roam…for the times they are a-changin'." Billy Primm played baseball all his life. He had a four-year scholarship at Wake Forest University, became a Textile League star, fought in World War II, and later became president of Home Federal Savings and Loan. Combat veterans looked at the world differently. Heather Shores quoted Primm as he explained his mindset in postwar, "After what I had seen overseas, baseball just didn't seem that important anymore." Also the boom for textile goods decreased; many mills changed ownership, lessening their economic importance. The GI Bill made it possible for workers to move to better-paying jobs with improved working conditions; consequently, the traditional mill village life began to diminish.

Yet six decades later, memories still live on in Lindale with reunions, newspapers articles, and stories handed down through four generations. At present, thirteen members of the Rome/Floyd County Sports Hall of Fame have direct connections with the Textile League. But after 1954, the amateur pastime faded along with the men who played the game. However, they left a huge legacy that endures even today.[123]

ERNEST OLIN "SHORTY" HALL (SEPTEMBER 1, 1911– FEBRUARY 5, 1993)

The sun beat down on a hot, lazy Sunday afternoon as Shorty batting fifth in the lineup belted a first inning homerun.
—Grandson and historian David L. Allen

On September 1, 1911, Ernest Olin Hall was born in DeKalb County to Thomas Henry and Emma King Hall; he was the youngest of ten children to the farm family in Valley Head, Alabama. This small hamlet was nestled in the valley between Lookout and Sand Mountains astraddle the railroad to Chattanooga. Large families were the norm in that day and time, for children performed as ready labor in the fields and barnyards. To this day, no one knows how he acquired the misnomered nickname Shorty. Olin, as he was called by family, was a six-two-tall handsome, lanky athlete who performed on the gridiron as well as shortstop on the diamond.

There was certainly nothing short about his game, for after graduating in 1931 where the senior class voted him president, most popular, and best looking, he reported to the University of Alabama freshman football team with another tall country boy—this one from Moro Bottom and Fordyce High School, Arkansas. Paul William Bryant and Ernest Olin Hall a.k.a. Bear and Shorty were first-year scrimmage players for the Alabama Crimson Tide. Years later, Olin spoke fondly to his grandson of young Bryant's colorful metaphoric language, i.e., "He's a running piece of thunder!" Afterward, Bear, who was the eleventh of 12 children, stayed on and made a name for himself in Tuscaloosa. Our subject stayed around for one year and a quarter before moving north to Chicago for the World's Fair of 1933. Pumping a bicycle-powered rickshaw around the 427 acres provided cash as well as adventure. When the fair closed, he moved back South seeking permanent employment. Lindale, Georgia, located 50 miles south of his hometown, was the logical choice. From its beginning in 1896, former farm families manned the weave rooms of Pepperell Manufacturing. The new destination featured steady employment at an established cotton mill, a comfortable village for living in addition to extra money playing Textile baseball. More importantly, there was a personal connection to this community. Five years earlier, sophomore Carl "Curly" Clements had transferred to Valley from Lindale Junior High. The most credible story is that the Lindalean was recruited by first-year head coach E. D. "Chink" Lott who heard of his prowess as an up-and-coming boxer. At that time, it was not unusual for high school athletic departments to arrange room and board for players living outside the district. During the 1929–1930 VH School terms, Curly was a teammate of Shorty Hall; a year later, Clements would follow Coach Lott to Anniston before returning home to Lindale.

Calling on this youthful friendship, Olin arrived at the 207 Park Street duplex of Howell S. and Ada Fowler Clements who were older brother and sister-in-law of his buddy Curly. A middle-of-the-day knock at the door surprised the young lady inside, for both parents were at work. After identifying himself, the quiet young man asked for accommodations. Marguerite Clements said later, "He was the most handsome man I ever saw. I knew in an instant, he was to be my husband." They were married on September 27, 1934.[124]

Although he ultimately retired from Rome's General Electric Company, Olin spent many years with Pepperell, rising to supervisor in the Sanforizing Department. The family spent happy times in the Jamestown section of the village while Dad played for the well-known mill baseball team. Early on, the infielder had performed well enough for the Detroit Tigers to offer a professional contract which he turned down, saying later, "I didn't want to drag my wife and daughter, Marguerite and Suzanne, around the country," adding, "That's not a life for a family."[125] However, the Alabama native's claim to fame occurred on June 15, 1947, at the local field against Northwest Georgia Textile rival Tubize. Grandson and historian Dr. David L. Allen wrote, "The sun beat down on a hot, lazy Sunday afternoon" as Shorty batting fifth in the lineup belted a first-inning home run. Coming to bat for the second time, the right-handed slugger belted another four-bagger—this time off a relief pitcher. The ensuing third inning against pitcher number three was described by grandson Dr. Allen, "Mr. Spaulding [the ball manufacturer] was given another ride out of the park." Eleven-year-old Suzanne Hall remembered the excitement building as her father went through the hitting progression that hot June day. On Shorty's fourth trip to the batter's box, the crowd began to realize the moment and began "to cheer him up." Was another homer possible? The fourth hurler wound up and let fly; the powerful third baseman proceeded to hammer the pitch over the outfield fence. Four straight round-trippers off four different pitchers in four consecutive innings! The feat had never been accomplished in baseball history. The fifth at bat was a mere single; later, he confided to his grandson (Dr. Allen) it was the only time he tried to hit the ball out of the park. The last time up, Tubize manager Dan Milner wisely ordered an intentional walk. The final score was 25–4.

Peeping though a knothole of history that day in 1947 was fifteen-year-old Lewis Allen who watched through a crack in the fence, for he did not have money for admission. He would eventually return from the Army in 1955 and propose to nineteen-year-old Suzanne; their children David and Beth Allen are thankful. Another fifteen-year-old village lad, Bob Baker, shouted encouragement from the stands; luckily, he had retrieved a foul ball in exchange for admission. Bob Baker would remain in Lindale for most of his life; he played four seasons (1951–1954) in the outfield for the mill team, later becoming a revered community coach and resident historian of the league and village. He has mentored the research and writing of *Lindale, Lint, and Leather*.[126]

Word of the feat spread to the local paper where *Rome News-Tribune* reported the next day on Monday, June 16, 1947, "Lindale…whips League foe Sunday…Third Baseman Shorty Hall hung up a home run performance Sunday afternoon that would probably make Robert L. Ripley sit up and take notice." *New York Post* cartoonist Robert Ripley (1890–1949) did take notice. The entrepreneur began featuring trivia in the early 1920s and especially enjoyed hearing from small-town sports enthusiasts. The series eventually grew to eighty million readers worldwide. Almost three months later, on September 6, 1947, he added Shorty Hall's feat to his famous "Ripley's Believe It or Not" collection. The entry is still there today and reads, "Shorty Hall, Lindale, Ga., Hit 4 Home Runs in 4 Consecutive Innings Off 4 Different Pitchers—Georgia Textile League."[127]

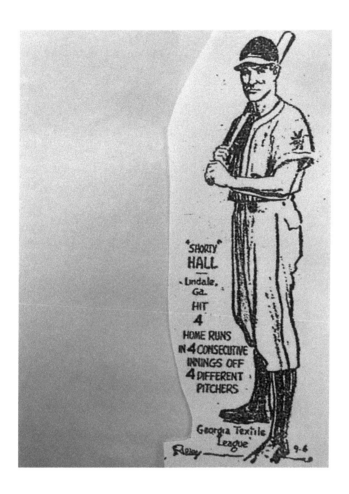

WILLARD LEE NIXON (1928–2000)—THE YANKEE KILLER

There are different ways to measure the impact a man's life has on the world. Perhaps the best way is to take stock of what life meant to the man. For Willard Nixon, it was simple—his family, his friends, his community and baseball.
—Rome News-Tribune sports editor Jim O'Hara

As a ten-year-old youngster in the midst of the Great Depression, Willard Nixon would roam up and down the local railroad tracks carrying a broomstick handle, looking for grade rocks to hit. As anyone who has tried this knows, it is not an easy task, for there is a small bat surface with a miniature target tossed up and whacked on the way down. Had he not possessed a golden pitching arm, the young man would certainly have been an everyday position player feared for his sweet left-handed swing. While walking along the railroad bed that spurred into the Pepperell Manufacturing Company, he assumed his destiny was like other boys living in the quiet cotton mill town of Lindale, Georgia; they all would follow those steel rails into the unloading docks and toil the rest of their lives in the noise and lint of weave rooms. At no time did he envision throwing, running, and swinging as a twenty-two-year old in a "whooping and hollering" Fenway Park or Yankee Stadium. Later he would tell friends, "It's been more or less a dream. I was from a small mill town in Lindale. How in the world did I get involved in all this?" Well, it makes for a most interesting story.[128]

At the turn of the century, grandfather William Franklin Nixon (1880–1941) was living in Broomtown, Alabama, while working as a conductor for the Chattanooga Southern (later TAG) railroad that ran nearby. This small community (present population 182) is located snug against the Georgia state line thirty-seven miles from Lindale. The area was named for Chief Broom of the Cherokee Nation who occupied the lands prior to Indian removal. It was here that William met and married Martha Ola Hardin; this occurred sometime around 1900. Although the Hardin family lineage traces from Cherokee County, Alabama, into Chattooga County, Georgia, Martha Ola was from nearby Floyd County, Georgia. The couple's first baby, Wesley, died at birth; however, a daughter, Thelma Ann Francis, was born in 1902, and then a son, James William Thomas "Tommy" Nixon, was birthed three years later in 1905. We assume these first three were born in Broomtown. The fourth child, Robert Lee, came into the world on March 11, 1908, but his obituary shows birthplace as Farill, Alabama. This small community is located between Cedar Bluff and the Georgia state line fourteen miles due south of Broomtown. The Hardeman Cemetery near Farill is also the resting place for William Franklin, Martha Ola, Thelma "Tay" Ann Francis, and Tommy.

As a young man, Robert Lee relocated to Rome and worked for Anchor Duck mill located near the present site of Rome/Floyd County Health Department. It was here he met future wife, Eva "Mother Lou" Brownlow, whose people lived on a family farm in Bartow County's Taylorsville community. They married on June 11, 1927, and moved into a duplex on Blanche Avenue where R. L. also worked part-time at a filling station. The couple had two children, Willard Lee Nixon, born on June 17, 1928, and Mable Virginia, birthed February 4, 1934. Willard's birthplace is always listed as Taylorsville, for Mother Lou's dad, Cicero Brownlow, owned land and country store on Chulio Road close to Euharlee; evidently she moved there to have her first baby. In later life, she returned to the farm and built a home near her parents. Sister Mable Virginia was birthed six years after Willard but on Rome's Blanche Avenue.

After thirteen years of marriage, R. L. and Lou divorced; in 1940, their children moved to Rome's Noble Street with paternal grandparents, William F. and Ola Martha. It was on this street that the future major leaguer was introduced to baseball courtesy of Uncle Tommy. At this home, the kids developed a special relationship with their grands. Daughter Dawn Nixon Brock believes her father's "huge heart" came from time spent with Martha Ola, yet he also had a good relationship with William Franklin. Unfortunately, the latter passed away prematurely at fifty-three when Willard was thirteen. Although divorced, Mother Lou and Papa Nixon remained a loving part of the family, and the kids never questioned the separateness.[129]

At the onset of World War II, R. L. gained employment at Pepperell where he met and married Bert Cason; they set up housekeeping in the village on D Street and later bought a house on Eden Mountain across the road from the Eden clan. But this was an unhappy union, which ended in divorce. R. L. then met Nora Masters Caldwell Abney also in the mill. The couple wed and lived together until his death at age seventy. Prior to that, R. L. sold the Eden Mountain home and moved a trailer to Sunset Drive in Lindale to property owned by son Willard. These were happy times for the Nixons, a time in which Mama Nora became a treasure of the family. After leaving the mill, the elder Nixon ran a paper route for years with his wife accompanying him along the way. On July 4, 1978, R. L. died of a heart attack in the trailer. The widow stayed for a while on Sunset and then moved to Durham, North Carolina to be near her son Dale. She died there in 1991.

In 1942, with the cancellation of NWGTL play, fourteen-year-old Willard played sandlot baseball with the Silver Creek Wildcats. Shortly afterward, he entered high school at McHenry and performed with the school squad. At the same time, manager Earl Donaldson formed a small minor league version of the Pepperell Textile team. The stated purpose was to "keep baseball alive despite wartime conditions." The squad was financed by the mill and rostered with those under or over military age. By 1945, young Willard was the ace of the pitching staff, compiling an 8–1 record for the league winners.[130]

The first postwar year saw the Textile squads reorganize, reload, and respond to a community starved for entertainment. It was a breakout year for the seventeen-year-old soon-to-be phenomenon as he opened the season with thirty-four consecutive scoreless innings and three shutouts. In two playoff series, he pitched in six of ten games and won the deciding game in each set for the champion Pepperell team. In the other four contests, he played left field and batted .519 (19 for 37), including a game-tying home run in the final game.

Willard graduated in 1947 from McHenry High; the *Cardinal Classic* yearbook of that year (courtesy of Bill Howell) reveals "Nick" had transferred from Cave Spring in 1944. As a Cardinal, he starred in football for Coach Hollis Smith as a captain and QB wearing red jersey 24 with a leather helmet. The squad was a conglomerate of thirty players from Tubize, Lindale, Harmony, and Alto Park. However, the annual class prophecy stated that "Willard Nixon is winning fame in professional baseball."[131] And true to form, the Detroit Tigers offered the four-year letterman and high school graduate a pro contract; however, he opted for scholarship to Auburn instead. In his first game against Mercer, the Lindalean faced only nineteen batters in five innings for the win. He finished the year at 8–2 as the Tigers placed second in conference. After the initial collegiate season, he found summer work with the mill and went 8–1 on the Textile mound. Although Atco won the championship, Willard won three, saved one, and lost one in the postseason; he also batted .364.[132]

The rising sophomore pitcher returned to Auburn in the fall of 1948 as a newlywed. On October 5, Nancy Jane Logan (1930–2007) and Willard Lee Nixon were married at Silver Creek Presbyterian Church. Nancy Jane's mother, Eunice Glenn Sproull (1903–1978), and father, Harry Brown Logan (1891–1943), had met while working for the mill; the latter was a longtime purchasing agent for Pepperell dating back to his personal friendship with Captain Henry Parish Meikleham. Mr. Logan was another of the very able people employed by the captain; he possessed a fine "genial disposition and optimistic outlook." Harry was a former Darlington and UGA football athlete who came on board the mill in 1921. The Logans set up housekeeping at 10 Terrace Avenue, usually called the house on the corner, before going over Eden Mountain. Nancy Jane and Sister Anna Glenn were both born in this house. On August 3, 1943, when the former was thirteen years old, father Logan suffered a fatal heart attack while home for lunch; he is interred at Myrtle Hill Cemetery. Afterward, mother Eunice Glenn continued employment in the mill as well as operating the Tea Room. Thirteen-year-old Nancy, who was now attending Rome Girls High, also helped Mom out in the room. The Nixon boy would come in with friends after football or baseball practice at McHenry High, which was located on the west side of Eden Mountain. It was here that romance bloomed. After nuptials, the new couple moved in with Grandmother Eunice on Lindale's Terrace Avenue but soon they relocated to a Nixon-built cabin on the Sproull farm property located off Kingston Road.

They remained there until Willard was called up to big league in 1950; shortly afterward, the husband bought a home on Sunset Drive. The three Nixon children, Bill, Nan, and Dawn, were born and grew up on Sunset. William "Bill" Franklin came along in 1950, Mary Dawn in 1953, and lastly Nancy "Nan" Lee in 1961. It was a happy home with family members always around. Fannie "Aunt Beck" Sproull (1901–1987) who taught school at Pepperell for forty-five years would come by in the mornings and pick up the kids. As the children grew, Willard purchased an old Civil War home just west of Cedar Creek toward Cave Spring (when the kids were older, they laughed about how many houses Dad bought). By the early sixties, son Bill was a student at Darlington School. Dawn was attending the local C. S. fifth grade while baby Nan was still a toddler. The adjacent Cox farm provided "riding horses and outdoor working on the farm." In 1965, the family moved back to Lindale at 17 Central Avenue where Dawn entered sixth grade under Mrs. Motes and where she met her future husband, Tommy G. Brock. Bill was participating in baseball and soccer with growing interest in theater and music, so much so that he formed a band that performed locally. The kids spent summer hours accompanied by Mom at the Lin-Valley Country Club swimming pool. In 1968, Bill graduated at Darlington and enrolled at Auburn, completing his studies in 1972; he married Connie Brown in 1984 and now resided in Lanett, Alabama, close to his appraisal business in nearby Lafayette. Dawn finished at Pepperell in 1971, later attending Floyd Junior College before marrying Tommy Brock in 1980. They built and lived in a house on Pleasant Hope Road in Silver Creek for years before moving to Florida. They have two boys, Tommy Daniel from her husband's previous marriage and their son Charles Willard (C. W.); Nancy matriculated from Pepperell in 1979 and Macon's Wesleyan College in 1983; she married Mike Gillespie in 1984 and settled in Macon. The Gillespies have two sons, both UGA graduates. The Nixon daughters now live close by each other in Florida. They reminisce today what fun it was growing up in the Lindale area and recall that Dad was "the center of us all and so much fun to be with...our house was a happy, loving place to grow up in."[133]

Back in the Plains of Auburn in 1948, Nixon stuck out 20 Ole Miss batters to set a conference record. Next, he threw a no-hitter against Tennessee while striking out 18. In the return game with the Volunteers, only an eighth-inning scratch hit prevented another no-hitter. In the same contest, he contributed 4 hits, including a 370-foot home run. Following this feat, the *News-Tribune* said, "Folks in Knoxville think that Nixon is the greatest college player of all time." He finished the year with a 10–1 record and set a 39-year record of 145 strikeouts in addition to batting .448 for the schedule. Fourteen major league scouts watched his final victory against Vanderbilt, and two days later, Willard signed with the Red Sox. All but two organizations had bid for his services. He chose not to accept a $30,000 bonus which would have placed him automatically in the major league, opting instead for the $6,000 standard offer. He told writer Wynn Montgomery later that "nobody in the world needed the money more than I did, I just didn't think I was good enough to start at the top. I was afraid I might get that money and go up to the majors and flop. Then, that bonus money might be all I'd ever get out of baseball."

The Sox sent the rookie to Class D Scranton one day before his twentieth birthday; there he closed the regular season with six straight wins, finishing 11–5. Spring of 1949 saw him up to Triple-A Louisville, but after three losses, they moved him down one letter to Birmingham. Three losses there brought about a derisive "War Eagle" chant from the Crimson Tide fans as he warmed up against the Lookouts; however, he pitched a three-hitter and proceeded to win thirteen of seventeen decisions to end up 14–7 in addition to a .345 batting average. The highlight of the season happened on August 15 in Atlanta's venerable Ponce de Leon Park. Hundreds of Lindale faithful showed up to cheer their hero take the mound against the Crackers. All he did was pitch nine innings and drive in all the runs in a 5–4 victory. Lang Gammon wrote later, "He was the whole show, producer and star."[134]

Spring training of 1950 saw him struggle with control; consequently the twenty-one-year-old began the year in Louisville. By the middle of summer, the record stood at 11–2. With the Red Sox mired in fourth place, new Red Sox manager Steve O'Neill decided to bring up the Georgian whose ninety-seven strikeouts led the association along with a .345 batting average. He joined the squad on July 7 in New York and was directed immediately to go sit with relief pitchers behind the left field fence. Shortly word came to warm up. The game was already lost when he was summoned to the mound. He reminisced later, "I started walking in and Ted Williams walked two-thirds of the way with me, talking all the time and telling me that they weren't that good, that I could do it." After two or three pitches, Nixon added, "It became just a game again." The mound in Yankee Stadium was very comfortable, even facing Joe DiMaggio who swung and missed a fastball. The next pitch was a curve taken for strike two. The catcher called for another fastball which Willard shook off. "I came in with a great curve ball," he said later, "and Joe hit it like a bullet into the left field screen—and I cussed him all the way around the bases." The humor of the play occurred later in the Sox's dugout when Dom DiMaggio (Joe's brother) sat down next to the rookie, put his arm around him, and said, "Don't worry about it Kid, he's hit that pitch off of good pitchers...'course, he was just kidding me." Six days later, he pitched a victory in Fenway Park against the White Sox. When the season ended, Nixon appeared in twenty-two games including relief, logged an 8–6 record, and finished with a 6.04 earned run average (ERA). Many experts predicted him as an effective member of the staff and possible stardom.[135]

Williams took an immediate liking to the laid-back Southerner; they spent off-hours together and often relaxed over postgame meals. Soon, Ted discovered his young friend was a master forger. Contracts required players to sign boxes of baseballs for the public; however, after the best hitter in baseball autographed several boxes, he would tire. Clubhouse manager Don Fitzpatrick told it this way, "We'd bring more Spauldings to him and he'd say, 'Give them to Willard.'" He added later, "That's why we thought Nick would never be traded or released."[136]

During the offseason, Willard did what he always did—worked at the mill, refereed high school basketball, and played golf to stay in shape. Although nagging injuries plagued him through the 1951 season, he still finished the first full year in the majors with a 7–4 record and a .289 batting average. New manager Lou Boudreau regulated him to the bullpen in 1952. He developed a new sidearm delivery along with a slow curve and managed to eke out a 5–4 slate, but he walked more than he fanned. However, sportswriters as well as coaches noted his temper was affecting the performance. The *Boston Post* even reported there was a "veritable frenzy when roughed up." Willard must have worked on his emotions, for 1953 saw him pitch 4 consecutive complete games which were all wins to go with 21 straight scoreless innings. Observers noted "added poise and confidence" in his game. But the rest of the schedule was a disappointing 4–8, resulting in his first ever losing season. The 1954 season began quietly with a start against the Yankees on April 19. In previous work versus the New Yorkers, Willard had been sporadic and unspectacular in throwing 20 innings and garnering 1 loss; there was certainly no indication of what was about to happen. This time, he allowed only 5 hits and fanned 10 in a 2–1 victory; although the year ended with an 11–12 record, he beat the Bombers 3 consecutive times. This was against a team that finished second to Cleveland with 103 victories.

Willard had a good spring in 1955, and his reputation as a Yankee Killer was growing, so much so that he was home opening-day pitcher. Nixon threw well and, combined with reliever Ellis Kinder, beat the Bronx squad for the fifth straight time. Next came a shutout against the Senators followed by 1–0 two-hitter in Yankee Stadium for a sixth. The *Atlanta Constitution* bragged, "Dan Topping and Del Webb may think they own the Yankees, but it turns out that Willard Nixon...does." But a dry spell occurred to even the season at 4–4 before he downed the Yankees again which started a five-game win streak. The last game was 4–1 decision over Whitey Ford. As August began, he was sitting on twelve victories; however, Nix did not win another that year, even losing two games against the New Yorkers. Also his temper resurfaced. After giving up four runs in the ninth against Detroit, he "splintered Fenway's locker room door with a metal chair." The anger was understandable as a very promising season turned south to 12–10.

In spring training, pitching coach Dave Ferriss suggested developing a knuckleball and a new curve for the upcoming 1956 schedule. There was talk that the 6-foot-2-inch, 195-pound Georgian could be a 20-game winner during the 1956 season. However, a freak accident occurred before the Sox broke camp for Boston. Ringling Brothers Circus winter quarters was in Sarasota close by the team's practice facilities. During a photo shoot request, Willard climbed aboard a circus elephant which unexpectedly dumped him to the ground unfortunately on his pitching-arm side. He was able to shrug off the fall but not the underlying pain. Baseball players are notorious for nicknames and kidding; Nixon gained the name Sabu, famed as Hollywood's Elephant Boy. A few puns also followed, the best being, "He has developed a trunkful of new curves." The manager thought enough of him to give him the ball in the Yankee Stadium opener which turned into a third consecutive loss to the Bombers. The team orthopedist began treating him for calcium deposit and tendonitis in the right shoulder. But on May 29 against the Yankees, Willard carried a no-hitter into the eighth before a fielding error ruined a shutout in the win. The ailing back pain persisted, but the arm felt better on August 7, 1956, when he dueled Don Larsen at Fenway before 36,350 standing-room-only fans. For 10 innings, the two matched each other in the scoreless contest. In the eleventh, Ted Williams dropped a routine fly ball which drew the wrath of the faithful Bostonians; minutes later, Ted made a great catch to retire the side. As he neared the dugout, the Splendid Splinter showed his disdain toward the fickle fans by spitting in their direction (the "great expectorations" cost him $5,000 in fines). In the home half of the eleventh, Willard drew a walk that led to the winning run. The next encounter with the Pinstripes resulted in a 2-hit shutout and brought the Yankee Killer's record to a dominant 11–5. Although he threw several excellent games, inconsistency plagued the rest of the year. He stated later that "the only consistent thing about me was my inconsistency."[137]

The new year of 1957 brought about chronic arm pain to go with a pulled tendon in his leg; nevertheless, by mid season, his quality starts led to an ongoing 7–7 slate. Eventually the season record would settle at 12–13. Hidden in his win-loss was a career-best ERA of 3.68, complete games were at 11 in addition to leading American Leagues pitchers with a .293 batting average. These maladies were somewhat lessened by family. During baseball season, wife Nancy, Bill, and Dawn would drive to Boston and spend most of the summer there. The son has vivid memories, keepsakes, and souvenirs of that special time in and around Fenway Park.

A milestone was reached at the start of the 1958 year as only Theodore Samuel Williams (1918–2002) ranked above Willard Nixon in tenure with the Sox. However, two early losses to the Yankees soured his mood. This was followed by a three-hit complete game against Kansas City (it would be his last major league win). A few days later pitching in relief against New York, he would weaken after three innings and took the loss. He said after the game, "I'm not worried about my arm...It's only a temporary thing." But the Yankee record now stood at 12–12. Although arm trouble persisted to a mid-season 1–7 record, it did not slow the bat down, for at the time he was leading the team in hitting with a .312 batting average. Three weeks prior to July 4 in Fenway Park, Willard threw daily batting practice, testing the arm; before a holiday-packed house, he relieved the starter in the sixth and retired the side. After getting one out in the seventh, three hits and two runs followed. He said later, "My arm's throbbing like a toothache...as things stand, I'm no good to...my manager, myself, the team—anybody!" Years later, Pepperell teacher Sandra Cooper and Willard were partnered together playing in a bridge tournament and at the same time watching a muted Atlanta Braves baseball game on the television. After a pitching change, Sandra asked the former major leaguer, "What did you say when the manager visited the mound?" Willard replied, "Our Father Who art in heaven Hallowed be Thy Name." By mid-July, he was placed on the disabled list for the remainder of the season. The season-ending 1–7 ultimately cost him a winning career record which ended at 69–72. Back in Lindale, he sold real estate and played golf to occupy the rest of the year.[138]

Reporting to Scottsdale, Arizona, for training camp in 1959, Willard was confident that "I can pitch again." Also securing a spot on the roster would bring additional pension benefits as a ten-year professional major leaguer. However, the arm continued to hurt in the spring whereas on April 4, the Sox were forced to outright release the Georgian. He immediately signed a minor league contract with Triple-A Minneapolis and threw respectably during the year. But as the season wore on, ineffectiveness plagued him again, necessitating a move from the mound to first-base coach. The Junior World Series finals came down to Havana Sugar Kings versus Minneapolis Millers. Midwest cold weather forced the games to be moved to warm-clime Cuba where Fidel Castro had just overthrown the Batista regime; the wide-eyed Lindalean later talked about armed soldiers manning the streets and even team taxi drivers packing automatic weapons. With three thousand armed soldiers inside Gran Stadium, submachine guns outnumbered the bats. For seven straight days, twenty-five thousand fans filled the stands along with their baseball-loving premier. They were treated to a well-played series with two games being decided in extra innings and two others in the ninth, including the Sugar Kings 3–2 championship win.

After the 1959 season, Willard told the *News-Tribune* there was "considerable doubt" of pitching again, yet he still hoped for a spot on the roster or as a coach. When Boston called to offer a position as scout, he accepted. For the next five years, he scoured the southeast for talent before retiring and returning to Lindale Mill as purchasing agent. Next, the Floyd County Commission named him clerk of the board; he resigned that position in 1971 to become court investigator. Two years later, the same board wanted him as chief of police. There was mirth attached to this position since he forged Ted Williams's signature on dozens of baseballs. Two years later, the local school system hired him as transportation director from which he retired in 1989.

As a youngster, Nixon learned the game of golf as a caddie. His baseball swing translated well to the smaller white ball. The latter years saw him become a par golfer until heart trouble slowed the pace; then in his late sixties, Alzheimer's disease came upon him. Willard Lee Nixon, born June 17, 1928, passed away on December 10, 2000, and is interred in Rome's East View Cemetery. The tall blond Yankee Killer is probably Floyd County's most famous athlete—most certainly Lindale's.[139]

With President-elect George W. Bush on its December 25, 2000, front cover, *Time* magazine posted this on page 53: "Milestones. Died. Willard Nixon, 72, 1950 Boston Red Sox pitcher who never won more than 12 games in a season but who routinely trounced the indomitable Yankees, after a battle with Alzheimers, in Rome, Ga. 'I have no earthly way of explaining my mastery over them,' Nixon said."[140]

Postscript: In 1971 and 1993, Nixon was elected to Rome/Floyd County and Georgia Sports Hall of Fame respectively. In 2002, Auburn University recognized him with a plaque on the Tiger Trail Walk of Fame, which represents an athlete that has brought "pride, glory and honor" to the Plains.

In 1950, thirty American League pitchers made their first appearance on the mound; only three, Lew Burdette, Whitey Ford, and Ray Herbert, lasted longer and won more games than Willard Nixon. Looking back, he said, "I'm happy with my career...I wouldn't have had anything if it hadn't been for baseball."[141]

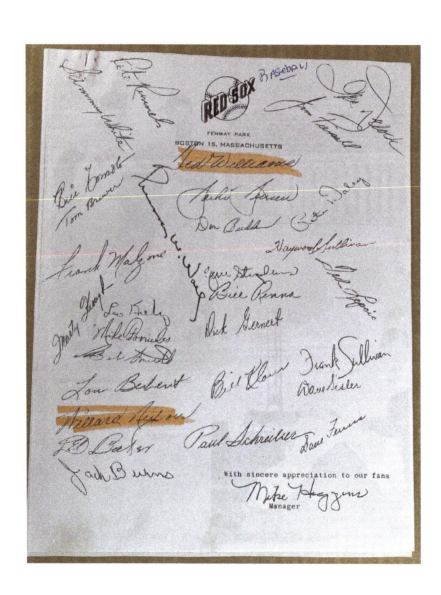

JACK BOWDOIN GASTON (1911–1994)

Writers in the later years characterize his pitch as, "a curve ball that almost changed zip codes on the way to the plate."

As far back as the fourteenth century, the Gastons were French Huguenots in Southern France; however, we pick up Jack Gaston, our third prominent player of the Northwest Georgia Textile League, at the turn of the twentieth century. His parents, William Maxwell Gaston and Linnie Lee Lanham, both Georgia natives, were married on September, 20 1899. The farming couple moved around a lot with children being born in Sugar Valley, Adairsville (Bartow County), and the river-bend community of Oostanaula in west Gordon County where Jack was birthed. Eventually, ten children, five boys and five girls, were brought into the world. Unfortunately, sometime in 1918, Mr. Gaston contracted tuberculosis or consumption which at the time had only a 50 percent survival rate. The desperate family then found a better tenant farm on Burnett Ferry Road in Rome, leaving behind tubercular William Maxwell in the care of his thirty-year-old sister Betty and ma Cythia Ann, whose husband, Thomas Gaston, had passed away in 1902 in Oostanaula. William's granddaughter Patricia (Jack's daughter) has preserved twenty-six letters written between Oostanaula and West Rome dated May 29, 1919 to November 21, 1919. The missives from Linnie Lee to William cover his attempt at healing and eventual death. Pat has graciously permitted us to cite these informal family records.

Gaston Letters (1919)

> One-hundred years later Patsy said, "They give a glimpse of the problems, fears and everyday life of the family."

The first letter from Burnett Ferry Farm to father Bill was dated May 29, 1919, and speaks of a good-looking corn and cotton crop. The cows were well, the children caught rabbits to supplement the protein of chickens. When Linnie moved the family to Rome, six-year-old Joe stayed behind with his ailing dad, Aunt Bettie (Betty), and grandmother Cynthia Ann Gaston in nearby Plainville area; all the while, nine-year-old Jack missed his younger brother terribly. Throughout the exchange of letters, it is apparent seventeen-year-old Thelma was doing a man's job in the fields, plowing with a mule in the cotton, corn, sorghum, watermelons, and garden plots. Consequently the hot weather sapped her strength which cut the days shorter, yet she found time to help other farmers with hoeing in return for them plowing her cotton, corn, and peas; still Thelma found time to write her father. The other children did their share in the fields with ten-year-old Billie being a good cotton chopper; Jack helped out some, but mostly he toted water to the field hands. By the middle of June, Linnie Gaston was beginning to have trouble with teenagers Irma (fifteen) and Lois (fourteen) as they wanted to play too much, which brought about a whipping for both. She didn't have much trouble with twelve-year-old Verna. The youngest girl, Mary Bess (four), sure missed her dad and said every day or so, "I wish Daddy would come home." By the last of June, the cotton had lapped the middles, and it looked like it would be better than last year. Word from Plainville was that husband Bill was in bed most of the time while in Rome, Linnie was expecting another child soon to be named Willard Maxwell if it were a boy. Meanwhile, little Joe kept the Oostanaula household guessing with his questions. This Saturday he was going to walk two hundred yards to the Hardshell (Primitive) Baptist Church and take in their foot washing; undoubtedly, questions would follow. Twelve-year-old Verna wrote to Daddy in middle July that she hired out to Messrs. Holbrooks and Walraven to chop cotton; the former paid $1.50 per day while the latter came in at $1.25. Neighbor Mr. Pyles said he would give them $2.00, but they had to work their own crop now. The bad news in August from Plainville was that Dad could hardly walk except in the mornings; he was in serious condition according to the doctor. Bill signed his letter of August 20, 1919, as "Your old sick suffering man." All this was happening twenty miles away just as Linnie became confined on the Burnett Ferry Farm with the expectant baby. The last child's birth happened sooner than thought as William Maxwell came into the world on August 22, 1919; he would be called Max. By the twenty-seventh, there was talk of moving to another tenant farm; oldest son, Thurman (eighteen years old), headed the search, but his mother thought the son could be more forceful in dealing with the likes of owners Gunn, Bradshaw, and Mitchell. In the second week of October, the children were busy gathering the crop while on "cotton picking" vacation from school. Prices were good as it was, bringing 34¢ per pound. At the same time, Linnie and new baby Max trekked to Oostanaula/Plainville for Bill to see his newborn. Thelma was disappointed she didn't make the fair this year; however, "she could see the airplanes good from the farm" as well as the balloon. On October 19, Bill wrote the family that Aunt Bettie was not doing well and might have to have another operation; also Grandma was in bad shape. Bill sent word to Thelma to run an ad in the *News* and *Herald*, which would cost a dollar or more: "Want to rent a good two-horse crop. Not subject to overflows. Not less than 4 large room house and other necessary building; it has own stock and feed. State distance from church and school. Signed W. M. Gaston Rt. 7." Bill wrote to "the whole bunch" on Sunday, October 26, 1919, that a chance at a Freeman Ferry Farm for two years was possible; he encouraged the kids to pick the cotton dry, which brought best price, and thought it would go to 40¢ if they could hold on to it. Of course, it was better to sell and pay off everything to protect credit. His health was not much better; staying in bed weakened the legs and cut the appetite also. He complained the kids in Oostanaula were all redheaded or towheaded, said it would be nice to see a black-headed one. The family found a place on River Road west of Rome that suited them exactly. The cotton ground was red, and the corn earth was fox-fur gray; the house had five downstairs and two up, large porch, servant house, garage, washhouse, and shop. School was one mile, and church was close by. Mr. R. M. Pattillo had recently bought the spread and planned to live there also. On November 2, 1919, a neighbor, Ms. Hattie Lynch, had to write Linnie and kids because William did not feel able to do it; neither did Ma Gaston or Bettie. The father encouraged the family to fight for the Pattillo place. The final letter was dated Friday a.m., November 21, 1919. It says the kids were still picking the cotton; however, the Gastons' search for next year's tenant farm was not successful.[142]

Bad news continued toward the end of the year as William Maxwell Gaston passed away from his tuberculosis on December 9, 1919. Wife, Linnie Lee, would survive him by almost thirty-five years, passing away in 1954. Aunt Betty remained in Gordon County for the rest of her life, becoming an icon in the community; she never married and lived to be eighty-three. After the crops were gathered on Burnett Ferry, a neighbor suggested to the now thirty-five-year-old widowed Linnie Lee that her two oldest children (ages sixteen and eighteen) could gain employment in the Lindale cotton mill. A move to 216 Grove Street was forthcoming with the entire brood. The oldest son and daughter immediately went to work at Pepperell. The regular paychecks were a blessing to the large family, which also made extra money with truck farming and livestock. In the meantime, a children's home representative offered to take the three youngest children. This "infuriated" mother Gaston who replied, "If we starve, we will all starve together, no one is taking my children away."

When the younger Gastons grew to the age of millwork, they helped with household expenses. As the decade of the 1920s faded, the family established and maintained a happy existence in the village; however, another tragedy occurred in 1928 when next to the oldest daughter Vera Gaston Holdbrooks died in childbirth at age twenty-three. The baby son named Houston survived, and Linnie took him in as one of her sons. Linnie Lee Lanham Gaston would live to be seventy years old, dying in Lindale on February 1954.[143]

The benevolent mill manager Captain Meikleham saw to the needs of his workers daily. However, as the next decade began, so did the Great Depression. The Gaston children were older now, ranging from early teens to the oldest, Bud, who was thirty. The unexpected death of Henry Parish Meikleham in the summer of 1937 caused consternation in the community. But his successor, Robert Donald Harvey, quickly proved more than capable of running the company. He temporarily cut workers' hours but reduced house rent and costs on fuel supplies; Mr. Harvey held periodic town meetings to keep everyone informed, advising the families to be frugal with their earnings.

Captain Meikleham's favorite pastime, Textile baseball, came along in the early 1930s and provided relief to a working public; in addition, extra money went to players who also worked shifts at the mill. Bill, Joe, Jack, and Max Gaston all played the game well while the oldest, Bud, became the team's official scorer; Bill later became an umpire in the league. Years later, the youngest child (Max) reflected on the heritage of Floyd County, Georgia (1833–1999), "Small towns are capable of offering the opportunities of a well-rounded lifestyle, a life full of health, happiness, love and lots and lots of fond memories." And then December 7, 1941, occurred. A family member remembers: "Everything rocked along very smoothly…then 'blam' World War II! We had just survived the Great Depression. Now the war was beginning to disintegrate our family." The Gaston boys answered the call. Thirty-one days after the Japanese attacked Pearl Harbor, Bill and Joe enlisted in the US Army; Jack quit the Weave Department and followed his brothers. The *News-Tribune* reported on Wednesday, February 25, 1942, that "a group of Lindaleans left today for Fort McPherson…those departing included Theo Sartin, Henry A. Bruce, Jack Gaston, Johnnie Stroupe, Ernest Bobo, Raymond Stowe, Joe Sills and Joe William Roach." Grandson Houston was already in the Navy when Max was sworn into the Marines a year later. A worried Mama Gaston displayed five front-window blue stars, each representing a son overseas in the ETO, Aleutians, North Atlantic, and the South Pacific. She had reason to be concerned, for Joe was to see duty in the Normandy Invasion as well as Germany's Siegfried Line battle. He received a Purple Heart (October 1944) for action in Belgium as an ambulance driver for the Thirtieth Division. In February of 1945, Max was a gunner on Saratoga when a kamikaze (suicide plane) crashed into the carrier just above his gun emplacement. Following basic training, Bill was assigned to a medical attachment; he was "fighting in the Aleutians, seeing action on Attu, Adak and Kiska." On Wednesday, July 15, 1942, Lang Gammon's "News of Lindale" reported Private Jack Gaston arrived overseas and was now serving "somewhere in England" with the Fighter Command Headquarters Squadron of the Eighth Army Air Force. The World War II exploits of the Gaston boys is available in section "Lindale Goes to War."

One of Jack's first letters home in 1942 had survived; it was addressed to Coach E. Russell Moulton:

> Hello, Slick. Received your letter and was more than glad to hear from you. I guess I am doing pretty well over here…I was really glad to hear your school children were helping all they could buying War Stamps. I think everybody over there is helping what little I get to read in the papers. I sure hate to hear you won't have much of a ball club this time, but you know you just can't

help it in these days…We may get to play some softball, but I'm pretty sure there will be no baseball. I got a nice letter from Mr. Harvey on my birthday. Tell him hello for me, and I hope he has a job for me when I get back; say hello to Ish [Williams] and ask Earl [Donaldson] to hold me a uniform because this thing isn't going to last much longer for our boys have too much on the ball for them. Well, Slick, there isn't much over here I can write about so, until later, I'm wishing you lots of luck.[144]

On January 15, 1942, President Franklin Roosevelt recommended Commissioner Kennesaw Mountain Landis continue professional play. In a "green light" letter, FDR said, "I honestly feel that it would be best for the country to keep baseball going." However, would the troops support an activity that took able-bodied men from the battle area to play baseball? The men responded wholeheartedly in favor, believing the four-cornered sport is part of the American way of life that should be played for the morale of, not only soldiers, but also America itself. Jack Gaston's commanding officer, Major General Ira Clarence Eaker, leader of the Eighth Air Force, agreed with the president that recreation, especially baseball, would be a great morale booster for his men. The general's background mirrored small-town America. He was born on a tenant farm in Field Creek, Texas (130 miles due north of San Antonio) on April 13, 1896, the same year Massachusetts Mills of Georgia began production. He entered the Army Air Corps after infantry service in World War I and advanced quickly between the wars. He achieved brigadier rank in January of 1942 and then received lieutenant general stars as head of the Eighth Air Force based in the UK. He agreed with Commissioner Landis and President Roosevelt to continue baseball in wartime. This command reached 750,000 troops by 1943, and young men faced the upheaval, rigors, and anxiety of serving in a foreign country. English historian Gary Bedingfield later wrote, "The servicemen needed a morale booster and baseball fit the bill." The general officer proceeded to organize teams chosen from a wealth of talented amateur and professional players coming into the services. The Eighth Air Force nine quickly became competitive against other military units. But the All-Stars, which included Lindale's Jack Gaston, chosen from former professional players, became the commander's favorite. With 21,500 fans watching in Wembley's Empire Stadium, Air Force pitcher Bill Brech threw a 1–0 no-hit victory against the US Army Ground Force. A local dignitary threw out the first ball much to the pleasure of the press; however, the British print media struggled with American vernacular when describing the action as "wonderful catching" and "spirited dashes from one base to another behind the pitcher's back." The winning commanding officer rewarded his squad with a 30-day tour of the military bases around Great Britain. Wearing red uniforms, they achieved 22 victories without defeat. In a personal letter dated October 9, 1943, Commanding General Ira C. Eaker of the Eighth Air Force wrote to Jack:

Dear Sergeant Gaston,
I am enclosing an autographed copy of a picture of the best baseball team I have ever seen in action and of which you were a valuable member. I took great pride in this team and its exploits and have said repeatedly that it

played the best baseball game I have ever seen, and I have seen all of the big league teams in action.

You and the other members of the team contributed materially to the morale and high spirit of the Eighth Air Force by your personal example and your great professional skill while a member of this team and for this I wish to thank you on behalf of the whole Eight Air Force.

Sincerely,
Ira C. Eaker

As the summer ended, the squad returned to their military duty. Jack's children remember Dad reminiscing about his years in England. Postwar baseball historian Gary Bedingfield wrote about those times in his *The Boys of an English Summer.* The work included biographies of the important players. An inquiry letter posted to mayor and town clerk of Lindale were returned. Luckily a second missive, dated May 1995, was addressed to the mayor of Rome, Georgia, and found the Gaston children. Daughter Pat responded with, "We were delighted to receive your letter...it saddens me to say that Dad passed away last September...I know he would have enjoyed communication with you for he enjoyed those times with the British. He felt they had it rough during the war, but were very brave and hospitable to American Soldiers...I am sending various articles and pictures from our scrapbook for your history."

Exactly how Jack Gaston was picked to play Army ball is undocumented; perhaps it was at a tryout camp or information taken from induction questionnaires that listed the 31-year-old Lindalean's résumé in the NWGL (see pages 53–54). The right-hander carried 180 pounds to go with his 6-foot-1-inch frame; this was coupled with a strong arm, foot speed, and a good batting eye from the left-handed box. His pitching prowess may have been helped by a playground accident in elementary school when he suffered a broken bone to the right arm; the break was set and wrapped rigidly in chicken wire with cotton padding underneath. More than likely it was a greenstick fracture which occurs when a bone bends and cracks rather than breaking completely. All was well until later when a schoolmate pushed him into a ditch on the way home from classes. This fall was not checked for further injury. When the make-do cast was eventually removed, Jack's pitching arm was permanently crooked. Family members believe his effectiveness as a great pitcher came from this mishap, causing him to rely more on wrist movement when throwing curveballs and sliders. A reporter in England described his expertise on the mound, "He's a master workman on the hill. He has speed, hooks, a dipsy-doodler, floaters and almost anything else that goes into the makings of a superlative heaver." Another writer said, "Jack Gaston is one of the cleverest hurlers ever unveiled in these parts...his slow ball is a honey and will cause many a strained back this season." A local newspaper added, "The Washington Senators have first call on the bomb-ball artist when he again dons civvies...they could use him now." Perhaps the boyish shove into the ditch years earlier by an anonymous schoolmate did Jack a favor.[145]

Twenty-seven months after he arrived in the UK, Sergeant Gaston was transferred stateside to Newburgh, a small town northeast of New York City where his reputation as a fireballer for the

Eighth Air Force All-Stars preceded him. The family has preserved several write-ups of the day courtesy of local sports editor Bo Gill's piece "STRAY BOOTS," which paralleled Lang Gammon's "News of Lindale." The Air Force media also added to this with pictures and write-ups in their section called "PROP WASH." These features gave the public a print history of military baseball in the summer of 1945. Playing for the Stewart Field Airmen, the Lindalean dominated the headlines: "GASTON IN NO HIT, NO RUN GEM AS AIRMEN WIN 5–0"; "GASTON HOMERS, DRIVES IN FIVE RUNS"; "GEORGIA JACK GASTON SNAG 1–0 DECISION OVER PANTHERS"; "GASTON SLATED TO FACE LYNCH ON MOUND"; "ADMIRAL GASTON FAILS AFTER TOSSING STEADY BALL FOR 7 INNINGS"; "GASTON IN FORM, WHIFFS 11 BATTERS"; "GASTON'S MOUND MAGIC WASTED AS AIRMEN FLUB HOME OPENER"; "GASTON TWIRLS, BATS AIRMEN TO SIZZLING TIE WITH KILMER"; "GASTON VERSUS LYNCH IN TITLE DUEL TOMORROW"; "GASTON LEADS AIRMEN WITH TERRIFIC .571 BATTING AVERAGE."[146]

Early in the season, a teammate from Stewart Field arranged double dates for himself and the young Georgian. Jack and twenty-five-year old Anna Marie Gibb were paired together before and after the game; a friendship first then romance developed. In August prior to Jack's transfer home for discharge in late September, they were engaged to be married. The November 1945 issue of *Home Front News* belatedly noted that "Sergeant Jack B. Gaston has returned to Lindale with an honorable discharge from the U. S. Army." He immediately returned to the weave room at Pepperell as a loom fixer. After a six months' engagement, Jack and Nan (the bride's grandmother bestowed this pet name) were united on January 13, 1946, at Saint Mary's Church, Rome, Georgia. The newlyweds moved into the Lindale Hotel for a while before finding a four-room house at 120 Garden Street. Their first child, Patricia Ann, was born here in 1947 with son, Jack Charles, coming along in 1955. Five years later, with both children now attending local schools, the couple built a home at 306 Garden Street. Nan worked briefly in the mill's cloth room before moving to Advance Glove on Maple Street. Her husband retired in 1973 and for a while was employed at Lin Valley Golf Club. Although he was an excellent amateur at Lin Valley Golf Club, who frequently shot his age, it was forever baseball prowess that brought fame. Following the war, Lindale welcomed their fan favorite back as though he never left. And in 1988, he was elected to the Rome/Floyd County Sports Hall of Fame. In his opening remarks to the group, local broadcast icon Lee Mowry noted that Jack Bowdoin Gaston began Textile play in 1931; he was a terror at the plate and in the field who once led the league in batting at .422 in addition to topping the home runs lists. Just prior to the war breaking out, the young man "signed a contract with the Washington Senators who agreed not to assign him below Class A ball—something unheard of at the time."[147] Serving in England during World War II, Jack was a brilliant pitcher for his service team, winning more games than he can remember, including a sparkling no-hitter and numerous shutouts. With Gaston as its star, his team introduced baseball to the English during wartime. Returning home, he patrolled the garden for Slick Moulton and was the 1948 MVP of the league playoffs while batting .428 and pitching to a 7–0 record. His 1946–1954 exploits, along with others, are recorded in Tom Klenc's Research Guide, pages 187–299.

Lindale was the Gastons' home until they passed away in the early 1990s. They settled here because Jack's family was quite large and lived close by. Furthermore, he was a true Southern boy who loved the village. Nan returned two times to Newburgh over the years—the occasion of the 1964 New York World's Fair and Grandmother O'Mara's funeral in 1968. In a recent interview, daughter Pat wrote this tribute to her Mom, "Mother was well liked by everyone who knew her. It wasn't easy moving to the Deep South from New York in 1946, but she adjusted and was able to 'fit' in. She was a very friendly and helpful person who was also a hard worker. Dad was lucky to have her."

NATHANIEL MCCLINIC
(1924–2004)

Nathaniel "Nath" McClinic was born near the substation in Silver Creek, Georgia, on April 26, 1924, to Samuel and Sarah Jones McClinic. He attended the Floyd County school located directly behind the mill proper to the point of being drafted in 1942 as an eighteen-year-old; afterward, he completed GED requirements while in the service. The self-professed country boy was immediately sent to Camp Lee, Virginia, for basic training and then shipped out to Camp Stone, California, and then to Hawaii. During an air-raid drill in Honolulu, he sustained burns to the arms; then the Army transferred him to the Forty-Third Amphibious Trucking Battalion bound for the invasion of Iwo Jima in February 1945. Nath remembered later that Pacific storms had prevented Navy PT boats from landing provisions to the beach and tragically many of the onshore Seabees were killed or wounded, "so they commandeered us and our amphibious crafts (Ducks) to ferry much needed equipment to the desperate 4th Marine Division...My outfit was not supposed to be in combat yet we were under constant enemy fire for several hours."

He added, "We lost the majority of our men in that action." The entire island battle took seven thousand American lives in addition to several thousand casualties. The Forty-Third Amphi was scheduled for another island fight, but the battalion was so depleted, the able troops remained bivouacked on Iwo. Yet they were not idle. The surviving remnant soldiers, Marines, and sailors got together and formed a baseball league in which the Forty-Third proceeded to win the 1945 Iwo Jima Island Championship tourney with the young Georgian hitting two home runs and stealing three bases.

Samuel McClinic's other son Sergeant John L. McClinic served with distinction in the European theater Quartermaster Corps. On page 7 of the Sunday, January 21, 1945, *Rome News-Tribune*, commanding officer Lieutenant Colonel Max W. Goodman issued a citation praising the Lindalean for "high soldierly qualities, fine spirit of co-operation, loyalty to duty and leadership over men." A copy of the printed award, which was sent home, informed the parents that "your fine son is a great credit to the military service." An accompanying letter stated, "This is an honor which any soldier would be most proud to possess, and few receive."

When the war ended, Nathaniel was honorably discharged in December of 1945; he returned home to pursue his first love—baseball. The youngster grew up around the ballpark his father kept in Lindale while hoping one day to be a good player. He would tag along while his dad, who had a crippled leg, maintained the "best diamond in Northwest Georgia." Upon returning to South Floyd in postwar, he restarted the local baseball team, which was segregated at the time. This squad rotated the use of West Point Pepperell field when the white nine were on the road. Floyd County native Earnest Long played for the Chattanooga Choo-Choos, and it was he who suggested a team scout come to Lindale to look. Nath signed and played outfield in the Negro Southern League until the middle of 1947; at that point, he and Long moved to the Cleveland Buckeyes for a couple of seasons where the twenty-five-year-old lived out his childhood dream. The Buckeyes were part of the twelve-team Negro American League which produced some of the greatest players in baseball history, namely Jackie Robinson, Hank Aaron, Willie Mays, and Satchel Paige. He remembers facing Paige by saying, "Well, let's just say I went up to the plate against him." The future Hall of Famer was using the hesitation pitch which today still makes Nath shake his head about trying to make contact. "I didn't hit too much cover—had trouble with the curve." More than likely, the modest Lindalean pounded his share of crooked balls. But even Nath admitted he could run. The October 1948 issue of *Pepperell Fabric-cator* noted on page 17 that he stole fifty-five bases during the season; the squad (Dragons) won forty-three of fifty-three games that year. And he could throw. For those who watched, McClinic was one of the best center fielders around, possessing an excellent arm from all parts of the garden. In a Sunday, November 19, 1995, interview with *RNT* staff writer Mark Wilder, he attributed success to the following: "I never smoked and never drank whiskey and have tried to live a pretty decent and clean life." Although playing professional ball was a childhood dream, the twenty-four-hour bus rides and paper bag lunches tempered the good times of playing a segregated game. By the late 1940s, he had returned to Lindale and married Lorine Inez McClinic; the two parented one daughter and three sons. However, the love of the sports continued with the Lindale Dragons as player and manager in the eight-team semipro

Josh Gibson League, which culminated with a championship in 1960. Citing success against local white teams, he believes several local players could have played major league if "given a shot."

In 1991, the surviving legends of the Negro leagues were transported to Cooperstown, New York, where they were honored at the Hall of Fame. The crowd's reaction at the event was amazing, remembers Nath, "We came out of the meeting room and there were 4,000 fans all asking for autographs. To me, when someone wants your autograph, it's an honor. Here's a man who grew up a black man in the South with a GED education and people want me to sign my baseball card...to me, that's great." In a *RNT* "Past Times" interview on July 1996, he added, "You would be surprised by the mail I get from people sending me baseball cards, wanting autographs." In 1995, former players attended a Negro League Hall of Fame ceremony in Kansas City; some had not seen one another for forty or fifty years, which made it very special. Reporters asked the attendees one main question: "How do you feel about not being able to play in the major leagues because of your race?" McClinic recalls most replied, "That's the way it was...We weren't angry at the white players." In essence, he thinks these gatherings have brought to the forefront what the nation missed.

In 1965, McClinic became the first African American police officer in Floyd County. Retired county policeman George Lemming partnered with Nath from 1974 to '75 and again in 1980 to '81. An insight into the latter's character came in two personal interviews on October 2022. George remembers when father Samuel began to age, the son traveled every day to the house near Silver Creek's Liberty View Church on Spur 1E. On occasions, the sergeants would stop by Bobo Street in East Rome where Inez cooked lunch for her husband and partner; these were good days for the two policemen, and despite seventeen years' difference in age, they became as close as brothers. Some incidents brought them even closer. While cruising on US Highway 27N on a Sunday afternoon in January, the pair blue-lighted a car speeding toward Rome. As the driver exited his vehicle, it was obvious he was distressed, for his wife was moaning in the front seat with serious labor pains. The two policemen quickly moved the expectant mother into the back seat of the cruiser with George in attendance as Nath raced toward Floyd Hospital. Officer Lemming said in an October 11, 2022, interview, "We didn't make it! The crying baby boy was birthed in the back seat with me assisting." At the hospital, emergency personnel took charge, and all was well with the mother, father, and child. Nath was visibly shaken by the event. As he pulled back out into traffic back on patrol, he turned to his partner and said, "I'm thinking about taking up drinking."

Jack Ozment is an eighty-three-year-old retired deputy sheriff who was a third grader when he first saw Nath working around the village. Following World War II, father Joe Tom Ozment moved his family from Farill, Alabama, into the spacious house of sister Eunice Payne; it was here on Cedar Avenue that McClinic first noticed big Jack's baseball athleticism. For the next decade, the Negro Hall of Famer would quietly (so as not to anger white teammates) coach him on the finer points of the sport. It must have worked for Jack (teammates called him Beanie as in "Jack and the Beanstalk") played on back-to-back—1957 and 1958—state championships for PHS. In the 1957 deciding game versus Habersham, Ozment singled and came around to score the only run in a 1–0 victory. Nath liked his protégé's dedication to baseball, which eventually led to a professional contract. Like most Pepperell kids, Beanie worked summers in the mill doing odd jobs; he recalls Nath working in the cloth room where Joe Tom also worked. After a stint with the US Army in Bavaria, Jack joined the county police force in 1967; while chasing a bootlegger in the Armuchee area that same year, he was involved in a multicar accident that left him with serious injuries. At the time, Inez McClinic worked at Floyd Hospital; following her shift, she would come and sit with the injured officer for hours but refused compensation from the family, saying, "I won't take money for this—I practically raised that boy." Ms. Inez passed away in October 1987. Jack Thomas "Beanie" Ozment retired in 1996 and resides in Old East Rome. In a long personal interview on October 19, 2022, it became obvious Jack Ozment still reveres his silent coach.

Milton Slack III was born in Rome on September 7, 1943. The talented athlete graduated from Main High School in 1961; however, he turned down a scholarship to AME-associated Wilberforce University in Ohio in order to help his mom raise four other siblings, all of whom are now college educated. Prior to finishing school at Main, the youngster performed as an underage player by using an older person's identity in order to play for Nath McClinic in the Josh Gibson League. Once of age eighteen, he retrieved his own name with the Lindale Dragons. In an October 20, 2022, interview, Milton fondly remembered calling the big manager Daddy. The squad would play on Lindale field or use East Rome's Cole Stadium, which was located at Fifteenth Street and Flannery complete with wooden bleachers and fences. It is now Orchard Place homes. Milton describes his manager as fun loving but serious about baseball. He added that Nath retained the same easygoing demeanor after joining law enforcement in the mid-fifties. There was no attitude of superiority about him probably because he knew everybody around. The two remained close through the years, serving in the Army Reserve together with local 5435 Quartermaster Corps on Redmond Circle. Milton retired from Sears after thirty-four years of service and resides off MLK Boulevard in the Fair Grounds area of Rome. Sadly, McClinic passed away before his former second sacker was elected as a Rome City commissioner. When Nathaniel passed away in a Rome hospital after a short illness, *Rome News-Tribune* staff writer Lauren Gregory wrote on April 4, 2004, "Floyd County lost a seasoned athlete, an experienced law enforcement officer and a beloved friend and role model."

The 1946 Postwar Lindale Dragons

Pepperell's crack league-leading baseball team is not the only diamond outfit in this community "setting the woods on fire" this season—the colored team shown above is typical of other fine teams composed of employees of the Company. In the picture of the 1946 team above are: Jessie L. Ransom, secretary of the club, B. Harris, N. McClinic manager of the club, L. Carson, N. Fielder, Captain of the team, B. Carmichael, M. Ransom, assistant secretary, M. Wesley, C. T. Hight, D. Richard, H. Jones, J. W. Allen, W. Woodruff, and Charlie Hudson, Umpire. (*Lindale Bulletin*, April 1946, page 20)

Front row (left to right): John Henry Clifton, Charles Head, James Jones, Napoleon Fielder, and Marshall Wesley. Second row: Bud Ransom, C. J. Hight, Romus Crew, and Arthur Montgomery. Third row: William Woodruff, John McClinic, Nathan Riley, Isaac Richards, and Nathan McClinic, manager.

1948 Lindale Dragons
The 1948 company yearbook, page 126.

LINDALE SCHOOLS (1896–1926) AND PEPPERELL SCHOOLS (1926–PRESENT)

In 1908 Miss Madeleine John Sevier Wyly (1865–1952) assumed leadership of the school and its five teachers.

On May 6, 1945, Pepperell School librarian Ms. Sara Hightower wrote a five-page paper detailing "A Brief History of the Schools of Lindale." She reported that prior to 1896, Lindale did not have a school per se; small Floyd County one- and two-room buildings located in Barker, Dunahoo [sic], Reeseburg and Silver Creek communities nurtured the education of farm youths. Students of the latter section remember hiking from the south side over a mountain (Lakeview) and down to their daily studies. But when the mill opened in 1896, farmers flocked to the area for employment, bringing with them large families. Consequently, county superintendent Gwaltney coaxed Mr. C. H. Shiflett to come and establish a grade 1 to 9 junior high system in a recently built duplex at 102 Park Street (this residence was later occupied by Mr. Floyd Ridley). The first principal brought with him two competent teachers, Ms. Annie Morton who taught first-year students and part of the second. Ms. Bessie Maitland headed remaining second graders along with third and fourth classes. Mr. Shiflett instructed children fifth through the ninth. Surprisingly, 125 kids showed up at the house on Park Street. Ms. Hightower explained, "There were so many at times that the children sat on the stair-steps and recited their lessons." The three trustees, A. W. Hunking (agent of the mill), Mr. George Black, and Daniel W. Barnett oversaw the organization. Teacher salaries were paid by the Massachusetts Mill with the state and county having no input.[148]

In 1902, or the second year of H. P. Meikleham's reign as manager, construction of a new two-story elementary building was finished across the road from the brick mill. Earlier, the *News-Tribune* noted on page 2 of its August 14, 1900, issue that "Lindale will soon have one of the best schoolhouses in the County. Work has commenced, and when completed, it will be an ornament to any city." Although Mr. Shiflett stayed "only a few years" (1896–1901), he did much toward improving the system. A. N. Swain succeeded him until 1908. That same year, Ms. Madeleine John Sevier Wyly assumed leadership of the school and its five teachers. She quaintly added "John Sevier or J. S." to her signature in recognition of her famous ancestor who was an American soldier, frontiersman, and politician. He fought in the Revolutionary War, the Indian conflicts, and later became the first governor of Tennessee. Polly Gammon wrote that she was a "strict disciplinarian and when she clapped her long, slender hands from her office on the second floor, every child on the playground reacted—favorably." She was also Northwest Georgia's original suffragette who led several organizations for women's rights, especially voting. As vice president of the Georgia Suffrage Association, she wrote to the league president in Washington asking for advice to further the cause of Southern females: "We have to 'go slow' in the South… Conservatism originated and first sprouted in Dixie; it has always been our chief export, import, report and support…We may not at first do very big things and we are perfectly certain not to do spectacular things, but believe me…we are not dead." In 1935, after twenty-seven years, she retired as superintendent due to health issues. Mr. J. D. Fleming, former Cave Spring leader, was employed to "take charge" of all grades; he remained until 1941.[149] Under Wyly's reign, great strides were made including a new spacious annex to the main building in 1920, and more importantly, the school now housed twenty-five classroom instructors. Madeleine Wyly passed away at eighty-seven on December 22, 1952, and is interred in Myrtle Hill Cemetery.

SARA HIGHTOWER (1911–1991)—LIBRARY PIONEER IN THE STATE OF GEORGIA

Sara Hightower was born on April 14, 1911, in Cedartown, Georgia, and received her BA degree from the Teacher's College of the University of Georgia in 1928. She was most instrumental in creating libraries throughout Floyd County. After receiving a master's of library science from Emory University, the lady initiated bookmobile services in the county while still overseeing the entire book system of Floyd. After retirement, Sara was recognized when a new branch system was named for her in 1980. This Tricounty Regional network delivered reading materials to citizens throughout rural parts of Northwest Georgia, and her name became synonymous with *library*. Upon her death, Jim Doyle, reference historian, wrote, "Thousands of school children were on a first name basis with this pioneer of education and when she died April 8, 1991 the world lost a dedicated server of the people of Northwest Georgia."[150]

When H. P. Meikleham hired Russell Moulton in 1929, his instructions were "build a high school." The captain's motivation was the fact Lindale graduated only three students per year at Cave Spring. The high school movement began immediately in 1931 when Mr. Moulton organized and taught eighth-year courses (Lindale only schooled grades 1 to 7 at the time) to fifty-six students in the basement of the auditorium; four years later, forty of the fifty-six students from Moulton's '31 basement class moved on to and graduated from Cave Spring, McHenry, and Rome high schools. Their transportation as well as tuition was provided by the mill.

In 1935, Mrs. Clara Ellen Moulton took over the cramped belowground classroom. Consequently the crowded conditions in the existing buildings prompted mill manager R. Donald Harvey to spearhead an effort to improve the situation. With the support of Pepperell Manufacturing Company, a new junior high school was completed on December 2, 1940. In anticipation of the new structure, a ninth grade was added for the fall semester of 1940. The initial faculty included nine teachers led by forty-year-old Mobile native and Auburn graduate Edward Russell Moulton, who was appointed superintendent of schools. Now sixth graders through freshmen studied under the same roof. The present-day site of Pepperell High School exists on this original 1940 campus. By the first semester of 1945, thirty-three teachers were employed by Pepperell. Led by Ms. Sara Hightower, a grammar school (grades 1 to 5) library was established in 1941; it was one of the first of its kind in Georgia.

Academics were not the only concern of Lindale where records are replete with health care for its students. Skin tests for tuberculosis, typhoid inoculation, vaccinations for smallpox as well as dental health and eye care were all addressed by the community leaders. Valuable aid and assistance was provided by the mill with access to the clinic, the local doctors, the village nurse, and the county health department. Ms. Hightower noted on page 3 of her paper that Mr. Moulton believed in the 3 Rs of education but also citizenship, cooperation, and ability to live and work well with others. He believed the school should meet the needs of the children and community, develop the students by practicing democracy, honor the rights and property of others, and to respect constituted authority and live by the Golden Rule. In addition, the school purchased a "visual curriculum series" to acquaint all students with food, clothing, shelter, health, transportation, resources, and home. Ms. Hightower finished her paper with this statement on page 5, "The schools could not operate on their high standards of efficiency without the enthusiastic support of the Pepperell Manufacturing Company and Mr. R. D. Harvey, Manager." Dated May 6, 1945, she recognized the board of managers of the system: Mr. R. D. Harvey, chairman; Mr. Garland Howard Smith; and Mr. Robert McCamy. These three men were responsible for 34 professionals instructing 1,075 pupils.[151]

EDWARD RUSSELL "SLICK" MOULTON (1900–1979)— LINDALE'S INDIANA JONES

Slick was a friendly unassuming fellow...a fine athlete excelling in both football and baseball...he had a gift for music as well.

Even before Captain Meikleham hired twenty-nine-year-old E. Russell Moulton (1900–1979) in the spring of 1929, the young man from Mobile had experienced a colorful Indiana Jones–like career. While in elementary grades, he acted in Chataugua, was an underage bugler for the local National Guard unit, starred in high school and local collegiate football, served a stint in the Merchant Marines, and performed as an all-American end for Mike Donahue's Auburn Tigers where he also entertained teammates with his tenor voice and banjo playing. At the end of eligibility, he successfully coached schoolboy football in Mississippi and Alabama before returning to the Plains where he led his alma mater to a conference championship in baseball. He later played professional minor league baseball and found time to marry Clara Ellen Yarbrough. Young Moulton was easily Mobile's Indiana Jones.

In 1939, father John Lewis Moulton wrote a thirty-three-page narrative of the family dedicated to his wife. The front page shows, "To the Meritorius Queen of Song. Annie Powers Moulton 1939." The entire work may be viewed in the author's files. The fascinating history stated the first Moulton sailed to America aboard the *Mayflower*. Many years later, when confronted by a smart granddaughter that the 1620 voyage failed to show a Moulton on the 102-passenger manifest, Great-Grandmother Elizabeth Cleveland retorted, "I'll have you know Missy—the *Mayflower* made more than one trip." The elder matriarch was the youngest daughter of General Moses Cleaveland (sic) who founded Cleveland, Ohio, in 1796 along the Cuyahoga River. Readers may take note of the very successful and entertaining Paramount/Twentieth-Century Fox sports film *Major League*; the opening minutes of the 1989 release tours the city with several shots of the general's statues.

One of these other *Mayflower* voyages (1629) brought a man named Thomas Moulton who became a settler in the Virginia colony at Jamestown. With him came a younger brother James and nephew Robert. The elder was entrusted with all the shipwright tools sent to the settlement; the same were used later to build vessels in Salem and Medford. In 1906, another family historian stated in his annals that the surname was of French derivative, meaning "first-class citizen." Embracing this description, the recorder qualified this by saying, "At present, we have not advanced beyond conjecture."

As the Moultons migrated westward into the hinterland, some moved into Canada, and a few settled near Pavillion in upstate New York. It is here we pick up our subject's great-grandfather John Jay Moulton (1836–1910). While in his midtwenties and for no known reason, he adventured down the Ohio River, floated the Mississippi to New Orleans, and then traveled east to Mobile. When the War Between the States erupted in 1861, John Jay joined the Confederate Army. Two years after the war, he met and married the twenty-nine-year-old widow Anna Lewis (1838–1893), mother of five children. Four years later, she gave birth to their only child, John Lewis Moulton (1871–1941), father of our E. "Slick" Russell. Upon reaching manhood, John Lewis courted and married Annie Eleanor Powers (1873–1965). The nuptials occurred at Saint Francis Street Baptist Church on October 24, 1893, to a standing-room-only crowd. The groom was to spend his entire life in Mobile working for the Mobile and Ohio Railroad. He lived by the axiom that there are two kinds of folk, "the people who stand and the people who lean." The bride became an accomplished and well-known musician (the Meritorious Queen of Song) and civic leader in Mobile. These leadership traits were passed on to four sons, George Lewis, John Callaghan, Edward Russell, and William Patrick.

Our subject was the third son; his father wrote that "Little Rutch arrived at 41 South Ann Street in Mobile, Alabama—in the last week or so of the fourth moon in the good year 1900." Upon birth, the two midwives, Gussie Hargrove and old Lady Hart, announced "a Big Beautiful Boy." The baby was named for a good, kind, and considerate railroad man who afterward always asked about "his boy." With two older brothers, Little Rutch "did some tall following." His first thespian appearance occurred as a seven-year-old Hiawatha in the Citronelle, Alabama Chautauqua; scholastics at Mobile's Leinkauf Elementary and Barton Academy stood as well as anybody. When trouble broke on the Mexican border in summer of 1916, older brother George was a member of Machine Gun Company in the Fourth Alabama Infantry Regiment of the National Guard. Prior to leaving, George was commissioned lieutenant and evidently took Edward Russell with him where "he became a 'Bugler of Noble Birth' in Company M—but after going all the way to Battalion 181 with the troops—the Army sent him home account of his age." The youngster returned to hometown and got a job with Mobile Ship Company, giving all his salary to his mother. When school started about the same time as the work played out, he went back and graduated at downtown Barton Academy in 1918; afterward, he spent the summer in Sheffield on a war job, earning family money before a scholarship was offered at the Hill the following year. At Catholic-supported Spring Hill College, which is the state's oldest institution of higher learning, the 18-year-old excelled at football. As the outstanding player on the 1918 squad, Russell pulled a couple of games "out of the fire" for SHC. The Mobile *Register* reported him as being an athletic 6 feet, 4 inches, 175 pounds who as a team passer could flick the oval 50 yards with a receiver right there to catch it; he also handled the kicking chores for the eleven.

Although the World War I armistice had been signed, he was picked in the fourth draft and was anxious to join George in Europe. There was some doubt with his impaired sight—too much football—if he could have passed the physical. Regardless, the draft was annulled to the relief of the Moultons.

Undeterred, he stretched his age and joined the homeport Merchant Marines. As part of the black gang, the youthful seaman eventually shipped out of Pensacola on three different vessels, the SS *Tarpon, Monganza*, and the Mobile-built SS *Daca*. All told, he served a combined seven months at sea. Daughter Cissy Rogers provided documentation that confirmed Slick's service aboard the latter ship from July 8 to September 23, 1919. A shipping board card shows that "the S.S. Daca anchored in New York; liberty launch leaves pier A."[152]

By the fall of 1920, brothers George and John were waiting at Auburn, sweet Auburn, loveliest village on the Plains. Both were engineering students at Alabama Polytechnic Institute who recruited their little brother to "Iron" Mike Donahue's Tigers.

A team picture of the Orange and Blue dated December 8, 1920, shows one a row uniformed squad facing the camera. Slick is easily identified as he is 4 inches taller than teammates; Coach Donahue is the shortest. In his first season, Russell kicked off and played defensive end, earning a letter, which was a rare feat. The *Montgomery Advertiser* wrote that "he was a hard and conscience fighter, who goes in the game to give all he has." As a favorite of the campus dining hall staff, the youngster was given extra helpings of traditional fish on Fridays. They assumed the rangy end from Spring Hill was a devout Catholic; however, truth is Slick was actually a Mobile Episcopalian who simply enjoyed seafood. The 1921 year saw Russell excel on both sides of the ball. The Tigers lost at Georgia Tech and to visiting Centre College. In the Praying Colonels contest, Russell suffered a fractured skull. The 1922 schedule saw Auburn go 8–2 with close losses at Army and Tech. The Grant Field game numbered 24,300 fans grossing $45,000 in gate receipts—a record for the conference. He was also a gentleman. After the 6–14 loss, Slick presented Tech star halfback Red Barron with a gift from the Auburn squad—a silver service in honor of his wedding which occurred the evening following the game. Slick said later that "we liked to have never have nickled and dimed paying for that gift."[153]

The Army contest was special for a kid from South Alabama. In 1981, the Atlanta Historical Society documented the train ride to West Point which began on October 11, 1922; stops along the way included Atlanta, Washington, and New York. A young man with a last name Reynolds and his dad occupied the Pullman car next to the team, giving both access to mingle freely with the squad. On page 86 of his journal, the son wrote, "Of all the players I met on the trip, the one who made the greatest impression on me was 'Slick' Moulton. A friendly, unassuming fellow, he was not only a fine athlete, excelling both football and baseball, but he had a gift for music as well. He had a good tenor voice, could really play the banjo, and kept us entertained on the long journey…On the return trip, he gave us quite a few laughs imitating a ditty picked up from the famous Ziegfeld Follies routine."

In the capital, a tour of the White House was on the agenda. In one of the large gracious rooms, the Tigers and company were lined up for a reception when lo and behold, a smiling President Warren G. Harding walked into the chamber. Reynolds recorded, "He shook hands with each player, coach and followers. What a treat that was!" After a brief stop in New York City for sightseeing which revealed the natives to be friendly, the entourage moved north.

The last link of the trip was up the Hudson Valley, which was pristine in the autumn air. The manicured parade grounds surrounded the football field. There was no stadium, just wooden bleacher-type stands twelve rows high on both sides of the gridiron; no admission was charged. After the 6–19 loss, *Birmingham News* sports editor Zipp Newman wrote that "Moulton could play the wide open stuff as well as sneaking in to hit the Army backs in their tracks. He was a fine pass receiver, a most intelligent end that Donahue utilized to pass and on end-around runs. If there are any better ends in the South, we surely would like to see them in action." In the postseason, Slick was named all-Southern end as well as honorable mention on Walter Camp's all-American team. Eleven years later, sportswriter Gasper Green noted in the January 10, 1933, *Tuscaloosa News* that Coach Donahue named Russell to his all-time Auburn football team. In 2016, Auburn University and the *Birmingham News* voted him to the school's all-nickname team. Slick joined such notable names as Cadillac, Bo, and Shug. There are three stories related to the acquiring of this moniker. One refers to him as a slick runner on the field while the second comes from his boyhood ability to swipe extra milk at school; finally, a close friend in Lindale offered he was a slick talker.[154]

With his eligibility used up, the young man spent much of 1923 summer earning extra money playing baseball in the Cotton States League and working for Dr. Isham Kimbell at the World War I rehabilitation camp in Pascagoula. More than likely, this good work led to an offer to coach a local prep football team. In his first and only season in Mississippi, Slick's Pascagoula Panthers won the Gulf Coast Regional Class A Championship, finishing at 7–2 while scoring 122 points and giving up only 25. He then returned to Lee County Alabama football for the 1924 and 1925 seasons as head coach for Auburn High School. The Alabama historical website shows a 3–4 season in 1924 followed a year later by an excellent 7–1 campaign. In May of 1926, Edward Russell Moulton received a BS degree in education from Auburn. Also graduating was his fiancée Clara Ellen Yarbrough (later known as Cool), daughter of the team doctor. Two months later, they were married. For the next three years, Clara Ellen taught school while her husband held three jobs as PE instructor, assistant football, and Auburn head baseball man. His 1928 nine logged a 22–8 record while winning the Southern Conference championship.[155]

In the spring of 1929, the time had come for E. Russell Moulton to decide on a life's work. There was serious consideration of a career in insurance. In February, New England Mutual Life officer Earle Brailey wrote, "We understand you are giving serious consideration to the matter of Life Insurance as a life work." A month later, the general agent addressed him as Slick with an informative letter, "We are making a very definite and determined effort to increase our man power in the field. Every help in attaining that desired result is welcome." Yet athletics continued to be the first love. Earlier he had joined the American Football Coaches Association and pursued the head football job at Mercer University in Macon. A number of letters quickly filled his résumé. A business friend wrote, "He is a man of fine personality and good character…qualities so necessary in work of this kind." The superintendent of Panama City Schools made this offer by telegram: "Would you be interested in position of Athletic Director of our high school?" His old coach Mike Donahue, now AD at LSU, praised his former player, "E.R. never gave the slightest trouble…he has a pleasing personality and has character and habits above reproach." Dr. Isham Kimbell of the Mississippi US Veterans Bureau wrote, "Mr. Moulton is entirely sober, has no bad habits whatsoever."[156]

JOHN WILLIAM "J. W." SUTTON JR. (1919–1975)

He remembered later, "Papa insisted upon a well-rounded education and I tried mighty hard to do just that...scoring better-than-average-grades."

Slick Moulton, Otis Gilbreath, and J. W. Sutton formed the modern age of Lindale schools. Mr. Moulton dated back to 1929 when Captain Meikleham hired him from Auburn University while the latter two came on board in the postwar complements of the GI Bill. Honorably discharged veterans with at least ninety days of service could benefit from low-cost mortgages, business loans, and receive payment of tuition and living expenses to attend high school, college, or vocational school. Longtime principal Sutton was a recipient of this program. But as the reader should have realized by now, there is more to Lindale's leading notables than education and training. Christian upbringing and family values were passed along to all students and parents during their reign.[157]

The youngest of ten children was born on June 9, 1919, in Cedartown; however, home was a medium-sized farm that stood on Cave Spring Road four miles out in the Friendship community. Parents were Roxie Anna Brock and John William Sutton Sr. who married on Christmas Day

1898; Senior was principal in a two-teacher building a few yards from the homeplace. It was an idyllic location for the close-knit family accommodating a country store, cotton gin with corn, and wheat mills. Today the peaceful community is still pristine; the quiet is broken only by the gurgling of Cedar Creek (Sutton's Mill) and a few passing cars. Friendship Baptist Church sits on high ground east of the road; its whitewashed buildings welcome visitors to the immaculate cemetery where at the top of a rise rest many of the Suttons. At the grave site, we discovered mother Roxie and father John Sr. were birthed in the middle 1870s. Yet long before the sound of their son's voice resonated in the halls of Pepperell School, the family placed a premium on education. Three members of the family were college graduates and teachers including daughter Lucille, son Taft, and John Sr. Significantly beneath the latter's name and before the birth/death information, the pink headstone is etched with a simple word "Teacher."[158]

Six surviving children (three boys and three girls) worked the farm business and attended the nearby two-room schoolhouse before moving on to higher grades. Of course, the youngest, J. W. Jr., had to walk "the chalk line" during academic time, but idle hours were spent Tom Sawyer–like helping out at the store, playing around the mills, swimming the creek, milking, and cutting wood. Fifth grade brought about a new world with a nine-month town school (country schools instructed seven months) in nearby Cave Spring. However, the pressure of scholarly excellence continued because young John sat in classes taught by his two older siblings. As a Yellow Jacket, he excelled at football, track, and baseball, and admitted to "specializing in sports and girls." Yet the monthly report card was religiously inspected by parents.

The time for advanced education came in 1935; however, a less expensive two-year State College of West Georgia was chosen. Following four semesters in Carrollton, where he participated in baseball, wrestling, and boxing and part-time instructing, the young man enrolled at the university in Athens. This would have been difficult had not all the older siblings matriculated. While pursuing a course of study in education, he was on the Bulldog football squad, worked various summer jobs including cotton mill, measuring agricultural land, and lifeguarding at swimming pools. In June of 1939, Georgia bestowed a bachelor of science upon the country boy from Friendship. In the fall term, he began teaching science and mathematics at Canton High School, Cherokee County's first secondary institution, which is located 100 miles west of Athens. Afternoons and Friday nights were spent as an assistant football coach. The handsome young man enjoyed this time of his career. However, he was soon smitten by an attractive English teacher at CHS. Mildred Lee was raised in the small town (population 3,900) of Covington located 75 miles due south. She was born on January 29, 1920, to Pearl Mitchell Lee and Fitzhugh Lee of Newton County. The young lady also attended West Georgia College and then received a BS degree at the university in 1941. Over the next two years, young John Sutton faced competition from five other unmarried male faculty members, but he prevailed, and plans were made for matrimony. December 7, 1941, changed their world. A letter from the local draft board began, "Greetings. Uncle Sam needs you!" And as he stated later, "Get me he did." At Fort McPherson on October 8, 1942, John William Sutton Jr. raised his right hand in the air and took the oath. He said, "I was sick. All I could think of was leaving Canton and Lee—mostly Lee." While his fiancée continued teaching at CHS during the next two years (1942–1944), the recruit reported to Air Corps basic training at Keesler Field, Biloxi, Mississippi; from there, he was assigned to instrument trainer school at Chanute Field, 130 miles south of Chicago. A background in science and math was paying off because the next move was permanent. For the next three-plus years, Airman Sutton taught critical instrument flying at Biggs Field, which is located within Fort Bliss, San Antonio, Texas. There was one respite during this time. While on furlough in the spring of 1944, John and Lee were married on March 5. At the end of the academic year, the bride spent the summer in Texas. However, living spaces in the area were so primitive that in late August, Lee moved back to Covington with her folks where on March 24, 1945, first child, Judy Lee, was born.[159]

World War II had been over for almost four months when on November 25, 1945, the discharge came through. It was a happy day, one that "rivaled wedding day and birth of first child." Before military service ended, the plans were a return to Canton and resume employment there; however, the housing situation was again a problem. While "loafing around" prior to returning to work, John ran into another Floyd Countian, Mr. E. Russell Moulton, who was head of the Pepperell Schools, Lindale. He offered the former Technical Sergeant a position as the junior high assistant principal and coach in addition to teaching physics and geometry. The salary was much better than Cherokee County, so on February 1, 1946, a contract was signed. Page 1 of the *Lindale Bulletin* dated March of the same year announced that "ATHLETIC INSTRUCTOR ADDED TO FACULTY OF PEPPERELL SCHOOL." The article noted that the new hire was experienced in all types of recreation and physical education; it also mentioned his prewar work in Canton as well as military service. During the remaining winter and spring months, Lee and baby Judy lived in Covington because of the ever-present lack of lodging. At the end of the term, the veteran enrolled in the postgraduate program at the university. When classes in Lindale resumed in late summer 1946, the small family finally came together. Mr. R. Donald Harvey graciously found the couple an upstairs apartment at 108 ½ East Third Street, Rome. On December 22, 1946, a Christmas baby and second child, Mildred Jeanne, was birthed. In the fall of 1949, the mill manager provided them with a house at 4 Central Avenue in the village where on September 26, 1952, John William "Johnny" Sutton III was born. Three years later, the family of five moved to 12 Central Avenue, which remained their residence until children were grown and parents passed away.[160]

Early on, Mr. Sutton began to organize the junior high athletic program. From his personal files, we have a look at 1948–1949 basketball. Fifteen boys and twenty girls reported for practice on December 1. Coaches were Mr. Hollis Smith for the Dragons and Mr. Sutton, the Dragonettes. Pepperell Manufacturing bought new gold shorts and shirts with warm-ups and jackets. The Pepps were the "best dressed team in Georgia." A first team roster consisted of the following:

	Girls		Boys
Forward	Bobbie Jean Walker	Forward	Larry Joe Duncan
Forward	Betty Jean Milton	Forward	Jimmy Bell
Forward	Mary John Bagley	Center	Dewey Shiflett
Guard	Marjorie Tucker	Guard	Bobby Joe Dillingham
Guard	Dorothy Bruce	Guard	Harold Dillingham
Guard	Patty Ruth Shiflett		

The season record for girls was 8–7 while the boys won 10 and lost 6. Bobbie Jean Walker and Dewey Shiflett were singled out for outstanding play as was manager Billy Bowman for his dedication to the team equipment.

Mr. Sutton's files then give us a short report on other sports. The junior high football squad played a 10-game schedule and finished with a 4–5–1 record; the track team finished second behind Model but won first in 220- and 440-yard dashes, high jump, and pole vault; the spring baseball nine was competing at a .500 level in early season.

The physical education program at Pepperell was exemplary. Each day, 250 students gathered in the playground area for 30-plus minutes of active competition. From the viewpoint of students, this was the most interesting part of the day. The schedule rotated every day, according to different sports with one class competing against another. Freshmen leaders acted as coaches and referees.[161]

OTIS FORREST GILBREATH
(1924–1993)

Otis developed a love of sports early in his life. As a youngster, if there was a ball game going on in Lindale, he was somewhere around.

Coach Otis Gilbreath

The third dominant member of Pepperell schools/athletics was Otis Forrest Gilbreath who came on board after the war and stayed until the early 1980s. He also had a biography to match other Lindale famous persons. Coach was born in the village on April 30, 1924, to Madison Norris (1891–1956) and Maude Barton (1895–1982) Gilbreath. Like many locals, they gave up farming for a regular check at the mill. Their farm in Gordon County lay near the Pocket area of Floyd County where Otis's grandparents Alexandra LaFayette Gilbreath (1868–1940) and Mary Matilda Joyce (1872–1937) lived and worked after marrying in 1890. For reader's information, Grandmother Mary's parents were also farmers from the Pocket being J. P. Joyce and Laura Brown. The next older generation was Oliver Washington Barton and Martha Elizabeth Chitwood Barton.

Otis was the third of five children born in Lindale to Maude and Norris. On that Wednesday morning of the last day of April 1924, Dr. Moore delivered the big boy at the family home. Because the good doctor's scale topped out at ten pounds, a next morning trip to the postal package scale logged him in at an even twelve pounds. He never resided anywhere but in the village. Son Charlie identified five homes occupied by the Gilbreath family: 123 C Street, 105 B Street, Walnut Street, 202 Garden Street, and 1 South Fourth Street. As time passed, each family member was employed in the mill beginning with father Norris who logged forty years as a loom fixer while Maude worked over thirty-five years in the weave room.[162]

Son Charlie Gilbreath described his dad's early years in the village:

> Football, basketball, baseball and boxing were favorites; however, he developed a particular love for baseball as a bat boy for the Lindale textile team. As an 18 year old now nicknamed "Woppie" a nickname he never cared for, Otis became the player/manager for the local amateur nine that reported to the Recreation Director Ish Williams. His squad was comprised of Donald Green, Ralph Jones, Charles Schram, Melvin Stamey, John Forrester, Methvin Bruce, James Treglown, Otis Gilbreath, Carl Morgan, Wilburn Holsomback, J. W. Duke, Baldy Stager and Donnie Donaldson. Prior to electric refrigerators, the teenager delivered ice to the local homes. He was extremely proud to be awarded Eagle Scout Badge from then President Franklin D. Roosevelt and later helped construct Boy Scout camp Sidney Dew in north Floyd.[163]

Education began in 1929 with grade 1 and ended eight grades later. With no formal secondary classes available in Lindale, Rome High provided three years of academics; a transfer to Darlington Prep provided the final term. High school football, baseball, and track provided extracurricular activities. Unfortunately, December 7, 1941, brought tremendous change to all graduates. On July 11, 1942, Otis married his childhood sweetheart Evelyn Pauline "Polly" Timms (1923–1996), daughter of Al Burl Timms (1893–1967) and Mary Etoyl Smith (1905) and granddaughter of preacher/farmer George Washington Timms and Mary Susan Barkley Timms of Sand Mountain, Alabama. Maternal grandparents were Benjamin Franklin Smith and Sarah Elizabeth Turner. The former came to the mill in 1901 as one of the first hands and logged in forty-five years of service according to the 1947 mill book. Sarah's relatives were Irish, Dutch, and Native American (Cherokee).[164]

Polly was educated in the local schools until ready for high school in Cave Spring. Afterward, she enrolled in Rome Business School studying secretarial skills. While her husband was overseas, the young bride worked in the laboratory department before moving to timekeeper (payroll) for the mechanical division. After retirement, she worked for a local heating/cooling company.

Shortly after marrying Polly, Otis volunteered for the Army. For thirty months, he was attached to the 439th Army Air Corps Signal Battalion, serving in major campaigns including North Africa, Sicily, Italy, France, and Germany. It was in the push toward the Rhineland that he ran afoul of General George S. Patton. Telecommunications operators were required to string their own lines. While the unit was atop a pole connecting wires, the general's convoy drove past. Always a stickler for properly dressed soldiers, Patton stopped and berated the lead officer because the men were not wearing leggings. The officer explained the wraps caught on splinters. The general replied he did not want excuses and ordered all the men placed on report and placed in the stockade for twenty-four hours. As soon as the convoy moved on, Otis and his communicators were released; however, they continued not wearing Army-issue leggings.[165]

The military has traditionally promoted athletics, especially boxing. In 1953, Hollywood released *From Here to Eternity*. The award-winning movie revolved around post competition in Hawaii just prior to the attack on Pearl Harbor. In a script made only in Columbia studios, Otis was a light heavyweight who fought his way to the Corps championship match against an officer from the Panama Canal Zone—his brother Herbert Gilbreath! Lindaleans loaded up two passenger cars at the depot and drove 740 miles to Camp Crowder, Missouri, where they watched two favorite sons compete.[166]

No one individual had more influence upon the youth of Lindale than Otis Forrest Gilbreath. At the end of the war, the veteran returned to Park Street environs and began working at the mill while taking night and weekend courses to complete a teaching degree. Mr. Sutton immediately put him to work coaching elementary school squads. Pepperell's first 2 years as a high school (1951–1952) lists Otis as physical education teacher and line coach for football varsity. By the 1953 gridiron year, he was listed as head football coach—a position he retained until 1975. His record for the period was 97 wins, 96 losses, and 10 ties. However, his real passion was Dragon baseball. In a 33-year tenure, Otis recorded an amazing 551 wins, 117 losses with 6 state championships ('54, '57, '58, '70, '78, and '80), 4 state runners-up, 16 region titles with 24 subregion trophies. Accolades included being named Georgia coach of the year 6 times, Southeastern area once, and national high school COTY for 1982. He was eleventh in number of wins among national-wide managers. Hall of Fame credentials included Rome-Floyd County, Georgia Sports, and Georgia Coaches Athletic Association. Coach Gilbreath was presented with the Dwight T. Keith award for outstanding coaching career, sportsmanship, and dedication. Mr. Keith was founder of *Coach and Athlete* magazine as well as the Georgia Athletic Coaches Association. The recreation/community building in Lindale Park was posthumously dedicated to the coach for his "mentorship of generations of youth in Lindale and Pepperell Schools."

The city of Rome has a levee built to prevent annual flooding; it was dedicated in 1939. Inside the levee is a narrow alluvial plain fronting the banks of Coosa River. The area was perfect for youth baseball and football fields which soon became known as *behind the levee*. Pepperell teams here became legendary with one squad winning fifty straight contests. Along with his second-in-command, Wilbur "Pee-Wee" Coffia, Otis dominated play. Rumor was that any team that defeated Lindale was treated to the best steak dinner in Rome. Few teams enjoyed sirloin.[167]

Lindale Enters the Modern Era (1951–2001)

Change came to the village after the war. It began slowly and then moved rapidly in the second half of the twentieth century. Southerner Rick Bragg cited a veteran who reclaimed his place in a mill, "The war shook something loose in him, shook it so hard it broke tradition." The parochial-nature mills began to wane. In South Floyd, no new houses were built after 1940. A good postwar economy and mobility occurred simultaneously. Folks could buy junk cars for $100 and drive to other plants; some of them were even looking all the way to Detroit, where it was said a man could get rich on the assembly line. Nowhere was individualism more evident than the railroads that coursed through the village. Lindale native Charles Brock noted that Central of Georgia discontinued passenger service in 1953. Its depot which was built in 1903 was retired June 27, 1963, and torn down the following May. Brock's grandfather C. J. Logan became agent/operator on April 12, 1912, and retired on November 9, 1962. The depot in Lindale spanned sixty years with Mr. Logan logging fifty as its manager. The elder railroad man recalled every day at noon a mill employee would call the depot and wait for Washington (Naval Observatory) to send a Western Union telegraph message pinpointing noon; at that moment, boiler room personnel would become official keepers of mill time by blowing a steam whistle, thereby allowing villagers to synchronize clocks. For connection accuracy across the nation, railroads had led this push for establishment of time zones.[168]

Twenty-two years after H. P. Meikleham hired Slick Moulton (see page 122-123) to build and start a secondary school in Lindale, PHS opened for business in the fall of 1951 with John W. Sutton as principal. A good omen came on August 10 when Pepperell general manager R. Donald Harvey announced a contract for Navy denim totaling 3,733,333 yards of 37.5-inch cloth. The mill had been operating on a 3-day workweek for some time due to high customer inventory. On the first day of senior high, panoramic photos of the campus show 2 brick structures in tandem at the terminus of Dragon Drive. The back structure housed grades 9 to 12. The front building with its antiquated chimneys educated grades 6 to 8. The cavernous-like Russell Leonard gymnasium also with a visible chimney anchors the north side while the expansive baseball field complete with removable bleachers lies due south; the Boy Scout hut sits aback several feet from the first base line of the diamond. The remaining area we know now as the PHS complex is covered with underbrush and trees.

The 1952 yearbook (published by Taylor Company of Dallas, Texas) is dedicated to Superintendent of Schools E. Russell Moulton who "has distinguished himself as a leader, an educator and a speaker WHO ABOVE ALL IS OUR FRIEND." Principal Sutton oversaw twenty-seven teachers. The student editor and associate Barbara Goodwin and Earnestine Hale produced a very organized all black-and-white annual which consisted of eighty-one pages; the interior reveals nineteen various clubs and organizations ranging from the student council to athletics. The padded hardback covers are white with gold trim displaying a prominent Dragon. Eighty-six senior pictures are highlighted after pictures of the faculty. Boys are wearing coats and ties while girls pose in sweaters with string of pearls. Supporting advertising listed in the back lists eighty-five different patrons.[169]

For the next twenty-two years, J. W. Sutton walked the halls and kept order at 3 Dragon Drive, Lindale. The following excerpt is paraphrased from a paper written by 1961 PHS graduate Betty Burkhalter Shiflett in June 2020:

> In September of 1954, graduated 5th grader Betty Faye Burkhalter departed the old two story elementary building at terminus of Grove Street and prepared for academic life on the main campus. The front building housed 6th

and 7th students while the back structure corralled the rest. Superintendent Moulton possessed a kind fatherly demeanor; however, it did not take us long to hear about Principal Sutton. The word spread that you don't get in trouble with front office officials for there awaited a "big and bad" paddle with holes which would leave blisters on your butt. Thankfully, it was a few weeks before the man was spotted in our part of the school. Betty remembers him walking down the hall with his head down and classmates whispering "there he is." The stern and non-smiling face was met with apprehension and avoidance especially by 6 graders. But in the upper grade halls, he knew everybody and happening. In senior year 1960 most of my required classes were complete leaving me free after lunch. Miss Clara Mitchell had taught me well in the business department stressing typing and shorthand. One morning Mr. Sutton asked to see me. I was confident there was no trouble as I entered his domain; would I work as student secretary on half days? The pay would be $.75 per hour; silently, I am calculating 20 hours per week equals $15.00. I had honestly never held anything larger than a fiver so consent was immediate. In the next several weeks I got to know a fine man. Although he did not smile much, behind the stoic face was someone qualified and comfortable to the assignments. He missed nothing and expected perfection. In a world with of no copy machines, word processors or spell checks secretarial life could be difficult. Still, he was very involved with teachers, students, extracurricular activities in addition to GHSAA and Region 3-A official business. Added to professional duties were family responsibilities; he was very proud of wife Lee and the three children Judy, Jeanne and Johnny. When Mrs. Sutton visited the office, she would usually leave saying, "Now Sutt, when will you be home?" That year I learned how an honest and hard-working man can do a tough job. Generally, no one comes by the office or calls except with problems. He took them on with integrity.[170]

In July of 2020, Mrs. Sandra Cooper gave us this look at J. W. Sutton; her missive is paraphrased below:

On June 7, 1938, Sandra Gayle Midkiff was born to Ralph and Lucille Stevens Midkiff in Mount Airy, North Carolina. The small Southern town is well-known as the home of actor Andy Griffith. Her father worked various jobs over the years while Mom held two jobs most of the time, one being millwork. This was necessary to support the family of five, which included twin brothers, Ronald and Donald, three years senior to Sandra. Mom Lucille had graduated high school and was an avid reader all her life and passed along a love of learning to her offspring. In the early 1950s, a chance at further education seemed financially impossible for the boys and their sister. But the mother never discouraged the dream. Destiny appeared in the family's minister who had attended Rome's Berry College. He told of the school's work program that fulfilled the tuition requirement; consequently, in the spring of 1953, the twins applied and were accepted. Afterward, in time the boys completed teaching degrees at Berry as did their wives.

In May of 1956, the youngest child graduated from Mount Airy City High School with hope of following her brothers; Sandra immediately applied and was accepted to the freshman class, fulfilling her mother's prophecy, "God will provide a way." Four years later on June 6, 1960, the pretty young senior earned a degree and a husband (John Cooper) on the same day. After stops at East Rome Junior and Johnson High Schools where she met her lifelong best friend Shelby Chandler Talley, the young mother applied to the Pepperell school system. The customary interview ended with Assistant Principal Gene Byrd saying, "I see no reason you should not be hired." However, he added that the headman was at McCall Hospital for minor surgery, and as no teacher was placed on staff without his consent, a visit to South Rome would be necessary. From his bed, Principal J. W. Sutton Jr. met and approved Sandra Cooper to teach eighth-grade science beginning in September of 1963. She remembered later, "He was a very good principal...who led with a business-like authority. He controlled every aspect of the school...at class changes or assembly, he was always visible...any problem with an unruly student was handled promptly." In her three-page recollection, Mrs. Cooper remembered a faculty meeting in which she and two fellow teachers were giggling and whispering. He called them out. They never did that again! Mrs. J. W. Sutton was a cherished colleague who also taught eighth grade (English). When her husband passed away in 1975, Mildred Lee Sutton did not drive; thereafter, Sandra provided Lee with driver's education and later transportation to the motor vehicle licensing department. The popular teacher retired from Pepperell High School in 1992; now she and John spend time with old friends, grandchildren, and church functions in which Mrs. Cooper teaches Sunday school to numerous former pupils. Midkiff family gatherings are humorously described as faculty meetings, but none of the three graduates ever forgot the opportunities afforded them at Martha Berry's College.[171]

INTERSCHOLASTIC COMPETITION—FOOTBALL

1937 Football Season

The Georgia High School Football Historians Association website (GHSFHA) documents home and home football games played between Bremen and Lindale. The opposing coach was listed as Ernest Goldin; Earl Donaldson is thought to be coach of Pepperell. Neither local newspaper reported the contest. Since Pepperell was not a high school at the time, it is probable the game was a scrimmage-type event for the benefit of Bremen HS football, yet important enough to draw attention of town folks.

    10/15: Bremen, 6–Lindale, 0
    11/25: At Bremen, 33–Lindale, 0[172]

1951 Season

After World War II, some of the hill people just went home, back to the pines. Park Street seemed to lose interest in the adult Textile League and moved their loyalty to youth games. For easier reading, each of the three major PHS sports is hereby presented as a unit itself; sources for game write-ups are contained within reports and are presented chronologically in pages 155–520.

Game details: 7–3
Coach J. W. Sutton

09/13: At Trion W 14–13
09/22: Cumming W 34–0
09/28: At Bremen W 32–0
10/05: At Carrolton L 19–25
10/13: Murray Co. W 58–0
10/19: At Acworth W 39–0
10/27: Ga. S. Deaf W 52–0
11/02: At Canton L 12–20
11/10: Austell W 13–0
11/16: Model L 6–13

It all began on March 5, 1951, when the *News-Tribune* announced that "spring football drills will be inaugurated by Pepperell School Monday afternoon as soon as classes are over for the day." The groundwork for the upcoming year in Region 3-B lasted from four to six weeks according to Coach Sutton. In September, the new varsity and some 350 classmates walked the halls of a brand-new building costing $120,000. The 10 classrooms are part of a county-wide construction program. The cornerstone was laid by the Mason's Lindale Lodge No. 455 on June 2.

The "Leather" portion in the first Dragon yearbook is nothing short of astonishing, for the initial 1951 football squad of thirty-four led by cocaptains Bob Toole and Howard Smith went 7–3 with narrow losses to Carrollton, 19–25; Canton, 12–20; and Model, 6–13. The seven victories included six shutouts with only Trion managing points (13). Accolades went to all-region players Wallace Kelley and Bud White positioned at end and running back respectively. It should be noted that PHS followed that with a 6–3–1 season. The well-dressed team wore black jerseys highlighted by wide gold band atop the shoulders which matched the game pants. Head Coach J. W. Sutton was assisted by Otis Gilbreath and summer-hire Olan Cosper. Other local high schools' first schedules cannot compare with Pepperell. Model High School began sporadic play in 1931 but did not reach a seven-victory season until 1948. The start-up 1955 Coosa Eagles managed 4–6; a year later, the Johnson Wildcats began a 4–12 record for three years. In 1962, Armuchee established a permanent squad which lost all nine games; even the new 1958 East (5–4) and West (6–3) Rome squads could not match the Dragons. Although the exact date is unknown, the musically inclined E. Russell "Slick" Moulton penned the alma mater lyrics for Pepperell High School's beginning year. We think it appropriate to present now:

> 'Midst the rolling hills of Dixie,
> 'Neath the sun-kissed sky,
> Proudly stands our *Alma Mater*,
> Our own Pepperell High.
> Gold and White for thee we fight,
> Our pledge is "Always True,"
> For your trust will e'er be with us
> All the ages through.[173]

1952 Season

Game details: 6–3–1
Coach J. W. Sutton

09/10: Canton W 26–0
09/20: Carrollton T 6–6
09/27: At Model W 14–6
10/04: At LFO W 13–19
10/10: At Villa Rica L 13–19
10/18: Buchanan W 52–0

10/24: At Gordon Lee W 27–13
11/01: Trion L 19–27
11/07: Dallas W 41–13
11/14: Avondale L 13–21

Following our first varsity action in autumn of 1951, the enthusiasm was football high on August 13, 1952, as coaches J. W. Sutton, Otis Gilbreath, and Maurice Culberson issued uniforms to twenty-seven football players. Six starters and four more standouts were lost from the 1951 eleven; however, this varsity squad would proceed to go 6–3–1, losing close games to Villa Rica, Trion, and Avondale while tying Carrollton 6–6. They averaged 22.3 points offensively and allowed 11.7 on defense. Backfield strength came from Bud White, Jim Yarbrough, Baltimore Smith, Bob Toole, Jack Pence, and Jo Jo White. On the line, Beefy Teat and all-region, all-state guard Jimmy Green provided the blocks; Jack Bolton and Arkansas transfer Claude Cox also performed well on the O line. Injuries probably cost the Dragons a chance to go undefeated. Darlington Field served as home stadium for the Dragons; the 14–6 Shrine Game victory over Model at Barron Stadium was a highlight for 1952. Trailing 0–6 with three seconds remaining in the first half, Jo Jo Stephens threw six yards to Bud White for a touchdown; Thompson's PAT was good for a 7–6 lead. Well into the 1990s, this was locally the most important football game of the year, surpassing even East-West in attendance and excitement.

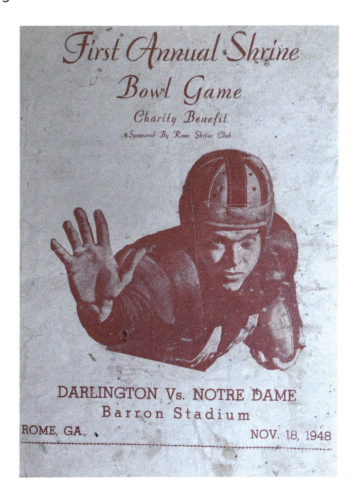

1953 Season

> Game details: 5–5
> Coach Otis Gilbreath
>
> 09/04: At West Point L 6–21
> 09/11: At South Cobb L 6–32
> 09/18: At Carrollton L 0–33
> 09/26: Model L 6–16
> 10/02: At LFO W 26–6
> 10/09: Villa Rica W 12–6
> 10/16: Avondale W 20–7
> 10/23: Gordon Lee W 20–7
> 10/29: At Trion L 6–7
> 11/07: Dallas W 19–12

There would be no "slipping up on opponents" during the 1953 football season. The squad opened spring training with Coach Otis Gilbreath being "assigned the duties of handling" the Dragons during early March practices. He would be assisted by Maurice Culberson and J. W. Leach. Nine returnees formed the nucleus for the coming fall including cocaptains Jo Jo Stephens and J. W. Bennett, Ronald Formby, Jack Pence, Bobby McCoy, Joe Ozment, Claude Cox, Lloyd Allen, and Beefy Teat. The Dragon Club advertised season tickets for the coming fall. The coaches started issuing equipment on Tuesday, August 4. As the season got underway, PHS lost in a gallant effort at West Point 21–6; three more road losses brought their record to 0–4 before the youngsters began to play like veterans and ran off four consecutive wins. They upset Villa Rica 12–6 behind a lineup that included ends McCoy and Gresham, tackles Teat and Taylor, guards, Connell and Allen, center Ozment, and backs Stephens, Pence, Duke, and Formby. The same group romped over Gordon Lee 48–6. In week four, the second annual Shrine Game saw Model claim the trophy 6–16 behind the running of speedster Mitchell Shellnut. On October 2, our own speed back, Jack Pence, raced through host LFO's defense for four TD runs in a 26–6 win. By popular vote, the student body named Ms. Barbara Jackson as homecoming queen for the second consecutive year; she presided over the team's November 7 victory over Dallas 19–12. Tough losses to Carrollton, South Cobb (a new school in Austell), and undefeated Trion could be attributed to injuries and six road games. A week after home standing, PHS defeated Class 2-A Avondale 20–7 in Lindale. The GHSA in Thomaston elevated Pepperell into a Class A team (400 to 650 students) for the 1954 season; classification is based on average daily attendance. Five days before Christmas, the GHSA honored all-region 3-B players, which included Jack Pence, Bob McCoy, Billy Teat, Lloyd Allen, and Jo Jo Stephens. On January 2, 1954, Superintendent E. Russell Moulton expressed appreciation to the Dragon Club for their support during the past football season. In a letter to club president Sharon H. Williams, he wrote, "The faculty and students join me in this note of appreciation." The group handled concessions, seat cushions, programs, and public address system.

1954 Season

    Game details: 6–4
    Coach Otis Gilbreath

    09/03: At LaFayette W 20–6
    09/11: Model L 7–20
    09/18: Newnan L 13–24
    09/24: At Douglas Co. W 14–0
    10/02: Cartersville W 19–0
    10/08: At Canton W 13–9
    10/16: Summerville W 7–0
    10/23: South Cobb W 27–13
    10/29: At Rockmart L 0–12
    11/05: At Buford L 7–25

The 1954 gridiron squad surprised the pundits. When the dust had settled following the final game, this team had won six games; four losses were to Class B state champion Model, runner-up Class A Rockmart, second-place Class C Buford (an 18-point deficit was the largest of the year), and Newnan, whose only loss was to the Polk County Yellow Jackets. Impressive victories were to Douglasville, Cartersville, Canton, Summerville, and South Cobb. Record attendance (6,000 for Shrine Game) showed up during the year to see seniors Harold Gresham and John Brown, Emory Moore, Fred Mathis, and cocaptains Jo Jo Stephens and Ed Duke perform. The largest crowd ever to witness a football game in Lindale occurred on Saturday night, September 18, when Newnan visited. Although the highly touted Cougars downed the Dragons 25–13, the 1,300 paying customers were pleased with the play of their squad. A revamped lineup consisting of ends Ted LaRue and Harold Gresham, tackles William Burkhalter and Emory Moore, guards Jerry Lee and Wesley Connell, center John Vaughn, and backs Jo Jo Stephens, Ed Duke, Hilton Arnold, and Charles Reynolds. They proceeded to defeat Douglas County, Cartersville, Canton, Summerville, and South Cobb. The community had fallen in love with their Dragons; to wit, another record crowd (1,400) watched them pound the Purple Hurricanes 19–0 and then down undefeated and unscored-on Summerville 7–0. With less than 3 minutes to play, Stephens hit Burkhalter with a 31-yard TD pass for the victory. Against South Cobb, RB Jerry Bolton hit pay dirt on romps of 12, 31, and 46 yards that led to a 27–13 victory. Unfortunately, Rockmart and Buford ended our good run with 0–12 and 7–25 wins. At the postseason banquet on Saturday, January 12, 1955, Auburn coach Ralph "Shug" Jordan was guest speaker before a large group.

1955 Season

    Game details: 6–4
    Coach Otis Gilbreath

09/02: LaFayette W 46–2
09/10: Model W 13–0
09/16: At Newnan L 0–27
09/24: Douglas Co. W 21–16
09/30: At Cartersville L 0–13
10/07: Canton W 13–7
10/14: At Summerville W 24–0
10/21: At South Cobb L 0–13
10/28: Rockmart L 3–16
11/04: Buford W 33–7

Five months before the 1955 regular season began on September 2, Coach Gilbreath and staff prepped the boys with three weeks of spring training. Fifty-two players divided equally sited up for the traditional intersquad game Saturday night, March 18. At four o'clock, the school band paraded down Park Street as a warm-up for the scrimmage. It was announced on March 4 that Coosa High School would field a football team in the fall. Already 49 players were out for Coach Mac Bolton's squad. The fall schedule lined up favorably for PHS oblong ball in 1955; six home games, three on the road, and one neutral site. Among Coach Gilbreath's varsity players, 21 lettermen were returning; the starting lineup was ends Weyland Burkhalter and Roger Greer, tackles Wesley Connell and Bobby Roberson, guards Al LaRue and Jim Colquitt, center Hugh Ware, quarterback Jerry Bolton, fullback Billy Joe Scoggins, and halfbacks Charles Reynolds and Lowell Curry. They were boosted by Dragon Club president Elmer Dillingham and 652 dues-paying members. The many highlights of the season included a 13–0 victory over consecutive (1953 and 1954) Class B state champion Model in the eighth annual Shrine Game and a 33–7 thrashing of visiting Buford in the finale; in between, they won 24–0 in Summerville. However, many observers believe the peak performance was the 3–16 homecoming loss to Rockmart on October 28. The undefeated/untied Jackets needed a desperation fourth down pass completion from QB Coalson to Hardin down to the 1-yard line, which set up a TD sneak and a 7–3 lead just before intermission. Jerry Bolton's 15-yard field goal in the first stanza put the visitors behind for the first time all season. In the third quarter, another fourth and long was converted by the same players which almost replayed the earlier second-quarter action. In 10 contests, the Dragons' offense tallied 153 points while the defense allowed only 91. This was a tribute to Coach Gilbreath who was forced to play 3 different quarterbacks (Jerry Bolton, Lowell Curry, and Wesley Connell) due to injuries. In postseason, the *News-Tribune* cited Lindale's 11 as having an impressive year, reporting on November 15 that "Pepperell started off at a winning clip and ended the same way…to finish with a 6–4 record." As the year progressed, 500 additional seats were added to the field. Afterward, 42 players were guests of new mill general manager G. Howard Smith at the annual Thanksgiving Day gridiron classic involving the freshmen teams of GT and UGA at Grant Field.

Early in the above football season, Langdon B. Gammon wrote in the *News-Tribune* that longtime Lindale Mill general manager R. Donald Harvey has resigned due to ill health. The paper continued two days later in an editorial that "Mr. Harvey's life work has been in Lindale and for Lindale. He has always put first the interests of his company, its employees and their families. No man could want greater recognition than is in the love and affection in which Mr. Harvey is held by his fellow workers and his neighbors." He succeeded to the position upon the death of Captain H. P. Meikleham in July of 1937 and was responsible for establishing a junior high, senior high, gymnasium, and a fenced-in lighted athletic field. On September 18, both the Rome and Atlanta newspapers reported that Pepperell Manufacturing Company president Brackett Parsons named twenty-six-year veteran Garland Howard Smith to replace Mr. Harvey. Mr. Smith has been assistant general manager of the division since January 1, 1946.

1956 Season

Game details: 4–6
Coach Otis Gilbreath

09/07: At Cartersville L 13–20
09/15: Newnan L 6–32
09/22: Davis W 34–0
09/28: At Ringgold W 31–13
10/06: Ellijay (Gilmer) L 13–24
10/13: Cass W 18–0
10/19: At LFO L 0–6
10/27: Summerville L 13–33
11/03: Model W 8–6
11/09: At Rockmart L 0–51

In 1956, the Dragon Booster Club was four years old. President James W. Jordan promoted preseason membership and planned first home game festivities for our opponent Newnan HS. On August 20, football coaches Otis Gilbreath, Bill Boling, and Olan Cosper greeted 34 suited-up Dragons. Only 8 lettermen returned from last year's squad; they would be led by eleventh-grade captain Lowell Curry and senior end Joe Abney. The latter would receive all-state accolades. On the morning of September 7, Coach Gilbreath told the *News-Tribune* he would start Lowell Curry at quarterback, Albert Burkhalter at right half, Kenneth Harris at left half, Homer Mathis at fullback, Joe Abney and Roger Greer at ends, Jim Colquitt and Butch Packer at tackles, Paul Carroll and Joe Marion at guards, and Roger Carney at center. The schedule began with two losses to tough opponents, Cartersville and Newnan. In Bartow County, the Hurricanes scored TDs in each of the first three quarters and outgained their visitors "by a large margin." The team from Coweta County traveled 75 miles north to Dragon Field on Saturday night, September 15, and topped us 32–6; scatback Jimmy Hammon was practically unstoppable as he sped around our perimeters almost at will. Fullback Homer Mathis scored our only TD with a 3-yard-line buck. Next we romped 31–0 over Davis HS of Trenton with Lowell Curry accounting for 3 TDs before halftime. The junior back scored on a 4-yard burst, a 30-yard pass reception, and finished with a 65-yard keeper. The Dragons then shut out visiting Ringgold on September

28 while putting 30-plus points on the scoreboard. However, a disappointing and surprising 13–24 home loss to visiting Ellijay left our record at 2–3 entering the Cassville game the following Saturday. Fortunately, the Lindale 11 evened its slate at 3–3 with a convincing 18–0 shutout of the Colonels. Home-standing Lakeview Fort Oglethorpe won 0–6 on October 19; perhaps we were thinking about next week's opponent, Summerville. The always tough crew from Chattooga County left a Lindale homecoming crowd deflated with a convincing 13–33 victory. A Dragon fumble which was caught in the air and returned 80 yards to the end zone started the onslaught; a 30-yard TD pass combined with 269 yards rushing did not help our cause. On the bright side, Ms. Peggy Cornelia Nickles was crowned queen; the senior had a résumé that included being elected/selected class officers, Letter Club, band, majorette, basketball, softball, cheerleader, and Miss Pepperell.

On Saturday night, November 3, we entered Barron Stadium for the Shrine Game at 3–5 slightly worse than Model's 4–3 record. The five thousand spectators anticipated a high-scoring affair—it did not happen. On page 11 of the Sunday, November 4, edition, *News-Tribune* staff writer Don Roberts wrote that "Dragons Win 8–6 behind Mathis, Burkhalter before Capacity Crowd." Accolades also went to Lowell Curry, for he quarterbacked an early fifty-three-yard drive which led to Mathis's four-yard smash for the TD. The deciding two points occurred in the third stanza with a high punt snap into the end zone, resulting in a safety. The dreaded road trip to Polk County turned out to be just that for the 7–1 Jackets romped 51–0. The hometown led 13–0 at the break; however, they added 25 and 13 markers in the final two quarters via six touchdowns.

1957 Season

Game details: 5–5
Coach Otis Gilbreath

09/07: Cartersville W 19–13
09/13: At Newnan L 7–25
09/21: Davis W 48–12
09/28: Ringgold W 33–6
10/04: At Gilmer L 14–26
10/12: Cass W 25–0
10/19: LFO L 7–20
10/26: At Summerville L 6–46
11/02: Model W 19–13
11/09: Rockmart L 6–33

A record Dragon Field gate receipt was reached when Coach Gilbreath's squad opened the 1957 football season with a rousing 19–13 victory over Class AA Cartersville. There were 1,533 paid admissions or 111 more than the previous count established last year against Newnan. All told, a throng of 1,800 watched the high school game. Two other milestones were noted when

Lindale School superintendent E. Russell Moulton announced a record enrollment of 1,455 students in grades 1 to 12; in addition, Dragon Club president Jim Jordan also reported 1,017 boosters have joined up. Membership drive chairman J. D. Mathis proudly stated this was "an unparalleled success" for the club and school.

However, the following Friday the thirteenth proved unlucky in more ways than one for the home-standing Cougars of Newnan HS downed Pepperell 7–25; furthermore, the Dragons lost starting left HB and cocaptain Lowell Curry to an injured foot. Regular QB Don Ingle had been moved to Curry's post while Clinton Green was now under center. Other changes were Joe Marion from guard to end with Darold Green replacing him; Wayne Sloan would now start at tackle and Donald Melton at fullback. Davis HS of Dade County provided the next week's competition, and the Dragons took their frustrations out on them 48–12. Right half Albert Burkhalter scored on runs of 6 and 7 yards; he also caught a 17-yard TD pass from Dink Green. The latter tossed a 47-yard strike to Roger Greer in addition to a 20-yard scoring toss to Donald Melton. Following an open date, Ellijay once again broke our short win streak despite superior play on both sides of the ball by senior halfback Burkhalter and sophomore Charles Morgan; the home-standing Indians overcame a 12–14 deficit in the last 4 minutes to defeat PHS 14–26. The following week, Lowell Curry returned to the lineup against Cassville at quarterback. He ran for an 11-yard score and later caught a 45-yard halfback pass from Highfield for another 6-pointer; Albert Burkhalter ran for almost 100 yards to lead all rushers. On October 19, LFO visited and defeated Lindale 7–20. The Warriors of Coach Jack Wade were really good; one week earlier, his squad moved to the top of Region 1-A with a 7–0 home win over Summerville. They were very strong defensively, allowing only 7 points per contest during an 8–2 year. On October 26 in Chattooga County, the number 2 team in Region hammered us 46–6. Summerville's Marnell Rickets and Tommy Hall each crossed the double stripe 3 times for the winners while our only score came on Burkhalter's 55-yard jaunt. On Wednesday, October 30, 3 days before the Shrine Game, an ominous post in the *News-Tribune* said, "EIGHT FLU ABSENTEES MISS DRAGON DRILL." Coach Gilbreath called off Monday practice because of missing players. The same paper also reported that Rome, Model, and Darlington have numerous gridders out with influenza. It reached a point where Rome and Darlington postponed games with Griffin and Columbia Military Academy, prompting the local paper to add that "OUTBREAK OF FLU, VIRUS FORCES SCHOOL OFFICIALS TO TAKE ACTION." Superintendent Russell Moulton shut down Lindale schools on Friday, November 1, after 465 students were reported sick. Although the virus was called Hong Kong or Asian Flu, it originated in Guizhou, China; it peaked in October '57, and the pandemic caused 116,000 deaths in the United States. Nevertheless, Model kicked off to Pepperell at 8:00 p.m. on Saturday night, November 2, in Barron Stadium. On the fourth snap, Cocaptain Albert Burkhalter broke off left tackle and scampered 48 yards for the TD. Late in the first quarter, Roger Carney blocked a Blue Devil punt; on the ensuing snap, QB Lowell Curry sprinted 16 yards for a touchdown to put his team up 13–6. He would do one better after Shannon tied the score at 13–13 in the third stanza. Late in the game, with 1:51 showing on the clock, Curry rolled out and "journeyed" 38 yards for a 19–13 Shrine victory.

Homecoming is an event in Lindale; the excitement starts with a parade down Park Street followed by lunchroom barbecue suppers; after the new queen is crowned at halftime, a postgame alumni dance is held on campus. Pretty Ms. Betty Ruth Callaway reigned as 1957 queen. She had been a member of PHS band, majorette, basketball, cheerleader captain/cocaptain, school chorus, and held membership in Future Teachers of America. Betty was the daughter of Mr. and Mrs. Porter Callaway of 102 Linden Street, Rosemont Park.

Ringgold versus Pepperell football was played on a "sea-like playing surface." However, wet conditions did not affect Lowell Curry who had a career night in the 33–6 victory; he returned a punt ninety-nine yards for a score and then threw a sixty-one-yard scoring toss to Roger Greer before sprinting eight yards for our final score. Fellow classmate Greer added another TD on a seventy-five-yard interception return. Ten seniors hung up their cleats: Burkhalter, Melton, Greer, Robinson, Curry, Highfield, Brannon, G. Green, D. Green, and Wayne Sloan.

1958 Football Season

Game details: 6–3–1
Coach Otis Gilbreath

09/05: At West Rome W 7–6
09/11: At Coosa W 14–0
09/20: Gordon Lee W 27–0
09/27: Model L 12–26
10/04: Summerville L 6–12
10/10: At Pickens T 13–13
10/18: Cass W 65–6
10/24: At Cartersville W 24–0
10/31: At Trion L 7–33
11/08: Gilmer W 33–14

On January 7, 1958, the *News-Tribune* reported, "New Rome Schools Open with Model, Pepperell." This headline referred to the division of Rome City into East and West high schools. Two months later, 52 candidates reported for Dragon spring training. Coach Otis noted only 9 lettermen returned from 1957, which posted a 5–5 record. Post drills ended with a senior-class-sponsored scrimmage game against last year's players. PHS would now compete in Region 3-A. Four days before the September 5 kickoff against West Rome, Langdon B. Gammon headlined, "1,512 Pupils Enroll in Local Schools" with a few more expected with first and ninth grades leading 147 and 140 respectively. Also, new band director Phyllis Norton Cosper presented a 55-member ensemble complete with new uniforms led by drum major Leslie Hatch.

As the 1958 football season grew closer, new West Rome coach Paul Kennedy told the *News-Tribune* he inherited several experienced linemen from the former Hilltopper squad. He also had a "flock" of backs that had been showing well recently as they "cavort" from the single-wing type of attack. Lindale countered with ends Clayton Byars and Ronnie Corntassel, tackles Charles Morgan and Eddie Morris, guards Dale Caldwell and Paul Carroll, center Albert Shiflett, quarterback Clinton Green, halfbacks Jerry Brumbelow and Joe Marion, and fullback

Roger Carney. On Friday night, September 5, PHS defeated WR 7–6 at Barron Stadium. *Rome News* said on Sunday a "top bracket defense" slowed Coach Kennedy's single-wing attack. It appears opposing coach Otis Gilbreath had a knack at stopping this type of offense. However, according to the GHSFHA website, victories over the Chieftains would be few and far between with wins occurring in 1968 (26–14), 1990 (14–12), and finally 14–7 in 1991. Another newly established school provided the competition in week two; however, Coosa, which opened in 1955, was no match for PHS, losing 14–0. Yet until Lynn Hunnicutt established his program in the early eighties, the Eagles would dominate the series with nineteen wins and six losses. But by the last Saturday of September 1958, Pepperell was unbeaten and had won four Shrine Game contests against three defeats. Coach Ralph Tuggle's Model squad played well and evened the series with a 26–12 victory. Six nights later, one-loss Summerville came to Dragon Field and won 12–6. In Jasper on October 10, the green and white Dragons of Pickens County met Pepperell's gold and white Dragons for the first time; nothing was settled in the 13–13 tie. Our homecoming game opponent was "good ole Cass." The Colonels are known for their basketball prowess rather than oblong ball, and true to form, we hammered them 65–6. The game was almost secondary as a parade, barbecue, and postgame dance with refreshments in the Leonard Gymnasium highlighted a fine Friday evening in Lindale. Halftime excitement peaked when Ms. Jewel Cox was crowned queen. Event planners Jean Palmer and Phyllis Cosper were responsible for a successful homecoming '58. The following Friday night, state-ranked number five Cartersville High School waited in Bartow County. Coach Gilbreath was always confident when playing the Purple Hurricanes, and his team responded with a 24–0 shutout. During the last week of October, Otis labeled his eleven as in the best shape of the year. Yet winning in Riegel Cotton Mill country (founded in 1845) was difficult. Trion's largest employer (1,700) was nestled around the Chatooga River, and the resulting village took its football seriously. The Bulldogs were last year's Class B state champions with a sparkling 13–0 slate. And they aren't bad this season—Bulldogs, 33; Dragons, 7. In the finale of 1958 against Gilmer, QB Clinton Green put on a clinic in the 33–14 win. The "ace sharpshooter" hit Ronnie Corntassel with a seven-yard TD, Clayton Byars on a thirty-yarder; a seventy-five-yard pass-run to Jerry Brumbelow, and then a twenty-one-yard "looper" to senior Joe Marion. The last touchdown of the year was a thirty-two-yard exclamation run by Marion. Pepperell's 33–14 victory enabled the fourteen seniors to finish 6–3–1 behind Region 3-A South–unbeaten Model. Junior receiver Ronnie Corntassel was honored with All-State honors.

1959 Football Season

   Game details: 6–4
   Coach Otis Gilbreath

   09/04: At East Rome L 7–27
   09/12: Coosa W 41–6
   09/18: At Gordon Lee W 14–0
   09/26: At Model L 6–7

10/02: Summerville L 0–7
10/10: Pickens W 32–0
10/16: At Cass W 43–6
10/24: Cartersville L 13–20
10/31: Trion W 12–7
11/07: At Gilmer W 33–0

By the middle of the 1959 football season, Pepperell's record stood at 2–3; they would lose only once more. In retrospect, the caliber of the teams dealing losses to PHS was worth noting. East Rome tied for first place in their region; Summerville ended at the top of the heap in 3-A while Model finished second. Cartersville managed to eke out a 20–13 victory over Lindale en route to the title of 3-A South. Veteran head coach Otis Gilbreath with assistants Olan Cosper and Bill Bolling agreed the '59 squad accomplished the "mostest with the leastest." Led by only five returning starters, this inexperienced group was hard-hitting and possessed "a wealth of spirit that never dimmed" from the opening loss to final game 33–0 romp over Gilmer County.

It all began in the heat of Pepperell practice field at four o'clock on Monday, August 17; however, it was players rather than weather, stadiums, schemes, coaching, headlines, or boosters that made this bunch of Dragons special. Springtime mononucleosis was thought to ground all-state end Ronnie Corntassel for the fall but the 6-foot-4-inch, 172-pounder fought through and was ready for the opener. Tri-captains Clayton Byars, Corntassel, and 145-pound junior RB Billy Studdard provided daily leadership. Clyde Cox converted from tackle to fullback and back to tackle all for the good of the team; steady and dependable Ralph White took over at center snapping to QB Kenneth Shiflett, whose throwing ability prevented teams from playing eight-in-the-box. The youngster could also run the football. Although he retained his defensive lineman position, all-state Sonny Mathis was shifted to the backfield to add depth and more size; Harvey Brown took his place at pulling guard next to starter Ray Peugh. Sophomore Wallace Shiflett spent much of his time switching between fullback, tight end, and elsewhere; young starting tackle Johnny Mills nursed an injured arm that cost him much of the season. By the end of September, future Dragon head coach (1975) Scott Green had filled in at tackle opposite Clyde Cox; running back Steve McRay worked his way up from the JV to start at right halfback. Reserve QB Larry Gresham, who did not even make the roster in early September, was discovered late in the season as an excellent dropkicker. In the Cassville game, the junior made three PATs and a 25-yard field goal. This was before soccer-style placekicking evolved in the 1970s. Coach Gilbreath regularly bragged on FB Charles Locklear for his outstanding play on both sides of the ball. Last year's JV players provided depth and scout team opposition for the starters; later, many would make the 2-deep rotation. Eddie Turner, Paul Kilgo, Doyal Peek, Bob Sewell, Edward Spears, Gary Brannon, Johnny Shamblin, Carl Smith, Jerry Green, Ralph Stansell, Jimmy Long, Dan Bohannon, Howell Kerr, and Kenneth Nichols all made their older teammates better. Offensively, Otis's crew put up 41, 32, 43, and 33 points against Coosa, Pickens, Cass, and Gilmer respectively. On 8 occasions, the defense surrendered 7 points or less. Although the boys finished third in the region, this band of Dragons made school history by scoring 201 points while allowing only 80. With that said, all accomplishments were not confined to the gridiron. At halftime of the 32–0 victory over Pickens County, Ms. Sylvia Anne Nelson was acclaimed Homecoming Queen. The pretty young lady was editor of the 1960 Dragon yearbook and vice president of the National Honor Society. She was a member of Christian Council and was elected secretary/treasurer and chaplain of student government; Sylvia had been a cheerleader, football sponsor, and senior class officer. The twelfth grader was a member of the First Baptist Church of Lindale and the daughter of Mrs. Frank Nelson of Gaither Park.

A postseason epilogue occurred on Friday morning, January 22, 1960, when Pepperell Mill manager G. Howard Smith presented twenty-three letter jackets to the varsity squad in the Russell Leonard Gymnasium before an assembled student body. Fortunately, eleven of these veterans would return for the 1960 campaign.

1960 Season

As local schools moved into a new decade, Region 3-A football welcomed Carrollton and Rockmart to its ranks. On April 4, halfway through spring training, Coach Gilbreath worried about no returning lettermen at defensive tackle or linebacker; it proved to be a prophetic concern. However, on April 13, his underclassmen downed graduating seniors 19–13 in the final scrimmage. Afterward, he praised Mathis, Peugh, Bohannon, McGregor, Gresham, and Studdard as "looking good."

Otis, Olan Cosper, and Bill Boling returned from the summer GACA coaching clinic and began to prepare for a rugged ten-game schedule starting on September 2 in Calhoun. Four days prior, the veteran mentor again warned, "We just don't have the depth necessary to play our tough schedule." Yet his crew "scared the pants off" a hefty and highly favored Yellow Jackets before losing 13–6. The big play for PHS was Wallace Shiflett's end around fifty-four-yard TD pass to halfback Billy Studdard. The following week at Barron Stadium, Coosa scored twice before intermission and shut out PHS 12–0. We managed to move inside the red zone twice after halftime but were thwarted by determined defensive play. Vaughn, Mathis, and Studdard received praise for their efforts. On September 13, the *News-Tribune* featured our cheerleading squad as they prepared for first home game in Lindale Saturday night versus Gilmer County. The young ladies were Sherry Echols, Sandra Lloyd, Glenda Smart (cocaptain), Ruth Price, Betty Burkhalter (cocaptain), Jane Smith, Pam Polifka, Donna Halton, Donna Murdock, Rosella Sewell, and Amy Willis. Versus the Bobcats our first two quarters looked promising as the youthful defense held Gilmer without a first down and took a 7–0 lead into intermission courtesy of Larry Gresham's twenty-two-yard option run. Unfortunately, a ten-yard TD run after break combined with a forty-eight-yard sweep put GHS ahead 12–7 and victory. Yet if not for a penalty on Billy Studdard's eighty-one-yard punt return, a win could have been Lindale's. Again we had trouble "punching it over" in the shadow of the goalpost.

On September 24, both Shannon and Lindale entered the thirteenth annual Shrine contest without a victory. In games versus ER, Calhoun, and Coosa, the Blue Devils scored only 1 touchdown. With over 5,000 watching the biggest sports event in Floyd County, Model tallied 3 times to extend their series lead to 6–4. The ball-controlling winners shut out PHS 21–0 while running for 190 yards; they scored all TDs on short yardage plunges. Pepperell's deepest penetration faltered at the blue and white 28-yard line. Seven nights later, it did not get any easier as East Rome won 33–12 at Barron. The Gladiators jumped to a 25–0 lead at the half by virtue of Coach Wallace Wilkinson's pregame orders to "pass, pass and pass." His instructions produced 3 TDs by midway of the second quarter and enabled him to play youngsters going into intermission. Dragon junior tight end Grady Brannon was a bright spot for the losers, catching a 7-yard aerial from freshman Johnny Mathis and later intercepting and returning a batted ball for a 23-yard score.

There was hope the following week when the 1–4 Polk County Bees came calling to Lindale Field. Lang Gammon reported on Friday that three freshman backs, Johnny Mathis, Steve Barnett, and Jerry Henderson, would start for Coach Gilbreath. On a soggy field with showers, Rockmart scored twice in the first half and then added two more tallies in the final stanza for a 25–0 victory over the "banged-up" Dragons. The only highlight of the evening was Ms. Betty Faye Burkhalter being named 1960 homecoming queen which was voted on by the student body; the crowning was held in the Leonard Gym following the game due to inclement weather. The pretty senior was a member of Christian Council, annual staff, basketball cheerleader, football cheerleader cocaptain, chorus, FHA, and Future Business Leader of America.

Lindale superintendent E. Russell Moulton announced on Monday that a record-breaking 1,518 students have enrolled this year; this is 70 more than last term. But the increased enrollment did not help on Friday night, October 14, on East Third. Thanks to a 7–6 victory over West Rome in 1958, Lindale owned a 1–0 slate over Paul Kennedy's 11, and he told the *New-Tribune*, "I respect Otis, he plays the gambling type ball and you have to worry about that." However, we were our own worst enemy on this night, giving up 2 long punt returns, losing 2 fumbles and allowing a 61-yard run from scrimmage. Kennedy's crew scored 3 times before all patrons found their seats and coasted to a 33–7 win. In the game's waning minutes, senior Howell Kerr returned an interception 80 yards to account Pepperell's only score.

In Cartersville, the 'Canes added to our woes 25–0 for an eighth consecutive loss but their seventh win. Quarterback Don Swanson threw two scoring passes and ran for another; the losers totaled less than sixty yards of offense. A week later, host Trion won their sixth straight victory 33–0 while the visitors lost for the ninth time. Five players tallied for Coach Sam McCain's chargers in the rout. Not only were the Dragons young, but also they were "injury jinxed," which accounted for our lack of offense (first downs and three yards rushing). The newcomer to Region 3-A football was undefeated and untied when they welcomed PHS on Friday, November 4; two hours later, Coach Charlie Gresham's Carrollton squad remained so with a 32–0 win and a Region 3-A South crown. The Trojans had little trouble scoring three TDs before the break and two more later.

1961 Season

Interest in the 1961 season started early with the third annual coaches' clinic in Rome. On March 10, more than 80 coaches watched and listened to lectures by UGA and Tech staffs. On the schoolboy level, Charlie Gresham of Carrollton High talked about his single-wing offense which had dealt misery to several teams in our region. One week prior to this, Pepperell opened spring drills. Coaches Gilbreath, Cosper, and Boling welcomed some 37 players that "lean toward the youthful side." After 2 weeks of practice, the headman said, "Most of our boys are freshman but more importantly, they want to play football." He noted Dan Bohannon was manning the center position well; Johnny Mathis looked like a quarterback, David Erwin, 130-pound halfback, had performed well in drills while Archie Vaughn was a good tight end. These youngsters should fit well into a two-platoon system which was being installed for the coming season. On Tuesday night, April 4, the returnees scored a 19–0 decision over last year's seniors; the scrimmage closed out spring training.

The third week of August came quickly in South Lindale as fall practice began with Coach Otis saying his youthful squad had only one way to go after losing all 10 games last season—up! The Dragons' last victory occurred on November 6, 1959, against Gilmer County, 33–0. On September 2, Calhoun (Region 3-AA) was hosted in Lindale. The Jackets were coming off a 5–4–1 year, losing close games against East, West, and Cedartown. With 7 sophomores starting, PHS played determined ball; however, an early fumble at their own 36-yard line led to Calhoun scoring the only points in a 7–0 win. Pepperell's only threat occurred in the second half when sophomore QB Johnny Mathis threw 42 yards to Wallace Shiflett; a later fumble ended our chances. The losing streak continued the following Saturday night at Barron Stadium as Coosa triumphed 33–6. Pepperell shocked the 4,000 spectators when Wallace Shiflett "picked up" a loose punt and traveled 90 yards for the game's first marker. The winners retaliated quickly behind QB Ted Goss who engineered 2 running scores and a 21-yard TD strike before intermission. After band performances, Coosa's Eagles passed for another 6-pointer and ran back a Dragon interception. Before our team visited Region foe Ellijay, Otis and assistants made some changes. Dan Bohannon was moved from center to quarterback, Grady Brannon from end to center, and Shiflett from the backfield to end/flanker. Consequently, Lindale played hard-nosed ball, but so did Gilmer County in winning 6–0; the 'Cats rolled up 184 to 49 yards offensively and logged 16 first downs while allowing only 3. It could have been worse, for we bucked up and stopped the 'Cats several times inside our red zone.

After thirteen consecutive losses, the Shrine Game loomed Saturday night at Barron Stadium. Injuries and illness had slowed the Blue Devils whereas, according to newspaper opinions, a scarcity of material was Pepperell's malady. As a consolation, neither Shannon nor Lindale had scored a touchdown this season. Thankfully, *Rome News-Tribune* reported on Sunday, September 24, "Pepperell Wallops Model, Snaps Long Losing Skein." Before some "5,000 screaming fans," PHS dropped the Blue Devils 26–6; Johnny Mathis threw sixteen yards to Wallace Shiflett; then David Erwin ran a punt back sixty-five yards to give our boys a 13–0 lead at half. Per the local paper, "tempers flared for a brief period after intermission which seemed to arouse Dragon spirit." A replay of an earlier Mathis-to-Shiflett pass resulted in a fifty-four-yard touchdown and a 20–0 lead. With 1:31 showing, QB Mathis sneaked over for a three-yard TD. Model's only score was Latimer's thirteen-yard pass to Gary York. Region 3-AA East Rome welcomed 1–3 Pepperell to Barron Stadium on September 29; the Glads had yet to win a game with losses to Coosa, Cedartown, and Dalton in addition to a scoreless tie with Calhoun. We evened up their win record with ours in a 12–0 loss. The loss to ER preceded a visit to Polk County. There, the odds were almost even as Rockmart was winless for 1961. But after Friday night, October 6, their record improved to 1–5 with a 14–7 victory. Next up was four-win West Rome from Region 3-AA. We were outclassed and outmanned, losing 36–7. Saturday night, October 21, was homecoming in Lindale.

Coach Otis Gilbreath was quoted in *RNT* on Wednesday that "for the first time in quite a while, the Dragons are ready physically for a tough game." Highly ranked Cartersville, loser of only one game (Carrollton), would test them. Yet history shows Coach Otis seemed to have a knack for beating the Purple Hurricanes. He told the Rome paper one day before kickoff, "I honestly think we've got a chance to win this ball game." Obviously the veteran mentor had not given up on his youthful squad. After playing six consecutive games on "foreign soil," the Dragons would tee up on Lindale Field. His team responded with a 7–6 upset. In the third quarter, Jerry Henderson gathered up a visitor punt and scooted sixty-eight yards for the TD; Johnny Mathis "rammed" over for the PAT. In the final stanza, FB Norman Dabbs bulled over from six yards out to make it 7–6; fortunately for us for the 'Canes extra point was wide. The special night at Lindale Field continued as Ms. Sandra Faye Sharpe reigned as homecoming queen by last year's queen Mrs. Betty Burkhalter Shiflett; a dance for students in grades 9 to 12 followed in the Leonard Gym. On Saturday night, October 28, Class A number-5-ranked Trion came to Dragon Drive with a 7–1 record. Only a two-point loss to LaFayette High in the first game kept them from being undefeated. Traditionally, the Bulldogs have a bevy of fast backs and good strong linemen, and they cruised 27–7. Two weeks later, they would lose the Class 3-A Region Championship game 21–6 to Carrollton. And speaking of the Trojans—it did not get any easier for PHS when Gresham's crew visited a week later; they departed with a 32–7 victory and their record intact. One month later, they would down Ware County 21–0 for the state championship.

1962 Season

A few days after Pepperell opened spring practice on Monday, March 12, some eighty-five coaches from Alabama and Georgia high schools attended the fourth annual clinic held in Rome. For the first time, basketball, baseball, and track were added to the agenda. The Georgia Tech staff along with accomplished high school mentors provided their expertise. Noted among that group were Waymond Creel, Sam McClain, Ed Pharo, Bill Keller, and Al Mariotti. The two-day event ended at Barron Stadium for a scrimmage between East and West Rome high schools.

By the first day of April, Coach Otis was pleased with his troops, saying, "This has been the best spring we've ever had." He praised center Dan Bohannon as being "a much better polished player." In the three weeks of work, backfield mates David Erwin, Charles Waldrop, and Jerry Henderson had excelled. Linemen Studdard, Maxwell, Cook, and Jordan had added weight; hopefully this group would be 20 pounds heavier than last year. The all-important quarterback position would be handled by veteran Johnny Mathis while Jerry Boatner would work in his shadow. Coaches' optimism was rewarded on August 6 when 30 candidates, including 19 lettermen, showed up for first fall practice to perhaps begin Pepperell's "long uphill climb." The community was certainly fired-up as a king-size campus pep rally took place on Friday evening, August 24, before the Johnson High Wildcats and Pepperell Dragons kicked off on Saturday, 8:00 p.m. Don Leithauser's band generated enthusiasm while the cheerleaders provided spirit.

This group included Judy Betts (captain), Sandra Lloyd (cocaptain); Sheila Knight, Ruth Price, Jeanne Sutton, Linda Allen, Judy Sutton, Ellen Tillery, Jane Knight, and Janis McBurnett. The local booster club fed the kids a steak supper after the festivities. A standing-room-only crowd at Lindale Field watched as FB Jerry Henderson ran 13 times for 131 yards and 2 touchdowns. Johnny Mathis sprinted 63 yards on a keeper; Charles Waldrop cracked over from 2 yards before skinny sophomore Jimmy Brumbelow scored on a 20-yard reverse for the final TD in a 31–6 victory. Opening-game jitters resulted in 130 yards of penalties.

The first day of the 1962–'63 school terms began on August 30. Superintendent Moulton announced enrollment for grades 1 to 12 soared to an all-time high of 1,603, and it was expected to increase next week. One day later, an inexperienced and underdog Calhoun squad hosted PHS. However, it only took twelve seconds for the "greenness" to disappear. Jacket halfback Terry Woods electrified the capacity crowd with an eighty-five-yard kickoff return—untouched. Following a Dragon fumble, QB Tony Black scooted five yards for a 13–0 lead. Pepperell responded quickly when Johnny Mathis hit David Erwin for forty-seven yards; suddenly, it was 13–7. After intermission, another visitor fumble resulted in a fourteen-play drive to pay dirt and a 19–7 advantage. With game clock time fast clicking off, Dragon quarterback Mathis took to the air with seven consecutive passes, culminating with a thirteen-yard strike to Ricky Stephens; a successful extra point made it a disappointing final 19–14. Calhoun players were so jubilant, "they tossed full-clothed coaches into a nearby swimming pool." Alas, the Yellow Jackets would not win another contest, finishing 1962 with a 1–8–1 record. One week later in Barron Stadium, Coosa received a 12–6 upset jolt. Dan Bohannon performed viciously on defense with several tackles for loss; however, it was QB Johnny Mathis's unscripted run with seven seconds left before halftime that ultimately gave us the win (earlier he had thrown to end Ricky Stephens for our first TD). Finding all receivers covered, he scrambled past goal, giving us a six-point lead and victory. The ensuing Shrine Game between Lindale and Shannon was billed as "youth against youth." Coach Ralph Tuggle played thirteen sophomores while Coach Otis's gold and white suits up only one senior. Model was looking to revenge last year's 28–6 "thrashing." Most observers predict an evenly matched battle; however, this contest, which was usually the largest attended game in the county, can often go against the odds. And it did, for Model won handedly 27–0. Actually they were pretty good that year (7–2–1), especially on defense giving up a total of thirty-six points all year. On Friday, September 21, *Lindale News* feature writer Langdon B. Gammon speculated that Pepperell's next game against North Cobb would be an in game. He noted the squad had alternated wins and losses this season. Johnson was an in, and Calhoun, an out; Coosa was in, and Model, an out. If this analogy holds true, the game at Lindale Field Friday night would be an in. The invaders from Cobb County would be a Region 3-A South counter. A 1957 bond issue funded a new high school for Kennesaw and Acworth to be called North Cobb High. Versus the Warriors on September 22, 1962, Coach Gilbreath listed his starters: ends Glenn Studdard and Ned Beard, tackles Frank Martin and Robin Harris, guards Ronnie Baldwin and Larry Cook, center Dan Bohannon, quarterback Johnny Mathis, halfbacks David Erwin and Charles Waldrop, and fullback Jerry Henderson. Our opponent at Lindale Field on Saturday night was decent during the season, recording a 5–5 slate, but the Dragons won 12–0.

Valley Point High School of Dalton visited Lindale for homecoming on September 29. In all honesty, they were pretty bad, having won just eight games in five years while we were sitting at 3–2 overall and 1–0 in Region. Coach Otis had made more changes to his lineup with Jimmy Brumbelow and Tony Taylor starting at halfbacks and Bobby Jordan at tackle. Homecoming queen Ms. Judith Ann Champion, a 17-year-old senior, presided on Pepperell's 34–0 romp over the visiting Green Wave from Whitfield County. She was a member of Spanish Club, FHA, vice President Christian Council, majorette, Ms. Pepperell Court, and Future Business Leaders of America. Following a tough 6–0 home loss to a tough Cartersville squad on October 6, our boys rebounded with a 20–14 road win over a Dallas high school that was destined to consolidate after the 1968 season. On October 26, Lindale made a long trek on Federal Highway 41 South to, as Lang Gammon wrote, "storm the bastions" of one-loss Carrollton High School. Comparable scores, i.e., one point wins over North Cobb and Cartersville, suggested a winnable contest. Guard Ronnie Baldwin's hand injury kept them from being at full strength. Nevertheless, Carroll County's Trojans shut out PHS 29–0. PHs finished 1962 on November 3 at Lindale Field when Subregion 3-B champs' Trion visited, sporting a 6–3 record. Ronald Day's 6-yard plunge gave them a 6–0 lead at intermission; afterward, Day's second TD and Harold Bryant's 2-yard run, put them up for a final of 19–0. We could have led at the half but for two red zone stops by their defense; another drive was thwarted late, which closed 1962 with an even 5–5 slate.

The local Kiwanis Club recognized all-area football players with a banquet on November 24. Unanimous captains were Bucky Ayers of Cedartown and Dan Bohannon. Previously, team parents hosted and fed a hot dog supper to hungry Dragons. For the occasion, Mrs. Laura Arnold baked a beautifully decorated cake, which was consumed at the Girl Scout hut. On Thanksgiving Day, plant manager G. Howard Smith, who was an accomplished athlete at Auburn, chaperoned thirty-five athletes to Tech's Grant field for UGA versus Tech versus annual freshman football game.

1963 Season

On July 5, 1963, the Lindale nation was saddened by news of Robert Donald Harvey's passing. The popular former plant manager had retired in 1955 due to poor health. "His death cast a pall over Park Street Village and brought messages of sympathy and sorrow from hundreds of people in all walks of life," spoke *Rome News-Tribune*. Mr. Harvey was a native Roman who joined Massachusetts Mills in Georgia in 1920 after graduating from Georgia Tech. He was an affable and friendly Darlington alumnus whose lifework was for Lindale. Mr. Harvey guided the company through tough times and later led post-depression improvements which included a new elementary school, a new high school, a gymnasium, a fenced-in lighted athletic field, scout huts, and a new American Legion building in addition to promoting employee wage increases. Two years before retirement, the corporation's 102nd annual report reported net earnings of $3,861,002 or $7.69 per share.

In preseason, coaches Otis Gilbreath, Bill Boling, Jim Mullins, Olan Cosper, and Jack Carroll attended the annual coaching clinic in Atlanta. All learning sessions climaxed on Thursday night, August 8, with a North-South high school all-star game in Grant Field. On Monday, a dozen

Dragon lettermen reported for conditioning drills led by entire returning backfield from last year; however, only one first-team lineman returned—guard Ronnie Baldwin. In desperation, coaches converted offensive backs Jerry Brumbelow and Jerry Boatner into tackles; newcomers Roger Goss and Earl Robinson were competing at center. Flankers/ends would be handled by Stephens, Penson, Hardy, Maxwell, and James Rush. Although quarterback was set with four-year veteran Johnny Mathis, youngster Larry Kenney was also capable; veteran halfbacks Brumbelow, Locklear, Boatner, and Taylor would line up alongside 210-pound "bull of a fullback" Jerry Henderson. The latter was also described by Coach Otis "as good a high school kicker as there is in Georgia." On defense, Henderson and fellow 200-pound ball carrier Tony Taylor would shift to tackle positions. Obviously athleticism would reign on our offensive side. On Thursday, August 29, those lazy, hazy, crazy days of summer were over as classes began at PHS. Two nights later on Lindale Field, we made 3 sustained drives that fostered a 19–0 shutout victory of Johnson High. Mathis, Locklear, and Taylor each had running touchdowns; however, Wildcat fullback Ricky Gresham was exemplary as he romped for 136 tough yards. On Saturday, September 7, in Lindale, a "record throng" watched visiting Calhoun go down in defeat 26–0. The paid attendance was 1,890 or 910 students and 980 adults, sending school officials scrambling for additional bleachers. A corps of "fast stepping backs" led the romp over a Region 3-AA opponent. A first-period blocked punt set up Johnny Mathis's 4-yard TD pass to Ricky Stephens; then Mathis ran an option play for 9 yards and a 13–0 lead. After intermission, Henderson crossed the double stripe for 4 yards; then scatback Brumbelow scampered in from 34 yards out, giving us a score in each quarter. Defensively, our goal line had not been breached.

Although the Dragons topped Class B Coosa last year 12–6, Coach Branch Bragg's eleven was a vaunted opponent. A light rain fell in Lindale on September 14, and it turned both team's strategies into defensive struggles, which was won by Coosa 6–0. The lone score occurred just after halftime when Eagle quarterback Jimmy Hudgins scooted ten yards to paydirt around right end. Statistically, Pepperell led in first downs 6–2 and passing yards 11 to minus 2; rushing was almost even at 75 to 80. Illegal-motion penalties, fumbles, and a muddy track stymied Otis's crew most of the first half.

For Saturday night's annual Shrine Game versus Model, Coach Gilbreath announced his starting lineup: ends Gaines and Penson, tackles Millican and Taylor, center Robinson, halfbacks Brumbelow and Locklear, fullback Henderson, and quarterback Mathis. In their opening game, Ralph Tuggle's squad scared East Rome mightily before bowing 6–0. If that was not enough to worry Lindale's coaches, last year's 27–0 thrashing by Shannon still haunted them. Well, the game wasn't a revenge blowout, but our boys won 13–6 as Johnny Mathis slammed over from 3 yards out for a 6–0 lead at intermission. Blue Devil Ed Murdock's short yardage run tied it at 6–6 after break. The winning points occurred late fourth quarter with a 13-play 73-yard drive culminated by a Mathis-to-Gaines 6-yard pass. The winners led in first downs 11–5 and rushing 115 to 68. Penalties were fairly even. At halftime, some 6,000 fans were treated to "high stepping" Pepperell majorettes, namely Sherry Echols, Judy Edwards, Carolyn Sheppard, Vera Huether, Judy Gilreath, and Louis Jordan (head). With season preliminaries completed, a 5-game subregion schedule awaited. In North Cobb on Friday night, September 27, Jerry Henderson broke away for a 32-yard jaunt despite "soaked underfooting." Jimmy Locklear followed that with a

36-yard scamper down to the one; QB Johnny Mathis's sneak and PAT gave us a 7–0 victory. The rugged Dragon defense allowed only 56 yards rushing and 5 first downs; neither squad completed a pass. Penalties were 50 yards for Pepperell but zero for old Acworth High School. Region opponent Valley Point was up next on October 4. As a courtesy, *Rome News-Tribune* printed directions for traveling fans: "Valley Point is located south of Dalton and west of the highway." It was a happy trip back to Floyd for Coach Gilbreath's "fire breathing" Dragons who put up 20 second-period points and followed that with 25 more after break. It was a night when nothing went wrong, for we logged 19 first downs with 248 rushing yards and 208 passing. The Green Wave was fairly inept offensively, managing only 10 yards running and 63 passing mostly by reserves late.

Rome's newspaper waxed eloquent on Tuesday, October 8, printing Pepperell's Dragons, the winningest team in Floyd County, "head into the Face of big wind" on Friday.

Team scouts confirmed this with alarming reports of Cartersville's 21–6 victory over East Rome. However, we scored two early, and they scored two late for a 13–13 tie. On second snap and before fans had time to settle in, QB Johnny Mathis hit Ricky Stephens for 49 yards and a TD. Just before intermission, Jerry Henderson scampered 39 yards down near goal. One hike later, he plunged over for a 12–0 2-touchdown lead. Meanwhile, our defense gave up only 1 rushing yard in 24 minutes of play. But a change in Hurricane strategy occurred after break which led to 204 yards passing; QB Bradshaw threw to Roberts for a 52-yard TD pass to cut their deficit to 12–6; they followed that with a 20-yard TD run by Latimer. Thankfully, Johnny Mathis blocked the PAT, producing a 13–13 tie as time expired. Coach Gilbreath and staff faced a problem on October 19—how to play Dallas with Carrollton on your mind. Yet Lindale took care of business with a 32–8 victory. They scored 4 touchdowns before intermission, of which 2 were courtesy of interceptions by Mathis and Robinson. A late-game 7-yard scoring run by senior John McKay Mathis closed it out.

The Single-Wing/Notre Dame Box offensive set would visit Lindale on Saturday night, November 2. Coach Gilbreath believed this Carrollton's 7–1 squad, who were ranked fifth statewide, was superior to last year's state runners-up. With that said, Otis believed this group of Dragons was potentially just as good and very capable of stopping Charlie Gresham's bunch. He said, "We're healthy and I know what they are going to do but it's hard to stop." Before a packed house in Lindale, triple-threat tailback Billy Whitworth threw a 28-yard TD pass to Max Skinner for the only score before half. Whitworth then threw 8 yards for another marker and then ran a short yardage TD to close out a 20–6 victory. A tough visitor defense basically shut down our offense except for a late 45-yard aerial gainer Mathis to Locklear down close where Johnny sneaked over for Pepperell's only points. After a record crowd of 2,156 (1,169 adults and 987 students) passed through school turnstiles, a local booster said philosophically, "We might not have won but we made some money tonight."

A final contest for 1963 ended in Trion on November 8 with 170-pound hard-charging fullback Randy Martin running for touchdowns of 4 and 9 yards to win 13–0 over Pepperell. Our own FB, senior Jerry Henderson, gave a "stellar performance" by rushing for 128 yards on 10 carries; however, a determined Bulldog defense refused to surrender a point. During a postseason chapel period on November 26, trophies were presented to outstanding players. Johnny

Mathis was MVP; halfback Jimmy Brumbelow was tops on offense while guard Ronnie Baldwin collected for defensive excellence. Dragon coaches presented a "Best Hustler" award to senior end James David Penson.

1964 Season

On Monday, March 9, football managers and staff began issuing equipment in preparation for monthlong spring training. Previously, Pepperell butted heads with Region South powers Carrollton and Cartersville; now with a move to 3-A North, our schedule looked better as Valley Point, Pickens, and Gilmer counties would provide competition. Although 13 veterans are gone, many good players returned, including Earl Robinson, center; Ronnie Pajor, Rex Puckett, and Doug Meers, guards; Jim Millican, tackle; Larry Kinney, quarterback; Jimmy Brumbelow and Eddie Garrett, halfbacks; and Dan Turner, fullback. Many of these athletes would perform both ways. Coach Gilbreath cited two players from this group, "Offensively, Kinney and Brumbelow have got to make us go." The former is a 6-foot-3-inch senior weighing 185 pounds who grew up as a linebacker; he must now do double duty at quarterback. Brumbelow was a 170-pound speedster described as "there is not a better halfback around." Four weeks later, 50 aspirants finished drills, prompting Otis to say, "We've been well satisfied with the results." As spring turned to summer, Lang Gammon announced Charles Abrams had been elected as president of Pepperell Dragon Club. Other officers included Bryant Henderson, vice president; Bob Tillery, secretary; and F. D. Hand, treasure. Mr. Gammon then noted a list of recent club accomplishments: paving of sidewalk at elementary school as well as blackout curtains for classrooms, helping with cost of new film projector, purchased award jackets for varsity baseball, and funded equipment for Mite and Midget football teams. These project outlays were north of $2,700. On August 18, *Rome News-Tribune* sportswriter Orbie Thaxton headlined: "Dragons in Rebuilding Job...of the 11 men who started in Lindale's opening game last season, none are returning." Nevertheless, several pundits picked home-standing PHS over Johnson by 2 touchdowns on the last Saturday of August. They did not miss it much—Pepperell, 13; Johnson, 6. Senior Jimmy Mathis broke a 6–6 deadlock with a second-half kickoff return of 90 yards; QB Kinney sneaked over for point after. Meanwhile, our defense allowed only 50 yards rushing. Up next, underdog Armuchee came to Lindale; early on, Lindale speedster Jimmy Mathis slanted off tackle for a 10-yard score; Steve Bennett ran point after for a 7–0 lead at halftime. Following intermission, a bad punt gave them a short field whereas HB James Reonas pranced 11 yards around left end to score; pressure mounted as J. W. Bridges "slammed" his way into a 7–7 tie. Coach Homer Mathis's (1957 Pepperell graduate) squad played well in logging 8 first downs to our 7; net yardage favored them also 152–116. They incurred no penalties throughout a much "heated struggle." The Sunday morning *Rome News-Tribune* headline read, "Armuchee Rally Ties Dragons in Thriller." Although Coosa lost their opener to West Rome 14–0, game predictors chose them over Pepperell by 20–6. In trying to get some punch to his offense, Coach Otis moved Kinney to fullback and promoted lanky junior Steve Johnston to quarterback. We still struggled to a 6–0 loss. The annual Shrine Game between Lindale and Shannon usually brought out the best in sportswriters. Lang Gammon of *RNT* waxed eloquent on September 18, "The fires of an ancient, spirited rivalry will be rekindled at 8 o'clock Saturday night when Model and Pepperell come to grips on the turf of Barron Stadium." Region 3B Blue Devils were 1–1 after losing to East Rome before nipping a good Calhoun 11 6–3 last week. Our starting lineup was announced as ends Tommy Bright and Scotty Farrer, tackles Randy Roberts and Jim Millican, guards Doug Meers and Rex Puckett, center Earl Robinson, quarterback Steve Johnston, halfbacks Jimmy Brumbelow and Eddie Garrett, and fullback Larry Kinney. Two days before game time, an interesting note appeared in Rome's gazette which said, "The State Board of Education turns down proposed 9–12 grade consolidation at Johnson and Model." Soon after opening kickoff, on September 19, we fumbled near midfield Blue Devils recovering. A steady drive goalward ended with Jerome Gray crashing over from 1 yard out; Latimer's run converted point after for a 7–0 lead. After intermission, it was another Dragon miscue that spelled defeat. Flip Latimer scooped up the bouncing ball and returned it 26 yards untouched for a 14–0 edge. Down 2 touchdowns early in the final period, PHS marched 32 yards to paydirt. Fullback Larry Kinney ran 5 straight times before moving to quarterback for a 1-yard TD sneak; back at his regular FB spot, Kinney's PAT run was stopped short by that man Flip Latimer. Unfortunately for us, several opportunities to move the scoreboard numbers failed in the 14–6 loss. Statistics showed first downs, rushing, and passing yards pretty well even as were penalties. Seven nights later, Valley Point came to South Floyd for a subregion battle. Although Whitfield matched a 1–2 record with our 1–2–1 slate and totaled 51 points to our 26, they provided little resistance in losing 32–19. On the first Friday of October, *RNT* said, "Pepperell left their artillery [zero passing] at home but brought their road machinery [221 yards rushing by Kinney, Brumbelow, and Garrett] to Ellijay in a convincing 19–6 win." Host Gilmer County High showed reverse stats with only 53 ground yards off their favorite outside tackle and end sweeps; however, they did complete 16 passes for 197 yards.

Cartersville at Pepperell pitted both subregion leaders in Lindale on Saturday night, October 10, which projected to be a preview of postseason competition. The former had a "hard-charging" undefeated defense to go with ample offensive power. A standing-room-only crowd was expected just off Park Street to watch their Dragons who recently blew out Valley Point and Gilmer. However, PHS lost 21–9.

Another good team was next. Host Calhoun was riding a four-game win streak and picked as a seven-point favorite over Pepperell. Occasionally a punter can really determine the outcome of the football game; this happened last Friday night in Gordon County when Bobby Tamplin pinned the Dragons on the one-, eight-, twenty-, twenty-five-, twenty-eight-, and thirty-eight-yard lines. With that said, our defense outplayed CHS in the 6–0 loss. Although a short visitor punt just after break gave them a short field, it took a fourth down twenty-three-yard pass completion and three line bucks to win 6–0. Total yards gained favored us as did first downs and lack of penalty yards.

In the preseason, Coach Gilbreath had predicted some struggles for 1964, but he also thought this bunch would be scrappy. He was dead right, for on Saturday night, October 24, PHS blasted Pickens County 53–8 to wrap up Subregion. It was pretty much the Jimmy Brumbelow show, for the shifty halfback ran for 180 yards and 2 touchdowns; he also intercepted a pass and returned it 99 yards for the score—all in 2 quarters of play. On Monday evening, Rome Quarterback Club feted and recognized Jimmy as Back of the Week. Following his first half gridiron performance, Ms. Jane Shields Knight was named 1964 Homecoming Queen. The pretty blonde had been a member of Christian Council, Spanish, and Letter Club; served as Class President, Football Cheerleader, MVP of women's Basketball squad, Chorus, Future Teachers Association, and Girl's State Delegate. Members of Jane's HC Court were Misses Joyce Sutton, Carolyn Boatner, Sheila Knight, and Carolyn Sheppard. In Bartow County on the last night of October, Pepperell was favored by 7 over Cass Colonels; surprisingly, we lost by 20–14. Nevertheless, our North Region Champion boys prepared to visit South's 7-2-1 Carrollton on Friday, November 20. Charlie Grisham's Trojans were playing in 7 straight region finals. They were led by triple-threat tailback Bobby Sullivan who had amassed 1,193 yards of total offense; to make matters worse, Dragon starting QB Steve Johnston broke his collarbone in practice and was out of action. Sophomore Steve Dodd at 135 pounds, but with "with abundance of competitive spirit," would attempt to replace Johnston. Fullback Larry Kinney could also revert back to quarterback if necessary.

Yet with less than five minutes to play, PHS had the upper hand in a 7–7 contest by virtue of statistics and penetration inside opponent's twenty-yard line. All we needed was some time off the clock. We had reached this point by blitzing interior linemen that wreaked havoc with single-wing off-tackle and end sweeps. Middle backer Earl Robinson had clogged up running lanes all night, freeing up guards Doug Meers and Granger Poe to make eleven and seven individual tackles, respectively. But with the clock ticking down, halfback Danny Akin accounted for forty-one of sixty-six yards in a winning TD drive. *Rome News-Tribune's* Orbie Thaxton posted on Sunday that "Trojans Pushed to Limit, Whip Pepperell, 14–7." At season's end, Rome Kiwanis Club named its area all-star squad, which included Pepperell's Robinson. Other good news was a state championship won by girls' volleyball; also freshman football was undefeated at 8–0. Two weeks later, Carrollton downed Fitzgerald 20–7 to win state.

1965 Season

On March 21, page 14, Rome's newspaper interviewed Coach Gilbreath who predicted his 1965 squad, which numbered 62 players, would be tough defensively because "this bunch loves to hit." In addition, it would be more experienced and bigger at tackles with Randy Roberts and Jim Millican weighing in at 250 and 230 pounds, respectively. Offensively we were small at halfbacks with Scott Farrer, Gary Wingo, David Barton, and Steve Bennett; fullback came down to Mike Edwards and Terry Bolton. Steve Johnston, who started most of last year's games, returned at QB.

Football season '65 came quickly in Lindale where we hosted and shut out North Cobb High 7–0 on Saturday night, August 28, with a tough defense as predicted. Kennesaw was allowed only 3 first downs, 67 yards rushing, and 10 passing. Gary Wingo immediately dashed 20 yards off tackle, and Bennett ran point after; subsequently there were no more scores. Last year, Armuchee tied Pepperell 6–6, but most pundits now marked PHS as 6-point favorites for Saturday night in Lindale. An overflow crowd watched Blue receive and march to our 1-yard line where Eddie Willerson plunged over goal. Wingo answered with a 7-yard TD dash before Bennett bulled over for point after touchdown. A few minutes later, Bennett tallied on a 28-yard reverse for a 14–6 edge. Following halftime, Bennett added a 13th point to his stock, this time receiving a 27-yard pass from Johnston. A final-quarter AHS fumble was claimed by Bo Firestone at midfield; 10 plays later, Steve Dodd scored on a short charge with senior Vaughn Terrell running point after for a 29–6 victory. Coach Otis was pleased with Larry Tate and Adrian Martin who filled in at tackles. After 2 contests, Steve Bennett claimed the area, rushing lead with 228 yards. Coosa was always tough on Dragons; ominously, the Class 3-B Eagles tied West Rome 0–0 prior to visiting Lindale on Saturday night, September 11. Yet the black-clad squad were 6-point underdogs. A second standing-room-only crowd watched the smaller Eagles take advantage of a fumbled punt and an intercepted pass to win 13–0. They logged 11 first downs to our 5; rushing and passing sticks favored them 145–73 and 21–0. Traditionally Floyd County's biggest football game of the year was the Shrine Game—Pepperell versus Model or Lindale against Shannon. An overflow crowd stood most of the night of September 18 in Barron Stadium where 2 defensive squads forced a 0–0 deadlock; still with 26 seconds left, there was excitement galore for 6,500 paying customers. They watched officials spot the oval at Model's 12-yard line. One half moaned while the rest cheered as senior Dragon Jim Millican missed a winning field goal. Next week was better as our boys tallied 4 touchdowns on 276 yards rushing in a decisive 33–7 victory over host Valley Point. Steve Johnston, Wingo, Farrer, and Bennett each ran past goal for 6-pointers; for a finale, Johnston tossed 21 yards to Tommy Bright. Going into Gilmer County at Pepperell on October 2, Coach Otis announced a starting lineup: ends Vic Freeman and Tommy Bright, tackles Randy Roberts and Jim Millican, guards Toby Hamby and Powers Garmon, center Bo Firestone, quarterback Steve Johnston, fullback Terry Bolden, and tandem halfbacks Wingo and Bennett, who raced for 152 and 142 yards, respectively. It was a good group, for they waxed Ellijay 28–0. Wingo barely edged his running mate for Back of the Week locally. On October 8, host Cartersville packed 8 defenders up close, forcing us to throw; QB Steve Johnston completed 7 of 16 passes for 129 yards, but it was not enough in a 21–7 loss. Eight nights later, Class 3-AA Calhoun scored twice to down home-standing Pepperell 14–0. The bigger Jackets stymied our run game completely, allowing only 14 yards on the ground; our only bright spot was Johnston's 85-yard passing. Yet on Sunday, October 24, *Rome News-Tribune* headlined, "Dragons Breathe Fire, March to Sub-Region Title." The Gold and White traveled to Jasper on Friday and came away with a 27–2 victory over Pickens County. On first snap from scrimmage, Scotty Farrer galloped 41 yards; a few plays later, Steve Johnston, quarterback, sneaked a second score. Next, Farrer and Bright combined for 17 yards running and 28 in the air before Wingo dove over from 8 yards out. The third marker was razzle-dazzle as Wingo fielded a Pickens punt and handed off to Bennett on a reverse that went 62 yards to goal. The final touchdown was a halfback pass from Wingo to Victor Ray Freeman covering 42 yards. Region 3-AA Colonels at Class 3-A Dragons on October 30 looked easy at first; we received promptly marched 67 yards to score; however, Cassville countered when Roger Moore hit halfback Lamar Lowery with an 8-yard TD to tie 6–6. Gary Wingo countered that on the ensuing kickoff when he brought everybody to their feet with a 95-yard return up the middle. Millican toed PAT for a final score of 13–6. Still there was some suspense left as Cass moved inside our 10-yard line twice in the waning minutes but were thrown back by our "staunch" defense. At halftime, pretty senior Ms. Donna Gayle McChargue was crowned Homecoming Queen 1965. She belonged to Christian Council, Band's Color Guard, JV and Varsity cheerleading squad, and Future Teacher and Homemaker Clubs of America.

Because of scheduling differences, Region 3-A championship between Carrollton and Pepperell was played November 20 or three weeks after we defeated Cass. Other than trying to keep his squad focused, Coach Otis's major problem was obtaining enough seating for the expected overflow crowd. Defending state champion Trojans carried a 9–0–1 record and were heavy favorites. *Rome News-Tribune* speculated the game could be a match between Pepperell's Steve Bennett and Gary Wingo versus Carrollton's Jimmy Tuggle and Steve Traylor. On defensing a Notre Dame Box, Coach Gilbreath had stated on many occasions, "I know what their direct-snap offense is going to do—it's just hard to stop." Penny-wise, our defense surrendered only 7.63 points per contest. Well, we did a pretty good job as regulation ended 13–13. Just minutes before half, QB Johnston hit Vic Freeman for 6; Terry Bolden rammed for 4 more and a first down at the 35. With 3:33 showing, Johnston decided to go for the bomb. The senior dropped back, waited momentarily, and then rifled a bullet downfield. Number 80 Tommy Bright "reached as far as he could, pulled the ball in at the 8 and stumbled past goal for a 6–0 halftime lead." After intermission, CHS used 20 snaps to drive 61 yards for a TD; point after made it 7–6 for visitors. But if standing-room-only folks thought "game over," they were sorely mistaken. Scotty Farrer hauled in the ensuing kickoff and handed it to number 23 Wingo who reversed down the sidelines to midfield; he then dodged his way for a 90-yard return. Millican toed point after, and Pepperell led 13–7. With 3 minutes to play, it was Lindale's game to win, and it appeared so for the feared Single Wing faced a desperation fourth down and 10 at Dragon 42-yard line; changing tactics, backfield mate Steve Traylor used a throwback pass to 145-pound tailback Jimmy Tuggle who gathered it in at the 25 and scampered into paydirt with 2 minutes remaining. Fortunately for us, Bone's try for PAT was low and wide left, leaving us tied 13–13. Otis's crew did not quit as Steve Johnston's passes clicked for 2 first downs before that man Tuggle intercepted. *Rome News-Tribune* explained tiebreaker rules on Sunday, November 21, "Under Georgia High School Association rules, one point each is awarded for most first downs, total offensive yards and times penetrated inside opponent's 20-yard line." Carrollton garnered 2 points on first 2 while both squads were even on red zone penetrations, therefore giving them a 15–13 victory. In the postseason, the *Atlanta Journal-Constitution* named Steve Johnston, Jim Millican, and Steve Bennett honorable mention All-State in Class 3-A. The 1965 season was a landmark for Pepperell High School. On page 60 of the 1966 yearbook, there is a picture of Coach Billy G. Reynolds standing behind 28 suited members of his freshman team; in the third row were Billy Woodruff and Rickey Langston, our first Black football players.

1966 Season

Back in the spring, Pepperell Coach Otis Gilbreath and staff put seventy youngsters through gridiron drills; all told, the veteran mentor was "pleased but cautious" about his squad. He told the local newspaper, "We are blocking much better and our ends and halfbacks have looked really sharp." News from the college ranks indicate many schools were moving to the I formation, which is a tandem fullback and running back as opposed to a full house set of two halfbacks and a fullback. John McKay's success at Southern California running off tackle both directions along with sweeps (called student body right and left) and QB sprint-outs had begun to take the day.

Four months and 20 days later, all players were requested to meet at the gymnasium for football physical examinations. However, 2 happenings took some of the luster from the weigh-ins. On the first Thursday of August, 2,204 employees of the Lindale plant of West Point Pepperell Manufacturing Company voted (2,254 were eligible) whether to accept the Textile Workers Union of America as their collective bargaining representative; it was approved by a margin of 1,139 in favor and 917 against. This was the fourth referendum in the plant's 71-year history as the union was turned down in 1947, 1955, and 1965. This ballot was ordered by the NLRB under charges that the company had threatened to close the plant last year if workers approved joining the TWUA. The second news event occurred on August 4 with the annual North-South All-Star football game in Atlanta. The *News-Tribune*'s Orbie Thaxton bemoaned the lack of support (only 7,300 fans turned out) for the high school classic. He considered the number a disgrace when compared to the 25,000 attendance of 1964. Orbie blamed Atlanta traffic, professional sports, and weather for the dwindling interest. Prior to Pepperell's opener versus Armuchee on August 27, Coach Gilbreath's squad received a boost when halfback Steve Bennet returned from knee surgery. The senior had been high in rushing and scoring when injured last season. He would team with junior Gary Wingo again at the speed positions; Charles Gilbreath and David Jones would back them up. Kent Millican and Lamar Ashley would fight it out at fullback while Steve Dodd would be the field general. On the flanks, Chambers and Cox were leading; Larry Tate and Adrain Martin were returning tackles while Toby Hamby and Mike Abney manned the guards with help from senior Roger Mull and junior Byron Green. The man Bo Firestone would anchor the center spot along with Jimmy Dudley. The local paper forecast a Dragon victory Saturday night at Barron Stadium, but Coach Otis was wary of Namon Wiseman's 11. The latter felt his Indians could win the matchup. "It'll be a tough ball game," he said. Pepperell quarterbacks Steve Dodd and Jimmy Morris were first-year men as were Armuchee's Darrell Lowery (later Dr. Lowery) and Charles Rickman. Before 6,000 fans, the Dragons did almost everything right in a 33–0 victory, especially Steve Dodd who completed 4 of 7 passes, 2 for touchdowns. The attending sportswriter said, "He threw hard, spiral passes right on the target." Cheerleading for each score were spirited ladies Kathy Black, Martha Henderson (captain), Cynthia Rayburn, Delores Brewer, Janice Scoggins (cocaptain), Linda Pilgrim, Carolyn Harrison, Patricia Dawson, Sally Shell, and Lynn Hinton. After a 43–13 romp over host North Cobb, the Gold and White were no longer considered a dark horse in Region 3-A. But for Bo Firestone's tenacious play at linebacker against Cass High, the Dragons would have been down more than seven points at the intermission. His hard work and eight individual tackles, combined with "sparkling play" by Wingo and Jimmy Dudley, made it possible for a home team touchdown in the final minutes to win 13–7. Lindale went into the annual Shrine Classic with Shannon undefeated at 3–0; we also had the top rusher, scorer (Wingo), and passer (Dodd) in the area. Our boys won on Saturday night, September 17, in cold drizzle of Barron Stadium, but it looked doubtful midway through the final stanza with Model in front 7–6. However, with 5:30 showing on the clock, the Blue

Devils were forced to punt from their own 2-yard line; they never got the kick away as Jimmy Dudley rushed and blocked it for a 2-point safety "which settled the issue" at 8–7. For his effort on a "twisting, driving" 14-yard touchdown run just before halftime, Gary Wingo was named area back of the week. In addition to gaining 89 yards from scrimmage, the junior halfback also made several key plays on defense. We pretty much dominated the statistics with 10 first downs to 8, 209 total yards as opposed to 120, and penalties were almost even. With only 1 loss between them, Coosa versus Pepperell at Barron Stadium on Saturday night—what more could fans ask for? In a game that named him lineman of the week, Eagle tackle Bill Reed was relentless on both sides of ball; it paid off with a 7–6 victory. The youngster made 4 individual stops and 8 assists; on offense, he consistently opened holes for team running backs; accordingly, Coach Bragg's 11 moved to top of Region 3-A North. We were not without outstanding effort as LBs Bo Firestone and Jimmy Dudley excelled as did linemen Byron Green, Adrian Martin, Larry Tate, Toby Hamby, Mike Abney, Roger Mull, and offensive end Steve Cox. But tomorrow was another day, and Coach Gilbreath stressed to his squad that next week's road opponent Gilmer County was "real tough." In blanking Model 12–0 last Friday night, Ellijay displayed a wide-open offense with the quarterback in a shotgun set, and receivers spread all over. We were cautiously favored by 2 touchdowns but covered the line easily, winning 40–14. Cartersville came to Lindale on Saturday night, October 28, with 1 loss and featuring Northwest Georgia's best running backfield; however, they had scrimmage line problems which might explain why local media picked PHS 20–14. After 48 minutes of play, the 'Canes returned to Bartow County with a second defeat courtesy of Pepperell's gut-checking 6–3 victory. Once again, Gary Wingo garnered back-of-the-week honors as he ran for 118 tough yards, including the game's only touchdown. He outgained their best back Larry Henderson by 60 yards. A week later, local gurus favored PHS over host East Rome; an earlier 28-point loss to Cartersville, a squad we bested 6–3 may have figured in. On statistics, we averaged more offense 315 yards to 227; furthermore, their defense gives up 274 compared to 163 for Lindale. However, Coach Otis was having none of that as he told *Rome News-Tribune*, "They are bigger and will be as tough as any team we meet this year." A wet Barron Stadium turf hampered our speed and quickness and helped the home squad to a 19–0 victory. Coach Larry Muschamp said afterward, "It was as near perfect a defensive game as we have played in a long time." His entire 11 was named Linemen of the Week for Rome area. Two gridiron casualties underwent knee surgery on Tuesday; backfield mates Charlie Gilbreath and Kent Millican chose to have same-day operations, ending their junior-year season. They now occupied the same hospital room.

Homecoming (Spirit Week) in Lindale brought Pickens to Floyd County for a Region 3-A game. A gala parade began marching up Park Street at 4:00 p.m. accompanied by floats, school clubs, cheerleaders, band, and Mite and Midget football squads. At 8:00 p.m., the Gold Dragons matched against Green Dragons. According to *RNT*, Christian Saint George would have a heyday Saturday night hunting the mythical beast that sought to sacrifice a princess in the fourth-century Roman Empire. Fortunately, our mascot was favored by four touchdowns, and like Saint George, we slew the Green Dragon 33–0. In the game, junior Gary Wingo boosted his lead in area rushing and moved ahead in scoring. At halftime, lovely Ms. Donna Jean Mitchell was crowned Queen; she had been a football sponsor for two years, is a member of the Band's Color

Guard, a member of the Christian Council, the Future Business Leaders of America, and Student Council. Donna is the daughter of Mr. and Mrs. Robert Mitchell of Route 1 Aragon; last year's runner-up, Ms. Sue Garrett, assisted with the crowning. Sporting a fine 7–2 record, we finished 1966 hosting Rockmart on Saturday night, October 29; it was "a thrilling and hard-fought" game that stalemated 0–0 at the half. Following intermission, Wingo faked a punt and ran deep into Jacket territory; three snaps later, Dodd hit him over the middle, and the swift HB took it to goal for a 7–0 lead. However, Polk County's Bees opened up a passing attack in final quarter, forcing a 7–7 deadlock. We finished a game back of Coosa for Subregion North. In postseason, tackle Larry Tate, center Bo Firestone, and halfback Gary Wingo were honorable mention All-State.

1967 Season

The Dragon yearbook prefaced its feature about gridiron 1967 with "Pepperell Dragons, A Very Good Year, 7–1–2." It actually started on March 10 at West Rome High School with the ninth annual Rome football coaching clinic. Vanderbilt head coach Bill Pace headed a program that included French Johnson of Marietta, Jack Wills of Tucker, and Bob Allen of Bradley County, Tennessee. Coach Otis Gilbreath and staff began spring training earlier on Monday, March 6, with approximately 70 candidates. The veteran mentor expressed concern about method of attack with no returning letterman at quarterback; he even suggested Lindale could operate out of something other than the T formation. Seniors Larry Tate, Adrian Martin, and Gayland Green were returning as tackles; the guard slot was depleted with only senior Byron Green there. Last year's fine linebacker Jimmie Dudley now handled center snaps. All six ends that suited up last year either moved or graduated. But excellent running backs seniors Gary Wingo, Kent Millican, along with Charlie Gilbreath carried the load. By middle of March, some things began to settle in; many observers saw a bright future for rising freshman QB Phil Baker while Donald Stamey and Johnny Kiser showed promise at halfbacks. Guard had been shored up with Richard Stager, Donald Bragg, young John Kendrick, and Ronald Stamey; freshman Don Studdard moved to backup at snapper while ends and flankers had no experience. It was a good group consisting of Lynn Hunnicutt, Donald Jackson, David Roper, Jackie Littlejohn, and Joel Howell. An afternoon scrimmage game closed practice on the last day of March. Coach had yet to mention his defense. It was a short summer as posted by *Rome News-Tribune*'s August 6 issue that Pepperell practice started at 5:00 p.m. Speculation was it was possible Gary Wingo could join West Rome's Roger Weaver in the 1,000-yard rushing club. Gary just missed with 961 last year. Our first public appearance scheduled on August 28 in Barron was delayed by rain, forcing a Monday-night battle with Region 3B Armuchee. Thirty-five hundred fans showed up on a school night to watch our 20–0 victory. Surely many of the crowd was part of newly announced 1,798 Lindale enrollments. In the second quarter, Pepperell linemen blocked a punt at the Indians' 27-yard line; 3 snaps later, freshman QB Phil Baker lofted a strike to Lynn Hunnicutt for the first score of 1967. Before halftime, we used 13 plays to travel 60 yards, ending with Johnny Kiser's counter trap for a 13–0 lead. With 7:30 showing on the third-quarter clock and facing long yardage on Armuchee's 25, Baker sent both ends down and out to drawn DBs; Gary Wingo slipped down the uncovered middle to catch a perfect pass for our first victory of '67. Noteworthy in Don Biggers's game report was Spence Millican's booming 57-yard punt over the deep man's head. A short 5 nights later in Lindale, we downed North Cobb 34 to zip. Touchdowns were recorded by Terry Kiser who ran 7 yards off tackle and Gary Wingo who sped 52 yards with a Warrior punt; Wingo bulled over twice for short yardage tallies before halftime to give us a 27–0 advantage. Late in the fourth quarter, Stamey, Kiser, and Wingo alternated to drive 58 yards for a final score. Our defense limited North Floyd to less than 100 yards of offense.

In third week, PHS rushed for 345 yards over Cassville; Gary Wingo accounted for 173 and 3 TDs while Billy Woodruff garnered 71 but did not score. Early on QB Baker hit Lynn Hunnicutt for a 32-yard scoring pass; reserve Randy Lloyd finished the 6-pointers with a short run in the fourth. On Sunday morning, September 17, *Rome News-Tribune* summed up the twentieth annual Shrine Game between Shannon and Lindale as "a Phil Baker-to-Lynn Hunnicutt pass and a driving power-sweep by Tommy Nasworthy produced the game's only touchdowns Saturday night in a 7–7 standoff before 7,000 fans at Barron." The stats reflected the score as PHS netted 192 total yards against 190 for Model; halfback Gary Wingo was lost to an injury before intermission, which certainly affected game strategy. The consolation prize was the pass-catching end (Hunnicutt) and hard runner (Nasworthy) winning the Lineman and Back of the Week. The following Saturday night, it was same song, different verse when Coosa and Lindale tied 3–3 in Barron Stadium; field goals from Dragon Larry Tate and Eagle Bubba Keith before halftime ended all scoring. On three occasions, fumbles stopped Pepperell drives.

Gala homecoming events were planned for September 30 when Gilmer County came to Lindale. A parade with floats, band, cheerleaders, majorettes, and color guard moved down Park Street at 4:00 p.m. A postgame alumni dance for couples only at Pepperell Elementary cafeteria, and music to be provided by Jaywalker and the Pedestrians. Boys should wear coats and ties while ladies were to be in "dressy attire." In pregame notes, both squads were undefeated but twice tied; Lindale had not scored a touchdown since Gary Wingo went down against Model with cartilage damage. Converted center to running back Jimmie Dudley ran 26 yards in the first stanza for a 6–0 lead; Larry Tate kicked a 24-yard field goal, and Kent Millican, who had 11 tackles on the night, bumped it to 11–0 with a safety. However after intermission, the Bobcats scored on a 3-yard plunge and a 70-yard punt return to go ahead 14–11 with just minutes left. That's when freshman phenom QB Phil Baker, who completed 14 of 18 throws, went to work and earned the headlines: "Baker Passes Dragons by Gilmer, 17–14." With the overflow crowd on their feet, he maneuvered his team downfield, finally hitting likewise phenom Lynn Hunnicutt with a 6-yard winning touchdown. The lanky end caught 6 throws for 127 yards, which netted him a second Lineman-of-the-week award; in his first attempt at halfback, Jimmie Dudley gained 75 yards on the ground and snagged 6 catches for 61 yards to go with 7 individual tackles at linebacker.

Pepperell visited and beat a good Cartersville squad 13–0 on the first Friday of October; Phil Baker had a hand/toe in all points as the freshman threw 1 touchdown, kicked 2 field goals, and a PAT. Our "rock ribbed" defense kept the Bartow boys bottled up all night. With his team leading by a single third-quarter field goal, junior DB Allen Baldwin's interception led to a short TD pass Baker to Dudley for some fourth-period insurance at 10–0. Minutes later, Baker hit a

20-yard kick to make it 13–0. To win against East Rome is good—to beat them 31–9 is better. More than 5,500 fans watched in Barron Stadium on October 14 as Jimmie Dudley scored 1 running and 2 receiving TDs. QB Phil Baker kicked a 17-yard field goal and threw a third scoring pass to Lynn Hunnicutt. In doing so, he merited successive area Back-of-the-Week accolades. Sports editor Don Biggers noted on October 18 that former center Jimmie Dudley was a "sure-bet" for all-star honors before he was moved to running back. He added, "He's probably done more to provide leadership than any other player." Our underrated defense limited the Gladiators to 133 total yards; this fine performance moved PHS into a number nine ranking in Class A schools just behind Westminster. Good news on Thursday before a road trip to Jasper was Gary Wingo returning to the lineup; bad news was fullback Kent Millican underwent knee surgery on Monday. Senior end Joel Howell was hurt, and a sprained ankle had safetyman Ray Hines hobbling. He was being replaced by Charlie Gilbreath. However, we persevered, beating Pickens County 34–14 with Dudley, Wingo, and Kiser receiving kudos for their play. Jimmie Dudley ran for 106 yards and was our most consistent performer. Wingo and Johnny Kiser both scored TDs. Phil Baker threw an easy 7 completions in 15 tries for 119 yards and a score. Charles Gilbreath relieved and completed 3 tosses for 57 yards. Pepperell was so dominant that the Green Dragons had only 18 running and 18 passing plays that yielded a meager 98 yards. In 16 years of playing, PHS had never experienced an undefeated season; observers thought this might be the year (we were 6–0–2 at the time) if host Rockmart could be dealt with on Friday night, October 27. The quarterback battle between freshman Baker and senior Williams was as close as the final score; Andy Williams's Jackets won the game 16–12 with 3 completions, rushing for 43 yards, kicking a 21-yard field goal, and intercepting 2 passes, 1 of which he ran back 33 yards while the other stopped a Dragon's last-minute drive. On the other sideline, Phil Baker completed 11 of 23 passes for 154 yards including a 10-yard last-quarter TD strike to Lynn Hunnicutt; the young field general also caught a 17-yarder from HB Gary Wingo prior to his scoring on a 4-yard sweep just before the intermission. Pepperell's 248 total yardage slightly favored them as did first downs; the home team was not penalized.

On November 18, a "smooth-running, well-oiled" Carrollton football team came to Barron Stadium to face PHS for the Region 3-A crown. After twice turning them back at our goal line, the Trojans put seven on the board before intermission and then added seventeen more in the last two quarters to win handily 24–0. Our offense was hampered all evening by poor field position, for we never started outside our own twenty-five-yard line. Coach Charlie Grisham's squad had now won nine straight (they would extend the streak to ten in 1968) Region 3-A championships. However, there were rewards for our fine season. Otis Gilbreath was named Rome Area Coach of the Year. Lynn Hunnicutt and Roger Weaver were unanimous cocaptains of the All-Star eleven. Gayland Green was honored at tackle along with guard Jimmie Dudley and Gary Wingo at safety. The latter was also picked for the 1967 Class A All-State football team. On Sunday, December 17, the *News-Tribune* announced, "Wingo Signs Pact with Georgia Tech." The all-purpose athlete was a star, rushing, catching, tackling, and defending passes. To close out the year, GHSA reclassification moved Pepperell and Cartersville into Region 6-AA along with East and West Rome.

1968 Season

On Sunday, March 10, 1968, Coach Gilbreath explained to the local newspaper that he and staff "have a major rebuilding job on our hands." He welcomed 64 boys to spring training, many up from ninth grade in hopes of finding replacements for twenty graduating seniors. The interior line of scrimmage had no lettermen except center Spence Millican; however, last year's Lineman of the Year Lynn Hunnicutt returned and would pair up with big Raymond Smith at end position. Quarterback would not be a concern as rising sophomore Phil Baker was entrenched there after a sensational freshman year. Donald Stamey and Randy Lloyd had some experience at offensive backs, but much was expected from 210-pound senior Donald Bragg; on the other side of the ball, Billy Woodruff, Allen Baldwin, and Ray Hines were excellent D backs. Because of increased enrollment, Pepperell High School would compete in Class 7-AA this year which meant subregion foes would be East Rome, West Rome, Cartersville, Cedartown, and Cassville.

The GHSA mandated Monday, August 19, as first day of fall practice and forbade any regular season play until the first week of September. On Thursday, September 5, area play began when Cartersville came to Barron Stadium versus Pepperell. The squad from Bartow County was expected to be mostly a running offense while PHS should depend on an aerial game, which was precisely how the contest played out. CHS ground out 239 yards, and QB Baker threw for 206 yards mostly to Hunnicutt who caught 15 throws for 176 yards. However, as fans filed out onto Second Avenue, the dual scoreboards at Barron still glowed 21–6 in favor of Cartersville. The following week, Chattooga with QB Lee Lenderman leading was a 20-point favorite over the Gold and White; they won 13–7 but did not cover the spread. Phil Baker scorched their secondary for 149 yards passing, which upped his area lead to an amazing 355 yards in 2 games; Hunnicutt caught most of his throws. When 2 teams with 0–2 records lined up and one of them had scored only 13 points on the season, not much of a crowd was expected. However, Barron Stadium was mostly filled on Saturday night, September 21, when Pepperell and Rome's largest Black school, Main High, played for the first time. PHS logged almost 500 yards of offense in winning 46–12. *Rome News-Tribune* opined on page 1C that "Little Billy Woodruff raced up and down the field for his finest performance to date for Lindale." Dragon QB Phil Baker was not far behind with 15 completed passes. Main Panthers were not without accomplishments collecting 276 total yards; senior HB Edward Cole ran for 1 TD while Stanley Bailey hit a wide-open Jarvis Daniel for a 52-yard TD pass. When we faced Coosa the following week, they had won 2 games by a total of 10 points and lost 1 by 3. The pundits picked CHS by 4 in a close battle. Instead, Coach Bragg's crew scored 5 TDs in a 31–13 victory. Still it was not decided until late after they converted an interception and fumble recovery into touchdowns that added 14 points to a 17–13 lead. An overflow crowd of 7,000 was expected for the twenty-first annual Shrine Game at Barron. Both teams had diversified their attack somewhat with Model halfback Tommie Nasworthy playing some at quarterback and Pepperell's Billy Woodruff running and catching well. Pepperell led 7–0 most of the game thanks to a Billy Woodruff (he totaled 107 yards on the night) 3-yard run with 5:57 left before band performance. However, midway of the final quarter, Shannon recovered a Lindale fumble at the latter's 10-yard line. Three running plays later, it was fourth and goal at the 4. After a time-out, Nasworthy found Haggard all alone in the middle of the end zone. James Barrett went off tackle for point after and ultimate 7–7 tie. Next we went to Cass on October 11; each squad had two wins between them, indicating a toss-up. Senior flanker Raymond Smith could not have picked a better time to become more than the "other end" on his team. The *News-Tribune* wrote, "Smith weaved in and out of the Cass secondary, hauling down passes from Baker." At the end of 4 quarters, he was credited with 10 receptions for 201 yards and a touchdown, turning an even chance game into a 44–6 rout.

Heading into seventh week of fall, we had managed a 2–3–1 record while Saturday night's October 19 opponent was 3–3; however, East Rome was ranked first and undefeated in the Class 7-AA Subregion (for almost 30 years this region was feared across Georgia). Local football gurus predicted a battle between QBs Phil Baker and Jerry Purcell was imminent; the former led the area with 1,076 through the air, and the latter was a distant number two with just over 500. Also in Pepperell's favor, as published in the *RNT*, was leading scorer Billy Woodruff with 48 total points; added to that was top flanker Lynn Hunnicutt with 614 yards. Nevertheless, Powder Blue and Gold dealt us a 28–0 loss. Actually the contest turned on 1 play in the third stanza with ER leading 7–0 but Pepperell 5 yards away from tying. Our backfield fumble was scooped up by 126-pound Joe Fowler who never looked back on his 95-yard run to the opposite end zone.

With our season slowly slipping away, heavily favored Rockmart came visiting Barron on October 26 with the best defense around. With Joe Fowler's game-changing play last week still in our memory bank, PHS converted a critical fourth and fourteen situation into a 7–6 upset victory. With 3:37 remaining, Phil Baker hit Billy Woodruff near the right sideline, and he dashed eighteen yards to paydirt; Phil kicked a decisive point after. Woodruff was honored as player of the week; the "lightweight, slithery-hipped" halfback added to Rockmart's demise by rushing twenty-two times for eighty-three yards and snagging three passes for thirty-seven. His closest BOTW competition was teammate Phil Baker who hurled a game-tying touchdown and then kicked decisive point after. Were West Rome and Pepperell on divergent paths?

Local sportswriters were asking this question prior to November 2 in Barron. Two weeks ago, WR was breezing along at 6–0 while Lindale had lost mightily to East Rome; then Marietta and Cartersville upset Green while Coach Gilbreath's boys knocked off mighty Rockmart 7–6. Illness and injuries had forced Nick Hyder to realign his backfield; Roger Weaver had been moved to fullback while replacement QB Jimmy Edwards was a drop-back instead of sprint-out type.

However, there was nothing ailing David Watkins who had 31 tackles last week. The Gold and White had their problems also, for Lynn Hunnicutt was out with mononucleosis; fortunately, Raymond Smith had moved up to second receiver in 3-AA South area. "Pepperell Stuns Chiefs, 26–14 on Baker's Razor-Sharp Passes." After this headline, the *News-Tribune* wrote, "If Phil Baker had used a scalpel instead of a football he would have qualified as a surgeon Saturday night." Five thousand fans watched him rally Pepperell from a 14–6 halftime deficit to win by 12; if not for junior defensive end Randy Lloyd's spectacular deflection and interception at the Chiefs' 12-yard line, the intermission score could have been worse. But Lloyd's work led to a 4-yard TD catch by junior Danny Wilson, which changed the game momentum. Following intermission, WR punted right away, and PHS came out in a shotgun attack, leaving no doubt as to what they intended to do. Baker would hit on 9 of 15 passes for 216 yards. He proceeded to hit Billy

Woodruff with passes of 39, 31, and 15 which carried deep into enemy territory. This combination clicked again on a nine-yard TD to cut it down to 14–13. After our defense held them, the offense marched 58 yards mostly on a 43-yard aerial Baker to Woodruff and Baldwin's short line buck to go up 20–14.

However, we were not through when young Donald Studdard snared an errant Chieftain throw at the twenty-nine-yard line as time expired in third period. Five plays later, POTW Baker found Woodruff alone and uncovered for an eighteen-yard touchdown.

Our victory gave 4–1 East Rome the Region 7-AA South championship. After a particularly bad week of prognosticating last week, local Sports Editor Don Biggers decided to let his wife choose winners and losers for upcoming games; she picked Pepperell to win over Cedartown because "they throw the ball so pretty." But her husband wrote pre-kickoff, "Cedartown is not to be taken lightly." They came into Barron on Saturday night, November 9, with veteran QB Wendell Rhodes and two strong receivers, which they did not need because of daylong torrential rains. On a miserable Barron Stadium cold night, five hundred fans watched Black and Red kick a twenty-yard field goal with 5:07 left before halftime, which was actually all they needed in the 17–0 win. Our downfall was a quagmire field, wet footballs, two blocked punts, a pair of fumbles in addition to an opponent that came to play and allowed us to cross midfield only once. In the postseason, Phil Baker, Lynn Hunnicutt, and Billy Woodruff were named to the Area All-Stars squad sponsored by *RNT* and Rome Kiwanis Club.

1969 Season

The National Alliance Football committee voted to approve 2-point conversion options for the 1969 season. An experiment to place posts on the goal line was abandoned, for it made little difference. All local coaches agreed the new points-after-touchdown system would drastically reduce tie games. One local mentor said, "I had rather lose than tie," while another thought the rule would just give armchair quarterbacks "more ammunition." Coosa's Branch Bragg indicated he would do what "the situation calls for." East Rome's David Patterson planned to "go for two every chance we get." Before football season began, successful coaches Jack Shamblin, Larry Muschamp, Bill Keller, and Paul Kennedy tendered their resignation; most sought better-paying jobs. Into his second week of March spring training, Coach Gilbreath was missing 20 former players. He was concerned about a lightweight backfield and only 1 top-notch receiver returning, Lanny Ely; however, B team players were encouraging. Bright spots on the line were tackles Randy Johnson and Steve Murdock, guards John Kendrick and Danny Hutchins. Ray Davis was moved from tackle to halfback, helping out Randy Holland and Donald Blankenship as well as fullbacks Ray Hines and Randy Holland. Of course, Phil Baker returned for the junior year sporting 2,500 career passing yards. At defensive tackle, Johnson played both ways while Don Studdard suited up as linebacker again. Kicking and snapping left was senior Spence Millican; even so, the Coach was "real satisfied with spring drills" including sophomore flanker Donald Jackson who caught a winning touchdown in spring scrimmage.

We opened the season in Cartersville, September 6, with a 14–3 victory; they returned nineteen lettermen and were picks in subregion. A large home crowd watched in disbelief as

Pepperell's Dragons took the game to their heavily favored hosts. After the Gold and White defense controlled play early on, we gained possession at our own thirty-two-yard line. A line buck was first, and then Baker dropped straight back and threw a strike to end Donald Jackson in stride; the Purple DBs hauled him down at the two. Phil scored on the next snap and kicked point after for a 7–0 advantage. Bartow stormed back almost to goal before we stopped them, forcing a short placement kick and a 7–3 score. But we were not through, for Ray Hines returned the ensuing kickoff to almost midfield where a pass interference penalty and two short throws moved us to the CHS thirty-three-yard line. With just seconds left before halftime, Baker went to the shotgun and lofted a spiral toward Jackson at the seven; he literally snatched the ball away from two DBs and ran in untouched. Baker's point after made it 14–3. Following intermission, our defense stopped them on fourth and goal at the six-inch line, preserving an eleven-point victory. On September 13 versus visiting Chattooga County, our high-stepping majorettes were prepped and ready; these young ladies included Susan Head, Donna McDonald, Carla Lumpkin, Kathy Hatch (head majorette), Pam Rush, and Kathy Eden. Don Biggers set the spread at four points, and he was right on, for Joe Kines's Indians led by "one of the best tailbacks [Jimmy Linderman] in Georgia" downed us 24–20. However, it was our inability to score inside red zone that spelled defeat. To wit, Lenderman intercepted at the sixteen-yard line, and a five-yard field goal sailed off the mark; a first down inside the twelve was thwarted by a fumble. Finally, a fake field goal pass was batted away in the end zone. But we did have some success; just before half, passes to Ely and Jackson took us down close where Baker ran it into a halftime tie 7–7. After intermission, Lenderman ran four yards for a 14–7 lead, but we made par by marching seventy-three yards to tie 14–14 when Baker hit Jackson on a four-yard TD toss. Lenderman came right back with a six-yard scoring dash to make it 21–14; minutes later, a twenty-five-yard field goal pushed it to 24–14. Pepperell stormed back with Baker hitting Jackson for a seventeen-yard TD to cut it to 24–20. On one last gasp, a pass to Alonzo Chubbs could have won it but didn't. After an open date, we faced always tough Coosa High at Barron on September 27; they spotted us a 3–0 lead and then marched to a convincing 31–17 win. With 31–3 glowing on the scoreboards, the Dragons woke up and drove seventy-seven yards to score; passes to Jackson and Holland pushed the ball in the red zone where Ray Davis burst up the middle for an eighteen-yard TD. On a dwindling clock, Baker once again hit Jackson and Holland before once more lofting a strike to junior Randy Holland for our fifteenth point; a two-point conversion ended it at 31–17. Before meeting Shannon on October 4, Lindale sported leaders in passing and receiving with Baker and Jackson; we were not ranked in rushing or defense. Statistics in *Rome News-Tribune* show our eleven gave up about as many points as they scored. The twenty-second annual Rome Shrine Game was themed "Strong legs run so that weak legs may walk." Quarterback play on both sides was good, but Pepperell won 21–14. Coach Ralph Tuggle's crew tallied early when Richard Haggard threw four yards to Tony Studdard; a two-point conversion made it 8–0. In second frame, Phil Baker marched his team seventy-four yards using a variety of passes down to the one where he sneaked over; a short toss to Jackson tied it at 8–8. A Model interception and run back to our seven preceded Haggard's short run for a 14–8 edge. Following intermission, we used sixteen plays to tie with Lanny Ely's seven-yard touchdown catch, tying it 14–14. In the game's waning minutes, John Kendrick intercepted a Haggard pass at midfield; Baker went to work throwing twenty-five and twenty yards to Donald Jackson and Chubbs. Donald then ran it close in where Phil sneaked a touchdown; a kicked point after made it 21–14 Dragons. We were still undefeated in the Subregion 7-AA on Saturday, October 11, prior to hosting Cassville. Although the Dragons were favored by fourteen, Cass moved to 4–2 record with a 14–8 victory that was at least exciting. The Colonels mixed running and passing to march seventy-four yards to goal with 3:19 showing before half. Leading 6–0 after intermission, they drove eighty-four yards and scored with 00:17 remaining in third when Lamar Ray bulled over from a yard out; the two-point conversion was good for a 14–0 advantage. We used a long fourth period scoring drive sustained mainly with Baker-to-Jackson passes to narrow it 14–8. But a last-ditch effort to win was thwarted by an end zone interception.

Gold and White were 7-point underdogs to 5–1 East Rome on Friday night, October 17; some 4,000 Barron Stadium fans watched our homecoming battle which featured the area's top passing team versus one that had held four foes scoreless. On Sunday, the *News-Tribune* posted that "East Rome's Passes Beats the Dragons at Own Game, 23–6." It's true QB Bill Shiflett completed 2 TD throws, but their quick trap run game kept us off-balance; our only score was Baker to Jackson for a 15-yarder late in the contest. PHS led in total offense 198 to 107 yards; penalties were practically even, but our 3 turnovers made a big difference.

Yellow Jacket head coach Ed Pharo had this to say about his squad facing Pepperell's quarterback Phil Baker, "He's Archie Manning of the area football who does everything well... sometimes under adverse conditions." South Floyd visited Polk County on October 24 with heavily favored Rockmart winning 14–7. Pharo's game plan was to stop our passing game, but Coach Otis surprised them with a pounding ground attack that included Alonzo Chubbs's 59-yard touchdown run. A high punt snap in addition to an interception run back accounted for the Jackets' points. We dominated all statistics with 282 total yards to 126, first downs 11 to 5; penalties were even. End David Williams harassed our offense all night.

Next up, West Rome defeated Pepperell 21–13 in a game not as close as the score. An eighty-three-yard touchdown pass, a ten-yard run off the left side, and, of all things, a fourteen-yard quarterback sneak netted the Chieftains three six-pointers. Injuries to Nick Hyder's squad forced wholesale changes in the lineup, prompting him to say, "We're starting our second season tonight." He would get no sympathy from Otis who finished the contest with three major players in the first aid room including Lanny Ely, Donald Jackson, and QB Phil Baker.

Rome News-Tribune highlighted one of the finest catches of the year or any year when Baker sent halfback Randy Holland on a sideline wheel route and launched a high spiral in his direction. "Holland stretched out to the maximum to catch it on the tip of his fingers kept his footing long enough to dive into the end zone for the score." His reception tied the score 7–7 at intermission. We again won the statistics margin with 315 total yards to 305; first downs were 15 to 8. On Friday night, November 7, Lindale visited Gray Field in Cedartown where the Bulldogs' record was not exemplary at 0–8. We put up 20 points before halftime on TD throws Baker to Lanny Ely and Randy Holland. Game yardsticks slanted heavily toward PHS; first downs were 14 to 7; rush yardage 149 to 129; pass completions netted 150 yards to minus 24. Polk County did not cross goal until the second half.

The 1969 season ended with Region 5B Armuchee versus Pepperell on Friday night, November 14, at a freezing Barron Stadium. Only 500 fans were strong enough to brave a north wind and sub-20-degree conditions. The *News-Tribune* wrote that the secret to survival was to keep moving, and both squads adhered to that advice, putting up 70 points and over 700 yards of offense in a 42–28 Dragon victory. Both squads played better than their record with the victors racking up 31 first downs, 450 rush yards, 312 passing, and hardly any penalty yards. Pepperell's Phil Baker easily claimed his third consecutive quarterback crown with 3 14-yard TD throws to end Lanny Ely, the area's third leading receiver at 28 catches. He also threw a pair of scoring strikes to HB Randy Holland who occupied the number two position with 29 receptions. Although teammate Donald Jackson did not tally any points in the cold, he comfortably clinched the area total catches title with 38 for 630 yards. Baker's ending stats meant he entered the senior season 1970 with 3,935 career passing yards or 2.24 miles. However, at season's end, the number one story was Coosa High's Class A state championship run culminating with a 28–8 victory over Fitzgerald; the Eagles previously won the 1961 Class C title over Lincolnton 21–0. Ranking just below that news was the *News-Tribune* staff choosing Phil Baker as Athlete of the Year; the writers noted he won the award "hands down." Other accolades went to All-Star tackle John Kendrick and end Donald Jackson.

For reader information, an interesting article appeared on page 21 of the *Rome News-Tribune* Thursday, November 6, 1969, edition. It is paraphrased here:

> The P. E. Class 408 Test and Measurements at Berry College revealed that a total of 354 players make up rosters of nine area football teams; their average weight is 160 lbs.; only 22 of 354 boys weighed over 200 pounds; 18 scaled-in at less than 130 lbs. Surprisingly Cedartown has the smallest team at 152.15 pounds; Coosa at 165.30 has the largest. Most youngsters fall between 135 and 169 pounds. Only four teams averaged better than 150 lbs. per player; they are Coosa, Pepperell, Rockmart and West Rome in that order.

1970 Season

In the spring of 1970, several schools in middle and South Georgia had not completed their fall schedule because of probable consolidations as a result of integration mandates. *Rome News-Tribune* sports editor Don Biggers believed local schools would not be affected. One for-sure change was that Darlington would become a full-fledged member of the GHSA; consequently, the Tigers would be entitled to compete in state tournament structures. Region 7-AA expanded with the addition of Darlington, Paulding County, and Rossville to the ranks while Cartersville moved down one class. Biggers noted on August 16 that the emphasis on oblong ball reflects its ability to fund secondary sports, which traditionally breaks even or loses money. In July, many local head coaches were searching for assistants; however, Otis welcomed back Bill Boling and son Billy to Lindale. Also in August, rumors persisted that Pepperell's Phil Baker, who lacked only 65 passing yards to reach career 4,000, would be moved around to take advantage of his athleticism. Phil was one of the "most outstanding athletes to don a Pepperell uniform...he is considered a coach on the field." Premier tackle Randy Johnson would probably take his speed and quickness to fullback. A potential backfield of Baker, Johnson, halfbacks Randy Holland and Dana Burkhalter should give Pepperell a very balanced attack. Up front John Kendrick, John McGowan, Steve Carver, John Knowles, and Steve Murdock would provide blocking; junior Jim Morris would handle snapping. At ends, veteran Lanny Ely was top-notch while junior Steve Edge had speed to go with good hands. Gary Burkhalter might be undersized, but Otis believed his speed "will register plenty of playing time." An outstanding group of defenders were led by ends Jimmy Fitzpatrick and Wayne Robinson; depth chart were Russell Rogers, Dale Childs, Randy Cox, Harlan Smith, David Bruce, and Roy Gilreath; linebacking was led by Kendrick with good athletes Ronnie Newberry, Mitchell Crabbe, Don Jacobs, and Jim Strickland adding excellent depth. On Sunday, August 30, *RNT* predicted 30,000 to 35,000 fans would attend games this weekend.

Kickoffs began on Thursday night, September 3, with 4,000 watching Adairsville versus Pepperell in Barron Stadium; we pounded them 42–0 while accumulating 16 first downs, 180 yards rushing, 183 yards passing, and 87 yards in penalty mark-offs. Kendrick, Johnson, Carver, Robinson, and company limited the Bengals to 3 first downs, minus 10 yards rushing, and zero passing. The contest was a bit ragged and took a record 2 hours and 20 minutes to play partially because of 29 penalties. Before Phil Baker turned it over to back up Jimmy Farrer, he became the first area QB to surpass 4,000 pass yards at 4,082 with 5,000 in his sights. Eight nights later in Armuchee, the senior "took on a new role" by rushing for 126 yards and 3 scores; to top that, he opened the second half scoring gates with a 91-yard kickoff return; then in a span of 9 minutes, Pepperell added 3 more touchdowns to win easily 35–0. A week later, we were favored by 15 over Darlington in Barron. Coach Joe Campbell believed his squad could win a passing duel with Lindale's unbeaten team, but 2 days prior to kickoff, Otis was quoted as saying, "Other teams may think they throw the ball, we know we throw it." In a 54–0 runaway, we netted 341 yards of offense, including 3 rushing TDs by Randy Holland who "doesn't mind running in the thick of things" and 1 by Johnson; Baker hit on 10 of 19 passes with 2 scoring throws to Ely as well as receiving a HB-to-QB toss back for another. Gary Burkhalter helped out with a 40-yard interception return to goal; our Defenders allowed only 102 yards of offense. Playing in Coosa's Eagle Stadium is never easy; being behind 21–0 with 12 minutes to play is worse. This was what the undefeated Dragons faced on September 25, 1970. In a game that is still talked about in Lindale, we scored on 4 straight possessions in the last quarter to win 26–21. It happened when senior quarterback Phillip Marion Baker shifted to the shotgun offense and riddled Coach Bragg's defense with these statistics: "He ran the ball 18 times for 73 yards and a TD. He also hit on 16/27 passes for 162 yards and two more touchdowns. Furthermore, he punted three times for an even 38-yard average and contributed a pair of game-saving tackles from his safety position. His passes set up the final running six-pointer from two yards out." The local paper summed it up on September 29, noting, "At Least Coosa Won't Have to Face Baker Again." Needless to say, he was named area Player of the Week. The always exciting and colorful Shrine Game is traditionally the biggest football game of the regular season in Rome/Floyd County. Coach Ralph Tuggle's Model crew was 3–1 behind a big veteran line of scrimmage; halfback Bobby Ray had tallied 22 points on 89 carries totaling 412 yards. Shannon was healthy for this twenty-third annual charity classic while Pepperell was expecting the return of 5 players who were out against Coosa. Both squads had battled on close terms over the years; a huge crowd was expected on East Third. And true to form, more than 7,000 watched as the Dragons doubled up on Model 28–13. We "piled up" a large lead at halftime and "toyed around with Model" thereafter with both squads using reserves. Big fullback Randy Johnson "smashed" into the end zone for our first points; then 2 fumbles by the Blue Devils resulted in recoveries by Randy Cox and Wayne Robinson. Both miscues led directly to first half rushing touchdowns by Randy Holland and sophomore Mike Cabe. With 41 seconds left before intermission, QB Phil Baker hit 4 straight passes, the last to Lanny Ely for a 9-yard score and a 28–6 advantage. PHS celebrated homecoming at Barron Stadium on Friday, October 9; we were heavily favored against Cassville High as the Colonels had struggled to score; they had since gone to a passing attack as a remedy. A large crowd watched as Ms. Pamela Danette Rush was named 1970 Homecoming Queen, and a "converted" tackle led the Dragons to a 6–0 record. The Sunday paper featured the headline, "JOHNSON RUNS WILD AS PEPPERELL RACKS UP COLONELS, 23–8." The aforementioned Randy Johnson rambled for 109 yards on 25 carries, caught 6 passes and tallied 2 touchdowns against a tougher-than-expected Cass club. Three consecutive fumbles had Lindaleans nervous late, leading only 14–8; however, Phil Baker hit a 26-yard field goal. John Kendrick intercepted QB McPherson's toss, which led to Johnson's 9-yard TD reception from Baker. This throw pushed Phil to 1,071 total yards in offense for the year. Pepperell played a home contest at Barron Stadium against East Rome on Saturday night; there were no other weekend games in the area. Although PHS was favored by 12 points, we eked out a 21–14 win. Sunday's *News-Tribune* write-up featured top Northwest Georgia's running back Mike Hogan on a sweep right for an 80-yard TD; later the 181-pounder ran a punt back 75 yards. Our first score happened after 4 Baker completions to Holland, Johnson, and finally twice to Lanny Ely. A second 6-pointer occurred after Steve Murdock claimed an ER fumble at their 21; Baker's nifty QB keeper converted the miscue into a score. However, the biggest play of the game was defensively when Wayne Robinson returned a fumble for a touchdown. As it happened, QB Ches Chaffin attempted a toss sweep to Hogan, which was mishandled; junior linebacker Robinson, who had scraped inside the right-side blockers, scooped the pigskin and outran everybody for an 80-yard return and a 21–14 victory. On paper, Pepperell at Paulding County on Friday, October 23, looked like a cakewalk for the former. If there was any overconfidence, it did not show, for the Dragons won 41–14. Our first game outside Floyd County this season was described by *News-Tribune* as "two if by land, four if by air." Unbelievably Paulding County and Pepperell completed 38 passes for 571 yards. (Editor's note: This was 50 years before the spread offensives of the new millennium). QB Phil Baker enjoyed a career night connecting on 24 of 38 for 391 yards and 4 touchdowns; the senior whiz now had over 5,000 yards throwing since starting as a freshman. Randy Johnson, Randy Holland, and Ely all caught TD tosses, with the latter snagging 8 throws all told for 157 yards. He and Holland ranked one and two in area receptions. The ground game scored twice including when Ely pounced on our own fumble in the end zone. Defensively the visitors did not neglect their opponent's ground game, limiting them to 28 total yards. Honestly, the Patriots were not very good game in 1970 going 0–9–1. Hype for the most talked about gridiron contest of 1970 reached its peak two days before Pepperell visited West Rome on Friday, October 30. Don

Biggers tried to put himself inside the pregame staff meetings, thinking the Dragons would pass and the Chieftains would grind out a ball-control offense featuring RBs Sapp and Hatch. The visiting Dragons, who were ranked number nine in the state, had an explosive ball carrier also in 162-pound Randy Holland who also flared out for passes from Baker. The number-two-ranked Green-clads countered with a much improved QB David Love. On the morning before the game, the local paper posted the probable starting lineup, a tradition that had faded in recent times. Tickets were available at schools as well as Owens Hardware, Candler, and Garden Lakes Pharmacies. Although both 11s were 8–0, ultimately defense wins championships, and Mr. Biggers leaned toward the Chieftains' front 4, making a difference in his prediction of 20–14. However, it was no contest as Nick Hyder's squad won handily 51–0. They did it before 7,000 in the stands and another 1,000 hanging on the restraining fences of venerable Barron Stadium. They did it by "returning punts, picking off passes, recovering fumbles, executing and playing defense the way it is taught." The rout began with Love's 39-yard TD throw to Stan Green late in the first and finished with his fourth-quarter toss to Hatch. The performance garnered him Back of the Week. Sunday morning's write-up said that after the initial touchdown, Lindale was "really out of it." The winner outrushed PHS 148 to 24, led passing 202 to 160; penalties while first downs and penalties were about even. The travesty for losers is one region loss probably eliminates state playoffs contention. One week later, we returned to Barron hosting Cedartown. The game plan was run, run, and run some more to the tune of 3 touchdowns on 219 rush yards. Early on, Johnson scored twice and Holland once. With that strategy working to perfection, QB Baker elected to stay on the ground as he did not attempt a pass in the first 19 minutes of play. After intermission when the Bulldogs started putting 8 in the box, the senior threw 16 times, including a 14-yard TD strike to Holland late that ended in the game at 29–12. Because of a poorly designed system, 9–1 Pepperell did not qualify for region/state playoffs.

On page 2C in the December 20 issue of the local gazette, Don Biggers noted that Phil Baker "is the only player around that has lettered in *football, basketball* and *baseball* for four straight years." Although the Pepperell QB passed for over five thousand yards and fifty TDs, the right-hand column of said newspaper article announced, "Baker Decides on Baseball Grant." In eliminating a future in football, he did not reveal the college of choice. Senior linebacker John Kendrick inked a scholarship with East Tennessee State as did a pair of Rockmart tackles Randy Stone and Eugene Sigers.

On December 13, 1970, a large picture on page 1C showed Randy Johnson signing a football scholarship as his Grandparents and Mother looked on. An underneath caption reads, "Pepperell's Randy Johnson Joins the Bulldogs (Georgia)." *Rome News-Tribune* noted that "Johnson was a two-way performer at Pepperell. He worked as a fullback on offense and was a devastating blocker; when opponent possessed the ball, he moved in at middle guard and was just as effective." Robert Randall Johnson was born January 2, 1953, to Melvin Alphonso Jr. and Robbie Lou Redden Johnson. They had first met at Rome High prewar prior to Melvin joining the Army; while on an early leave, he and Robbie married. Postwar the veteran worked as a painter with father-in-law, Mr. Robert Redden; when Randy was eight years old, his father passed away from a heart condition. The youngster spent all of his early years in school at Fourth Ward Elementary in Rome followed by a transfer to West Rome Middle. Mom had remarried by this time, prompting the fourteen-year-old to move in with his grandparents Robert and Daisy Redden. The couple owned a large farm with wooded acreage on Lumpkin Road in Booger Hollow, which was located in Pepperell School District. Junior Lynn Hunnicutt recalled Randy first as a just-graduated middle schooler being around summer workouts with the varsity. Before coach-supervised training started, several squad members would choose to play kickback, which was a punt/placekick game between two groups. The not-yet ninth grader could actually drop-kick the pigskin farther than older boys could punt; off a tee, as a straight-on placekicker, he could boom the oval into the back of the end zone with ease. The following year, Johnson's natural strength and ability was showcased during a summer weight lifting session. Randy did not show up very often, bringing Coach Otis Gilbreath to ask one day if he was strong enough or should he come to more workouts. The youngster walked over to the tubular Universal Machine and squat-lifted it along with all the weights on board. A stunned Otis said, "Randy, we will see you when the season begins."

In his high school career, the young man participated in five sports, i.e., football, wrestling, basketball, baseball, and track; he was an All-Area fullback, won unlimited weight division wrestling crowns, and competed in State Track and Field discus and shot; he also lettered at PHS in basketball and baseball. Robert Randall's superlatives in Athens were mind-boggling. He started and lettered three years (1973–'75) earning All-SEC honors and garnering consensus All-American recognition senior season of 1975; he was named Offensive Lineman of the Year by Atlanta Touchdown Club and was awarded the prestigious Jacobs Blocking Trophy as the best blocker in the SEC. He was Bulldog offensive team captain in 1975. Johnson played in the Cotton Bowl, Hula Bowl, and the first Japan Bowl. Later, legendary Georgia Coach Vince Dooley had this to say about his former player, "Of all the players I've had the privilege of coaching, no one was more of a naturally-gifted blocker than Randy Johnson. He had all the basic fundamentals of an All-American." Master UGA recruiter Doc Ayers picked up on the sophomore's talents early and began making regular visits to the Lindale campus. Coach Gilbreath respected Doc, who was a former Cedartown coach, and the UGA program to the extent of discouraging other schools from looking at his prized lineman. Professionally Randy was drafted fourth round by the Seattle Seahawks, but later signed with the Tampa Bay Buccaneers and played in twenty-two games before a back injury sidelined him; afterward, he spent a month with the Edmonton Eskimos in 1980 before retiring from football. The thirty-one-year-old finished his education degree at UGA in 1984 and then served as assistant coach at Coosa, Pepperell, and Cartersville as well as head coach at Model. In 1977, the Pepperell star was inducted into the Rome/Floyd County Sports Hall of Fame. Four decades later, he became a member of UGA's Circle of Honor. The award is designed to pay tribute to extraordinary student athletes and coaches who by their performance and conduct have brought honor to the University and themselves, and who by their actions have contributed to the tradition of the Georgia Bulldogs. In 2016, Pepperell High School retired his jersey.

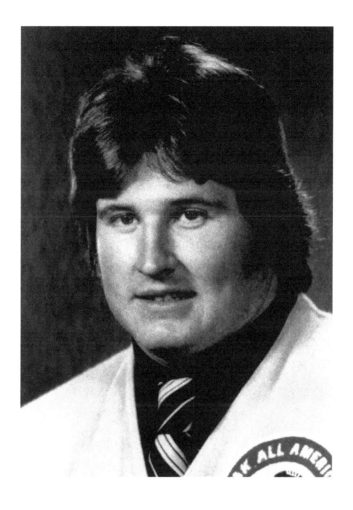

1971 Season

As baseball season wound down, two items of interest to local sports fans appeared in *Rome News-Tribune*. First, a new overtime system for football was being introduced, replacing the complex penetration rules which rewarded a victory to the wrong team in Pacelli versus Hogansville region championship game. This proposal featured red zone competition between squads with the scoreboard determining a winner. On Sunday, February 28, writer Don Biggers noted that Rome City Board of Education voted 3–2 to consolidate East and West into new buildings and campus. Thirteen years ago, there was opposition to this plan; doubtlessly, it would reoccur again. Biggers thought athletics should be better under one roof.

As the 20 days of spring practice began in early March, Coach Gilbreath and staff were attempting to establish a larger player rotation or 2-platoon system for the upcoming season; some 72 candidates including 18 lettermen could certainly fill the position ranks. For 2 seasons, rising senior Jimmy Farrer had been backup at quarterback for Phil Baker, and now he and Billy Boling manned that position. It would be a hard act to follow as the '70 Dragons were 9–1; a March 19 intersquad scrimmage should provide some answers. On August 22, Otis met with reporters to evaluate our region; reporters always appreciated his honesty and accuracy. The veteran thought West, East, Cedartown, and Pepperell would be the final four while some felt he was "throwing up a smoke screen." Plain and simple, the Dragon defense would match anyone's; nevertheless, offense was inexperienced at interior line with center Steve Barnes being a lone returning letterman. Nevertheless, a capable rotation would be Johnny Knowles, Drew Freeman, John McGowan, Ronnie Newberry, and Mitchell Crabbe. Hopefully QB Farrer should have a good complement of backs with Mike Cabe, Gary Burkhalter, Carlton Floyd, and Dale Childs; big David Bruce had trained all summer with UGA receiver Lynn Hunnicutt in hopes of having a great senior year. Wayne Robinson, who made plays on both sides last year, would again lead linebackers and ball catchers. On Saturday night, September 4, we met Adairsville in Barron; Pepperell manhandled them last year 42–0. To their credit, the Class C Tigers regrouped and finished second in the state; most of that team returned, and it showed when halfback Davis galloped 12 yards to goal with 6:10 left in the second quarter; he followed that with a surprise 30-yard jaunt off right tackle for a 13–0 lead at intermission. The Dragons made some adjustments and dominated thereafter; to wit, Jimmy Farrer executed a perfect bootleg down close to goal with 2:33 left in third; from there, Mike Cabe carried it over, but point after was no good. Trailing 13–6 under 2 minutes left in regulation, a short Tiger punt set us up 32 yards from tying or winning. From there, senior QB Farrer hit David Bruce for 22; 3 snaps later, the former sneaked over, leaving us down 12–13. Coach Otis and staff decided on a 2-point conversion. *Rome News-Tribune* reported on Sunday, "Farrer moved around end, was hit and fumbled into the end zone where PHS senior John Benton McGowan claimed the ball and victory 14–13." Our defenders held them to 86 total yards, yet Lindale was not much better with 97 gained. Seven days later versus visiting Class B Armuchee, we eked out another close win 13–7. In first period, Armuchee's Scott Holder blocked and recovered a Billy Ingle punt at the 16; Indian QB Danny Wiseman lofted a perfect TD pass to Larry Lumpkin for a 7–0 advantage. Early in second frame, LB Wayne Robinson reciprocated by stepping in front of a Holder throw and returning it to the visitor's 33; Mike Cabe tied the contest at 7–7 with several power sweeps, leaving 6:11 left before intermission. Pepperell regained possession deep in its own territory with less than 3 minutes to go. No one in the south stands was thinking another score; however, Cabe caught a 55-yard pass from Farrer and carried it to the 18 before being hauled down. At the next snap with 51 seconds showing, Farrer threw toward Billy Brown in the right corner of goal; the senior wrestled it away from a defender for a touchdown, giving us a final 13–7 lead. We pretty much dominated all statistics with 12 first downs to 6; rushing yards were 178 to 109, and passing 83 to 17. Lindale read on Sunday morning that Ronnie Newberry was "a thorn in the side" of Coach Namon Wiseman's offense.

In a rare Saturday afternoon game in Barron, we defeated Darlington with a hockey score 6–2. After a 0–0 tie at halftime, we drove 36 yards using 12 running plays, 3 of which were fourth and ones to score. Cabe ran for 3; Billy Fricks chalked up 4, and Cabe for 5 more on 2 line bucks; Fricks moved for 4; Cabe covered 7 on 3 more totes. Fricks picked up a first down with a 5-yarder; Cabe garnered 3, and Fricks 4 more before Cabe bulled over goal from the 4. All were power runs aimed at slant holes off tackle; point after was blocked, leaving Pepperell up 6–0. The Lakesiders threatened once as they marched to our 20 before senior DB Billy Brown outfought receivers at the 3 for a game-saving interception. With his feet on the goal line, Jimmy Farrer took the snap and maneuvered around in his end zone before going down as the horn sounded. Some 3,500 fans watched 1–2 Coosa win over unbeaten Pepperell 13–0 Saturday night, September 25, at Barron. When Lindale stopped his ground game, Eagle quarterback QB Randy Wilson went to the air (per *RNT*, Coach Bragg called most of the plays) for TDs in each half. First, he hit Jim Bragg for a 10-yarder and lastly Edmonds from the 4 to finish the scoring. Wayne Robinson gave us a chance to put fourth-quarter points when he blocked a Wyatt Nance punt and returned it himself to the 16; however, our offense advanced backward 5 yards. Model and Pepperell had opposite records, 1–3 and 3–1, when they met on Saturday, October 2, at Barron's Shrine Game. But Shannon messed things up for sportswriter and fan predictors with a well-deserved 14–0 upset victory; although QB Harold Crowder's clutch throwing and HB Billy Nasworthy's tough running/catching ruled the night, it was Donnie Bailey's second-quarter 68-yard punt return down the left sideline untouched that changed momentum and was enough points to win. Blue logged 11 more first and tens, plus 67 in rushing and 116 in pass yardage. With that said, Coach Ralph Tuggle refused to select a star performer, preferring to stress team instead. Reports from Athens and Atlanta were positive for Lindaleans Lynn Hunnicutt and Gary Wingo; the former was Georgia's top pass catcher with most of them in crucial situations while Wingo worked in Tech's defensive backfield.

At season's halfway mark, Coach Gilbreath's remarks in August rang true—the offense was rebuilding, but the defense could play with anyone. It was led by Ronnie Newberry, Steve Murdock, Don Jacobs, and Jimmy Fitzpatrick; to wit, we shut out Class AA Cassville 13–0 on Friday night, October 8, in Bartow County; Gold and White pounded out 174 yards, rushing with Mike Cabe claiming 140 of that on 28 carries. We added 89 yards passing to go with 11 first downs and no turnovers. Meanwhile, our defenders permitted their hosts only 42 yards of total offense and 3 first-and-tens. More than 4,000 fans packed Barron Stadium on Friday night, October 15, to watch Gladiator RB Mike Hogan carry 27 times for 152 yards and score 2 touchdowns; he was already approaching 1,200 yards for the season. Lindale was outmanned from the get-go as they managed only 58 ground yards to go with 87 aerial yards. East Rome was sitting at 7–0 while PHS slipped to 4–3. But we advanced to 5–3 on homecoming night, October 23, at Barron with a victory over Paulding County; we did it by racking up 323 yards of offense and taking advantage of 3 turnovers by Patriot players. In first drive, Farrer hit David Bruce twice for 56 combined yards; then Cabe rambled in from the 7 at the 5:58 mark. Paulding tied it 7–7 with less than 2 minutes before intermission; however, Jimmy Farrer countered with 2 straight throws to Cabe and 1 to Billy Brown before finally spiraling another toward Cabe for an 8-yard touchdown to give us a 13–7 advantage at the break. Pepperell received an early gift after intermission when Patriot HB Pugh coughed a fumble after a vicious tackle; Billy Brown scooped and galloped 43 yards for a 20–7 advantage. With a dwindling clock, Brown intercepted at midfield, and 13 plays later Carlton Floyd crossed goal from a yard out. Game stats showed Mike Cabe carried 23 times for 107 net yards, caught 3 passes for 52 yards, and scored 2 touchdowns. For his effort, the 161-pound junior, who just kept "plugging away," had been named Back of the Week in Rome area. The Lindale crowd gathered in Barron Stadium for a home game versus undefeated 7–0 West Rome on Saturday night, October 30; it was our eighth trip to East Third. Nick Hyder's Green Machine erupted for 23 points in second quarter and finished with a 36–0 win. Our only serious threat was an 82-yard punt return by Billy Brown; unfortunately, it was nullified by a clipping penalty. The statistics were askew toward the Chieftains who made 16 first and tens, rushed for 193 yards and threw for 159 aerial gains; they also played errorless ball. A 39–0 loss next week to the Polk County Bulldogs was explained by *Rome News-Tribune*, "The visitors seemingly could not do anything right." The Cedartown crew led 18–0 by halftime and added 21 more points afterward; both squads ended 1971 with 5–5 records. On page 1C on the December 12 Rome *News-Tribune*, it reported, with accompanying picture, that All-State tackle Steve Murdock signed a scholarship with UGA.

1972 Season

Football season started early in Rome when it was announced on February 13 that Jax State's Charlie Pell and staff would headline the fourteenth annual coaching clinic at West Rome High. Meanwhile, spring grid jamborees were set at twenty-four minutes' playing time with no more than half of that time against the same team. In the first week of March, Coach Otis Gilbreath welcomed seventy-six candidates to practice, with a vast majority being last year's B teamers. In order to build experience, Otis made the decision last year to let the boys play eight freshman contests in addition to seven B games rather than sit on the varsity bench. Returning starters from 1971 were scarce; backfield men Mike Cabe, Gary Burkhalter, lead reserves Billy Ingle, and Billy Fricks, they would team with LB/DE Mitchell Crabbe to form a small nucleus. The latter would also play offensive guard alongside senior Billy Trotter; however, "there is a big search for a quarterback." Last year, junior Mike McAteer and Todd Smith took snaps for the B team and freshmen, respectively; senior Fricks was working there also. Although interior linemen numbered twenty, the Coach said, "I just don't know right now." As practice reached third week, a senior, who had been around for a while, had shone in the backfield; Wayne Evans was now expected to contribute come fall. Freshman Gary Millican along with sophomores Bob Allen and Johnny Morris had upgraded the linebacker position; youngsters Greg Payne, Mike Ware, Tony Bradshaw, and Ronnie Sparks had added good competition to "grunt" (linemen) rotation. Defensive back Ricky Sitten was "a good player, a good athlete and will knock with anyone." He would team with Burkhalter, Darrell Wright, and Earl Spann on the defensive backside. On Friday night, March 17, we scrimmaged against 7-AA foe Coosa and lost 7–0, but with 3:38 left, Pepperell came quickly downfield with Mike McAteer's ten-yard toss to Evans followed by a twenty-four-yard completion to Fricks; with seconds left, at the five-yard line, McAteer's pass into the end zone "was knocked out of the hands of the receiver."

On a warm Saturday night, September 2, Adairsville came to Barron Stadium and defeated us 30–0. The story of the game was summed up in the *News-Tribune's* page 2C paragraph that began, "The Adairsville Tigers marched for a touchdown on their very first offensive series, then stopped Pepperell four times at the one-yard line." The Bengals, who led 22–0 at the intermission, rolled up 288 total yards while holding us to less than 100. Bright spots were D back senior Billy Trotter and running back Mike Cabe. We faced an "unknown foe" on Thursday night next when new head coach Buddy Windle brought Chattooga High to Barron; among his 35 players were 10 returning starters, rendering the Indians a 27-point favorite. Pepperell beat the betting line by 20 losing 7–0; at times, we appeared "businesslike" with Fricks and Cabe rushing for 138 yards combined. However, turnovers and penalties stopped us short of scoring. The only touchdown occurred on a 37-yard counter trap that completely fooled the home defense; we did manage to chase the runner down at the 2, but they scored next snap. On Saturday night, September 16, 2,500 Barron fans watched Darlington miraculously edge Pepperell 8–7 on the last play. Last year's final was 6–2 in favor of Lindale, and it appeared history was about to repeat with the Tigers in possession 42 yards away from paydirt; with one snap left and his team behind 7–2, quarterback Joe Holbrook faded back, sidestepped a defensive rush, and let fly toward end Tommy Nichols at the front edge of goal. He was not open, but "he went up and literally took the ball away from them." It was Holbrook's only completion of the night. Pandemonium ensued as winning Tiger fans swarmed Barron field. *RNT* wrote, "The celebration probably lasted well into the morning. It was that kind of game." In Barron Stadium again on September 23, we upset 20-point favorite Cedartown 7–6. The Dragons scored early with 4:54 left in opening frame when Mike Cabe bulled into the end zone from the one; Ingle kicked the point after which didn't seem that important at the time. Before the quarter ended, CHS reciprocated with a Michael Owens 1-yard burst past goal. Owens tried to run a conversion, but he was "nailed by Mitchell Crabbe," and this proved to be the difference as neither squad dented the goal again. It was a defensive struggle with the winners logging only 1 more yard—115 to 114—than the losers. The area's biggest game of the year was the annual Rome Shrine Club charity classic between Lindale and Shannon; this rivalry, which dates to 1920s textile mill baseball, surpassed East versus West for attendance and excitement. Although most pundits predicted Blue Devils by a touchdown, page 1C of *News-Tribune* reported on Sunday, October 1, "MODEL EXPLODES, COASTS PAST THE DRAGONS, 35–0." In a 3-column article with approximately 591 words, Blue Devil QB Harold Crowder's name was mentioned 12 separate times. Perhaps predictors should have heeded pregame reports from Coach Gilbreath who warned that "Crowder is an excellent player; he does about everything you could ask for...runs, throws and leads." The senior rushed and threw for 100 yards and led his team to a 15–0 advantage at intermission; our defense gave up 300 yards while the offense gained half as much due to 3 interceptions and 1 lost fumble. Next week with shades of the Darlington game lingering, Pepperell lost on a last-minute pass play versus Region 7-AA Cassville 18–13; a 10-yard completion turned into a 61-yard TD run on Saturday night, October 7, at Barron. Two plays prior, PHS had reclaimed the lead 13–12 and seemingly a victory for homecoming queen Ms. Angie Cox. Afterward, the yardstick confirmed the closeness of the score with each squad making 12 first downs; the Colonels led in total ground gained 253 to 221, but also in fumbles lost and penalties. Nevertheless, their record moved to 4–1 while we fell to 1–5. Unlucky Friday the thirteenth for Pepperell versus East Rome and it was. The local paper predicted a 21–0 victory for new coach Jerry Sharp's Glads; they bettered that by 30 points, winning 51–0 and improved to 5–1–1 (tied Calhoun 0–0) on the year. The best we could do was 64-yard rushing and 32 passing. The Dragons rebounded in Dallas on October 20 with a 14–6 win that was not as close as the score indicated. Mike Cabe returned to the lineup after several weeks of injury rehab and carried 12 times for 105 yards and a touchdown. Quarterback McAteer had a good night also with a 45-yard scamper for our first score. Our defense dominated in the first half by holding Paulding to minus 6 yards. Up next was West Rome who was tied with East in Region 7-AA; the two schools would meet in two weeks for the south crown providing neither loses. Sportswriters forecasted a 38–0 win over Pepperell for October 27; however, 1,500 fans sat through miserable weather to watch a rather lackluster 18–0 West victory. More than likely, Green was playing Gold and White with Powder Blue and Gold on their minds, a sometimes fatal attitude. WR scored touchdowns in the first, third, and final quarters while racking up a modest 203 total yards while holding PHS to 79, 2 first downs and forcing 9 punts. It didn't get any better in the season finale on November 3 on the Alabama Road as Coosa administered a 40–0 whipping. A homecoming crowd watched the Eagles improve to 8–1 by virtue of a 400-yard night in total offense; touchdowns were recorded by 6 different players, and along the way, winning QB Randy Wilson reached 1,000 pass yards. Although Pepperell was held to minus 25 yards rushing, they did complete 11 throws for 134 yards. Pepperell all-area linebacker Mitchell Crabbe, who measured 6 feet, 2 inches and weighed in at 215 pounds, was rewarded in the spring for a fine season by inking a scholarship with Auburn University. New classifications for 1973 season were announced by GHSA with Pepperell falling into Class AA once more; this group covered average daily attendance (ADA) from 700 to 1,050; we barely made the cut at 711.

1973 Season

In a mid-March spring training interview with *RNT*, veteran coach Otis Gilbreath spoke about his 1973 team. At the time, he and staff were working with sixty players of which seventeen were back from last year. Although most players would be extremely young, he believed "this is the best group of young athletes we've had at one time in the history of Pepperell. I've been here since the doors opened and they are good ones…the boys have speed, size and are winners." He then ran down the roster of lettermen starting with flankers Bradley Padgett, Phil Ball, and Greg Turner, interior linemen Tony Wheeler, Danny Dean, Craig Smith, David Burkhalter, and Randy Tillery played at guard and tackle slots while Ronnie Sparks and Randy Green were both sides performers at center and linebacker. Senior quarterback Michael McAteer had experience; he would be backed up by Todd Smith and Jeff Finley. His backfield mates would be Randy Clowers, Joe Henderson, Billy Ingle, Tim Holloway, and Bobby Allen. Much was expected of runners Henderson, Dennis Whatley, and Larry Beard. Youngsters counted on "to aid the team" were Gary Boling, end; Mark Turner, Jimmy Reagan, and Sidney Sheffield, backs; and Mike Ware and Kenny Green were doing well as linebackers. Underclassmen in the line included Tony Bradshaw, Glenn Easterwood, Greg Payne, Keith Baker, Gary Coffee, Greg Jackson, Randy McHaffey, Greg Bollin, and Mark Cosper. Otis reiterated that the '73 Dragons may be a year or possibly two away from excellence, but he liked them nevertheless. In the Friday night, March 25, spring jamboree, PHS lost 13–0 and 10–0 to East and West Rome, respectively, but played Coosa to a scoreless tie.

As the regular season approached versus Adairsville, sportswriters wrote of their improvement. Three years ago, PHS won handily 42–0; in 1971, it was a narrow 14–13 victory. Last September, the Class B Tigers prevailed 30–0. This current bunch would be dangerous, for quarterback Johnny Gulledge was, according to reports, "dangerous." Offensively a Dragon lineup would consist of QB Mike McAteer, halfbacks Randy Clowers and Joe Henderson, with Bobby

Allen at fullback; at flankers were Bradley Padgett and Gary Boling. Tony Wheeler and Danny Dean would be at tackles with Billy Ingle, Craig Smith, and Randy Green working at guards and center. The Thursday night area opener kicked off in Barron Stadium at 8:00 p.m.

There were 4,000 "first-nighters" in Barron Stadium Thursday night, August 30; although they watched a 7–7 tie, both squads could say "we didn't lose the game." Two things were established—Pepperell was an improved club, and Adairsville should do quite well against Class B challengers. In a tale of two halves, the Tigers dominated for 24 minutes as they ran 39 snaps to only 11 for PHS; with 11:53 left before intermission, RB McConnell, who would gain 100 yards rushing on the night, finished off a 50-yard drive-by slanting off tackle for a 20-yard touchdown. We received after halftime and marched to a tying score. Dennis Whatley broke off an 11-yard TD run with 7:37 left in third; Billy Ingle's extra point was perfect. However, it was a bit ragged for the squads combined for 167 yards of infractions and came close to double-digit penalties. We came out ready to play against Chattooga on Saturday, September 8, in Barron. The Indians fumbled 3 times in the opening stanza; however, we failed to capitalize as their defense stopped us in close twice. When Buddy Windle's bunch settled down, they unleashed a bevy of running backs to win convincingly 20–0. They scored touchdowns in second, third, and final quarters while holding us to less than 40 yards and 4 first downs; both squads had "fumblitis," losing 4 each; penalties were about even. On Saturday, September 15, Darlington was presumed the underdog as quarterback Joe Holbrook was missing due to injury; however, with his team down 6–0, replacement Mike Davidson led a late surge, culminating with his 11-yard TD pass to Ricky Sitten with 6:00 showing on the clock; Davidson calmly added the extra point for a 7–6 victory. Pepperell had led up to that point thanks to Dennis Whatley's 24-yard sprint with 1:16 left in the first stanza; later, we missed a short field goal attempt that would have sealed the win. The yardstick showed first downs and total offense about even; the disparity came on penalties as the losers were flagged for 100 yards to only 35 for the Tigers. For teams that pride themselves on offense, the last 3 contests with the Lakesiders had been more baseball-like at 6–2, 8–7, and 7–6.

Although Cedartown's varsity was "crippled up," they were still twenty-one-point favorites in Polk County on Friday, September 21. Diehard Dragon fans still held hope for the Dwags to bring out the best in our football teams. On Thursday, *News-Tribune's* Orbie Thaxton solicited predictions from his readers. Lindale supporter extraordinaire Bob Baker said, "I really feel that we have a good chance against Cedartown; I'll have to go with the Dragons in this one...I can't go against Pepperell." Bob's faith was justified as his beloved team fought back in the second half to "knot the Bulldogs, 6–6." The home squad easily marched sixty-two yards for a TD on its second possession; although point-after-touchdown failed, it didn't seem to matter as the half ended at 6–0. But Gold and White collected themselves at intermission and took momentum away from Coach Jimmy Carter's squad. Senior linebacker Ronnie Sparks was a prime mover as he was literally all over the field making plays. It was his fumble recovery early in the third that led to our score. From the thirty-six-yard line going in, Joe Henderson, Bobby Allen, and Dennis Whatley pounded inside tackle down to the fourteen where QB Mike McAteer swept outside for a fourteen-yard TD, but the ensuing extra point was low. We stopped two tie-breaking drives in the final period; Greg Smith recovered one of their fumbles at our fifteen while another bobble inside our 5 may have cost them the game. If not that, Mike McAteer's first down run from punt formation "took the final life out of the Bulldogs."

    Saturday night was the best night of the week especially if Shannon and Lindale were playing football. This year's Shrine Classic would be more special because Baseball Hall of Famer Dizzy Dean would be in town for the twenty-sixth annual classic. A breakfast and press conference were planned Saturday morning before the legend met and greeted folks on Broad and Second Avenue to sell game tickets. *Rome News-Tribune* promoted the game with a picture of four Dragon linemen including Tony Bradshaw, Billy Ingle, Keith Baker, and Greg Payne. Although the Dragons were 13-point underdogs, they scored early second quarter after a Model fumble; Dennis Whatley's 11-yard scamper finished a 62-yard drive. Ingle's point after was perfect for a 7–0 lead at intermission. Early in final stanza, QB Hughes hit Steve Finley on a 42-yard pass; he followed that with a 6-yard scoring toss to the same wide-out; the extra-point was good and with 10:24 remaining and game tied 7–7. The contest appeared heading toward a deadlock until a fake punt by Pepperell failed at the 25; 3 plays later, Hughes again lofted an aerial toward Finley who outfought the defender in the end zone for 6 points and a 13–7 victory. A second 13–7 loss followed us to Cassville on Friday night, October 5. Four turnovers—2 fumbles and a pair of interceptions—cost us the game. Cass scored with 18 seconds left in the third to lead 6–0; however, a steady offense led us toward goal late with Bobby Allen cracking over from the one; Ingle's kick made it 7–6, advantage Lindale. The 1-point lead did not last long, for the Colonels roared downfield in "chunks." A deceptive tailback sweep pass to James Owens plus the point after was good for a 13–7 win. Senior Ronnie Sparks was again all over the field defensively; offensively Allen was the game's leading rusher netting 106 yards on 26 carries. The staff cited Greg Jackson, Brad Padgett, and Dennis Whatley for their good play. We were prohibited underdogs against East Rome on Saturday, October 13, in Barron; however, despite a misleading 0–4–2 record, Coach Gilbreath was upbeat, saying, "Defensively Chattooga is the only team to beat us more than two touchdowns." Yet with oncoming games versus East, Paulding, West, and Coosa, the offense must get better. In the only Saturday night contest around, East took command early and never let up; they scored 3 touchdowns before intermission and 1 each in third and fourth quarters. After being beaten 13–8 last week by Carrollton, the Gladiators were focused; they gained 238 yards of total offense, 12 first downs, and no turnovers while limiting us to 108 yards, 3 first and tens coupled with three PHS fumbles and one INT. On Saturday night, October 20, a large gathering of 2,500 watched as Ms. Melissa Claire Sisson was named 1973 homecoming queen; she reigned as the Dragons won over Paulding County 20–14 with alert defensive play and clutch offense. The home team scored quickly in first period when Ronnie Sparks recovered a loose ball at their 21-yard line; on first snap, QB McAteer faked a running play and threw to Gary Boling falling into the end zone; Billy Ingle kicked point after with 8:55 left. The visitors took the ensuing kickoff and marched to our 3-yard line before Tim Holloway's clutch interception in the end zone; however, they later drove 62 yards to tie the contest at 7–7 with 4:22 left before intermission. Gold and White took the lead for good after halftime when Dennis Whatley scooped up a loose fumble and galloped 75 yards to paydirt, giving us a 13–7 advantage. On next possession, QB McAteer hit Whatley with a 43-yard screen pass down to the 5 where Bobby Allen cracked into the end zone; Ingle nailed the extra point for a 20–7 lead with 10:20 remaining. Paulding took the ensuing kickoff and marched to a TD; they were aided by 4 pass interference calls. The following week, we battled West Rome "tooth and nail" in a 6–0 loss; all action before halftime was played on their side of the field, but it ended scoreless. After the break, Green did not permit a single Dragon first down while they scored with 2:43 left in the third thanks to pass completions of 23 and 33 yards. The long season came to an end on Saturday, November 3, at Barron Stadium with a 21–0 loss to Coosa. A large crowd of 4,000 watched as Eagle Doug Ragland caught a Melvin Coheley 60-yard touchdown bomb in the first period; in second half, the speedster wide-out returned a punt with a twisting tackle-breaking 55-yard return to the end zone. Quarterback Coheley accounted for the other 6-pointer with a 1-yard sneak. The yardstick indicated the game was closer than the final score as the Dragons outgained the visitors 239 yards to 160; first downs favored us 14–8. Unfortunately, we also led in mistakes. Several times during the contest, PHS drove close to goal thanks to Bobby Allen's power runs up the middle coupled with Mike McAteer's throws to Phil Ball, yet we stopped ourselves with two dropped balls, one of which fell into the end zone. A disappointing season of 1–7–2 was lessened somewhat when 175-pound senior offensive center Randy Green was named to the 1973 Rome area all-stars team.

1974 Season

On Sunday, January 2, *News-Tribune* sportswriter Orbie Thaxton highlighted concern for high school athletic budgets; the rising costs for equipment, medical services, and travel were "far outstripping" gate receipts. Most local programs spent $20,000 to $25,000 on the above items; coaching salaries were not included in this outlay. As a consequence, Mr. Thaxton feared elimination or reduction of nonrevenue sports. Rome's Barron Stadium was scheduled for twenty-three "grid battle" this fall; perhaps fans would see an increase in admission prices which now were $2.00 to $2.50. The 1974 football season would see Pepperell move down to North Class 6-A where they would compete with Model, Darlington, Chattanooga Valley, Bowdon, Villa Rica, Central of Carrollton, and Haralson County. After twenty days of spring practice, a Barron Stadium scrimmage jamboree was held on Friday evening of March 22; Coach Gilbreath and staff experimented with a wishbone offense against three opponents. Model scored late and went for two-point conversion to win 8–7; a scoreless tie with Cassville was disappointing, for we fumbled on the one-yard line. Thanks to penalties, Darlington edged PHS 6–0 on Holbrook's short TD run.

On Monday, August 19, we suited up in pads in preparation for an August 29 game at Bremen; sixteen lettermen including seven sophomores would play against former Dragon Homer Mathis's Blue Devils. Our backfield looked solid with returnees Joe Henderson, Bobby Allen, and Dennis Whatley while Larry Beard, Billy Bradshaw, and Keith Pitts added depth. With one letter already, sophomore QB Todd Smith was the key to team success; fellow tenth grader Jeff Finley would provide backup. However, Jimmy Eddy, Spencer Lee, Chris Barnes, along with John Brown, were also competing there. Veteran linemen were guards Jim Reagan, who may start at center, and Greg Payne; support at that position were Claude Cash and Greg Holloway. The all-important tackle slot was manned by Greg Jackson, David Burkhalter, Gary Coffia,

Kenneth Jones, and Tim Hogan; there were four experienced ends, Phil Ball, Tim Holloway, Mark Cosper, and Gary Boling. Prior to kickoff on Thursday, August 29, heavy rain had soaked newly remodeled Bremen athletic field, which resulted in 7 turnovers during the 0–0 deadlock. Homer Mathis's Class 6B Devils, who were 9–1 last season, tallied 212 yards total offense against 155 for us; first downs favored them 14 to 10, and passing yards and penalties were pretty much even. Dennis Whatley led all rushers with 89 yards; we dominated after intermission and were on the home squad 11 at game's end. Last year, Adairsville recorded a 9–0–1 regular season; the one blemish was a 7–7 tie with Pepperell. At Barron Stadium on Thursday night, September 5, Don Biggers et al. picked the home team by 7 points. Tiger coach T. M. Tucker told the same, "Pepperell will probably play us down to the wire." Before 3,000 spectators, we played beyond the wire, winning 21–6. Highlights were numerous; for example, we limited their offense to minus 19 yards rushing; 13 times we downed them behind the line. Super ball carrier Michael McConnell gained only 20 yards on 16 touches; QB Kirk Alford was sacked 6 times. His team never once moved to a first down and played the entire contest on their side of midfield. With 6 seconds left in first, Dragon Jimmy Reagan's 34-yard field attempt was blocked; Henry Curtis scooped it up and sprinted 73 yards for a 6–0 lead. With 7:28 showing until half, Dennis Whatley broke off the right side and scampered 17 yards to the end zone and a 7–6 advantage. Late in third stanza, quarterback Todd Smith threw 28 yards to Phillip Ball for a touchdown. Reagan kicked true, and it was 14–6 going into last quarter. On next possession starting at midfield, Smith again went to the air, hitting sophomore Mark Cosper for a good gain; he then threw toward Gary Boling near the goal. Both receiver and DB tipped the football before it landed in the sure hands of Mark Cosper falling into the end zone. Reagan kicked point after. Coach Tucker cited a severe case of overconfidence for the loss; his squad watched the 0–0 game from the stands in Bremen last week. Another factor was a change in the Dragons' blocking scheme from previous week. On Sunday, September 22, *Rome News-Tribune* featured, "Dragons Edge Tigers on Penetration Rule." At the end of regulation play and 2 5-minute overtimes, neither squad was able to cross the other's goal. Rules state deepest penetration would then determine the winner. Football was literally a game of inches; to wit, Pepperell downed Darlington by less than a foot due to advancing the ball deeper into their territory. The final measurement showed the Dragons moved to the Tigers' 45-yard line while the Tigers' spot was between the 45 and 46, resulting in a 1–0 victory for Lindale. Game statistics favored the losers, but Todd Smith, David Burkhalter, Kenny Green, and Jeff Finley were mostly responsible for stopping critical penetrations. The recent history of this game is interesting:

    In 1971, PHS won 6–2.
    In 1972, DHS won 8–7.
    In 1973, DHS won 7–6.
    In 1974, PHS won 1–0.

The following Saturday night in Barron, Chattooga received a scare from the Dragons before winning 12–10. Jim Reagan gave his team a 3–0 lead late in the first quarter with a 31-yard field goal; the Indians inched ahead 6–3 on Clint McCary's short TD run with 6:47 left before intermission. Following an interception at midfield in third frame, Henderson, Allen, and Whatley pounded the ball downfield climaxed by the latter's 25-yard touchdown sweep right for a 10–6 lead. Lindale's "high" lasted only 2 minutes as McCary raced 67 yards down the right sideline for the final touchdown and a 12–10 victory. Coach Gilbreath said afterward, "McCary's scamper is the play that broke our back…the whole team played a real good ballgame against the Indians." The area's biggest game of the year occurred on October 5 with traditional foes playing in the Shrine Classic. Otis told a local reporter, "The record books can be thrown away… it will be a whale of a battle." He was right. The Blue Devils won 7–6 as they scored the deciding points with 6:21 left in the quarter one when Clifford Barrett took a pitch out and ran past goal from 2 yards out; Marshall Rice booted a critical point after. Our score came early in quarter four with a 69-yard drive; fullback Bobby Allen pounded the ball to midfield where QB Todd Smith ran the option, pitched to Dennis Whatley who raced past goal. But Jim Reagan's extra-point try was wide right, leaving the final at 7–6. Statistics wise, PHS dominated with 248 yards to 137.

We defeated Villa Rica on October 12 at Barron; a quick score in quarter one by Bobby Allen gave us a 7–0 lead that lasted until first snap of second period when Terry Collins raced twenty-eight yards around left end to tie 7–7. It stayed that way up to the final stanza when the Wildcat punt returner could not make up his mind to catch or let roll. His indecision was a fumble recovered by Mark Cosper at the two; QB Todd Smith sneaked over for a 14–7 lead and victory.

Cooler weather added to the "keen and friendly" region rivalry with Haralson County on Thursday night, October 17. A large crowd of 6,000 showed up on Thursday night in Barron Stadium anticipating a battle. The contest was billed as a running battle between Henderson, Allen, and Whatley up against one of the finest ball carriers around in 175-pound James Moreen. The latter rushed for 199 yards and scored 2 touchdowns, 1 of them a 72-yard gallop in the 28–0 victory. Perhaps overlooked was workhorse fullback Randy Carter who totaled 100 yards on the ground with 24 totes. Sportswriter Don Biggers, who witnessed the loss, felt Pepperell did not equal previous efforts, citing our 104 yards of offense. In Bowdon, Georgia, October 25, the scoreboard glared 0–0 with few seconds left in quarter three. Coach Gilbreath said later, "It was a whale of a game…That was when the ceiling collapsed and the Thomas boys fell right in with it." He was referring to halfbacks Robert and Bobby Thomas who scored 4 touchdowns in just over 12 minutes. The former took a pitchout and outran Dragon defenders as well as his blockers for 42 yards and 6 points. On first snap following a PHS punt, he did it again, only this time for 70 yards. After a PHS fumble, the other Thomas (Bobby) sprinted off tackle for 33 yards to make it 21–0; late in the game, he rambled 6 yards after our high punt snap was recovered inside the 7. For Lindale, running backs Dennis Whatley and Bobby Allen were cited for outstanding play. On Saturday night, November 2, Ms. Kira Sisson was crowned homecoming queen. The pretty senior superlatives were Spanish Club, Honor Society, color guard, class president, softball, basketball manager, Letter Club, yearbook, and student council. Gold and White gave all grads an easy victory over Chattanooga Valley 41–0. In 1989, this institution, which was located in Flintstone near the Tennessee state line, became a middle school as did Rossville; a new Ridgeland High was built to house these two feeder programs. In the action, we scored single TDs in the first and last periods with double 6-pointers in middle stanzas. Whatley ran for

3 TDs—a 21-yarder, a 59-yard end run, and topped it off with a 60-yard fly pattern touchdown reception from quarterback Todd Smith. Gary Boling also caught a scoring toss for 18 yards; early in play, youngster Larry Beard returned punt 58 yards. The season ended on Highway 27S Carroll County on November 8 when Central downed us 29–16. Although Coach Gilbreath was not happy with the loss, he was pleased by "one of the finest team efforts I have ever seen." We dominated the yardstick with 12 first downs to 7 and 309 total yards to 206. The Lions scored early, but the Dragons countered with a Todd Smith sneak just before half for a 7–7 tie. Jim Reagan booted a 14-yard field goal for a 10–7 advantage; the home team went ahead 14–10 at the end of the third stanza and increased it to 21–10 after recovering a fumble on the Pepperell 22-yard line. Todd Smith threw a pick 6 to add to our 29–10 deficit. Dennis Whatley boosted our morale when he bolted 46 yards for a final of 29–16.

1975 Season

    The last quarter century of the millennium was interesting to say the least, for there were momentous changes about in the area, especially 1975 oblong ball. On January 9, a press release from Floyd County superintendent Harold Lindsey announced fifty-one-year-old Otis Gilbreath has retired from football to coach baseball only. Otis came on board the system in 1946 following the war. He left the Dragons to former player and assistant Scott Green. After twenty years, Model's Ralph Tuggle gave way to former Pepperell basketball head coach Wayne Huntley. Following nineteen seasons at Coosa, Branch Bragg retired from athletics. He was succeeded by Leroy Jackson. The three veterans have a combined experience of sixty plus years and would remain as administrative consultants. Mr. Lindsey commended each for their faithful service. Other area changes were Ron Purdy and Mike Knighton were leaving Calhoun and Cassville respectively; tough Eddie Pharo of Rockmart quit but hinted at other coaching situations. Reacting to this, *Rome News-Tribune* sportswriter Orbie Thaxton wrote, "It was a shocker although rumors had been circulating." He later authored an op-ed piece (the opinions and editorial page) giving several reasons for the dwindling ranks of legendary mentors. First and foremost, he noted they receive 17¢ per hour for managing eighty youngsters and a half dozen or more assistants. Sessions in game planning, film evaluation, and practice schedules last well into the late night and early morning. The logistics of tending stadium grass and practice fields in addition to dressing room tasks take up numerous hours as does the purchasing of equipment and medical supplies. The financial burden of a first-class program is usually his charge; this entails all nonrevenue sports; basketball was considered the only break-even part of the budget. During school session, the staff carried a traditional load of day classes, for this provides 90 percent of salaries; this, in itself, was a tough assignment. The writer believed as it stood now, "It is a job for the man who has a lot of time, is willing to dedicate himself to the chore, make the sacrifices necessary and forsake his family to a great extent." The tremendous pressure of a top-notch football school was sometimes overwhelming, and "the money isn't that soothing." Mr. Thaxton believed this had led to a "new Breed" coming into the ranks, one who now looks at the paycheck first because they realize increased salaries led to a better homelife.

Coach Scott Green began conducting his first spring training at Pepperell the second week of March; he welcomed sixty-two boys, sixteen of whom were lettermen, and believed his squad would be strong at the flanks, backfield, and line of scrimmage. The spring jamboree was held in Barron Stadium on Friday night, March 21, with Pepperell edging Model 7–0 and Cass 6–0; in the third "game" against Darlington, a Dragon fumble allowed the Tigers to kick a thirty-two-yard field goal to win 3–0.

Lindale welcomed Bremen to Barron Stadium on Friday, August 29; although PHS alum Homer Mathis brought one of his better teams to town, the home squad was favored by 7 points, and true to form, Gold and White won 13–7 before 3,000 partisan fans. The winners outmuscled their opponent by running 63 plays to 29, outgaining them 243 yards to 143, and moving the sticks 15 times to 7; in addition, the winning defense caused 3 fumbles. While new coach Scott Green showed little emotion on the sideline, he relaxed in the middle of the field as told reporters, "Boy, it sure feels good." The offensive workhorse was junior Larry Beard who carried the ball 22 times for 107 yards; his running mate Mike Whatley added 65. The first wishbone score occurred on an option right pitch to Beard for a 5-yard TD. Tim Hogan kicked point after with 3:52 left in period one. The Blue Devils cut our lead to 7–6 just before intermission, but Hogan's high booming punts kept Bremen backed up most of the night. In the last 12 minutes, the Dragons added to their lead when Jackson recovered a fumble that led to QB Todd Smith throwing an 18-yard touchdown pass to senior split-end Sheldon Whatley who made a great catch on fourth-and-six play. The squad began preparing for Adairsville in the middle of a heat wave; the Friday, September 5, encounter took place at Barron Stadium following thunderstorms that soaked the field; however, PHS prevailed 26–0 behind a stout defensive effort that held the Bengals to 4 yards before halftime and only 59 afterward. Wet ball fumbles and bobbled center snaps thwarted their usually powerful offense while we accumulated 16 first downs and almost 250 yards. Larry Beard ran for a short TD early, and Todd Smith hit Mike Whatley for a 13-yarder to put PHS ahead at intermission 13–0. Two long drives of 64 and 60 yards in the last 24 minutes produced TDs; first, Smith found Mark Cosper for 21 yards. Midway of period four, Mike Whatley took an option pitch around left end for a 16-yard touchdown. Last season, Darlington lost the closest game in the nation 1–0 to Pepperell; they improved their scoring on Saturday, September 20, by 3 points in a 28–3 loss to the same Dragons. Speedy halfback Mike Whatley was the star as confirmed by *News-Tribune* headline, "WHATLEY RUNS WILD." While accumulating 255 yards rushing, the senior had TD runs of 72, 54, and 68 yards; his first TD in frame one posted a narrow 7–0 advantage at intermission. In the 2 final quarters, PHS used a crushing ground game that reaped 257 of their 381 total rush yards. Meanwhile, the Gold and White defense limited the Lakesiders to a single 31-yard field goal by Mike Davidson to go with 137 yards of offense. So far, Scott Green had not been behind as a head coach; his squad had reached the Associated Press number eight state ranking in Class A. Our next opponent, Chattooga, was ranked in the top ten preseason before Coosa upset them 29–0. At the Little Big Horn on September 26, the Indians edged us 16–14; Coach Buddy Windle remarked later that "except for the long run early in the game, I thought we did a tremendous job of containing…they have so much speed." He was referring to Larry Beard's 82-yard scamper on the third play of the contest; after the home team quickly cut our lead to 7–6, the 2 11s played scoreless football for 2 quarters. In the last stanza, Baker booted a 25-yard field goal for Chattooga's first lead 9–7; the backbreaker came with 3:31 left when Petitt (sic) sprinted 57 yards for a 16–7 advantage. Our second big play of the evening happened on the ensuing kickoff when a lineman fielded the ball only to see it "squirt" up in the air; along came Whatley who picked it out of the air and raced down the sidelines for 55 yards and 6 points. It was now 16–14 in favor of Chattooga with 3:15 to play. Both crowds stayed in their seats and watched as the Indian defense refused to "buckle under pressure" to preserve victory.

A milestone was reached prior to the Shrine charity event on October 4 which was the birthday of venerable Barron Stadium. Fifty years ago, a Rome City school coach changed Hamilton Field to Barron Field in honor of board member W. F. Barron who originated the drive to purchase ground from private owners for athletic use. Sportswriters predicted a huge crowd at Barron to watch squads with opposite records line up against each other; PHS stood at 3–1 while MHS record was 1–3; however, Shannon lead overall 12–9–3. The 1975 contest was not expected to be as close as last year's 7–6 Blue victory, but it was more exciting for 6,000 some odd spectators. Model took a 13–0 lead in quarter three only to see the Dragons cut it to 13–7 behind QB Todd Smith's passing and his 3-yard TD run; then the improbable struck on ensuing kickoff when HB Stevenson was trapped in the end zone for a safety. Pepperell had tallied 9 points in less than 10 seconds to trail 13–9. With less than 3 minutes to play, the Blue Devils fumbled back to PHS; Smith proceeded to hit Billy Bradshaw on a 29-yard TD strike with 16 seconds left, and the north sideline erupted in joy. Leading 15–13, Lindale kicked to the fleet-footed Harlan Stevenson who gathered in the pigskin at the 15 and raced against the clock 85 yards to paydirt; Rice tacked on point after for an upset final of 20–15. We opened the game versus Villa Rica with a vengeance when Beard scored in 4 plays; then Todd Smith ran a 41-yard option. Beard took a screen pass to the end zone from 40 yards out; FB Jimmy Eddy tallied twice and Steve Turner once all on 2-yard runs as we pounded the Wildcats 41–6. Kenny Green, Kenneth Jones, and Jerome Jones were singled out for outstanding defensive play. A road trip to Tallapoosa was next, and it proved to be as productive as the trek to Villa Rica; junior Larry Beard rushed for 195 yards on 25 carries; he notched 6-pointers as did Whatley and Eddy; we rang up 374 yards of total offense while limiting Villa to 89 and only 6 first and tens. Turnabout is fair play; Coach Ben Perkins' "power-laden" Bowdon squad rolled up 373 yards on the ground while holding us to 96 in a convincing 26–0 victory on October 25; they tallied 3 TDs before intermission and shut us out entirely. The loss eliminated PHS from contention in Region 4-A North. On the last day of October, Pepperell traveled north to Chattanooga Valley and came away with a 42–8 victory; the game write-ups were a reverse of the previous week, reading, "A crushing ground attack, aided and abetted by some stout defensive play…allowed Scott Green's eleven to bowl-over out-manned Valley." The victory assured Lindale of a winning season as we bolted to a 21–0 lead at the halftime behind running backs Larry Beard and Mike Whatley who combined for 298 of our 372 yards of total offense; meanwhile Billy Bradshaw, Greg Jackson, Kenny Green, and mates were limiting the Eagles to less than 100.

During the first week of November 1975, the McCord family of Randall, Joyce Anne, Scott, and Jamie moved from their Weiss Lake home in Centre, Alabama, to a new residence in the Midway Community of Silver Creek, Georgia; the boys who were first and fifth graders entered the local school located on Rockmart Road while Randall, who resigned as teacher and coach at his alma mater, began a new career in the forestry industry with his biological father, C. L. McCord. While their sons were attending PHS, Joyce would complete her elementary degree at Shorter College and teach at McHenry and Pepperell before retiring; Scott matriculated degrees at Berry College, UVM, and UConn while Jamie attended Alabama, Southern Tech, and Berry.

On Saturday, November 8, Central of Carrollton came to Barron Stadium for a finale. During halftime, Ms. Lynn Weems was crowned homecoming queen for 1975; her credentials were many, for the attractive senior was active in basketball, volleyball, Honor Society, yearbook staff, Letter Club, FCA, and Student Council. Unfortunately, her 6–3 Dragons did not perform well, losing 29–6 in a game that saw us commit 8 turnovers. The only home highlight was a blocked punt by Tim Hogan at midfield just before intermission; 8 snaps later, Larry Beard went off right tackle for our only points. Postseason accolades went to 210-pound center Kenny Green who was named all-area. Nonetheless, PHS finished the schedule with a respectable 6–4 record in Scott Green's first year as headman; sadly he would not coach another Pepperell squad.

In addition to high school all-star Green, another Pepperell Dragon was being groomed for honors. Following UGA's 400-yard rushing against Auburn on national television, Bulldog lineman Randy Johnson was "charged with the responsibility of opening those holes." He followed that with an outstanding effort versus Georgia Tech on a Thursday night broadcast in which the cameras kept zeroing in on an athletic young man. Consequently, the 6-foot-2-inch, 250-pound first team SEC offensive guard became Floyd County's first consensus (judgment by most of those concerned) all-American football player. The 11-game SEC schedule can be an emotional drain, so the senior was resting for a few days prior to preparing for the Cotton Bowl against Texas A&M. A trip home to Lumpkin Road for hunting and eating deer steak precluded a return to campus life; the prestigious Walter Camp honoree told *News-Tribune* sports editor Don Biggers that he wanted a chance to play pro ball because "football is a fun game…it's something I know how to do." In the postseason, the young man was recognized by the town folk of Rome and Floyd County with an official Randy Johnson week beginning January 26; the local Bulldog Club gave him both praise and gifts at its last meeting, which was attended by Georgia head coach Vince Dooley and assistant Doc Ayers.

Jerry Scott Green (1942–1976)

Rome News-Tribune associate sports editor Orbie Thaxton broke the news of Scott Green's passing to the general public on Sunday, August 8, 1976, three days after death. The page 2C article announced "Death Halts Green's Dream of Working with Youngsters." The first year head football coach at Pepperell had fought an abbreviated battle with cancer; a confrontation with the disease was as he lived his entire life, "never surrendering until the end." He was a Lindale man through and through, attending elementary and secondary schools in the village; military obligation in the US Air Force followed graduation in 1960. Afterward, the young veteran worked at General Electric Rome while obtaining his bachelor of science degree from Berry College and master's from West Georgia. He became a mathematics teacher by trade in 1972 at East Rome in addition to assisting with the football team. Two years later, the former Dragon lineman moved "back home" by joining the staff of his alma mater. In January of 1975, Coach Otis Gilbreath retired from football and Principal Dr. Gary Holmes immediately named thirty-two-year-old Scott Green as a replacement. Reflecting on his successor, Otis said, "He came through our program and was a hard worker and a very dedicated person athletically as well as academically…In addition, he is a good man. You can't really say much more about a person that does everything to the best of his ability." The season of 1975 was a testament to hard work for the squad recorded a 6–4 slate; it could easily have been 8–2, for Chattooga won by two and Model by five. The first-year coach publicly considered the 1975 season as just one step in climbing the "dream ladder" of excellence; however, cancer interceded. On February 23, 2021, Betty Burkhalter Shiflett wrote a vivid memory of the late coach, which is paraphrased here:

> The day is still clear after all these years. Sunday July 25, 1976 was my birthday and as of late morning no one in our family had mentioned it; thinking a neighborhood walk around Tremont might offset the memory loss of my husband, children and Dad, I strolled into the quiet Sabbath day street and immediately noticed Scott seated outside his carport. We chatted just a moment before he suddenly wished me a Happy Birthday and then asked, "How old are you?" When I replied, "thirty-three" he spoke slowly saying that he would never be older than me. In an instant I knew the cancer was overtaking his body. Together we experienced "a little cry from deep in our souls." The day was saved for both of us when his sweet sister Sandy Rickman Davis drove up with her newborn baby Elizabeth. Sadly Jerry Scott would live only 11 more days. My husband Kenneth came from a family that is large, friendly and welcomes anyone quite opposite to Scott's upbringing. The two high school athletes were good buddies and at every chance Scott could be found amongst the Shiflett clan. Forty-five years later Betty still remembers those days and the young man who was Driven, Determined, Dedicated, Direct, Dashing and sometimes Delicate.

Scott Green was the second child born to Leonard A. and Sara Frances Winkles Green on October 19, 1942; older sister Lynda Jeanette had preceded him in 1939. When the marriage dissolved, Sara Frances returned to the Winkles home until she met and married Fred Rickman. The couple had one child, Sandra "Sandy" Frances Rickman, in 1949; however, mom Frances died at childbirth before ever holding her baby. The infant was taken in by grandparents Glenn and J. W. Rickman who lived on South Broad for six years before moving permanently to the Bells Ferry area where Sandy began first grade in Model school district. The older children, Lynda and Scott, moved to father Leonard Green's residence in the Lindale area; at ages eight and ten, they began education in Pepperell schools. Upon graduation in 1960, Scott joined the military; while on furlough one year later, the airman married his sweetheart Diane Dorris, who was a senior at East Rome. Two children, Mary Ellen in '65 and Sandra Lynn in '67, were born to the couple before divorce occurred in 1969. Scott continued shift work at GE and classes at Berry where he met student Elizabeth Ann "Betty" Lam; they were wed in 1970, and a son,

William Scott Green, was born in 1971. A year later, an undergraduate degree was bestowed, which started a four-year progression to head football coach of the Dragons. At noon Saturday, August 7, 1976, the coach was laid to rest in Rome's Sunset Hills with the Reverend Jimmy Green officiating. A list of pallbearers read like a Lindale hall of fame with Jerry Green, Steve Johnston, Bill Boling, Guy Hall, Doyal Jackson, Kenneth Shiflett, and Terry Jones attending.

1976 Season

In February, reclassification placed Pepperell in Region 7-A along with East Rome, Model, Darlington, Haralson County, Bowdon, Villa Rica, Carrollton, and Central of Carrollton. Some improvement was made in qualifying for state playoff. The region decided that the top four teams would compete for a 7-A championship with one versus four and two against three. Still, we were playing one another all season and then doing it again following regular season. In early March, acting coach Guy Hall welcomed 65 candidates to spring training, 35 of which were returning players. The wishbone was the feature offensive set when Shannon and Lindale met on March 20 for a Barron Stadium jamboree. Unfortunately, we played second on a sloppy mess turf; actually, this was more suited to Pepperell's ground attack as opposed to Model's quick outside sweeps and passing game. And sure enough, PHS dominated by rushing for 241 yards and 12 first downs; Jimmy Eddy scored a TD from 15 yards out, and QB Jeff Findley ran a perfect wishbone option to paydirt from the 36 as we won 15–0.

In the first week of August, Guy Hall was named interim head coach; the veteran baseball and football assistant was also vice principal of PES. Pepperell opened the season versus West Rome on Friday, September 3, at Barron. Although Robert Green's club was fresh off a 21–7 win over Cartersville, he worried our big line and returning 1,000-yard rusher would be dangerous. On game day, *Rome News-Tribune* posted our starting lineups on offense as guards Greg Payne, Kenneth Jones, and Steve Clark; center Barry Henderson; tackles Greg Jackson and Tim Hogan; ends Mark Cosper, Gary Bowling, and Cris Barnes; backs Jeff Findley, Greg Holoway, Larry Beard, and Jimmy Eddy. On defense, tackles Greg Jackson and Ken Jones, ends Tim Hogan and Greg Holoway, nose guard Greg Payne, linebackers Jim Eddy and Gene Nelson, and D backs Steve Turner, Sammy Burdette, Mark Cosper, and Mark Dillingham. West prevailed in a hard-fought defensive battle 14–0; Williamson cracked short yardage over right tackle in period one. Before intermission, Johnny Tutt gathered in a Tim Hogan punt at the 39 and rambled 61 yards to goal. Gold and White could not get untracked but for 3 fumbles and 2 interceptions. Without Tutt's sprint, the game was pretty even with WR gaining 120 yards to our 115. First downs favored Green 9–5; passing was not a factor. Coach Hall was not overly pleased with his error-prone squad and expressed concern with the upcoming Coosa's defense that was "big, strong and quick that does not break down very often." With the game over on Alabama Road, September 10, Leroy Jackson's 11 was still undefeated and unscored upon winning 19–0. Neither squad dominated rushing with Coosa garnering 119 yards to PHS 97; the difference was 84 critical yards passing, which gave them a 6–0 lead at intermission and improved to 12–0 at the end of quarter three. At halfway point of final frame, Mansour "rammed over" to close out a 19–0 victory. Facing their first region game against visiting Villa Rica on September 18, the Dragons practiced, worked to improve pass offense because opponents were crowding the line of scrimmage. Although we routed Villa 42–0 last year, Saturday night's encounter at Barron was predicted to be closer, and it was. We led 9–6, 22–12, 22–19, and finally won 35–19. Both squads rushed the ball well with PHS leading 226 yards to 212; Steve Turner was the star runner with 117 yards on the ground, including a long 55-yard TD sprint. In addition, the junior rang up a whole lot of kick return yardage. Our offense threw for 68 yards, which forced them away from an 8-man line. In Carrollton, Georgia, on Friday night, September 24, the Dragons rang up 312 yards of total offense and 14 first downs versus the Central Lions, only to lose 28–20 by virtue of spotting them 14 points before spectators found their seats. Thankfully, Steve Turner broke a 49-yarder to cut Central's lead to 14–6 at intermission. Midway period three, PHS marched the length of the gridiron to narrow it 14–12; the Lions countered with their only sustained drive ending with Neal's 5-yard TD run and 21–12 advantage. Disaster struck on the ensuing possession when a botched punt snap was fielded and returned 21 yards by Huckaby for a 28–12 advantage. Although we tallied a late marker, the game was already settled. The slender Steve Turner was exceptional as he ran for 158 yards, returned kicks for 46 more, and added 47 on a pass reception. The season did not get any better 7 days later as East Rome hosted us in Barron. The Gladiators had reeled off 3 straight region wins, allowing only 6 points in the meantime while we have combined for 55 markers the past 2 weeks thanks to Steve Turner's 277 rushing yards. East would counter with a trio of backs including Gordon, Gibson, and Kinnebrew. It was not a classic as 2,500 fans watched ER fumble 4 times to go with 150 yards of penalties. At the 10:56 mark before intermission, a bit of razzle-dazzle accounted for the initial score; the play started as a toss sweep to the TB who suddenly shoveled the pigskin back (flea-flicker) to his QB; Elkins then threw 28 yards to Ferguson in the end zone for a 6–0 advantage. There was no trickery in the second score; Gibson hauled in the second-half kickoff at his 11-yard line and sidestepped his way 89 yards to paydirt; Gordon ran for 2 points and a 14–0 victory. On several occasions, penalties and bobbled footballs killed promising drives for the losers; consequently, Steve Turner was held to 36 yards on 10 carries. A 1–4 Pepperell squad visited 5–0 Bowdon on October 8; we almost sprung Region 7-A's biggest surprise of the season before losing 10–7 in wet weather. Fumbles were "all over the field what with the slippery football." In quarter one, PHS went ahead on a short sneak by Findley following a fumble recovery; Hogan booted point after for a 7–0 lead. At the 10:45 mark of period four, Carroll County's Red Devils tied the game after we fumbled on our 7 where Ellis scooped up the loose ball and crossed goal to tie 7–7. Following the ensuing kickoff and another fumble deep in Dragon territory, Bobby Skaggs kicked a 22-yard field to lead 10–7; however, the game was not over, for on next possession, BHS dropped the ball again, and Pepperell recovered near their goal. We called our last time-out with 1:14 remaining with first and goal at the 5-yard line. As the clock ticked down, we bucked the line 3 straight times but ended a half yard short as the horn sounded. Coach Guy Hall promised Lindale faithfuls there would be no late kickoff runbacks this year. He was referring to Model's Harlan Stevenson's 85-yard sprint in last year's Shrine with 16 seconds remaining to give his team a 20–15 victory. He told *News-Tribune* on Friday, "We'll kick it out of bounds, if we have to." Opposing Coach Wayne Huntley noted, "We kind of throw records out the window on this one." For 6 consecutive years, Shannon had entered the contest an underdog or even and each time came out a winner; they would make it seven in a row on Saturday night, October 16, with a 14–3 win. The statistics would indicate a Lindale victory, for we led in rushing with 150 yards to 125 and first and tens 11–9; penalties and turnovers were even. Although the visiting Dragons threatened several times, a Tim Hogan 25-yard field goal with 7:22 remaining in stanza one was all our scoring. Meanwhile Blue edged ahead 7–3 in the last half minute before intermission when QB Rayburn hit Mathis with a 14-yard scoring toss. With rain falling in the second half, Model beat the final clock by just 1:30 when TB Justice bolted 18 yards up the middle for 6; nemesis Harlan Stevenson booted his second PAT for a final 14–3. The following Friday night did not get any easier for our boys in Carrollton where we lost 35–7. During the contest, Coach Hall gave some youngsters playing time, yet the team lost 4 fumbles, suffered an interception, and had 2 punts blocked. The Trojans capitalized with touchdowns in periods one, two, and three and then added a pair in the last quarter. A Jeff Findley to Steve Turner 26-yard scoring pass in the final minutes ended the game. But there were some bright spots for Pepperell as Greg Holloway rushed for 40 yards and Barry Henderson made 7 tackles; youngsters Greg Allen and Tim Burkhalter were cited for good effort after halftime. Homecoming and Darlington usually raised the hackles of a Dragon fan; the Saturday night, October 30, affair pitted 1–7 PHS versus 3–4 DHS. Pretty Ms. Beth Battles was crowned 1976 homecoming queen; her accomplishments were many with student and Christian council memberships, class president and favorite; Miss Pepperell, Golden Torch staff, and senior superlative. Although the wind and rain brought the smallest crowd of the season to Barron, Ms. Battles presided over her team's 20–0 victory over the Lakesiders. Tim Hogan booted a 37-yard field goal in early quarter two for a 3–0 lead; quarter three produced a long drive that ended with Turner's short TD run. Later Hogan's 22-yard placekick gave us a 13–0 advantage. Midway final quarter, Jimmy Eddy scampered 62 yards on a simple dive play that pushed the final to 20–0. Going almost unnoticed, except for winning coaches, Lindale limited the Tigers to minus 8 yards rushing after intermission. As a result, Coach Hall was coach of the week in local sports. Six days later, Pepperell trekked to Tallapoosa for a 1976 finale; it was a rousing success. Page 5 of the November 7 *News-Tribune* highlighted, "Dragons' 4ᵗʰ Period Surge Tops Haralson." Beneath bold print, it read, "Haralson County put points on the board and controlled the contest throughout the entire first three periods of play." However, all high school rule books say teams must play four quarters in regulation time—and we did. We gave up touchdowns in periods one and three to fall behind 12–0. Early in the contest, Jeff Findley had hit Mark Cosper for a 56-yard TD, which was called back on a penalty; now in quarter four, "it was *déjà vu* all over again" as they connected again for the same yardage without infraction. Tim Hogan toed point after to narrow the lead at 7–12. Nevertheless, the Rebels had possession at their 10 with just over 2 minutes remaining; a first down or good punt, and the game was probably theirs, but a Gold and White defender fell on a loose ball, netting us a first and goal. It took 4 tries before Steve Turner cracked the end zone from 3 yards out and a 13–12 victory. Although the opponent's failed PATs gave us room to win, 3 players on defense made a difference. Gene Nelson had 7 tackles. Jimmy Eddy racked up 6. Warren Barton tacked on 5 in the second half alone. At season's end, 230-pound senior tackle Greg Jackson was cited as an area all-star on offense; also Jimmy Eddy, a senior 198-pound linebacker, was named to the all-star defense. Also in the postseason, Greg

Jackson, Chris Barnes, and Jimmy Eddy signed scholarships with Tabor College in Hillsboro, Kansas, a 4-year liberal arts Christian institution.

1977 Season

In early 1977, local sports editor Don Biggers addressed the issue of playing fields for high school football or rather the lack thereof; he noted that Barron Stadium hosts nineteen to twenty varsity games each season. The venerable site had become home venue to East, West, Model, Pepperell, with Darlington and Coosa also choosing select contests. Late-season wet weather doubleheaders leave the grass surfaces slippery at best. Rather than building a countywide complex which some have suggested, the writer believed smaller on-campus fields are the answer; these sites would benefit all school activities as well as the entire community. Mr. Biggers's interest and comments may have prodded Floyd County Board of Education into action, for in late May, they agreed to work for a stadium on Model's campus. In the meantime, the GHSA approved Thursday night football games for facilities such as Barron that are overtaxed. In an attempt to save energy, the committee mandated starting times for football at 7:30 p.m. The reason being some contests can be played almost without use of lights; basketball now must start at 6:45 p.m. with ten minutes between girls' and boys' games. Also heating controls for gymnasiums would be set at sixty-five degrees for night use and vacated buildings at fifty degrees. Donald C. Biggers (1932–2007) was born in Polk County and began newspaper work while a student at Cedartown High; after a stint in US Air Force, he attended Georgia State and UGA majoring in journalism. The veteran joined *Rome News-Tribune* in 1959, and for the next thirty-eight years, he held many positions including sports editor, managing editor, and vice president of news for the *RNT*. He has served on the Floyd County Commission and was a member of the Rome/Floyd County Sports Hall of Fame. Exactly a month after the above article appeared, his newspaper announced, "Pinson Is Selected as Pepperell Coach." He succeeded interim coach Guy Hall who served following the death of Scott Green. Principal Dr. Gary Holmes made it official a day earlier. The 1967 East Rome graduate came from the Gladiator staff where he tutored football as the offensive coordinator and head track coach. He received a history degree from West Georgia in 1971.

In the spring of 1977, Coach Pinson welcomed a squad that was missing 28 veteran gridders; needless to say, he and staff exercised much patience while installing a new system, yet there had been good player enthusiasm so far. In the spring scrimmage versus Model on Saturday night, March 19, there was some leather popping and strong running. The Devils won 12–7 behind William Mitchell's 160 rush yards which included a 64-yard TD gallop in second stanza; fullback Lindsey accounted for the other touchdown on a short plunge in quarter three. Pepperell's offense came to life when Joe Marion hit John Kelly with a 14-yard completion on third down and long followed by TB Steve Turner's 49-yard sprint to paydirt; Greg Everett booted point after to make it 12–7. We had a goal line stand and picked off 2 passes to keep victory within reach which almost happened late as we just missed on a "TD bomb."

To begin the season, Coach Pinson had to deal with daunting Class 7-A competition including East Rome, Carrollton, Bowdon, Central of Carrollton, Model, Darlington, Haralson County, and Villa Rica; although West Rome and Coosa were Class AA, they were also part of the schedule. Of immediate concern was a shortage of players. "We're down in numbers to just a little over 30 people out for pre-season practice," Pinson told writer Darrell Black 4 days before kickoff. Perhaps the Dragons would be known as the Dirty Thirty, he added. However, the squad had great attitude and hustle about them, which should lead to continuing improvement. Certainly there would be no 2-platooning this year, for only 2 starters returned from last year, center/linebacker Barry Henderson and halfback/defensive back Steve Turner. Most positions were open to competition, especially quarterback where junior Joe Marion and sophomores Greg Gentry and Danny Barton were battling for the number one spot. On Friday, August 26, the Pinson era began with a 7:30 p.m. kickoff at Barron Stadium versus Haralson County. The Dragons were 13-point favorites and would start with their third head coach in 3 years. Using variations of the East Rome power I set and 4-4 defense, Pepperell ran up 264 yards of offense to win 22–8. Senior tailback Steve Turner carried mostly power sweeps 17 times for 116 yards while his backfield mate Greg Everett scored on a 35-yard scamper and a TD sweep for 13. Rebel Emerson Bridges returned the ensuing kickoff 90 yards after Everett's sweep to make the score 14–8 at intermission. At 4:33 mark of stanza three, QB Joe Marion pitched the oval to Turner who in turn "flicked" it back; Joe then hit left end Van Westmoreland for a 40-yard scoring pass. Up next on September 3 was West Rome, a team we had knocked out of region championships twice. The Barron Stadium Saturday night crowd watched as the Chieftains marched 67 yards on their first possession to a 7–0 lead at 6:54 in quarter one; a 38-yard pass completion covered most of the drive. Late in frame two, West attempted to punt inside their 20; however, senior Barry Henderson and Ricky Ingle broke through and blocked the attempt with Ingle falling on the pigskin inside goal. At 1:41 remaining before intermission, Pat Mulrennan's point after kick tied it 7–7. A spirited second half defense kept Green at bay thereafter thanks to 5 turnovers. Traditionally Coosa High had been difficult to defeat for PHS, and they proved to be again on September 10 in Barron, outscoring us 21–14. Gold and White capitalized on an opening kickoff fumble to drive 29 yards for a 7–0 lead even before CHS had run a play. They tied it 7–7 with 3:29 left in period one and then followed it up with another touchdown at 7:02 mark of quarter two to go up 13–7. They weren't through, for after recovering a fumble deep in Pepperell territory, Mansour "burst up the middle" to put Coosa ahead 21–7 at halftime. Once again, Coach Pinson's defense pitched a shutout in second half. The final tally came after a short Eagle punt; several sweeps later, senior HB Samuel Burdette ran behind center Barry Henderson from 15 yards out to a final of 21–14. Associate sports editor Orbie Thaxton followed the Dragons to Villa Rica on Friday night, September 16; the *News-Tribune* writer watched Steve Turner run 1 yard (he had 92 for the night) to score with 5:40 left in the third period and Danny Barton pass 11 yards to Van Westmoreland for a 14–0 advantage. Late in the game, Villa countered with a short TD run and 2-point conversion, making it 14–8; then with 1:29 remaining, tenth-grade quarterback Danny Barton noticed their middle guard shading to one side, and he proceeded to sneak opposite for a 39-yard TD with 1:29 remaining. The 20–8 victory "mustered PHS a 2–1–1 record for the year." Seven days later, we upped that by 1 victory in downing Carrollton Central 21–7. Coach Frank was pleased especially with his defense, which did not allow a first down after intermission. An 83-yard kickoff return in quarter four spoiled our shutout after a youthful coverage team was inserted and failed the test. Pepperell dominated statistics with 282 yards of offense compared to 88 for Maroon and Gray; Steve Turner rushed for 110 yards as we ball-controlled for a full 20 minutes after half. Our scoring was Danny Barton on a 3-yard run in first, Turner's 1-yarder in quarter three, and Van Westmoreland's 32-yard TD pass to Barton in last stanza. On Saturday, October 1, it was pupil versus teacher or Frank Pinson against Jerry Sharp. "I raised him, he leaves home, and takes my offense and defense with him." The teacher laughed one day before game time. Although Pepperell was obviously rebuilding, the important fact was both squads were atop the region standings at 3–0. East Rome came in on Saturday night, October 1, top-ranked in Georgia Class A. Our adrenaline was "pumping," for we fought to a 7–7 draw at intermission. However, Coach Sharp's bunch adjusted their blocking and started giving the oval to I back Greg Gordon; he responded with 27 totes for 132 yards and a 28–7 victory. Gordon, Elkins, and Tutt accounted for 3 TDs in the last 24 minutes. Actually, Pepperell scored initially after a home team fumble. Danny Barton hit Joe Marion for 10 yards; then Steve Turner tossed a slotback around pass to Stanley Hale for 19 yards and a touchdown aided by their DB stumble. Until then, no team had crossed East's goal line; as evidence, their defense shut Lindale's ground game down at 51 total yards. There is an old football adage that says special teams can win three to four games in a season. These percentages can be increased with extremely wet fields of play. Chalk up one for Bowdon High School as they partially blocked a punt in muddy Barron field that led to an early 7–0 advantage; then just before intermission, ten Red Devil rushers once again got to our punter, which netted a 27-yard field goal and 10–0 score. Pepperell adjusted at the half with personnel changes and once kicked on third down; late in period four, Bowdon coughed it up for a third time whereby Joe Marion scooped and rambled 45 yards which set up Sammy Burdette's 5-yard plunge for 6 points. Now trailing 10–6 with 5:03 remaining, Pepperell's cover team failed to defend the middle, letting Red Devil Clay Walker run it back 80 yards for a final of 18–6. A disparity in game stats was that Bowdon punted 4 times for a 43-yard average while PHS kicked 6 times for 27. For 26 years, Shannon and Lindale have played in football's Shrine Classic. Prior to Saturday night, October 15, *Rome News-Tribune* listed 3 reasons why Pepperell High needed to win. First was to keep playoff hopes alive. Secondly, seven consecutive losses to Model was approaching a jinx point, and lastly, twelve months of "braggin' rights" would accompany a victory. Gold and White accomplished the trifecta with a 7–0 win to improve their record at 4–3–1. At the 1:02 mark before intermission, QB Danny Barton threw a flat pass to Sammy Burdette that turned into an 11-yard TD. A strong second-half defensive effort was settled when Greg Everett intercepted a Devil pass inside our 20-yard line with only ten seconds remaining; previously a fumble and 2 errant throws kept Blue from scoring. The PHS ground attack netted 160 yards with Steve Turner getting almost half of that on 27 carries. One week later, 46-year-old Cullman, Alabama, native Charlie Grisham brought Carrollton to town, seeking a twentieth straight region playoff berth; they successfully departed Rome but with a hard-fought 15–14 victory. However, Black and Gold were forced to come from behind twice to win. At 11:45 mark in second period and following a 1-yard visitor punt, Danny Barton hit Joe Marion with an 11-yard TD pass, giving us a 6–0 halftime advantage. Grisham's crew came out of intermission like a team possessed, for they ground out 63 yards to go ahead 7–6, but PHS recovered a fumble and countered 5 snaps later when

Greg Everett ran 5 yards to paydirt; Sammy Burdette bulled over for 2 points and a late third-period lead. However, last-period penalties and a dropped football resulted in a 69-yard TD march by Carrollton; their power sweep right netted 2 points and the game 15–14. In the '77 finale, Pinson's Dragons traveled 4 miles west to Lakeside seeking a region playoff spot; however, Darlington was after the same. A 28–6 verdict on Saturday night, October 29, improved Darlington's record to 7–2 and moved them into second place in Region 7-A; the losers finished at 4–5–1. Tiger halfback Earl Gibson rushed for 62 yards on 11 carries and scored from the 8, 2, and 1; Tommy Barron accounted for a 33-yard pass interception run back late in the third quarter. Bruce Hunter was successful on all point afters. Senior Steve Turner tallied Lindale's only points on a short plunge; he was also a force on defense. Game statistics were pretty much even as DHS had only a 3-yard advantage in total offense; first and tens were also close. The losers committed 25 yards more in penalties. The abovementioned Turner received recognition as a DB on the area all-star squad.

1978 Season

In the spring of 1978, school consolidation, Georgia High School Association change of command, and a *News-Tribune* survey of local coaching supplements were newsworthy. A recommendation by Georgia Department of Education that Cave Spring and Pepperell combine was being considered locally. The ideal size of secondary student bodies was determined to be a thousand; therefore, redirecting funds to three county high schools would meet this criterion as Pepperell, Coosa, and northern Floyd would house what are now five facilities. Superintendent Dr. Nevin Jones indicated we would immediately be eligible for $1.7 million in capital outlay funds. It did not sit well with many of those present at the board meeting. One citizen said, "We ought to tell them to keep their damned money." Most felt large was not necessarily good; a Cave Spring parent balked at busing her children to Lindale; a bond issue must be approved for these changes. A second option was proposed for South Floyd, Armuchee, Coosa, and Model.

In April, a major change in GHSA hierarchy, Pepperell High School principal Dr. Gary Holmes was selected as its new president. He replaced M. E. Nichols who served twenty-one years in the position. Forty-four-year-old Dr. Holmes has a background in athletics and administration which should serve him well. As a 1952 Model graduate, he excelled in football, basketball, baseball, and track before obtaining degrees from West Georgia, Appalachian, and Mississippi State universities; Dr. Holmes ascended to PHS in 1974 after serving as a classroom teacher and principal of Johnson Elementary. On the job, later he said, "I'm just beginning to realize the work load involved in presiding over the most powerful group in prep sports."

Sportswriter Darrell Black posted this in Sunday's May 28 *News-Tribune*, "Wanted. College-educated young man to clean floors, mow football fields, wash uniforms, file equipment, discipline students, act as part-time guidance counselor, serve in concession stands, be gate attendant, and do some coaching, pay scale negotiable, but under 50 cents an hour." Perhaps this paragraph was the seed that led associate editors Don Biggers and Orbie Thaxton to survey Rome area coaching supplements; their findings are quite revealing:

(1) Basic pay for coaches is generally the same.
(2) The supplementary pay is not as great as some believe.
(3) Some systems do not pay for minor sports.
(4) Head football pay is $2,500 to $3,600. Fifteen years' experience could increase to $6,000.
(5) Athletic directorships in Floyd County range from a base of $500 to $1,000.
(6) Top assistants begin at $1,200 and reach $1,700 after fifteen years.
(7) Basketball's top men and women earn $1,200 to $1,700 per year.
(8) Wrestling is $600 to $850.
(9) Baseball pays $500 to $750.
(10) Track is same as above.
(11) Tennis is $150 to $400.
(12) Golf is same as above.

As schools add to their athletic programs with soccer, tennis, cross-country, golf, and even swimming, these figures are at best inadequate.

Football season began for PHS on Saturday, August 26, at Barron versus Adairsville. We pretty much dominated the Green-clads 14–0 by accumulating 236 total yards to 63; first and tens favored the Dragons 9 to 5. Turnovers were even; unfortunately, the winners led in penalties also 55 yards to 15. Much of the victory credit should go to our defense which did not allow a second half first down; senior linebacker Greg Allen was responsible for 8 solos and several assists while Vernon Godfrey pitched in 7 individuals. With 1:08 left before half, Allen burst up the middle to block a visitor punt which teammate Buster Knowles recovered for 1978's first touchdown; Pat Mulrennan was true on point after and a 7–0 advantage. At 8:48 left in quarter four, RB Benjie Shiflett swept left for 14 yards and a 2-touchdown lead; the sophomore led all runners with 105 yards on 18 carries which enabled our offense to sustain time-consuming drives after intermission. Seven days later, West Rome coach Max Dowis worried about run-oriented Pepperell, and "you never know how a squad is going to play that first night with a crowd watching." Green shut our ground game down to 57 yards, but we responded with QB Danny Barton passing to Joe Marion for 17 yards, and then he hit 210-pound receiver Buster Knowles with a 44-yard strike to tie the game 7–7 going into halftime. The senior outjumped two defenders and "lugged" one of them into goal for a touchdown. At this point, "water-bug style runner" Sam Person took over by rushing for 166 yards on 23 totes; he scored from 11 and 23 yards out to lead a WR 20–7 victory. Our nemesis Coosa was next up for September 9. *Rome News-Tribune* began its Sunday morning write-up with, "In trench play…inch by inch, yard by yard, and first down by first down, the Coosa Eagles slowly and methodically produced almost 300 yards of offense defeating the Pepperell Dragons last night 20–6." It appears they did it with defense also, for Lindale managed less than 50 yards' running and throwing. The game was tied 6–6 in second quarter at 10:06 mark thanks to Greg Allen's 11-yard burst off left tackle; however, Coosa went ahead 13–6 just before half on a Downs-to-Payne TD pass that covered 22 yards. Post-intermission, QB Downs repeated his feat by throwing 21 yards to Ballard who outleaped defenders for a score; the local paper declared game over with 4:02 left in the third period. On Friday night, September 24, it was mentor versus pupil as Sharp and Pinson faced off for a second time.

East Rome pretty much dominated statistics and scoreboard, winning 36–0; total offense favored ER 345 yards to 116; first downs 16 against 6. The three Tutt brothers, Eric, Greg, and Johnny, combined with Warren Gibson to record all Gladiator points while Brown and Campbell excelled on defense. Yet Pepperell had its moments, for they came out in a shotgun formation with Danny Barton throwing to backs Sims Gordon and Joe Marion for almost 130 yards; Greg Allen played well for the defense. The following week, he made the mid-season all-star checklist at linebacker. We traveled to Buchannan on October 6 searching for a win and got it 12–7. It was Danny Barton's show as the junior signal caller ran for 107 yards, including a long TD jaunt, and threw for an additional 68 yards. Benjie Shiflett recovered from a recent injury to help out with 70 yards on the ground. But it was defense that made the play of the game with less than three minutes left; trailing 12–7, Haralson County marched downfield and reached a fourth and one at Pepperell's 15-yard line where our defenders "stopped Haralson County in their tracks." Coach Pinson said afterward, "We just needed this one." Shrine week is always special in Floyd County. Lindale was set to meet Shannon in Barron Stadium on Saturday night, October 14; they had played for 27 Shrine games with Model holding a narrow 14–10–3 advantage. Most classics have been decided by a touchdown or less (16 of 27); in recent history, underdogs have won more than not. Wayne Huntley had witnessed multiple games on each sideline while Frank Pinson only once; the former knows emotions likely determines outcome. Although the Blues' record stood at 5–1 and Pepperell's is 2–4, the latter had faced several strong football teams. The money raised by the charity event went to help Shriners with their great work minus a set fee for each school. On Sunday morning *RNT* reported, "Model Grinds Out 418 Yards on Ground as They Top Pepperell 40–12 in Shrine Game." Underneath this headline, they added, "See Model run. Watch Model run." It was the highest point total ever. Fifty-two points scored was a Shrine record. Five Blue Devil backs ran for 60 yards or more while amassing 25 first downs. A bright spot for the Dragons was RB Benjie Shiflett's 91 yards on 17 attempts and QB Barton's long completion to Westmoreland which set up a 1-yard TD pass in closing minutes. On defense, Greg Allen led us in tackles while Barton, Brannon, and Westmoreland had interceptions in the first half. Shannon's small backs caused problems throughout with their combination Wing-T, Veer, and Power I which used trappings, misdirection, halfback crosses, and bootlegs to fool defenders rather than trying to power over them. Bowdon High School came to Barron Stadium on Saturday night, October 21, and won 28–6 over PHS; they scored TDs in periods one and two and added 2 more right after halftime in accumulating 248 rushing yards without completing a forward pass. Our points came from Benjie Shiflett who swept left with 4:48 remaining; Joey Rickman supplied some offensive punch late with 3 good throws for 35 yards. A road trip to Villa Rica on October 27 ended in pain and a 7–6 loss; Pinson's squad "won the battle; however, in the long run, the war was lost." Pepperell doubled their hosts in total yards and first downs but unfortunately threw four interceptions. A long sustained first period drive ended with a Johnny Mack Terrell 2-yard TD run, plus a perfect PAT gave Villa enough points to win. With 5:12 left in stanza three, Joey Rickman hit Pat Mulrennan on a 54-yard touchdown which cut the advantage to 7–6, yet point-after-touchdown try was no good. Our defense, which was paced by Greg Allen, Vernon Godfrey, and John Bennett, allowed the winners only 118 yards of offense. Ms. Dedra Cox was crowned homecoming queen at Barron Stadium halftime on Saturday night, November 4; the pretty senior had participated in various groups while at PHS including basketball, FHS, FBLA, Nutrition Council, Miss Pepperell Court, and four years on Projects Committee. Unfortunately, the young lady presided over a 26–0 loss to rival Darlington. Henry Chubb's 130-yard rushing on 24 carries plus Tiger touchdown passes that covered 25, 14 and 18 yards, all in the first half, pretty much sealed our fate and a 2–8 record. Pepperell's offense was "unrhymatic" against a top defense which allowed only 62 yards rushing and 27 through the air. On December 9, Jerry Sharp's East Rome Gladiators downed Claxton 25–9 to complete a 15–0 state championship run in Class AA. They won last year's Class A crown with an identical record.

1979 Season

Spring game in Shannon on Friday night, March 16, pitted experience against youth—and the former prevailed 39–0. These types of contests are considered training grounds for upcoming year and seldom foreshadow anything to come. However, in Model's case, it did, for they won the Class 7-AA state championship. Winning coach Wayne Huntley was philosophical, saying, "It has nothing to do with the upcoming season. We'll make some changes and so will they, so you can't judge a team on one game." For youthful Dragons, Greg Shiflett, Sims Gordon, and Labron Newberry were team leaders. Some rule changes for 1979 were actually minor. Home teams would wear dark jerseys except in mutual consent. Two players would participate in coin toss. Identical jersey numbers were "allowed as long as they're not on the field at the same time." Since last December, *News-Tribune* staffers had been working on a fourteenth annual "Pigskin Preview." Projected defensive all-stars listed Pepperell's 6-foot-1, 175-pound senior Danny Barton as a defensive back. In preseason, Coach Frank Pinson bemoaned his team's lack of size, noting, "We will be the smallest team in the area…Our offensive line will average about 165 pounds…Senior Tim Herrington is the only player over 200 lbs. but this is his first year." As kickoff time neared against host Adairsville, some writers predicted an "exciting contest." Although PHS won last year 14–0, it must now face a veteran squad led by future star Vic Beasley Sr. It was a rainy night in Georgia on Friday, August 24, and Pepperell led 6–2; with 4 minutes left, Beasley started an end sweep, and 57 yards later, his Tigers were out front 8–6. The junior was "hit a number of times but was undented by the effort." The home team tallied another TD late to make a final 16–6. Lindale took a 6–0 first-period lead on Greg Shiflett's 2-yard run; a high punt snap cost us a safety just before intermission, but still Gold and White had a 6–2 advantage. For the next 20 minutes, a wet field slowed play until Beasley's long run and another late TD pushed it to 16–6. Bartow Green outrushed their visitors 149 to 81; otherwise statistics were pretty much even. Three weeks later, undefeated Adairsville vaulted to sixth in state Class 6-A. West Rome coach Mike Hodges, who scouted "rainy night in Georgia," evidently learned some things for his squad and downed us 23–8. On September 1, 9 running backs outrushed PHS 315 yards to 9; they lost passing stats 14 to 106 and were almost tripled us in first downs 17 to 6. Penalties probably cost them more points. With 50 seconds left in quarter one, QB Joey Rickman completed a 54-yard throw to Pat Mulrennan down to 1 inch of goal line; Joey sneaked over for 6. A fake kick on point after went from holder Greg Gentry to Charlie Ball for 2 points and a 8–7 Dragon lead. But 7-AAA Chieftains were too strong and won 23–8. In Barron Saturday night, September 8, Pepperell offense was "just plodding along" while the D was limiting Coosa to 26 yards rushing, 2 first downs, 6 pass completions, all the while forcing 7 punts and catching 2 Eagle passes themselves in the 10–0 shutout. *Rome News-Tribune* summed it up on Sunday morning, "Defense Does the Job, Pepperell Stops Coosa." Almost lost among the accolades was Pat Mulrennan's 28-yard field goal at 3:40 in second period; afterward, a 12-play drive that began late in third and ended with 9:06 left in regulation gave us breathing room and a 10–0 victory. QB Rickman hit Greg Shiflett for 15 and Jeff Brannon for 14 yards before Greg Gentry busted through a gap-8 defense into goal with 9:06 left in the game. An elated Coach Pinson said later, "It was just a great team win and I can't cite any one person." After an open date and Coosa's surprising 0–0 tie against East Rome, Lindale had a chance versus consecutive 2-time state champs ER. And we fought "toe-to-toe" with the powerful squad from Turner McCall Boulevard, allowing them 1 first down in the fading minutes of period two. The Dragons took the second-half kickoff and, behind the blocking of seniors Jeff Wolfe and Steve Cauthen, drove the ball goalward where Patrick Mulrennan kicked a 24-yard field goal at 2:03 mark. Almost as famous as East's 32-game win streak is their toss sweep; however, we found the key to stopping it by allowing 1 first down in 24 minutes. Mulrennan kick and lead held up until midway period four when Sharp's Gladiators discovered tailback Tim Spivey up the middle behind all-area center Charles Smith; with most of his 21 carries and 92 rushing yards coming on 2 long marches to goal, the youngster led a 13–3 victory. Sophomore LaBron Newberry and senior Greg Gentry were defensive standouts. On Friday night, September 28, hometown Carrollton Central High kicker was wide left on his PAT attempt, and visiting Pepperell High's Pat Mulrennan was wide right; therefore, regulation play ended tied 6–6. As it played out, Central advanced to PHS 35-yard line and won on penetration 7–6. The home squad scored on a 6-yard run with 3:40 left in period two while PHS crossed goal with less than 4 minutes remaining when Greg Gentry bulled his way into goal from 2 yards out. The losing offense showed up well, gaining 214 yards on the ground with Danny Barton, Sims Gordon, and Benjie Shiflett carrying the load while Coach Chuck Taylor's squad managed 158; with the exception of Greg Shiflett's interception, turnovers and first downs were pretty well even. Carrollton improved its record to 4–1, reverse of Lindale. Saturday night next in Barron Stadium, "Pepperell swept Haralson off their feet 27–4." In first 2 periods, we tallied 4 touchdowns; Benjie Shiflett ran a power sweep 32 yards. On a flea-flicker, QB Joey Rickman hit Pat Mulrennan for 32 yards; Danny Barton halfback-passed 28 yards to Mulrennan for our third 6-pointer; Greg Shiflett intercepted and ran back a Rebel pass 40 yards to the 7; 3 snaps later, Rickman sneaked into goal with 10 seconds left before intermission. Although we led 27–0, 9 second-half penalties hampered play calling. Fighting this malady with an aerial game (Rickman was 6 of 9 for 89 yards) helped but bad field position prevented more scores. Haralson managed 2 safeties after halftime consequences of a low punt snap and then a bad pitch on tailback sweep. Model took up where they left off in the middle of March, defeating Pepperell 29–0 on Saturday night, October 13. Running back David Stone came into Shrine Game at Barron Stadium needing 81 yards to become

Northwest Georgia's first 1,000-yard runner for 1979; he surpassed it by 31. However, PHS did hold Wayne Huntley's vaunted ground attack under 3 football field lengths. Nonetheless, Shannon tallied points on 2 running plays, a forward pass, and a blocked field goal return. At the same time, their defense limited us to a little more than half a hundred. Poor field position plagued Lindale after halftime. On Friday afternoon next, Dragon football boarded a "yellow bird" and picked up Highway 100 South in Cedartown en route 50 miles to Bowdon, Georgia. Thank goodness, Danny Barton was saved a seat as he rushed for 118 yards on 27 carries. Number 21 scored on a short run to tie 7–7 in period three and, following a critical fourth-period fumble recovery, helped move the football close in allowing Greg Shiflett squirt over with 1:49 remaining. Then as the band and home crowd came to life for a last-minute comeback, he made a timely interception to secure Lindale's 14–7 win; his defensive mates included Labron Newberry and Eddie Davenport. With Villa Rica and Pepperell both shooting for a playoff spot Saturday night in Barron, a packed house was expected; it was also homecoming for PHS. Ms. Dedra Cox was crowned queen for 1979. She had been a member of JV basketball, FHA and FBLA, Nutrition Council, Miss Pepperell Court, and Projects Committee. The lowlight of October 27 was a surprising 42–14 visitor triumph. They outrushed us 256 to 29 yards, logged 21 first downs against 8; however, Dragon Air (senior QB Greg Gentry) threw for 120 versus 43 mostly to Barton and Mulrennan. With that said, Villa led 21–0 at the half and stymied our attempts to catch up with fumbled recoveries and interceptions. The season ended at Lakeside on Friday night, November 2; Darlington celebrated homecoming and defeated Pepperell 7–0 to clinch a playoff spot in Region 7-AA. Tailback Henry Chubb surpassed 1,000 yards rushing for 1979 and scored the game's only TD. Only one Dragon was mentioned in Sunday's paper. "Sophomore tackle Dave Stager paced Pepperell defense." On December 9, *Rome News-Tribune* chose senior Eddie Davenport as all-area offensive guard. Although he stood in at 5 feet 10 and weighed 170 pounds, Eddie could have been picked on defense as well; he was not big but good. Later Danny Barton and Davenport were named to the Kiwanis all-county team. In spring football signing period, Danny inked with Jacksonville State to play defensive back. He was expected to be a "strong performer" for the Gamecocks.

1980 Season

As Coach Frank Pinson began year four at Pepperell, he cited experience at key positions. Quarterback would be manned by Greg Shiflett with Robbie Robinson, Ben Shiflett, and Tommy Gentry in the backfield; Labron Newberry moved from fullback to center but would team with Gentry at linebacker slots. Greg Earle was a tight end with good hands and blocking size. Although fall ball would begin in Class AAA, Model provided competition for spring scrimmage and won 41–0 on Friday night, March 14. As Class AA defending state champions, they rushed for 404 yards, accumulated 18 first-and-tens, and had a bevy of running backs cross goal; Pepperell's offensive leaders were QBs Jeff Brannon and Greg Shiflett who managed 94 passing yards to go with 48 on the ground.

Georgia state prep season began on August 22 with high temperatures; 8 days later on August 30, Pepperell lined up in Barron Stadium against Adairsville. We were 15-point underdogs and lost 12–7. Greg Shiflett ran for over 100 yards while freshman Randy Jackson excelled on 11 carries for 68 yards; Dave Stager and Lebron Newberry were leading "line" players for Lindale. The thirty-third annual Shrine Game kicked off early on September 6 at Barron before a sellout crowd. One million dollars had been raised in Rome area since 1948 to fund expenses incurred by handicapped children. Although most Shrine battles have been competitive, Blue holds a 16–10 advantage; 3 have ended in ties. The average total points pretty much tell the story of the game with Shannon at 13.9 while Lindale was at 8.6. Because of so many offseason variables, a spring game normally does not replicate a regular season encounter; however, on Saturday night, it did as Model took us to task 47–6. Star athlete Norris Allen gained 90 yards on 10 totes, received 2 passes for 16, and carried back 2 interceptions for 99 yards and 1 TD; he also kicked 5 extra points. Model went ahead 33–0 at intermission and coasted thereafter. Our only score came after Randy Jackson scampered 28 yards, and Shiflett hit Tim Wright for 28; then Jackson finished the 74-yard drive with an 8-yard sweep around left end. Number 55 Labron Newberry was a highlight on defense. Pepperell came back next Friday night in Barron to rousingly defeat Calhoun 34–14. A "spirit night" theme had inflamed our community, and nearly 100 varsity/midget cheerleaders, a marching band, and fans celebrated our first Region 7-AAA victory. The issue was never in doubt as PHS dominated with 240 yards rushing to go with 186 passing and 24 first downs; meanwhile, our defenders were holding them to 177 yards. Greg Shiflett, junior Tim Wright, freshman Randy Jackson, and junior Bob Griffin led our offense. With a dwindling clock, sophomore QB Bryan Griffin hit fellow tenth grader Mark Wheeler with a 16-yard TD pass. On September 19, Coosa downed us 20–6 in a contest where neither team punted. They scored TDs in the first 3 periods while accumulating 300 total yards against our 189. QB Hal Williams was a thorn in our side, running and throwing. His scramble from sideline to sideline in third quarter ended with a completion and a disheartening touchdown. Vernon Wilkes's Eagles improved to 2–2; Lindale fell to 1–3. On Friday night, September 26, Cedartown used a pair of running backs in defeating Pepperell 28–6; Clarence Calhoun tallied on runs of 6, 4, and 9 yards while mate David Barrow totaled 188 yards on 19 carries and 1 TD. Pepperell played "gritty" and refused to quit against a strong visiting defense that allowed only 52 yards on the ground and about that in passing while giving up 4 first downs. A bright spot was Greg Earle's interception near midfield followed by Bryan Griffin's short touchdown toss to Mark Wheeler. The Dragons traveled to Dallas, Georgia, on October 10 as a 1-point favorite over Paulding County and lost 31–15. At first, the game seemed winnable for QB Greg Shiflett and Mark Wheeler connected on a 42-yard throw and catch with 7:00 left in period two; Kenny Shaw kicked point after for a 7–0 advantage. However, that play must have awakened Paulding, for they scored 2 TDs and a 39-yard field to go up 17–7 at intermission. An 8-yard scoring pass late in the third pushed the advantage to 24–7. We got back on the board with 21 seconds showing on quarter-four clock when Bryan Griffin passed to Greg Earle for an 11-yard touchdown; he then hit Wheeler for a 2-point conversion. Game statistics were almost even with total offense favoring Dallas 268 to 244 yards; however, it was interceptions and fumbles that probably cost us a chance at victory. The Cass Colonels came to Barron Stadium on Friday night, October 17, with one of the area's top defenses, yet it was Pepperell's tackle Dave Stager who "spearheaded the Dragons' sack attack" that limited the visitors to 24 total yards. In the second stanza, QB Greg Shiflett finished a drive that started at midfield with a 9-yard score on the option play; Shaw converted the PAT for a 7–0 advantage and the only points we would need to win. Shiflett closed it out with 2:43 left in the game when he bootlegged around end for 6. Running back Randy Jackson was an offensive force carrying 23 times for 90 yards. On the first day of November, Pepperell hosted Chattooga County on homecoming in Barron Stadium; the Indians' quarterback and tailback accounted for 324 offensive yards while scoring 6 touchdowns in their 57–14 victory. Junior halfback Charlie Ball gave us a 6–0 lead when he swept around end for 20 yards at the 8:39 mark of the first stanza; however, the visitors quickly retaliated with a score and then bolted to a 28–6 advantage at intermission. Late in the third, Randy Jackson finished a 63-yard drive with an 11-yard power play up the middle; Greg Shiflett threw to Ball for the conversion and our final points. At halftime, pretty Ms. Wanda Faye Smith was crowned queen of the 1980 class; the senior's accomplishments were varied and many. They include class favorite, FBLA, football and basketball cheerleader with captain honors, Governor's Honors, Math League, Miss Pepperell contestant, secretary in the student council, yearbook staff, National Who's Who, Fellowship of Christian Athletes, class treasurer, and junior and senior Honor Society. Wanda's crowning was the highlight of the evening. It was a short 16-mile drive on Georgia Highway 101 South to Rockmart; traditionally, the Polk County Bees have been difficult to beat. On Friday, November 7, they were true to form, for with 6:00 remaining in quarter four, Coach Pinson's crew held a tenuous 14–7 lead. We had scored minutes before halftime with a long pass completion down close where Randy Jackson bulled into goal; however, Kirk Stallings's 11 responded with 2 aerials for 46 yards to inch ahead 7–6. After break, Pinson's crew drove 58 yards with Shiflett running it in from 13; Jackson converted a 2-point conversion to lead 14–7; it stayed that way until Rockmart marched 43 yards to tie 14–14 with a dwindling clock. With less than a minute remaining, the Jackets intercepted an errant Dragon throw and drove in close where a chip shot field goal wins. However, with 16 seconds showing, a high center snap forced holder Rodney Haynes to catch and ad-lib his way to goal for a 21–14 victory. Game statistics were pretty much even as RHS garnered 310 total yards to 237 for PHS while first and tens favored them 11 to 9; penalties were a wash. In the postseason, Dave Stager and Greg Shiflett were part of *News-Tribune* all-area squad. A month later, Dr. Holmes accepted Coach Pinson's resignation. Frank thanked his principal and other county administrators for their excellent cooperation during these past months; he indicated a move into private business was next.

1981 Season

A new coach, a new offense, and a "new feeling" comes to Pepperell in the person of Charles Bryant (C. B.) Cornett. He was born into a railroad family in Athens, Tennessee, on April 27, 1948; after graduation from McMinn County High in 1966, he enlisted in the Marine Corps. Two years later, he was assigned to a recon helicopter as an open-air door gunner in Vietnam where he received a Purple Heart, which is for wounded or killed military personnel; it is our nation's oldest military medal established in 1782. Coach Cornett also merited a Silver Star for valor and gallantry in action in addition to thirty-two Air Medals for meritorious achievement in aerial flight. After active-duty discharge in 1968, C. B. retired from the Corps as a reservist. In

1970, the twenty-two-year-old enrolled at East Tennessee State where he walked on the football team. As a 1975 graduate, he coached high school ball in Southwest Virginia and Penning Gap schools. In years 1978–'80, he was an assistant coach at Villa Rica High as well as Pickens and Madison County. Charles is married to Kim, and they had three grown children.

The newly hired headman welcomed back several veterans from last year; however, he pointed out that none could be considered "returning starters." Offense had been a problem lately in Lindale; hopefully a newly installed inverted wishbone would solve many shortcomings. A spring game versus highly regarded Armuchee was won 8–0 using a "straight ahead style." Two bullish two-hundred-pound runners, Randy Jackson and LaBron Newberry, gained fifty-nine and forty-four yards respectively; Jackson scored on an eight-yard dive with 3:24 remaining while Newberry led PHS defenders from his linebacker position.

On August 3, local football teams were permitted to don pads. All summer prep squads had been hard at weights and conditioning. Pepperell completed a week of rigorous camp on August 21 and were feeling good about themselves. Coaches had put together their version of a "wishbone" offense, which came from several states and had several ways of doing things. Coach Cornett noted his runners do not have great speed but excellent size; this described linemen as well. He made no predictions to *RNT* sportswriter Darrell Black, saying, "Region 7-AAA is as good as anywhere in the state…We're stressing teamwork and hardwork…It's going to take the whole school and community working together to get the type program we all want." In Adairsville on Friday night, August 28, the coach watched his Dragons overcome mistakes to take a 12–7 lead with 2:00 left in regulation. With time running out, Lindale marched "picture-perfectly" 85 yards to take a 12–7 advantage when Randy Jackson, who rushed for 127 yards and 2 scores, carried for 21, 11, and finally 12 yards for the TD. Then lightning struck! On Adairsville's next center snap, they completed a quick throw and catch that turned into a 69-yard touchdown run to victory 13–12. Opposing Coach Danny Wiseman said afterward, "We certainly feel fortunate to win on a last-minute play…This is the best Pepperell team I have seen in several years." On Sunday, September 6, *News-Tribune* reported on Shannon and Lindale, "Model Keeps Shrine Streak Going with a 20–0 Triumph." It marked 4 straight wins for Blue and 10 out of past 11. Model played with good defense and good offense; they gained 230 yards but gave up only 78. Winning coach Namon Wiseman was "pleased with the way his squad hung in there because Pepperell is so physically tough." In first frame, a 15-yard run inside guard netted a 6–0 advantage; Wiseman's crew upped that to 12–0 in late period three with a 6-yard TD pass. With 8:43 remaining, QB Nicky Sharp sneaked over from 3 inches out and then quarterbacked an option play for 2 points. In Gordon County, September 11, Pepperell dominated with almost 300 yards of offense against Calhoun. Labron Newberry led us on an initial 6 first down series to goal; he scored on a "student body left" from 4 yards out to lead 8–0. Jerry Smith's first team answered with 6:07 left before half to tie at 8–8. Then our best football occurred after kickoff on a 9-play 80-yard drive that ended with LaBron Newberry crossing goal from 33 yards out. Assistant sports editor Mike Pendleton of *RNT* wrote, "He was probably hit by every Yellow Jacket defender but refused to go down…finally he busted loose from a pile about 25 yards away and literally waltzed in for the score." Another 2-point conversion gave us a 16–8 advantage with 2:16 remaining before intermission. Following a PHS-fumbled punt late in stanza three, Calhoun crossed goal in 3 plays to cut our lead to 16–14; right after that with 7:00 showing to play, a critical fumble followed by a spearing penalty gave Calhoun momentum and a 12-yard TD pass on first down giving them a 22–16 win. A week later, on September 13, *Rome News-Tribune*'s Sunday morning sports page headlined, "Dragons Nip Eagles, 13–12." An ill-advised Eagle forward pass at their own 5-yard line was picked off by Dragon defensive end Greg Hancock who danced for 6 points; Greg Earle drop-kicked point after for a 7–0 lead at 1:25 mark of quarter one. Just before halftime, a short visitor punt enabled QB Brian Griffin to find Mark Wheeler on a 22-yard flag pattern for 6 points and a 13–0 advantage. Starting third Coosa came out determined and marched downfield to score on a short run but missed point after try. At 6:44 of period four, CHS used a dozen plays to drive 80 yards to score when QB Potts hit McClain on a 13-yard TD strike as time expired. A good PAT kick would tie, but Jack Jones and staff chose a 2-point conversion to win. The play choice was not unexpected—a sweep right with RB Eric Dupree, our D met and stopped him 2 feet short of goal for Pepperell's first 1981 victory 13–12. Dave Stager starred on defense recording 14 individual tackles. It was a "picture-perfect" evening in Polk County when Lindale visited on Friday night, September 25—at least it was for the "University of Cedartown" because they "buried" us 43–0. They led 29–0 at intermission while giving us only 1 first down, no passing yards, and 25 yards rushing. Red and Black added 14 more points after half. Calhoun, Whatley, Burger, Gammage, and Beavers were more than we could handle and probably marked them a dominant force in Region 7-AAA. Labron Newberry managed 64 yards for the Dragons. It did not get much better next Saturday night in Barron where Carrollton High School jumped to a 14–0 lead in opening quarter and then added 2 more TDs after halftime to win 27–12. PHS played tough with Labron Newberry, plunging past goal at 7:01 mark of quarter two, giving them a smaller lead 14–6; a deceptive 36-yard hook-and-lateral, Griffin to Earle to Newberry, brought the ball close in for Lebron's run. Lastly, Randy Jackson's 7-yard touchdown scamper with 2:06 remaining capped an 11-play march to goal for a final of 27–12. On a night when Jackson carried 22 times for 117 yards, Coach Cornett said, "We held our own physically...but we just didn't have the speed to keep up with the likes of Carrollton." Nor its vaunted Notre Dame Box, which featured a variety of misdirection plays. In a rare Friday-night Barron Stadium contest, Paulding County "plowed" past Pepperell 28–6; a slow drizzle that threatened to spoil the evening stopped 5 minutes deep into play. Maybe a wet field could have slowed the Patriots some, for they "ripped" our defense for 358 yards rushing. Our only points came in frame two when Randy Jackson swept right end from 8 yards out. An ensuing on-side kick failed which *Rome News-Tribune* thought was a pivotal play. In a battle for last place in Region 7-AAA, Cass and Pepperell met on Friday, October 16, in Bartow County with the Colonels prevailing on homecoming night 24–14. A 36-yard field goal with 4:51 to go before intermission and a 32-yard TD strike from Ivan Carter (he totaled 216 passing yards) to Hight made it 9–0 at halftime. Blue and Gold upped it to 16–0 in frame three; however, we "bucked-up" after that when Brian Griffin threw a 21-yard TD to Greg Earle. Then Randy Jackson intercepted, and three snaps later, Charlie Ball plunged over from the two. A Griffin-to-Wheeler pass was good for 2 points, which narrowed the lead to 16–14. But Cass answered with another long march and score with 7:33 remaining. Defensively PHS was led by Mark Wheeler with 8 individual tackles and 1 interception; seniors Dave Stager and Earle added 6 take downs and 3 assists. Two weeks later in Summerville's Little Big Horn Stadium, Chattooga celebrated a 43–12 victory over Pepperell; the October 30 affair also witnessed quarterback Kip Allen break Phil Baker's 11-year-old season passing mark of 1,521 yards. The tall, slender junior completed 11 of 17 for 222 yards to total 1,582. Randy Jackson led his team with 116 ground yards on 15 carries and a touchdown in period three; senior Michael Barwick scored on a 15-yard run with 18 seconds remaining. Monday's November 9 write-up in *News-Tribune* began with, "It was a game that Pepperell thought it had in the bag." Yet after 48 minutes plus 1 overtime, the visiting Rockmart Yellow Jackets prevailed 22–21. Lindale jumped ahead early when QB Bryan Griffin threw 24 yards to Van Vaughn for a touchdown; freshman Tom Curry toed first of 3 PATs for a 7–0 advantage. David High scored on a short plunge with 7:54 left before half to tie 7–7. Following intermission, Griffin once again hit Vaughn, this time for 8 yards and a TD; Curry converted for a 14–7 edge. The Polk Countians did not give up and tallied 6 points as quarter three ended; however, point after was no good, leaving PHS up 14–13. With 1:19 showing in quarter four, the game was essentially over after Randy Jackson ran 11 yards to goal. Curry nailed his third PAT for a 21–13 advantage. But it was not over as RHS received and returned to midfield where they promptly mixed runs and passes to score with 14 seconds left. As Park Street fans looked on in disbelief, a 2-point conversion pass tied it at 21–21. In overtime, Pepperell penetration of the ball stopped at yard line 45 while Rockmart moved 8 yards deeper to a 22–21 victory. The highlight of the evening, at least for Lindale, was the crowning of Ms. Angel Carnes as 1981 homecoming queen. The senior excelled at PHS as a basketball and football cheerleader, Christian Council, class favorite, Projects Committee, Who's Who, Thespian Society, and Teen Board.

Ms. Marsha Jordan was crowned homecoming queen; her accomplishments were many including marching band captain, Nutrition Council, concert band, Honor Society, class officer, Projects Committee, Governor's Honor, student council, Miss Pepperell Court, Who's Who, and Optimist Youth Award.

1982 Season

In the second week of March, Coach C. B. Cornett welcomed fifty-eight players, half of which were sophomores, to spring training 1982. A scrimmage took place on March 19 versus Darlington where a Pepperell short punt and a long pass completion allowed the Tigers to come away with a 12–0 victory. The Dragons' second-year coach was pleased with his defense but disappointed in overall strength and speed; we threw eighteen times and caught five for fifty-one yards; rushing was held to less than a hundred yards.

In the third week of August, Georgia High School Athletic Association reclassification once again placed Pepperell in Triple-A, which falls between 550 to 874 average daily attendance. Three days before opening game in Bremen on Friday, August 27, Coach Cornett told *News-Tribune*, "We'll be very, very young…They worked hard all summer…We will do a lot better than a lot of people think we will We'll be a surprise." Conversely the local writers did not agree reporting on August 24 that "things don't look much better for this year," especially since losing top player RB/LB Randy Jackson, who transferred to East Rome. Furthermore, Lindale was showing a minus record every year since Scott Green's squad recorded a 6–4 slate in 1975. When PHS de-bused in Bremen, they were 21-point underdogs and lost 40–0; we also lost total yardage 323 to 41 and first downs 24 to 4. Gold and White attempted 15 passes, completing 4 for 35 yards; meanwhile, Larry Weatherington's crew scored once in period one, 3 more times before intermission, and twice in quarter four. Coach Cornett said afterward, "We came down to play our young kids and that was what we did." A home game played in Coosa stadium on Friday, September 3, resulted in a 23–6 loss to Northwest Whitfield. Although NW logged 271 yards, PHS coaches were pretty much pleased that we reached 155. But for an interception and fumble, the contest could easily have been much closer. Freshman Carl Hammond ran for 34 yards on 6 carries; Todd Maxwell added 31 yards with 16 totes. Van Vaughn and Mark Wheeler were cited for their defense. Whitfield were no slouches, for they recorded an 11–2 season with close losses to Adairsville and Buford. The biggest game of the year featured Model versus Pepperell at Barron for the thirty-second annual Shrine Classic on Saturday night at 8:00 p.m. The unscored on Devils were 14-point favorites by virtue of winning 4 straight years and 9 of last 10. Coach Cornett put the game squarely on his offensive line, saying, "We haven't had very much line play…it will be the key to the game." Inside positions were manned by center Todd Wheeler. Joe LaRue and Wilson Couey were guards. Barry Williams and Ronnie Baldwin were at tackle spots. This game would be 1 of 14 played this year in venerable Barron Stadium which PHS used mostly as a home venue. Shannon could not breathe easily until a late interception sealed their 13–7 win. Trailing 13–0 at intermission, Lindale began a comeback following a fumble recovery by senior Gary Bryant at midfield. With 16 seconds showing in third, sophomore QB Todd Maxwell threw "a floater" to Van Vaughn, who took it to goal from 20 yards out, which were the first points allowed by Model this season. Maxwell booted point after. With 1:12 left in period four, a fumbled punt was claimed by PHS senior Pat Bagley on Model's 34; Maxwell, who was playing with an injured hand, immediately hit Vaughn for 13 yards. Unfortunately, his next throw was intercepted by Johnston. Although Lindale threw for 104 yards, the game difference actually rested with Blue's ability to stifle our rush offense which showed minus 9. In West Rome's 65–0 victory over Pepperell Saturday night, September 18, in Barron, public address announcer Lee Mowry identified many of the Chieftain's playmakers: Tyrell Wofford, Keith Green, David McCluskey, Eric Floyd, Emory Chatman, Rob Monford, Tim Glanton, and William Kent were primarily responsible for 390 yards rushing and 48 passing. The above group received and scored in 11 seconds; it did not help that Gold and White threw 6 interceptions and fumbled twice. Well, preparations for upcoming game on September 25 were a little different for PHS because Calhoun had lost a game whereas all other previous opponents were undefeated. At present, Gordon County's Bees were sitting at 4–1, much better than last year when their sole victory was 22–16 over Pepperell. Dragons' coaches seemed confident our kids would be mentally ready for this battle; two freshmen, running back Carl Hammond and safety/RB Mike Dublin, had received praise for recent performances as had upperclassmen Van Vaughn and Mark Wheeler. However, the Yellow Jackets extended Pepperell's losing streak to 11 straight with a 20–0 shutout on Saturday night in Barron. Statistics pretty much told the outcome; we fumbled 5 times and threw 2 interceptions while gaining 40 rushing yards and 100 passing. Although Calhoun ran up 252 offensive yards, they dribbled the oblong ball on 4 occasions themselves. It seemed PHS could not sustain a ground attack, for Mike Dublin led with 24 yards on 7 carries.

A visit 12 miles south to Cedartown was next up for winless Lindale. On Friday, October 1, John Hill's top-ranked Class AAA squad used a "powerful offense and a strong defense" to win 51–0. If published statistics are correct, Pepperell fumbled 10 times, threw 2 interceptions, rushed for minus 12 yards while making 2 first downs. John Hill's Bulldog machine ran up 425 total yards of offense; our biggest play of the night was Van Vaughn's 74-yard pass reception. In a home game played Friday night, October 8, at Coosa stadium, Gold and White faced Black and Gold or a squad they had never beaten; Carrollton came in ranked fifth in the state and a prohibited 27-point favorite. Although they won 35–12, Coach Cornett was mostly pleased with his squad for allowing only 69 first-half yards to the Notre Dame Box. However, they compensated by throwing 2 touchdown passes before halftime and led 21–6. With 1:20 remaining before intermission, Dragon Gary Bryant recovered a fumble at his own 34; quarterback Mike Googe quickly hit Mark Wheeler for 20, 12, and 28 yards. The last went for a touchdown, which cut our deficit to 14–6. Pepperell's other score occurred with only 3:41 left following another fumble recovery. Googe threw 34 yards to Wheeler down close, and 2 snaps later, senior James Garmon bulled over as it ended 35–12. The legendary Charlie Grisham recorded his 248th career victory. On Friday night, October 15, we returned to Alabama Road and faced Coosa on their homecoming night; it was a battle of "beatens" for CHS was 0–6 and PHS was 0–7. We had not won since downing them 13–12 4 games into 1981. Coach Cornett saw some maturity developing in his football team; he cited skilled players Mike Googe, Mark Wheeler, Carl Hammond, and Michael Dublin as well as linebacker Barry Williams and end Bradley Wilkins for excellent effort. However, our old bugaboo of fumbles and penalties led to a 36–6 loss. Winning coach Jack Jones was proud of the win but said, "Both ball blubs played sloppy and referees were flag-happy." Again, statistics told the tale as PHS gained 101 total yards with 6 first downs, fumbled on 3 occasions and committed 12 infractions. Meanwhile, Coosa netted 274 total yards but coughed it up 4 times to go with 8 penalties. Dragon Carl Hammond scored on a 20-yard sprint with 2:32 left to play; Mark Wheeler rushed for 24 yards on six carries. This all-around athlete began playing some quarterback 2 games ago and continued to do so Friday night; Bradley Wilkins helped the offense with 2 receptions for 51 yards. It was Pepperell homecoming on Friday night, October 30, at Barron where 1 squad would try for first season victory while another attempted a winning season for the first time in 13 years (8–2 in 1969). For Lindale to be victorious, they must stop Cassville's QB Ivan Carter who was first in passing and sixth in rushing (580 yards) for Region 7-AAA. Cass entered as a 16-point favorite and covered the spread plus 4 with a 28–8 win. On this Halloween eve, Ivan Carter proved to be as good as reported; he threw 25 forward passes, completing 10 for 192 yards (James Schmick caught 4 for 124 yards) and 2 touchdowns in addition to rushing for 56 yards on 6 carries. PHS trailed 20–0 at intermission but took advantage of a bad punt snap in quarter three to score; from 9 yards out, Googe hit Wheeler for a score. He then hit him again for 2-point conversion. Other than a Wilson Couey interception, there weren't many highlights for a defense that surrendered 367 yards. Offensively, freshman Carl Hammond ran 17 times for 61 yards. On a lighter note, 1982 homecoming was a success. Ms. Christina Marie Roberts was crowned queen at halftime. Page

117 of Dragon yearbook 1983 revealed Marie excelled in cheerleading (captain and cocaptain), cross-country, Miss Pepperell Court, Governor's Honors, top 10 percent of the class, baseball manager, Math League, junior and senior Honor Society, class favorite, yearbook staff, class president, student council, Who's Who, and Best All Around. Our season ended in Summerville on Friday night, November 5, where Chattooga came in at 1–8 and finished with a 28–0 victory over Pepperell. Again, the statistics pretty much tell the tale. Chattooga's offense gained 313 yards while PHS mustered 97; they more than doubled us in first and tens, 16–7. We fumbled twice and threw 2 interceptions. No Dragon player was mentioned in Sunday write-ups.

Jeffrey Lynn Hunnicutt Sr.

On Tuesday, January 25, 1983, *Rome News-Tribune* sports editor Kerry Yencer announced to the Pepperell nation that Lynn Hunnicutt had been named head coach in Lindale. The former Pepperell star (1966–1969) came from Fitzgerald City School where he piloted that program for seasons 1981 and 1982. It was not considered a homecoming as such because "I've moved around all my life." First, there was eight years in Macon; eight in Alabama; Rome area, 3; Athens, 4; Warner Robins, 8; Fitzgerald, 2; and now a return to South Floyd County. Nevertheless, it was definitely a returning home for wife, Margie Moss Hunnicutt, who was a Cedartown native. As soon as replacements were found for his coaching position and business education classroom responsibilities, the couple would settle in Lindale with sons Jeff, five, and Greg, two. Lynn understood bringing Pepperell athletics back to respectability was a tremendous challenge, and it would take time. However, "there is interest. They [the community] want to turn the program around."

Jeffrey Lynn Hunnicutt was born in Macon on February 21, 1951, to World War II veteran Second Lieutenant Dewey Clangman Hunnicutt (1921–2004) and Mary Elizabeth Carter (1922–2004). Mr. Dewey was a railroad man who moved his family along with him. After Lynn completed third grade in South Georgia, the family, which now numbered five children (Judy, Gary, Dane, Lynn, and Beth), relocated 125 miles west to Opelika, Alabama; it was here that remaining elementary and middle school terms were completed. In the first part of freshman year, Lynn worked part-time jobs at Jordan-Hare Stadium, hawking Cokes and later renting seat cushions to Auburn fans. At Christmas of 1965, the Hunnicutts transferred to Lindale where they established residence at 107 Hawthorne Street in Rosemont Park. In a new fall term of 1966–'67, it did not take long for Dragon coaches to realize the now sophomore athlete could be special. In back-to-back January 1967 wins versus Cartersville and Coosa basketball squads, *News-Tribune* reported, "Last year's freshman transfer Lynn Hunnicutt was a demon on the boards for the 10th grader hauled down 15 misses…in the Coosa win he claimed 14 rebounds." Following 3 varsity years as a multisport letterman, Lynn Hunnicutt graduated Pepperell in 1969; by this time, he was a highly sought-after football receiver who was offered and accepted a scholarship to UGA where he excelled as a tight/split end for Vince Dooley. As playing time increased, Coach Dooley noted that "Lynn is one of our most consistent and reliable athletes…and is not only a good pass receiver but also a sure tackler…he is dedicated and one of the most reliable players I have ever coached." After 4 outstanding athletic years in Athens, in addition to maintaining a 3.0 GPA, he was named permanent captain of the 1972 Bulldog offensive squad. Soon, an offer was extended and accepted from Houston County's Warner Robins High School AD and HC Robert Davis to tutor offensive linemen. Coach Davis's Demons would win a mythical national championship in 1976 with Lynn on board. In 1981, as a 31-year-old assistant, he interviewed at Pepperell following the resignation of Frank Pinson. Instead, the former alumnus decided to accept a first head coaching position in Fitzgerald, Georgia; 2 years later, his alma mater called again.

Coach Lynn Hunnicutt with his first playoff quarterback Jamie McCord

1983 Season

Going into their third week of spring practice on Monday, March 7, Pepperell's coaching staff had been working with 90 "young hopefuls." So far, there had been little attrition, which was heavy with freshmen and sophomores. Our first-year coach was getting to know his kids, saying, "It's been pleasant up to this time; we've been real satisfied." He added, "This is a team that has one senior listed on the top of the offensive depth chart and four or five on defense… It'll be a year of reconstruction and restructuring." Junior Mike Googe was running first at quarterback; he was teamed with junior Chuck Abney and senior Kenneth Huckaby in the backfield. Abney was a wide receiver/safety "with speed and great hands and is an honor roll student." Huckaby was a tough tailback who would benefit from guard Greg Dobbins, tackle Todd Wheeler, and tight end Mitchell Locklear's ability to open running holes. On defense, Wilson Couey, Larry Cook, and Danny Franks were making strides; Joel Dillingham, Lee Fortune, David Swanson, and Tom Curry were secondary prospects. A multiple scheme would be "well-balanced" and would play to players' strengths. A scrimmage game was scheduled for this Friday, March 11, versus Coosa on Alabama Road. And on a bitterly cold night, 350 fans watched as JV and varsity lost 14–0 and 30–7 respectively. In the first varsity 30 seconds, Chuck Abney broke a middle trap for an 83-yard TD sprint; Alan Kelley converted point after for a 7–0 lead. We rushed 28 more times, but a swarming CHS defense gave us only 73 more yards. Meanwhile, big running backs and a good passing game put them in front 22–7 at intermission en route to victory.

A New Stadium for the Dragons

Although our football team used Barron Stadium as a home venue, we actually play ten games on the road each year. But according to Floyd County Board of Education minutes of March 2, 1983, this was about to change. A feasibility study by Georgia Education Department approved building new PHS structures on its current location. Previously West Point Pepperell had given Floyd a five-year option on thirty-two and a half acres located south and west of current owned land; this parcel, which was free of charge, must be used solely for school purposes. On August 3, Superintendent Dr. Nevin Jones requested and received deeds from Mr. Richard Wolfe. On March 7, 1984, site work for a new Pepperell athletic facility was completed, and bids for the new stadium were advertised. They were received on-site March 20 and consisted of the following:

B&S Construction	$371,823.50
Double Diamond Construction Co.	$391,843.00
J. O. Kendrick & Associates	$439,515.00
Snider Development Company	$359,651.00

The board gave the contract to B&S Construction. McCord Enterprises submitted the only bid for tree removal at $2,983; the timber money was received, and according to B&S, work would begin immediately with 120 workdays specified.

One hundred and sixty-five days after spring scrimmage, *Rome News-Tribune*'s eighteenth annual edition of "Pigskin Preview" filled paper boxes in Northwest Georgia. Lindale was well represented on the first-team all-area defensive squad with Todd Wheeler "anchoring" a spot. Defensive end Wilson Couey, linebacker Kenneth Huckaby, and safety Chuck Abney were designated as "others to watch."

In 1983, PHS began a team tradition of pregame meals at Hotchie Millican's restaurant located in company-owned former Knights Department Store building. Bremen High School came to our homesite Barron Stadium on Saturday night, August 27. They were fresh off an 11–2 campaign that included Region 6-A championship and "whipped" visiting Pepperell 40–0 last year. However, we were ready and prepared on this night, for earlier, with support from boosters and others, our Dragons spent a week at football camp in West Georgia University facilities. Seventy-two players got off the bus there, including thirty-three freshmen. If not for this sequestering, Coach Hunnicutt said, "We would not have been ready." And ready we were, for Pepperell won 14–6! Or as *Rome News-Tribune* reported on Sunday, "The drought ended Saturday night…and a new era is ushered in." In quarter one, Wilson Couey caused their punt returner to fumble inside the red zone where Terry Wheeler recovered; 7 plays later, QB Googe hit David Swanson for a short 4-yard TD. Lance Hulsey's conversion made it 7–0. Bremen scored 6 points just before intermission, but we retained our edge 7–6. Turnovers carried period three, but early in stanza four, PHS started a 58-yard drive that ended when backup quarterback Glenn Atkins sprinted left and hit Todd Maxwell for a 5-yard TD with 10:06 showing. Apparently Blue defense did not notice he was left-handed; Hulsey toed point after for a 14–6 advantage. Bremen received and flew down the field but self-destructed at our red zone with fumbles on 3 consecutive center-quarterback exchanges. After we punted it out to midfield, there was 42 seconds remaining. *News-Tribune* reported on Sunday morning, "An incomplete pass, a one-yard gain, a penalty and a no-gainer found them still at mid-field and it ended there with players and fans streaming onto the playing field." This win was costly, however, for QB Mike Googe was lost for the season with a leg stress fracture. "That really hurts," Coach Hunnicutt said. "We feel comfortable with Glenn as replacement there but Mike was also one of our better defensive players at strong safety." A few days before going to Tunnel Hill as 7-point underdogs, Carl Hammond and Todd Maxwell earned a spot on the weekly Honor Roll for their previous week performances. A very good (8–3 season record) Northwest Whitfield squad won out 25–0 on September 2; they scored on opening drive and converted a 22-yard field goal for 10 points at intermission, but it was talented QB Greg Hargis who put the game away in period three with a 22-yard TD run. Coach Hunnicutt was disappointed in our overall intensity and enthusiasm, which we must have to win. We were favored by a field goal on September 10 against Model in the thirty-sixth annual Shrine Classic. Although Namon Wiseman's Blue Devils were 0–2, former Dragon Lynn Hunnicutt understood the significance of Shrine play and was worried about their quickness and misdirection-type Wing-T offense. Wiseman noted Pepperell was playing several young kids, which helped team morale. Lindale had not defeated Shannon since 1977. After Model scored early, it was all Pepperell 20–13 in Barron Stadium. Or perhaps it was all Carl Hammond for the 155-pound sophomore RB carried 29 times for 106 yards and tallied all 3 touchdowns (he also made 8 tackles with 6 assists on defense). Senior cornerback Joel Dillingham helped Carl's chances with 3 interceptions. Thirteen seconds into quarter four, and Pepperell leading 20–7, Kenneth Finley picked off an Atkins pass and returned it 78 yards. Then Model caused a turnover near midfield with 2:38 to play, which caused some consternation on the Dragon sideline; however, not to worry, for Todd Wheeler and Joel Dillingham made back-to-back plays of a QB sack and an interception to win by 7. *News-Tribune*'s Kerry Yencer praised the slender DB on Sunday morning, saying, "Catching three passes for 28 total yards is usually not a reason for jubilation but three interceptions in 48 minutes are exemplary. It's like opposing quarterbacks are using Joel for target practice." West Rome is a top-tier team in Georgia prep circles; in the 1980s, so far they had recorded a 34–1–1 record. Rome's media observed that "they are bigger, stronger and faster than anything Pepperell can line up." On September 16, we had some success throwing, but early mistakes and turnovers plagued us against this top-notch Chieftain 11—final score on Friday night in Barron was 42–0. In week five, Pepperell was a homecoming opponent in Gordon County. Although our good effort was in a 21–12 loss, Calhoun coach Jerry Smith was still pondering how a well-prepared Dragon squad almost came back and won, for his squad did a poor job of blocking shooting linemen and linebackers. Smith credited his wide game as decisive in winning. On opposite sideline, Coach Hunnicutt thought his squad played well until they "ran out of steam" late. He said later, "Calhoun was better than I thought." Our next opponent was as good as advertised. Most staff members believed Cedartown would be our toughest game to date; they were a major power in the area and "rolling pretty good." If not for 2 upset losses to Dalton in '81 and '82, they could have claimed state championships. Polk County's Dawgs led 22–7 at intermission and added 20 more markers afterward to win, going away 42–7. Although PHS ground game was stymied, we had some success throwing as witnessed by a 42-yard TD pass by Atkins to Chuck Abney with 10:02 left in stanza two. In 1983, we seemed to be competing against squads with outstanding QBs. Carrollton triple-threat John Driver was a talented Notre Dame tailback, who scored on a 75-yard punt return, threw a nine-yard TD pass, and kicked 5 extra points in the Trojans' 35–7 victory over Pepperell. On September 7 in Carroll County, Lindale played pretty well; statistics showed 199 total yards for CHS versus 194 for PHS. However, 2 interceptions and a fumble probably cost us points. Trojan headman and Cullman, Alabama, native Charlie Grisham would finish his career with a 261–69–13 record; his tenure spanned parts of four decades (1958–1986) with 5 state championships and 16 region crowns. Next up was Coosa at Barron Stadium. They featured 3 large running backs returning to a squad that beat us 3 touchdowns in spring scrimmage. In a complete turnaround on October 14, Coach Jack Jones's visiting team threw for 236 passing yards while holding our aerial game to less than 40. Coosa's secondary caught 4 of our throws in a 35–14 victory. Pepperell's Carl Hammond rushed for 95 yards on 20 carries while Todd Maxwell led receivers with 27 yards. A much-needed off week allowed 2–6 Pepperell to rest before traveling to Cassville. We got off the bus as 19-point underdogs on October 28. Once again, an outstanding quarterback, who at one time led Region 7-AAA in rushing and passing, carried his team to victory 41–20. Senior QB Ivan Carter carried 9 times for the length of a football field; as there was no need to throw, their run game totaled 3 times that distance. Kenneth Huckaby scored 2 short touchdowns, and Hammond broke a 61-yarder in period four to account for Dragon points. In 1983, Cassville fielded their best football team with a 6–0 Region mark before being upset 28–0 by Marist in the first round of state.

Chattooga County was a narrow favorite on November 5 in Barron; they more than covered the line with a 32–20 victory over Pepperell, leaving both squads at 2–8. Running back Tony Adams accumulated 194 yards rushing with 3 TDs; PHS quarterback Glenn Atkins also put on a show with scoring passes of 14 and 15 yards to David Swanson and another short throw to

Kenneth Huckaby. In the meantime, Carl Hammond kept their defense honest with runs of 6, 14, 12, 8, and 7 yards. A halftime highlight was when Ms. Holly Lynn Mazurek was crowned queen for 1983. Holly had excelled in band, majorette, FHA, FCA, Science Club president, Projects Committee, class secretary, Dragon Tales, Miss Pepperell contestant, varsity basketball cheerleader, Who's Who, senior superlative, concert band, and Drama Club. Prior to the Chattooga game, Coach Hunnicutt recognized his 6 seniors for their effort in reestablishing our football program; they were Ricky Bonds, Wilson Couey, Keith Shelly, David Swanson, Kenneth Huckaby, and Joel Dillingham. When the dust had settled on the 1983 season, several Lindale kids were recognized by sportswriters; 250-pound junior tackle Todd Wheeler was listed as first team on *RNT* all-area offense. Honorable mention selectees were QB Glenn Atkins, RBs Carl Hammond and Chuck Abney, split end Todd Maxwell, and tight end David Swanson.

1984 Season

Second-year coach Lynn Hunnicutt told sportswriter Kerry Yencer on March 8 that his kids "understand the system more, are a little stronger and carry more size than last season." An 8-man front on defense had been installed with more stunts and quickness to help our secondary, which gave up too much yardage last year. The return of cornerback Tom Curry and safety Mike Googe would help tremendously as would the added poundage of linemen Wheeler, Dobbins, Shiflett, Kelley, and O'Neal; this group weighed in an average of 225 pounds. Spring practice began mid-February with a roster of 125 candidates, counting freshmen; through normal attrition, this had been trimmed to 90—still a sizable number. Although there was a good group of sophomores, the coaches were looking for senior leadership from Abney, Wheeler, Maxwell, Wilkins, Franks, Clark, Cook, and Dowdy. Spring scrimmage took place in Gordon County on Friday, March 16, where Calhoun scored in quarters one and three to lead 12–0; we fought back with 3:11 remaining when Todd Maxwell raced 61 yards for a TD; point after was unsuccessful, and the game ended 12–6. A month later, Mr. Yencer printed word of a new stadium in Lindale. For several months now, local media people and others had referred to Lindale as homeless Pepperell or Floyd County's team. On top of this good news was GHSA's new classification that dropped us down one notch to Class AA. Now PHS would align in Region 7 South; nevertheless, the schedule would still be daunting with Cartersville, Carrollton Central, Haralson, Rockmart, and Villa Rica.

In late August, *Rome News-Tribune* picked potential 1984 all-area players. SE Todd Maxwell and tackle Todd Wheeler were first-team offense; others to watch were QB Glenn Atkins, RB Carl Hammond, and safety Mike Googe. It also noted that 52 area players from 17 local high schools were contributing to collegiate squads. On the last day of August, we visited Pickens County and received this headline on Sunday morning: "Pepperell Plummets Pickens." A final score of 30–0 happened when we scored in every quarter with TD runs of 7, 4, 2, and finally Todd Maxwell's 48-yard sprint; Terry Wheeler, John Allen, and Mike Earle played well on offense, but the surprise for Pickens was 255-pound Todd Wheeler lining up at fullback (à la 1971 PHS graduate Randy Johnson) where he scored twice and rushed for 58 yards. When asked about this later, Coach Hunnicutt explained that Todd was as fast as our other backs and had a good hand-eye coordination also. The FB quick trap ended up being very productive in 1984. On defense, senior Brett Brumbelow drew notice while Danny Franks had 5 tackles, 6 assists, and a fumble recovery; Corey Osteen made 5 tackles with a like number of assists. RB/tackle Todd Wheeler contributed 11 tackles, a sack, and 2 fumble recoveries.

Next up were the West Rome Chieftains who had won 34 straight victories and consecutive state crowns. Pepperell coaches believed Green and White was the best team in Georgia regardless of classification. We were 24-point underdogs on September 7 in a game played at Coosa field. WR covered that line and more with a 36–0 victory. Although we "hit them good," their team speed was too much to overcome. Seven days later, PHS again played a game on Alabama Road where Coosa dominated us 20–8 while rushing for 336 yards. We tallied late when Glenn Atkins hit Mike Earle with an 8-yard TD pass. It did not help that Googe, Hammond, and Wilkins were out with injuries. Tom Curry continued his excellent punting with a 40-plus average.

Everybody in media chose Model by 4 points in next week's annual Shrine Game in which Blue held a 19–11–3 advantage. Originally (1948), Darlington and Notre Dame schools were event opponents. Going back a ways, Lindale and Shannon were competing mill villages in Textile baseball. After both teams were paid expenses, all money collected was used for crippled children. On Friday, September 21, 1984, sports editor Kerry Yencer provided his readers with a win-loss ledger:

1951	Model, 13; Pepperell, 6 (not a Shrine Game)
1952	Pepperell, 14; Model, 9
1953	Model, 16; Pepperell, 0
1954	Model, 20; Pepperell, 7
1955	Pepperell, 13; Model, 0
1956	Pepperell, 8; Model, 6
1957	Pepperell, 19; Model, 13
1958	Model, 7; Pepperell, 6
1959	Model, 26; Pepperell, 12
1960	Model, 21; Pepperell, 0
1961	Pepperell, 26; Model, 6
1962	Model, 27; Pepperell, 0
1963	Pepperell, 13; Model, 6
1964	Model, 14; Pepperell, 6
1965	Model, 0; Pepperell, 0 (tie)
1966	Pepperell, 8; Model, 7
1967	Model, 7; Pepperell, 7 (tie)
1968	Model, 7; Pepperell, 7 (tie)
1969	Pepperell, 21; Model, 14
1970	Pepperell, 28; Model, 13
1971	Model, 14; Pepperell, 0
1972	Model, 35; Pepperell, 0

1973	Model, 13; Pepperell, 7
1974	Model, 7; Pepperell, 6
1975	Model, 20; Pepperell, 15
1976	Model, 14; Pepperell, 3
1977	Pepperell, 7; Model, 0
1978	Model, 40; Pepperell, 12
1979	Model, 29; Pepperell, 0
1980	Model, 47; Pepperell, 6
1981	Model, 20; Pepperell, 0
1982	Model, 13; Pepperell, 7
1983	Pepperell, 20; Model, 13

When Lynn Hunnicutt came to Lindale in 1983, Shannon's dominance on West Third would diminish. On Sunday morning, September 23, *Rome News-Tribune* highlighted, "ABNEY LEADS DRAGONS TO 20–7 SHRINE GAME WIN." To say the game was a spirited affair is an understatement. First, Todd Maxwell caught a twenty-five-yard strike from Atkins; Model's Allen quickly matched that on a like TD run. Tempers began to flare following intermission, and with the score tied 7–7 late in period three, "another major penalty" on Model caused fighting to break out. Order was restored, but both elevens' hackles were up. With possession at midfield, Atkins hit Chuck Abney for fourteen yards; a fifteen-yard penalty was tacked on, and we set up twenty-six yards away from goal. Early in quarter four, PHS had pounded inside Blue's four-yard line where Abney went over right guard for a touchdown with 10:59 to play. Leading 13–7 after an exchange of punts and a recovered fumble by sophomore John Allen, Pepperell started a ten-play drive with 4:37 showing that ended with Abney taking a handoff on fourth down from thirty-one yards out with 27 ticks left; Mike Earle converted for a 20–7 win.

Despite all 10 snaps being a run inside guard, Chuck's TD provoked another round of fisticuffs that took officials somewhat longer to quell. Glenn Atkins had a good night throwing with 9 of 14 for 92 yards; not unnoticed was Todd Wheeler's 18 carries for 76 yards, which netted him offensive honors, nor were Brett Brumbelow's 8 tackles, 4 assists and 2 caused fumbles. Coach Wiseman's Devils may have been their own worst enemy being assessed 90 yards in penalties and committing 5 turnovers. It has been a while, maybe never, since a winless East Rome squad faced a 2-2 Pepperell squad. Nevertheless, we were 9.5-point underdogs in a game to be staged at Model field. Pepperell did not play well as opposing sophomore RB William Spivey scored 3straight rushing touchdowns to put his squad up 21–0 early. At game's end, ER had logged 396 yards rushing and 119 passing. Our lone score occurred with 3:54 remaining on backup QB Jamie McCord's 25-yard TD throw to senior Terry Ray Wheeler who made an acrobatic catch. With prohibitive favorite Villa Rica coming to town (this time in Armuchee stadium) on Saturday, October 12, Lynn Hunnicutt remarked, "I don't mind playing a tough one right off the bat, but playing the top three [state Class AA ranking] is a bit much." Yet his young Dragons gave Villa all they wanted before falling 16–10; we led 3–0 at the intermission thanks to Mike Earle's 30-yard field goal at the 2:00 mark of period two, but Villa responded with 16 points in stanza three. Our last marker came with 50 seconds left in regulation with Glenn Atkins's

21-yard TD throw to Terry Wheeler; an ensuing on-side kick failed. Glenn threw for 214 yards with Wheeler catching 82 and Maxwell 73. Mike Googe returned from an injury to record 7 tackles and a fumble recovery in addition to grading 90 percent at safety. With a road trip to Cartersville upcoming on October 19, Coach Lynn told the local media that "we're more competitive; we're just not doing it in the won-loss column." Gold and White entered Friday night lights a 3-touchdown underdog; however, Rome's Sunday paper headlined on page 6B that "Pepperell Turns Hurricanes into Zephyrs [a soft gentle breeze]." It was referring to the Dragons stunning 24–17 victory over their hosts and noted we played well for 4 quarters and did not make any big mistakes. Although we trailed 10–0 at half our fortunes were about to change with 6:19 left in quarter three mark when sophomore Jamie McCord recovered an end zone fumbled punt to narrow the deficit at 10–7. With 1:42 left in third, PHS needed only 5 plays to inch ahead thanks to an apparent defensive busted coverage which enabled Atkins to throw a 47-yard TD strike down the middle to TE Mike Earle; his PAT pushed it to 14–10. A few minutes later, Earle also toed a 27-yard field goal to make it 17–10. But an ensuing long touchdown run from scrimmage by Stevenson made it even again at 17–17; however, Jeff Rickman proceeded to answer with a 52-yard kickoff return. Five snaps later, aided by a face mask infraction, Chuck Abney "dove over" from the 3; Earle's PAT finalized it 24–17. Terry Wheeler and Earle combined for 141 receiving yards, but clutch time was Tom Curry's 4 punts averaging 41.7; his last kick rolled out almost at their goal line, essentially ending the game. Coach Hunnicutt praised his special teams, saying, "Our kicking game was awesome." Mike Googe continued his fine execution at safety with 9 tackles and 6 assists. Homecoming week opponent Central of Carrollton was replete with potential college athletes; many think Dennis Wallace, Terrance Parks, Tim Holt, and company were good enough to be region champs (West Rome would defeat them in overtime for Region 7-AA crown). Central's Lions blitzed us 38–14 (31–0 at halftime) before we recovered to play with "great effort" in the final 24 minutes. Early third period, Carl Hammond smothered a Lion fumble in red zone; 6 snaps later, Chuck Abney scored from 2 yards out. Our last points came with 7:00 left when Glenn Atkins connected with Terry Wheeler on a 46-yard TD pass. All was not unpleasant on Saturday night as Ms. Rebecca Lynn Harper was crowned Queen during halftime festivities. The senior's superlatives were Marching and Concert Band, Basketball and Football Cheerleader Captain, Science Club, Student Council, Honor Society, Baseball Manager, Top 10 percent in Class, Class President, Who's Who, Best All-Around, and Drama Club. Tough Dragons were in "firm command" 37–0 in Tallapoosa on Friday, November 2; we ran up 430 total yards versus Haralson County while holding them to a meager 142. Chuck Abney, Hammond, Dublin, and Clowers each had rushing touchdowns; Todd Maxwell added to his résumé with a TD catch while fellow WR Terry Wheeler recorded 87 yards receiving. Junior QB Glenn Atkins totaled 113 yards on 6 of 8 completions. Seven nights later in Polk County, the 4–5 Gold and White lost 15–14 via penetration in overtime. A fourth down reception gave 3–7 Rockmart enough ball advancement to win. *News-Tribune* reported on Sunday morning, November 11, that each team "put on a good show" for fans. We trailed 14–7 at intermission; however, Carl Hammond rambled 43 yards to goal early in quarter four to tie 14–14 and set up overtime. Seniors Terry Wheeler and Chuck Abney closed out their careers with 50 and 27 yards receiving. Postseason all-area accolades went to punter Tom Curry who averaged 38.2 yards;

tackle Todd Wheeler was chosen defensively this year. PHS honorable mentions were Abney, Terry Wheeler, Earle, Cook, Allen, Brumbelow, and Googe.

On college football's national signing day, February 13, 1985, Pepperell's 6-foot-3, 268-pound lineman/fullback Todd Wheeler inked with the University of Georgia. Although most fans thought the Dragon multisport (track and wrestling) athlete was headed to Athens, as late as Monday he wasn't totally sure of the college destination, for there were offers from Alabama, Auburn, Tech, Clemson, and Tennessee. Still UGA was probably a leader for some time. Todd, who was projected as an offensive guard, "drew it out" until signing day on purpose, saying, "I thought it might help some other players later if recruiters came to Lindale." With Wednesday's decision, a weight had been lifted from his shoulders. "I feel like I just lost a thousand pounds," he said. His coach, Lynn Hunnicutt, remained in the background of recruitment, but was there to offer advice if asked. Lynn's goal was "getting you into a good and stable program and set short and long term realistic objectives and dedicate toward them"—and Todd did. In a career that any athlete would envy, the business education major started 3 consecutive years and played in 36 straight games, including bowl games in 1986 (Hall of Fame), 1987 (Liberty Bowl), Gator Bowl 1988, and postseason Senior and Hula bowls. The 6-foot-3-inch, 257-pound team leader won Coffee County's Hustle Trophy and a True Grit Award for outstanding offensive play and work habits. Atlanta Touchdown Club recognized him as its top lineman. Needless to say, he was elected permanent team captain and would now be featured alongside such notable Bulldogs as Bill Stanfill, Fran Tarkenton, and Frank Sinkwitch in the yearly UGA media guide. With Wheeler as a big kid with speed in junior year, Coach Lynn Hunnicutt moved him from O line to fullback. Lynn said, "He's in 4.9 to 5.1 range on forties or as fast as our other backs." He continued, "Although Todd is an all-around athlete, he's the best long snapper from deep position I ever coached." This talent probably cost him a redshirt year in 1985 because Georgia needed him immediately.

In April 1989, Todd signed as a free agent with New Orleans where he moved from developmental squad to number three in depth chart before a broken tibia ended his career. Afterward, he finished a teaching degree and moved into high school coaching first as an assistant at Pepperell and then Model in addition to head jobs at Armuchee and Coosa. He had served all Floyd County schools with loyalty and class. Pepperell High School retired his jersey in 2020. Matthew Todd Wheeler was born on Blackweilder Lane on July 25, 1967, to Robert Marcus and Faye Don Cook Wheeler. Mom died in December of 1977 due to poor health; however, Robert lived another twenty-seven years before passing away on April 24, 2004. He was married to the former Pebbles Pace, and they had two daughters.

1985 Season

On Friday, March 15, Coach Lynn Hunnicutt told *RNT* sports editor Kerry Yencer that "it's the best spring we've had...We've got a lot accomplished." With eighteen lettermen, there was not much guesswork on this squad. That same night of his comments, a scrimmage game in Gordon County produced a 7–7 tie with Calhoun and a 19–16 victory over LaFayette. Both squads were Class AAA or one notch above PHS; although very pleased with spring game results, he qualified it afterward, "They are not West Rome."

With the help of hired contractors and a volunteer-labor program, the new Dragon Stadium field house ($318,000), press box, weight room, and concession stand were expected to be ready by fall. However, it was not ready for Pickens County on Friday, August 30, but we were in downing them 28–0 in Barron Stadium. Illya Dublin scored in quarters one and two as we took a 14–0 lead into intermission. After halftime, Robbie Cook ran for 16 and 36 yards before scooting into goal at 5:35 mark. Glenn Atkins hit Jeff Rickman with an 11-yard TD pass for final points with 9:33 showing in final stanza; Jamie McCord toed his fourth straight PAT for a 28–0 win. We pretty much dominated with 260 yards rushing, which was helped along by Pickens fumbling 7 times. A week later, West Rome coach Charles Winslette was concerned about Pepperell's size; actually his squad exceeded Lindale in that department and used their speed to win 35–0 at Barron. Running back William Kent scored twice in the first 3:16 minutes, prompting Coach Hunnicutt to say later, "I'm glad it's over with." Winslette's Chieftains were going to beat a lot of teams 35–0. Search as we might, there were no neutral fields on Friday night; consequently, the Dragons played a home game versus Coosa at Coosa. QB Chris Jenkins ran for 2 TDs and threw for another in defeating PHS 21–7. We made it interesting with 1:35 remaining when Atkins hit McCord for a 38-yard scoring toss that cut it to 14–7. After an on-side kick failed, Jenkins broke a 33-yard quarterback sneak; thus, a designated visiting team won 21–7 in their own stadium. PHS was "home" again on Barron Field on Saturday night, September 21, for Shrine Game 35. Receipts from record crowds and hoopla helped support 19 Shriner Hospitals, three Burns Institutes, as well as Scottish Rite Children's Medical Center in Atlanta. Thirty-four-year-old Randy Edwards of Lindale, whose son was a freshman for Pepperell, had served as club president and other various capacities. Randy believed his "chosen life goal" was to help heal children. Lynn Hunnicutt had played or coached in 5 events. Unlike his rival coach, Model first-year headman Tab Gable was new to Shrine Game hype. The event can sometimes overshadow gridiron play. But not for Dragon nation on Sunday morning, September 22: "DRAGONS WIN SHRINE GAME ON ATKINS-TO-RICKMAN PASS." The final score was 7–0 thanks to Atkins's 20-yard pass to Rickman who took it down his own sideline for a 73-yard catch and run midway stanza two; after McCord toed point after, there was no more excitement until Devils' quarterback Stacy Elliott started a desperation drive with 2:44 remaining. However, as they neared our red zone, Mike LeCroy sacked Elliott with 25 seconds showing; then lucky number 13, Steve Gladney, stepped in front of Elliott's twentieth forward pass for an interception and a Lindale victory. Glenn Atkins was voted offensive MVP, completing 8 of 16 for 150 yards; Jeff Rickman totaled 123 of those 150 pass yards. In Barron Stadium, October 4, there was much shouting and jubilation on Pepperell's sideline after QB Glenn Atkins connected on a 10-yard TD pass to Jeff Rickman with 7 seconds remaining. Coach Hunnicutt elected to go for a tie, and Jamie McCord's point after kick split the uprights for a 7–7 final. He said later, "They're an undefeated football team...This was for our program...We needed something positive." East Rome led 7–0 from the 6:16 mark of quarter two. And it remained a 1-touchdown game until 1:06 remained in quarter four when a high punt snap gave us possession below midfield going toward Second Avenue. From the 38, Atkins immediately looked to Rickman who was covered; he then went down the middle to McCord for 14 yards; the same pair completed another long gainer, falling out of bounds for 24 yards; next Rickman caught a toss and walked a tightrope down close to goal. Glenn was sacked, which used our last timeout; Lynn and staff called a new pass route which was put in only 5 days ago. Jeff Rickman went down and out to the left, planted, and pivoted back toward the middle as Atkins delivered a perfect TD strike. The senior receiver said later, "I turned around the loop, and nobody was there." On the other side, Dragons' nemesis from years gone by, RB William Spivey, was limited to 45 yards on 22 carries. Coach Jerry Sharp explained, "They stacked a lot of people near the line and squeezed everything to inside...We didn't do a good job on anything we did." Prep Honor Roll recognized Brad Bennett, Jeff Shiflett, and Glenn Atkins for their play. Going into week six of schoolboy football, Lindale had yet to face a team with a loss; this streak ended with a visit to 2–2–1 Villa Rica on October 11. Later, Lynn Hunnicutt marked it as the most important game in his 3-year tenure. His Dragons came from behind twice before subduing Ronnie Burchfield's Wildcats 29–28. We trailed 20–7 at intermission, but Carl Hammond caused an opening second-half fumble, which Jamie McCord recovered deep in Villa territory. "That set the tempo for the second half," said Coach Lynn Hunnicutt. And it did, for when quarter three ended, we led 21–20. Illya Dublin had a career night with TD runs of 3, 5, 50, and 3 in addition to a crucial 2-point conversion, which the coach reasoned later, "We decided to go for broke on the two-point try because our defense wasn't up to par." Pepperell's winning staff said afterward, "Villa never really stopped our offense." It credited our offensive line, which included tackles Steve Jackson and Mark Maxwell, guards John Allen and Jeff Shiflett, center Hank Jackson, and tight end Dusty Dowdy. On Friday night, October 18, Lindale hosted its first home game since 1967. Cartersville provided opposition in our new stadium sitting on 32.5 acres donated by West Point Pepperell Lindale Mill; it holds 2,500 home-side seats and 1,500 for visitors. However, weeklong hoopla and excitement took its toll, resulting in a 21–8 loss to Rodney Walker's Hurricanes. "All the fanfare took away our concentration," Coach Hunnicutt said later. We trailed 18–8 at intermission and just got whipped by a big, strong physical team from Bartow County. Pepperell fell behind 15–0 early before Glenn Atkins directed a 13-play drive to score with 4:33 left before half; he completed passes of 12, 11, 14, and 11 to Jeff Rickman before Dublin bulled over goal to make it 15–8. A field goal just before break and another in period three ended scoring at 21–8. Atkins, Hank Jackson, and Bo Langford were cited for outstanding play. The competition did not ease up the next week on a visit to Central Carrollton; they were undefeated at 7–0 while outscoring opponents 237–13. Although we lost 28–20, Lynn said, "We won the battle but lost the war." He added, "We played hard-nosed ball with great intensity and won everywhere except on the scoreboard...their speed and quickness is impressive...also the play of their QB Dennis Wallace." Robbie Cook, Illya Dublin, and Calvin Clowers rolled up 165 yards rushing while Rickman and Dowdy caught almost 100 yards in thrown passes. The Prep Honor Roll cited John Allen for 11 individual tackles and Hank Jackson who graded 97 percent at center. Back on Dragon Drive for homecoming versus Haralson County, coaches and fans hoped our "stage fright" was gone, and it was, for we downed the Rebels 27–6 on November 1. Robbie Cook and Illya Dublin put us ahead 14–0 at intermission with TD runs of 9 and 53 yards; at the 7:34 mark of quarter three, Carl Hammond "got loose" for a 28-yard sprint. Although a wet turf forced us to run inside tackle most all night, McCord ran a 54-yard option right for final points with 3:34 left. John Allen and Corey Osteen were outstanding on defense, which had gotten tougher each week. To close out a perfect night, Ms. Frona Jewel "Pebbles" Pace was crowned Homecoming Queen for 1985. Her accomplishments were many: football and basketball cheerleader including captain, perfect attendance, class officer, track, student council, yearbook staff, Miss Pepperell, Who's Who, runner-up Miss Floyd County, and Dragon Tales. On November 8, four Subregion South teams were sitting at 2–2 and battling for playoff spots; Cartersville, Villa Rica, Rockmart, and Pepperell were all still possibilities. But Friday night lights' final in Lindale was déjà vu all over again versus visiting Rockmart. Overtime games against RHS had not been kind to Pepperell as Marshelle Thaxton's Jackets claimed a 22–21 victory to go with last year's 15–14 win in extra innings. This OT turned during the first of 2 5-minute halves when "with 00:00 showing, quarterback Tommy Atha rifled a shot to his smallest receiver Corey Wood who battled a defender for possession at Pepperell's 10-yard line and won." It was deepest penetration and ultimately gave them a single-point victory 22–21. In regulation, PHS totaled 314 yards with Hammond scoring twice on short runs and Rickman catching a 15-yard TD from Atkins. Other than losing 3 fumbles to a single 1 for Rockmart, it was an even statistical game for the 4–5–1 Dragons. Shiflett, Dublin, and Atkins were mentioned on weekly Prep Honor Roll. On December 29, *Rome News-Tribune* published their all-area team with Hank Jackson listed as starting center. Honorable mention players were QB Glenn Atkins, RB Illya Dublin, end Jeff Rickman, O line Mark Maxwell, D-line Corey Osteen, and Jeff Shiflett, in addition to LB John Allen.

1986 Season

In early March, Coach Lynn Hunnicutt opened spring drills with one major goal—find a replacement for Glenn Atkins who led Region 7-AA in passing for three straight years. An heir apparent was rising senior Jamie McCord; only thing was he had been fighting flu-like symptoms and had participated in few practices; to make matters worse, backups Danny Robinson and Ken Hutchins were ailing with neck and knee injuries. But not to worry, for Lindale would be more ground oriented on offense this year due to 3 years of weight room work that had now produced several big, strong kids; this also boded well for a defense that returned almost intact. A spring scrimmage in Thomaston against R. E. Lee would determine if PHS could compete versus quick teams at their place. Despite losing 17 pounds recently, McCord caught the bus and passed 6 yards to TE John Allen with 39 seconds showing before halftime to tie 7–7. With 6:08 left in quarter four, R. E. Lee kicked a 25-yard field goal for a 10–7 lead. Driving 80 yards against a dwindling clock, Pepperell used 9 running plays to reach the 31-yard line where McCord ran a 12-yard keeper on third down to just inside their red zone. Three snaps later, Robbie Cook took it to goal from 16 steps out. Trailing 13–10, the Rebels moved to midfield quickly before Mike LeCroy took them out of field goal range with a quarterback sack—game over. John Allen was outstanding as he collected 13 tackles, a pass interception, fumble recovery, and a QB sack. Kevin Pruett recorded 6 tackles while LeCroy, Bennett, Shiflett, and Dublin finished with 5 each. Our offense ground out 141 yards and did not have a turnover. R. E. Lee was a very good football team in 1986 as witnessed by their 11–2 season. A year later, this group would go 14–1, losing in the finals of Class AA to Central of Carrollton.

On Tuesday, September 2, Lindale residents welcomed *Rome News-Tribune's* twenty-first annual "Pigskin Preview." Preseason all-area picks were guard Bo Langford and center Hank Jackson on offense while tackle Jeff Shiflett and cornerback Steve Gladney were picked on defense. Other players to watch were RBs Illya Dublin and Robbie Cook, tackle Todd Burkhalter, and linebackers John Allen and DB Matthew Smart. However, Kerry Yencer headlined, "Quarterback Key to Pepperell Hopes." Underneath, Coach Hunnicutt said, "We're excited. It looks pretty good; very few kids have missed workouts this summer; we have good size and the best speed we've had in a while; however, attitude is the biggest thing—it has been super." He continued to say that quarterback play would be key; Jamie had been in camps all summer and was bigger (180 pounds) and stronger; in addition, he had a really strong arm. Class AAA Rossville brought 95 players to Lindale on Friday, September 5, and lost 32–7. When a football team can successfully run, throw, catch, and commit only 2 5-yard penalties with a single turnover, the headman can be "jubilant," which was what Lynn Hunnicutt told *RNT* writer Bond Nickles after his squad thrashed a good football team. However, the visiting Bulldogs scored quickly courtesy of a Derrick Pullom 39-yard return on kickoff and Clemons's 11-yard run from scrimmage. McCord tied it with a QB sneak, and Robbie Cook scored from 5 steps out to take a 12–7 advantage. Just before intermission, McCord completed his first of 3 TD passes, this one a 17-yard strike to TE John Allen giving us an 18–7 advantage. Coming out of halftime, Allen caught his second touchdown on a slant-in to make it 25–7. A few minutes later, Illya Dublin and McCord hooked up on a well-designed screen pass for a 23-yard score. Allen, who played both ways and made 7 tackles at linebacker, said later, "We had a hard time adjusting at first…they were very fast. I guess after practicing against our freshmen all summer they looked especially swift." The Prep Honor Roll cited Allen and Brad Bennett for tackles and McCord for passing. In Summerville on Friday, September 12, Pepperell "demolished" Chattooga County 40–14, prompting Indian coach Buddy Windle to respond to Bond Nickles's question of "What would you do different?" He replied, "I wouldn't have scheduled them." An offensive line that featured three sophomores, Grodeman, Langford, and Spears, led RB Calvin Clowers to 112 yards rushing while Robbie Cook almost matched his mate with 109. Both ball carriers were on Prep Honor Roll on Wednesday. On Saturday night, September 20, "Strong legs run, so that weak legs may walk." This is the mantra of Rome Shriners who sponsor Shannon versus Lindale each year in Barron Stadium. Although Model was unbeaten, we were prohibitive favorites. Blue Devil coach Tab Gable was worried, for "they just line up and run behind big linemen." About his squad, Lynn Hunnicutt said, "We have a different type attitude than we've had in the past." Before a packed house, PHS won 34–7 to cut Model's overall series lead to 19–14–3. With 5:25 left in period one, RB Illya Dublin gave us a 7–0 lead; then McCord scored just before intermission to give us a 13–0 advantage. On our first snap after halftime, OC coach Steve Horne called Calvin Clowers's number, and he responded with a 71-yard TD run; next McCord found TE Michael Newman down the right sideline going east on a 54-yard scoring toss. Backup RB Brad Fuller's 1-yard touchdown run wrapped it up at the 1:34 mark. Clowers, Newman, and CB Matthew Smart were recognized by Prep Honor Roll on Tuesday. Prior to playing talented Adairsville on September 26, PHS was on the verge of being ranked in AP top ten of Class AA. Although Coach Hunnicutt seemed worried about their 2 backfield sprinters Marty Baker and Kerry Smith, we won 23–0. In game action, Illya Dublin carried 14 times for 79 yards while scoring on 2 short runs; backfield mate Calvin Clowers added another close-in TD and later tackled their runner behind goal for a safety. We scored 16 points in quarter four. PHS logged 20 first and tens and were forced to punt only once, which was negated by a roughing penalty. Prep Honor Roll named Shiflett, Allen, and Langford for accolades. On October 1, sportswriter Paul Marks wrote the truth, i.e., Pepperell had seldom played well versus Coosa with the 1970 come-from-behind victory being an exception. The last 2 contests had ended 21–7 and 20–8 in favor of Alabama Road; however, Gary Graves's Eagles were coming off an unemotional 14–0 loss to Darlington. Although we had allowed only 28 points all year, our staff was concerned about talented QB

Chris Jenkins throwing and running the football. Lindale came to Eagles' nest ranked number ten in Class 7-AA Associated Press poll and a unanimous pick to win; few fans can remember the last time this happened. Lindale won 14–0 behind superior line play and a mistake-free run game that produced 178 yards on 44 snaps. Our first possession saw Robbie Cook culminate a 15-play drive with a 4-yard plunge to goal; in period three, Clowers scored from 9 yards out; McCord kicked both PATs for a 2-touchdown victory. Our pass rush harassed QB Jenkins into 2-for-11 passing, 2 interceptions, and 159 yards total offense. Opposing coach Graves commented afterward that "they play as close to flawless football as you can." The weekly Honor Roll recognized DB Kevin Graves and LBs John Allen and Kevin Pruitt for their performances. West Rome was next on Friday night, October 10, in Lindale. Pepperell last defeated Green in 1968 or Coach Lynn Hunnicutt's senior season. He explained to sportswriters that "we are into the hard part of our schedule now and these games all count in sub-region standings." *News-Tribune* reporters unanimously predicted a victory for Pepperell. It did not happen, for West won 20–12. On Sunday, Paul Marks wrote that "the Dragons failed to answer their curtain call to center stage of area prep teams." With 11:07 showing in period two, Frederick Dallas skirted right end on a 20-yard TD jaunt with point after failing. Lindale responded with a 20-play drive capped off by Dublin's 3-yard run with 18 ticks left before intermission. A high snap on PAT ended quarter two at 6–6. Lightning struck on ensuing squib kick when Richard Sullivan fielded the pigskin and "disappeared momentarily in the middle phalanx of blockers and then reappeared with an open field 73 yards away." Our cover team did not maintain their lanes, assuming they would just fall on it; instead, Sullivan's play put us down 14–6 at halftime. Coach Hunnicutt bemoaned the missed PAT earlier as much as anything, saying, "We had them a little down but missed an opportunity to go ahead." In period three, PHS used 16 plays that ended with Calvin Clowers's 1-yard TD run 1 play into stanza four. A 2-point conversion pass to tie went through end Brian Corntassel's hands, leaving them with a 14–12 edge. We had 1 more possession, but a failed reverse put us in a bad field position; from there, Rolaundo Edwards intercepted McCord at the 20-yard line; RB Sullivan ran it into goal with 1:18 remaining. Coach Charles Winslette praised his squad, saying, "This is as fine a win as any of the 15 we had last year on the way to the state championship." Coach Hunnicutt said, "We've been flat at practice a couple of weeks…we've never been in a position where everybody is shooting at you." Lineman Mark Tanner and CB Steve Gladney received mention in Prep Honor Roll on October 15. Home-standing Adairsville did us no favors when they upset number-seven-ranked Carrollton Central 19–6 last Friday night, for it would surely motivate them. And the Lions were inspired to a 21–0 victory over visiting Lindale. It was an unusual game in that ground-oriented Pepperell High School threw 40 times and missed 26; junior Kevin Graves caught 8 throws for 83 yards on mostly hitch passes. It was out of necessity, for they bolted to a 3-TD lead before halftime, thanks to RB Walt Crowder's scoring runs of 41, 16, and 53 yards. Other than those plays, we played pretty well as Central barely topped us in total yards 260 to 243; we led in first downs 16 to 11 with no turnovers and few penalties. With mighty 5–1 Cartersville coming to Lindale on Friday night next, our situation was "very critical." A loss probably eliminated region playoff hopes. But on a cool, rainy October 24, "Pepperell Becalms Hurricanes 7–0." Sportswriter Bond Nickles explained on Sunday morning that "the 'Canes never penetrated Dragons territory while gaining a total of only 147 yards." Following halftime, our offense was "frustrated" after 2 failed tries inside Cartersville's 10-yard line, yet no more points were needed after McCord hit TE John Allen with a 51-yard TD strike down the home sideline late in the opening quarter. John said later, "It was a flag out which usually is a shorter route but I was open longer and Jamie put it right in there." He added, "It was rededication week for us." The two received accolades on Prep Honor Roll Thursday for throwing and catching. Pepperell's defense led by Allen's 14 tackles was cited for excellent play. Both Jerry Sharp and Lynn Hunnicutt agreed Halloween night, October 30, in Lindale between Darlington and Pepperell squads was really a playoff game with the loser staying home. A strong kicking game plus the area's top passing combination, Tim Morgan to Doug Braden, was formidable; also freshman RB Will Muschamp tallied 149 yards last week versus Haralson County. Nevertheless, Lindale won 14–7 by limiting DHS aerial game to 35 yards and forcing 2 interceptions. Gold and White defense gave up only 117 rushing yards while our runners gained 218 to go with 51 passing. Yet homecoming remained scoreless until midway of quarter three when Morgan scrambled for a 21-yard TD on third down; his run came after a controversial roughing their punter call. Down 7–0, Pepperell used 15 plays in marching 74 yards to tie; we converted 4 third downs including timely passes of 13 and 16 to SE Kevin Graves. TB Calvin Clowers, who accounted for 118 yards rushing, powered down to the 5-yard line; then on first down, QB McCord "faked beautifully" to Calvin Clowers's off tackle and scampered northward into the right corner of the goal. He tied it at 7–7 with point after kick. Darlington received an ensuing kickoff and was driving toward field goal range when Clowers forced a fumble recovered by Brad Bennett at midfield. Coach Sharp said later, "The turning play of the football game was the fumble." PHS moved quickly inside red zone where, on third and 7, Jamie McCord hit John Allen with a 17-yard pass down near goal; then with the clock winding down, it was déjà vu all over again as McCord faked once more to Calvin off right tackle and retraced his previous touchdown steps past the red flags with 9 seconds left; Lindale's west stands erupted in homecoming joy. *RNT* writer Bond Nickles's headline on Sunday morning summed it up, "McCord's Tricks Lift Pepperell to 14–7 Win." Lynn said afterward, "Darlington played our tails off, to be quite honest…but in the second half the kids did what they had to do." Four days later, Prep Honor Roll included Bennett, Clowers, and McCord. Michelle Sullins was crowned 1986 homecoming queen by last year's winner Pebbles Pace. Ms. Sullins had been a member of Projects Committee, Christian Council, Science Club, JV Football and Basketball Cheerleader, as well as Class Secretary. In Polk County Friday night, November 7, Lindale clinched a playoff berth by "pasting" nemesis Rockmart 27–0. We did it with dominating line play that netted 253 yards rushing; Calvin Clowers ran for 80, and Robbie Cook added 60. The visitors went up 21–0 with 9 seconds left in quarter two when QB McCord threw a 50-yard TD strike to SE Kevin Graves; Illya Dublin scored after intermission on a 15-yard scamper. Prep Honor Roll cited Shiflett and Clowers as well as McCord who sneaked for 1 score and was 8 of 10 passing with 1 touchdown.

On Wednesday, Bond Nickles wrote how the redheaded senior rose to Dragon quarterback. For three years, he played wide receiver and backed up Region 7-AA leading passer Glenn Atkins. Now he had "filled Glenn's shoes nicely." Although Pepperell was primarily a running team, he ranked second in total passing yards with 656 on 111 attempts with only 5 interceptions while leading in TD throws with 6. McCord's coach explained, "Offensively, he's the leader, no doubt about it...he's an intelligent ball player who makes things happen for us in clutch situations. The big games are where he's played best and excelled." Added to the job was handling placekicking chores, blocking on punting downs, and increased time at cornerback.

Unlike basketball and baseball where squads might play two or three times in a season, football the second time around can be fatal—and it was on Friday night, November 21, in Bartow County. Adairsville defeated us 24–8 using long end runs of eighty, twenty-one, and forty-six, which revenged a late September 23–0 shutout in Lindale. Coach Hunnicutt commented afterward that "we were outplayed...committed too many turnovers [five fumbles and an interception] and failed to contain end runs on defense." Despite this game, Lynn believed his program made strides this year. Pepperell lost two regular season contests, one being to four-time defending state champion West Rome and another to eventual 1986 Class AA winner Central of Carroll. When this group of seniors began ninth grade in 1983, our previous football record was 0–10.

On Sunday, February 12, *Rome News-Tribune*'s all-area football team was featured. Leading was Player of the Year John Allen, a 6-foot-2, 225-pound linebacker who led his team to 8–3 and a spot in Region 7-AA playoffs. College recruiters thought John was "one of the top, if not the top LB prospect in the South." He was deceptively fast for his size and clocked at 4.8 in the 40-yard dash to go with 350 pounds on bench press. Pepperell coach Lynn Hunnicutt praised his versatility and leadership and believed the best was yet to come. Joining John on the squad selected by area coaches was "fierce blocker" guard Jeff Shiflett at 6 feet 1, 260 pounds. The senior anchored a Dragon line that led all local schools in offense with 2,757 yards. A third member of elite eleven was our punter. Sportswriter Paul Marks described this choice: "Robbie Cook, 5-11, 170 averaged 39 yards per kick with 6 of 29 placed inside 10 steps of goal...there was a long boot of 67 yards; none of Cook's kicks were blocked and there was less than five-yard average returns." The 1986 squad also produced 3 honorable mentions including DB Steve Gladney, RB Illya Dublin, and QB Jamie McCord. At 1:00 p.m. on Wednesday, February 11, 1987, John Allen signed with UGA as parents Nancy and Robert Allen as well as many well-wishers looked on.

1987 Season

In a scrimmage game played in Lindale on March 13, host Pepperell lost to Coosa 20–9. Of more significance was GHSA eliminating spring football at least for now. Local coaches differed on this policy. West Rome's Winslette thought overall program quality would suffer. East of town, Danny Wiseman believed it would mean better baseball, track, and tennis. PHS athletic director Lynn Hunnicutt knew football receipts paid for all other sports except basketball; a "diluted caliber" of football would mean less money available for other athletics. States that did not permit practice in March–May tended to be not as good on Friday night lights as Georgia. He also noted that most clubs were finished with drills before decent spring weather began.

On August 25, Coach Hunnicutt evaluated his 1987 squad for *RNT* sportswriter Ruth Hughes. There were fourteen seniors present, but few had experience; however, a complete coaching staff returned intact with veterans Steve Horne, Jimmy Farrer, Gerald Payton, Joe Knight, and David Jones; Jamie McClendon and Ricky Naugher were in their second year. They were all excellent teachers. The same issue cited above selected a preseason all-area team, which was prefaced by Ms. Hughes's statement: "It doesn't take much to put together this team i.e., a list of top returnees, some statistics, a few coaches' suggestions, a good memory and—presto—instant all-star elevens." For Lindale WR Kevin Graves and OL Rodney Langford were chosen; defensively Calvin Clowers was at end. Honorable mentions were CB Matthew Smart, OT Mark Tanner, and RBs Illya Dublin and Brad Fuller. By the fourth week of August, two-a-day practice was over; now specialty sessions preceded afternoon workouts with multiple water breaks and cooling ice for thirst and injuries. Coach Lynn recalled, "Back in the day water breaks were rare and injuries were treated by rubbing a little dirt on it and go back to work." Another change was the elimination calisthenics; most programs now did more stretching as a group.

Pepperell boarded the ole yellow bird on September 4, 1987, bound for Walker County as a prohibitive favorite over Rossville. As they did last fall, Larry Flemming's Bulldogs scored first; however, converted running back now QB Calvin Clowers galloped 55 yards to tie 7–7 at intermission. A high punt snap into their goal netted us 2 points and a 9–6 advantage at intermission. They took a brief 12–9 lead in stanza three before Clowers dived over from close in to end scoring at 15–9. Coach Hunnicutt praised Class 7-AAA Rossville as being much stronger than last season (RHS would consolidate with Chattanooga Valley High in 1989 to form Ridgeland High School). He complimented 270-pound DL Rodney "Bo" Langford for being dedicated as he was all over the field, making 7 tackles with 2 assists. Langford and RBs Dublin and Clowers were recognized in *RNT* for their play. We were again heavy favorites next week versus Chattooga and delivered a 20–6 victory. Contained within 279 yards rushing were TD jaunts by Matthew Smart of 44 yards; Illya Dublin, 61; and sophomore Ron Robinson's 80-yarder. Pepperell tackled well on a slippery field; a key hit by CB Danny Robinson "picked our team up" after halftime. Those Dragons receiving newspaper accolades were RBs Dublin, Robinson, and Smart; Mark Roberts at center graded almost 80 percent while DB Robinson played well. In the "Strong legs run so that weak legs may walk" game on Saturday night, September 19, PHS was a solid favorite. Yet Model came in matching their opponent at 2–0, and "they are a much improved squad," according to Coach Hunnicutt. The *RNT* Sunday sports page explained later, "Elliott Bedevils Pepperell, 26–14." In a 7–7 tie game with 11:05 remaining, Blue Devil QB Stacy Elliott led his team on 3 scoring drives to win at Barron Stadium. Before a standing-room-only crowd, a roughing-the-kicker call against Pepperell tipped momentum. "Model came prepared and answered everything we did. Tonight they were the better team," Coach Hunnicutt said later. QB Ken Hutchins and receiver Kevin Graves were cited for their play. In a poll on Thursday, September 24, 3 of 5 local sportswriters picked visiting PHS over Adairsville. They were right but barely, for white-jerseyed Lindale won with a 6–2 baseball score; at 2:30 left in stanza four, Calvin Clowers, who finished with 141 rushing yards on 26 attempts, caught a wheel route pass at midfield from QB Hutchins and carried it to goal. "My coaches had been trying to get me to call it all night," reflected a happy Lynn Hunnicutt afterward. As a reminder, the play called throwback-fullback had been drawn up on a chalkboard at halftime. Chamlee Stadium's losing crowd was sullen as they filed out, for their team suffered 3 interceptions, lost 2 fumbles, shanked a 34-yard field goal, and nullified a TD run with a holding penalty.

Senior Calvin Clowers was named *RNT* offensive player of the week on Thursday next. He was joined by honorable mention teammates DB Kevin Graves, LB Tony Hall, and DT Bo Langford. A week later in Lindale, PHS was a unanimous pick to win versus Coosa.

However, it took a blocked extra point by senior CB Korey Popham with 5:19 remaining to "stifle" an Eagle comeback effort and win 7–6. The game was scoreless at intermission before RB Illya Dublin ignited a 60-yard drive culminated by QB Hutchins's 10-yard TD toss to WR Graves (the youngster also caught one of their passes) with 1:20 remaining in period three; Gary Huckaby converted PAT to lead 7–0. A huge homecoming crowd needed respirators thereafter, for we fumbled twice going in. Then Brad Fuller coffin-cornered a punt one play before "sensational sophomore" RB Eric Miller (192 yards on 23 rushes) took a handoff, got stood up by 2 defenders, shook loose, and sprinted 91 yards to score. It was time to cue Popham who had a knack for kick blocking. Afterward, a happy but drained Lynn Hunnicutt was proud of his kids for rare consecutive wins over Coosa. In complimenting Miller, he said, "If Pepperell sees a better running back than him later, we're in trouble." Thursday's *RNT* gave accolades to Popham, Dublin, Hutchins, Smart, freshman LB Tony Hall, and tenth grader William Ford. Although Pepperell had not defeated West Rome since 1968, they were favored to break Green's string of victories. Unfortunately, we were "upset" 14–7 on Friday night, October 9, at Barron. Gold and White defense performed well enough; however, "offensively, we did not block them." To wit, PHS gained only 83 total rushing yards well below their 188.1 average. In spite of that, Lindale led 7–0 at intermission, thanks to a Ken Hutchins 25-yard TD toss to freshman Ken Irvin. But following intermission, the winner's wishbone kicked in to score twice thanks to 122 yards rushing and good field position. Hutchins, Graves, Irvin, and Clowers were cited later for good play. Defending 7-AA champion Carrollton Central came visiting Lindale on October 16. Mostly because PHS had scored only 1 touchdown per game in 3 weeks past, sportswriters picked Lions' speed and quickness to win, and they did 26–0. A South Floyd crowd saw good hitting by our defense, but we came up short on 3 potential scoring drives, which prompted Coach Hunnicutt to say, "When you move up and down the field like that, dad-gummit, you've got to score." Korey Popham did his part again, blocking 3 PATs.

On occasion and when deserving, *Rome News-Tribune* features accomplishments of local athletes. On Thursday, October 22, 1987, the topic heading read, "Popham Lights Dragons Specialty Teams Attack." Beat writer David Wichard gave readers insight into Corey. He was not an imposing football player, weighing in at 165 pounds, measuring 5 feet, 10 inches with 4.9 speed, but he had an uncanny knack for affecting PAT kicks. In fact, Korey had blocked 4 and caused another to go awry. Only Adairsville had escaped his wrath. He was always stationed on the right perimeter of rush line before slicing through a gap. He told the *RNT* interviewer that "we work on it diligently in practice with Coaches Hunnicutt and Farrer." His coach explained that "he won Coosa game and gave us a chance to against West Rome." Also since the fourth game, Popham had established himself as a starter at cornerback. While playing with a broken hand in last week's contest against Carrollton Central, he made 7 tackles with 1 assist and blocked 2 kicks. Consequently, an October 23 road trip on US 411 east to Bartow County resulted in an

18–0 shutout loss to Cartersville. Statistics showed a much closer contest as PHS logged 14 first and tens to their 12; rushing yards were 165 to 142 in PHS's favor. They barely nipped us in passing 87 to 60 while penalties and turnovers were almost even. On Wednesday, October 28, page 1B of *RNT* headlined, "Pepperell Facing Forfeit of Four Games." An unfortunate oversight on an eligibility list submitted to GHSA on June 9 failed to flag an overage player. Although a return letter from Thomaston did note Illya Dublin's ineligibility, it was filed without being scrutinized; Illya had no knowledge of this. A minor police report in *News-Tribune* on October 21 alerted Coach Lynn Hunnicutt who then found and confirmed the mistake in school files. He immediately reported this to Principal Steve Johnston and Superintendent Terry Jenkins. As a result, Pepperell would forfeit victories over Rossville, Chattooga, and Coosa. Adairsville would stand as a win because the senior RB was injured and did not participate.

We traveled to Lakeside on Friday, October 30, with 1 win and 7 losses. Darlington shut us out 23–0, which added to our dozen scoreless quarters. Jerry Sharp fielded a very physical football team which featured his trademark I formation using fullback traps, tailback powers off tackle, and toss sweeps. With Calvin Clowers back at quarterback due to an injured Hutchins, DHS packed 6 men up close with 2 outside backers to counter Calvin's option runs. In Thursday's newspaper, 3 Dragons were noted, including Matthew Smart, Danny Robinson, and Calvin Clowers. The final game of 1987 occurred in Lindale on Friday, November 6, against Rockmart. They scored 21 points in period one and then added another TD before halftime. Yet we did fight back behind junior QB Fabian Hall who threw TD passes of 14 and 10 yards to senior WR Kevin Graves, but halftime closed at 28–14. Polk County's Jackets added a field goal in quarter three to finish scoring at 31–14 and close our year at 1–9. Still game statistics indicated a much closer contest. PHS logged 17 first downs to their 14; Rockmart outrushed us by 5 yards at 160 to 155, but did complete 212 passing yardage to our 135. Turnovers and penalties were a nonfactor. Calvin Clowers, Kevin Graves, and sophomore tight end Kevin Hunt were media mentioned for their effort. On Sunday, December 27, *News-Tribune* recognized a 15-school all-area team. The chosen 11 offensive stars averaged 6 feet 2 and 209 pounds while defenders measured the same height but 19 pounds heavier. Pepperell High School placed 5-foot-11, 160-pound senior WR Kevin Graves as first team. Although multitalented 6-foot, 180-pound senior Calvin Clowers ran for 647 yards on offense, he was picked as a defensive back.

1988 Season

On Monday, October 19, of last year, GHSA voted overwhelmingly to reinstate spring practice for football but restricted it to fifteen days provided it did not interfere with other outdoor sports. This would not affect Pepperell, which traditionally used inclement-weather February for workouts.

In August, Coach Hunnicutt decided to camp his squad at home in expanded campus facilities. Players reported at 8:30 a.m. and were dismissed at 9:00 p.m. The Dragon Club provided logistical support. Nevertheless, he still preferred out-of-town (West Georgia College in Carrollton) sites because it eliminated distractions. He wanted wins to keep this season and tried to forget 1987 when "we just folded our tent." Prospects were good, for there was excellent size and body strength with a solid offensive line and wide-tackle-six linebackers. Region 7-AA South would consist of Central Carrollton, Cartersville, Rockmart, Darlington, Haralson, and Pepperell. *Rome News-Tribune* preseason team included senior OL Brian Spears; DL Rock Pace, and LB William Ford. Others to watch were Fabian Hall, Ken Hutchins, Kevin Hunt, and Tony Hall.

Pepperell was a solid pick to win in Blue Ridge on Friday, September 2. We used power running and aggressive defense to down Fannin County 27–7. RB William Ford scored on runs of one, twenty-four, and two yards while we held them to zero rushing. Meanwhile senior CB Gary Huckaby intercepted two passes and claimed one fumble. He merited praise in *RNT* "Best of the Rest" feature on Wednesday along with lineman Brian Spears, who graded high on offense and defense. We came out firing against visiting Adairsville on September 9; to start, Hutchins threw thirty-three yards to junior Kenneth Graves. Then on fourth down, Steve Milhollan sprinted thirty-four yards down to the eight where Frankie Fletcher ran across goal two snaps later; Kelly Fountain's PAT made it 7–0 at 5:45 mark of quarter one. In quarter two, a twenty-five-yard field goal cut into our lead 7–3. With one second left before halftime, we missed a counter field goal from twenty-five yards out. At 8:21 mark of stanza three, Tigers running back Woodard busted inside, was stood up, then bounced outside right and rambled thirty-four yards to goal; a good point after ended all scoring at 10–7. A late fourth-quarter interception on a broken route near midfield killed our chances to tie or win. Coach Larry Parker said afterward, "We made our field goal and it gave us an edge." In historic Barron Stadium, September 17, Lindale and Shannon played for the thirty-eighth time. In pregame, first-year coach Jimmy Bennett commiserated with Model fans that his starting QB was out with injury, and Pepperell had eighteen seniors versus his half that. On opposite sideline, Coach Lynn Hunnicutt was concerned with a "super quick" team which could cause trouble for larger squads. Nevertheless, hometown media unanimously picked PHS to win. On a damp night, Dragons' might prevailed 25–0. A soft turf and hard hitting by us caused eleven fumbles.

We held Model's offense to 52 total yards while racking up 272 ourselves. QB Ken Hutchins completed TD passes of 13 and 69 yards to Crabbe and Graves to go with short scoring runs by Ford and Fletcher. This particular Saturday night event was special for Lindalean Jerry Collins who had been a Shriner "since I was two years old." He was stricken with polio as an infant and spent most of his first 12 years at Scottish Rite Hospital in Atlanta. Yet "he fought the crippling disease, grew up, got married and now has three children." Jerry had been an official Shriner for 17 years, and in 1974, he received Noble of the Year award. In addition, Shrine Game 1988 was dedicated to him. As Lindale celebrated victory, son Joel, who was a junior lineman for PHS, presented Dad with a souvenir game ball. On Tuesday next, Crabbe, Hall, and Irvin were honored in *RNT* for their performance. A day later, Pepperell was ranked number one in area defense and five on offense among 15 schools. A 60-mile drive due north to Tunnel Hill, a waxing moon, and a running back that scored on runs of 9, 64, and 68 yards spelled defeat on Friday, September 23. Northwest Whitfield's Brad Bowman led his team to a 27–12 victory under a harvest moon. We led early at 6–0 before falling behind 13–6 at intermission. After a scoreless third, Frankie Fletcher scored his second TD to make it 13–12; however, point after was blocked. Whitfield's Bruins then broke a long TD run and followed with a 73-yard drive for another. Coach Hunnicutt remarked later, "When it was 13–12, we didn't take the fight to a well coached team." And he added, "We couldn't hold on to the ball." Indeed, Lindale lost 3 fumbles while still grinding out 359 total yards. On a cool breezy last night of September just off Park Street, Pepperell found itself down to number-three-ranked Class AA Cartersville 10–6. The south scoreboard clock showed 8:39 remaining, and the downs marker showed 88 yards to paydirt, a difficult task, for we had gained a total of 2 yards in the second half. But at that moment, as their coach said, "We took the fight to them" by getting out of double tight ends set while maintaining our interior size. Two undersized young running backs, Tony Hall, 5–7, and Frankie Fletcher, 5–9, pounded goalward while QB Hutchins hit WR Ken Irvin with a clutch 14-yard first down completion into red zone; 6 snaps later, he followed that with a perfect left-side slant-in once again to Irvin for a 12–10 edge. Knowing Cartersville's kicker was reliable, we went for 2; Hutchins threw complete to sophomore Scott Crabbe for a 14–10 victory. In four quarters of play, we had no turnovers. At Barron Stadium on October 7, East Rome's Danny Wiseman planned to use a new offensive formation to offset anticipated pressure from visiting Pepperell. When it did not work, he reverted to old standby "student body left" to down PHS 20–7. Following intermission, Wiseman's Gladiators ran 21 of 28 snaps using power sweeps to gain 229 yards rushing. Lynn said later, "They blocked us and used speed to win; they also stuffed us defensively." Wiseman added, "The 6 fumbles killed them." On. Tuesday next, *RNT* recognized senior John Baker, Huckaby, and Pace for their play. On Alabama Road, October 14, RB Frankie Fletcher gained 146 yards on 36 totes in Lindale's 13–0 victory over Coosa. The sophomore scored his sixth and seventh touchdown for season 1988 while our defense held counterpart RB Eric Miller to 31 total yards. "In the past he has made us look silly, but not tonight," said a happy Lynn Hunnicutt. He added, "An intense defense and error free O-ball helps too." On a chilly Friday in late October, Darlington's 5–9 tailback weighing 165 pounds made a winning play; Joseph Gray turned a simple sweep into a 70-yard touchdown sprint that won it 20–13 for Jerry Sharp's Lakesiders. Coach Hunnicutt was disappointed in his defense for not hitting and tackling. Furthermore, offensively we gained only 47 yards and 1 first down rushing before halftime. *Rome News-Tribune* cited Greg Dutton, Tony Hall, Frankie Fletcher, and Brian Spears for their performance. Homecoming in Lindale is a happening made more so when our team wins. With tough defensive play and a new starting quarterback, Pepperell defeated Haralson County 12–7 on the last Friday night in October. Fabian Hall took snaps and handed off to Frankie Fletcher for 131 yards on 21 carries; Frankie scored our first TD from close in. Hall then threw an 11-yard slant to Scott Crabbe for a 12–0 advantage at intermission. Haralson tallied late in period four on a long run and were threatening again before we stopped them on fourth down inside our red zone. Gold and White season record improved to 5–4. Four Dragons were cited for good play afterward, including Chris Gilmore, junior Tim Garrett, Ken Irvin, and Fletcher who maintained his area rushing lead at 938 yards.

At halftime of HCHS versus PHS, pretty Ms. Leana Lambert was named and crowned Homecoming Queen 1988. Leana had been a Varsity Football Cheerleader, Track athlete, Cross-country, Class Vice President as well as Class President, Senior Superlative, Most Popular, Who's Who, FCA, Christian Council, and JV Basketball.

Pepperell High School Homecoming Queens To Date

1953	Barbara Evans
1954	Freida Tyson
1955	Roma Kiser
1956	Peggy Nichols
1957	Betty Callaway
1958	Jewell Cox
1959	Sylvia Nelson
1960	Betty Nelson
1961	Sandra Sharp
1962	Julie Champion
1963	Joan Greer
1964	Jane Knight
1965	Donna McChargue
1966	Donna Mitchell
1967	Jackie Barron
1968	Gail Bennett
1969	Karen Landers
1970	Pam Rush
1971	Anne Dudley
1972	Angie Cox
1973	Melissa Sisson
1974	Kira Sisson
1975	Lynn Weems
1976	Beth Battles
1977	Amy Mull
1978	Deidra Cox
1979	Wanda Smith
1980	Angel Carnes
1981	Marsha Jordan
1982	Chris Roberts
1983	Holly Mazurek
1984	Becky Harper
1985	Pebbles Pace
1986	Michelle Sullins
1987	Kelley Brumelow
1988	Leana Lambert

The final contest of 1988 occurred after a short drive south on Georgia Highway 101. Rockmart, which was seeking its first playoff slot in 10 years, was very concerned with "the biggest, most-physical team in Region 7-AA and its No. 1 rusher." However, local sportswriters gave Polk County's Black and Gold a solid vote to win. Coach Steve Cordle's crew responded with a 35–19 victory. After falling behind 7–0 early, the Four Horsemen of the Apocalypse, Riley

Jones, Jason Van Zant, Geno Thompson, and Joseph Alexander, scored 21 points before halftime and 14 afterward to offset Fletcher's 178 yards on 27 carries. PHS finished with a 5–5 even record. Greg Dutton, William Ford, and Fletcher were acknowledged on Tuesday next for their finale performance. Frankie finished 79 yards (1,181) behind Coosa's Miller in individual rushing and trailed the Yellow Jackets' Alexander by only 5 (1,107). Rockmart finished first in 7-AA South at 8–2, which gave them playoff home field advantage. To realize just how good this bunch was is to read their record. In '88, they lost to triple-A squads Cedartown and East Rome; in the second round of state, Washington-Wilkes (defeated in double-A finals 17–16 by R. E. Lee) nipped them 10–15 at home. The following season saw them go 10–0 but lose in the first round to West Rome 19–16.

1989 Season

PHS began a new season September 1 in Lindale versus Fannin County. We were missing 17 graduated seniors and were projected to play 2 eleventh-grade quarterbacks, neither of whom had ever taken a snap in high school competition. Fortunately, we returned junior RB Frankie Fletcher who ran for 271 yards and 2 TDs. After the 41–7 beatdown, Coach Lynn Hunnicutt said, "We have some new schemes, new coaches and new players—a completely new team...I am pleased with our victory." For his effort, Fletcher was named *RNT* offensive player of the week. Others named for outstanding effort were Gilmore, Hall, and Kines. Next week's opponent, Adairsville, was coming off a 16–6 road loss to Cass High, prompting Coach Larry Parker to say, "The only thing we did right last week was get off the bus. We didn't even run through the sign right coming onto the field." Visiting Pepperell was a solid favorite on September 8 and won 14–7. However, Lynn's staff thought we got pushed around defensively early on by a surprise wishbone set that used wide splits and an unbalanced line. On offense, RB Fletcher took constant hits from their 6–2 defense but still accumulated 122 yards on 17 carries. He told writer Thomas Monigan afterward, "That was the longest football I've ever played in my life." Yet with the game tied 7–7 in quarter three, he took a short pass from QB Ken Irvin and, using "superb open-field moves," turned it into a 30-yard winning TD. Next week's notable players in print were Crabbe, Dowdy, Fletcher, Gilmore, Graves, Hall, and Irvin. Although Lindale was a heavy favorite in the thirty-ninth Shrine Game on September 15, Shannon still held a 20–15–3 advantage. Eight thousand fans showed up and watched Pepperell dominate Model 33–14. Sportswriter Paul Marks summed it up on page 1B the next morning, "A pounding run game led by Frankie Fletcher's three touchdowns, pinpoint passing by QBs Irvin and Crabbe and a relentless defense" brought the Gold Ball home to South Floyd. PHS ran up 306 yards of total offense while allowing 156. Fletcher and senior Kevin Hunt were named MVPs by event officials. A disappointment on this football Saturday was news from Athens that former Dragon and UGA sophomore starting linebacker John Allen had been lost with a season-ending knee injury. In our tradition of defense, LB Tony Hall was named player of the week. The 5-foot-6, 180-pound junior made 12 tackles, including 3 for losses; he also combined for 3 assists. Other player recognitions featured 2 new names—TE Chris Wright and safety Brandon Davis. Last year in Tunnel Hill, Lindale went down in defeat 27–12 to Northwest Whitfield. In Friday night's September 22 return game, local writers predicted another Bruin win, yet this was a new season with different players. Playing as underdog hosts, we took control by scoring 15 points in quarter four to win going away 34–20. Our runners pounded Whitfield with 356 yards. QB Ken Irvin (player of the week), freshman RB Germaine Roberts, and Fletcher gained 113, 103, and 96 yards respectively. Losing coach Don Murray said afterward, "We could not keep up with their quickness." Pepperell was behind 20–19 at intermission but got inspired in early third by a tremendous hit by senior DT Joel Collins. On Friday night, September 29, in Bartow County, their Purple Hurricanes rallied to win 28–21. Poor field position plagued us all night; still we led 14–6 at intermission and 21–20 with 8:29 remaining in the final stanza. In a steady rain, Cartersville changed offensive strategy going from Wing-T to power football. In the final 24 minutes, they ran 28 times for 148 yards mostly to right side of their line while grinding out 9 first downs. Coach Hunnicutt explained it later, "We didn't play great defense all night long and we didn't play great offense all night long." WR Kenneth Graves and LB Marshall Payne received postgame honors for their play. East Rome came to town on October 6 with "11 good athletics playing at all times." Local sportswriters predicted a toss-up, and it was tied 6–6 with 7:34 left in regulation. At this point, we had sputtered offensively with 4 fumbles, 1 interception, and a blocked punt. However, Black and Gold blockers began moving Powder Blues' defense, and we began a 13-play 91-yard drive that ended with Frankie Fletcher's short TD run; Ken Irvin ran for 2 points to give us a 14–6 edge. Earlier junior DB Jonathan Price blocked their extra point, preserving a 6–6 tie, and in waning minutes of play, freshman Brandon Davis "closed the issue" with a recovered fumble. A relieved Coach Hunnicutt remarked afterward, "I know it wasn't pretty...but we will take it in a heartbeat." LB Tony Hall was again selected defensive player of the week by writers. Defensive coordinator Mike Hensley said of his prize backer, "In a pair of loose-fitting street clothes, you wouldn't think Tony is an athlete but once you see him in a tee shirt and shorts, you know he is." Hall was accompanied by 5 teammates in receiving recognition in print on October 11, including Crabbe, Dowdy, Garrett, Hunt, and Fletcher who continued to lead the area in rushing yards and points. Although upcoming opponent Coosa had "always given us fits," local media gurus gave Pepperell an edge in Friday night's October 13 game in Lindale. Thomas Monigan's Sunday morning sports headline featured the headline, "Dragons Fly Over Eagles." Instead of grinding out long drives, we scored 3 times from 40 or more yards in winning 29–13. PHS rolled up 405 yards of total offense, which prompted Eagle coach Gary Graves to remark, "We didn't execute at all in the second half and overall we did not come to play." Those Dragons cited for playing well were Crabbe, Gilmore, Irvin, Payne, and Shayne Sledge. Another successful event occurred at halftime with the crowning of Ms. Stephanie Kennamer as homecoming queen. The pretty senior had also been named Miss Pepperell, Miss Floyd County, and Miss Coosa Valley Fair. Her other accomplishments were Christian Council, Who's Who, VICA, class treasurer, senior superlative, and prom committee. We were a solid pick 7 nights later versus Darlington. Sports editor Jim O'Hara did the Sunday honors: "Dragons' Defense Tames Tigers 22–0." We tamed them by running for 242 yards and passing for 47. Meanwhile, our defenders were allowing the Lakesiders 40 rushing and 34 throwing. Fletcher scampered 10 yards off right side with 11:51 left in frame two for a 7–0 lead. And then with 30 seconds before intermission, QB Scott Crabbe tossed a 9-yard TD to counterpart QB Ken Irvin who lined up at wide receiver. Yet it was defenders that carried the show by allowing them only 74 yards of offense; they did it by stopping power running and preventing big plays. Six Dragons merited honors on Wednesday next in *RNT*, including Crabbe, Davis, Mark Dowdy, Gilmore, Hunt, and Marshall Payne. Lindale was heavily favored in Tallapoosa on October 27, and they should have been. We scored TDs on a kickoff return and 6 running plays which equaled 344 yards of offense to win 54–31. Meanwhile, Dragon defenders limited them to 207. RB Frankie Fletcher continued to lead area in rushing with 1,088 yards and in scoring with 118 points. Overlooked this season by some but not coaches was sophomore Chris Wright's placekicking. Against Haralson County, he converted 7 consecutive PATs. During open week November 3, sportswriter Thomas Monigan wrote of Pepperell football's current condition. Two years ago, Lynn Hunnicutt faced a grim task after discovery of an ineligible player resulted in 3 forfeits and ultimately a 1-win season. He said, "There was probing and questions by parents; some kids lost confidence, too…there were doubters." Prior to that, Pepperell had won 12 of 15 and were a playoff squad. Now Dragon football had "risen from the ashes" to take an 8–1 record into next Friday against defending Region 7-AA champion Rockmart. In dressing room jubilation following Haralson's beatdown, word began to trickle in from Rome's radio stations that East Rome had lost 21–20 to Haralson. Oh, woe is us! A Gladiator victory would have ensured a playoff berth for Pepperell. Now we must defeat state-ranked-number-two Rockmart next Friday night to make postseason. A philosophical Lynn Hunnicutt said, "We've got to do it ourselves. We've learned not to count on anybody else." Twenty-four hours before kickoff, *News-Tribune* writers called RHS versus PHS "even-steven." On Sunday morning, November 10, Thomas Monigan said it all, "Watching a dream die numbs the heart." Underneath that quote was "Rockmart 12, Pepperell 7." The Jackets scored a touchdown in period one but missed point after. Early in quarter four, Tony Hall completed a 14-play march to tie with a 1-yard blast; Chris Wright's extra point made it 7–6. Polk County's Jackets retaliated in less than 2 minutes with QB Bryan Culver's short option run from 3 yards out; Ken Irvin slapped down a conversion pass, giving them a 12–7 edge but leaving us with room to win via a single touchdown. Using up 7 minutes of clock with 16 snaps, we were at Rockmart's 18-yard line with 2:47 left. As 6,000 fans held their breath on fourth and 13, QB Irvin put the football "on the money" at the 5-yard line but it was not caught. When asked about the play, Coach Steve Cordle thought carefully and said, "What do you want me to say on that, other than they don't give points for dropped passes." In the PHS dressing room, Co-Coach of the Year Lynn Hunnicutt thought we played well enough to win. Later he recognized the Magnificent Seven seniors which included Chris Gilmore, Tim Garrett, Kevin Hunt, Shayne Sledge, Joel Collins, Kenneth Graves, and Britt Chandler, and dedicated assistants David Jones, Jimmy Farrer, Mike Hensley, Randy Johson, Brian Henderson, Steve Horne, and trainer Betty Silver. A quote on page 152 in class of 1990 yearbook by veteran Coach Lynn was revealing: "This football season was the most enjoyable and successful endeavors that I have personally experienced." Senior leader Kevin Hunt added, "I will always remember the love and unity of this team and I will never forget my Pepperell teammates." On December 24, *Rome News-Tribune* honored Frankie Fletcher, Chris Gilmore, and Eric Dowdy as first-team all-area offense. On defense, Tony Hall and Ken Irvin were on premier unit. Also important were honorable mention players Tim Garrett, Kevin Hunt, Scott Crabbe, and Brandon Davis.

1990 Season

In May of 1990, *Rome News-Tribune* wrote on page 8B that "Lynn Hunnicut is difficult to please but 17 seniors and a host of proven, talented veterans at skill positions is making it tough for him to do his usual Vince Dooley routines." Though not as hefty as last year's squad, they would still play a high-pressure eight-man front defense to go with a punishing ground attack. However, beware, for Pepperell competed in Region 7-AA, long regarded as the toughest league in Georgia.

Prior to kickoff, PHS was ranked sixth in Class AA; other rankings include Early County, Lovett, Cartersville, West Rome, Rockmart, and Morgan County—all schools we would see up close later. Coach Hunnicutt said, "It's an honor to be chosen and quite a bit to live up to." Green Jerseys and Silver pants visited Lindale on September 7. We had not defeated the "most tradition-rich football program around" since 1968 or 2 years before Bo Payne was born. On Friday night, September 7, the 185-pound senior nose man "single-handedly" preserved our 14–12 victory with a quarterback sack that prevented WR from a tying 2-point conversion and later stopping a fourth down rushing attempt with 56 seconds remaining. On that last play, Payne used his quickness (4.7 on the 40-yard dash) and strength to whip the snapper and stop RB James Mackey cold. His coach said, "He's a big-play guy." One week later in North Floyd, Armuchee gave up 396 yards rushing to the "finest backs in the area" and fell behind 27–3 at intermission prior to losing 41–3. Statistics showed scoring by Fletcher, Fletcher, Roberts, Irvin, Irvin, and Drew. A road trip to Villa Rica followed where 2 short Wildcat TD passes put us behind at half 14–0. Fortunately, our defense did not allow a first down after halftime, and Pepperell's offense "broke loose" for 27 points. Fletcher ran for 2 touchdowns while Irvin tallied 1 and also caught a 22-yarder from QB Crabbe for a final of 27–20. Shrine Game number forty was played on September 29 in Barron Stadium. Shannon versus Lindale was built on tradition; for Dragon senior Scott Crabbe, it was more so. The 6-foot-2, 185-pounder's 23-year-old sister Cheri suffered from a degenerative nerve disease; for half of her life, she had received financial and emotional aid from this benefit game. On September 27, Scott told *RNT* sportswriter Michael Alpert, "I feel fortunate to have the ability to play football and this game makes me want to play harder." Six thousand fans watched as Pepperell "rolled the dice" twice in the first half and scored 14 points. Ken Irvin scrambled outside for 46 yards on third and 5 deep inside our own territory that led to a 7–0 advantage with 11:28 in the second. Next on a fourth and 4 play call at Model's 31, QB Crabbe passed to Irvin for 9 yards. On the following snap, he found Brandon Davis for a 22-yard TD with 1:07 left before intermission. Junior Chris Wright converted both PATs for a 14–0 advantage. For Cedartown High School, the 13.7-mile trip to Dragon Stadium was almost like a home game. On October 5, great plays by good athletes enabled Pepperell to down the Polk County 'Dogs 21–15. Both coaches were somewhat in awe. John Hill said, "I thought our kids played good enough to win." Lynn Hunnicutt agreed, "It was a great game. I wish I could have sat in the stands and watched that one." Passing and running by Bulldog QB Brian Burgdorf versus all-purpose Ken Irvin's kickoff return, pass receiving, and defending were exciting and entertaining. With PHS leading 21–15 at the final 1:00 mark, Burgdorf, who would later star at Alabama, threw toward his favorite target Myron Pace 7 steps from goal. Irvin made a super pick to seal the victory. In our third home contest, Coosa fell to Pepperell 42–14 primarily because the visitors could not stop 394 yards of rushing. Fletcher (2 TDs), Hall, and Irvin all scored running while Crabbe returned an interception for 6 points. The winning coach said later, "We were a little flat in the first half." Intensity spiked quickly after break when Gold and White tallied 3 times in less than 3 minutes. On October 19, a short road trip south on Rockmart Road was next. Coach Ronnie Crabtree's Jackets were sitting at 3–4 prompting him to say, "If anything, the pressure is on Pepperell. We have everything to gain and nothing to lose." He was correct, for with 4:00 minutes left, it was tied 7–7. However, at that point, we scored 15 quick points to close out a 22–7 victory; by doing so, PHS retained its number three Associated Press state ranking. At 7:55 p.m. on October 28, the public address announcer in Cartersville's Weinman Stadium notified a large crowd, "Ladies and gentlemen, this stadium is now under a hurricane watch." Visitors in the East stands glanced uneasily skyward as Bartow's Purple Hurricanes sprinted to midfield. State-ranked-number-eight Cartersville hosted number-four-ranked Pepperell. "It is a game that can determine a playoff spot; loser drops out," said opposing coach Mike Earwood. His game plan was "stop Fletcher and know where Irvin is at all times." Lynn Hunnicutt's strategy was simple—ball control by running inside tackles. The final score was PHS, 14; CHS, 0. Lindale Dragons had several 8-minute drives, prompting Earwood to say later, "Every time we got the ball, we felt pressed to do something...they 2, 3, and 4 yarded us to death." Fletcher carried 26 times for 136 yards and a TD; Irvin bootlegged around end for a score. Meanwhile, PH's defenders gave up only 145 total yards. Still Lindale must defeat visiting Darlington on the first Friday of November to clinch Region South subregion title. Tiger coach Jerry Sharp had adapted to the rigors of 7-AA South jungle and brought his squad into Lindale at 6–2. On game day, he said, "This is probably one of the best coaching jobs my staff has had in a long, long time." One Lakesider in the East stands said before kickoff, "I hope we're not overmatched." They were; Pepperell passed and ran to a final score of 42–28, which delighted our "steadily growing fan contingent." Offensively, PHS put up 434 total yards, allowing Coach Hunnicutt to play reserves most of the second half. In quest of Pepperell's first ever undefeated season, *Rome News-Tribune* predicted Pepperell's Dragons would down Chattooga County 24–14. Home field advantage and a stunning upset of LaFayette last Friday night could make this contest interesting. Coach Hunnicutt explained it this way, "There are a lot of bigger things, like winning in the playoffs, than being undefeated in the regular season." Nevertheless, his principal, Steve Johnston, said, "When your football team is having a great season, it spills over into everything else at the school." Booster club vice president Steve Murdock added, "There's a certain excitement to going where nobody else has ever gone." At 10:30 p.m., November 9, there was dancing in Summerville and on Park Street, for Lindale gained 440 yards in an almost effortless romp over CHS 49–12 to complete their first ever unbeaten regular season. A touchdown roll call included Fletcher, Fletcher, Davis, Irvin, Roberts, Fletcher, and Hall in that order; Chris Wright kicked five PATs. Frankie Fletcher said afterward, "I don't think we dodged anybody this season. We played all the tough teams and beat them all straight up." In the first round of Region, 7–3 LaFayette High School came visiting South Floyd on November 16 with a team, according to PHS defensive coordinator Mike Hensley, that likes to "line up and play 'smackmouth' football." *Rome News-Tribune* picked Pepperell in a close one over Rayvan Teague's

Ramblers 21–17. And for 24 minutes, everything went according to that script, for it was tied 7–7 at intermission. Fletcher blamed himself, saying, "In the first half I was stumbling over my feet." But he corrected that flaw and "hit another gear" in scoring on runs of 51, 1, and 42 yards plus a 2-point conversion. Furthermore, the senior tailback was inserted at defensive end late and sacked their QB, killing any chance of a LaFayette comeback. Despite being 11–0, Pepperell traveled to 4075 West Paces Ferry Road on November 23 to face 10–1 Lovett, a school that has "made the football playoffs 9 years running." They featured a "slingshot" quarterback Spence Fisher who had 1,729 passing yards with 12 TDs. However, Pepperell's big victory on the Chattahoochee River rested in *RNT* sports editor Jim O'Hara's headline on Sunday morning. On page 4B was highlighted, "Treglown, Pepperell Shut Down Lions 28–0." Mr. O'Hara described how senior Scott Treglown "had the kind of game he will be able to boast to his grandchildren about in years to come." The 5-foot-10 defensive end was a one-man wrecking crew on Friday night; to wit, he recovered 2 fumbles, returning 1 for a 32-yard TD, intercepted a Fisher pass, and recorded a pair of sacks. Scott said afterward, "I don't know what got into me tonight…All I know whatever I had for Thanksgiving dinner last week, I'll eat the same thing next week." Pepperell's offense scored all their points before intermission and kept it simple afterward to protect their big lead. Our defenders played just as well on this damp Southern evening with the river at their backs holding an explosive squad to 55 total yards including minus 18 rushing. Losing coach Bill Railey commiserated later, "They got momentum early and it just snowballed." Coach Hunnicutt remarked, "I felt we were ready to play." The next week, another long road trip awaited PHS. It was 125 miles out I-20 East to Madison, Georgia, where Morgan County High School was located. The 10–2 Bulldogs were not finesse oriented like Lovett but straightforward wishbone power. This should play to our strength and philosophy of "run, and then stand up against the run." Local Rome sportswriter Michael Alpert noted that Coach Hunnicutt was nervous prior to kickoff maybe because stadium front-row seats hovered 10 feet from players and coaches' boxes. They also held loud marching band members. A moderate Lindale contingent concerned him too. Furthermore, word filtered in from the hometown bleachers that Fletcher was going to be limited to 44 yards rushing on 22 carries. He dispelled that rumor before halftime by running through gaping holes to score touchdown sprints of 13, 27, and 42 yards. Losing coach Alvin Richardson said afterward, "Fletcher put on a show." In the meantime, the Bulldogs' vaunted wishbone attack was held to 5 total yards and no points in our 21–0 victory. Way back in August, our next opponent, Early County, was AP ranked second in state with Pepperell sitting at number six. Now they were preparing to meet in Blakely, Georgia, for the semifinals of Class AA. Although Early preferred Friday night lights, PHS had asked for a Saturday (December 8) contest owing to 4-plus hours' drive time from Lindale. On Tuesday, GHSA approved our request. In midweek, Coach Hunnicutt spoke with Jim O'Hara about his staff. In the paraphrased statement presented here, he said, "I'm doing just what all good head men do—let the assistants do the coaching. We have a good blend this year; some are laid back, others really get excited." Steve Horne coordinated the offense; Randy Johnson handled the line. Jimmy Farrer and Mike Hensley took care of the receivers and tight ends; David Jones was charged with the backfield. On the flip side, Hensley was defensive coordinator with the same group of position coaches; however, the largest unit was secondary. Here it took Farrer, Brian

Henderson, and Bill Curtis to work this group. Immediately following a game, we'd grade film until about 3:00 a.m. At 9:00 a.m., Saturday morning, team review took about 2 hours. On Sunday, we'd meet on campus at 2:00 p.m. to go over next opponent's scouting report and begin preparing. As the interview ended, Lynn offered a bit of blue-collar values, saying, "It's nothing special. In this day and time, the community will tell you they do the same thing week after week." He finished with "There's a mutual feeling and rapport between staff and players. We've just got a good thing going." The Dragons departed Lindale at 8:30 a.m., Saturday, checked into a Columbus hotel by early afternoon before leaving for Blakely in time for pre-game at 4:00 p.m. Many of Lindale's twelfth-man contingents were already traveling after booking motels in Albany and Dothan, Alabama, which was 30 miles away. A team spokesman said, "There will probably be a lot of people in the stands." The battle would pit "hulking" Early County featuring super running back Ted Yarbrough (1,970 yards) and quarterback Jason Brackin (706 rushing and 1,100 passing) versus a Dragon squad who were more quick than big. Hometown coach Ed Pilcher was very perceptive in a Friday interview, saying, "Our chances are best in a low scoring affair...hinting that a late score might be decisive."

In what many Lindaleans think is the single most important play in Pepperell football history, our defense hit Early County QB Jason Brackin low and high, causing the pigskin to roll loose. Sophomore safety Brandon Davis fell on it to preserve a 21–20 victory. The significance was that it occurred 12 inches from goal with 45 seconds left. With Pepperell leading precariously 21–20, Early used 18 plays to cover 84 yards—a score here and Bobcats win; a stop here and Dragons win. *Rome News-Tribune* sportswriter Michael Alpert wrote next morning, "**If you blinked, you might have missed it. Late Fumble Lifts Dragons to Come Home For Title**." Indeed, much happened in about 5 ticks of clock. Prior to snap, D linemen Eric Dowdy and Bo Payne guessed QB Brackin might run veer left to their side and keep it. One Dragon planned to go low, and the other would charge high over scrimmage. And it happened just that way, for on "hike" Eric leaped over his blocker at the same time Payne and staunch LB Mike Robinson penetrated and hit faking halfback Yarbrough just as Dowdy reached and slapped at backside of Brackin's arm, causing a fumble. Sophomore safety Brandon Davis said, "Mike hit him, and I just saw the ball laying there and fell on it." All losing coach Ed Pilcher knew was, "There was some penetration and the ball popped out." And then he asked reporters in jest, "Do you have a gun? I have the bullet." Coach Lynn Hunnicutt was more realistic. "Their veer offense is high-risk and that was what hurt them tonight." Everything that happened before the final snap was almost mundane. The host squad scored all 3 of their touchdowns before halftime, but on the last one following Yarbrough's 6-yard TD run, Ken Irvin blocked point after try. The visitors from Floyd tallied a 3-yard run by Fletcher in quarter one and twice in quarter three on Frankie's 49-yarder and Irvin's 3-yard rush. Reliable Chris Wright converted a trio of point afters while punter Kelley Fountain averaged 41 yards per kick. There was one last hurdle left after Saturday night lights in South Georgia, but thank goodness, Pepperell would finally get to play at home. Brown High (12–2), which was located just west of downtown Atlanta, had enrollment of 635 and a shared home field at Lakewood Stadium; there was no active booster club. Neither opponent was a preseason choice for state playoff and had "dark-horsed" their way into the finals. Nevertheless, Coach Jacob Hodge would bring his 12–2 Jaguars into Lindale where 10,000 fans showed up and filled all parking spaces by 6:00

p.m. Reporter Michael Alpert wrote, "Were there not firm, sturdy soil beneath Dragons Field, it may have fallen of its own weight Saturday night." Vice Principal Marlin Gilmer said, "I've seen some big crowds at games, but nothing like this. It's students, parents, alumni and community." One thousand game programs were sold out well before kickoff. Dragon Club president Lanny Ely, a receiver on the 9–1 squad of 1970, noted, "We have great fans, even during lean times." And they bring rock-filled milk jugs, foghorns, and cowbells with them. At the traditional head coach meeting at midfield, Coach Hodge commented on the throngs of people inside Dragon stadium. And then in a minute, he said to Lynn, "Win, Lose or Draw Coach, we're going to make some money tonight." Michael Alpert posted this headline on Sunday, December 16, 1990, with comments "**Dragons claim state crown, 42–8**." The game itself was anticlimatic, for we won in a rout. Lindale's scoring cannon went "boom in the night." The game was anticlimactic—Pepperell won in a rout 42–8. Fletcher scored on runs of 7, 1, and 9 yards; Irvin quarterback sneaked in for a short TD and a 7-yard rush. Jonathan Price capped it with a 2-yard blast. In quarter four, Coach Hunnicutt's biggest problem was not to embarrass others. Frankie told *RNT* afterward, "We deserved what we worked for...as freshmen we played on the 0–10 team." On Sunday morning, undefeated Pepperell Dragons joined storied programs Valdosta, Cairo, and Lincoln County as 1990 state champions. Twenty-four hours later, Lynn Hunnicutt was feeling sad and melancholy over losing his 16 seniors. "I'm really getting wrapped up in losing them," he told Jim O'Hara on Sunday night. On the first Wednesday of February, Eric Dowdy signed a scholarship with Furman University. Frankie Fletcher inked with Memphis State. Scott Crabbe chose Jacksonville State while Ken Irvin also chose Memphis Tigers.

Kenneth Pernell Irvin

Professionally and otherwise, Ken Irvin's accomplishments rival Lindale's first and foremost professional athlete Willard Nixon. Ken is a rare individual who combined athleticism with extraordinary drive and determination; these attributes are shared behind a modest, soft-spoken personality. Upon graduation in 1991 from PHS where he helped his alma mater win 1990 state championship, he excelled in college at Memphis State. The youngster started four years as defensive back, earning team Player of the Year and MVP in 1994. In sophomore year, the youngster used up a whole career of blocked punts against Arkansas with four in a single afternoon. The NCAA record performance drove the visiting Razorbacks staff nuts. Head coach and Cedartown native Joe Kines said afterward, "If we hadn't fought defensively, they would have scored 100." On Sunday morning, Arkansas media explained that "number-one block was attributed to security setup; second time it was a skilled culprit; the last two were just embarrassing." For his play on September 26, 1992, the sophomore from Rome was recognized National Defensive Player of the Week by *Sports Illustrated* and the *Sporting News*. As a junior in 1993, Irvin was exemplary in registering fourteen tackles, three pass breakups, plus an interception during a Miami University ESPN telecast. In 1995, NFL draft Buffalo selected him in the fourth round. Ken became a starter in the second season wearing number 27 (he would have the second longest tenure wearing this franchise number) and averaged nearly sixteen games per season for seven straight years. Buffalo coaches once described him as "one of the Buffalo Bills best conditioned athletes." As their starting cornerback, Irvin told a sportswriter, "I never take anything for granted. If you prepare for the worst, you give yourself the best." Kenneth Pernell Irvin attributes success to his mother, Karen, who gave him "a solid foundation in values and instilled in him patience and hard work." In 2002, Irvin signed a free agent contract with New Orleans and played one season before inking with Minnesota. Retirement came in 2005, ending an eleven-year career. However, the former Dragon is not all about athletics. Outside football, he supports many charities and has received multiple awards. But the former Dragon has not forgotten his alma mater or the Lindale community. In 2012, Ken helped establish a scholarship fund for former PHS teammate Tony Hall who was tragically killed. In 2009, Ken Irvin was inducted into Rome/Floyd Sports Hall of Fame. His HOF biography noted, "Irvin's accomplishments are attributed not only to skill developed through hard work, but also to his tremendous depth of character." Pepperell High School retired his jersey in 2010. During Dragon Club after-banquet cleanup time following the 1986 fall sports ceremonies, I asked Coach Lynn Hunnicutt casually if we had any prospects moving up from middle school next season. Without hesitation, he said, "Yes, there is an eighth grader named Irvin who could be special."

1991 Season

What does a football team do after completing a 15–0 state championship year? In spring, Coach Lynn Hunnicutt said, "It's going to be a real challenge...we're reloading so to speak." But he explained later that there were twenty-nine freshmen and forty-seven upperclassmen on a squad that should be more solid in the trenches. Prophetically, he predicted an interesting year and thought whoever made it out of tough Region 7-AA should be a state playoff favorite. By late August, Pepperell had retained its number one ranking, and *Rome News-Tribune*'s preseason all-area selections were Scott Treglown (defense), Brandon Davis, Gabe Goggins, and Chris Wright on offense.

The '91 opener was not easy. A packed house at Barron Stadium waited anxiously for kickoff Friday night, September 6. Sportswriters established PHS as a two-point favorite versus West Rome. And with 6:00 remaining, the score was tied at 7–7; then Dragons' fullback Mike Davis, who had spent most all evening running inside, took a quick pitch wide left, shook off two tacklers, and raced seventy yards to paydirt. When Chris Wright converted PAT, Lindale claimed a 14–7 victory. Davis said later he had been hoping OC Steve Horne would signal it in. Opposite sideline, Coach Sam Sprewell explained, "They blocked us and he made a great run."

Lynn Hunnicutt noted that "Mike does a lot for us; he starts at defensive tackle and punts also." Next week's Honor Roll listed Ryan Blair, Mike Davis, Will Drew, Mike Robinson, and Scott Treglown as outstanding. On lucky Friday, September 13, in Lindale, Pepperell led "hapless" Armuchee 28–0 with over 6:00 left before intermission. Multiple visitor fumbles led to a final of 49–0 before a smaller crowd than last week. Writer Michael Alpert observed the winning coach was "soberingly subdued" in postgame comments despite his squad limiting Blue-clads to 18 rushing yards to 263 for PHS. "We're nowhere close to where we want to be," he said. A peek at our upcoming schedule was no doubt worrying our head coach because unbeaten Carroll County Wildcats came to Lindale in 7 days. Last week, Prep Honor Roll accolades were given to Ryan Blair, Frankie Cronan, Trent Farrer, Jamie Kinard, and Jermaine Roberts. Villa Rica against Pepperell came down to a late interception and a questionable conversion call by Coach Frank Vohun. With 2:30 left and his team leading 14–13, Dragon junior Brandon Davis caught a tipped pass at midfield and returned it deep into Wildcat territory, preserving a hard-fought 1-point victory. Davis had earlier returned a punt 71 yards to give us a 14–7 advantage at intermission. But with 5:48 left to play, Villa scored on an 8-yard touchdown pass; their sidelines decided to kick for a tie, play defense, and try to win with a 2-minute drill. Even after an offside penalty spotted the pigskin nearer to goal, their PAT man lined up but missed it "barely wide" to give PHS a 14–13 win. Coach Vohun said afterward, "I probably should have gone for the two-point conversion." Then he added, "Hindsight is always better than foresight." Our number one state ranking held going into Saturday's Shrine Game where 2 undefeated teams would square off in Barron. A fractured thumb to starting QB Kyle Rush would likely affect Model's offense, yet Coach Hunnicutt thought another good athlete would step up and take snaps for Coach Randy Johnson's squad. Johnson was a former Dragon and recently was line coach for 3 years in Lindale. Pepperell won its nineteenth consecutive game 34–8; Lindale led throughout courtesy of touchdowns by Mike Davis, Germaine Roberts (3), and Brandon Davis. Statistics were close with PHS tallying 260 total yards of offense to Blue Devils' 194; first and tens favored us 13 to 11 while turnover and penalties were almost even. Sportswriter Michael Alpert noted that Lynn Hunnicutt did not smile until final horn ended the crippled and burned children's benefit game. We toted our number one ranking to Cedartown on October 4 and, in what both coaches described as "the toughest game ever," came away with a narrow 8–7 victory. With 7:27 to play, Bulldog RB Frazier raced around left end for an 11-yard TD and 7–0 lead. Pepperell answered in 3 plays. At midfield, it was Drew to Drew when reserve QB Will scrambled around before hitting TE David behind a fallen safetyman for 49 yards; Will Drew's next throw was caught by Germaine Roberts for a 2-point conversion and ultimate 8–7 win. On October 11, *News-Tribune* reported GHSA was debating a move to Atlanta's Georgia Dome for all championship games. Pepperell coach Lynn Hunnicutt was opposed, citing last year's game in Lindale made between $30,000 and $35,000. He believed "local flavor" would be taken out of the contests, and a change would "take out of your community what should be there." Traditionally Coosa had been tough for PHS to beat. However, on October 11, Scott Treglown blocked 2 second-half punts leading to touchdowns in our 41–0 shutout on Alabama Road. His coach said afterward, "Anybody who's followed his career has seen he's always near the ball." We rushed for 167 yards in addition to 94 passing while Dragon defenders limited them below 90 total yards. The following week's Prep Honor Roll highlighted Brandon Davis, Will Drew, Scott Treglown, Jevard Williams, and Chris Wright. Although next week's opponent Rockmart was dealing with injury problems, Coach Hunnicutt still expected them "to play their best ballgame...just like everyone else has...We've learned to expect that." And they did. Polk County's invading Jackets went into halftime tied 7–7 with number one in Class AA. However, junior DB Will Drew intercepted 4 enemy passes and made 7 individual tackles while our offense put up 17 points after halftime in a hard-fought 24–7 victory. Sometimes a team would play against one colored jersey with another on its mind. Perhaps Gold and White was thinking about next week's Purple-clad number-nine-ranked Cartersville. "It ought to be a good one. Every time we play Cartersville it's been a war...they have a very talented group of athletes—I can't remember when they haven't had those kind of players," said Coach Hunnicutt. "Hurricanes End Dragons' Streak" was page 1 of the *RNT* sports page on Sunday, October 27. Badly timed turnovers spelled defeat for Pepperell. In quarter three, an interception and fumble gave visiting Purple a lead 12–7, yet it was the third miscue that was costliest. Trailing by 7 with 22 seconds left, running back Jermaine Roberts fumbled going in 8 yards from goal whereas Cartersville recovered for a 22–15 win. The winners scored all their points after intermission, prompting Coach Hunnicutt to comment, "A lot of untimely things happened." We totaled 230 yards of offense to CHS 185; first and tens were almost even as were penalties; PHS committed 4 turnovers while Bartow County played errorless ball. At Darlington next week, it came down to winner takes all for the second slot in Subregion 7-AA South. The Lakesiders had Jason Payne at quarterback, whom most believe was Region 7's best passer. And he proved that on game night with 169 yards of completions; 2 went to Brad Bohannon and one to Watson. The Tigers also rushed for 165 yards.

Yet the 35–21 loss did not start that way, for we led 14–0 late in stanza two behind Chris Wright's 5-yard TD pass to David Drew and Mike Davis's short scoring run. But woebegone Payne threw for 2 touchdowns in less than 3 minutes to tie at intermission 14–14, and they outpaced us 21–7 in final quarters to claim a playoff berth. Statistics actually favored PHS with 158 yards rushing to 165; passing was 184 to 169 advantage to Pepperell. We also led in first downs 18 to 12.

Coach Hunnicutt said, "They out-executed us. We just got beat." Jerry Sharp said, "This is one of our biggest wins, without a doubt." Lindale played for character and pride in Summerville seven nights later. We completely dominated Chattooga County 46–8, which prompted Lynn Hunnicutt to say, "This is an awfully good team not to get to go anywhere." And then he wished our two playoff teams good luck and said, "They don't realize how fortunate they are to be there." Perhaps the veteran mentor saw Region 7-AA survivor as a favorite for Georgia Class AA championship. Cartersville Purple Hurricanes "ran the table," defeating Cedar Grove 28–19 to win state. Three days before Christmas, the *News-Tribune* announced all-area offense, which included OL Brian Powell of PHS; the defensive squad featured DE Scott Treglown and DB Will Drew. An epilogue to the season was many Dragon fans thought the 1991 squad was better than last year's state winner.

1992 Season

In the upcoming season, local 7-AA coaches had agreed to eliminate subregion format in favor of a round-robin slate. Play everybody head-to-head and promote the best four teams. Pepperell had been victimized recently with two squads recording 8–2 years but missing post-season. Coach Lynn Hunnicutt said, "Obviously the stronger elevens have been in South Region; a full schedule makes things more even." Another subject came to light in early summer with "no pass, no play" eligibility rules coming out of Texas. However, Lynn said PHS had not been victimized by academic failures. His program had an exploratory system that reached out to all potential middle school athletes. Players and parents were made aware of being organized, keeping up with studies, and knowing your responsibilities. By fall football practice, Pepperell was already facing adversity. All-area safety Will Drew, who was also slated to be our starting quarterback, would miss the entire season after surgery was required to fix a wrist injured in spring training. His coach said, "He was one of the best quarterbacks we've had since Ken Irvin." And the hits just kept on coming. Blue-chip safety Brandon Davis had opted to attend school in North Carolina coached by a relative. Additionally several other players had moved from Rome area. Seven returning starters on defense had now dwindled to three. In addition, we now had a new defensive coordinator in Lindale native David Jones.

First up for Lindale was a home contest against Adairsville on September 4. It was billed as Dragon ground game versus Air Parker. Last season, QB Chad Parker threw for an "astounding" 1,711 yards in a sophisticated system; his coach and father, Larry, said pregame, "If we don't throw the football 40 times Friday night, I'll be disappointed…they will be lucky to see five running plays." Although PHS lost 14–2, "Air Tigers" netted only 72 yards on 17 attempts with 1 4-yard TD pass late in quarter four. They countered with 124 yards rushing which included 1 12-yard rushing TD. A rain-drenched field and wet football slowed Adairsville but also bothered us into 5 turnovers. It was 65 miles via I-75 North to Ringgold, Georgia, which was nestled against Rocky Top. After Pepperell fell behind 7–0 and 14–7, we fought back with "enthusiasm and intensity" to tie each time before RB Jermaine Roberts scored on a 4-yard run late (RHS stadium game clock malfunctioned for the last 3 periods) to win 21–14. Statistically, we doubled their offensive output 256 to 115 yards; if not for their punter who averaged 54 yards per kick (he had boots of 59 and 62), it could have been worse. Losing coach Don Patterson said afterward, "They've got a good ballclub…Roberts is exciting." Next week, Villa Rica High School's head coach Frank Vohun said he did not believe Pepperell was down and rebuilding, saying, "They always have a very good team…their guys will line it up and come after you hard, straight up." Gold and White visited Carroll/Douglas counties on Friday, September 18. Elusive quarterback Phillip "Pops" Johnson led his team to a 21–6 victory over PHS. He ran for 8- and 17-yard touchdowns and threw a 59-yard TD pass. Dragons' runner Jermaine Roberts carried 22 times for 150 yards, and it was his 65-yard sprint in quarter four that gave Pepperell hope; however, Johnson countered with a long TD pass and Wildcats victory. Coach Hunnicutt bemoaned our poor punting that averaged only 26 yards on 8 tries against their 7 kicks for over 43 yards. A few days later, Memphis State sophomore Ken Irvin blocked 4 Arkansas Razorback punts, tying a 50-year NCAA record. Ken explained later, "They were letting me come in free. I was sure they'd change their blocking scheme after that first blocked punt, but they didn't." Pepperell had a new field general in freshman starting safety Jeff Hunnicutt, who had taken on quarterback responsibilities owing to injuries at that position. Head coach Lynn Hunnicutt didn't think his son wanted to play quarterback, but in the best interest of the team, he agreed. The dad said, "I try to coach him like anybody else...most times I get caught in a game and don't watch him that closely." In Lindale on September 25, it was Maurice Brown (4) and Germaine Roberts (3). Two premier running backs duked it out all night in a battle won by Chattooga High 29–20. Germaine rushed for 157 yards on 22 carries and 3 TDs while Maurice went for 218 on 16 totes and 4 scores. Chattooga's Indians were fast and physical. Lynn analyzed later that after we went up 14–0, "his youngsters turned their motors off." On October 2 at number four ranked Cartersville, the Dragons went up 7–0 on Germaine Roberts's opening 85-yard kickoff return; however, Mike Earwood's Hurricanes benefited from 4 visitor turnovers to reel off 5 straight TDs in winning 29–14. With Pepperell sitting at 1–4, LaFayette came visiting Lindale on October 9. In a hard-fought battle in which we played tremendous defense, PHS shut down Rayvan Teague's Ramblers 20–0. We held the Walker County contingent to less than 90 total yards of offense while Germaine Roberts, Ike Smith, and Jevard Williams scored touchdowns. Teague said later, "Their backs make people miss." Because of a scheduling conflict, Shrine game number forty-five would be played on Friday, October 23. Model still held a narrow lead in the 42-game series 20–18–3. However, Ike Smith needed only 13 seconds to cover 78 yards on opening kickoff for a 7–0 Pepperell lead. With 2:51 left in period three, he returned interception 48 yards for another TD; these 2 plays netted him offensive POTG. In quarter four, Jermaine Roberts sprinted 38 yards for a 21–7 victory that cut Model's overall lead to 20–19–3. PHS senior Rickey Davenport claimed defensive accolades in a hard-hitting emotional contest that produced little offense but 150 combined yards of infractions. Coach Hunnicutt said later, "I'm proud of our kids, the staff and the whole community." *Rome News-Tribune* reported on Wednesday, October 28, that no Greater Rome football team was ranked in Associated Press top ten polls.

A homecoming game can be a distraction to teams competing for a playoff berth. Yet it did not seem to bother Lindale as they dismantled Northwest Georgia High (Dade County) 42–20, eliminating them from contention while retaining a spot for us. We amassed an amazing 406 ground yards with Jermaine Roberts scoring on runs of 72, 23, 2, 34, and 16. His coach said afterward, "Jermaine can be as good as he wants to be." At halftime on October 30, Ms. Cissi Rene Chester was crowned PHS queen. Cissi's achievements were many and varied. She served on the student council, varsity football and basketball cheerleading squad, Fellowship of Christian Athletes, Leadership of Rome, class officer, senior superlative, most popular, and Who's Who. On selection as queen, she said, "It was a great feeling to be chosen by my peers."

Our next opponent, Coosa, was ahead of us in region standings. We visited Eagle Stadium on November 6 without senior linebacker Mike Robinson, who was lost for the season to injuries. However, Jermaine Roberts caught the bus and rushed for 160 yards and 4 TDs. Homecoming on Alabama Road must have been a distraction for CHS because they fumbled 8 times in losing 42–10 to Pepperell. Rockmart High School visited Lindale next week in both squads' last regular season game; it was a "scrappy game with plenty of hard knocking" won by PHS 35–7. We clinched a playoff berth behind RB Roberts who had first-half scoring runs of 13, 12, and 1 while freshman TE Brian Smith caught a 19-yard TD throw from QB Jeff Hunnicutt. Meanwhile, Coach David Jones's defense was holding the Yellow Jackets to 72 total yards. In the first round of postseason, Lindale traveled for a second time to Villa Rica, needing to stop outstanding quarterback Phillip Johnson once more. Coach Hunnicutt and staff devised a variation of Oklahoma 5-4-2 defense with athlete Ike Smith mirroring Pops's elusive pass/run abilities. But great players make great plays. On an option he pitched at the last moment to trailing back Chuck Walker who scampered 34 yards for the TD. With 4:19 left before halftime, he ran 80 yards for a 13–7 lead at intermission. Johnson struck again in period three with a 10-yard run. We had a good ball control plan which enabled us to make 17 first downs; actually Villa never really stopped us. But Coach Hunnicutt explained later, "They just big-played us into a 23–7 victory." On Sunday, December 27, the *News-Tribune* all-area team was announced. True to what Coach Hunnicutt said publicly at season's end, Jermaine Roberts was Offensive POTY. His consistency and explosiveness set the 5-foot-9, 175-pound senior apart from all others. He ran for 23 touchdowns and added 1,504 yards rushing to a career total of 3,500. O lineman Jeremy Swafford joined Roberts on the squad. On defense, two freshmen, DE Brian Smith and DB Jeff Hunnicutt, were recognized on first team.

1993 Season

The Dragons had lost 9 games total in the past 4 seasons. They began 1993 ranked number eight in Class AA. Coach Hunnicutt "feels like our program is pretty well established and we are building some tradition out here." New Adairsville head coach Gary Graves, who began his tenure on September 3 hosting PHS, agreed with the above statement. He said, "Playing against Pepperell, I don't know that anybody looks forward to that." Lindale won 13–6 in a contest that was as close as the score. Holding a precarious 7–6 lead with 5 minutes left in quarter four, we exchanged fumbles with Adairsville before rover Jevard Williams scooped up a loose ball and sprinted 82 yards to a 7-point victory. Needless to say, Jevard was the player of the game for Lindale. We pretty well dominated the stats with 12 first and tens to only 5, and 191 yards of offense to 141; penalties were even.

Pepperell was a 3-point favorite going into Class AAA Ringgold game on September 10. We covered that spread and more, winning 28–6 in Lindale. It was a ragged game of turnovers, for they lost 5 fumbles and threw an interception; PHS lost 3 fumbles and threw 2 picks. RB Brian Smith and QB Jeff Hunnicutt scored 2 rushing TDs apiece. Lynn thought his defense was "quicker than their offense." Pepperell moved up a notch in the polls coming in at number seven with always tough Villa Rica coming to South Floyd on September 17. We endured 2 heart-wrenching losses to Villa last year. They came in at 0–2 but qualified that because both losses were to powerful Carrollton and Central of Carroll. *RNT* Sports Editor Jim O'Hara watched on Friday night's 21–6 win and wrote on Sunday's paper that Hunnicutt's team "struck quick and then defended." Two rushing TDs gave us a 14–0 edge at intermission while our defenders limited them to 118 yards total offense. Junior Wright Edge substituted for injured Brian Smith at DE and received praise for making several big plays. Next week in Summerville, it was said, "Chattooga can score some points, they just can't stop anybody." Coach Ron Williams critiqued his upcoming game on September 24 with visiting PHS as "as always, they're big, strong and well-disciplined—the type of team that gives us trouble." The Floyd County contingent was favored by a field goal; they won by 5 touchdowns at 42–6. We played great defense/offense as our linemen did their job. Our staff's game plan worked to perfection, for Brian Smith scored 4 touchdowns while sophomore kicker Justin Allen nailed each PAT. The following week against nemesis Cartersville, we were picked to win 14–12; we won 21–20. With 9:34 remaining in quarter four and tied 14–14, QB Jeff Hunnicutt hit Wright Edge with a 20-yard TD strike; Allen's kick made it 21–14. However, Neon Winters returned our ensuing kickoff back 95 yards for a score. A penalty on PAT gave Cartersville a chance to win on a 2-point play. But our Dragons stuffed their runner short of goal and handed Purple and White their first loss of 1993. Brian Smith rushed for 176 yards on 25 carries, prompting Coach Earwood to say later, "He was the difference in the game; we just could not tackle the guy." The "co-difference" was QB Jeff Hunnicutt who completed 5 of 9 passes including 3 for touchdowns. His head coach said later, "Jeff had by far his best game; every time they played a 9–10 man front, he showed that we can throw the ball." In Walker County next week, we were, according to sportswriter Jim Jaquish, perhaps a bit overconfident, and certainly dealing with injuries. In addition, LaFayette High was a very good football team that was coming off an open date. Although tied 7–7 at intermission, LHS Ramblers went ahead via a 55-yard interception return en route to a 23–7 victory. They led us in total offense 204 to 171 and had no turnovers as opposed to Pepperell's 2 lost fumbles. Winning coach Teague said afterward, "I tried to break all of our tendencies...what we would normally do and change it." Lindale had an open date prior to Shrine Game versus Model on Saturday night, October 23. Pepperell's rested squad responded with a 42–10 victory over Blue. It marked our sixth consecutive charity title and 10 of 11. Dragon offense was efficient and dominant in rolling up 21 first downs with 431 yards rushing and 122 passing. Jeff Hunnicutt had settled in at QB and had another good night with 2 rushing scores to go with a pair of TD throws; Justin Allen kicked 5 extra points. Meanwhile, Shannon gained just 108 total yards. Before traveling to Dade County on October 29, PHS moved back into the state rankings at number nine. Local media picked PHS to win 21–10, and we covered the spread with a 21–7 victory. Dade managed only 128 yards of offense. Brian Smith scored 2 TDs in his 26 totes for 153 yards. Pepperell's seventh victory clinched a 7-AA playoff berth. On November 5 in Lindale, PHS was favored by 14 points over Coosa. A different offense for them had no effect as we won easily 48–7 on a soggy turf. Five different Dragons scored touchdowns while D gave up only 46 yards rushing. Late in the game, Coach Lynn Hunnicutt took a shot to his chin on a sideline play that he was unable to avoid. Later in his office while being stitched up, he expressed happiness over Coosa victory. "We're glad to get this one out of the way." Lindale closed out their regular season in Polk County. *Rome News-Tribune* wrote on Sunday, November 14, that "a strong first half, a power defense and an offense that turned in sustained scoring efforts enabled Pepperell to win 38–14." Brian Smith, Jevard Williams, and Darrell Clowers were scoring leaders; we led 21–0 at intermission, tallied twice in quarter three, and added a field goal late. Polk County's Jackets crossed our goal once on a short run in period three and a long pass with minutes left. Because of a 3-way tie in Region 7-AA playoffs, a coin flip determined seedings. LaFayette and Cartersville placed first and second with 9–1 Pepperell coming in at three; Gold and White would visit Cartersville first on November 19. Coach Hunnicutt was not concerned with this system, saying, "It doesn't matter who we play or where, you've just got to play." Then he quipped, "I don't know how to coach a coin toss." With the game of chance eliminated, Pepperell's Dragons scored twice before halftime while our defenders allowed only 1 score late in quarter four in a 14–7 victory. In period one, QB Hunnicutt hit Darrell Clowers for 20 yards deep into enemy territory; then Clowers "burst up the middle" for a touchdown at 7:26 mark. In quarter two, big sophomore Brian Smith took a handoff, blasted past scrimmage, and sprinted untouched 69 yards to goal. Coach Earwood remarked later, "He is physically imposing…a man among boys tonight." Defensively, we gave up a meager 117 yards rushing while our backs were rolling up 241. Home field advantage came with the 14–7 win. Number-five-ranked Greene-Taliaferro came to Lindale on November 26; they were coached by former West Rome mentor Charles Winslette who led WR Green to their last championship in 1985. The combined county schools were located in Greensboro 140 miles east of Rome and just south of Athens. They were as strong and physical as advertised and used a pick 6 and a 52-yard run in winning 22–0. Two untimely fumbles cost us momentum and points, yet it was their defense that was exemplary. We managed only 56 yards rushing on the muddy field of Dragon stadium and 57 passing. Coach Winslette said, "We didn't let No. 48 [Smith] get going…he's been up and down all season." Coach Hunnicutt agreed, saying, "They just took Brian away from us." Defensively, it was not bad surrendering a meager 125 total yards. There was one consolation; Greene-Taliaferro continued to win and downed East Hall, Houston County, and finally Mary Persons to win Class AA championship with a 13–2 season record. *Rome News-Tribune* announced on December 26 that Darrell Clowers was named POTY on defense; DL Don Rush and DB Jeff Hunnicutt were first team also. Offensively, RB Brian Smith and OL Clay Graham were honored for their play.

1994 Season

In April, the GHSA approved a move to Atlanta's Georgia Dome for four northern semifinals. There was hope for forty thousand paying customers. Southern squads would play at local sites. On Monday, August 15, full pads were donned by local schoolboys in preparation for fall football. A week later, *News-Tribune*'s preseason all-area elevens were announced with OL Scott Wilson, RB Brian Smith, and kicker Justin Allen representing Pepperell. On defense, DL Austin Goggins, LB Jevard Williams, and safety Jeff Hunnicutt were first team.

On August 23, Dragons' mentor Lynn Hunnicutt stated a fact that Pepperell could possibly start at 0–2 this year, a tough road trip to Stevenson, Alabama, to face defending 4-A champion North Jackson High School followed by hosting Cartersville next. However, he received an endorsement from two former players now performing for Memphis State; in an interview, RB Frankie Fletcher reflected about his time in Lindale, "Coach Hunnicutt has a lot of dedication. That's what it takes on the college level. It wasn't as much of an adjustment for Ken [Irvin] and me as it was for some of the other players we came in with. We were very well prepared."

Citing their recent record (14–1), Rome *News-Tribune* predicted a 21–20 loss for Class AA number-six-ranked Pepperell. But they had to print a retraction in Sunday's September 4 issue, saying, "So much for a Georgia high school football team respecting an Alabama state champion." Pepperell rolled up 295 yards rushing and 35 passing in a 21–0 shutout while holding Coach Phillip Lolley's crew to 121 total yards. Brian Smith scored on a short run but went down with a sprained ankle shortly after; RB Kodi Keith filled in admirably with a 27-yard romp for our second TD. In quarter three, QB Corey Rhodes took advantage of single coverage and threw a 29-yard strike to WR Desmond Irvin. Cartersville was next on September 9, bringing to mind an old adage, "Better strap 'em on tight, boys, 'cause this is going to be a war." We were favored by 3 points and covered 13–10. Sportswriter Jay Stone wrote later, "Somebody in Lindale is living right." He was referring to a sure touchdown pass dropped by their wide-open receiver that would have given them a lead with 2:36 remaining. Coach Hunnicutt said, "It was just a tough break for them." Brian Smith ran for a short TD in stanza two to put us up 6–3 at intermission. A great second-half kick return by Irvin prefaced RB Eric Wells's 8-yard TD run, giving us breathing room. PHS had now won the last 5 of 8 versus Cartersville. Number-five-ranked Lindale took a week off before facing 2–0 Coosa in the forty-sixth annual Shrine Game; the Eagles replaced Model because of a scheduling conflict. A huge crowd was expected, possibly one that could exceed record the 8,500 in 1991. The inaugural game in 1948 receipted $900 for Shriners. Last year, it netted $27,000. In the past 8 years, 6,000 Floyd County children had benefited at Scottish Rite Hospital in Atlanta. A healthy squad from Lindale was favored by 7 points; they won by 35 and cruised to a 50–15 win. We rang up 580 yards of offense and allowed only 15 in complete domination. Senior RB and newcomer Patrick Floyd had runs of 63 and 70 yards in period four to ice it for his team. On September 30, Haralson County came to Lindale. The head coach thought we might be a little "flat" after 3 tough games, and perhaps he was correct. But his Dragons shook off a lackluster first quarter to score 5 touchdowns, 4 running and 1 passing, in 3 remaining quarters to win 35–0. Although offense got most ink, our defense was very good as they limited Haralson to 62 total yards. Coach Tommy Sosebee thought Rockmart was better than its 0–4 record. However, on Friday night, October 10, Patrick Floyd caught the opening kickoff at his 11, headed upfield, veered left, and sprinted 89 yards to score in a convincing 42–0 victory. After that, Jeff Hunnicutt ran for 1 short and 1 long (23 yards) touchdown; Irvin caught a 16-yard scoring pass from Rhodes. Brian Smith rumbled 46 yards to goal; Floyd completed his bookend night with a 1-yarder. Justin Allen continued to solidify his reputation as best place-kicker in Region 7-AA with 6 PATs. Meanwhile, our defenders held Polk County Jackets to less than 100 yards of offense, prompting losing headman to say afterward, "Pepperell was too strong throughout and their depth was a major factor." On October 14, we were 17-point favorites versus host Chattooga. Floyd County's Dragons won by 21 in posting a 28–7 win. Kodi Keith ran for 125 yards on 19 carries and a touchdown; Justin Allen kicked field goals from 32 and 23 yards. Wright Edge caught an 18-yard score from Corey Rhodes, and in a little razzle-dazzle,

Kenneth Davenport snagged a 6-point halfback pass from Desmond Irvin. Again, our defenders limited an opponent to just over 100 yards of offense. Three years ago in 1991, Darlington upset Pepperell, which resulted in an 8–2 squad staying home for Christmas holidays. It almost occurred again on October 21 in Lindale. We were favored by 2 touchdowns and won 28–27 when a Tiger 2-point conversion try failed with 1:40 left in the contest. Jerry Sharp defended his decision to go for 2-point conversion, saying later, "We had momentum and the kids wanted to win." But veteran safety Jeff Hunnicutt picked off a Jonathon Formby pass over the middle (they had scored on the same play earlier) to preserve a 1-point victory. "We knew they would go for two...we had open field defense in there...they completely dominated us in second half...we didn't play well enough after intermission to win," said Lynn Hunnicutt. Nevertheless, PHS dominated with 4 touchdowns in the first 24 minutes. Jerry Sharp's Lakesiders shut us out after halftime and tacked on 2 TDs of their own. They outdid us on offense 322 yards to 290 with 177 of their real estate covered by aerials. Yet 100 years from now, it would still be Pepperell, 28; Darlington, 27. Next week at Central of Carrollton, we escaped with a 16–13 win over 1–6 Lions. Lynn evaluated his squad afterward, saying, "We are not committed like we need to be...Our intensity level isn't good at all." It was a game of fumbles—Dragons lost 4, and Central, 2. This undoubtedly explained why visiting Gold and White gained only 138 yards of offense and less (103) for them. Pepperell High against Carrollton High was like playing yourself. Both squads were 8–0 overall and 7–0 in region; one was ranked number two in state while the other was number five; each squad wore Black and Gold. Their schemes were similar with I formation offenses and 5-3 defenses. Local sportswriters thought PHS would lose by 3 points but CHS won 28–12; Lindale's crowd was still stunned by a reversal call in the last quarter that would have given us a lead and possible victory. On a Pepperell pass completion, a defensive back collided with a receiver, causing a fumble. Fellow WR Desmond Irvin scooped and ran 45 yards to score. No one heard a whistle, and the near referee even threw his bean bag at the recovery spot. They (officials) ruled it an incomplete throw, thereby nullifying Desmond's score. Bottom line, striped shirts gave us no breaks in 48 minutes. They told Lynn, "We got it right." Of course, Carrollton's sideline agreed. Postgame, Coach Hunnicutt took time to praise 2 of his players, saying, "I know he's mine but Jeff had 21 tackles from safety and had a 60-yards pick-six...Desmond Irvin played probably his best high school game." As fate would have it, a final regular season game at Villa Rica was to determine playoff home field advantage. Unfortunately, on Friday, November 11, Villa "throttled" us 23–0 for our first shutout in 7 years. Coach Vohun's Wildcats outplayed us 14–0 before intermission. They ran up 410 total yards at Sam MacIntyre Stadium while Pepperell was "not making plays." Now Villa Rica would host first round against, you guessed it, Pepperell next week, same time, same station. Lynn Hunnicutt was not ashamed about successive losses to combined 19–1 Carrollton and Villa; to win the next game, he thought his crew just needed some breaks. Most coaches would tell you that unlike baseball and basketball, it is very difficult to defeat a good football team twice in a season. Coach Frank Vohun could attest to this principle for his 11 lost 26–20 in overtime. It was a momentous football war. The Dragons allowed them only 17 total yards before halftime on just 9 offensive plays. It was same players and defense (base 50) as last week that gave up 410 yards. On Friday night, November 18, TB Brian Smith hammered their defenders with 54 carries (a state record) that netted 184 yards and a touchdown. Quarterback Jeff Hunnicutt's yardage was almost as good, for he riddled the opponent with 160 yards on 8 of 12 passing and 2 scores. Yet it took a dramatic rally to win. Late in final quarter, with possession and holding a 17–14 lead with running clock, Brian Smith fumbled, and VRHS defensive back Jermaine Thrash scooped it and "bolted" 69 yards to score. Finally, first break in over a month—Villa missed point after try! Frank Vohun thought, "Oh, curd." We went to 2-minute drill with 1:09 showing and drove 65 yards to set up a 38-yard field goal attempt by Justin Allen. As new ball holder senior Eric Henry knelt down, Justin told him, "Don't be nervous." The center pass and hold was perfect, and Allen nailed it with 12 seconds left to tie 20–20. At the 2:54 mark, Jeff Hunnicutt "notched" a 57-yard TD pass to Wright Edge down the left sideline in overtime for a 26–20 lead; however, Purple and Gold quickly marched downfield where on fourth down, 36 inches from goal, our defenders stuffed RB Eddie Jones to take a 26–20 win. Coach Lynn Hunnicutt said afterward, "I'm just so proud and elated for our staff and kids." Our season extended 1 more week. On a cold and sleet-filled evening on Atlanta's Lakewood Stadium's artificial turf, Crim High School defeated Pepperell High 19–6. No doubt, Coach William Lester's 9–0 Eagles who last played 15 days ago versus Grady were a fresher 11. Senior running back Frank Bailey, who stood at 5-feet-8, 170 pounds, had world-class speed that he used to accumulate 1,200 yards rushing with 25 touchdowns this fall. On Saturday night, November 26, he scored on runs of 10, 63, and 40 yards. With that said, Lindale had its chances. We had several dropped clean passes on 4 different occasions and fumbled once. Coach Hunnicutt thought we "didn't play our best ball" on Saturday night. Early in quarter three, a huge penalty play swung momentum in favor of Crim. Trailing 7–6, we had a big stop on third down at their 22 but an unsportsmanlike conduct penalty gave them a first down; then on next hike, Bailey went 63 yards, and we never recovered. Coach said, "That penalty was huge, we had them stopped with field position." In the remaining quarter and a half, Pepperell never got consecutive first and tens. On December 26, 1994, Associated Press announced its all-state team. Dragons' safety Jeff Hunnicutt was named best defensive player. The youngster led Region 7-AA in interceptions with 10; he blocked a punt and totaled 104 tackles with half a dozen preventing touchdowns. Honorable mention accolades went to RB Brian Smith, OL Chris Jenkins, and LB Ed Cox.

1995 Season

In a non-counter preseason jamboree Friday night, August 25, in Barron Stadium, Pepperell downed Rome by 14–0 and Coosa 25–0. Seven days later, Coach Phillip Lolley brought his North Jackson, Alabama, squad to Lindale. Last year's 21–0 loss was his Chiefs' only regular season defeat. On September 1, this year's Alabama/Georgia outcome was closer, but PHS "out-fought" their visitors 9–6. On a sloppy field, Dragon defense held them to 100 total yards; our offense doubled up with 204. Brian Smith scored on a short run, and a Justin Allen PAT made 7–0 in period one. A safety added a deuce to our final tally. Coach Hunnicutt was extremely proud of his defense's play, especially linemen. Their only points came on a 58-yard fumble recovery and return. Next week, we hit 411N for Bartow County and downed always-tough Cartersville in a "frenetic" 36–34 victory. Lindale came from behind on 4 occasions using a Jeff Hunnicutt-to-

Desmond Irvin 14-yard touchdown pass with 40.3 ticks left to win by 2. It was a track meet as PHS ran for 297 yards compared to 164 for Hurricanes. Coach Earwood's new passing offense favored them 170 to 90; turnovers, first downs, and penalties were almost even. In Lindale's fourth straight win over Bartow's 'Canes, Brian Smith carried 35 times for 230 yards. When it was over, the losing coach said, "Brian Smith's the difference…He's hard for us to tackle." Although Georgia's number-two-ranked Class AA squad prepared to face Coosa in Shrine Bowl 47, most hype went to needy children. Charity committee chairman Stanley Payne hoped their biggest fundraiser would net $15,000 for local kids. Pepperell was an 8-point favorite over undefeated Eagles, but it was a 49–0 rout on Saturday night, September 23, in Barron. Brian Smith was "unstoppable" as he logged 176 yards rushing and 4 TDs; running mate Kodi Keith was not far behind with 160, which included a spectacular 80-yard run late. Meanwhile Dragon D picked off 3 passes. Coosa was hampered without their leading rusher who was suspended. In an understatement, Coach Hunnicutt said, "I thought we played well." He praised his 6-foot-2 running back, saying, "Brian played hurt last season but is well now. His first step's pretty quick. He has good feet for a big 230 lbs. kid, a lot better than you'd think for a person that size…he reminds me of a large Tony Hall [a star on the 1990 state championship squad]." On the last Friday night of September, PHS downed Haralson County 50–6; Brian Smith got his usual 100 yards rushing. Jeff Hunnicutt garnered 71 on the ground and 74 through the air; Kodi Keith ran for 99 on 8 carries. Lynn said afterward, "We did everything well."

On Monday, October 2, 1995, head coach Lynn Hunnicutt self-suspended himself from teaching and coaching without pay for Rockmart game next week. Accusations surfaced several days ago pertaining to the use of performance-enhancing drugs among Dragon players, field profanity, letter jacket policy, lack of playing time for some athletes, postgame improper meal money given to athletes, in addition to booster club money funding a $5,000 bonus to assistant coaches after its state championship in 1990. The state regulatory agency (Professional Practices Commission) investigated all charges beginning with steroid use. Every student who had their names brought forward was voluntarily tested, and all came back negative. It was confirmed that occasional uses of the words "damn" and "hell" happened at practice. However, PPC, in fact, found Coach Hunnicutt chastised players for such language, saying, "And that's the same mouth you kiss your Mother with?" The committee made no comments about the enforcement of a written contract pertaining to letter jackets. Qualified athletes were given the apparel provided they (student athletes) maintained proper conduct, passing grades, and "participated" in at least two sports. Failure to do so waived their right of a free garment in which case the item may be purchased by reimbursing Pepperell High School. Professional Practices did not address complaints from some individuals as to the amount of playing time given some players. As to the matter of meal money after games, the agency found parents and boosters did, in fact, give $5 to $10 to hungry players and to those who performed well during games. However, the evidence here was "inconclusive" that Lynn Hunnicutt knew of these practices. Acting Dragon Club president Bradley Padgett stated he had never seen nor heard of this occurring. Investigators did confirm that bonus money had been given to PHS coaching staff after the 1990 season ($1,000 each to four, $400 to two, and $50 to one assistant) and regularly each football year since. The report stated that although this is accepted practice elsewhere, it is a violation of Floyd County Board of Education guidelines (Alabama communities had been amused by these investigations). School officials said this type of perk should be routed through proper accounting channels. Local superintendent Jackie Collins said the committee did not recommend punitive action against Coach Hunnicutt; however, it determined better and clearer guidelines for support groups should be worked out. Collins mailed a report copy to Executive Director Tommy Guillebeau of GHSA for review. On Thursday, October 12, *News-Tribune* sports editor Jim O'Hara quoted Mr. Guillebeau as saying, "No action may be taken…I don't see any problem."

On field preparation before traveling south on Highway 101, Friday, October 6, interim HC Steve Horne said, "Not much has changed. We're moving right along and preparing for our next game like we do every week. Our guys will be ready to play without a doubt." And ready they were to the tune of 49–0. Junior QB Jeff Hunnicutt had a career night as he scored 4 TDs running and threw an 8-yarder to Joey Shiflett. Dragon defense held winless Rockmart to 39 total yards. Friday, October 13, was unlucky for Chattooga County but lucky for pretty Ms. Nikki Rampley and QB Corey Rhodes who were named queen and king on homecoming. Pepperell, which had not played at home since September 1, enjoyed a 48–8 romp over Summerville's Indians. Neither a chance of rain nor a Friday the thirteenth kept a huge crowd from enjoying alumni night. Last year's winner, Nikki Adams, returned and crowned a tearful Ms. Rampley. And then Class AA number-one-ranked Dragon football took over and clicked for 16 first downs, 333 yards rushing, and 107 throwing while limiting them to only 110 total yards of offense. Afterward, when asked what he thought about his team being ranked number one in Georgia, Lynn quipped, "It's better than being 30." He would take Lindale to Lakeside on October 20 favored by 15 points but knowing Darlington would be ready to play like always. Jerry Sharp said Pepperell was the best football team his squad had faced this year, and that line of scrimmage would probably be a determining factor. We were caught off guard in the first quarter as Darlington jumped ahead 13–7; however, we scored 21 points in stanza two and then added a TD in each of the 2 remaining periods to win convincingly 42–13. Brian Smith "hauled the ball" 32 times for 197 yards and 4 touchdowns. Sharp said afterward, "My kids came out and played hard, but we never could slow them down." Coach Hunnicutt said simply, "I'm pleased." Central Carroll came to Dragon Stadium next fresh off a 70–33 rout of Coosa. Bill Bailey's Lions ran for 788 total yards out of their Notre Dame Box formation. Hopefully the film library at Pepperell still had some 16-millimeter cans of Otis Gilbreath's 1963–1964 teams versus Carrollton High's Charlie Grisham Box. Lynn evaluated it as being "scary" because nobody saw it anymore; it was a very deceptive offense that enabled them to defeat Villa Rica and play even with Cartersville. Coach Hunnicutt explained that the pigskin was hiked back to a tailback 4 yards deep, so his linemen must get upfield. They did, for Maroon and Grey netted only 32 total yards of offense while we ran for 256 yards, passed for 156, and logged 19 first and tens. The losing coach said, "They played us like the No. 1 team… I was real impressed with their O-line and defense." Jim O'Hara wrote on Sunday morning, "So much for Central of Carroll's 'Notre Dame Box' offense." Based on our 2-point win over Cartersville earlier and Carrollton's recent 20–13 home loss to them, Lindale was established a 3-point favorite in Carroll County Friday night, November 3. However, before a packed house, Black and Gold dominated 30–8. Their defense allowed us 82 yards rushing, 13 passing, and 4 first downs while they countered with 317 total yards and 18 first and tens. Lynn remarked afterward, "It was a long night. We got away from our game plan and totally got beat." Next week, PHS fell to number seven with 5–4 Villa Rica coming to Lindale. A win over inconsistent Wildcats would give us home field advantage in 2 weeks. However, it was not meant to be, for VR won 7–0. Coach Hunnicutt thought our offense "sputtered" with bad timing, missed blocks, and penalties. On opening series, sophomore QB Denver Pate, getting his first start, engineered the Dragons to Villa's 7-yard line before a fourth down incomplete pass stymied our offense; we never threatened again. In Georgia's high school football playoff system, which has since been changed, "You play each other all season and then play each other again in region playoffs." Consequently, it was Dragons at Carrollton part II. Ben Scott remarked later that Pepperell came out "smoking" tonight. Before a stunned home crowd, Pepperell took a 10–0 lead in period one courtesy of a Justin Allen 25-yard field goal and Brian Smith's short TD run; Desmond Irvin set up Brian's run with a midfield fumble recovery and return inside their red zone. However, CHS refused to panic and scored on QB David Rooks's 2-yard run with 14 seconds left before halftime. With Lindale leading 10–7 in third, a Trojan punt bounced inside midfield. Because a football is oblong, it caromed against a blocking Dragon and was recovered by a punt coverage player—first and ten Carrollton! They scored 3 snaps later to make it a 14–10 final. With a dwindling clock, an interception ended our season. Coach Hunnicutt was philosophical afterward, saying, "We out-played them all over the field in my honest opinion… This team's full of character and they deserved better."

When *RNT* all-area team came out on Tuesday, December 26, safety Jeff Hunnicutt was named Defensive Player of the Year (on January 23, he would commit to play for Tennessee Tech's Golden Eagles). His dad and coach reflected later, "Jeff's been a great player for four years and been a great person for every bit of that same time." Brian Smith was named on both sides of the squad as a linebacker and running back (Brian would later sign a scholarship to play linebacker at UAB). Justin Allen was easily chosen as all-star punter. Justin would walk on at West Georgia University thinking he would be redshirted, but soon found himself punting, kicking off, and placekicking. Coach Hunnicutt praised him for doing a great job and being mature beyond his years. Desmond Irvin was picked as offensive triple-threat player. Gordon Central's Vernon Jackson was named Coach of the Year by virtue of leading his school to their first AAA postseason. Former Dragon running back and 1992 Offensive Player of the Year Germaine Roberts ran for 2 touchdowns as North Alabama University won its third straight division II championship against Pittsburg State 27–7.

1996 Season

In the second week of May, PHS finished spring drills; Coach Lynn Hunnicutt told sportswriter Kevin Eckleberry of *Rome News-Tribune* that we had good skill position prospects, number one of which was Desmond Irvin. He was a three-year senior starter who would catch passes, return kickoffs and punts, as well as man a cornerback slot. Yet Lynn believed his defensive line would be outstanding in 1996. Pepperell played one of the toughest schedules in Georgia including Carrollton, Villa Rica, Cedartown, and Rome High.

Dragon season began in Tallapoosa by blasting Haralson County 63–0. Quarterback Denver Pate threw for 157 yards while new faces appeared in the lineup, i.e., Zack Battles, Greg North, and Ernie Moses all scored TDs. Next week in Lindale, we were 4-point favorites over Rome High but lost 17–10 in a non-region contest. We led by 10 points just before intermission, but the Wolves cut it to 3 with a 79-yard TD pass. "That was the play of the ballgame," Coach Hunnicutt said later. He also thought Pepperell dropped a lot of passes and committed too many turnovers. QB Denver Pate threw for 134 yards in spite of facing "a variety of blitzes and stunts." Seven nights later, Lindale was an underdog by 2 points in Villa Rica; we lost by 7, 19–12. After giving up 19 points to big plays, we shut them out in the second half. Game statistics showed PHS dominance. To wit, 343 total yards to 265, and first downs and penalties were even. On a "soggy, rainy Friday night," September 27, in Lindale, our Dragons were in a foul mood, and Dade County paid the price 49–2. PHS led 35–0 at intermission and cleared it bench afterward. Sophomore running back Sidney Ford rushed for 139 yards and 3 TDs on 11 carries. Denver Pate had another good night at quarterback throwing for 100 yards and running 61 for a score. Prior to our playing in Cartersville on October 4, Lynn Hunnicutt refused to give the game a "must-win" status. He did concede that "we're not supposed to beat them on paper." The local media predicted a close contest with Purple Hurricanes winning by 5 points. Sportswriters were correct about a small margin but missed on winning prediction as the Dragons won 8–6. Number-seven-ranked Class AA Cartersville led 6–0 at intermission, but Sidney Ford tied it with a 2-yard run with 34 seconds left in quarter three. However, when ensuing extra-point snap was high, sophomore kicker Jonathan Kilgo "rolled away from rushers" and threw to Matt James near goal; he fought his way in for a 2-point score and victory. Coach H. said philosophically, "We'll take it any way we can get it." Gold and White outplayed Purple in statistics, recording 291 yards of offense to 121; first downs favored us 13 to 7. Fumbles and penalties were dead even. We dispatched Sparta Georgia's Hancock Central 35–12 on October 11 homecoming night. A standing-room-only crowd watched as PHS ran up a 28–6 lead before halftime, which started with Desmond Irvin returning first kickoff 90 yards. Sidney Ford rushed for 108 yards in 24 minutes and sat out most of final 2 quarters. Sparta was a 3-hour drive covering 165 miles on I-20 East to near Lake Oconee. Our only game relationship with Maroon and Gold was the 1985 baseball finals. At halftime, Ms. Jennifer Anne Trotter was crowned HC queen 1996. The pretty dark-haired young lady was a senior superlative, served on Miss Pepperell Court, performed as JV and varsity cheerleading for basketball and football as well as varsity competition squad. She managed for the track team and was a member of the FFA and FCA. Senior Ace Amerson was elected king. On October 18, local media predicted a 17–16 loss to visiting Carrollton; they got the margin correct but not the final as we lost 21–20. On Sunday morning, *News-Tribune* sportswriter Kevin Eckleberry began his take on the game this way, "As surely as the sun rises, Pepperell will lose to Carrollton. It doesn't matter how good the Dragons are, or how well they play, they simply cannot beat the Trojans." Yet with just over 4 minutes to play, Denver Pate hit Joey Shiflett with a 17-yard TD. An unsportsmanlike penalty moved the ball 1 yard closer to goal, bringing about a try for 2 and probable victory; however, Pate was stopped on a keeper, and Ben Scott's Black and Gold had another win. Lynn said later, "We played their fannies off." Against visiting Chattooga the following week, Dusty Bright was "a one-man wrecking crew."

He tallied 3 TDs on 139 yards rushing before halftime. Greg North relieved him after intermission and rushed for 91 yards with 2 scores. PHS put up 22 first downs and almost 500 yards of offense while the Indians managed less than 100.

Coming into the November 2 Shrine Classic, Coosa was 0–12 recently; conversely, the Dragons were 5–1 for 1996. Prior to Lynn Hunnicutt's arrival in 1983, Pepperell had lost 11 of 12 charity contests; since then, there had been only 1 defeat (1987). Lindale would add another victory on Saturday night with a 49–0 shutout. Sidney Ford was recognized as offensive player of the game, scoring 3 touchdowns. Coach Buddy Knapp's squad did not help themselves with 5 turnovers. After an open date, PHS prepared to invade Cedartown on November 15; surprisingly, 8 of 11 region teams still had a chance at playoffs. Kevin Eckleberry wrote of this, "It's more intriguing than a soap-opera, more unpredictable than the plot of an Alfred Hitchcock movie." Coach Hunnicutt thought we could finish second or be eliminated depending on what happened Friday night. *News-Tribune* predicted a classic with 8–1 Bulldogs winning 15–14. Polk County's squad was after a region championship while our South Floyd contingent was just hoping to survive. Coach John Hill said of Dragons, "They're as good as any team we've played all year." Lynn countered with, "He's got a great program and is one of the winnings coaches in Georgia." On Sunday morning, *RNT* headlined, "Wheat (Johnny Ray) Sows Win for Dragons." With 3:01 remaining, Bulldog and UGA commit Reggie Poole grabbed a deflected pass and rambled 49 yards to put his team up 17–14. Celebratory high fives and cheering erupted in the home stands and sideline; however, an ensuing kickoff sailed westward out of bounds. Pepperell immediately requested another kick which this time hit and skipped toward Cedartown's eastside bench. Because seats were so scarce across the way, a small group of Pepperell fans were seated with Black and Red fans directly in front of the bouncing pigskin when Wheat scooped it very near his own 34-yard line. Just as Johnny Ray began his "dash for the roses" southward, a small gap opened for a split second at midfield directly in front of their player box; Johnny Ray slipped through and sprinted to paydirt and history—Dragons, 21; Bulldogs, 17! Speaking as a former player and coach in Lindale, Lynn marked the return as "that was probably one of the greatest plays we've ever had at Pepperell." Coach Hill said simply, "They made the one play, we didn't cover the kickoff." With that kickoff return, PHS clinched postseason play. Gilmer County of Ellijay came to Lindale in the first round on November 22. The Dragon nation was grateful to host a game in late November. Mike Thompson's Bobcats came in with a 6–5 record and running a wishbone offense, which was now rare in Northwest Georgia. We countered with a QB that had passed for over 1,000 yards, a WR who had caught 500 passing yards, and 2 running backs who combined more than 1,100 rushing yards. On Sunday morning, *News-Tribune* said this one was over early as PHS took a 27–0 lead into intermission. Our runners racked up 251 yards while passing netted 156; we led in first downs 20 to 6. Meanwhile, Dragon defenders gave up only 126 total yards. Our next opponent, Chattahoochie River's Lovett School, had won 9 straight games after losing on opening night to Darlington. We traveled to West Paces Ferry Road on last Friday in November and lost a heartbreaker 44–34. Although Lindale led by 9 with just over 4:00 minutes remaining, the Lions outscored us 25–7 down the stretch courtesy of a pair of turnovers. Superb quarterback John Portman was the catalyst as he ran for 2 and passed for same. A Lions' assistant coach said afterward, "John won this game in August with his high work standards." One day after Christmas, Georgia High School Association released all-state honors. WR Desmond Irvin received first-team Class AA honors while OL Clay Hyde and DL Brad Allen were named to honorable mention group. On December 29, *News-Tribune* announced its all-area squad. Desmond Irvin, who would soon sign to play at Tennessee Tech, and Clay Hyde were listed as starters on offense; Denver Pate, Michael Perrien, and Zach Battles were on second squad. All-area defense was headed by DL Brad Allen (Brad would later commit to play for Georgia Military Academy); second teamers were Joey Shiflett and Johnny Ray Wheat.

1997 Season

When Lynn Hunnicutt began his fifteenth spring practice in early March at Pepperell, little did he know this squad would play fourteen games and win eleven. But this squad was different. The headman explained to *News-Tribune* assistant sports editor Rick Woodall, "We're not really an I-formation team anymore like we have been. We utilize our fullback a lot now running and pass receiving."

On September 5, visiting Haralson County felt the brunt of this spread offense, losing 59–14. Fullback Dusty Bright rushed for 143 yards. RB Sidney Ford collected 77 while quarterback Denver Pate threw for 237 with almost half of that going to freshman speedster Pedro Holiday. Next week before a capacity crowd in Barron Stadium, PHS nipped Rome High 17–16. Sidney Ford carried 26 times for 136 yards and 3 touchdowns. Sam Pickett's Wolves played our wide game, forcing a more inside tackle power game which netted 228 yards. Our offensive line of Brian Huckaby, Ryan Thacker, Justin Nichols, Seth Murdock, Jonathan Stamey, Patrick Sisson, and Joe Knight drew high praise from Dragon staff members. With less than 5:00 to play, Rome scored to cut our lead to 1; however, point after TD smothered a low kick. The number-eight-ranked Class AA 11 welcomed Villa Rica to Lindale on September 19. Coach Hunnicutt said of them, "They may be the best team I've seen." Local media agreed, but we were a slight favorite 22–21. Both evaluators were correct as VR Wildcats won 24–14. Their wishbone offense confused our defenders with long runs of 80, 68, and 54 yards. A stunned standing-room-only crowd witnessed the winners pile up 452 total yards to a squad not playing its best. The northernmost town in our region is Trenton, a treacherous 2-lane blacktop winds 75 miles through Georgia mountains and valleys; it takes two hours on a yellow bird to get there. Furthermore, if they can schedule you on a Saturday night homecoming affair, distractions for a visitor are enormous. Although we played them on Friday, September 26, and won 33–13, the coach said, "It's hard to win up there." Quarterback Denver Pate had a good night completing 7 of 14 for 111 yards; his last toss went to Pedro Holiday for a score. Top-notch rushing (259 yards) enabled Lindale to take a 26–6 advantage at intermission. The end of an era accompanied Cartersville to Lindale on October 3. The former would move up in classification and to another region. Pepperell had not lost to Purple since 1992 and were media favored by 9 points. We did better than that with a 21–0 shutout in which Dusty Bright rushed for 149 yards on only 14 tries. Greg Hunnicutt and Bubba Owens had interceptions as our D gave up a mere 144 yards total. A scheduled travel trip to Hancock Central on Friday, October 10, changed with a negotiated and rewritten contract approved by GHSA to change contest site whereby winless Hancock comes to Lindale for a share of gate receipts. Assistant Sports Editor Rick Woodall of *RNT* noted sadly, "While the home side of Pepperell stadium was teeming with fans as usual, not a single supporter of Maroon and Gold could be seen in visitor bleachers." Coach Hunnicutt said later, "That's the first time I've ever seen that, to be quite honest." No one in Bulldog fandom traveled 165 miles to Lindale, possibly sensing a rout, and it was, 45–0. Perhaps one day Pepperell would defeat Carrollton High, but it was not on October 17 in Carroll County. Georgia's Class AA number-two-ranked Trojans raced to a 27–3 lead at intermission and won going away 40–10. Terrell Walker broke 2 long TD runs, and Reggie Brown caught 2 touchdown throws from star QB David Rooks who led his squad to 497 yards of offense. New coach John Starr and his Chattooga Indians were a slight favorite to defeat visiting Dragons on Friday, October 24. They had been "red-hot in recent weeks" with 4 straight victories. Running back Keyson Morman led the Northwest Georgia area in rushing with 908 yards; still PHS had 2 good ball carriers and an excellent quarterback, which might make it "a shootout at the Little Big Horn." On game night, Sidney Ford carried 37 times and scored 24 points to lead Gold and White's 31–19 victory; in addition, our defense caused 4 fumbles and intercepted 1 pass.

Summerville moved up and down but could not overcome turnovers and 100 yards in penalties. A pair of Chattooga TDs came with a dwindling clock and PHS leading 31–7. The annual Shrine Classic had become a "stomping ground" for Lindale since Lynn Hunnicutt came back home in 1983; only a 26–14 upset loss to Model in 1987 kept it from being a clean sweep. In season 1994, Coosa agreed to replace Blue who requested to opt out; however, Pepperell dominance had remained. Although attendance had been down lately, event leader Jerry Collins hoped for a revival this weekend which would mark the fiftieth anniversary. The football game played out to script with PHS downing Coosa 53–13. Touchdown stars were many for Pepperell including Ford, Pate, Hunnicutt, and Jeremy Whiteside; Jonathan Kilgo kicked 2 field goals and several PATs. In pregame of November 14, Cedartown coach John Hill said, "Pepperell has a very successful program, a very successful coach and we're playing at their place, so we really have our work cut out for us...they shift in and out from wide open to straight-on power attacks." We won in South Floyd 27–16 mostly by rushing; 1-2 punchers Sidney Ford and Dusty Bright covered 257 yards on 43 combined carries. Across the line of scrimmage, senior Bubba Owens caught 3 enemy passes which were 2 more than any Bulldog receiver.

On October 2, Gilmer County hosted Lindale and their first ever home playoff game. Despite foggy air and muddy ground in Huff Mosley Memorial Stadium, Sidney Ford still ran for 181 yards and 3 TDs; his cohort Dusty Bright kept Gilmer off balance with counterplays and pass catches. Quarterback Denver Pate completed 78 yards of his throws and had several drops because of field conditions; wet did not seem to bother Jonathan Kilgo who converted 5 PATs. The Bobcats "really hit us hard," Coach Hunnicutt said afterward. Their 182 yards of rushing proved his point. Still smarting from last year's second-round 44–34 defeat at Lovett, Pepperell prepared to welcome an equally good 8–3 Creekside High, which is located in Fulton County 70 miles almost due south of Lindale. The Seminoles boasted 2 1,000-yard rushers and tremendous speed on defense. Yet our triumvirate of Pate, Ford, and Bright posed problems for any defenders. But it was our defense that provided a key play in winning 21–14 victory. With the score knotted at 7–7 late in stanza three, Sidney Ford ran for a short touchdown to give PHS a 14–7 lead; a few minutes later with 9:58 remaining, Dragon senior Orlando Johnson had a 31-yard pick 6 for insurance. Coach Amos McCreary said of the play, "That interception kind of deflated us a little bit." All told, Dragon D had 4 picks and a fumble recovery by Hershel Waddell. Coach Hunnicutt remarked, "That was two good football teams. It's a shame anybody had to lose." In preparation for the quarterfinals at 9–3 Dacula next week, Coach thought his team had not peaked as yet, and on film, the Falcons were similar to Pepperell except in playoff experience, for Kevin Maloof's host squad had made it this far in 9 of 12 years. Both had running backs with 1,200-plus-yard résumés and quarterbacks with almost 1,000 throwing. Lindale matched and bettered their hosts with 495 yards of offense, winning 28–21. They (Falcons) had no answer for Sidney Ford (TD runs for 5, 6, 60, and 15 yards) who had a "monster" night carrying 28 times for 212 yards in addition to Dusty Bright's 101. Pepperell's offensive line was "blowing" them off scrimmage, which took its toll late. A few weeks ago, there were 8 teams from Greater Rome playing for a state football championship; when the stadium lights dimmed at Falcon Stadium last Friday night in Dacula, there was only 1 left—Pepperell. Now Lindale's Dragons were bound for Atlanta's Georgia Dome and a semifinal battle with Region 4-AA 13–0 Washington County. But first, there must be film swaps and meetings with dome officials; those were minor problems compared to dealing unfamiliarity of the venue. None of our kids had played on artificial turf or inside a vast arena. Rick Tomberlin's Golden Hawks had no such anxieties, for they ripped Westminster 35–7 in the dome last year before nipping Americus 21–20 in finals. Coach Hunnicutt was worried. "If we go in 'googly-eyed' we might be down three touchdowns by the time they get over it." Lynn pretty much nailed it, for Washington bolted ahead 34–0 en route to a 42–14 victory. "Take that first quarter away, and it was a different ballgame," he said afterward. We recovered somewhat just before intermission when Pate hit Pedro Holiday in back of the end zone. Coming out of halftime, Sidney Ford sprinted 53 yards to make it 34–14; however, a failed fourth down conversion inside Washington territory reversed momentum. The winning coach was satisfied, saying later, "I was pleased. I thought we were getting after it. We were very intense." When the *News-Tribune* all-area squad was announced on Sunday, December 28, RB Sidney Ford was named Offensive Player of the Year; he was joined by lineman Brian Huckaby. On defense, Ryan Thacker, Dusty Bright, Joey Shiflett, Bubba Owens, and Jonathan Kilgo were first team. Pepperell finished state rankings as Class AA number four team.

1998 Season

Number-five-ranked Pepperell began 1998 by hosting 0–1 Rockmart, which had just lost 21–6 to Darlington. Although his team won 30–0, Coach Hunnicutt was not happy, for penalties negated 3 touchdowns. In addition, misalignments, passing, and kicking were a very real concern heading into Shrine against Coosa on Saturday night, September 19. Eagle coach Buddy Knapp was not buying any of the above, saying, "The only reason Pepperell is not ranked No. 1 is because Carrollton's ranked No. 1...It's a tough, tough draw for us." However, the 26-game losing streak was over with last week's 28–22 upset of Model. Hopefully that victory would bring new life to Alabama Road; still PHS won 56–7. Seven nights later in LaFayette, another struggling team faced a Lindale squad averaging 43 points per game. We increased that total by winning 70–21. Running back Sidney Ford, who recently committed to Georgia Tech, scored 6 TDs; quarterback Greg Hunnicutt ran for 2, and Jeremy Whiteside crossed goal once. On October 2, Georgia's number-one-ranked double-A squad hosted and downed number ten Central of Carroll 28–0; Sidney Ford tallied 205 yards and 3 touchdowns. Early in quarter four, QB Greg Hunnicutt suffered an ankle injury; he was replaced by backup Jonathan Neighbors. Last week against LaFayette, our defense lost end Wayne Groves to an injured knee. Rome physician Dr. Sidney Bell performed successful surgery on Greg one day later. Wayne Groves visited renowned sports doctor Jim Andrews in Birmingham on October 8. Coach Hunnicutt told the *News-Tribune* that "we lost two key players and two outstanding leaders. They're both captains and great kids." Sports editor Jim O'Hara noted young Hunnicutt "had already made a sacrifice by having to move to quarterback to fill a hole on offense." Villa Rica coach Rick Tolleson was making a name for himself; last week, his squad upset number one Carrollton 9–7; this Friday night, his tenth-ranked Wildcats would have another chance at beating a first-place double-A squad when Pepperell visited Sam McIntyre Stadium. And they were not doing it with smoke and mirrors as Lynn Hunnicutt evaluated. "They're good, like they are every year with speed and quickness; I've been here [PHS] 16 years and I haven't seen a bad Villa Rica team." On October 9, Villa completed their back-to-back sweep of top squads with a 17–0 shutout. Pepperell had its opportunity to make plays but couldn't because of an overthrown pass, a missed field goal, and a sack inside the Wildcats' 10-yard line. Yet Lynn thought, "We have a good team and have nothing to get down on ourselves about." We hosted our nemesis that wore Black and Gold (Carrollton) on October 16 as 3-point underdogs. Ends Blake Sabo and Georgia's leading D-1 receiver prospect Reggie Brown were a gridiron force; we countered with Sidney Ford who had rushed for 1,119 yards and 16 touchdowns this year. The Trojans duplicated our previous week's loss to Villa, 17–0. They led 3–0 at intermission but passed for 135 yards after intermission by moving Sabo (1 TD catch) and Brown into inside slots and running cross field patterns with them; they also rushed for 85 yards with QB Johnson scoring on a 23-yard run. Dragon O struggled to 52 yards of offense. In spite of 2 17–0 losses and a vastly improved Cedartown squad "looming on the horizon," Coach Hunnicutt told *RNT*, "We are as down as you think." Visiting Lindale was a 2-point favorite in Polk County on October 23. At postgame, South Floyd County fans filed out of Bulldog stadium in a happy state following their Dragons' 37–0 victory. Coach John Hill was mystified by his team's 1 first down in the first half and told reporters he thought "we could win this game." Game statistics revealed what happened, for PHS led in first downs 24 to 5; rushing yards were 321 to 14. Turnovers and penalties were a nonfactor. Actually the contest was a Kilgo and Ford show as Jonathan kicked field goals of 38, 50, and 21 yards plus 4 PATs while Sidney ran for 2 scores; Matt James and T. J. Wilson also added a TD each. On October 30, PHS found its passing game versus visiting Chattooga. Jonathan Neighbors, who had settled in as Dragon QB, completed 5 of 6 throws for 130 yards and 2 touchdowns (57 and 28 yards) both to Pedro Holiday; in addition, Sidney Ford rushed for 131 yards and 4 scores. DB Matthew Johnston set up 2 TDs with an interception and a punt return; Kilgo converted 7 extra points. Next game night, November 6, was good to Lindale. Pepperell defeated Haralson County 45–7; our upcoming opponent Dade County Wolverines lost to Cedartown and Ms. Haley Michelle Fricks was named 1998 homecoming queen. Between the lines Sidney Ford rushed for over 300 yards and 5 touchdowns. Our passing continued to improve as Neighbors had now connected on 8 of 11 throws in past 2 games for 224 yards and 3 TDs. Dade's 38–27 loss at Polk County Bulldogs eliminated them from region playoff contention and gave PHS a postseason spot for 7 consecutive years. At halftime on a freezing Friday night, 1997 winner Takila Wilson crowned Ms. Fricks who had been a member of student council, French Honor Society, football and basketball cheerleading, competitive cheerleading; track, student mentor, Who's Who, senior superlative—most popular. Friday the thirteenth was not unlucky for Pepperell's next stop in Trenton, Georgia, which is located in an Appalachian valley between Lookout on the east and Sand Mountain on the west. On a team yellow bird, it took almost 2 hours to travel 75 miles. Once there, our defense was stalwart, allowing Dade 3 points in a 21–3 win; furthermore, Dragon D was stingy elsewhere giving up only 114 yards rushing (24 in the second half), no pass completions and 5 first downs. Meanwhile, Sidney Ford ran for 186 yards and 3 touchdowns; in doing so, he totaled 2,037 or 1.15 miles of gridiron real estate in regular season. Sidney's very much appreciative of Dragon O line. In Southern football vernacular, "He knows who puts the butter on his bread." First round of state playoffs began in Morgan County. In Friday afternoon Atlanta traffic, Lindaleans must navigate a tough 125-mile drive on I-20 east to reach the stadium in Madison. Fans have fond memories of this historic Southern town in 1990 where we came away with a 21–0 victory en route to the state championship. This November 20 almost matched last visit, for PHS won 21–9; we led 14–3 at intermission courtesy of Ford's 52-yard run and a Jonathan Neighbors short TD throw to Pedro Holiday. The visitors opened stanza three with Matt Johnston returning a punt to the Bulldogs' 36. Then from 10 yards closer, Neighbors hit Holiday for a 24-yard touchdown on third and 11 to make it 21–3. Morgan's Bulldogs scored once in period three, but our defense stopped 3 drives deep inside our territory in final quarter. Losing coach Kenny Moore assessed the winners. "They're a good team. You can't make mistakes against a team like that." Next up was old rival Cartersville who moved into Region 7 last season. They were undefeated at 11–0 and ranked number 8 in state; they presented the same problem as before. They were "big, strong, physical and well coached." Coach Hunnicutt spoke with *News-Tribune* sports editor Jim O'Hara on November 24 about the upcoming battle. He began with, "At this time of year you've got to have a stronghold in the trenches." Offense center Seth Murdock was a 3-year starter while 2-year men Jonathan Stamey and Justin Nichols were forces at guard. A trio of tackles included Jason Hawk, Brian Dudley, and Patrick Sisson; good blocking tight ends were Jimmy Hillis, Paul McCoy, and Herschel Waddell. Lynn stated that although this squad had good experience coming back, "it all starts with the teachers." In this case, former Dragon Todd Wheeler and assistant Mike Moore carried this load. On defense, Jeff Shiflett mentored Waddell and McCoy at ends; Sissom and Nick Swindle gave strength at tackle. Interior linemen consisted of Derrick Campbell, Kevin Boatner, and Hawk. But it was a D back that gained notoriety on Sunday morning, November 29, when *Rome News-Tribune* heralded, "JOHNSTON, PEPPERELL DEFENSE STAND GROUND AGAINST 'CANES." After home team Cartersville scored first on a 17-yard run, UGA commit Jonathan Kilgo kicked a 32-yard field goal with 10 minutes left before intermission. However the defining moment of this game occurred with 48.2 seconds left before halftime when senior DB Matt Johnston caught an errant Purple Hurricane pass and returned it 38 yards for a score. When Kilgo converted, we had the lead and eventual 10–7 victory. A happy winning coach said, "I can't say enough about how stellar Matt played tonight during the game...We needed him because we had a rough time on offense." Sidney ran 35 times to gain 128 yards; Cartersville keyed 3, 4, and even 5 tacklers each time he handled the pigskin.

Seven days later in state quarterfinals, Lindaleans took their gold rock-filled milk jugs to Manchester, Georgia, which was near Warm Springs; it took about two and one-half hours to motor 125 miles south to Blue Devils' stadium. The 1997 Class A champions had since moved up a notch and sported an 11–1 record. The Devils had never lost at home under Coach Greg Oglesby that covered 37 straight games. Lynn critiqued them. "They're just a lot bigger team than we're used to playing." We were a 1-point underdog at kickoff but won by 2, 17–15. It was a war that came down to a great defensive play with 1:29 remaining. On fourth and 9 at our 31, Blue Devils' quarterback Shea McInvale dropped back and let fly toward WR Sandreal Carter where DBs Johnston and Wilson were defending; T. J. said afterward, "The ball was thrown and he dove and I dove with him...As he caught it my hand was under the ball and was able to push it back out." Sunday morning's newspaper said, "It could be called the most crucial play of the year." A Ford run and Kilgo field goal gave us a 10–7 advantage at intermission. In period three, Sidney ran 6 yards for a 17–7 lead. Yet shortly after that, a 62-yard run and 2-point conversion narrowed the margin to 17–15, which set up the game saver by Wilson. On Wednesday, December 9, Coach Lynn Hunnicutt was in a pensive mood while sitting in his office at PHS football building. He read from the Bible to sportswriter Scott Chancey. "I use passages from the Good Book about believing in your self. It's about running and not getting tired, walking and not becoming weary and about gaining new strength." He noted that at one time or the other this season, Pepperell and our semifinal opponent, Carrollton, had been ranked number one in Class AA. Since 1958, Black and Gold had won 18 consecutive games versus Lindale. Coach was 0–6 since taking over in 1983. Pepperell was not intimidated by either the Georgia Dome or Trojans, for they "played their hearts out," but Carrollton made more plays than we did and, consequently, won a hard-fought 26–7 victory. This group of seniors had excelled, and they would be sorely missed. Lynn had always been very astute in sizing up future opponents; he felt if we could get past the dome, a state championship was obtainable. To wit, one week later, Carrollton beat host Early County 37–18 to claim Class AA crown. On Sunday, December 27, *Rome News-Tribune* published all-area for 1998. For consecutive years, RB Sidney Ford was named Offensive Player of the Year. He accumulated 5,337 rushing yards (3.03 miles) and 77 touchdowns (462 points). The Georgia Tech commit reflected on his career, "It was a fun ride...Coach Hunnicutt, I loved playing for him. As far as coaching, he's the greatest man I ever met in my life...I'm going to miss it." Joining Sidney on the O squad were WR Pedro Holiday and OLs Jason Hawk and Seth Murdock. Second teamers were Justin Nichols, Jonathan Stamey, and Jimmy Hillis. On defense, DL Patrick Sissom, DE Herschel Waddell, LB Matt James, DB Matt Johnston, and punter Jonathan Kilgo were with first group. Honorable mention went to DB Luke Sheffield. These student athletes helped Pepperell finish number three in final poll of 1998. On signing day, Wednesday, February 1999, 4 Dragons signed football scholarships. Jonathan Kilgo went to UGA. Sidney Ford inked with Georgia Tech. Greg Hunnicutt joined his brother Jeff at Tennessee Tech, and Seth Murdock chose Presbyterian.

1999 Season

    Dragon nation news began early in 1999 when *RNT* announced on March 18 from Orchard Park, New York, that former Pepperell player Ken Irvin had resigned with Buffalo. Last season, Ken started every game at left cornerback where he made 65 tackles and broke up 25 passes with 1 interception. Ken originally signed out of Memphis University in 1995. Before a full house in Rockmart's Hilburn Field on September 10, Lindale won 13–6. Sophomore QB Roderick Ware ran for 2 short TDs and passed for 90 yards; the Jackets were their own worst enemy, fumbling 6 times, losing 4. In Floyd County's biggest football game, a huge crowd turned out for the 1999 annual Shrine Classic in Barron Stadium. Last year's benefit affair raised $17,000. Coosa High coach Buddy Knapp was wary of Pepperell's change in offensive philosophy, saying, "To begin with, they are one of the elite teams in Georgia and now Coach Hunnicutt's squad no longer depends on three-yards and a cloud of dust mentally." Conversely, Lynn was cautious about their improved team speed. Yet Coach Knapp was right about Air Pepperell. PHS scored on 4 of 7 possessions while using a variety of slip screens, curls, fades, and deep routes. Behind excellent blocking, Roddy Ware threw for 233 yards on 13 of 21 completions, 2 of which were TDs to junior Pedro Holiday and sophomore Justin Bruce. Holiday and T. J. Wilson also had running touchdowns, as did Ronnie Waddell who scooped up a loose ball and returned it 56 yards. However, Eagles' speed put up 324 total yards against our defense, which did not please the headman. A week later on Friday, September 24, Lindale was heavily favored on homecoming night versus LaFayette; we won 39–14 with 424 yards of offense, which was equally divided run/pass. Pedro Holiday caught scoring passes of 36, 55, and 9 yards; Breon Ford, T. J. Wilson, and junior QB Matt Wheat ran for TDs. At halftime, pretty Ms. Summer Elizabeth Lloyd was chosen and crowned 1999 queen from a field of 16 other contestants. Patrick Colum and T. J. tied for HC king. We continued good balance on offense by running for 219 yards against host Central of Carrollton. Most of our critical points were made by T. J. Wilson who rushed 3 yards late in regulation for a 20–20 tie; then in OT, he found goal with an 8-yarder to win 27–20. Freshman RB Breon Ford added 84 yards on 16 carries. On October 8, PHS prepared to meet visiting 2–2 Villa Rica as 18-point favorites. Coach Hunnicutt was not buying it, saying, "They always seem to possess big play capabilities—this year is no different." *News-Tribune* wrote on Sunday that it was "rush hour" in Lindale Friday evening, meaning quick Wildcat running backs rushed 55 times for 257 yards and 3 touchdowns in winning 21–16. Because their starting quarterback was out with an injury, VR attempted only 1 pass. Breon Ford and T. J. Wilson recorded rushing TDs for Lindale. By consensus, both 11s actually played well on defense. As Carrollton loomed on our radar, October 15, word came out of Polk County that John Hill's Bulldogs had whipped the formidable Trojans 41–7. Most schools had 1 team they struggled to beat. Cedartown was that school for Carrollton; we don't know about such, for Lindale had never won over Black and Gold dating back to 1958. Furthermore, when Coach Hunnicutt's squad de-bused on-site, they were 7-spot underdogs to Ben Scott's squad.

    But this betting line was wrong, for the final was Dragons, 13; Trojans, 7. *News-Tribune*'s Sunday morning headlines explained, "Finally! Dragons Stop Trojans." It continued with, "Pick a cliché...the monkey is off their back...the dark cloud has been lifted...the drought is over." Junior

Pedro Holiday did it all Friday night as he rushed, caught, and threw for a combined 168 yards. He was simply "the best player on the field." Yet others contributed as Corey Hutchins had a 10-yard TD run; Breon Ford carried the ball 13 times, and Shane Forsyth sealed it with an interception. The winner's defense allowed only 27 yards rushing and forced 8 punts. As Lindale's jubilant crowd mingled with their heroes, 2 boosters sliced a plug out of Trojan natural turf; 5 days later, it occupied a place of honor in the PHS trophy case. However, 7 nights later, the schedule toughened even more. For whatever reason, Pepperell had traditionally played well against Cedartown. Yet in all honesty, this year's contest in Lindale on October 22 looked like a mismatch because Coach Hill's Bulldogs decisively defeated Villa Rica 49–8 and Carrollton 41–7 while we lost to VR by 5 and beat CHS by 6. Coach Hunnicutt evaluated Polk County's contingent as a veteran group with a college size O and D line to go with big skilled players. Indeed, many Lindaleans referred to them as University of Cedartown. But the Sunday morning *News-Tribune* writeup began with, "And a Ford will lead them." Young Breon carried 18 times for 97 yards and a TD as number-three-ranked Dawgs went down 13–0. Dragon D, led by 5 tough seniors, allowed their option offense only 113 yards. Coach Hill said later, "We were ineffective tonight and they played well." Lynn reasoned afterward, "In a region like ours, it's like college football; anybody can beat anybody on any given day." In Summerville on October 29, Roddy Ware completed 8 of 12 throws for 110 yards and 2 scores; Pedro Holiday ran for 51 and caught 57 yards of offense. Breon Ford rushed for 130 yards and a pair of TDs. Chattooga lost 4 fumbles, which turned into same amount of touchdowns for PHS. Shane Forsyth, Kevin Popham, and Luke Sheffield all claimed loose balls. Coach John Starr said later, "They were much better prepared." Pepperell defeated Haralson County 28–7 in Tallapoosa on November 5; our defense limited the Rebels to less than 120 yards of offense, only 5 first downs in addition to recovering 2 fumbles. Meanwhile, QB Ware was hooking up with receivers Jonathan Neighbors and Mark Middleton for touchdowns; in addition, Breon Ford rushed for 103 yards. Lindale was 1 win away from a Region 6-AA championship. Friday night, November 12, Dade County yellow bused into Floyd County sporting a 7–2 record but fresh off a 33–7 home loss to Cedartown. Again, Coach Lynn Hunnicutt was an astute evaluator of upcoming opponents. He said, "Dade is the most experienced, most mature team in our region." George Hoblitzell's squad had roughly 95 percent seniors starting. In addition, super athlete Darian Jordan was region 6-AA's leading rusher. Apparently, no one was listening to the coach, for the Wolverines stunned us 42–14. They jumped out 21–0 before intermission and then tallied 21 more markers in the second half. Coach Hunnicutt thought our defense was on "roller skates" all night long because we could not stop a ground game that put up 356 yards. Lynn commented later that "in truth, the score could have been even worse if they wanted it to be." Now instead of playing at home for the first round, we must trek 170 miles to Hartwell, Georgia. The small town (4,200) is situated lakeside just over the state line from Anderson, South Carolina. Hart's Bulldogs were undefeated region champs for a reason; a talented quarterback led excellent receivers and a strong running game. Defensively, top college prospect DE Carlos Bates along with 5 other potential all-state players led a team that had allowed opponents a meager 10.4 points per game. In team speed, they resembled Villa Rica. In 1997, William Devane's Orange and Black lost to Creekside in the first round and a year later to Mary Persons in the quarterfinals. However, this year on November 19, his squad would advance to second round by virtue of a 35–12 victory over Lindale. Although we cut a 21–0 halftime deficit to 21–12 in quarter three, Dragon O "hit the skids" in final stanza. Statistically, Hart rushed for 330 yards to our 71; first and ten advantages were 19 to 5. Neither threw the ball well. Our hosts would play into state finals where they lost to Cartersville 27–21. In his last comment about an 8–3 season, Coach Hunnicutt said, "Tonight, we just got beat by a good football team." On Sunday morning, December 26, 1999, the *RNT* all-area squad was announced. First squad on defense were seniors Jonathan Neighbors at DE and repeat member T. J. Wilson who started at cornerback; a backup group featured LB Ronnie Waddell, DB Corey Hutchings, and punter Cody Ball. Honorable mention awards went to Paul McCoy, Shane Forsyth, Jimmy Hillis, Luke Sheffield, and Nick Swindle. Team offense recognized WR Pedro Holiday and OL Justin Nichols as starters; both were eleventh graders. Second tier were freshman RB Breon Ford, sophomore QB Roderick Ware, and junior OL Bubba Dudley. Honorable mention went to junior Kevin Popham.

First Wednesday of each February was designated national signing day for senior football players; on February 3, 2000, *News-Tribune* reported that T. J. Wilson had inked a full-ride scholarship to continue his career at Furman University. Although young Wilson was known for his athleticism on both sides of scrimmage, he projected as a DB for the Palladins. Position coach Jimmy Farrer spoke to his character, "He has been a joy to work with, is dependable and always did what you told him to do; in addition T. J. is a quick learner who sports a 3.5 grade point average."

2000 Season

Much to the delight of sports fans, *Rome News-Tribune* publisher B. H. Mooney announced on Sunday, March 19, 2000, that the paper would now print 7 days a week, which added a Saturday issue; also morning delivery would supplant long-standing afternoon time frame. Eleven days later, hometown news was Todd Wheeler's hiring as head football coach at Armuchee. Principal Tony Bethune said this about the former Pepperell Dragon, "Everybody I talked to had good things to say about him." In late summer, there was a buzz in Lindale and North Floyd about Hunnicutt versus Wheeler jamboree to be played on Indians' field on Friday, August 25. However, the contest turned into a typical preseason scrimmage with turnovers, penalties, and sloppy play. Although PHS scored twice, Coach Wheeler was pleased with his defense against a tough offense. Coach Hunnicutt was also happy with his team, saying, "We looked quick and tackled well." We opened football season on September 1 on Alabama Road against a much improved Coosa squad that went 6–4 last year. Normally, Dragons versus Eagles occurred in Barron Stadium Shrine Classic, but reclassification and scheduling conflicts had eliminated them both from the fray. PHS was favored by 12; they won by 33 (47–14) mostly because RB Breon Ford carried 24 times for 195 yards and 5 touchdowns. The battle took more than 3 hours to play and totaled 20 penalties and 7 turnovers. In a new millennium, some things never change as Cartersville visited Lindale on September 8. Coach Hunnicutt told sports editor Jim O'Hara, "If I was a spectator, I'd come to this one." Gold and White led by 8 at intermission, but Purple took "complete control of the tempo" in second half to win 28–21.

They rushed for 340 yards with zero passing; for us, Roddy Ware and Breon scored on short TD runs, and Holiday returned a fumble 35 yards. Next against North Cobb High School of Kennesaw, host Pepperell repeated last week's scoring plays of Ware and Ford TD runs coupled with Hutchings's 35-yard interception return to win 20–0. We totaled 364 yards of offense, and it would have been worse but for 4 fumbles. As the crow flies, it is 70 miles due east on Georgia Highway 20 to Cumming where 1-loss Forsyth Central played error-free ball, excepting 1 fumble, on Friday night, September 22, yet were beaten by visiting Pepperell 21–17. In quarter one of a well-played and entertaining contest, Pedro Holiday returned a punt from midfield to goal; in period three, he caught a 20-yard toss from Ware for another score. But the Dragon faithful crowd were holding their breath as Forsyth's Bulldogs scored a touchdown late in third stanza to pull ahead 17–14; not to worry, QB Roddy Ware led us downfield on a final-period 50-yard drive capped off by Breon Ford's short winning TD run with 3:12 remaining. Coach Hunnicutt thought we grew up and came together as a team at that point. Coach Bob Herndon's crew would win their next 7 games to qualify for Class AAA playoffs. Region 6-AAA opener for Lindale occurred in Carrollton's Charlie Grisham Stadium on September 29 where Coach Ross New had replaced the late Ben Scott. Same old scouting report said his squad was strong, fast, and well coached. Yet just when it seemed we could never beat Black and Gold, PHS now had defeated them in consecutive years 13–7 and last Friday night 16–0. Breon Ford had 96 yards rushing, Pedro Holiday caught 9 passes, and Corey Hutchins snagged a 24-yard TD reception; still it was field general Roderick Ware who led us to a 16–0 victory. He threw for 217 aerial yards and ran for 40 more. The losing coach said later, "Pepperell showed a phenomenal amount of balance offensively." Prior to Hiram Hornets visiting on homecoming night, October 6, Lindale's Dragons shot to number four in Class triple-A rankings; it seems when you beat Carrollton, people take notice. Despite having 3 touchdowns called back for infractions, we still won 35–21. Paulding County's contingent fell behind 28–13 at intermission thanks to Ware's TD tosses to Justin Bruce and Kevin Popham plus a short scoring run by Breon. Eighteen first downs netted 364 total offensive yards for the winner. At halftime, senior April Jeanette Maddox was chosen as homecoming queen 2000. Ms. Maddox was a member of honor chorus, FBLA, Drama Club, Miss Pepperell Court, and National Creative Society. Paul McCoy was elected homecoming king. On Friday the thirteenth, Cedartown came calling to Lindale. Both coaches were quoted in local media as saying, "We have played very well at times this year." Coach Hill added that "in the past we haven't matched up well against them, we think it will be better this year." Bulldog defensive coordinator Everett Kelley critiqued Gold and White as very much like old Carrollton teams in that they would show you 20 odd formations (against Hiram, we Dragons ran 11 different formations in the first quarter) with a power I back set that pounded the scrimmage line, and then they went 4 wide-outs. Polk County's Bulldogs used a 95-yard kick return, a 67-yard pass, and a 20-yard TD run to lead at intermission 20–7. They would not need any more points, but it did take a batted-away pass (they tipped 7 passes and had 1 interception) with 1:25 left to preserve a 20–14 victory. Statistically, Hill's troops outplayed us 346 to 222 total yards to go with a 12–7 advantage in first downs; penalties and turnovers were almost even. An open date followed Cedartown with a road trip to Villa Rica next.

Much of off week was spent on conditioning in hopes of solving our second-quarter swoon that had bedeviled the squad all season. Coach Hunnicutt was concerned, saying, "I do not know what the problem is as we have not tired in the fourth period like most teams." As usual, Villa's Wildcats were a good, quick squad loaded with talent; however, Dragon O scored 20 points after intermission to win 34–27. Pepperell was up 21–8 in quarter third only to see the Wildcats knot it at 21–21. With a final quarter remaining, QB Ware hit big tight end Justin Bruce for 7 yards and a TD. But the home 11 stormed back with a quick touchdown that was set up by a 57-yard pass. But their PAT was wide, leaving PHS ahead 28–27 with 5:00 remaining. Then Gold and White made 3 critical plays. Freshman Marcus Dixon tipped a throw over the middle, and Justin Bruce intercepted; Pedro Holiday put a "final nail in Villa Rica's coffin" when he sprinted 12 yards to goal with 56 seconds left. The losing squad led in total offense 369 to 253 yards, but they also fumbled several times. There was a time when Central of Carrollton football team put fear in the hearts of opponents; however, since a 15–0 state championship in 1987, Central had gone 61–63 with only 5 winning seasons. This year's contingent was sitting at 3–5, yet they were to be respected. Unfortunately, playmaker Corey Hutchins was sidelined with a broken collarbone suffered last week. We were 14-point favorites in Carroll County on Friday, November 3, and almost covered the line winning 28–15. We gained 218 to 74 yards rushing but fell behind in passing with 160 against 78. Breon Ford scored on running TDs of 26, 5, and 20 yards; Roderick Ware benefited from Central's keying on Ford and Holiday to rack up several all-purpose yards.

Senior night on November 10 in Lindale wrapped up the regular season. *Rome News-Tribune* sports writer David Dawson wrote on Saturday morning that Matt Wheat got some "PT." Starting quarterback Roderick Ware got some "R-and-R." Wideout Pedro Holiday got a pair of TDs, and Pepperell got a "W" that clinched home field advantage in next week's first round of state competition. Our offense put up 466 total yards and led comfortably 28–7 at intermission. Fresh names filled the statistics chart as Wheat completed 4 of 7 for 42 yards and a score; Mark Middleton caught a touchdown pass from Ware. Chris Davenport rushed for 57 yards on 10 carries that included a 6-pointer; Willie Robinson contributed 28 yards on 8 rushes. Meanwhile, our defenders caused 4 turnovers, including interceptions by Kevin Popham and Will Sullins. Coach Hunnicutt happily rested his starters and got nobody hurt. Playoff games for Lindale had become commonplace, yet home court advantage was fleeting. It had been the second round 1997 since we hosted. On November 17, Towers High School visited South Floyd. The institution is located in DeKalb County just east of Atlanta, and a trip can be made in about 90 minutes in non–rush hour. The Maroon and White was established in 1963 and used Avondale Stadium for home games. Their defense was exemplary, recording shutouts in 7 of their last 8 victories while allowing only 4.3 points per outing. Titan offense was no slouch either, averaging 4 touchdowns per contest. Both squads sported 8–2 slates in Class AAA. Matt Sanders had replaced injured Jim Hellriegel at center for Friday night's contest, and senior Justin Lee Nichols was scheduled to start at offensive tackle for 50 straight times. Pepperell ran for 3 touchdowns, kicked a PAT, and collected a safety in winning 22–0 over Towers. Breon Ford ran 91 and 9-yards to goal while Chris Davenport crossed it once from 4 yards out. But it was our defense that made the play of the night. Trailing by only a 2-point safety midway of quarter three, Towers marched down to our 3-yard line where QB Brian Anderson attempted an option keeper off tackle for a go-ahead score; however, Paul McCoy penetrated and disrupted, forcing a lateral pitch to an unprepared trailing back who bobbled the pigskin. Mark Middleton and Justin Bruce pounded him loose from the ball which rolled inside goal; a large pileup occurred with PHS recovering. Coach Hunnicutt said later, "That was a great play Paul McCoy made on their quarterback back down there. It turned the game around." Ultimately, Dragon defenders gave up only 86 yards of real estate. Three snaps later, Breon Ford dashed 91 yards to paydirt for an 8–0 lead. As our depth began to take a toll, Ford scored again this time from 9 yards out. With a dwindling clock, PHS special teams blocked and recovered a punt; directly Chris Davenport made it an official 22–0 win with a 4-yard TD jaunt. The second round would take place in Hart County again. Pepperell beat writer David Dawson asked his Lindale readers where they were on Friday, November 19, 1999; the answer was easy: in a cold, blustery Herndon Stadium 3 hours away from South Floyd where we lost to the Bulldogs 35–12.

Some 370 days later on November 24, Hunnicutt's Dragons would get a chance to redeem near Lake Hartwell. This group of unbeaten Bulldogs was state ranked number one and rated better than last year's contingent, which lost last year in finals to Cartersville 27–21. Lynn felt "really good about our chances." He was feeling even better after Auburn commit Pedro Holiday returned their opening kickoff 71 yards and Breon Ford scooted into goal from the 4 to give us a 13–0 advantage in period one. However, local sportswriter Anthony Dasher summed it up afterward, "But back came Hart County." Incredibly, in a steady rain, Hart scored 21 second-half points behind star QB Jeff Leard who completed 14 of 23 throws for 232 yards (they rushed for only 41 yards) and 4 touchdowns; there were no fumbles. Winning QB Leard gave major credit for the 28–19 victory to a group of sideline boys who kept the game balls dry all night. Coach William Devane's 12–0 crew hosted Swainsboro next week. Unfortunately for them, Rayvan Teague's Tigers pounded out a 48–20 victory. On December 16 in Fitzgerald, these same Tigers would win Class AAA championship 6–0 to close out a great season at 14–1.

On Christmas Day 2000, *Rome News-Tribune* published all-area. Sophomore Breon Ford was first-team running back; Pedro Holiday lined up at wide receiver, and Justin Nichols repeated as offensive lineman. Second-squad quarterback was Roderick Ware along with end Justin Bruce; freshman Marcus Dixon made it for all-purpose player. Defensively on first team was senior Brian Dudley at D end as was Paul McCoy at linebacker and junior Corey Hutchings, D back. Second teamer was Luke Sheffield as DB.

"COACH HANGING UP HIS WHISTLE" BY JIM O'HARA (DECEMBER 12, 2006, *ROME NEWS-TRIBUNE*)

Lynn Hunnicutt's 24-year run as head coach at Pepperell High School included a state championship in 1990. Football and Pepperell High School have always been close to Lynn Hunnicutt's heart. On Monday night, at the football team's postseason banquet, he told those who share that love he is going to ease the strain on that Dragon-filled heart. After being Pepperell's head coach for 24 years, Hunnicutt announced he will be hanging up his whistle for good.

"It's a good time to do this," Hunnicutt said of his retirement, one that brings to close a stellar career that includes a 186–94–1 record, three region championships, two state semi-final appearances at the Georgia Dome and a state championship in 1990. We've got a new school, a new guy, a new track—things that have been great additions for the school—and then there's the health issue," said Hunnicutt, who suffered a heart attack earlier this year, "I want to enjoy the rest of my life."

Hunnicutt will remain as a teacher at the school and as its athletic director according to Principal Phil Ray. "I consider coach Hunnicutt a valuable member of the faculty," said Ray, who added the job will officially be posted after Christmas. "He is committed to every student and every sport at Pepperell High School. He has the good of the school in mind. The close bond between the school and the coach is a lifelong one, with Hunicutt developing a love for football as a 10th grader, finally convincing his mother he wanted to play. By the time he was a high school senior, the youngster had emerged as a prized college recruit, opting to play for Vince Dooley at the University of Georgia, where he became a key member of the team; he was picked the offensive team captain as a senior. "I still consider that to be one of the greatest things that ever happened to me," the former Bulldog said, "being selected by my teammates."

It was during those years in Athens that Lynn decided to become a teacher and a coach. Before that however, the Dallas Cowboys came around with what was like an IQ test; they were really ahead of their time and Lynn had some hope to be taken in the late rounds. Yet, he was 6-2 225lbs. and according to him with marginal speed. He was not chosen during the draft but both Philadelphia Eagles and Los Angeles Rams expressed interest in him as a free agent. But Margie and I married in December of senior year and those offers were not all that attractive, so I just decided it was time for me to go on to other things. In 1973, the 22 year old began teaching and working as an assistant coach for Robert Davis at Warner Robins High. In 1981 was named the head coach at Fitzgerald High 70 miles south of his first job. Two years later the top position at Peppereall became vacant and Hunnicutt returned to Lindale, not only to take over the football program but also to help revamp the school's entire athletic program and facilities. "At that time all we had was a baseball field and a gym," Hunnicutt said. "We had no football field and either used Barron Stadium – when East Rome or West Rome weren't in town—or play on another county school's field."

Getting everybody on the same page was a major task," he said. "It took a strong commitment by the coaches, the community and the booster club, and they stayed with me." Just six years after coming back to Pepperell, Hunnicutt directed the Dragons to the 1990 state championship, a season that remains special to him. "That was a very special year, but at the same time, some of the best coaching we did as a staff was when we had teams that didn't have such a good record. They were overachievers."

Hunnicutt realizes some outside the Pepperell community consider him a tough, gritty and emotional coach, a trait that was his trade-mark on the sideline. "I know that I have that Billy Goat Gruff label but a coach's relationship is unique, something a lot of people on the outside do not know about. It took a strong commitment to play for me. Sacrifice commitment and discipline—these were the only way we could be successful."

Hunnicutt, a member of the Rome-Floyd Sports Hal of Fame, is quick to point out he was not alone during his tenure, noting the friendship and support he received from all of his assistants, including Ken Mitchell, Charles Kelly and Joe Knight and two current assistant coaches who have been with him for most of the 24 years Jimmy Farrer and Steve Horne.

More than anything, Lynn said, his wife of 34 years, Margie, has been the one person who has been by his side throughout it all. "Every coach's wife has to go through so much, the good and the bad. When I came back to Pepperell, Margie raised our two sons by herself for six months. I know it was hard. She has been real special to me."

INTERSCHOLASTIC COMPETITION—BASKETBALL

1951–'52 Inaugural

Just as amazing as its success at football, PHS's inaugural 1951–'52 basketball squads were equally competitive. The school's first yearbook shows boys varsity basketball featured thirteen varsity members coached by Olan Cosper and captained by Larry Joe Duncan; our JV also numbered thirteen. The women's 1951–'52 combined rosters totaled twenty-seven players led by Barbara Jean Mathis. A coach identified as Ms. Owsley was present in team pictures. The *News-Tribune* posted on Thursday, November 29, 1951, that Pepperell's inaugural varsity squads would open tomorrow night at seven thirty in Russell H. Leonard Memorial Gymnasium. However, there was more to the name than a brick arena.

Russell H. Leonard (October 4, 1888–November 5, 1949)

Russell H. Leonard, President

This large and imposing building was funded in the late 1940s, compliments of its namesake who was president and treasurer of Pepperell Mills. Company executives enjoyed annual trips south to escape New England winters. While escorting such a tour of Lindale assets in 1948, smooth-talking school superintendent Slick Moulton recalled to the Massachusetts group Captain Meikleham's 1929 directive "build us a high school." Now twenty years later, there were no plans for such; furthermore, outdoor grounds had to be used for all physical education activities and also interscholastic sports, weather permitting. In the walkabout, Mr. Leonard and associates took note of these inadequacies, especially a lack of covered spaces; whether planned or not, Mr. Moulton thought out loud, "I wonder how much it would cost us to build a gymnasium?" Russell Leonard responded, "It won't cost you anything—I will build it." This reflected his belief that balance sheets were figures but no more important than human beings. Before the day was over, he had promised Lindale a state-of-the-art building. In relating this story to me, local historian Bob Baker said, "They didn't call E. R. Moulton Slick for nothing." Construction began in early 1949, and when completed, it met all expectations and dominated the campus.

Sadly, Mr. Leonard did not live to see his namesake, for on Saturday, November 5, 1949, president and treasurer Russell H. Leonard died suddenly of a heart attack at his home in Brookline, Massachusetts, a suburb of Boston. The sixty-one-year old was survived by his wife, the former Helen E. Case of Springfield; one son, Dr. Fields Leonard; and two daughters, Mrs. George Brownell and Mrs. Marion Caryl. Ten weeks after his passing, page 1 of *Rome News-Tribune* in the January 16, 1950, Monday edition featured, "Pepperell Opens Huge Gymnasium." Underneath, an article told that "yesterday afternoon before an audience that taxed the capacity of its bleachers, plant general manager R. Donald Harvey noted this dedication of Russell H. Leonard Memorial Gymnasium was a sad and proud occasion—proud that the building would add to existing amenities already provided by our deceased president/treasurer." He then described Mr. Leonard as "best business coach ever." Lindaleans were treated to a background of vocal music by our boys' choir directed by Ms. Evelyn Harle; invocation was offered by Reverend T. R. Morse, pastor of Lindale Church of God. Benediction was pronounced by Reverend J. W. Stephens of Lindale Methodist; before and after dedication, Pepperell's band was heard in concert directed by Ralph Champion Jr. From 2:30 to 5:30 p.m., the building was open for all to see. In later years, our younger generation shortened the gym name to just "the Leonard."

Russell Leonard was born on October 4, 1888, in Somerset, Massachusetts, into an old Massachusetts family that came from Wales during the great Puritan migration of 1620–1640. The family quickly found employment in local ironworks, which led them to establish their own metal-fabricating business in Bay Colony where there was ample ore, timber, and water power. This industry smelted, cast, or wrought household utensils, fireplace implements, and a myriad of products; it operated much like tobacco plantations in Virginia with living/working areas complete with cottages, schools, churches, and company stores. By the first decade of the twentieth century, three life events occurred to young Leonard. First, he graduated from Harvard College in 1910, and his grandfather Job and father, Henry, died; furthermore, their company was no long profitable. In 1912, he chose to liquidate assets. He then turned from metals to "cast his lot" with the rising textile industry in New England; as a new college graduate, Leonard saw a great opportunity for able, aggressive young men not bound by former ways of doing business.

He believed that a factory system or a concentration of industry brought about by improving technology (steam) was the future. Twenty-four months later in 1914, he became treasurer and chief executive officer of Wampanoag Mills in Fall River; within a decade, his aggressive ability made him a marked man for any company seeking growth.

Post–World War I economy changed dramatically fostered by style-conscious clientele led by the automobile's annual "new" models; staple merchandise no longer sold itself. The great China trade was lost to cheap and unscrupulous Japanese competition; pent-up military demands were no longer available, leaving domestic markets oversupplied and fighting for survival. The Pepperell executives were not oblivious to this trend; they needed a leader and were attracted to the record and personality of the young man from Fall River. Unfortunately, it was a hard sell; when approached, he was very reluctant to enter the "rough and tumble" battles that were imminent. Finally, on November 5, 1924, after repeated interviews, the thirty-six-year-old agreed to become treasurer and president of Pepperell with one basic stipulation—he was to have "an absolute free hand to formulate new policies and choose his own lieutenants," all of which ultimately brought unparalleled growth. Page 90 of *The Men and Times of Pepperell* states, "He brought to the management of Pepperell the most pragmatic and realistic mind in the Company's long history." With foresight of an older man, he understood that textile factories must adapt to "incisive changes" occurring in human affairs. Women were becoming emancipated politically, socially, economically, and physically. They cast off yards and yards of clothes and wore only scanty short garments, thus reducing demand for ginghams and ruffled petticoats. In addition, Americans began to substitute paper for cotton towels and napkins; foreigners began to compete in our export market. He clearly saw a "rough and tumble" battle that lay ahead for cotton mills. It was against this grim background that Russell Leonard built Pepperell into a closely knit sales and manufacturing organization with a solid *esprit de corps* that grew from one mill in a single state to five in four states. Mechanical and inventive skills of some combined with organizational genius of others to produce a spirit of trust, comradeship, and profit. Its output went seven times greater; major products increased from six to twenty-two. They sold widely across America and thirty-two different countries, making the Red Dragon trademark known in hemispheres as well as states and territories.

Corporately, the Massachusetts cotton mills of Georgia (Lindale) had not shown extensive profit for several years; therefore, in 1926, its capital stock was offered to Mr. Leonard's group and quickly accepted. It was a match made in heaven, for the Floyd County plant was actually well equipped and well managed by Captain H. P. Meikleham. On December 13, 1926, the Lindale operation became a "vital and integral" part of Pepperell Manufacturing. The same year saw introduction of a line of sheets called Lady Pepperell (the first bedsheets stamped with the Pepperell name was sold in 1851).

Drawing on his earlier professional knowledge of ironworks and tobacco communities, Leonard promoted a model for Lindale (see page 312). Although the financial collapse of 1929 brought havoc to cotton textiles, Pepperell continued to grow fueled by rumors of war. In the last prewar year of 1939, the company sold 308,000,000 yards of cloth—more than 175,000 miles of fabric. Through genuine leadership and devoted teamwork, company shareholders reaped some $9,000,000 in dividends for the fifteen years prior to Germany invading Poland in 1939. To put it another way, on page 102, Dane Yorke in *The Men and Times of Pepperell* explained these figures as lived through on Park Street, Lindale, USA: "They spell homes kept together, marriages made, children born and educated, churches maintained and communal business helped. The whole interlaced structure of the Pepperell communities felt these wholesome influences."

During World War II, Lindale and parent company received three Army-Navy "E" awards for such various products as parachute cloth, sheets for barracks and hospitals, herringbone twill for soldiers, and sturdy chambray for sailors. In 1943, Russell Leonard closed out his annual report, which also marked the company's centennial birthday with typical foresight. He believed change was inevitable and would rule the postwar world, but it should be a period of opportunity for all; it would be driven by returning men and women who would be abler and better. Then he struck a keynote for Pepperell's second century, saying, "It is age that dreads change; it is youth that welcomes it and finds its prospect heartening and encouraging."

Leonard's gymnasium was christened on Tuesday evening, January 17, or one day after its dedication, when Pepperell Junior High girls and boys defeated Celanese 20–6 and 16–11 respectively. In opening round, Marie Norris, Ducky Stansell, Peggy Godfrey, Ethel Smith, Nancy Wood, and Margie Tucker were starters. Subs were Joyce Turner, Alice Pence, Sara Givens, Maxine Nickles, June Knowles, Barbara Smith, Nancy Sheppard, and Katheryne Crump. Our girls outclassed Celanese by holding a 12–3 advantage at halftime and 16–3 after period three. In the nightcap, our boys lined up with Charles Wood, Bud White, Howard Smith, Jack Pence, and Donald Ridley; subs were Ray Treglown and Jimmy Green. This game was knotted several times before we pulled away.

Fast forward 22 months to first high school varsity action in Leonard Gymnasium. Cassville HS of Bartow County was first competition on Friday, November 30, 1951. *Rome News-Tribune* suggested 3 transfers each from McHenry would play important roles in success of both girls' and boys' teams. We would compete in Class B Region 6. Coach Olan Cosper's men dropped a 62–59 double overtime to Cass in a game that left the large crowd limp afterward. To wit, with 3 seconds to play in regulation, Captain Larry Joe Duncan intercepted a pass and scored to force overtime 53–53 in a battle that was knotted on 9 occasions and saw a lead change 16 times. Bobby Turner led us in scoring with 27 markers. The ladies led at all stops in winning 43–28; Captain Barbara Jean Mathis "flipped" in 17 points while Christine Miles and Peggy Godfrey contributed 14 and 12 in order. On Friday next, same gym, Rockmart fell in a doubleheader; girls won 42–20 behind Barbara Mathis's 19 points and Christine Miles 14. In the nightcap, it was 45–24 as Turner hit for 14 and Duncan 11; the first half was competitive, but we still led 16–12 at intermission. In the second game versus Rome High on Tuesday, December 11, home crowd fans were treated to "the half court shot of the year" by a tall lanky sophomore named Robert Marcus Wheeler (RM). In bold print, *News-Tribune* featured, "**Last-Second Goal Gives Dragons Win over Rome**...Wheeler's Long Toss Cops 54–53 Overtime Tilt." Tensions ran high for four quarters, and at times the contest resembled a "miniature football game." Two Hilltoppers and a Dragon fouled out with 5 personals; also referees disqualified 1 apiece for "excessive roughness." PHs girls completed a 39–7 sweep over City High. Next evening, as a good omen, Pepperell's gigantic electric Christmas star shone for the twenty-first time. Our undefeated

6–0 sextet ran roughshod over Trion on Tuesday, December 18, 1951, in the Leonard; Miles and Mathis chalked up 14 markers each while Sara Givens contributed 11. PHS boys held up their end with a 55–21 pasting of the visitors in which we led 30–13 at half; Bobby Turner had 20 points while Duncan and Olaf Bergwell followed with 11 and 9 respectively. In the new year, we visited Cedartown on Friday, January 4, and swept them 49–19 in girls and 57–24 for boys. Christine Miles netted 19 for Pepperell, which led at all stops 13–2, 28–6, and 39–7. Bobby Turner "blasted" for 30 points in our 33-point win. Armuchee felt our wrath on the fifteenth in the Leonard as our girls won 38–14 and boys, 63–30. In the first game, substitute Jerry Denise Holbrooks was high point with 12 followed by Mathis with 11; we were now 9–1. Coach Olan Cosper's men ran away and hid in their 33-point victory. *News-Tribune* wrote on January 16 that Duncan, Turner, and Bergwell were "swishing them in from all angles" to the tune of 18, 17, and 16 markers respectively. We traveled to Calhoun on Tuesday, January 22, and came away with 2 victories. Our sextet romped 59–36 with Mathis and Miles bucketing 25 and 21 markers apiece. Pepperell's quintet hammered the Jackets 57–30; more than a dozen Dragons played and 11 scored. In Chattooga's County's Trion High School gym, the "shooting twosome" of Miles and Mathis hit for 21 and 17 to win going away 51–25. In the nightcap, Cosper's crew shot 12 of 15 from the foul line to go with Bergwell and Turner's 18 and 17 buckets. Both PHS squads were now 12–2 on the year. We swept Cedartown again on February 1 with the boys winning 57–39 with Duncan "peppering" 14 markers; all starters were represented in the scoring column. PHS women won 43–28 with Miles netting 18 and Godfrey 16. Speedy forward Mathis managed only 2 points, her lowest output of the season. The Class B tourney began the week of February 11 with girls' bracket first. The boys followed 7 days later. The *News-Tribune* reported on Tuesday, February 6, that "high-stepping" PHS Dragons trounced Calhoun to run their combined records to 15–2. The girls romped 44–29 with Barbara Mathis rebounding with 20 points after 2 subpar games; our men played "firehouse" ball leading 41–8 at intermission and 52–18 going into the final quarter. Bobby Turner bucketed 16 while Bergwell added 14. Outstanding play on our part had given both squads the top seeds in the seventh district tourney which began on Monday, February 11, in Calhoun. On Tuesday, Pepperell sharpshooters Mathis and Miles poured in 48 of their team's 52 points in a 52–39 win against Lake View High. In the second round, we downed Valley Point 53–44. But basketball is a tournament game as attested to our third-round 38–21 loss to West Side High of Whitfield County on Thursday, February 14. Our top scorers, Barbara Mathis and Christine Miles, were held to 11 and 9 points respectively; nevertheless, our first-year girls squad won 16 of 19 games. While the women were playing in Calhoun, Cosper's boys were upset in the Leonard Gym by Darlington 44–43. The nip and tuck affair was tied 8 times in the second half and changed hands on a dozen occasions. Fighting a dwindling clock, we rallied from 5 down when Wallace Kelley hit 2 free throws to tie at 40–40. Seconds later, Darlington had to tie at 43 all; then with the clock stopped, Sonny Corum sunk a foul shot to win. On Wednesday, February 20, after a first-round bye in the seventh district Class B tourney in Calhoun, Pepperell boys led comfortably all the way in defeating Armuchee 70–42; Bobby Turner hit the nylon cords for 23 points. One night later, Cass "turned on the heat" and downed Gold and White 65–45; we trailed 32–29 at intermission but could get no closer as they began to "click from all angles." Olaf Bergwell and Larry Duncan led us in scoring with 15 and 13; we missed a chance to play in the finals Saturday night at Leonard Memorial. On Thursday, July 31, Lang Gammon's *Lindale News* reported forwards Barbara Mathis and Christine Miles would compete in the all-star game held during Atlanta's annual coaching clinic.

1952–'53 Season

Following outstanding first year of varsity basketball, the Dragons began the 1952–'53 season practice on Monday, November 17, 1952. Maurice Culberson had been named the boys' mentor while Mr. Sutton led the girls with Alabama graduate Carey Ann Skinner assisting. Both squads lost double-digit seniors from last year but retained a good nucleolus. Coach Culberson returned Swafford, Wheeler, and White who were rangy under the basket while Norris, Bennett, Toole, Yarbrough, and newcomer Charles Williams were backcourt men expected to play vital roles for our quintet. Coach Sutton's ladies would feature Tucker, Norris, Stansell, Smith, and Godfrey back for another season of half-court competition. PHS men finished last year at 17–3, and the women racked up an impressive 16–2 slate. After winning 2 from Cave Spring, the Dragons ran into a buzzsaw in Jasper on Friday night, December 5; our quintet had no answer for 6-foot-9-inch center Hulsey, losing 49–37. The women's 54–19 loss was not so much a surprise, for Pickens won its 128th straight regular season game. On December 16 against host Rome, big Swafford bucketed 21 points; the team hit 17 foul shots while Wheeler and White controlled backboards to win 63–53. Dragonette Peggy Godfrey "couldn't miss" as she scored 26 in our 45–21 win. On the first Friday of 1953, Dragon men nipped Berry HS at the Leonard 49–48 behind White's, Williams's, and Swafford's 10 markers each. Four days later, they swept a twin bill at Cave Spring. The Jasper Dragons visited the Leonard on Friday night, January 9; in the past four years, their women's team had an overall mark of 135 victories and only 2 losses. In an earlier meeting, they won 54–19 in girls' play and 49–37 for boys. It was same song, different verse as they downed our girls again, 65–37, and Lindale men, 52–36. For Pickens, Peggy Taylor and Bob Hulsey swished the nets for 43 and 21 points respectively in the twin killing. Marie Norris and Peggy Godfrey netted 16 and 12 for PHS while Charles Williams was our best scorer with 11 buckets. Coach Culberson used 10 men while the winners played "iron man five" throughout.

The Lindale crew turned back the favor on Trion nights later. Williams, Wheeler, and White hit most of our baskets in a 47–40 victory; Trion forward Clyde Cobb scored once at the wrong basket but led all shooters with 20. Mss. Norris and Godfrey collected 12 and 11 in a slow-moving 37–21 affair. As the season began to wind down, Pepperell got shellacked at home on Tuesday, January 27, by Rome 56–33 in which their defense allowed only 10 goals while holding our leading scorer Swafford without a goal from the field; however, Dragonettes nipped Hilltoppers 39–35. The "ancient flame of rivalry" was rekindled on Friday night, January 30, when Shannon came visiting. It was a split decision as Blue bested our boys 53–46; Charles Williams and J. W. Bennett kept the game close with 13 and 11 markers. Lindale women prevailed 45–31 behind Marie Norris's 32 points. On. The first Tuesday in February at Trion, we swept the home team 63–41 girls and 50–42 boys. Marie Norris shot lights out with 33 markers while Charles Swafford netted 18 points for boys. On Saturday night, February 7, at Cassville, our men scratched out a 50–49 victory behind Charles Williams's 23 buckets; despite a determined effort in waning minutes, Cass girls downed us 60–52; Marie Norris hit for 24 big points. After a February 7 1-point win over Cassville, the men were 12–8, and the women showed 13–6. In Dallas, Georgia, on Monday, February 16, Marie Norris sank 2 field goals and a free throw inside 37 seconds of play to help defeat McEachern 52–50 in the first round of seventh district tourney. But the following night, we ran into a rangy Dallas High School sextet that administered a 64–48 whipping despite Marie Norris's 27 markers. The boys fared much better at Cave Spring in the first round of their tournament; the *Rome News-Tribune* said it all on Wednesday, February 25, "Pepperell Rips Buchanan 108–35 in Cage Tourney." The game set a new scoring record for District 7; Swafford, R. M. Wheeler, and Troy Coffia with 17, 15, and 14 respectively. The following evening, we gained semifinal round with a 58–2 hard-fought win over Acworth who led on into the second half. Charles Swafford, Wheeler, and Charles Williams collected 15, 14, and 10 points; Williams got 8 of his markers in critical period three. On Friday evening, February 27, Pepperell and Cassville "tangles" in the semis to see who faced Lakeview in the finals. And it was Cass behind J. B. Bearden's 20 points in the 63–41 win over PHS; for us, Wheeler, Bud White, and Williams tallied 14, 10, and 6 markers.

1953–'54 Season

The 1953–'54 roundball squads traveled to Coosa on Friday, November 20. The boys' outfit coached by Maurice Culberson returned only 3 lettermen, Charles Williams, Sam Bennett, and R. M. Wheeler. The lack of veterans did not affect the outcome as the tall visitors romped 62–47, "wheelhorse" Troy Coffia netting 24 and Wheeler 15. Coach J. W. Sutton's girls lost a nip and tuck affair 44–38. This group returned 4 with playing experience, Sybil and Sylvia Packer, Elsie Terhune, and Alice Grissom. On Tuesday, November 24, we traveled to Dallas and split the wins; the girls "took it on the chin" 44–24 with Alice Pence being top scorer with 8. The Dragon quintet edged the home squad 49–45; we managed to stay ahead all the way because of R. M. Wheeler's 19 markers and Sam Bennett's 10. Cave Spring came visiting Russell Leonard Gym on first night of December and edged the men 54–53; Wheeler hit for 17 points while Jo Jo Stephens contributed 13. But the women claimed their first victory 29–28 as Sybil Packer canned 12 markers. On December 4, the PHS quintet trounced visiting Coosa 73–41; we had good scoring from Troy Coffia's 24 points, R. M. Wheeler's 15, and Jack Pence's 11. The visiting women "tripped" our girls 38–34 in a game tied at half 16 all; they managed a 30–28 advantage at the end of three periods; Barbara Brown netted 17 for Lindale. On Tuesday, December 8, we invaded Summerville and swept a doubleheader; varsity girls won 43–33 with Elsie Terhune ringing up 27 markers. Varsity boys triumphed 43–33 with Wheeler and Stephens bucketing 16 and 15 points together. We also won a B game with Wesley Connell hitting for 8 points. Playing a rare Thursday (December 10) night game so as not to conflict with Model's Class B football championship quest, Pepperell traveled to Rome's junior high gym and dealt their boys a first loss in 3 outings 51–31; the Dragons' R. M. Wheeler and Coffia controlled both backboards which helped R. M. Wheeler sink 21 points to go with senior J. W. Bennett's 4 "long range swishers." Our girls completed the sweep by edging their hosts 35–33 in a "bitter battle" that was tied at 30–30 with 1:30 to play in period four; Elsie Terhune and Sybil Packer hit for 16 and 15 in order. The slate now stood at 5–1 for Culberson's boys and 3–3 for Sutton's girls. Visiting Coosa won 1 and lost 1 on Tuesday evening, December 15; the PHS quintet defeated the Eagles 58–53 with our 2 leading scorers (Wheeler and Coffia) getting 19 and 17 points; Coach Sutton's women led 13–8 at intermission, but Coosa doubled us 33–16 in the 2 final quarters to win 41–29. It is always nice to beat Model in basketball, and that was what both our squads did on December 18 at Leonard Memorial. Sunday's December 20, 1953, paper headlined, "PEPPERELL EDGES TO TWIN CAGE VICTORY OVER MODEL." In all honesty, Ralph Tuggle's quintet had few practice hours due to football play; nevertheless, they made it interesting before losing 58–51. In our seventh win of the season, Wheeler hit 20 buckets to go with Coffia's and Stephens's 14 and 11. J. W. Sutton's women led 19–14 at halftime on the way to a 35–29 victory; Elsie Terhune was a high point for us with 16 markers. The boys continued winning on January 5, downing Cedartown 56–50; we led at all stops 17–8, 25–22, and 43–41 up against the Bulldog "two platoon" style of play; again, leading scorers were Coffia, Wheeler, and Stephens with 16, 14, and 12 respectively. Lindale girls were not so lucky, losing 45–32; after an 11–11 tie at the end of period one, we trailed thereafter despite Elsie Terhune's 16 points. On Friday, January 8, Troy Coffia "wore out the hoops" with 22 points leading us to a narrow 44–43 victory over Rockmart; it was his hook shot in the waning minutes that put us ahead to stay while Jo Jo Stephens added a bucket late and helped "freeze" the ball for the last 30 seconds. The girls trailed 18–16 at intermission before rallying for a 36–30 win; Elsie Terhune again led us in scoring helped by Packer's and Brown's 9 and 7 points. On Tuesday, January 12, our boys revenged their only loss by edging host Cave Spring 44–43. Coffia and Bennett spearheaded our offense with 19 and 13 markers in order. It was Coffia's 9-point third quarter "splurge" that put us ahead to stay. Our girls improved to 6–5 downing the Springers 36–32 behind Terhune's and Barbara Brown's 16 and 11 markers respectively. January 15 saw Pepperell boys run their record to 12–1 with a 57–43 victory over visiting Dallas. Four of Troy Coffia's baskets came in the final quarter and kept pressure on the Tigers; he finished with 20 markers while Wheeler and Bennett chipped in with 13 and 8 in order. Elsie Terhune hit for 18 points in our 27–26 loss to the Lady Tigers; our downfall was inability to score only 2 points each in periods three and four. Pepperell men edged Rome 53–51 in OT on Friday, January 22, at the Leonard. It took Coffia's 16 first-half points, plus R. M. Wheeler's tying free throw sending it to overtime and J. W. Bennett's two-point "icer" in extra time to settle a game which resembled a football game at times. The girls' game, which was won by Rome 33–32, was equally exciting; it was deadlocked 23–23 at end of period three. With a minute left, Elsie Terhune "found the hoop" to put us ahead before Hilltopper substitute Coffman sank the winning basket. In Russell H. Leonard Memorial Gym, PHS outfought Trion boys 60–47 on Tuesday, January 26. The 15–1 Dragons trailed at the end of first, second, and third quarters before rallying midway in period four. Troy Coffia "swished" the nets for 22 big ones followed by Wheeler's 10. The Lindale lassies also trailed most of the game before inching ahead 26–25 at the end of quarter three; senior Barbara Ann Brown hit for 13 points in our 39–36 victory. At Berry's gym on Wednesday, January 27, PHS men improved to 16–1 with a 53–41 win. *Rome News-Tribune* reported, "Machine-like Pepperell pivotman Troy Coffia scored more than any Dragon this season by hitting for 29 markers." We ran away in the final period by holding Berry to only 3 points. Two streaks came to an end on Model's home court Friday, January 29; the Blue Devils stopped our 14-game winning streak 54–49 while the Devilettes won their first of the year 34–32. In the nightcap, Blues' Jerome Webb netted 26 markers, but it was his defense that shackled Pepperell's Coffia into only 4 total points, which made the difference. Wheeler and Williams kept us in the game with 18 and 11 buckets in order. In girls' action, Model led most of the way despite Elsie Terhune's 22 buckets. Tournament time on Monday, February 22, in the Leonard Gym saw us down Bremen before facing nemesis Model on Wednesday, February 24. A hard-fought verdict favored us 55–48; although PHS led at all breaks, we actually won without a field goal in the final quarter. However, as we slowed (freezing) the game, diminutive sophomore Jerry Bolton kept getting fouled and kept hitting free throws as the clock ticked down; in all, he sank 7 of 8. A trip to Cartersville was next to meet Cassville in the semifinals; unfortunately, we trailed 31–24 at intermission and had no answer for defending champion Cass, losing to them 65–55. Bennett and Bolton netted 10 markers each to close out the season. The following night before a standing-room-only crowd in the Leonard, Bearden hit for 36 in leading the Colonels to district crown against Calhoun.

1954–'55 Season

On November 10, basketball practice was wide open in preparation of a 26-game schedule. Men's coach Maurice Culberson welcomed Jo Jo Stephens, Jerry Bolton, and Harold Gresham back from last year's squad; Ted LaRue and Wesley Connell were expected to fill out the quintet. Olan Cosper would tutor the girls who finished at 8–12 last year; visiting Coosa would provide first competition on Friday night the eighteenth against a lineup of guards Aline Leach, Roma Kiser, and Shirley Cook in addition to forwards Freida Tyson, Jacquelyn Green, and Faye Cook. The boys had little trouble with the Eagles winning 52–33; however, the girls lost. A buzz saw Dallas squad came to the Leonard on the twenty-second and left with 2 victories; the girls lost 39–14 as the Tigerettes led at all stops. Roma Kiser was high scorer for PHS with 8. The men came up short 60–51 despite Jerry Bolton's 18 points. We trimmed a 24-point lead down to 9 late but could get no closer. For the ninth consecutive year, Pepperell's 2,800 employees were treated to a sumptuous Thanksgiving meal courtesy of General Manager R. D. Harvey and cafeteria supervisor Ms. Dorothy Scurry; the event began in 1946. Saturday night, November 27, or two days after Thanksgiving, our men dealt host Berry High a 48–44 loss with Jerry Bolton scoring 18 points again. LaFayette visited Lindale on the last night of November and were defeated 48–33 by our boys behind Jerry Bolton's 23 markers; the ladies lost 39–28 with Roma Kiser hitting for 14.

On Thursday night, December 2, Rome High Hilltoppers opened their season against Pepperell Dragons in a new home venue. Their new $10,000 ($95,500 in today's market) memorial gymnasium is located adjoining Barron Stadium; it has a regulation-size court with rollaway seating for 1,200 fans. A record turnout watched as the Dragonettes eked out a 43–37 victory, and Lindale men won a thriller 50–47. Another record likely fell as 100 fouls were called on the night—61 in the girls' contest. Four visiting players and 2 Romans were disqualified in the ladies' opener, and 3 boys were tabbed in the finale. It didn't seem fair that Lindale competed against

Marietta, yet the Cobb County version of a Blue Devil came to Leonard Memorial on Saturday night, December 4, and departed with 2 victories over the boys 55–38 and the ladies 28–15. The next Tuesday, we rode 13 miles west to Cave Spring where the ladies narrowly lost 42–36; Aline Leach and Roma Kiser topped our scorers with 15 and 11. Although junior Jerry Dan Bolton continued to rip the nets (20 points), our boys didn't fare much better in the finale, losing 61–51. Berry High School did not field a women's team; consequently, a junior and senior squad competed. On Wednesday, December 8, PHS's B team won by 55–52, and the first five downed the visitors 72–62. Bolton scorched the nets for 27 markers supported by Gresham and Stephens with 17 and 11. South Cobb High School of Austell visited the Leonard on Wednesday the fifteenth and split a doubleheader with Dragon girls losing handily in the opener 33–18; Roma Kiser and Aline Leach scored 8 points each. We trailed at all stops and never got untracked. In the nightcap, both squads employed a zone defense resulting in a low scoring affair won by Pepperell 37–33. Jerry Bolton's 19 buckets equaled more than half of our points.

In a precursor to the now popular Rome/Floyd County Christmas Tourney, a new and annual basketball tourney would begin in Rome's new Memorial Gym on Monday, December 20. Officially called Northeast Georgia High School Invitation Basketball Tournament, it was sponsored by Rome Recreation Department and the *Rome News-Tribune*. The meet was organized and sanctioned to promote basketball in our area. In the first round, PHS downed a tough Cedartown 43–39 and then faced Coosa in the semis. The Eagles provided no competition as we romped 56–29 with 10 different Dragons in the scoring column. Through the semis, an average of 450 paying customers had witnessed the games. The headlines on Thursday, December 23, per the *News-Tribune* was "**BOLTON LEADS PEPPERELL TO CAGE TOURNEY CROWN.**" With Bolton hitting 22 points and Harold Gresham adding 13, Gold and White never headed in trouncing highly regarded Springers 56–38. The top three squads were presented trophies by tournament chairman and recreation director W. F. Montgomery. After a yule season rest, we visited and defeated Summerville boys 49–43 with senior Harold Gresham netting 14 markers, but our women lost by 10 with Kiser and Barbara Sue Treglown netting 5 buckets apiece in a 37–27 loss. On January 11, 1955, our quintet downed visiting Douglasville 62–36, yet the big news was Jerry Bolton's school record 31 points which bested Bobby Turner's 1952 mark by 1. PHS girls lost their eighth contest in 11 starts 37–27; Roma Kiser led in scoring with 15 buckets. Playing without 2 regulars Jo Jo Stephens and Wesley Connell because of injury and sickness, we traveled south to Rockmart on Tuesday, January 18, and came away with a 65–60 victory; Bolton and Fred Mathis accounted for 44 points combined. Although Roma Kiser "found the nets" for 15 baskets, the women lost 42–22. At Douglasville on the twenty-fourth, a same pattern developed, for the Dragon boys won 49–36 with Stephens collecting 22 markers total, 16 coming after intermission; cohort Bolton pitched in 15 swishers; it was our thirteenth win in 19 tries. The ladies got measured 41–28 with junior Katheryn Darnell netting 14 points. One night later in Trion, the Dragons improved to 14–6 while the girls won their fourth game in 17 tries. Although 10 players made the scorecard for Coach Culberson, Jerry Bolton stood out with 27 markers in the 70–52 win. The Dragonettes were "impressive" as they led all the way in a 44–41 victory; Roma Kiser logged 25 markers. Visiting Coosa girls romped to a 69–54 victory over PHS on February 2; Katheryn Darnell was big gun for us with 28 points. Turnabout is fair play, for we responded with a defeat of their Eagle men 66–57; Harold Gresham and Jerry Bolton combined for 40 points. In a makeup game the next night at Summerville, the Indians dealt our boys a 62–59 defeat despite us leading at all breaks; Bolton swished 27 big points. All good things eventually come to an end, and they did in a trek to Summerville on February 2; the boys lost 62–59 after leading for 3 quarters while the ladies were on the short end of 44–25; Roma Kiser and Katheryn Darnell netted 10 markers each.

The next road trip was a good bit longer. At 8:00 a.m. on Friday, February 11, an entourage of Dragons including 12 players, 2 managers, and coaches Maurice Culberson, I. R. Burch, and J. W. Sutton loaded in automobiles for a 190-mile adventure to Montgomery. Waiting in the state capital was Sidney Lanier High School, one of Alabama's top basketball programs. Along the way south, the travelers stopped in Auburn and toured Alabama Polytechnic Institute (Auburn) campus, which is the alma mater of Superintendent Slick Moulton and soon-to-be-named (September) plant manager Jack Smith. Then the Lindaleans continued west for an hour to Montgomery's Maxwell Air Force Base for a night's lodging. Basketball tipped off in early evening at Garrett Coliseum, the state's largest basketball arena. First-period jitters caused us to fall behind 16–9 before we settled down and "gave a good account." However, we had no answer to the Poets' rangy 6-foot-4-inch post Henry Marcus who swished in 20 points and rebounded with ease in the 65–53 victory. Underclassmen sharpshooters Jerry Bolton and Stephens were not intimidated as they hit for 21 and 13 markers. Six other Dragons scored including Larue with, 5; Gresham, 5; Connell, 2; Mathis, 3; Austin, 3; and Burkhalter, 1. After sleeping, over the team visited historical sites around the city; they arrived back in Lindale late Saturday afternoon. Players making the trip were Jerry Bolton, Jo Jo Stephens, Wesley Connell, Ted LaRue, Harold Gresham, Fred Mathis, Jerry Austin, Weyland Burkhalter, Jackie Padgett, Larry Tidwell, Joe Abney, and Harold Jones. Managers going were Jerry Melton and Ned LaRue.

Returning to action in Georgia on Monday, February 14, 1955, our women "fell by the wayside" in the first round of Region 3-A against a strong Canton sextet 54–22, thus ending their season. In the men's tourney in Rockmart one night later, our quintet edged tough Cartersville 61–53 in a game that ended near midnight. It did not seem to bother Bolton, Stephens, and Gresham who swished 20, 16, and 12 in order. But our run ended on Wednesday the sixteenth in the second round when machinelike Ted Denny "fed 31 points through the hoops" as Newnan High nipped us 58–54 in "a well deserved verdict." We just could never sustain a run at the Cougars who led at each quarter break. Jerry Bolton was our top performer with 22 markers. Edward Hendrix, president of the Dragon Club, announced on March 2 that a limited number of public tickets were available for the annual sports banquet. The March 12 event honored varsity athletes and band. This year's main speaker would be Auburn head football coach Ralph "Shug" Jordan.

1955–'56 Season

The 1955–'56 boys basketball team was exemplary. In only 5 years of varsity competition, Pepperell finished the year with a 27–8 record, which included the Region 3-A crown and a first ever trip to the state tournament. Led by senior sharpshooting guard Jerry Bolton and post Joe

Abney, the Dragons swept through their schedule and into the Northwest Georgia Invitational Tournament with only one loss. At Memorial Gym, the Lindaleans disposed of Johnson, Adairsville, and Cedartown before losing the finals to pretournament favorite Pine Long. As the January schedule developed, our boys lost 4 straight primarily because Jerry Bolton's "infected throat." He returned toward the end of January and went on a tear, averaging almost 30 points per contest while his cohort Joe Abney provided rebounds and markers.

On February 10, 1956, Sidney Lanier High came to Lindale for a return match; in part 1, the Poets won last year in Montgomery and sported 11 wins in a dozen outings. Again, they had a dominant post player; 6-foot-2-inch Tommy Ragsdale carried a 21-point game average. Ragsdale was as good as reported, "looping" 24 points in the 70–58 road to victory. Post center jump part 2 was similar to last year's 65–53 loss. Our boys stayed close and trailed narrowly at intermission but faded somewhat in the second half. Jerry Bolton wore out the nets with 30 big markers.

By Sunday, February 13, the brackets were drawn for Region 3-A tournament with PHS slated to face Cartersville in the first round. Gold and White then raced to the 3-A crown with decisive wins over Douglas County (Abney, 23 points), Calhoun (Bolton, 39 points), Newnan (Bolton, 20 points) and North Whitfield (Bolton, 28, and Scoggins, 20 points). At 27–7, the next stop was Macon in search of a state crown. On Thursday, afternoon, February 23, 1956, Chamblee edged out Dragons 64–60; Jerry Bolton was high scorer with 24. He was named to the state all-tourney team while Joe Abney garnered honorable mention. Years later, Jerry explained the loss to a bad defensive start, saying, "We had to battle back the whole game." Starters on the most successful basketball team in PHS history were Bolton and Wesley Connell at guards; Joe Abney was the center while Billy Joe Scoggins and Ted LaRue manned the forward positions. As a tribute to the aforementioned all-state Jerry Bolton, Coach Otis Gilbreath named him as one of the two best all-around athletes in Pepperell history.

1956–'57 Season

The bold caption on page 10 of the Wednesday, November 21, 1956, issue of *Rome News-Tribune* reported that "1956–57 DRAGONS ARE MINUS EXPERIENCED HARDWOOD STARS." The team coached by Olan Cosper returned one starter, center Joe Abney, and one sub, Jackie Brooks; gone were leading scorer Jerry Bolton and 6 others. Dragonettes were no better off as they had only 3 players back from last year, guards Peggy Nichols, Leota Melton, and Sandra Beck. Coach Otis Gilbreath would mentor the ladies. A complete schedule was listed beginning at Berry on November 26 and ending on February 15 at Cedartown.

The Gold and White would again participate in the Northwest Georgia Invitational along with 15 other quintets; the boys were defeated in last year's finals by Pine Log 57–54. As the season got underway, a surprise loss to Berry boys was followed by a 3-point defeat to Cave Spring while the women lost 29–17. PHS boys were still searching for a victory on the first Wednesday of December at Cass; alas, our Dragons lost handily to the Colonels 47–32 with juniors Beanie Ozment and Donald Ingle bucketing 10 and 9 markers respectively. Meanwhile, the girls narrowly lost a thrilling overtime contest 21–19. On December 16, Dallas High Tigers won a doubleheader at the Leonard; adding to our woes was another two-headed loss to Rockmart the previous week. But it's always nice to beat Rome, and that's what the Dragon men did on the eighteenth; Lowell Curry hit 4 long shots before intermission while Ozment and Abney contributed an even dozen apiece in the 52–40 victory. The ladies won by 8 with senior Leota Milton and junior Sandra Mull netting 19 and 16 in order. It's always nice to beat your friends, and Pepperell did that, downing Shannon's boys 44–43 in the Leonard Memorial Gym on December 21; Joe Abney led with 4 of his 15 points in the last 45 seconds. Junior Ann Rush and Sandra Mull led the girls' 40–25 triumph with 13 and 10 markers. The boys' record now stood at 4–5 while the girls came in at 2–5. Pepperell's quintet raced its way to the finals of the Christmas Invitational Tournament by virtue of a Joe Abney "fielder" and his free throw in the last 10 seconds. Jack Ozment led his team with 20 swishers while Hugh Green matched that with 20 for the losers. A capacity crowd saw the game tied on 13 occasions; last year's total record of 2,130 paying customers would surely be broken when Lindale faced Rockmart next for the crown. Unfortunately, the Yellow Jackets threw up an impregnable zone defense to win the third annual tourney 46–38. Senior Abney, Ozment, and junior Curry garnered all-tournament accolades. On January 3, Coach Cosper called for holiday practice to prep for upcoming rugged games. It was good strategy, for our boys proceeded to down Adairsville, Coosa, and Rome. On Friday, February 8, 1957, the old tune "We're Alabamy Bound" was being hummed by Olan Cosper and his team as they departed for Montgomery to face Sidney Lanier High School part 3. The Poets, who were fresh off a Christmas tournament championship, were sitting at 12–4 and had 3 players averaging 14 points. The visiting Dragons could almost match that at 15–9. However, once again, the "sharp shooting" Poets had little trouble with the Lindaleans in winning 79–43 to bring our regular season to a close. Back on Park Street, it was time for the Region 1-A tournament being held at Cassville. Jack Ozment sent us into the semifinals when he dropped in 2 free throws to nip Ringgold 41–39. However, Bartow's Colonels knocked us out of the championship game 42–29 which was the Dragons' smallest number of points of the season. The girls fared better as junior Ann Rush swished 22 markers in eliminating Summerville 36–24. In the women's finals played Saturday night on February 16 at Cassville gym, Ms. Rush scored half of our points in a 28–20 losing effort to host Cassville.

1957–'58 Season

Pictures in the 1958 yearbook show 26 men players coached by Olan Cosper; the women, who were mentored by Coach Phyllis Norton, suited up 23 prospects. Six lettermen returned, including Roger Greer, Lowell Curry, Roger Carney, Don Ingle, Wesley Rusk, and Larry Hightower. Only 2 with letters came back for this year, but we expected Martha Jo Kell, Gerettie Oxford, Ann Bohannon, Carolyun Walker, Shirley Morgan, Patricia Rhyne, Carolyn Skelton, Linda Smith, and Faye Lawson to compete for playing minutes.

At the time, girls' basketball in Georgia played half-court three-on-three on defense and the same on offense rather than five-on-five full court like we have now. Some unknown reporter chose the synonym "sextet" to describe this system. The term comes from a musical ensemble or composition totaling six. The boys, on the other hand, were referred to as a quintet or five who perform together. The popular belief in 1892 or one year after Naismith invented the sport was that girls could not run an eighty-four-foot floor; therefore, the sport was a half-court competition. On change of possession, defensive players could not physically move beyond half-court, forcing short or long passes to a teammate across the midline. On change of possession, the action moved to the other end court with different three-on-three deployments. Of course, the advantage for coaches was placement of best defenders (guards) against best shooters (forwards). In 1958, a movement was started to ban six-on-six game led by the Office of Civil Rights. Yet it took more than three decades to completely phase out. Georgia went to a regular five-person game in 1970. At present, the only rule differences are the ladies basketball is a smaller ball and the three-point line is closer.

On Tuesday, November 26, 1957, the Dragons' sextet and quintet opened the season by splitting a doubleheader with Coosa inside the Russell H. Leonard Memorial Gymnasium. No scores were available other than Coach Cosper's boys who won, and Coach Phyllis Norton's women lost. The same scenario occurred on December 3 when the men won over Armuchee 44–38 with Lowell Curry hitting for 18 points followed by Gary Henderson and Wesley Rusk at 11 and 10 respectively. Girls' score was in favor of visiting Lady Indians 54–26; senior Myrna Puckett netted 13 markers while junior Ann Bohannon followed with 9. Cave Spring is a small town, but their kids could play roundball as witnessed on Friday 12–6; their girls improved to 9–1 by downing us 55–21. Ann Bohannon collected 10 buckets. In the nightcap, the Springers led 39–22 at halftime and came out on top 66–50; Lowell Curry and Gary Henderson scored 18 and 17 in order. Friday the thirteenth was unlucky for Rome Hilltoppers, for we swept a doubleheader at the Leonard. PHS girls led 17–15 at intermission but won out 45–36 behind Ann Bohannon's 25 markers. The boys did better outpacing Rome 59–32; Curry, Henderson, and Rusk hit the nylons with 17, 15, and 12 in order. Four nights later, Ann Bohannon showed the way to victory with 14 points in a thrilling 26–24 win over Model. The boys made it a double killing 46–38 over their quintet; eight players made the score book, but lanky sophomore newcomer Ronnie Corntassel led us with 12 points followed by Henderson's 11. At Armuchee on the twentieth, Ann Bohannon aced 23 markers, but it was enough as Blue won 61–30. Pepperell men moved to 5–2 with a 68–63 win; Gary Henderson led everybody in the gym with 27 big points. The invitational tourney began on Monday, December 23, in Rome's Memorial Gym. Our quintet eliminated last year's champ Pine Log quite easily 61–42 with sharpshooters Curry and Henderson logging 19 markers each. However, two nights later, we fell 59–48 to Cave Spring before a large crowd. Consequently, it was the first time in 4 years that we didn't make the finals. Henderson and Curry (second team all-tourney) again led us in scoring with 18 and 17 markers respectively. Adairsville would edge Fairmount 40–36 on Saturday night for the championship. In the first game of 1958, Cave Spring "swung a two-bladed axe" in Leonard Memorial, defeating our boys 49–37 and girls 44–21. Gerettie Oxford netted 10 swishers while Ann Bohannon hit for 9. For the men, Roger Carney and Lowell Curry bucketed 16 and 11 markers. Bohannon came back on January 8 to score 21 points in a 30–18 victory over Model. On Blue Devil hardwood, our quintet won a thriller 57–53; Henderson and Carney were leaders in the score book with 16 and 14 in order. At Lakeside on Wednesday January 15, Darlington topped our boys pretty good 55–30; Lowell Curry netted 9 points for the now 6–5 Dragons. On Saturday night, January

18, Pepperell Dragon Club assembled a "large, merry throng" for a gala dance honoring varsity athletes, band members, majorettes, cheerleaders, coaches, and band director. The event, which took the place of an annual banquet, was held on the newly renovated floor of the former picture show theater in Lindale Auditorium. On Friday evening, January 17, Ann Bohannon and Bobbie Rogers got into a shooter's battle with the former hitting 25 points against the latter's 23 markers; alas, Rogers's Armuchee sextet won 47–29. In the nightcap, Pepperell led at all stops and won fairly comfortably 59–48; Dragon guard Lowell Curry led the fast second-half action with 25 points while Gary Henderson netted 16. On Alabama Road Tuesday, January 21, PHS lost a twin bill to Coosa. Dragonettes Oxford and Bohannon scored 8 points each, but it did not help, for we lost 39–18. The men's game was a thriller but with the same results 56–50 in favor of Eagles; Curry and Henderson again led us in markers with 12 each. At Model on January 22, the Blue Devils' lassies triumphed 27–19; Gerettie Oxford scored 10 counters for Lindale. Our quintet edged Shannon 62–54 behind center Gary Henderson's 29 markers; we trailed the first 24 minutes before tying it 45 all at the end of period three thanks mostly to Henderson who "was swishing them in from all angles."

Langdon Gammon reported in his "Lindale News" feature on Friday, January 31, that Brackett Parsons, president of Pepperell Manufacturing, toured our operation and premises yesterday on an inspection tour; Mr. Parsons complimented company employees and general manager G. Howard Smith on the appearance and performance of Lindale Mill. He also noted everyone's friendliness and courtesy.

Armuchee swept a twin bill from Pepperell on February 4, but it took overtime in the boys' game to settle the score with AHS edging us 65–64; Lowell Curry swished the nets for 28 points. Although Ann Bohannon scored 28 counters, PHS women went down easier 51–38. At Berry on Thursday, February, 6 our hosts led 36–34 at the end of three quarters; however, Lowell Curry led an 18–6 run in last period to win 52–42. He finished with 22 counters followed by Gary Henderson's 11 markers. In the Region 1-A tourney being played at Ringgold, PHS girls and boys faced Ellijay on Tuesday, February 11; our lads held a 9–10 record while the lassies came in at 3–14. The Bobcats from Gilmer County eliminated both our squads. The Pepperell sextet went down 47–30; Bohannon and Oxford closed out the season scoring 13 and 11 respectively. In the nightcap, our quintet trailed 32–30 at intermission but fell behind 47–38 at finish of period three, and we never recovered, losing 63–53. Ronnie Corntassel and Lowell Curry were our last leading scorers of the year with 14 each.

1958–'59 Season

On Monday afternoon, November 10, the varsity basketball squads launched drills for 1958–'59. Coach Olan Cosper expected 6 returning lettermen including Gary Henderson, Roger Carney, Clinton Green, Ronnie Corntassel, Tommy Climer, and Jerry Brumbelow. Mrs. Phyllis Norton Cosper would mentor the women with expected returnees Sylvia Dillingham, Ann Bohannon, Jewel Cox, Carolyn Walker, Marie Henderson, and Gerettie Oxford. Coaches Bill Boling and Otis Gilbreath would lead the boys' and girls' JVs respectively. Opening the year on Tuesday, November 18, the squad split with visiting Armuchee; the Dragons won 51–44 behind Gary

Henderson's 25 points while the Dragonettes were nipped 29–25. Four days later, Henderson hit for 19 markers in a 52–34 win over Cave Spring; Kenneth Shiflett chipped in 17 counters. Our girls were not as fortunate, losing 38–22 with Oxford netting 8 markers. On November 24, plans were firmed up for the fifth annual Christmas Tournament to begin in Memorial Gym on December 22. Defending champ Adairsville and runner-up Fairmount would defend against 14 other quintets. Lindale had captured the championship once and had been runners-up twice. In the meantime, our boys lost to a tough home-standing Cass squad 47–45; Henderson and Shiflett swished 18 and 13 points while the Colonels' big man James Abernathy canned 19. Regrettably, the Dragonettes lost by 15 with Bohannon swishing 20 points. On December 2 in Trion, the boys came from behind in quarter four to win 53–47; Gary Henderson and newcomer Dink Green scored 16 and 14 markers. The girls lost a low-scoring thriller 21–20 after leading 10–5 at intermission; Marie Henderson scored a dozen counters for PHS. Two nights later back in the Leonard, our men took a well-deserved victory over West Rome 49–40. After a close first half, senior Dink Green, who did not start, came on to "furnish a winning spark" with 20 buckets, which included several long-range shots. Our girls edged WR 32–25 behind Ann Bohannon's 18 big points. Next on December 9, visiting Darlington nipped Pepperell men 60–58 in overtime despite Green's 24 markers. On the twelfth, Cosper's men "lashed" invading Coosa 45–31 with Byars, Corntassel, and Green each scoring 10 points; however, the girls lost by a baker's dozen 36–23 with Bohannon and Oxford netting 13 and 10 respectively. Four nights later in Mount Berry, Georgia, Clayton Byars and Ronnie Corntassel continued their fine play by sinking 17 and 15 markers to win over Berry boys 57–44.

In the fifth Annual Invitational Christmas Tournament, the Dragons "vanquished" Coosa 51–38 and Pine Log 57–51 with Corntassel leading the way with 18 buckets in each contest; senior Tommy Climer and Clayton Byars supported him in each battle, sharing 37 points. But the semifinals on December 26 proved fatal as East Rome Gladiators downed Pepperell 56–40; ER took the lead at 5–4 and "were never headed," pushing our record to 9–3. Roger Carney, Green, and Corntassel tallied 9, 8, and 7 markers in order. In a nip and tuck consolation game, we edged Rockmart 46–45; we were down 43–37 with less than 4 minutes to play when Clayton Byars came on to score 7 of our last 9 markers to win; Green and Corntassel shared high point honors with 12 each. Losses to Coosa and Darlington followed before a 48–39 home win against Trion; Corntassel and Carney led in the score book with 16 and 11 counters. In the opener, Gerettie Oxford scored 12 in a losing 29–24 thriller for the girls. On Tuesday, January 27, visiting Cass swept a doubleheader from Pepperell with the boys losing 42–33; Byars led Gold and White with 11 points but could not match rangy Colonel center James Abernathy's 27 markers, most of which came after intermission. Our lassies lost by 14 (38–24) to complete the sweep; Marie Henderson tallied a dozen counters in defeat. Pepperell boys proceeded to lose to East Rome and Summerville before hosting Berry High on Tuesday, February 3; Tommy Climer sank 16 counters to lead us followed by Byars with 13 markers in a 48–28 victory. Prior to the Region 3-A tournament, the boys "carded" their highest points of the year defeating host Armuchee 75–43 on February 6 to end the regular season at 14–8; Clinton Green and Byars hit for 17 and 16 counters. The Dragonettes lost 3–30 to finish with a 7–11 slate; Bohannon, Oxford, and Henderson all scored 10 points. Unfortunately, both Pepperell squads were one and done in the first round of Region 3-A playoffs played at Pickens County; the boys fell 49–39 to Cass with Clinton Green closing out the 1959 score book with 20 big points. The same Cassville crew beat our ladies by 24 (59–35) with Pepperell's Ann Bohannon managing 13 markers.

1959–'60 Season

Basketball's second decade began with the 1959–'60 squad. Coach Olan Cosper welcomed 8 returnees to his team including Clayton Byars, Donald Satcher, David Vanhorn, Ken Shiflett, Billy Studdard, Ronnie Corntassel, Greg McGregor, and Jerry Lambert. Coach J. W. Sutton's Dragonettes listed only 3 letter winners from last year, Gerettie Oxford, Marie Henderson, and Glenda Smart. Another trio consisting of Sue Kilgo, Donna Helton, and Joyce Luker would be depended upon. The season opened on November 19 with a 55–19 romp over visiting Trion when 9 players scored; Coach Cosper's veteran quintet possibly showed it was to be reckoned within the area; we put 9 players in the score book led by substitutes David VanHorn and Benny Rampley with 11 markers each. The ladies swept to a 34–17 win behind junior Charlotte Bain's 14 points. A trip down Georgia Highway 101 South on Tuesday, November 24, produced a 43–42 victory over Rockmart men; Clayton Byars hit 14 markers to lead us in scoring. Despite 19 points from Gerettie Oxford, our girls lost by 15 or 45–30. One night later, the boys claimed another 1-point win in Shannon 39–38; Byars and Kenneth Shiflett led scoring with 9 counters each. Corntassel was next with 8 swishers. In the opener, Oxford sank 17 points in a 50–30 losing cause. After a 45–34 victory over Cave Spring and a 9-point win over West Rome (40–31) on December 6, the Dragons were officially tabbed as the team to beat locally. Three nights afterward, Ronnie Corntassel hit for 11 markers; however, visiting East Rome "punctured Dragons' Balloon" 48–35. The girls fell by 14.

PHS men cruised into the sixth annual Christmas Tourney with wins over Coosa, Cass, and Armuchee. The *News-Tribune* noted on December 20 that our boys had been the event's most consistent performer, winning the 1954 title with runners-up in 1955, 1956, and finishing third last year. Over 2,000 paying customers had watched the games each year. Tournament proceeds after expenses went to participating squads in proportion to games played; 16 teams with 250 players and managers competed for the championship. Roundball is a tournament game, and any squad with the "hottest streak" can win; in the opening contest, Rockmart became the favorite with a 48–37 upset of Lindale. It was close until near intermission as Polk County Bees edged ahead 32–26; however, Pepperell faithful thought our big men Byars and Corntassel could still take us to victory, but RHS's "race-horse" style of play combined with "all-around good floor play and accurate shooting" enabled them to pull away and beat us 48–37. Along the way, Rockmart downed Pine Log, Pepperell, and Model before winning the crown over East Rome 45–37 in front of a standing-room-only crowd.

January 8 was a new year and a leap year when we dumped Coosa and Cave Spring again with Corntassel supplying steady scoring, and rebounding; guard Kenneth Shiflett and forward Clayton Byars improved their game to double digits. This trio continued their good work when the Dragons routed visiting Cartersville 57–39 and nipped Rockmart 62–58. The Purple Hurricanes got us back a few nights later 62–55. The Dragon men won their twelfth in Cassville

49–38 and then claimed a 62–58 victory over Rockmart in Leonard Memorial. It was our thirteenth win and revenged an earlier tourney loss. Pepperell men sported a 13–2 regular season record while our ladies were reverse at 2–13. On Friday night, February 5, the hot and cold West Rome Chieftains were hot in pounding PHS 61–35. The women lost also 36–20 to close out their year at 2–15. However, the most disappointing boys' loss of the year occurred 2 nights later in the first round of Region 3-A tournament in Pickens County. Leading 54–52 against Model with 30 seconds remaining, the Blue Devils' Wyatt Webb made good 1 of 2 free throws allowing the Gold and White to rebound the miss and head toward their basket up by 1 point; regrettably for us, "Joe House stole the ball, drove past a neat screen by Donnie Morrison for the deciding goal" and a Shannon 55–54 win. A season's worth of write-ups in the local newspaper revealed that Ronnie Corntassel and Clayton Byars controlled the backboards as well as leading in points for their alma mater. Yet there was hope for the future when Coach Bill Bolling's junior varsity boys breezed undefeated through the year and captured the JV tournament crown to finish 12–0; this group hit the hoops for 482 points and gave up only 258.

1960–'61 Season

Participation was certainly not down for the 1960–'61 season as 50 kids evenly divided reported for practice in early November. On November 22, 1960, both squads won over Trion with the girls snapping a 13-game losing streak 36–23; Charlotte Bain led all scorers with 25 points. Three nights later, Coosa swept 2 low-point games in the Leonard; we followed this with a split in Cave Spring as the boys won by 15 and girls lost 61–32. Two nights into December, Cartersville visited and received the Dragons' best offensive effort so far, 60–52; Wallace Shiflett, Greg McGregor, and Larry Gresham led the winners' charge with 13, 12, and 10 markers. The Dragonettes played well but lost by 7. On the first Tuesday in November, Olan Cosper's 4–1 crew shocked unbeaten Berry 60–51 despite their Bryner's and Weller's 18 points each. The scoring for the winners was more balanced with Shiflett and Gresham hitting for 21 and 14 markers. The *News-Tribune* on Sunday, December 11, posted, "Pepperell's Dragons refused to give an inch Saturday night" before a large crowd and downed host West Rome 39–31. The visitors from South Floyd led most of the way thanks to Wallace Shiflett's 11 points and numerous rebounds while the girls struggled for baskets in losing 38–12.

On Monday, December 12, 1960 (the second week of the month), Pepperell's gigantic electric star was hoisted between the two huge mill stacks known affectionately as Bread and Butter. Since 1933, the Christmas Star had glowed above the village, measuring 12 feet across from tip to tip with 160 standard light bulbs 210 feet in the yule air as a symbol of Christ's birth. The 400-pound sphere was constructed by Clifford Bryant, Henry Holcomb, Bill Sealock, and Jim Mathis the week before Christmas 1933. Captain Henry Parish Meikleham placed the symmetrical body above the village to foster community and goodwill. The star also added to the decorated yards and homes of workers. Their efforts now gave the place a homey Southern beauty and stood for "Peace on Earth—Goodwill toward men (Luke 2:14)." Gammon noted on page 53 that "for around two weeks during the Yule season, the lights of the star are turned on at dusk, allowing the historical emblem to cast its majestic glow over the community until dawn of the next day." Daniel Scott Wilson grew up in Lindale; on page 111 of Lisa M. Russell's *Lost Mills of North Georgia*, he states that "at the time it was a symbol of hope for the employees to look toward during the hard times of the Great Depression. Cap'n hoped the star would draw people to the Village—just as the star brought the three wise men to the birthplace of Jesus." Wilson added, "Nothing happened in Lindale...that did not benefit the Company and... actually the mill star outlived the company that constructed it." In later times, former employee and Restoration Lindale president Tim Reynolds continued to oversee the annual event. Eighty years after the first hanging, Donna Greene Johnson traveled 2,000 miles from California to visit family and friends and watch the lighting celebration off Park Street. Her father, Ottis L. Greene, worked at the mill and always helped raise it using pulleys attached to each stack. In a December 8 page-1 *News-Tribune* interview, staff writer Carolyn Grindrod described how Donna fought back tears in the cold night thinking about the tradition. "I can imagine my Dad climbing up those smokestacks to hang the star. It's very emotional."

Keeping with the yule spirit 24 hours later, coaches Cosper and J. T. Bishop welcomed East Rome to the Leonard; however, the hospitality was overdone as the Powder Blue and Gold boys and girls won 64–39 and 62–14. On the eighteenth, the boys dispatched visiting Model 53–34, but the ladies faltered 32–26. The following week, 16 teams signed up for the seventh annual Northwest Georgia Invitational Tourney; Pepperell drew Cedartown in the first round and played a scrappy man-to-man defense that held the Bulldogs to 38 points in the 50–38 victory. In the semifinals, 1,400 fans watched West Rome eke out an overtime win 35–33 over PHS. In regulation, Wallace Shiflett "grabbed a rebound and calmly dropped it in to tie the game 32–32"; then Chieftain guard Don Law hit a 20-footer and 1 free throw in OT. On Christmas Eve, WR lost the crown to crosstown rival East by 47–35. On December 28, the Dragonettes tried the Cave Spring Invitational but lost the first round to East Rome 32–21.

The new year of 1961 brought a 48–44 overtime win over rival Model. When Wallace Shiflett fouled out late, substitute Grady Brannon's putback tied the game at the horn, allowing the Dragons to win the fifth period. Holcomb, Gresham, and Shiflett garnered most of their team's points with 13, 11, and 10 in order. On January 11, 1961, Pepperell visited Turner McCall Boulevard and came away with a big 52–48 win over East Rome; Johnny Holcomb swished 15 points for the boys while Charlotte Bain hit 8 markers in a 43–18 losing cause. Seven nights later, in a "smoothly played" contest, PHS nipped host Coosa 58–55 with Johnny Savage netting 14. The girls lost 39–22 as CHS never trailed. On Thursday, January 26, the *News-Tribune* printed on page 9 that "the Seventh District Principals' Association has endorsed a recommendation calling for the elimination of classifications in Georgia prep basketball." The administrators cited excessive travel and loss of classroom time as prime reason. Under a proposal, which resembled the state of Kentucky system, 16 teams or 2 each from 8 regions, regardless of enrollment, would compete for a true state championship. The term "Sweet Sixteen" evolved from the 1932 high school tourney bracket and was a trademark phrase of the KHSAA. On the first day of February, the Gold and White pulled a mild upset of visiting West Rome 43–31 with Savage and Holcomb hitting for 13 and 10; the girls competed but lost 30–25. In the last regular season schedule, home-standing Trion upset a contingent of our younger players 58–53 to finish the regular season 13–7; the ladies lost by 17 and struggled with a 2–16 overall record. In the first round of Region 3-A South tournament staged on Russell Leonard floor, Pepperell downed formidable Cassville 69–61 with 4 Dragons hitting in double figures; alas, the 20–2 Falcons of Berry HS waited. Behind sharpshooting of Rennie Bryner and Dickie Weller, who combined for 21 and 17 points respectively, the Birds won comfortably 57–42.

1961–'62 Season

On November 11, full-scale drills began for Pepperell varsity clubs. Gone from last year's team which won 13 out of 20 regular season games were 7 veterans; however, Coach Olan Cosper returned 5 lettermen including Wallace Shiflett, Johnny Savage, Archie Vaughn, Grady Brannon, and Jimmy Hinton. Girls' mentor Jim Mullins was encouraged by his squad's improvement in early workouts. Returning letter winners were Louise Jordan, Jane Jordan, Judy Betts, and Judy Sutton as forwards and Donna Murdock and Pam Polifka as guards. Following an upset at the hands of Cave Spring, PHS men rebounded with a 35–31 victory over host East Rome; the outclassed women lost 61–12. At Model on the twenty-second, our quintet won 44–38; Wallace Shiflett and Grady Brannon led scorers with 16 and 13 points respectively. The Dragonettes could not get over "the hump" in losing 40–25. The Polk County Jackets visited Leonard Memorial on the twenty-eighth and lost 51–32; Savage with 23 and Shiflett 15 led our scorers. Rockmart girls, who were Region 3-A champs last year, dished out a bitter 56–17 defeat to the home sextet.

Pairings for the eighth annual Christmas Tourney which would be held at Rome's Memorial Gym were announced on Sunday, December 3. Dragon men won their fourth of five games by nipping Berry School 57–52 behind Savage's and Grady Brannon's 17 and 14 points. However, on December 12, the "west of the river" squads swept a home doubleheader 50–40 and 57–15. Shiflett was high-point man for Lindale with 13 while Lady Chieftains "smothered" our girls 57–15. Returning to the Dragon den didn't seem to help as *News-Tribune* posted on December 13, "Cedartown Nips Dragons on Vincent's 1-Pointer." All-state fullback Dennis Vincent hit a free throw that provided a 41–40 margin of victory for Polk County Bulldogs. After Johnny Savage's 25-footer brought the Dragons within 1 point of the lead, frustration set in for us in the final 45 seconds as we missed on 5 consecutive shots which kept fans standing. In the opener, Cedartown's sensational Jeri Burgdorf ripped the net for 32 points in a 53–19 victory. As our basketball teams left for Armuchee on December 15, the yule star mounted between the "lofty Mill smokestacks" and shone down on them for the thirty-first year. Once in North Floyd, Pepperell's Johnny Savage "scored from all angles" to tally 32 points in a 63–56 victory; junior Judy Sutton and tenth grader Louise Jordan netted 8 and 7 markers respectively but in a 29–19 loss.

Our quintet opened Christmas Tourney play with a Wednesday afternoon game in Rome's Memorial Gym versus Johnson High Wildcats. *Rome News-Tribune* sports department had characterized our boys as "Dragons running hot and cold and play unbeatable ball at time." And on December 20, it appeared we might be running cold with 1:30 to play until "sure-fingered" Johnny Savage stepped to the line and sank 4 crucial free throws to win 47–43; he tallied 24 points to go with Wallace Shiflett's even dozen. The following afternoon, Wallace "grabbed the scoring reins" from sidekick Johnny (16 points) with 22 markers in a 56–35 win over Cave Spring to reach the semifinals.

In a low-scoring affair, Fairmount edged Pepperell 34–31. The mountain team's star player Carl Serritt was hit with 4 quick fouls, forcing him to the bench for almost 3 quarters; however, he returned to tally 19 total. Conversely, turnabout is fair play when 3 Dragons fouled out in closing minutes. Savage led all scorers with 23 long-range shots. He was named to the 10-man all-tourney team; Wallace Shiflett came in at 11, just missed being picked for 2 consecutive years. Consolation games are no fun, but they count—Pepperell, 42; Rockmart 36. PHS jumped out front and stayed there against Rockmart, winning 42–36; Savage and Shiflett led us in the score book with 17 and 9 respectively. Meanwhile, the girls lost to East Rome 33–16 in the Cave Spring Invitational.

The new year brought about double losses for our squads with Armuchee High boys winning 36–32 and their sextet 29–23. In a split location, host Berry High downed our boys 48–43 while up in Summerville, the Dragonettes dropped a 36–25 decision. On Tuesday, January 17, the girls lost to Mary Lou Cantrell (20 point barrage) and Coosa 39–22; the men nipped the Eagles 58–55 behind Shiflett's 17 markers. Three nights later, Lindale exploded for 63 points against East Rome on their way to a 63–39 victory; Jimmy Hinton, Bill Studdard, and Savage all netted double figures. Alas, the women lost 55–14. The next game at Cedartown was a squeaker, for we trailed most of the game until tying it at 47–47; with 12 seconds to play, Johnny Savage hit 1 of 2 foul shots for the 48–47 victory. But much credit went to young Glenn Studdard who with less than 5:00 to play tied it at 38–38, then put us up 40–38 and finally 42–38. Bulldog Jeri Burgdorf put up 40-plus points for a 69–33 win over the Dragonettes. In the last game of January, Johnny Savage, Wallace Shiflett, and Bill Studdard scored 23, 16, and 10 points respectively for a 60–46 win over Johnson High. Although Judy Betts and Louise Jordan topped the scoring with 15 and 14, our girls lost 53–40 to the Lady Wildcats. On Tuesday, January 30, at WR, lightning struck twice; the boys went down 52–32 with no player scoring in double figures; PHS girls lost 33–22, but Louise Jordan managed 10 markers. February 7 started right with a 47–35 victory over host Cave Spring. The boys' record improved to 16–7 overall, but the girls did not, losing 43–22. In Rockmart's Scoggin Hall in the first round of Region 3-A tourney on Tuesday, February 13, the Dragons were upset by the local Yellow Jackets 56–48; Shiflett and Savage closed out the score book for 1962 hitting for 19 and 18 markers. Our boys had previously beaten the Polk County squad by 19 and 6 points. Before an overflowing crowd in Russell Leonard Gym on Saturday night, February 17, Valley Point boys and Cartersville girls claimed Region 3-A championship.

1962–'63 Season

The Dragons began their season on Tuesday, November 27, at Johnson with a double loss; the boys were defeated 48–41 and the women 31–21. Sophomore Tony Taylor and junior Billy Mathis netted 13 points each while senior Judy Betts scored 11 for the girls. However, 3 nights later, we rebounded somewhat with a 57–44 victory over the visiting Armuchee quintet; Glenn Studdard and Johnny Mathis paced the home team with 12 and 11 points respectively. The Dragonettes lost 46–31 with Jane Knight being the leading scorer at 13. Next up, North Cobb dealt us another double loss; the men went under 43–34 and the women 45–26. On December 4, the home-standing Coosa Eagles were not very hospitable, dealing out a 41–32 loss to our boys and a 49–28 defeat to the girls. Glenn Studdard and Joe Knight hit for 11 and 8 markers while Mss. Jane Knight and Jeanne Sutton bucketed 11 and 10. For 32 years, Lindale's yule star had been a traditional symbol of Christmas; it was mounted between the 2 huge Pepperell mill smokestacks and cast its "majestic glow" over the village. Fans hoped its hanging would bring good luck to our basketball team as they prepared for the Rome area invitational tourney on Monday, December 17. At present, the Gold and White boys were 1–6 on the season with recent losses to Cave Spring, 28–26; Rockmart, 47–42; and Cedartown, 48–39. In the first game, a "spine-tingling thriller" against Chattooga wasn't settled until the clock struck zero. Our boys had battled back from a 10-point deficit to take a 1-point lead thanks to Tony Taylor's free throw with 14 ticks left. But as baseball great Yogi Berra once said, "It ain't over 'til it's over." Summerville's Mike Baker's rebound and putback with a second to play sent the Dragons home in the red 35–34. The squad would return to action on January 4. Model's "Cinderella" squad won the ninth annual tourney by downing Rockmart 45–39. At least there was good news economically in Lindale where plant manager G. Howard Smith wished all a joyous Noel; he then announced bonuses and 5-day paid vacations for all employees in appreciation for their cooperation and loyalty. Oh, woe is us; by mid-January, the men had lost 9 of 10 games while the women were 0–11. On January 15, the Berry hardwood brought some relief 53–38 over the Falcons with Glenn Studdard hitting for 16 baskets and Johnny Mathis and Steve Barnett at 15. On Tuesday, January 29, Lang Gammon wrote in the *News-Tribune*, "Coach Olan Cosper's Dragons seemingly have taken a new lease on life, capturing their last two starts, while Coach Jim Mullins' Dragonettes are riding a three-game winning streak, which has the players and their supporters alike jumping with joy." Although consecutive game double losses to Rockmart and Cartersville dampened our momentum some, the girls upset Carrollton 31–27 in the Region 3-A tourney. Louise Jordan and Jane Knight bucketed 18 and 11 points in order. But our ladies bowed out the following night 53–24 to the Purple Hurricanes. North Cobb quintet made quick work of our men in the opening round 40–26. In the finals at Leonard Gym on Saturday night, February 16, Murray County boys and Cass High girls claimed the Region 3-A crown. A paid attendance of 1,255 broke the old record of 1,201 set last year. Total souls in the memorial building were estimated at 1,500. In the spring, Coach Jim Mullins conducted 20 days of drills and fundamentals for his lady squad. He was very pleased with the progress toward next season, especially Louise Jordan, Jane Knight, Jeanne Sutton, Vera Heuther, Myra Littlejohn, Crissie Chambers, Marynan Boggs, Donnice Bohannon, Joyce Sutton, Sheila Knight, Patsy Gaston, and Judy Sutton.

1963–'64 Season

On December 12, 1963, *Rome News-Tribune* sports editor Don Biggers concluded in the preseason this would be a lean year for basketball in Floyd County. He noted 20 teams competed in the sport with 11 schools fielding men's teams while 9 high schools suited up women squads, Darlington and Berry being the exception. Biggers criticized fellow sportswriters who often neglect the 3-on-3 game. He praised Cave Spring coach Graham Woodell for providing the most consistent ladies program in Floyd County. In early November, Coach Olan Cosper began drills for the coming season. He welcomed lettermen Steve Barnett, Johnny Mathis, Tony Taylor, Joe Boggs, and Billy Mathis. Up from the JV were Steve Johnston, Sheely Wilder, Mike Kizziah, Steve Gilbreath, and Joe Knight. The season started well enough on Friday night, November 22, as the men won over visiting Trion 48–30, and the ladies "ran roughshod" over the Lady Bulldogs 42–21; senior Joe Boggs had 14 points to lead us while junior Jane Knight netted 18 big markers. Coming out of the Thanksgiving holidays, Lindale's quintet lost big to visiting Cave Spring 49–28; Joe Boggs again led the boys with 12 points. The ladies put a scare in the Springers before losing 31–30; Jane Knight had 11, and Jeanne Sutton hit for 9. By Tuesday, December 10, the Dragon quintet record was 1–4 while the women were 1–2. Hopefully the hanging of the Yule Star in Lindale on the thirteenth would change our luck as the Christmas tourney would begin in 4 days. This year, there was no clear-cut favorite in the ninth annual chase for the Gold Ball. Over 3,000 paying customers witnessed last year's invitation; rumor was that figure would be surpassed this holiday. Pepperell boys' record had sunk to 1–8 when they faced 9–1 Berry Academy on the first night, Wednesday, December 18. Coach Jerry Shelton's Falcons eliminated us easily 63–40; they sprinted to a 12–2 lead quarter one and never looked back. Joe Knight and Johnny Mathis bucketed 16 and 10 points respectively. On December 26, the Dragonettes lost to Cedartown 47–36 in the opening round of the Cave Spring Invitational; Louise Jordan and Jane Knight led scorers with 22 and 9 markers. Back at the boys' invitational, more than 1,000 fans watched as Rockmart's Jimmy Wuenach leaped high with 7 seconds showing on the board and knocked home a jumper to win the Gold Ball 41–39 over West Haralson. The new year brought about a split decision with visiting Rockmart; the boys lost significantly 52–28 on Tuesday, January 7, while the ladies eked out a 37–31 win. Johnny Mathis and Joe Boggs led the boys in points with 10 and 8; Jane Knight and Louise Jordan were tops for the winning lassies. On the fourteenth, Cartersville invaded the Leonard and went home 65–46 victors in boys and 58–38 in ladies; Joe Boggs led our quintet with 18 counters while Louise Jordan netted 25 for Dragonettes. Four nights later, Cave Spring administered a close 46–44 loss to the men; the women lost narrowly 44–40. The Dragonettes' season chart was 6–5, but the Dragons stood at 1–12. At Johnson on January 28, the girls increased their wins by 1 with a 48–25 victory, but the boys lost big 73–27; sophomore Steve Johnson was high-point man with 13 counters while Louise Jordan again led our girls with 25 counters. Thank goodness for Trion! We visited north Chattooga County on Saturday, February 8, and came away with double victories—men, 44–33, and women, 60–57. Joe Boggs hit for 12, and Johnny Mathis, 11; Louise Jordan netted half her team's points at 30 while Jane Knight and Jeanne Sutton scored 16 and 14 respectively. In the Region 3-A South tourney, our girls lost to Carrollton in the opening round played at Cartersville court. The north and south division winners would meet for the finals and semifinals at Leonard Memorial on Friday and Saturday, February 21 and 22. Neither Dragon squad made the cut.

1964–'65 Season

Pepperell basketball prepared to open its season on Tuesday night, December 1, hosting Rockmart. Women's coach Mildred Moore and boys' coach Olan Cosper were hoping for a better record than last year when the Lady Dragons posted a 10–11 slate and our quintet lost 22 of 24. However, 4 contests later, PHS boys were beaten by the Yellow Jackets, Gilmer County, Johnson, and Cave Spring; the girls salvaged a game versus Gilmer before breaking a 10-year losing streak to the Springers 37–34. In that contest on December 8, Jane Knight led all scorers with 25 points, many coming from the free throw line; the boys lost by 13 markers 51–38. The eleventh annual Christmas Tourney was scheduled to start a 6-day run on the seventeenth at Rome's Memorial Gym; Calhoun lassies and Berry lads were considered favorites. Two nights before the men's invitational began, our girls almost pulled out a win over host Valley Point but fell 40–39; Jane Knight again led her team with 19 baskets. Although the men got hammered 80–46, Wilder scored, 12; Popham, 11; Mathis, 10; and Cox, 7. On December 19, Berry Academy became the first two-time winner of the annual invitational, defeating West Rome 56–48. Both of our squads were one and done in the yule season. The first win in a rebuilding season came on January 8, 1965, versus Coosa 51–47. The final quarter was pivotal as junior Robert Gravitt led the rally with 15 points. Jane Knight pumped in the same amount of markers in the girl's 45–27 victory; it was our first doubleheader win since last year. It happened again on February 2 in Lindale when the boys beat Coosa 34–31 and the ladies won a thriller 39–36. Jim Mathis hit for 17 markers while senior Marynan Boggs "ripped" the nets for 25.

The *News-Tribune*'s Don Biggers editorialized on February 4, 1965, that basketball was being upgraded in Northwest Georgia; he cited as evidence the large number of teams now contending for a region championship. He wrote, "Maybe that's because basketball is now a sport all its own." Youngsters now played early and often; many worked year-round to improve. "This is in contrast to the past when football players made up the bulk of rosters." However, we had a ways to go to match Kentucky schoolboy enthusiasm which drew 18,000 paying customers for a March district championship game. In Jasper on February 5, "it was same song, 16th verse" for the men of Pepperell, losing 59–41 at Pickens County. Yet Coach Cosper was encouraged by the play of underclassmen Steve Johnston and Sheely Wilder who tallied 18 and 9 counters against a taller opponent. However, the ladies won by 10 when Marynan Boggs "erupted" for 20 points; junior Linda Chambers helped out with 11 markers. In the final week of February, Region 3-A play took the forefront. Valley Point ladies and Berry boys were favored in the north subregion with Rockmart and Cartersville in the south. In girls' play north first round, Pepperell crushed Pickens 58–30 with Marynan Boggs hitting for 20 points; Jane Knight and Nancy Mathis helped out with 17 and 9 respectively. However, both of our squads were later eliminated; the boys were defeated handily by Valley Point in a game played mostly by substitutes. They led 29–6 and 50–26 in the first two breaks. The girls succeeded in fighting their way to the 4-team region finals before bowing out to tournament favorite Valley Point 38–27; Jane Knight closed the score book on 1965 with 11 counters.

Also bowing out of basketball was longtime official Gene Baggett. In a career that spanned 29 years, the end came in Region 7-C girls' tournament in Rome. He decided it was time to make way for younger men. But as luck would have it, the last game went into overtime and was decided by a single point! In 1934, Baggett was assigned to the Sixth Cavalry at Fort Oglethorpe when he was "ordered" to call battalion roundball games alone. He completed Army duty in 1937 primarily to play baseball for Pepperell Mill (see pages 48–49); yet local gymnasium work always followed the diamond offseason. In a March 12, 1965, *News-Tribune* interview, which is paraphrased below, he recalled the game was different then as girls were allowed only one dribble/bounce, and a technical foul was called if a team tried to tie up the ball. After each bucket in the boys' game, the ball was returned to center court for a jump. Of course, this resulted in low scoring contests. He remembered one game with a 7–6 ending; many finished under 20 markers. The first player he disqualified was in 1938; Monty Montgomery who later became Rome's recreation director, roughed up an opponent who was holding him. With blood flowing, he said, "I had no choice than to put him out of the game." Once, Gene ripped his britches and had to finish work with a towel wrapped around his waist. Another time, a female fan attacked him with her pocketbook for picking on her boys. A very unusual incident happened one night in Alabama. The home squad was behind 1 point and shot just as the horn sounded. The ball stuck between the goal and backboard, and everything was at a standstill until a player tipped it in. Baggett disallowed the basket and almost got mobbed, including a local photographer throwing a camera at him. Following the 1-point home loss, the head coach sent "a couple of old graduates" to see him with the purpose of whipping the referee. Thankfully the old veteran talked them out of it. Identical twins once posed a problem until Gene hooked a safety pin on one jersey in order to tell them apart—but they kept switching tops. Pay was not much in the old days. First time to Cave Spring for a doubleheader paid $1.50. State tournaments including AAA, AA, A, B, and C were regular occurrences. The retiree recommended officiating to young people today, for it is a good way to offer guidance to youngsters but only if they treated it as a profession and not a moneymaker. Gene Baggett's character was validated by a female fan letter to *News-Tribune* sports editor Don Biggers on Sunday, March 14, 1965: "All these years we have watched Mr. Baggett and I've said a few hard thing to him, but he has never even given me a hard look. It's always been a smile…he has never lost his temper with any of us and has always been fair, firm and honest…we are very proud to have a man in our town like this."

News from the village on Friday, March 5, 1965, reported some 2,000 Pepperell Manufacturing Company employees were casting their votes for or against unionization. The voting concluded at 7:00 p.m. This was the third attempt in 70 years to bring the workers under Textile Workers Union of America. They were rejected in 1947 and 1955; total Friday night votes were tabulated at 2,192 with 1,155 against the union and 959 in favor. The mill closed immediately and scheduled a start-up on Sunday's third shift. General Manager G. Howard Smith thanked the employees for their vote of confidence and said, "The victory is yours…This is Lindale's finest hour." It was also noted that in 3 weeks (March 26, 1965), the company would merge with West Point Manufacturing Company subject to stockholders' endorsement to form West Point–Pepperell Inc.

1965–'66 Season

    Coach Olan Cosper told the *News-Tribune* on Tuesday, November 30, he expected a better squad this year especially toward the end of the season. A few hours later in Polk County, the Dragons lost 63–31 to one of the top teams in Region 3-A. Bill Keller's defensive-minded Rockmart quintet held the visitors to 8 points in the first half; seniors Robert Gravitt and Steve Johnston hit for 10 and 9 respectively. Conversely, the Dragonettes won a thriller 39–36 behind junior Nancy Mathis's and senior Linda Chambers's 20- and 12-point effort. The boys turned it around offensively at least on Saturday, December 3, in a 60–55 overtime loss to Model. If not for sophomore Sonny Chambers, who hit 2 foul shots with 8 seconds remaining, we would have lost in regulation 50–48. The girls' contest was close for 3 quarters before we pulled away to win 53–44; Mathis and tenth grader Terri Johnson were top scorers with 27 and 18. On December 15, visiting Valley Point went down to our ladies 43–37; however, it took a furious 18–8 rally led by Terri Johnson and sophomore Martha Henderson to win. Our boys fell behind early and never recovered in a 58–44 loss to the Pointers; Morris and Chambers scored 7 counters each.

    The brackets were drawn up for Rome area Christmas Tourney at Memorial Gym on December 20–23. Although Berry was defending champion, our Dragons must face the favorite and last year's runner-up, East Rome, in the opening round. Their front court measured Gary Mitchell, 6 feet, 7 inches; Jerry James, 6 feet, 6 inches; and 6-foot-5-inch Woody James, not to mention 3 other Gladiators who averaged 6 feet, 4 inches. Yet our squad "hustled" to the lead for most of the initial half before falling 67–44. Robert Methvin (a.k.a. Pete) Gravitt led us in baskets with 11. However, Powder Blue and Gold were upset on Thursday, December 23, by Calhoun 56–49. Interestingly, Coach Charles Faulkner rushed from Dalton where he coached his girls to the North Georgia Invitational championship over Murray County 57–55. Then a police escort accompanied the 40-minute dash to Rome. Faulkner's Calhoun quintet, referred to in the press as a bunch of racehorses, played fast in beating East Rome 56–49 to claim the Gold Ball. The new year started bad for our boys on January 4 when Region 3-A Cartersville scored 50 points after intermission and breezed 80–36. Other than Steve Johnston's 12 markers, no Dragon broke double digits. In all honesty, the Hurricanes were as good as their undefeated 11–0 record. In the women's contest, junior Nancy Mathis and senior Linda Frances Chambers netted 17 and 10 baskets in a 40–36 losing effort. On Tuesday, January 11, our quintet led all the way in beating visiting Armuchee 43–32; Sheely Wilder was the only player on the floor with double figures at 19. The Lady Dragons had to fight back from a halftime deficit to top the AHS 44–37; Mathis and Chambers again were top scorers with 17 and 13. The big news from the Leonard on January 25 was junior Nancy Mathis; the junior guard scored 44 points as our girls downed visiting Rockmart 61–39. In doing so, she broke 1964 senior Louise Jordan's mark of 39. The Jacket boys came to Lindale with a 14–2 slate and left at 15–2. In the 64–27 win, visitor Donnie Harris hit the nets for 22 markers while the losers' top man was substitute Sonny Chambers with 11. The same scenario broke on Friday night, January 28, on Highway 53 North where our lassies won by 13 points in Shannon, stretching their record to 13–4; we had big scoring from Mathis, Chambers, and senior Nancy Ann Williams with 24, 17, and 10 buckets.

But Model's quintet carded their fifth win of the year 52–41; Steve Johnston was our only double-digit scorer at 14.

Scenario part 3 occurred in Armuchee on Thursday, February 3, as the "high flying" Dragon girls, one of the finest teams in Region 3-A, won 54–48; the game's top scorer was Nancy Mathis with 24. The Springers of Coach Graham Woodell upset us 5 nights later 53–44; the win ran their record to 24–1. For most of the season, Woodell played Cheryl Pledger at guard/defender, but last week, she crossed the mid-court line and had averaged 29 points a game. Our fast improving men avenged an earlier loss to CSHS by whipping them 53–33; Steve Johnston was the only player on either squad with double digits at 22. At Gilmer County earlier in the season, Olan Cosper's crew lost 54–52 on a last-second shot in overtime. The February 11 return game did not appear heading in that direction; nevertheless, the Bobcats managed a 62–62 tie at zero on the clock. In the extra period, it was all Sheely Wilder; the senior collected 6 of his 24 points in the 70–64 victory. Steve Johnston backed him up with 18 regulation markers. In the opener, Ms. Nancy Mathis continued her "torrid scoring" with 43 points to lead the Lady Dragons to a 61–40 win.

There is an old schoolboy basketball adage on Sand Mountain, Alabama, that says, "If you hit 70% of your foul shots and 70% of your lay-ups, you will win 70% of your games." That was certainly true for Pepperell boys on February 15 versus visiting Cartersville. Although the Dragons lost 56–51, an upset victory could have been theirs but for missing 5 straight one-and-one attempts and 3 putbacks in the final 4 minutes of the battle. This, the *News-Tribune* speculated, could have added 10 more points to the scoreboard. Mildred Moore's women rolled to their seventeenth victory of the season 44–37 in the opener Friday night at Leonard Memorial; Nancy Mathis led her team with 19 tallies. Class 3-A subregion tournament north began in Lindale on February 21 with the Lady Dragons eliminating Gilmer 43–27; the other Nancy (Williams) sparked her squad with 17 points. In the ensuing contest between Berry and Pepperell, which lasted an extra 35 minutes because of OT, "thrills came in bunches" as the Falcons eliminated us in a 68–64 overtime victory. Gold and White senior Steve Johnston netted 17 points. However, Pepperell ladies won the north subregion division with victories over Gilmer (43–37) on Monday, February 21, and on Wednesday night, they easily defeated Valley Point 59–49 as Nancy Mathis hit for an amazing 35 markers; Linda Chamber chipped in with 15. On "Saturday night live" in Rockmart for the final round, all members of Region 3-A South swept their north opponents and would represent our area in Macon. Regrettably on Saturday, February 26, our Nancy Mathis experienced a "cold" night shooting with only 16 points as North Cobb won 34–31, ending the Dragonettes' season. Hopefully there was more help coming, for in early February, the Dragon ladies and lads both claimed the annual Floyd County junior varsity tournament played on the West Rome court.

1966–'67 Season

Coach Wayne Huntley made his high school coaching debut on Tuesday night, November 29, with a 66–49 loss at Rockmart in a game that was never in doubt after the early minutes; however, he was not dismayed by the score using his entire roster to evaluate players. Veteran

Bill Keller also used all his Jackets in a game that saw the Dragons play stubborn late behind Bo Firestone's 15 points to go with Larry Sheppard's and Sonny Chambers 13's counters each. In the opener, our girls took an early lead and rolled to a 53–39 decision behind Nancy Mathis's 24 buckets. Two days after the Rockmart defeat, Coach Huntley, who had been charged with bringing PHS back into the basketball spotlight, was interviewed by *Rome News-Tribune*; overall, he was pleased with his kids' game competitiveness and their determination and hard work in practice. The former all-conference performer at Shorter College predicted a bright future for Lindale, saying, "We're going to be hard to deal with before this season is over." He critiqued three seniors, saying Sonny Chambers and Larry Sheppard were tall enough at 6 feet, 2 inches with the former a good rebounder and the latter a good shooter who also had great ball savvy; Jimmy Morris was an excellent defensive player either starting or coming off the bench. Junior Larry Tate should help on the boards while sophomore Lynn Hunnicutt was little known but should be a surprise as he had "good hands, is quick and agile." Other future prospects included Gary Easterwood, Larry Hester, Mike Abney, Wayne Chastain, Gordon Boggs, and Albert Sullivan. The knowledgeable tactician has installed a wheel offense against man-to-man defenses and a 2-1-2 set versus zones. Pressure-type man-to-man with varying full- and half-court presses would hopefully limit opponents scoring. In part 1, host Model came from behind on Friday night, December 3, to edge Lindale 63–59; a large crowd was treated to a "fine exhibition of basketball." College teammates Huntley and Robbie Weir coached their players to great effort. With 45 seconds showing on the clock, Sonny Chambers hit a crip shot, cut the Blue Devils' lead to 61–55; Lingerfelt then hit a jumper before Chambers and Firestone hit driving layups to make it a 4-point loss. The girls' game was even closer; with 14 seconds left and fans on their feet, Sheila O'Neal sank both ends of a one-and-one to put the Lady Devils up 51–49. But Pepperell had its chances when Mathis fired 1 from top of the key which missed; they rebounded and shot, rebounded and shot again before Mathis on the fourth try finally tied the game with a putback just as she was fouled; 1 free throw and the contest was over, yet the ball wouldn't go in the basket. She made amends by scoring all 4 markers in the overtime for a 55–51 victory. The excitement did not let up Friday night in Ellijay; with 30 seconds remaining, the Dragons led by 3 before their James Moore went to the foul line and hit both ends of a one-and-one. Still we led by 54–53; unfortunately, Gilmer stole the inbounds pass and scored a layup to win 55–54. The ladies' contest was not a cliffhanger as they won 43–27 to improve to 5–0. Martha Henderson took the spotlight with 18 big points with Mathis and Chambers netting 14 and 11 in order. December 13 proved to be unlucky for Armuchee as the Dragons came out shooting and rolled to a 32-point win; they hit 50 percent in the second half and claimed a total of 55 rebounds in the 63–31 victory. Sonny Chambers did most of the damage with 23 markers while Dudley netted 10. Darrell Lowery was tops for the Indians with 7 counters. The ladies stayed unbeaten at 6–0 with a convincing 51–36 win; Nancy Mathis and Martha Henderson led the scorers at 31 and 15 markers. Lindale boys carried a 4–3 record to Jasper on Friday, December 16, and lost 64–70; the women did not fare much better, losing 41–34 for their first loss of the season. The thirteenth annual Christmas Tourney began the following Tuesday and again brought Model versus Pepperell excitement to some 800 fans, part 2. The lead changed hands no less than 8 times in the last quarter; with 4 showing and his team trailing 60–59, Model's lanky Lin Redden calmly sank 2 foul shots. However, it took a last-second Dragon miss for the Devils to win 61–60.

Moving into the new year our squads awaited the always tough Cartersville athletes; the Hurricane men had lost only once this season while we logged in at 4–5. Yet when the dust had settled on Tuesday, January 3, it was Pepperell 49–45 in overtime. Wayne Huntley was extremely proud of his group especially since they had lost several contests in the last few seconds. Bo Firestone and Larry Sheppard were cited for their offensive play in the fifth-quarter victory; last year's freshmen transfer Lynn Hunnicutt was "a demon on the backboards" as the sophomore hauled down 15 misses. Our girls "smashed" the visitors 55–33 with Nancy Mathis and Martha Henderson again leading the scoring at 31 and 16. On the tenth we won a doubleheader from Coosa; the men coasted to a 63–47 margin with Sheppard, Chambers, and Dudley the top scorers at 18, 12, and 11; we scorched the nets with 48 percent shooting and 70 percent from the free throw line; Hunnicutt again won the rebound battle with 14. Nancy Mathis hit for 50 points in our ladies' 80–15 romp over the Lady Eagles—honest.

Controlled revenge is sweet, and that was what we got against Pickens on the thirteenth when our ladies hammered the visitors 68–32; although Mathis swished for 43 points, the real story was our guard corps of June Scoggin, Gail Presley, and Cynthia Rayburn completely shutting down the opponent's offense. The *News-Tribune* posted on January 18 that with a 78–33 victory over Armuchee last night, the 9–7 Dragons "must now be dealt with" in the coming 3-A tourney. Prophetically first-year coach Wayne Huntley vowed in the preseason his squad would finish above a break-even record. Sheppard again led our scorers with 22 with Dudley and Chambers bringing 12 each. The ladies won 54–39 behind Mathis's 40 markers. Needless to say, she was the top scorer in the area with a 33.1 average; incredibly the score book showed her last 4 games were 52, 50, 43, and 40 points! The Pepperell coaches had high praise for their defenses after logging 52–37 and 56–36 victories over Dallas High's women and men in order. It was the best effort of the year, prompting the roundball mentors to say, "Offense gets the headlines but defense wins ballgames." On Friday, January 27, part 3 of Weir's and Huntley's squads going at it on the Shannon hardwood ended with Model again winning "a bruising, fast moving" contest 62–57. The visitors led for three quarters with Sheppard hitting for 24 points; Blues' Jim Edwards was the difference with 17 markers to go with his great board work mostly in quarter four. The Dragonettes escaped an upset when they tied the game 43–43 late in period four to force OT; Mathis led all scorers with 29 with a trio coming in the 48–45 overtime win. On the first day of February, our ladies pushed their record to 15–2 with a 62–40 win over West Rome while the men measured the Chieftains 56–42 to improve to 12–8. With a defense designed to stop Nancy Mathis, Martha Henderson took advantage by scoring 21 to go with Carol Lewis's 9; however, the area's top point-getter still netted 29 total markers. The men who were still irked about a loss to Rockmart cranked up a running offense and pressing defense to down WR 56–42. Larry Sheppard was the big gun with 21 baskets; Lynn Hunnicutt contributed 12 to go with "a basket of rebounds." After we won a doubleheader against hapless GSD, the Polk County Bees visited on February 7. Our boys led until Black and Gold starting hitting "from all corners" which brought them a 44–38 victory; it was their twentieth win of the season.

Sheppard knocked down 12 points, and Lynn Hunnicutt pulled in 16 rebounds; the Dragons were now 14–9. Our girls raced to their eighteenth win, 62–53. Lewis and Mathis tallied enough markers between them (55) to defeat the Jackets. Three nights later, Nancy Mathis was at it again scoring 44 points in a 77–40 victory over Chattooga. In the nightcap, we never trailed while winning 56–43 in Summerville; although Chambers hit for 15; Dudley, 13; Sheppard and Hunnicutt, 11 each, defense won the night. Cartersville's Dennis Baker was the second leading scorer in Region 3-A; on Valentine's Day, he put up 23 markers against visiting Pepperell 63–49. The Hurricanes led early and refused to relinquish the "frontage." Jimmy Dudley's 11 markers was our highlight. After losing to WR last Saturday night, our sextet beat Purple in overtime 47–43; Carol Lewis led the road win with 17 counters followed by Mathis's 16. The regular season ended in the Leonard 3 nights later on February 17 with East Rome boys claiming a 45–33 victory and our girls nipping the Lady Gladiators 37–35. On Monday, February 20, the opening round of Subregion 3-A in Pickens County was exciting, to say the least. Coosa was ahead 55–52 with 19 seconds showing and Pepperell in possession as Larry Shepperd was fouled; the senior calmly "put through" a one-and-one effort to narrow the margin at 55–54. The Dragons quickly stopped the clock with a personal infraction; fortunately, the ensuing Eagle free throw missed with Sheppard again controlling. Down 1 point on the other end, our leading scorer drove hard to the basket as the horn sounded and was fouled once more; he proceeded to "dump in" 2 more charities for the 56–55 squeaker. The girls had an easier time of it against Coosa (71–29) behind Nancy Mathis and Martha Henderson's 36 and 17 counters. Basketball is a tournament sport whereby fans usually turn out and remember the victors—and woe to the 20–1 squad that was upset in opening round. Case in point, favorites Pickens and Rockmart men were downed on the first night of tourney competition while the Dragons continued to suit up. It was a hungry bunch of Lindaleans who "picked on Pickens" Tuesday night to the tune of 59–56; Sheppard and Hunnicutt did most of the damage with 23 and 17 swishers. On Wednesday evening after beating Coosa 24 hours earlier, our girls lost in a mild upset 39–30 to a sextet from Jasper. There was no upset later that same night when Model once again beat our boys 67–59 in part 4 of Dragons versus Devils. In 2 tournaments and 2 regular season games between the textile villages, Shannon won 4 times over Lindale by an average of 4.5 points per contest. Still we made the Friday night semifinals against Carrollton on February 24 played in the Leonard Gym. Against the Trojans our crew fell behind early, yet the score was never out of reach, but we could not recover in losing 60–54, thus ending our season. Also in Friday's action, our girls beat Dallas 48–44 to set up a Saturday night special on February 25 versus North Cobb for the Region 3-A crown. Nancy Mathis and Carol Lewis combined for 45 points, but the Cobb County women won a close one 48–46; nevertheless, on Thursday, March 2, the runners-up qualified for state play in Macon's City Auditorium for the first round. The Lady Dragons who were coached by Mildred Moore included forwards Nancy Mathis, Martha Henderson, Linda Pilgrim, Cecelia Chambers, and Carol Lewis, and guards June Scoggins, Gail Presley, Cynthia Rayburn, Dolores Brewer, Donna Bing, and Melinda Edge. Team managers were Vicki Formby and Lyn Hinton.

The Macon *Telegraph* reported on page 27, Friday, March 3, that Pepperell downed Swainsboro 44–38 behind Martha Henderson who "dropped in" 5 points in the last minutes of play. In the first-round evening on Thursday, Mildred Moore's Floyd Countians led at all the breaks but could not quite shake the persistent Tigers of Coach Jimmy Harper who nudged ahead late. With 4:21 showing, Nancy Mathis sank a field goal that put the Lady Dragons ahead. The daily paper then noted, "From this point it was all Pepperell." Mathis and Henderson led in scoring with 17 and 13 counters along with Carol Lewis who came off the bench to net 10 buckets. The following evening, Central Gwinnett fought its way into the finals of Class A girls state tournament with a "pulsating" 43–37 victory of Pepperell. The Black Knights went ahead early in period two and stayed there. However, the *Telegraph* declared on Saturday morning that "this was a lot harder than it sounds." Central led 26–18 just after intermission, but the Dragons "stormed" back to trail 32–31 at third-quarter break. The final period was nip and tuck until Gwinnett hit back-to-back field goals with 3:20 remaining from which our ladies could not recover. Nancy Mathis scored 21 markers; Martha Henderson and Carol Lewis followed with 10 and 6 counters respectively. The daily paper mentioned that Cynthia Rayburn, June Scroggins, and Gail Presley were "equally outstanding for Pepperell." Thomas County Central girls would win the championship with a 56–40 victory over Lawrenceville. Lindale's group finished with a 21–3 record; they scored over 100 points in a single game and were the top offensive squad in area in addition to being third in defense.

On June 2, PHS principal W. E. Byrd presented Ms. Nancy Elaine Mathis the outstanding student award for 1967; she was the daughter of Reverend and Mrs. John Mathis of Lindale. In the past three years, the graduated senior had participated in many extracurricular activities including Future Homemakers and Teachers Club, the Christian and Student Councils, Women's Basketball squad to which she was named All-State forward, Volleyball, Tennis and Softball squads; the Letter Club, the Spanish Club, Girls State, and the Junior and Senior Honor Society. Nancy was on the Yearbook Staff and was a member of the Homecoming Court last fall. Ms. Mathis was a member of the Bush Arbor Baptist Church and was church pianist. Past winners of the award went to Roger Goss, Jane Knight, and Powers Garmon.

1967–'68 Season

Head coaches Mildred Moore and Wayne Huntley both expressed optimism for the coming season to the *Rome News-Tribune* on page 11 of a Sunday, November 26, article. The latter thought his boys had "the raw talent for a good team." He specifically mentioned 5-foot-11-inch Jimmie Dudley, 6-foot-6-inch Kenneth Mitchell, and 6-foot-2-inch Lynn Hunnicutt as lettermen with star quality. Sophomore Steve Hatch, junior guard Gary Easterwood, and freshman Phil Baker were also noted. The girls, who were defeated in the state semifinals last year, returned scorers Martha Henderson, Carol Lewis, and Cecelia Chambers; guards Gail Presley and Cynthia Rayburn were also back. Coach Moore predicted, "We plan to be right there with Model and Pickens." The schedule started on December 1 at East Rome where we lost both contests; however, the squads rebounded to defeat West Rome, Armuchee, and Coosa. Versus the Alabama Road Eagles, Jimmie Dudley netted 18 counters in the 57–39 win. The ladies triumphed 66–19 with Martha Henderson getting 25 points. On Tuesday, December 12, Model defended our men 54–31; we had 1 shooter barely with double digits. The Lady Devils sank a short basket and free throw with 18 seconds to go for their 37–33 victory; Henderson and Lewis led in scoring with 18 and 15. The men rebounded 3 days later with a solid win 64–44 over Pickens; freshman Phil Baker led PHS with 18 points. However, superior backboard work probably won for us as Hunnicutt and Hatch had 18 and 14 rebounds between them. The women almost pulled a big upset before losing 51–49 to Pickens; Henderson and Lewis collected 28 and 23 for Pepperell. That same night, the village glowed with the hanging of its yuletide electric star; 2 "lofty smokestacks" had supported the sphere every year since 1931. Another tradition began Monday the eighteenth at Rome Memorial Gym when the fourteenth annual Holiday Festival began at 5:30 p.m. The Gold and White began the men's-only tourney on Tuesday, December 19, with a convincing 57–37 victory over Chattooga with balanced scoring from Hunnicutt, Hatch, and Dudley (14, 14, and 13), yet it was our defense that almost shut them out in the last quarter. In the second round, we ran into a buzz saw from Walker County and lost 55–37 on Wednesday, December 20. The Ramblers fell behind in the opening minutes but cruised after that with Bill Cross netting 15 points and a like number of rebounds; Jimmy Dudley netted 13 for Lindale. On the other hand, it doesn't hurt as much when your loss is to the tourney winner—Friday night final score was LaFayette Ramblers, 52; Model, 50.

Going into the first week of the new year, area statistics showed Pepperell girls leading in team offense at 48.7 per contest while the men were tops in defense, allowing 43.9 points a game. The boys upheld their status on the ninth by whipping Coosa 56–35; the girls kept pace downing the Eaglettes 73–21. A tradition came to an end on January 14, 1968 when local independent write-ups ceased in the *News-Tribune*. For more than a half century, a daily feature in the paper reported on the happenings in Lindale. Judge C. W. Bramlett began as the first reporter in the early years of the twentieth century. Charles J. Ogles then wrote news beginning in the second decade; Langdon B. Gammon joined the mill in 1928 and became editor of "Lindale News" in 1935.

On Tuesday, January 16, Coach Bill Keller turned our reputation against us as his Rockmart Jackets "out-defensed the top defensive team in the Rome area" in winning a 55–39 decision, but with the game close going into the final quarter, the Rock turned up their shooting and outscored us 17 to 9. Steve Hatch was game high for us with 19 counters. The Dragonettes had an easy time of it winning 51–31 behind Henderson's and Lewis's 25 and 15 markers. On the twenty-seventh, Pepperell "virtually nailed Pickens County to the wall" with a lopsided 74–47 victory; Dudley, Hatch, and Baker led the way with 19, 18, and 16 counters. Although Henderson, Chambers, and Carol Lewis connected for a combined 53 buckets, the girls "fell to the wayside" 64–55. Fans sure got their money's worth when Huntley went against Weir. It happened again on Tuesday, January 30, with the Dragons leading 58–57 with 11 ticks remaining. Model's Scott Howell "charged through" with a short jump shot, and the scoring ended for the night with a 59–58 Devil win. Freshman Phil Baker led us and all scorers with 25 points. The Blue Devils completed a sweep by downing our girls 53–48; they hit 25 of 28 free throws. On February 6, the free throw syndrome spread from the Dragonettes to the Dragons as top-ranked Rockmart hit 17 foul shots to collect their sixteenth season victory 57–46; Baker and Hatch led us with 14 and 12 markers while their Ronnie Green burned the nets for 28 counters. In the opener, seniors Carol Lewis and Martha Henderson shot "lights-outs" with 24 and 23 baskets to lead PHS to an easy 58–31 win. Next game out on February 13 in Bartow County, Cartersville surprised both squads, first the girls, 45–33, and then boys, 43–37. Coach Huntley was not happy; he cited poor offensive play that did not warrant a victory. Junior Allen Baldwin was our top scorer with 11. The women were not much better shooting as Henderson and Chambers totaled 23 points together.

Basketball is a tournament sport; fans really get "pumped" for the postseason and treat the regular schedule as merely a warm-up. On February 19 in opening round of Region 3-A North competition in Lindale, the Dragons had little trouble with Pickens 62–35 as Phil Baker swished the nets for 28 points; he had help from Dudley and Hatch with 11 and 10. The "high flying" Dragonettes won as easily as the men, topping Gilmer County 63–32; Martha Henderson was high point in the score book with 28 on Monday night while Cecelia Chambers was next with 20. Twenty-four hours later, the boys won the second round versus Coosa 60–33; Lynn Hunnicutt paced the winners with 21 points. In a gratifying game for the ladies, Pepperell gained revenge for 2 earlier losses in defeating Model 51–39; it was Henderson and Chambers again leading with 25 and 18 counters. There was pregame excitement galore in the Leonard on Wednesday night, February 21, when the Dragonettes lined up against top-seeded Pickens. Although our ladies were down only 1 point at intermission, the bunch from Jasper played tough defense aided by Vansant's 33 markers to measure us 55–40; Henderson and Lewis combined for 35 counters in the losing cause. In the 9:00 p.m. nightcap, perseverance finally paid off for Wayne Huntley as his squad upset nemesis Model 52–45; the Blue Devils were never able to overcome a 17-point second quarter by the Dragons. Phil Baker provided scoring "punch" with 20 in the score book; Hunnicutt followed with 13 and was cited for his defense against star Jimmy Edwards holding him to 4 points. After disposing of Carrollton in the semifinals, we lined up in Cartersville for the championship game of Region 3-A versus a Rockmart quintet that had previously eliminated Model; Bill Keller's crew had defeated us twice in regular season, and they made it a trifecta on Saturday night, February 24, with a 70–54 victory. But the Rome newspaper posted the Dragons did not go quietly as Steve Hatch, Lynn Hunnicutt, and Jimmie Dudley pumped in 17, 15, and 12 markers; in addition, Lynn was especially "tough on the boards." However, the Jackets pushed their overall record to 23–2 with 4 players in double figures; big 6-foot-6-inch post Aaron Nix had the best game with 21 points. Nevertheless, PHS qualified for the state tournament versus top-ranked Rockdale County; the Bulldogs are located just east of Atlanta on I-20. The battle began in Macon at 4:30 p.m., Wednesday, February 27. The valiant Dragons could not overcome the deadly shooting of the Bulldogs and fell 62–51; the winners hit 67 percent of their first-half shots and 10 of 11 free throws. Pepperell finished the schedule with a fine 17–10 chart. Accolades for the season went to Wayne Huntley as Rome Noon Optimist Club Coach of the Year with Lynn Hunnicutt joining him as an all-star.

1968–'69 Season

On November 17, 1968, Coach Wayne Huntley told the *Rome News-Tribune*, "We'll have the best team we've had at Pepperell in the past few years." We had 4 starters back from last year's team that advanced to state competition including Phil Baker, Allen Baldwin, Lynn Hunnicutt, and Larry Hester; in addition, 6-foot-5-inch junior Steve Hatch was a fine shooter who had made strides in preseason practice as had sophomore Preston Cain. Senior Hunnicutt was a proven scorer/rebounder; Huntley expected senior Allen Baldwin to be the floor leader for PHS. Depth would come from seniors Spence Millican who missed roundball last year because of a football injury and tough Raymond Smith; junior Wayne Chastain was not tall but could be a contributor.

The Dragons had abandoned the Shorter College offense of ball control to a more aggressive style. However, a bump up in classification into tough Region 7-AA could challenge that change. On Tuesday, November 26, Coach Mildred Moore's rebuilding Lady Dragons fell at Model 61–48 despite senior Donna Jackson's 26 points and junior Brenda Poole's 16 counters. In the nightcap, Pepperell romped to a 60–48 victory; we were tied at the end of quarter one but never trailed after that as Baker tallied 21 markers to go with Hatch's 12 points. We remained undefeated on 12–10 versus Coosa as our boys won 67–37 with Hatch and Baker both scoring 20 points; Coach Moore's girls triumphed 40–32 behind Donna Jackson's 25 counters. Going into the fifteenth annual *Rome News-Tribune* Christmas Tournament, our boys were set at 4–0 and were considered a favorite to win a Gold Ball. On December 20, we came on strong against defending champion LaFayette, winning 70–55; strong inside play by Hatch and outside work by Baker produced 22 and 26 points respectively. Rossville was next with the tallest squad in the tourney, but we used a fast break and tight defense to win by 22 points—75–52; Baker got 20 markers mostly before intermission while Hatch tallied 22 with 15 after halftime. West Rome was waiting on Thursday, December 26; although the Dragons had defeated them earlier in double overtime, the Chieftains took us down 60–51 by jumping out to a 19–9 lead and were never headed. Raymond Smith led us with 14 counters while Hatch and Preston Cain scored 12 each. In the consolation contest, East Rome nipped us 51–45 by virtue of hitting 8 of 8 foul shots while we were 2 of 2. After Christmas, fans at East Rome gym on January 17 witnessed two different games. Although junior Fonda McKelvey netted 23 points and Donna Jackson 29, the Lady Glads outscored us 68–55 with "tension felt throughout the building." Iris Kinnebrew felt no tightness, for she had a career night bucketing 57 points. The men's game was completely different with host ER winning a squeaker 38–37; Hatch and Hunnicutt led us in the score book with 18 and 11 counters. Rockmart came to the Russell Leonard Gym on Tuesday, January 21, sporting a 10–3 record and averaging 65 points per game. On top of that, we played without 2 regulars, Hunnicutt and Smith; not to worry, for Huntley's Dragons "ran past" the Jackets 78–62. Allen Baldwin picked up the slack with his finest game of the season, scoring 21 to go with Baker's 20; our girls made it a clean sweep winning 41–30. Jackson led the way with 24 points. A strong Cassville crew came to the Leonard on Friday, January 24, and left defeated 74–43 by Huntley's quintet who "extended themselves a little bit further." Illness had bothered our team lately, but the *Rome News-Tribune*'s Sunday edition said it all, "Hatch Leaves Sickbed to Guide Pepperell by Cass in a Shocker." The 6-foot-5-inch senior scored 17 points mostly from the foul line and claimed 13 rebounds; also Preston Cain who usually was in the shadows of older teammates had 20 big markers plus a good share of rebounds against the taller Colonels. Coach Wayne was especially proud of Spence Millican "who performed like a real veteran on the boards and defensively." Our girls almost made it a sweep but lost in overtime 47–43; Jackson tallied 21 while junior Teresa Smith contributed 15.

Twenty-four hours later, we lost twice to West Rome; the girls went down 44–36, and the boys, 70–58. Preston Cain came on again and led us in scoring with 22 markers. In an earlier meeting, Huntley's crew knocked off Rockmart by 16 points, prompting the local paper to note, "The losing crowd left Lindale with a wait until the next time look on their faces." The next time came on Tuesday, February 4, and was much worse than the first. Steve Hatch, Preston Cain, Phil Baker, and Spence Millican tallied 28, 20, 13, and 10 points in the 80–52 shellacking. The Yellow Jacket women gained revenge in beating our girls 40–35 despite Donna Jackson's 26 counters. Four nights later at the Leonard, an up-and-down Cedartown squad came visiting; they departed down with an 88–58 beating.

On the last full weekend of February 1968, 7-AA South finalists met to determine the championship. In order to get there, Pepperell had to play Cartersville first on Monday, February 17. We "cashed in" 2 quick baskets and proceeded to hold them without a field goal for over 7 minutes en route to a 66–47 victory. A tight man-to-man defense, fast breaks, and great backboard work did the trick. Hatch and Cain scored 20 points each while Lynn Hunnicutt netted 14 to spark us. The following evening before a packed house of more than 1,000, Pepperell jumped a good Cass High squad by 23–6 and increased it with steady play to win going away 77–59. Sophomore guard Phil Baker scorched the Memorial Gym nets for 29 counters; another tenth grader, Preston Cain, added 15 while senior Lynn Hunnicutt sunk 14. East Rome downed rival West by 63–45 and faced up to the Dragons on Wednesday night, February 19. Although we had 3 players in double figures, Cain with 17, Hunnicutt with 16, and Hatch with 14, the Gladiator defense kept us off-balance most of the evening in winning the South subregion 63–54. They led 14–9 at first break and increased it to 48–32 after 24 minutes. Then with a dwindling clock, we made a run cutting the deficit to 8 points with 3:44 remaining in quarter four, but it was as close as we got. Dragon O had 3 players in double figures—Cain, Hunnicutt, and Hatch with 17, 16, and 14 in order. However, 4 teams, LaFayette and Calhoun (North champs) tipped off against South quintets East Rome and Pepperell for the region crown that weekend. Being a second seed, we lined up with number one Calhoun on Friday night; Wayne Huntley's strategy was to "let the air out of the ball" or stall on offense, trying to keep the Jackets at bay. Coach Hamp Alexander's crew was one of the highest scoring teams seen in a while as they hit the century mark on 3 occasions this season in recording a 20–3 slate. The final score of 35–30 bespoke we had a chance to win, yet baskets were at a minimum with Baker, 5; Hatch, 8; Hunnicutt, 1; Chastain, 1; and Cain, 15. On Monday, March 3, at downtown Forrest Hotel, the Noon Optimist Club named boys and girls all-star basketball teams which included Phil Baker and Steven Hatch.

1969–'70 Season

On December 6, 1969, Wayne Huntley began his fourth year as men's basketball coach at Pepperell. The opponent was West Rome. The home crowd at the Leonard sat in anticipation after the young mentor evaluated his squad to *News-Tribune* 2 days before. He started by saying, "I don't down-grade my kids; I honestly think we've got a good bunch—it's the best personnel we've had and they've worked harder so if we don't win, then you can blame it on the coaching." Mike Brownlow, who had made "remarkable improvement," was a 6-foot-5-

inch, 185-pound junior and would start at forward. Four veterans returned including big Steve Hatch and 6-foot-1-inch Preston Cain; floor leaders would be eleventh grader Phil Baker and senior Wayne Chastain who would man the point in a 1–4 offensive set. The bench would be good with junior Tom "the Bomb" Brock who had excellent leg spring and a knack of finding the basket; others were seniors Mitch Cordle, Alonza Chubb, and Ray Hines. This group featured quickness over height. Huntley, a former Shorter College player who performed for Bill Foster, had vowed his team would run and shoot because they were better suited to this type of game; he even predicted some 100-point contests along the way. Well, the home team put up 77 points against the WR Chieftains and followed that up with a 98–83 win over Coosa in which Steve Hatch logged 18 minutes, scored 39 markers, and claimed 27 rebounds. On Friday night, December 12, our quintet romped over rival Model 76–57 with Phil Baker hitting for 20 counters.

The sixteenth Holiday Festival began on Friday afternoon the fourteenth in Rome's Memorial Gymnasium with Calhoun as the favorite; Hamp Alexander's defending champion Jackets were hardly tested last year, blasting West Rome in the finals for the Gold Ball. In a preview of what might happen, Calhoun hosted Pepperell in a regular season game prior to tourney play. A packed gym in Gordon County watched Steve Hatch score 22 points and snatch 22 rebounds in our 78–72 victory, prompting veteran coach Alexander to say, "Hatch thought the ball belonged to him the way he played," and then added with tongue in cheek, "But I'm sure we must have paid $18.50 for it [the Spaulding]." PHS had 4 in double-figure counters; however, their Vaughn Robbins was not too shabby, making 35 markers. In the first festival game versus Fairmount, Huntley's century prophecy came true as his squad netted a 107–61 victory. But the rematch against Hamp's bunch came next at 8:30 p.m. on Monday, December 22, described as, "Pepperell-Calhoun Clash Spotlights Tourney Play." The Lindale quintet "demolished" the Gordon County Bees 96–67 before a crowd packed to the Memorial Gym rafters; they went ahead early and stayed there while building a 101.5-point average for the tourney. All 5 starters were scoring in double digits. After Christmas break, the games resumed on Friday, December 26, with PHS downing Chattooga 88–45; a full-court press bothered the boys from Summerville immensely. The inevitable happened in the nightcap as East Rome won over Adairsville, setting up a Floyd County matchup for the Gold Ball. The Sunday paper said, "Cain's Jumper Breaks Tie, Gives Pepperell Holiday Festival Title." The headline was referring to senior Preston Cain's memorable 12-foot fadeaway jump shot with 18 seconds left on the clock to break a 55–55 deadlock and give the Dragons possession of the 1969 Gold Ball. It was one of the few times Wayne Huntley's team led due to foul trouble and the tremendous play of East Rome's Rodney Aldridge who netted 22 points and many rebounds. Dragon big man Steve Hatch carried 4 personals for most of the game but still hit for 17 counters; he and Aldridge were named cocaptains of the 10-man all-tourney squad.

After Christmas, we "chewed up" highly regarded Cass on Friday, 96–74, and came back the next night to down East Rome again 61–52; veteran Phil Baker combined for 58 points in the 2 wins, many of them on outside jumpers. On the following Wednesday, January 7, we polished off Cedartown 92–69 for our twelfth consecutive win; although Steve Hatch scored 29 and pulled down 24 rebounds, Coach Huntley was not exactly pleased, saying, "They scrapped us into lots of mistakes." The Dragonettes lost in overtime to the winless Bulldogs; Fonda McKelvey netted 18 counters. We were 12–0 visiting Cartersville on Friday, January 9, and came away with a 64–59 victory. Hatch and Cain led our attack with 22 and 17 markers respectively. Postgame comments by the winning coach indicated the Hurricanes had as much manpower especially rebounding as any team in the area. We were sitting at 13–0 on the thirteenth as Calhoun visited for a third encounter versus the Dragons; when the Jackets departed, the good guys were 14–0 by virtue of a thrilling 70–69 final. No one in the Russell Leonard Memorial Gym dared leave until Wayne Chastain sunk a pair of free throws late. Afterward, Coach Huntley said, "It was a great game to win." A major shocker occurred 3 days later in the same building when East Rome nailed us 61–46, prompting the losing coach to say, "Maybe the pressure of a long winning streak is taking its toll." That and a really good Gladiator defense led by Rodney Aldridge, Strickland, Andy Akin, and Fletcher Parks. At least the girls were productive in winning easily 38–20; junior Ann Littlejohn and Fonda McKelvey carried the load for us, scoring 19 and 11. The men recovered and won comfortably against Rockmart 83–58 while the girls nipped the Jackettes 39–38. A third home game played on the twenty-eighth resulted in an 85–65 win versus Coosa; Hatch, Baker, and Cain swished for 21, 20, and 14 baskets while junior Tommy Brock hit for 12. The girls completed a double-victory night as Ann Littlejohn scored 16. In Shannon on the last Friday of January, a slow game turned fast when Pepperell's full-court press forced several turnovers which led to a satisfying 70–57 win. The *News-Tribune* wrote that the victors played sound ball despite losing floor leader Phil Baker in the second quarter to an eye injury; Hatch and Cain logged 24 and 21 baskets. The lady Blue Devils "went wild" in the last period, defeating our girls 59–42 to improve to 16–2 for the season. At Cassville on February 6, PHS boys changed to a 1-2-2 zone press that put 12 quick points on the scoreboard in a hard-fought 80–64 win. The local paper noted, "Cass can be just as stubborn as any team when it comes to surrendering a victory." The trio of Baker, Cain, and Hatch led us to a twentieth victory with 25, 22, and 18 counters. The following night in Lindale, we were coasting along at 20–1 when the Purple Hurricanes visited and nipped us 66–64 even after we raced to a 23–9 first-period lead. Terry Jones paced the winners with 26 points while Hatch, Baker, and Cain hit for 27, 15, and 14. We were now tied with East Rome in subregion. After the heartbreaking loss to Cartersville, we rallied and dominated host Cedartown 74–58 in spite of a "siege" of virus that had plagued the squad lately. It was a game of free throws and rebounds as we hit 24 charities and corralled 53 misses; Baker, Hatch, Cain, and Mike Brownlow all tallied double figures in points.

A flip of the coin may have cost Pepperell its first state basketball championship. Legendary Pepperell football coach Lynn Hunnicutt, who was a member of our 1968–'69 squad, once said, "I don't know how to coach a coin flip." We had finished in a dead heat with East Rome in South Region 7-AA; by virtue of winning the toss, East Rome elected the number two seed versus the West Rome–Cass winner, which enabled them to dodge talented Cartersville. Consequently, this put PHS's first round opponent as Cedartown-Cartersville survivor. The worst-case scenario happened to us as the Bartow County quintet had little trouble subduing the Bulldogs, and then they proceeded to upset/eliminate the Dragons 81–76 on Tuesday night, February 24. Next, East Rome's tough 1-3-1 defense helped them to the South 7-AA crown with a resounding 61–38 victory over our nemesis, the Hurricanes. At this point forward, Aldridge, Akin, Parks, and Strickland dispatched Calhoun and Athens Burney Harris High School in preliminaries to state. East Rome eased into Georgia Tech's Alexander Memorial Coliseum on March 12 virtually unknown to the city's sportswriters; 72 hours later, Coach Kingery's bunch was king of Class AA basketball. Victims North Springs, Central of Newnan, and Newton County were fine teams. However, *News-Tribune* sports editor Don Biggers explained on Wednesday, March 18, "The truth of the matter is that East Rome was untested in the state tournament. They met tougher opposition during the regular season right here on their own backyard." Case in point, Pepperell had defeated East Rome twice in 3 meetings. Coach Wayne Huntley finished his first 4 years (1967–'70) at PHS with season records of 17–12, 19–10, 15–9, and 22–3. He was named area coach of the year in 1968 which saw the team advance to state play against Rockdale County; his quintet also won the Christmas Tourney in 1970 as well as rising to number ten in Class AA state polls in late February.

1970–'71 Season

Spotlighting the coming roundball season on November 29, the local paper thought Pepperell would again be "cream of the crop" in the area but not as much as last year's 23-win squad; a rebuilding East Rome and veteran Cassville would provide ample competition. The area schedule started on the first week of December with 29 games on the agenda. Although we won 52–45, a rebuilding Rockmart quintet gave us all we could handle on December 5; however, Coach Huntley warned his team would start much slower than last year when we peaked at mid season. "The boys played about the way I expected them in the opener," he said afterward. On the eighth, we knocked a fine Model ball club from the unbeaten ranks 54–48; the coach felt his boys looked more like a ball club, especially on the backboards. Three starters were in double figures with junior Mark Leach and senior Mike Brownlow coming in at 8 and 9 counters. The girls completed the home sweep with a narrow 36–34 victory as seniors Linda Ross and Ann Littlejohn led us in scoring at 10 and 8. On December 11, Darlington welcomed us to Lakeside and their run-and-shoot offense which averaged 79 points per outing, yet PHS claimed a controlled 59–51 victory. Coach Jim Van Es commented afterward that "they are a well disciplined team and really put the defense to us." Offensively, the Dragons were up 4 markers with less than 3 minutes remaining when they decided on a "freeze" effort; Phil Baker and Preston Cain took control and used "easy charity points" to put the game away. On December 15, visiting Coosa, which had been "up and down" in early contests, was up in upsetting us 56–51. "It was no fluke...they wanted the game a little more than we did," remarked the losing coach. The Eagles' fine sophomore guard Mike Glenn did most of the damage with 26 points; Preston Cain matched him while Baker netted 14. The Dragonettes tied their game late and went into overtime where they hit for 6 markers to win 37–34; Linda Ross led us with 10.

In a prelude to the holiday tourney which was cosponsored by the *News-Tribune* and Rome Parks and Recreation Department, sports editor Don Biggers wrote in a feature article that after years of talking, the Recreation Committee of the Rome Chamber of Commerce had approved an inaugural Sports Hall of Fame. Nominees were now being accepted and would undergo a thorough screening as the requirements for consideration were extremely high. Also a committee unanimous vote was prerequisite to being named a member. Project chairman Horace Anthony explained that persons may qualify as amateur, professional, or meritorious service; also the individual must have brought state or national recognition upon themselves and the community through achievements. They must be of high moral character and have been a resident of Floyd County during or before the time of accomplishments. The first inductees would be honored during a banquet on January 21 at Berry College. Subsequently, seven persons were named with Willard Nixon being Lindale's representative.

The seventeenth annual tourney would begin at Memorial Gym on Friday, December 18, with 16 teams vying for the Gold Ball; the opening round would feature last year's champ Pepperell High School versus talented Berry Academy at 8:30 p.m. Afterward, sports writers thought the Dragons looked mighty good while "taking Berry apart" 83–62. Preston Cain, Mike Brownlow, and junior Mark Bennett scored double figures, 22, 17, and 10 respectively. On Monday the twenty-first, we got revenge on Coosa 68–58; after being tied at intermission, PHS started on a scoring spree and put the game away. Cain and Brownlow combined for 52 of our points or 76 percent in the score book. The following night a near-capacity crowd watched as Van Jacobs and East Rome led us 14–5 early; however, Wayne Huntley ordered a full-court press that cut the lead to 28–27 at intermission. The final quarter belonged to us with Preston Cain and junior Mike Gilbert leading the surge of a 25-point frame. Baker and Cain were steady at the basket with 23 counters each. Twenty-four hours later on Wednesday, December 23, LaFayette claimed their second crown in 4 years with a 78–72 victory over Pepperell; the Ramblers ran out to a 64–38 lead in the third quarter, prompting 1 veteran coach to remark, "The finest one quarter I've ever seen a high school team play." But Lindale exploded for 34 markers in the last 8 minutes and cut the visitor's lead to 6 points late in the game. Cain and Baker carried us with 24 and 18 counters. On the last day of 1970, the local newspaper recognized East Rome (basketball) and Pepperell (baseball) for state championships as well as kudos to West Rome's Chuck Kennebrew as Athlete of the Year. Reporter Orbie Thaxton noted that many area schools have reported an increase in basketball attendance; he attributed this to "the closeness of play, high scoring games combined with great defensive action." Also the men had several college prospects, namely Coosa's Mike Glenn, Robert Williams of Rockmart, the Dragons' Preston Cain, Ben Ansley of Berry, and Darlington's David Lacey. This was happening as the 1970–'71 girls' competition was weakest in a number of years due to change of rules format and youth of the squads.

Back from Christmas break on Tuesday, January 5, visiting Cedartown surprised PHS 62–55, convincing Wayne Huntley the Bulldogs were for real; Baker and Cain combined to score 41 counters. In the girls' contest, our ladies were tied 40–40 at the end of regulation; we only scored 1 basket in overtime, but it was enough to win 42–40; Linda Ross led us with 11 buckets while Ann Littlejohn and senior Annette McCoy added 10 and 7. In the Russell Leonard Gym 3 nights later, the boys remembered how to play defense by allowing highly regarded Cass only 37 points while our O tallied 52. The winning coach was effusive in praising his defenders, "It was the best defensive game we've played since I've been at Pepperell." Although Preston Cain knocked down 16 markers, first-time starter 6-foot-5-inch junior Mark Leach was cited for his 9 points and several crucial rebounds for the 9–3 Dragons. Baker and Smith also netted 9 each. First-year Pepperell coach Bill Wood's ladies almost matched the men, downing the Polk County sextet 48–39; senior Linda Faye Ross was a sharpshooter bombing the nets with 27 points. January 12 saw PHS men win in overtime versus West Rome 58–57; in free basketball, Phil Baker hit a jumper, and Cain sank a free throw for the winning margin. Those 2 also led us in points with 19 and 16. The women were not as fortunate, for we fell behind in the final quarter and lost 54–36. The men lost at East Rome on Friday night and then on January 16 rebounded in Polk County with a last-second shot by Preston Cain to win 56–54. We had led Rockmart most of the way until the "frantic fourth" was decided by number 32's jumper, which was airborne when the horn sounded; the senior led in scoring with 17 followed by Baker and Leach with 16 and 10. The women also played well after overcoming a first-quarter deficit to win 51–40 on the road; Ann Littlejohn netted 19 counters for the winners. On Tuesday morning, January 19, the men's record was 11–5 while the girls logged in at 7–5. That evening, both squads visited Alabama Road where the host Lady Eagles won 50–32 in the opener; we had no player score in double figures. The men "thrashed" Coosa 74–67 for our twelfth victory; Preston Cain put on a show with 22 points and a dozen rebounds for the winners. Phil Baker was not far behind with 20 markers, and junior Marc Bennett netted 10. On Saturday night, January 23, the men ran their record to 14–5 with a 62–48 victory over Paulding County; Baker and Cain both hit for 21 markers. The girls were on the short end of a 54–39 game; senior rover Annette McCoy and Linda Ross collected 13 and 6 points. Cedartown is a tough place to play as witnessed on the twenty-sixth of January; the Dragons were down 17–15, 29–28, and 51–45 at the end of the first 3 frames. But the fourth quarter brought out our best especially from senior Phil Baker who canned 14 points in the 71–67 win; all told, the 4-year veteran put 24 in the score book. Pepperell now had sole possession of first place in the subregion. The ladies' game was just as exciting as the Lady Bulldogs led most of the way only to see the Lindale edge ahead late to win 34–33. Linda Ross topped our scoring with 16 counters. A late-season surge had brought victories over Darlington, Paulding, and Cedartown. Cass had pushed the Dragons to 16–5. Coach Huntley said after the 57–54 win over host Cass on Friday night the twenty-ninth that "I have no doubt that we have improved as a team during the past few weeks." And much of that improvement was the work of Marc Leach and Steve Smith who netted 11 and 8 against the Colonels; of course, team responsibility rested on the shoulders of seniors Phil Baker and Preston Cain who hit for 18 and 17 markers. The Cassville girls claimed a close victory over the Dragonettes in the opener 44–42. In a 55–49 nightcap thriller played in Shannon on Friday, February 5, the Dragons ran their record to 17–5. Model coach Jerry Gatlin commented afterward, "It was just a well played ball game, that's all you can say." Wayne Huntley agreed especially on his squad's defensive work. Once more, the combination of Cain and Baker did most of the scoring as they drilled 18 and 15 counters each. Because of heavy fouling in the opener, Model's Lady Devils finished the game with only 5 players to Pepperell's 6; however, Lindale had the lead with a full complement on the floor and won 38–31; Littlejohn and Ross shot for 11 points each. The following Tuesday evening, February 9, by virtue of a 71–64 victory over host Paulding County, PHS finished atop the 7-AA South rankings. We led narrowly in the first 16 minutes but pulled away after intermission mainly because of Baker's and Cain's sharpshooting as the duo scored 43 points together; Mark Leach added 14 counters and 12 rebounds in his finest effort of the year. The Patriot women nipped our girls 39–38. We closed the regular season schedule on Tuesday night, February 16, in Calhoun, nipping the Jackets 52–50. As indicated by the low score, neither squad burned the nets; the difference was at the foul line where the visitors hit 14 of 17 freebies to the losers' 8 for 18. The dynamic duo of Baker and Cain put 21 and 17 into the score book. We won the doubleheader by 3 total points when our girls edged the home team 41–40 by virtue of senior rover Ann Littlejohn's swisher with only 2 seconds remaining. In Sunday's February 21 issue, the *Rome News-Tribune* announced area all-Stars; Phil Baker returned from last year's list by averaging over 17 points per game in the back half of the schedule; his partner Preston Cain managed almost 20 points per outing to go with 10 boards.

In the South Region playoffs on February 23 at Cedartown, the Dragon men nipped a fine Cassville team 57–55; although we only trailed twice in the game, the Tuesday night victory did not come easy, for it took a huge play by Phil Baker to win; the senior muscled in a driving layup and ensuing free throw with 14 seconds showing on the clock. Prior to that, he had made a foul shot with 1:37 showing to push our lead to 54–51; a bucket by the Colonels cut it to 54–53 before Baker closed it out with his clutch 3-point play. Baker and Cain canned 19 markers each supported by Leach's 15. The next night's loss to East Rome was an anomaly for the Dragons. Baker and Cain led a rally that gave us a 38–30 advantage with 1:30 remaining in the third; then Trapp and Hogan hit two baskets each, and suddenly it was tied 38–38 as quarter three ended. Hogan started period four with another pair of jumpers, and it was 42–40 Glads' advantage; however, a late whistle under the goal sent him to the bench with a fifth personal foul with 4:14 left. The crowd inside Cedartown's spacious gym figured Pepperell was about to put the game away; instead, the Powder Blue and Gold ran off 8 straight points to make it 57–49 with 1:20 remaining. The Dragons needed a miracle; 3 times we fiercely forced turnovers but could not convert them into counters. The rest of the contest was inconsequential foul shots ending in a 64–59 East Rome victory. Still, both squads advanced to the Region 7-AA playoffs in Calhoun.

"The boys take a rest and the girls take over on the basketball front," wrote the local paper on Thursday, February 25. The South play would be at Rome's Memorial Gym tonight with East Rome versus Pepperell. Most thought this contest would be close, and it met expectations with Coach Wood's lassies winning a thriller 56–55; the game seesawed back and forth until the third stanza when the lady Glads poured 18 counters through the nets to take a 41–27 advantage. With the clock showing 7:00 to go, PHS started a 19-point comeback to lead by 56–54; at the 10-second mark, their Deborah Carmichael was fouled and sunk the first free throw, but her second was off the mark with the Dragons claiming the rebound and victory. Ms. Carmichael could not be faulted, for she scored 27 points on the night. Twenty-four hours later and twenty-four miles to the east, our boys faced Calhoun in the Jackets' home gym, and they came away with a 64–60 win plus a berth in the Class AA state playoffs. The winners had pretty much controlled the contest going into the final quarter with a 14-point lead. The momentum changed when Cain and particularly Phil Baker began to swish the nets; the latter hit for 12 markers in the surge that cut the lead to 4 but no closer. In their final game together for PHS, the two seniors fittingly hit 23 points each. At least our women continued to play. On the first day of March, we upset South tourney cofavorite Paulding 52–42 in Memorial Gym; newspaper reports used comments such as "onslaught," "did everything right," "out of reach early," "reserves saw action," and finally the 10-point victory "really wasn't that close." Ann Littlejohn was the leader in the score book with 16. McCoy and Ross followed with 14 and 12 respectively. Ann's sharpshooting at the charity line accounted for half of her counters. We lost the next evening to West Rome 55–49 due mainly to the shooting of Marie Mercer who "killed" us with clutch baskets at the top of the key and free throw line. Nevertheless, South number-two-ranked PHS girls still advanced to Calhoun for the Region 7-AA finals against number one North Whitfield. Both squads were competing for a berth in Class AA state play. The Lady Dragons failed to "make the grade" but for a bit of cold shooting in the final stanza enabled Whitfield girls to win 42–37; 4 straight makeable baskets rimmed out that could have reaped 8 points and possibly a trip to state. Senior Annette McCoy led us in the score book with 10 markers followed by junior rover Debra Wallace's 7 counters.

On Sunday, March 28, Shorter College coach Doug Rogers announced the signing of forward Preston Cain; the 6-foot-2-inch redhead joined former teammates Steve Hatch (basketball), Lamar Wright, Ken Kizziah, and Wayne Chastain in baseball. Preston led the Dragons by averaging 21 points and 9 rebounds per game; many thought he was an even better diamond performer at third base and pitching. The youngster was the son of Mr. and Mrs. Herman L. Cain of 302 Strawberry Lane, Lindale.

1971–'72 Season

If height is a good indicator of success, the Dragons should be a good basketball team this year. Seniors Steve Smith and Mike Leach were both 6 feet, 5 inches with playing experience; two other twelfth graders, Dale Childs and Mark Bennett, are 6-foot-2-inch scrappers. Mike Gilbert was 5 feet, 11 inches and led at guard that teamed along with last year's spot starter John McGowan. Coach Wayne Huntley believed his squad would get stronger as the season progressed, but this he knew, "We have more enthusiasm than any team I've ever coached." Women's coach Bill Wood also thought his ladies would get better as the year moved on because of a large group of seniors including Debra Wallace and Diane Ball; other returnees were Ellen Henderson, Kitty McNeal, Donna Smith, and Kathy Branton. On December 3, we traveled to Polk County and lost 66–45 to 6-foot-2-inch hot-handed Lanny Ealey who scored 30 points and claimed 16 rebounds. Although Mike Leach tallied 18 markers, Rockmart's press bothered us as they built up a lead. The Dragonettes were more than doubled up by the Jacket girls 52–20; our high shooters were Debra Wallace and Kitty McNeal with 8 and 5 counters. The eighteenth annual Christmas Tourney was scheduled to start on Friday, December 1,7 in Memorial Gym; 16 teams would vie for the Gold Ball with previous champion Lafayette described as the best team around. They narrowly defeated Pepperell 78–72 last year. Prior to the tourney, PHS downed host Paulding County 64–47 for our first win after losses to Rockmart and Model. We hit 50 and 88 percent from the field and foul line. Huntley's bunch numbered 4 starters in double figures with Leach, Smith, Gilbert, and Bennett hitting 19, 17, 15, and 11 counters in order. Twenty-four hours later, the crew from Lindale upset East Rome 43–41; many thought the Glads were "cream of the crop" in 7-AA South. Steve Smith was the offensive star for the winners with 22 big points; junior Louis McNeal netted 9 in support. On Tuesday, December 14, Coosa defeated visiting Pepperell 78–65 in a regular scheduled game. At the end of period three, the Dragons led 51–47; however, the standing-room-only crowd watched as the Eagles put up 31 points in the next 8 minutes. Jim Bragg netted 12 in the last quarter alone to go with Mike Glenn's game-high 32 markers. The women did not fare quite as well, losing 39–24 with Kitty McNeal leading our scorers with 12 counters. On Friday the seventeenth, the Dragons hosted and lost a doubleheader to Cedartown; the boys went down 59–54 behind a 36-point second-half barrage by the Bulldogs; Mark Leach merited scoring honors for the losers with 25 markers. The Dragonettes lost by 7, 34–27, as the visitors led most of the way.

Finally on Monday the twentieth, Pepperell versus Coosa took place at 7:00 p.m. in Memorial Gym to start the eighteenth annual *Rome News-Tribune* Holiday Festival; although the affair was a low-scoring 47–43 Eagle victory, the crowd was on its feet most of the way, for Lindale led until the last 3 minutes. Then Glenn and Jim Bragg scored 6 and 5 respectively for the win. On championship Thursday, Coosa was on the receiving end of a disappointing "roof-raising" 72–68 loss to LaFayette High School, giving the Ramblers possession of the Gold Ball for 2 years running. At the end of Christmas week, our ladies lost 50–17 to the Springers in the first round of the Cave Spring Invitational. Needless to say, we had trouble scoring, for Debra Wallace was high point with 6 markers. Although in the first week of 1972 Huntley's quintet was only 3–5, they sat near the top of the region by virtue of wins over Paulding, East, and West. In the 58–54 victory over the Chieftains, we played without Steve Smith who injured an ankle during Christmas play; thankfully, Mark Leach picked up the slack with a 21-point effort with Marc Bennett and Mike Gilbert adding 12 each. The scoreboard margin was very close with PHS leading the quarter scores 18–17, 30–29, and 50–47; to protect the small lead, we went to a controlled shuffle offense in quarter four. On January 4, visiting Calhoun won 71–60 over Pepperell; the first half was closely contested, but the Dragons faltered after the break probably because we were outrebounded 45 to 23; Mike Gilbert paced Lindale with 19 counters. The girls remained winless as the Lady Jackets coasted to a 49–24 victory; again, putting points on the board was difficult, for Debra Wallace was high with only 7 counters. Chieftain Chris DiLorenzo made 2 critical steals that led to fourth-quarter baskets in Pepperell's 63–42 loss to West Rome on Tuesday, January 4. The 2 squads had battled on even terms prior to his thefts. The winner had 12 players make the score book while Mark Leach hit with 16 counters for Lindale. The PHS ladies tallied a measly 9 points in their 40–9 loss to the Lady Chiefs. We scored single points in quarters one and two and managed only 2 markers in period three; Debra Wallace topped us with 3 counters. On Friday, January 28, Steve Smith returned to the lineup versus Paulding County and claimed 15 rebounds to go with 11 counters; Mark Leach bested that with 20 markers and corralled 15 misses. However, the Patriots won 57–51 due mainly to our 2 dozen turnovers and the visitors' 25 free throws. News from courtside was senior guard Mike Gilbert was injured and would not return this year. On the first day of February, 3-12 Pepperell faced 1-loss Coosa High School, the number-three-ranked team in Class A. Sportswriters expected no more than "token resistance" from the host Dragons who had lost 7 straight contests and had become "a doormat" in Region 7-AA; also at the final horn area, leading scorer Mike Glenn had tallied 28 counters. With that said, the crew from South Floyd won the battle 69–67 behind a career performance by senior Mark Leach who outshined Glenn by swishing the cords for 32 points and gathering 10 rebounds. Afterward, a smiling Wayne Huntley said, "It was a tremendous team effort—the boys came to play." Three nights later, we cashed in another close victory downing Cedartown 42–41; good defense especially against Vance Frew and our "key shooting" led the way. We never trailed as Bennett and Smith netted 17 and 12 markers. The Lady Dragons fell behind early and never recovered, losing 43–32; Kitty McNeal paced us with 18 points. The Region 7-AA tourney started and ended for us on Monday night, February 21, on Cedartown's court. East Rome Ladies led us 24–5 at intermission in their 50–16 romp over PHS. Later, Darlington edged Lindale boys 50–48 in a game that saw the maximum lead peak at 3 points. The victory was sparked by the Tigers' backcourt man Jim Bonham, who, with just seconds to play, blocked a shot and intercepted a Dragon inbounds pass to protect a 2-point lead. Mark Leach and Steve Smith scored their last career points for the home team with 13 and 12 markers; on June 5, they would receive diplomas with 159 other graduating seniors. Their head coach Wayne Huntley resigned after the 1971–'72 school year; he would be heard from later at another county program.

1972–'73 Season

The winter basketball season was not very rewarding for Pepperell High School; former coach Wayne Huntley moved on to Model High, being replaced by Doug Rogers. The 1973 yearbook shows only 9 varsity players with average height and weight with no accompanying schedule or comments; in addition, there is no sign in local media of the traditional and invaluable roundball preview of team's strengths and weaknesses. As the season moved forward, few scores, records, or accomplishments appeared in the local newspapers. The first mention of our men's quintet occurred in Sunday's December 10 issue which reported a Model 61–30 victory; 10 members of Jerry Gatlin's troops tallied while we had no player in double figures. The girls copied our lack of scoring in losing 48–21. Next we traveled to Polk County on Friday, December 15, where our women downed Cedartown girls 38–32; Terry Kisor pumped in 17 counters as the only double-figure player in the game. The boys got beat pretty bad 60–42; Holloway was our only meaningful scorer with 14 markers. The nineteenth annual holiday tournament began on December 18 with Pepperell versus Rockmart at Rome's Memorial Gym. PHS was competitive but one and done 46–41 with Doug Smith and Tim Holloway scoring 13 and 12 respectively. On Friday, January 5, 1973, the local paper listed us as "winless" prior to visiting Alabama Road where we lost 93–33 to Georgia's number one BB prospect Mike Glenn who netted 36 points. Sophomore center Phillip Ball led us with 12 markers while Holloway hit 7 counters. The home team completed a doubleheader sweep as the Lady Eagles downed our girls 47–16. Tenth grader Tanda Norris was high scorer for PHS with 8; juniors Gina Rogers and Melissa Sisson each tallied 4 markers. On Saturday, January 20, we hosted split games with Darlington and GSD; our ladies won the opener 48–27, but DHS Tigers outscored our boys 66–56 in the nightcap game. Six nights later, East Rome came to Lindale and swept the women 51–30 and our men 74–58; in the first competition, Rogers hit for 12 while Jordan and Norris hit 6 each. The nightcap saw Ball, Smith, and Holloway net 16 markers each. On Saturday night the twenty-seventh, we know Rockmart tripped Pepperell in a doubleheader; however, no game scores were posted. On the first Saturday of February, Cedartown "roared" to a 19–6 lead in quarter one and defeated "winless" Dragon boys 56–49; sophomore forward Doug Smith, who was our tallest player, "burned the nets" for 33 points. On Tuesday, February 6, Model had to battle a Lindale team that was still searching for a single victory; following 24 minutes of play, we had cut the lead to 41–38. However, the Blue Devils pressed us into 3 straight turnovers to seal the victory 67–56; Phillip Ball led us in scoring with 15 while Smith followed with 10 counters. In the opener, Model whipped us 42–22 with Norris and Jordan each netting 6 markers. In the February 10 first round of Class 7-AA Subregion tourney, both Dragon squads were one game and out; East Rome dispatched our men 71–35 with 13 players getting points in the score book; Ball and Smith tallied 13 and 11 markers. The Gladiator women captured a "solid victory" over Pepperell 52–22; we had no player even close to double figures scoring. Unfortunately in 1972–'73, available documentation for Pepperell basketball reveals our men were winless while the girls recorded 3 victories.

1973–'74 Season

Pepperell's Doug Rogers welcomed a good roster of seniors and returnees for November preseason practice. Although they played in a fast league that contained West Rome, Cedartown, East Rome, Darlington, and Cass, the second-year coach said, "The boys are looking good and we feel they will be a contender." Supporting this statement was a trio of 6-foot-4-inch juniors including Doug Smith, Chuck Palmer, and Phillip Ball while Tim Holloway measured in at 5 feet, 10 inches. One of last year's starters was senior 6-foot David Langston who would be supported by fellow twelfth graders Sidney Sheffield and Randy Tillery; several underclass role players were Danny Pitts, Phillip Cooper, Danny Knowles, Joe Henderson, Kenneth Whatley, and Mark Gray; freshman Jerome Johnson was expected to log minutes on the floor. Women's coach June Scoggins was optimistic after last year's 3-win season; excellent depth could lead to victories as 10 girls, including 7 seniors, were capable of playing rotation. Leading the lineup were Gina Rogers, Terri Kisor, Penny Robinson, Susan Jordan, Tanda Norris, and Katrina Hogan; other experienced veterans were Melissa Sisson, Melody Billingham, and Sherelyn Burdette. Juniors Gina Bolton, Polly McGowan, and Katrina Hogan could help the team as could sophomore Peri Swafford. On November 30, we got the "monkey off our back" with double victories over Berry Academy. At the end of 48 minutes of roundball, the boys ended with a solid 79–42 win while the girls did even better, winning 50–19. Doug Smith and Phil Ball dominated the backboards with 21 combined rebounds; Smith also hit 15 counters followed by Jerome Johnson's 13. Mark Gray and David Langston chimed in with 10 each. Rogers, who played most of his roster, said after the game, "We found out one thing, these boys really hustle." Coach June Scoggins used most of her roster also in the 31-point victory. Although the Dragonettes made some mistakes, "It was a good opener for us," she said. On December 2, Wayne Huntley returned to Floyd County basketball as head coach of Model after a brief stay at Bremen; the Blue Devils proceeded to beat Pepperell men 56–42. The Dragons were up 6–8 and 29–22 at the first two quarter breaks, but Blue eased ahead 40–33 going into period four; Langston and Smith netted 12 and 11 for us. Lady Dragons never led at the breaks while losing 42–32; Kiser and Norris led us with 8 points each. However, on Friday night, December 7, in Lindale, PHS girls turned a close game into a 26–18 victory versus Cedartown; Katrina Hogan and Susan Jordan were outstanding on defense as they repeatedly stole the ball or batted it away from Lady Bulldog players. Meanwhile, Tanda Norris and Gina Rogers netted 8 and 6 points for the winners. Our boys had nobody in double figures scoring as the visitors took a 9-point lead in period three and won 46–36; Phil Ball and Danny Pitts each netted 9 counters. Our record was now 1–3. Two nights later, Paulding County scored at the buzzer for a tie in the first overtime period and then went on to win 65–61; juniors Doug Smith and Danny Knowles were top point makers with 17 and 15 respectively.

The twentieth edition of *Rome News-Tribune* Holiday Festival began in Rome's Memorial Gym on Wednesday, December 19; admission was $1.25 for adults and 75¢ for students. Although unbeaten West Rome had never won the tourney, they were the favorite. Rockmart versus Pepperell would tip off the second game at 5:30 p.m. We continued to struggle scoring baskets as the Yellow Jackets limited us to 21 points going into quarter four; they would take the victory 50–32; Knowles and Ball netted 7 counters each. On Saturday night, December 22, West "swept" past Cassville 62–53, claiming the Gold Ball for the first time. In post-Christmas women's invitational at Cave Spring, Dragon girls ran into a buzz saw from Atlanta; Greater Atlanta Christian, which had lost 1 game in the last 3 years, overpowered us 66–24. In the first contest of 1974, our boys put together a best performance in several seasons by downing Darlington 91–64. Indications were the Lindale quintet had jelled into a solid squad, for we put up at least 20 points in each quarter with 3 players getting double figures—Ball, Palmer, and Smith with 18, 15, and 11 respectively. It was the Tigers' seventh consecutive loss. However, their women gained some revenge with a convincing 54–38 victory; a 19-point fourth quarter "iced" the game. Rogers and Kiser netted 14 and 9 for the losers. Proof that our men were improving occurred on Friday night, January 11, when we edged East Rome 42–40 in a Class AA battle. The first quarter ended 11–11; the second, 24–24; and the third, 32–32. With a minute and a half left in the fourth, East led 40–38 before Danny Knowles sank both ends of a one-and-one free throw. The hero of the evening was another Danny (Pitts) who picked up a loose ball and dribbled the length of the floor for a layup to put Pepperell up 42–40; the Gladiators had 1 more shot but missed with the Dragons rebounding. Smith and Pitts scored 10 and 9 for the winners who were better than our 3–8 record. East eked out a victory in the girls' game 41–38 despite having the "upper hand" for almost 24 minutes; our lassies closed to within 34–35 with 1 stanza left, but the winners outscored us by 3 markers to win. Terrie Lynn Kiser led the ladies with 12 baskets. One night later, Rockmart downed the Dragons 58–51 despite Phil Ball's 20 points; the Jackets had taken us down by 18 markers 24 days earlier. The Polk County Bees tripped our ladies 34–25; evidently, we had trouble scoring, for Norris and Kiser were high point with 6 and 5 respectively. On Friday night, December 18, Cassville coach Jerry Gatlin's team "bowled over" the Dragonettes 57–33 and remained atop the standing in Region 7-AA with a perfect 13–0 record. They led 45–25 at the end of quarter three and coasted home. Gina Rogers and Tanda Norris scored 10 apiece for the losers. The PHS men did not fare much better, losing 59–42 to the 10–5 Colonels who ran out to a 13–2 lead in period one and never looked back. Pitts and Ball bucketed 10 each for us. The following Tuesday night against East Rome, we swapped leads until the final frame when the Gladiators eased ahead and maintained a 4-point advantage to win 44–40; Doug Smith netted 14 markers for Gold and White. On January 25, a nip and tuck game turned toward the host squad in the fourth quarter, which was posted in the *News-Tribune*'s write-up on Sunday, "Fouls Hurt Pepperell, Cedartown Wins, 63–49." A possible upset was averted when 2 Pepperell starters, Doug Smith and Danny Knowles, went to the bench with 5 fouls each; consequently, the Bulldogs ran up 14 points to win comfortably. We did have 3 players in double figures as Ball, Knowles, and Smith tallied 13, 11, and 10 in the score book. The Lady Bulldogs completed the sweep with a 46–29 victory; quarter three was the girls' downfall, for they collected only 1 point in 8 minutes while the host bucketed 18 markers. It was true on Friday night, February 1, in Lindale that Coosa boys were in a rebuilding mode post–Mike Glenn era. Actually, both quintets had suffered through inconsistencies and narrow losses during the season; therefore, it was no surprise the score ended a 57–54 Dragon victory due to last-second heroics. Despite Pepperell leading at all stops, we had only a 1-point lead late when Chuck Palmer connected on a hook shot followed by David Langston's steal and layup; the Eagles responded with a basket, cutting our lead to 56–54. At this time, however, with 3 seconds showing on the clock, Phil Ball iced the game (3-point shots were introduced in 1987–'88) with a free throw. Ball led his team with 16 counters followed by Knowles and Palmer with 14 each. In the girls' opener, "it was Coosa all the way" as they poured in 19 markers in quarter one and led 38–17 at intermission; Terrie Kiser netted 8 and Peri Swafford, 7 markers. In a girls-only contest played on Tuesday, February 5, in Cave Spring, the Dragonettes came from behind to down Berry Academy 41–39; senior Susan Jordan claimed scoring honors with 18 tallies while Tanda Norris added 10 to the score book. Friday, February 8, was Don Ingle Night in Lindale; the aforementioned was a member of the area officials association who died recently, leaving large medical bills. In support of his family, the PHS staff donated the entire receipts of West Rome versus Pepperell to a benefit fund. West was undefeated at 13–0 in the subregion and featured a top player in 6-foot-10-inch Larry Brewster. Dragons coach Doug Rogers's squad pulled out just about "every defensive play in the book" to slow the big man down; when they jammed the lane, he simply moved outside and flashed back in to score several "loft-baskets" on the way to a 20-point night. Teammate Alvin Ragland displayed his ability to score in the post, also netting 16 markers. The Dragons tried short jump shots in the middle to challenge the Chieftains' size to no avail as WR totally controlled the offensive/defensive backboards; in the end, height, scoring ability, and overall talent prevailed 72–54. Smith, Palmer, and Langston led the home team in points with 15, 11, and 10. The lady Chieftains completed the doubleheader sweep with a 43–30 victory over our PHS; the winners controlled the opening tip and led by 10 or more the rest of the way. Terrie Kiser netted 10 markers; Gina Rogers and Tanda Norris followed with 5 and 4 respectively. The Region 7-AA tourney started in Russell Leonard Gym 1 night later with both our squads playing Darlington. The *Rome News-Tribune* sports page headlined, "Darlington Double Winner in 7-AA South." In the most exciting game of opening round, DHS posted a 63–58 victory over Lindale girls; neither team had a safe lead as the game "rocked back and forth." We led 40–34 at the end of quarter three but got outpointed 13 to 6 in fourth period; Rogers, Jordan, and Norris tallied 14, 13, and 12 respectively. The Darlington Tiger men were frontage in the first three quarter breaks but then had to fight to win as Dragon Doug Smith hit a go-ahead basket with 4 minutes remaining, which was followed by 2 more lead changes before the Lakesiders took control again. Seniors Doug Smith, Danny Pitts, and David Langston scored 15, 13, and 11—their last points for PHS.

1974–'75 Season

The Dragons' season began early in December with games against Chattooga, East Rome, and Rockmart. In the preseason, Coach Doug Rogers was optimistic this year's squad would be "a stronger force" competing now in Class 4-A North subregion. However, on Tuesday, December 3, we lost by a single point, 59–58, to Summerville in Lindale. The Dragonettes also lost narrowly 40–37 with Haney, Norris, and Green combining for 33 points. Three nights later, in turnabout is fair play, the men faced East Rome in Memorial Gym and won by a single point 53–52. The Gladiators led until midway of the final period when their guests moved ahead and held on down the stretch for a victory. Johnson, Smith, and Palmer combined for 42 of our points. The girls made it a perfect night in winning by 3 points 39–36; it was their first victory over East in 4 years. Susan Green led the win with 15 big counters. On Saturday night, December 7, visiting Rockmart swept a doubleheader; PHS girls lost 41–37 despite the contest being tied at halftime. For the losing squad, senior Susan Green swished the nets for 15 counters. In the nightcap, RHS defeated us pretty good 68–51. They took control 36–26 at intermission and increased their advantage afterward; senior Danny Pitts was top scorer for Pepperell with 16 markers. In a regular season game on Tuesday, December 10, versus Coosa, the Dragons led narrowly at all quarter stops and then increased the advantage to a 64–56 victory; Phillip Ball was top scorer for the winners with 15 markers followed by senior Chuck Palmer and Knowles with 12 and 10. However, the women were whipped handily by the undefeated Eagles 73–33; Tanda Norris was the only Pepperell girl in double figures with 11. Friday the thirteenth was unlucky for Chattanooga Valley boys per the *News-Tribune* as "DRAGONS BLAST EAGLES ON 4TH QUARTER SURGE." We improved our record to 3–2 with the season's first home-court victory 73–66; it did not appear so at halftime for the visitors were up 36–26. Exactly what Coach Doug Rogers said to his players at intermission can only be speculation; nevertheless, we were a different squad in the last 16 minutes, scoring 26 points in the third frame alone. We added another 21 in the final stanza. Phillip Ball netted 22 counters with Chuck Palmer and senior Phil Hooper adding 13 and 10 respectively. The Valley girls got an early bit of revenge by winning the opener.

The Christmas Tourney opening round began on Friday, December 20; for the second time in December, Pepperell boys downed Coosa—this time 61–49. We led at all quarter breaks and finished with a 15–8 advantage in the last frame. Balanced scoring was the key as Doug Smith and Danny Pitts netted 20 and 14; Ball and Johnson added 10 each. In the following night semifinals, 1–4 East Rome revenged a 1-point loss earlier in the month to Pepperell and won easily 76–42 before a large Memorial Gym crowd; Doug Smith and Danny Pitts led us in points with 14 and 10. On Christmas Eve 1974, in front of a screaming crowd at Memorial Gym, the Gladiators won the Gold Ball by overcoming a 16-point deficit in upsetting Calhoun 60–56. The winners of the twenty-first annual tourney were led by underclassman Ray Donaldson who was the most outstanding player of the championship night; Lindale's Doug Smith was named to the 10-man all-tourney squad.

A January 3 road trip to Summerville resulted in a doubleheader loss; Coach June Scoggins's ladies lost a close 39–32 decision despite leading by 1 at intermission; Tanda Norris and Susan Green "hit the hoops" for 12 and 8 counters. The Chattooga men led all the way on deadly shooting to win 62–58; they hit better than 50 percent (11 of 21 in the first half alone) from the field and sunk 14 of 23 from the free throw line. The visitors countered with 4 players in double figures, including Mark Gray, Doug Smith, Jerome Johnson, and Chuck Palmer, but it was not enough to win. The Dragons traveled 12 miles on Highway 27S the following night (January 24) where the Cedartown men took our measure 64–47; Smith and Gray were leaders in the score book with 12 and 11 markers. Palmer and Ball added 8 points each. Pepperell then traveled out to Shorter Avenue to face West Rome on Friday, January 24, where the home teams treated us to a double loss; the Lady Chiefs took a 10-point advantage in the first stanza and increased it steadily for a 74–37 win. Tanda Norris managed 8 points in a losing cause. In the nightcap, Coach Rogers's Dragons played well in the first half leading 18–15 at intermission; however, the hosts inched ahead 33–28 at the third-quarter break and moved to a narrow 47–44 victory. Phillip Ball netted 14 for PHS. The Lindale men were riding a 4-game losing streak when they upset home-standing Rockmart 61–52 on January 28; of the 6 region games played that night, ours was the most impressive win, for we led all the way boosted by hitting 10 of 12 at the charity line. Hooper and Pitts swished 18 and 14 points respectively while Palmer added 10 for the improving 7–9 Dragons. In the opener, the Rock took a 23–12 lead at intermission and won 42–31; Norris was high point for PHS with 8 markers. On the first Tuesday of February, West Rome got good all-around double-digit scoring from 5 players to drop Pepperell boys 72–44; our top basket maker was Doug Smith with 10.

Invading Haralson County pulled off a late rally on Friday to win 62–57; the home squad led by 4, 9, and 3 at the quarter breaks but saw the advantage disappear in the last frame. Danny Pitts hit for a season-high 20 points while Doug Smith and Ball combined for 23 markers together. Our ladies continued to struggle with a 2–16 record as posted by the *News-Tribune* on February 6; the boys came in at 8–10. The sports section headline for February 12 featured, "DRAGONS SHOCK BLUE DEVILS." Underneath, the opening paragraph said, "When you're down by three points with only 10 seconds left to play in a basketball game, that's it. Or, usually that's the way it is." The article referred to Pepperell's unlikely 60–59 victory over Model. With 10 seconds showing on the clock, the Devils owned a 3-point advantage; however, the Dragons' Phillip Hooper was fouled and hit the front end of a one-and-one try. His second effort hit the rim and bounced to teammate Doug Smith who promptly shot a putback to tie the contest at 59–59. The Blue in-bounded and just missed a winning shot with 5 ticks left; that man Hooper grabbed the rebound and started toward his goal only to be fouled again. Once more, he hit the first free throw but missed the next; in the ensuing scramble for possession, the horn sounded for Lindale's finest win of the season. Young Hooper finished with 13 markers including the most important. For the winners, Phil Ball collected 16 counters while Doug Smith shot for an even dozen.

On Monday, February 17, the Region 4-A North tourney got underway in Shannon; the Model lassies had little trouble with the Dragonettes in winning 65–27. They jumped to a 12–2 first-quarter lead, and "it was all over at that point." The victors posted 4 players in double figures while the leader in a losing cause was junior Debra Acrey with 8. Pepperell men faced and defeated Chattanooga Valley 66–44 in the first round; we opened up a 16-point lead in frame two and won going away. The winners placed 4 in double figures with Hooper, Palmer, Smith, and Ball combining for 48 total points. The following night, Model won a thrilling second-round game 54–52 over the Dragons of Lindale. Blue Devil Harlan Stevenson scored but 1 field goal the entire night, but it was epic in Shannon basketball lore. His 25-foot jumper just beat the buzzer to give his team the North subregion crown; the losing squad placed 3 in double figures with Ball, Smith, and Palmer netting 14, 11, and 10. Nevertheless, the Dragons advanced to the second session of region playoffs also held at Model. On February 20, they faced up to Harris County High School from Hamilton, which is near Columbus. If not for foul trouble late in the contest, the boys from Lindale would have advanced to state play; as it was, the Tigers nipped PHS 50–47. The season ended with seniors Danny Pitts and Chuck Palmer scoring in double figures with 15 and 12 markers.

1975–'76 Season

In preseason, rule changes were in the forefront for area coaches. The Georgia High School Executive Committee voted girls' basketball would move to a full-court 5-on-5 game with 8-minute quarters same as boys; the new system was approved almost unanimously. For years, Georgia officials believed females could not run the floor; however, many other states went to a faster-pace sport without any adverse effects. Fast break offense is most exciting and has eliminated the advantage of a tall girl stationed on one end of the floor. In a later final analysis, *News-Tribune* reported, "The action seemingly is faster and more ragged at times, but the fans are not complaining." The men's game also experienced a revival of the dunk, which had been banned for almost a decade. In the past, any player dunking in warm-ups or games was hit with a technical; now only the former was forbidden. The reasoning being injuries were more apt to occur during shootarounds because youngsters try to overdo acrobatic shots. East Rome's Van Jacobs thought the reinstatement was "super," for it is part of the sport; he also would support a 30-second shot clock for high school.

The first reported roundball game of the new season was Sunday, December 7, when East Rome won a doubleheader from Pepperell. A lapse in quarters one and three was more than Coach Doug Rogers's boys could overcome in losing 67–43 to the Gladiators; Reggie Gordon swished the nets for 12 tallies while junior Barry Stephens scored 10. The Lindale women put up a fight before suffering a 37–35 loss. We surged ahead 8–4 in frame one, but opponent sharpshooting left us with a 15–10 deficit at the end of 16 minutes. The Powder Blue and Gold hit a "hot streak" after intermission only to see the Dragonettes knot the scoreboard at 33–33 and again at 35–35; by this time, both squads were playing with several substitutes, yet with 2 seconds showing on the clock, ER had possession and put up a final shot "and the ball went through the hoop." Karen Lane collected 8 counters for us while Treglown and Taylor netted 6 each. On Saturday night, December 13, Rockmart defeated our girls 45–33 and the boys 52–45. Although the Lady Jackets led by only 3 points going into period four, they moved to a 12-point frontage late; junior Zelda Gordon led our attack with 12 markers while Peri Swafford followed with 7. Yellow Jacket Phillip Davis's team led by 35–34 at intermission, but his 28 counters were a difference in the 52–45 outcome; Mark Williams scored 11 for the Dragons with Barry Stephens and Steve Green chipping in 10 each. Cave Spring girls won their eighth game in downing Pepperell 72–33; the Springers were in front throughout as they had 3 in double figures scoring with Julie Barnette netting 29 points; Swafford was high for the losing squad with 11 tallies. Edwards and Gordon combined for 18 markers. Coach Larry Bing's boys led 14–4 and 29–6 at the first two breaks, and the issue was never in doubt as we never got closer than 14 points; Reggie Gordon led our basket makers with 15. The twenty-second annual (1954) Holiday Festival began on Friday, December 19, in Memorial Gym with the defending champion East Rome quintet touted as the favorite; the 6–0 Gladiators faced and defeated the winless Dragons on Saturday night 63–33 behind Kondo Wiley's 17 first-half points; the 31–14 score at intermission indicated the winner's dominance. Reggie Gordon was our only double-figure scorer with 10. The tournament finals were played on Tuesday night the twenty-third with West Rome surging late to win 74–65; the game was a battle between the Ragland twins and East Rome's Ray Donaldson and Kondo Wiley; both pairs of players were responsible for most of the points and rebounds. One day after Christmas, the sixteenth annual women's tourney began in Cave Spring with the host team holding the Dragonettes scoreless in the first quarter en route to a 56–16 blasting; Sharon Edwards scored almost half our points with seven. Our men started the new year off wrong on Friday, January 4, versus Chattooga where we lost "a thriller" to the Indians; the following evening, the Cedartown boys' record moved to 3–4 with a 64–47 romp over us; Smith and Gray tallied 12 and 11 counters while Ball and Palmer added 8 points each. On January 6, West Rome's lassies handled us 36–24; they had the frontage by only 5 at halftime but increased the lead as the game progressed. Two nights later versus Coosa, it did not get any better as the Lady Eagles jumped to a 28–0 advantage and "glided through the game" 60–26. Peri Swafford was high point for us with 11 counters. The boys started quick in the first half only to fall behind later thanks to a Coosa half-court trap and foul troubles; Reggie Gordon "had 18 points and Steve Green had one less." On the seventeenth, Darlington won its eleventh contest by sweeping our girls 43–34; Peri Swafford again led us in the score book with 10. The men did not fare much better, losing 58–48; Gordon, Green, and Johnson netted 14, 9, and 8 respectively. At Model on Friday, January 23, the girls lost 58–30 as the Devilettes started slow and "steadily picked up speed to walk off with the win." Swafford and Gordon scored 8 points each. Doug Rogers's boys started to make a run at the home team, but foul trouble and lack of rebounding killed our chances for an upset win. Reggie Gordon was doing most of the damage to Wayne Huntley's squad until he fouled out; he and Jerome Johnson led Dragon scoring with 15 and 11 in the 58–46 loss. Finally, the Dragons won a doubleheader, sweeping Armuchee on the first Saturday of February; the women won first 50–42, and the men claimed the nightcap 54–48. The lassies moved ahead 35–26 in the third and "cashed" in on the victory; Peri Swafford scored 12 points for the winners. The boys led the Indians 14–6, 31–19, and 44–26 at the breaks and coasted home for the win; Steve Green and junior Mark Cosper had 16 markers each for us.

On Tuesday, February 10, Darlington went on a "scoring spree" against our host ladies, posting a 72–33 victory; Sharon Edwards and Justina Gordon netted 10 each for PHS. Coach Sherry Gatlin's Model girls moved into Region 4-A subregion playoffs with a perfect 6–0 record;

consecutive Friday night (February 6 and February 13) victories against Pepperell helped their cause; next, they downed Darlington 54–48 to win the crown. Wayne Huntley's boys were "traveling the same route" until this Friday the thirteenth when the Dragons upset them 48–42 in a regular season game. And lo and behold, Doug Rogers's late blooming Lindaleans came back in the first round of the playoffs versus the same Blue Devils to win 44–42. The February 13 battle was a nip and tuck affair with Shannon taking a 5-point lead with 3 minutes remaining in regulation; although PHS came back to tie, Blues had possession for a last shot with 27 seconds left. Now "it was Reggie Gordon time." As the clock hit 5 ticks with great quickness, the junior intercepted a pass and streaked down the court for the winning layup. He and Mark Cosper finished with 15 and 12 counters. Twenty-four hours later, the Lindale boys were determined there would be no letup in the finals against Chattanooga Valley as they took charge in the second quarter with an 18-point barrage and went into the intermission ahead 30–18. With Reggie Gordon, Mark Cosper, and Steve Green scoring 22, 18, and 16 markers, PHS won the Region 4-A North, proving that roundball is a tournament sport. Yet Floyd County teams suffered losses in the first round of region with the Model ladies bowing to Haralson County 49–30 and Pepperell losing 55–36 to the "running and gunning" Upson County boys.

1976–'77 Season

In Georgia, high school basketball postseason play was significantly changed in 1976; the GHSA voted in the spring to eliminate the region runner-up teams from state tourney bracket. Previously, two squads could advance which allowed better quintets who might be upset in the finals to advance. The association cited travel economics as the basis for change. One local coach blamed South Georgia schools who complained they had to travel great distances for tournament play; furthermore, state officials had concluded these games were losing causes and changes were needed to be made. Another reason for downsizing was academics. Many districts now used the shorter sixty-day quarter system, placing athletes and support groups at a disadvantage for makeup work. One concession to roundball was the approval of spring games similar to football.

Doug Rogers's club opened the season on December 3 versus visiting Rockmart; although it took overtime, the Dragons prevailed 46–43; big Steve Green collected 13 points in regulation and added 3 more at the charity stripe to lead his team; Mark Williams netted 12 in support. The Pepperell lassies lost 47–38 because they could not overcome a second-period 16-point surge by the Jackettes; Justina and Zelda Gordon led their squads with 14 and 9 counters with Sharon Edwards chipping in 8 markers. The Dragon boys ran their record to 3–0 with a 73–58 victory over Cave Spring on Tuesday, December 11. We had a 10-point lead at intermission and then "turned on the steam" to win easily. Steve Green and Mark Cosper led in baskets with 29 and 14 in addition to controlling the backboards throughout. Although the girls lost narrowly 41–35, they had a difficult time scoring 2-point baskets; the Springers held them to only foul shots (10) through the entire first half and 5 minutes into period three before we netted 19 markers in the final frame thanks to Zelda Gordon's dozen counters. The twenty-third annual Christmas Tournament began on Saturday, December 18, in Rome's Memorial Gym. Twenty-two years ago, the first Gold Ball was awarded to Pepperell's 1954–'55 basketball quintet; Jerry Bolton swished 22 markers to go with Harold Gresham's 13 in the 56–36 victory over a very good Cave Spring squad. This year, West Rome was defending champion of the 4-day single-elimination event; admission was $1 for students and $1.50 for adults. Eight days before tourney time, Coach Doug Rogers's boys ran their record to 4–0 with a 67–60 victory over West Rome and their 2-2-1 UCLA John Wooden zone press which gave them a 24–16 advantage at the end of the first 8 minutes. At this point, PHS solved the press and quit trying to play run and shoot; instead, the Dragons went to their postgame resulting in a 36–32 lead at intermission; Reggie Gordon, Steve Green, and Mark Cosper did most of the damage after quarter one with 23, 22, and 13 counters. Reggie also corralled 18 rebounds. The Dragonettes completed the doubleheader sweep of WR by virtue of a 47–44 win; for 32 minutes, we never trailed while keeping a narrow advantage throughout. However, it took some clutch foul shooting from Kay Treglown to "ice the battle." The senior hit 5 straight freebies in the waning minutes to even her team's record at 2–2. Coach Rogers's boys were making believers out of cage fans thus far, logging an impressive 6–0. He indicated in the preseason that size and experience would factor into a successful year. In the Eagles' den Tuesday night, December 14, it was Gordon, Green, and Cosper again leading the way with 19, 16, and 12 markers in an easy 69–50 victory over Coosa men; the trio also controlled the backboards. The Coosa girls made it a split decision by winning 50–46 over Pepperell coach Byron Nix's squad; Zelda and Justina Gordon led us in scoring with 14 each as we made a strong comeback in dwindling minutes. It is ironic that two local basketball powers had won state championships but no Holiday Festival Gold Balls. They would have an opportunity soon in Memorial Gym. When the game clock stopped Saturday night, December 18, 3 teams advanced to next round—undefeated Pepperell and Cass along with 1-loss Cedartown. In our contest, Lindale "turned it on" just before intermission and proceeded to down East Rome 64–45. Again, it was the "dynamic trio" of Green, Gordon, and Cosper leading the way as they netted 20, 19, and 12 markers; the taller and more experienced Lindaleans dominated the rebounding especially in the final frame. On Tuesday night, we faced West Rome in the semis; prior to this contest, all game margins were 11 points or more but not this one which went to double overtime before Silver and Green edged the Gold and White 64–60. The *News-Tribune* reported dozens of lead changes that left the crowd on its feet for most of the night. Reggie Gordon's foul shooting kept us in it as he hit 10 straight; meanwhile, the Chieftains were hitting from outside and countered by a Dragon postgame. Pepperell tied the contest at the buzzer but fouled in doing so; fortunately, they missed a winning free throw to force OT. West Rome took a quick lead at 56–52; however, Steve Green made a basket, and Daryl Buford came off the bench to hit a late shot that sent it into OT part 2. Although Buford hit a bucket, WR connected on 6 straight charities to claim the win 64–60. Green and Gordon were our top scorers with 20 and 18 markers; both were named to the all-tournament squad. In the seventeenth annual Cave Spring holiday tourney, Pepperell girls surprised East Rome 48–43; the winners led all the way. Zelda Gordon had 16 points; Sharon Edwards, 14; and Kay Treglown, 12. On Wednesday night, December 29, Model held off the Dragonettes 43–30 by sinking 17 free throws while we netted zero at the line; the contest was actually close until the Lady Devils posted a 15–8 in the third quarter. Justina Gordon led Lindaleans with 10 markers. In a match for third place, we upset host

Cave Spring 36–32 in a defensive struggle; the winners led by 15–14 at intermission and 23–22 at the third-quarter break. The Springers made several turnovers, and Pepperell made them pay; we were also good at the charity line hitting 8–12 on the night. Although the ladies failed to tally anyone in double figures, all 5 starters contributed with Z. Gordon, 7; Edwards, 6; Rush, 9; J. Gordon, 6; and Treglown, 8. On Friday, the seventh day of 1977, East Rome made 2 late-minute steals to upset Pepperell men 52–51. We recovered from a small halftime deficit to lead 43–37 in the third frame and had frontage until ER thefts gave them a 1-point advantage, yet a missed foul shot kept us from a last-second win. Cosper was high man for PHS with 15 followed by Danny Barton's 12; Green and Gordon scored 10 each. Although we led 15–14 at quarter one break, the Lady Gladiators went on a "scoring rampage," led by Barbara Kennedy's 30 points, and trounced our girls 61–34; the Gordon ladies, Justina and Zelda, finished with 11 and 10 markers respectively. One night later, host Rockmart took a doubleheader from Pepperell; the men led for the first half but not the second, losing 53–48; Steve Green and Mark Cosper had 16 and 14 for PHS. The ladies did not fare any better as the Jackettes enjoyed frontage at all quarter stops and won 40–37; Zelda Gordon netted 15 for the visitors. According to an article in the *News-Tribune*'s January 10 edition, there was some concern about Pepperell's quintet, for after winning the first 7 contests, they had lost 3 in a row; however, we remedied that problem with a 23-point win over Darlington on the twenty-fifth. The 7-A win came with ease as PHS led at all stops and had 10 players score; Cosper netted 20 while Green and Gordon chipped in with 14 and 11. On Sunday morning, January 28, the local paper featured, "Pepperell Upends Gladiators." The article referred our ladies' 50–44 victory capped off by the men's 65–52 win. The Dragonettes led throughout the first half only to see the visitors take advantage 31–29 8 minutes later; the frantic finish saw PHS outscore their opponent 21–13 for the victory. Zelda Gordon and Sharon Edwards were the "offensive masterminds" of the win with 22 and 21 markers respectively. In the nightcap, East edged ahead 13–10 at the first break; we reversed that at intermission 31–29 and went into the final frame ahead 41–39. Then we unleased a "surge of points" when Steve Green came downcourt 4 consecutive times to score baskets; Reggie Gordon added 2 quick buckets, and Mark Cosper "took control of the boards." When it was over, the Gold and White had piled up 24 points in the last stanza alone.

The energy crisis originally postponed the scheduled Model-Pepperell basketball game; in spite of that, we finally got together on the first day of February that ended in a double-overtime victory for the Dragons 59–55. The Devils led at all quarter breaks before going cold in the final 8 minutes, which enabled us to tie 47 all; both quintets managed only 4 markers in the initial free basketball. The local gazette wrote on the next day that "the Dragons played a solid game in every phase, but their free throw shooting under pressure was the main difference in the contest." To wit, the winning team hit 25–33 for the game, but 15 came in the fourth quarter and overtimes. Mark Cosper was a sharpshooter at the charity stripe and totaled 22 points for the contest while Steve Green and Mark Williams supported him with 13 and 10. In the girls' game, Cheryl Autry shot for 28 points for Model in a 53–33 victory over the Dragonettes; other than Justina Gordon's 17 markers, no one else helped much in the scoring column.

Pepperell High School held a big pep rally during sixth period on Friday, February 4; that evening, both varsity squads honored their parents at the Red Bud game. Then we revenged

2 early season losses to the Cardinals. In the opener, the Dragonettes evened their record at 10–10 by leading the entire game while holding the visitors to only 14 points in the first half; the 42–35 final was led by Zelda Gordon who hit 22 big counters. Our boys depended on a strong defense and a hot offense in the 60–39 victory; Reggie Gordon was the catalyst with a "whopping" 26 points to lead all scorers. The 6-foot-3 athlete also pulled down 16 rebounds. Mark Cosper contributed a dozen counters while Barry Stephens netted straight 4 markers that energized the rout. Region 7-A North tourney began play at Model gym on Thursday, February 17, with Pepperell boys as top seed. But the local paper reminded fans to "forget the 20–0 records, the 10–10 records and the 0–20 records," for all squads were back to 0–0. The Dragonettes started the event at 4:00 p.m. versus East Rome; the Lady Gladiators led narrowly at all the breaks, thanks to Barbara Kennedy's 32 points, and eked out a 44–43 victory. The last women's statistics of the year reported Zelda Gordon hit for 14; Edwards, 10; and Treglown, 8. The men's game was completely different with the number one team overwhelming Darlington 73–48; we led 20–8 and 44–24 at the first two breaks and were never headed. Steve Green, Reggie Gordon, Mark Cosper, and Barry Stephens all scored 14 points. On Thursday, February 24, region play began in Shannon; unfortunately, it was not a good night for area teams as 5 went down in defeat including Pepperell's loss to Bowdon 59–52. Most disappointing was the fact we led 12–7, 28–23, and 44–37 at the end of quarter breaks; however, in the last 8 minutes, 12 foul shots combined with 5 2-pointers by the Red Devils were more than we could handle. Rome area all-star Reggie Gordon led us for the final time with 18 counters while Steve Green netted 16 markers.

1977–'78 Season

"DRAGONS TURN TO DEFENSE," noted the *News-Tribune* on Sunday, November 27. This strategy seemed necessary for Coach Doug Rogers who must replace 4 tall starters from last year's 18–6 squad; Steve Turner, Danny Barton, and Mark Williams were the only returning lettermen. However, he was optimistic that bench strength should be improved by the moving up of a good JV team in addition to seniors Sam Burdette, Steve Gentry, Alan Howoren, and Turner. Juniors included Stan Coley, Buster Knowles, Chris Shiflett, and Van Westmoreland; they would be bolstered by sophomores Todd Brown and Pat Mulrennan. Dragonette head coach Byron Nix, who was a PHS graduate, was in a similar position with only starter Justina Gordon coming back for a junior year; the young lady was a gem who was one of the area's best players last season, but there was no experience behind Justina. Bridgett Long and Jane Lane were the lone seniors; 6 juniors, 4 sophomores, plus 1 freshman made up the roster. Although the ladies had worked hard and made great strides, the young coach noted, "I truly don't know what to expect until they get into a game." Our squads would begin their season hosting Cave Spring and Cedartown on successive nights, December 2–3.

As usual this time of year, the Christmas Tourney was most of the basketball talk; this year marked the twenty-fourth edition of the *Rome News-Tribune* Holiday Festival; it would get underway on Friday night, December 16, at Memorial Gym and finish on the twenty-third. The paper claimed a balanced field would compete for the Gold Ball but picked Cass boys and

Model girls as "class" of the area. The Dragons "have yet to get untracked" but were capable. The men opened with a good Rockmart team and lost 67–51; the Jackets ran out to a 36–22 lead at intermission and were never headed. Danny Barton was high man for the losers while Mark Williams netted 10.

PHS began the new year with a doubleheader loss to Coosa; the boys succumbed 63–52 when the Eagles bolted to a 16–8 first-period advantage and finished with 18 counters in the final stanza. Mark Williams led us with 14 points while Barton and Knowles added 13 each. The Dragonettes suffered a similar fate, losing 55–31; the winners led 38–22 at the end of the third stanza, and "it was more of the same" for the rest of the contest. Sherry Green and Gordon hit for 8 and 6 points. Rockmart administered another double setback on Saturday night, January 21; in the opener, our girls fell behind 24–5 at intermission; we then scored half of our points in the final frame before losing 32–23. Justina Gordon had 16 counters for Pepperell. In the nightcap, the Jackets outscored us 60–50; we took a 15–8 advantage in the first stanza but trailed 29–25 after 16 minutes only to falter at the end of the third 51–31; Mark Williams led us on the backboards with 22 rebounds to go with 13 markers. On January 24, the Tigerettes of Darlington kept running up a lead only to see PHS narrow it; unfortunately, our last rally fell just short 31–27. The losers' Justina Gordon led all game scorers with 15 counters. Thankfully, the men won 52–39; a loss would have set us back with 3 consecutive doubleheader defeats. We led at all the breaks 6–3, 14–13, and 31–21; Danny Barton matched Buster Knowles with 13 markers each while Mark Williams outshot Chris Shiflett 12 to 11. On Friday the twenty-seventh, both East Rome and Pepperell boys were unbeaten in subregion play. The Dragons went out front in the first period 13–8 and increased it to 26–20 at the break; the Gladiators began using a press that changed the tempo to forge ahead 44–40 at the end of 24 minutes. The last stanza was all East as they netted 21 points to put the game away 65–50; Williams hit for 18 markers while Barton and Knowles bucketed 13 and 11 respectively. Elkins was high for the winners with 17 counters. The girls' contest was no contest at all. It was a "scoring feast" for the squad from Rome, winning 60–20; Barbara Kennedy was unstoppable for the victors outscoring PHS herself with 27 points; Justina Gordon managed 10 for Lindale. On February 3, the Dragonettes upset Darlington 40–29 in the Leonard Gym. The home standers led throughout, leading 20–14 at the half, and outpaced the visitors 12–3 in the final frame. A pressing defense and Gordon's 9 field goals were the difference. Doug Rogers's Pepperell Dragons came into the Model gym on Tuesday night, February 7, and hit 50 percent of their shots in the first half to build a 34–17 advantage; they added 20 more markers in the final stanza to win going away 54–34. Mark Williams led all game scorers with 19 buckets while Steve Gentry followed with a dozen. When Doug Rogers's quintet welcomed Armuchee to the Leonard on February 10, the visitors were cruising along at 14–5 and ranked fifth among area boys' teams. But again, we were very efficient in shooting hitting 26 of 47 from the field and 20 of 27 at the charity line for the 72–56 upset; 3 Dragons scored in double figures with Chris Shiflett, 20; Danny Barton, 17; and Buster Knowles, 16. The girls played the opening game which ended with a 47–39 Indian victory; Sheila Nix led the winners with 25 whopping points. For the losing squad, Justina Gordon netted a dozen while Susan added 10 markers. On Valentine's Day 1978, Pepperell visited East Rome for the last regular season game. Coach Lanny Hamilton's Gladiators came away winners 72–42 by playing team ball that "worked the ball to the open man." They had 4 starters score in double figures and led at all quarter breaks to push their record to 16–6; Buster Knowles and Mark Williams teamed for 10 counters each in a losing effort. The Dragonettes ran into a buzz saw against the East ladies, losing 63–31; Barbara Kennedy and Cynthia Watters teamed for 51 points to increase their record to an impressive 18–3 going into the subregion tourney. Justina Gordon continued her fine play with 19 markers in the loss.

The Lindale girls ended their season on Thursday, February 16, with a 62–32 subregion loss to host Model. The once-beaten Devilettes used a pressing defense combined with a running offense to build an early 20-point advantage; this strategy "was too much for Pepperell." The boys fared much better versus Darlington, winning 60–46; we held a basket lead at intermission and increased it to 42–31 8 minutes later thanks to a zone defense and better play. In the fourth, we slowed play and used deadly foul shooting (18 of 24) to extend the lead. Chris Shiflett and Mark Williams combined for 18 markers each with the latter claiming a dozen rebounds. In the Saturday night finals, PHS played great before losing 68–63 to East Rome boys. The local paper said, "The boys' game was really too close for comfort all the way." The break scores bared this out as East led 16–12 after 8 minutes, 31–30 at the half, and 47–46 after 24 minutes of action; both squads "opened it up" in the final quarter with the Gladiators adding 21 markers to 17 for Lindale. For the latter, Danny Barton's and Mark Williams's had 19 and 15 counters while Shiflett and Knowles followed with 13 each. Both squads advanced next week to Region 7-A championship play. Haralson County boys treated us rudely in the region tourney played at Central of Carroll High School on Thursday, February 23. Although the initial period ended 20–13 in favor of the Rebels, it was all downhill from there as we lost 100–64; Barton netted 20 markers while Williams was 1 point below him; Shiflett added a dozen counters in the loss that ended the season.

1978–'79 Season

This time last year, Steve Horne was playing basketball for East Tennessee State University in Johnson City, which was founded in the early twentieth century as a state normal school; the young man was now the head basketball coach at Pepperell High School preparing for the upcoming season. Needless to say, he knew a little about area roundball, saying, "I haven't seen us or anyone around here play, so it's impossible to say how we'll do in competition. I do know that we've been working hard and we'll go after it." However, he was able to critique the squad to *Rome News-Tribune* in late November. Although there was not much height among the dozen varsity players, quickness should come from 5 defensive backs over from fall football; that combined with strong shooting meshed with the young coach's plan to have a running game and pressure defense. The boys returned 3 starters including seniors 6-foot-2 center/rebounder Buster Knowles and 5-foot-10 guard Chris Shiflett; Danny Barton was a 6-foot-1 junior guard who averaged double figures last year. Forwards Van Westmoreland and Todd Brown probably filled out the first 5; several others would merit playing time with sophomore Greg Shiflett and eleventh grader Bronson Payne leading. Also Stacy Hale, Joey Rickman, Justin Gordon, John Bennett, and Stan Coley would compete for rotation minutes. Dragonettes' Coach Byron Nix had been around for a while; he, too, returned several starters including leading scorer Justina Gordon, Penny Hipshire, Cheryl Gary, and Stacy Robinson; Brenda Treglown would most likely fill out the first 5, giving the team balance for this Friday's game versus West Rome in Lindale. The visiting Ladies unleashed a tall quintet on December 1 and downed us 44–35; thanks to Gordon's 21 markers, we trailed narrowly at the half and 30–24 at third quarter end, but our balance did not come through as Robinson's 6 points was our next highest scorer. The boys' contest seesawed through 4 quarters with the visitors ahead 45–44 and in possession with under a minute left in regulation; at this time, Greg Shiflett made the play of the game with a steal and pass to teammate Knowles who hit a 2-pointer to lead 46–45; next, as we claimed a caromed shot, Chris Shiflett was fouled with 3 seconds on the clock; he promptly sank his one-and-one for the 48–45 victory. The senior finished the night with 12 counters; Gordon followed with 10 while Knowles and Westmoreland tallied 9 each. On December 8, home-standing Armuchee girls hit 47 percent of their shots in a 44–37 win; Lindale girls got outrebounded 34–20 and outmuscled in the paint for a 7-point loss; Justina Gordon netted 20 markers, but she got little help from teammates who combined for only 13 counters. Although Armuchee shot 42 percent and we managed only 30 percent, PHS won 53–52. The 30 percent squad couldn't "throw it in the ocean" from the field nor the charity stripe (7–21). Pepperell trailed 16–11 at the initial stop but fought to a 37–37 tie at intermission mainly because a pressure defense caused multiple Armuchee turnovers and our shutting down the Indians inside game. In the 1-point victory, junior Danny Barton led scoring with 15 counters; Buster Knowles followed with 11 while Chris Shiflett had 10.

In Cave Spring on Tuesday, December 12, the Dragonettes fell behind at halftime 22–14 and 41–23 at quarter-three break to lose 52–41. Justina Gordon bucketed 19 of her 23 points in the second half, but it was not enough to overtake the Springers. In successive contests, the senior had put more markers on the board than her teammates totaled. On Friday night the fifteenth, Danny Barton was not the high scorer for Pepperell versus Adairsville, but he tallied the most important point. With the game tied 49–49 and in possession for a last shot, the junior was fouled just as the clock struck zero. He calmly sank the winning free throw to win 50–49 to even the Dragons' record at 3–3. Good scoring from Westmoreland, 22; Barton, 14; and Shiflett, 10, not to mention Knowles's 14 rebounds, contributed to an excellent win. The girls were "chugging along" in their game leading 15–11, 30–20 and 36–28 at the breaks; however, the Lady Tigers outscored us 17 to 4 in the final 8 minutes to win 43–40. Fourth-quarter foul problems and cold shooting from the field plus 2 of 17 from the charity stripe spelled doom. Gordon netted 15 markers followed by Hipshire's 11. The twenty-fifth annual Christmas Tourney was scheduled to start Monday, December 18, and conclude on the twenty-second; there would be 7 boys' and girls' teams vying for the Gold Ball. A total of 12 different schools had trophy-cased the sphere, yet Cedartown had never won (they would later claim the championship with a 56–55 victory over East Rome men). All games had been held at Rome's Memorial Gym. The Dragon men were set to meet Model on Tuesday, December 19, at 5:30 p.m., and the Dragonettes would follow at 7:00 p.m. versus West Rome. The local paper mused on the twentieth that the tourney for Model could be named "the double overtime silver anniversary." On Monday night, their girls topped Cedartown 53–49 in overtime; the following night, Van Jacobs's crew lost a thrilling

58–55 double-OT game to Steve Horne's Pepperell Dragons. PHS led most all the way, but turnovers allowed the Devils to tie at end of regulation. Trailing by 2 and with possession, the Blues missed a buzzer-beater, but Norris Allen got a "put back" to send the contest into second OT. With the game tied at 54–54, Van Westmoreland picked a good time to score 4 of his 14 points while Model managed only 1 counter. Buster Knowles led PHS with 17 markers which included 9 of 9 free throws while Danny Barton helped out with a 10 spot. The *News-Tribune* posted on December 20 that "the Pepperell lassies appeared headed for an upset win, but the West Rome got rolling in quarter three and dashed those thoughts" as they won going away 55–37. Justina Gordon and senior Cheryl Gray tallied 15 and 12 buckets. The Dragon men used good shooting from the field and sank 7 of 8 from the free throw line to take a 26–20 lead at intermission over the taller Cedartown; however, the Polk County quintet came out with a vengeance in period three to take a 36–32 advantage going into the final quarter; their top scorer, 6-foot-5-inch senior Robert Spurgeon (28 points), saw to it we never gained frontage again. Danny Barton and Todd Brown led in our score book with 14 and 10 points. At Lindale on January 12, 1979, the Dragonettes met and defeated Darlington 55–43; it was a game of free throw shooting as a total of 89 attempts were taken with the winners sinking 23 of 56, and the visitors, 10 of 33. The Lady Tigers fouled us 32 times, and we hacked them on 25 occasions. Justina Gordon scorched the nets for 27 counters while Penny Hipshire added a solid 17 markers. Steve Horne's quintet basically coasted to a 63–48 verdict over their Lakeside neighbors; we ran out to a first-quarter 18–2 advantage and led at the next 2 breaks, 32–23 and 45–27. We controlled tempo for 32 minutes by virtue of several defensive steals. Senior Van Westmoreland netted 21 big counters while Barton, Knowles, and Shiflett combined for 30 markers. The victors squared their record at 5–5 on the season. In the Russell Leonard Gym on Tuesday, January 16, Cave Spring "shot the lights out" at the charity stripe, hitting 20–31 tries which spelled a loss for Pepperell boys 68–60. The Springers led at all stops 19–11, 30–23, and 46–34; Danny Barton hit for 14 markers while Shiflett had 12 followed by Brown and Knowles with 9. On the nineteenth, Van Jacobs's Model quintet broke a 12-game losing streak to Pepperell basketball 58–53; after Lindale moved ahead early, the Devils surged to a 30–26 advantage at intermission and a 46–37 lead with 8 minutes left. Yet in the last 2 minutes, Steve Horne's 5 took a 51–50 frontage before clutch baskets and steals closed the game out for Model. Barton, Brown, and Westmoreland scored 13, 11, and 10 for the Dragons. Coach Sherry Gatlin's girls had little trouble with Byron Nix's Gold and White squad, winning easily 49–28; they entered the final quarter of play up 39–16 and coasted home. Senior Sherry Green topped our scoring with 7 markers. The ladies' next opponent was at rival Darlington on January 23; Coach Jim Van Es's group employed a pressure defense to take a 49–45 win over the Dragonettes. He said later, "It was as good a victory as we've had in a long time." The statement was certainly a compliment to Pepperell. Of course, Justina Gordon led us and all scorers with 20 markers. The boys gained some revenge in the nightcap winning 71–48. Van Es, who coached men and women varsity basketball at Lakeside, said, "Their [Dragon] pressure defense kept us out of our offense most of the night and they shot the ball excellently." Chris Shiflett's 17 points, Danny Barton's 15, and Van Westmoreland's 13 led the way to victory. On Saturday night, January 27, in West Rome's gym, Marshall Whatley claimed 30 rebounds plus scored 11 points in his team's 51–43 win over PHS; we held the advantage at intermission

19–17, but fell behind by 7 entering period four, and we eventually lost to the 8–7 Chieftains by 8. Westmoreland and Knowles were our leaders with 14 and 11 markers. WR completed the doubleheader sweep with a 63–35 win over our lassies; it was their fifteenth win in 17 tries; Justina Gordon tallied 18 counters for the losers.

The *Rome News-Tribune* printed on Sunday morning, December 11, that Pepperell boys stole a game from Adairsville. With 7 seconds left, the Dragons managed a steal and a basket to tie 55–55 in regulation. Then knotted at 57–57 in OT and with possession, Barton drove the lane and missed; the Tigers claimed the rebound only to let Buster Knowles steal the ball "out of the Tigers hands." He laid it through the hoop to win. The thief led all scorers with 20 counters; Barton and Westmoreland really helped out with 19 and 10 respectively. The home squad was led by Vic Beasley with 13 markers. The 14–7 Lady Tigers were in complete control of their 44–34 victory over the Dragonettes; turnovers plagued us especially in the third period 31–23 deficit. The winners Christa West was the sole double-figure scorer in the contest with 13 counters. In Lindale Tuesday night, February 13, East Rome nipped our boys 80–75 in a game that was close all the way; although the Glads led 21–15 at the first break, the Dragons matched them afterward. We made a late surge with a man-to-man full-court press that cut it to 3 but no closer. Pepperell had plenty of point makers with Westmoreland bucketing 22 while Brown and Knowles were right behind at 19 and 18 respectively. The PHS lassies lost 31–29 in a game that saw only 1 player in double figures; the 13–8 Lady Gladiators' Paula Kennebrew netted 11 markers that night. At the "M-Dome" in Shannon on Thursday night, February 15, the hosts Blue Devils overpowered the Dragonettes 63–20, knocking them out of Region 7-AA North tourney; a strong defense reaped 14 steals and limited our top scorer Justina Gordon to 8 points. The ensuing boys' game reversed course with Pepperell's defense holding Darlington to 46 points in the 77–46 opening-round victory. The local newspaper reported our "boys jumped on top 21–10 and raced to a win." Van Westmoreland scorched the nets for 30 big markers; Knowles and Barton helped him with 10 each. Saturday night's men's finals pitted East Rome against Pepperell. On Sunday morning, February 18, the *News-Tribune* reported, "Dragons Pull Major Upset in Sub-Region." The following write-up told of our 62–60 win which saw the Dragons score the first 6 points and then "cling steadfastly" to its lead; although the Gladiators never led, they tied the contest twice at 40–40 in the third stanza and 60–60 with 8 seconds left in the game. With possession, we sped down the court where Van Westmoreland let fly a 20-foot jumper at the buzzer to win. Fittingly, the senior led us in points with 19; Barton and Knowles followed with 19 and 17 counters respectively. Next up was 7-AA Region playoffs also at Model where we faced up against Central of Carrollton in the nightcap on Thursday, February 22. The scrappy Dragons fell behind 37–19 at intermission versus Central; however, a hustling full-court press cut the Lions' lead to 7 points late, but all in all, they just had too many "guns" and defeated us 82–71. Westmoreland netted 24 markers and Danny Barton, 22, while Brown and Knowles chipped in with 12 each to end the season. Postseason accolades went to senior standout Justina Gordon who was named to second-team all-area basketball squad.

1979–'80 Season

The Lindale girls opened the season with a 54–38 loss at Rockmart on Tuesday, November 27; the visitors led 13–12 at the first break but could not solve the Rock's defense. Free throw shooting spelled our doom as we sank only 8 of 25 chances; senior Penne Hipshire was high scorer with 16 markers. Two nights later, West Rome "staved off" a Dragonette rally to win 43–38; Penne Hipshire was again high pointer for the 0–2 Pepperell squad with 11 markers. The name Steve Horne was new to the Rome area because a year ago, he was playing basketball at East Tennessee State; last season, the young man led Pepperell Dragons to a surprising subregion title. Now the locals discovered he knew golf as well. On Saturday, June 2, 1979, at GEAA course, Horne was atop the leaderboard by 2 strokes shooting a 32 score in the first round of the Lester Martens Tourney. Six months later, WR Chiefs squeaked by 50–47 in the nightcap over Horne's Dragons thanks to a basket by Reggie Johnson with 1 second remaining. The winners were leading 12–11 and 22–21 at first 2 breaks; they increased it to 8 points only to see the visitors cut the advantage to 1 before Johnson's shot. Barton and Brown were high for PHS with 19 and 17 counters. The first Tuesday night of December was good to the Dragons as they won 46–44 over Cedartown; however, it took an overtime and Bronson Payne's 15-footer with 3 seconds left. The winning coach said later, "Our pressure man-to-man defense was the key to the win." Danny Barton led all scorers with 22 big points; Todd Brown added 12 for Lindale. In Adairsville on Friday, December 14, the home squads swept a doubleheader from invading Pepperell; the Tigerettes won 57–34 while the nightcap ended 75–50. Both visiting teams came out with a patient offense versus the stout fast-breaking attack of Adairsville squads; Penne Hipshire and Danny Barton led us offensively with 16 and 15 counters respectively. The *Rome News-Tribune* Holiday Festival classic started its second quarter century in Memorial Gym on Tuesday, December 18; the finals were set for Saturday night the twenty-second. Eight schools would pursue the Gold Balls last given to Cedartown boys and Model girls. Officials were hopeful a standing-room-only crowd would again watch the exciting final minutes of each contest. Opening action would pit Pepperell and East Rome girls at 5:30 p.m. The next evening, Cedartown men would face PHS at 7:00 p.m.; admission would be $1 for students and $2 for adults. The Dragonettes and Lady Glads did their part of thrilling basketball. After trailing 18–13 at intermission, we tied cold-shooting tournament host East Rome 42–42, forcing overtime. The contest was decided with 6 ticks left on the clock when junior Cindy Moore connected on a 15-footer to win for PHS 47–46. Penne Hipshire netted 18 counters, 14 in the second half before fouling out, to lead all game scorers; Moore's big shot gave her 6 on the evening. Cedartown men avenged an earlier loss to Pepperell by whipping us 54–41; the 'Dogs outscored us 17–6 in quarter three and led the rest of the way. Brown and Barton led us with 16 and 10 points. On Friday, December 21, our girls ran into event favorite Model and lost largely 62–30. The following night, Sherry Gatlin's Devils nipped West Rome 46–43 for the crown. In the boys' final, husband Jerry Gatlin led Rockmart to a 52–42 victory over rival Cedartown. The first Dragon documented game of 1980 occurred on Sunday's January 13 issue of the *News-Tribune*. The Lindale boys edged host Darlington 49–47 with Todd Brown hitting 20 points; Danny Barton and Bronson Payne chipped in 11 each. We won the game at the foul line sinking 19 of 25, including

8 in the final quarter alone. The Lakesiders were in a "tailspin" losing 6 consecutive contests while Pepperell's record was 4–6. New coach Cynthia Kiser's Dragonettes lost by 19 points in the first game of the evening; Penne Hipshire did not participate because of a slight concussion suffered last week against Armuchee. Stacey Robinson stepped up with 12 counters followed by Moore and Treglown with 10 apiece. We welcomed Cave Spring to Lindale on Tuesday, January 15, and they enjoyed our hospitality with a doubleheader sweep; the girls lost 43–33 to the consistent Springers who led at every break. Penne Hipshire hit for 13 counters with Moore adding 5. The boys were beaten by 8 points, 53–45; Coach Horne was mostly pleased as his squad "played some good defense...controlled the ball and kept the score down...but we had a little cold spell at the end of the game." Danny Barton was not cold as he netted 24 points for the losers. The local gazette noted after East Rome took advantage of the free throw line to nip the Dragons 52–44 on Friday night, January 26, that "there is a reason it is called the charity stripe." The Gladiators made 22 of 32 tosses with the clock stopped and without the defense getting in the way; conversely the losers made 6 of 13 attempts. The 6–9 Pepperell squad hung tough and made field goals by hitting 19 against 15 for the winners. Danny Barton and Todd Brown tallied 14 points each before the former fouled out as did teammate Bruce Banks. The Lady Dragons won 40–31 courtesy of the charity stripe as they sank 8 of 18 while ER managed only 1 of 12 tries. We led by only 5–4 at first break but "shot" to a 20–9 advantage after 16 minutes. Penne Hipshire sank 10 of 14 from the field in collecting 22 total points while Cindy Moore added 10. Our girls' record for 1979–'80 sat at 3–11. On Tuesday, February 5, Model clinched second place in the 7-AA North with a 56–46 win over Pepperell. Boys' coach Rick Howard said later, "We got a 100-per cent effort and did an outstanding job on the boards." Todd Brown and Danny Barton tallied 10 each for PHS; however, Greg Shiflett topped them with 16 markers. The following week, East Rome swept Lindale 42–41 in the girls' game and won easily over the men 65–39. The two women squads exchanged small leads throughout before the winners finally hit a free throw late to clinch. Penne Hipshire led Pepperell with 17 markers with Moore contributing 11. The Gladiators put together 2 scoring runs that turned a fairly close contest into a "rout." They put up 11 unanswered markers in the second stanza to go up 33–17 and then closed out the game with a 22-point surge. Brown and Barton topped the losing team scorers with 12 and 11 respectively. In the first round of subregion being held at Darlington on Thursday, Valentine's Day, the 6–15 third-seed Pepperell men took on 5–13 second-place Model. In what the local newspaper called "a mild upset," the Dragons won 33–30; although Shannon had the frontage at all the breaks 9–8, 19–16, and 26–19, Lindale got "red-hot at the charity stripe hitting all 8 tries in final period." Danny Barton sank 2 freebies with 1:06 left for the victory. Sherry Gatlin's Lady Devils "pounded" Lindale 64–42 to advance. Sherry said afterward, "We had an awful first half...but played beautifully after intermission." In the season-ending loss, senior Beverly Ewing led our girls with 11 points followed by junior Cindy Moore with 10. Steve Horne's crew faced East Rome in the Region 7-AA finals on February 16, and the Dragons took it to the 16–6 Gladiators. We slowed down the offense and held the advantage at all 3 quarter breaks. However, in the final 8 minutes, the winners began utilizing a strong press that caused several turnovers leading to a 9-point frontage; the Gold and White did not go quietly and responded with their own pressure defense to trail by just 2 with 17 seconds to go and in pos-

session. Greg Earl was fouled with 9 ticks left; on a one-plus-one charity attempt, he missed the first shot, which was rebounded by the defense's Jeff Wells who was immediately fouled. At the line, he sank both ends for a 44–40 lead; we scored at the buzzer but still short at 44–42. Nevertheless, next week PHS advanced to Region 7-AA finals at Haralson County on Thursday, February 20. On page 7 of Friday's newspaper, the Dragons' 45–32 loss to Haralson County was written up briefly, "Model, Darlington and Pepperell were all shot down."

1980–'81 Season

Pepperell began its season on Tuesday, November 25, with a 51–39 win over Armuchee men; what was looking to be a 20–20 "barn burner" at intermission turned into a comfortable victory. We had a "solid" shooting game from the perimeter as well as 21 of 29 from charity stripe; Micah Hamrick and Greg Shiflett led us in points with 11 and 10 respectively. However, the Lady Indians prevented a sweep by downing the Dragonettes 49–40; we led 15–6 at first break, but the home squad took a 34–31 advantage at the end of 24 minutes and coasted to an 8-point victory. Junior Lynn Osborne had a good night for PHS with 24 counters. One week later, West Rome boys visited Lindale and won 43–27 in a hard-fought contest that was close all the stops 11–8, 21–14, and 31–28. The Dragon methodical offense offset the Chieftains' size but not enough; Micah Hamrick scored 14 counters while junior Bruce Banks helped out with 11. On December 5, a "scrappy" bunch of Dragons held one of the state's top basketball players scoreless in the first quarter; however, Calhoun's Mike Nance recovered and tallied 23 points in his team's 58–51 victory over Pepperell. A part of his success was Bruce Banks's foul trouble which allowed Nance to maneuver his height inside. Steve Horne's crew held the lead 13–12 and 28–27 at the first breaks with 6-foot-5-inch Banks in the game. Leading scorers for 1–2 Lindale was Shiflett and Earle with 12 each. In the 51–46 loss to Calhoun girls, 60 fouls were called which netted 78 free throw tries; in the "rough and tumble" affair, the winners hit 20 while we managed 12. The Dragonettes made a couple of runs at Gordon County Bees, but they answered each time. Junior Lynn Osborne and senior Cindy Moore sank 13 and 11 points together for the winless Dragonettes. Coosa coach J. T. Bishop cited his team's 8 of 19 foul shooting, 0 of 6 in the final period, as reason for the 52–48 loss to Pepperell boys on Tuesday, December 16. The Eagles started strong leading at first 2 breaks 22–12 and 32–29 only to lose momentum in the second half. Our Greg Shiflett hit for 11 points with half a dozen in the last stanza and 4 in the closing minutes.

For the first time in a while, there was no clear-cut favorite in the Christmas Tourney; Pepperell girls took on Cedartown on Friday evening at 7:00 p.m., December 19; the men's nightcap at 8:30 p.m. would feature the same 2 squads. Pepperell's Steve Horne said, "I think we can beat them if we play well." Unfortunately, both of our squads went down in opening-round defeats; the girls lost 44–33 after the Lady Bulldogs bolted to a 25–9 halftime lead and were never headed despite senior Cindy Moore's 12 fourth-quarter points. In the following contest, the Polk County 'Dogs outscored Lindale in every stanza en route to a 61–43 win. Their three-quarter court press caused several turnovers that led to fast break points. Shiflett and

Hamrick had 14 and 12 markers for us. In the finals, East Rome claimed the Gold Ball in both the men and women divisions.

January of 1981 saw Cedartown claim another victory over Pepperell on Tuesday the sixth; once more, the full-court press brothered PHS in a 52–41 loss in Lindale; although the Bulldogs "sped" to a 16–6 opening quarter lead, we drew within a basket early in the final stanza but "let them slip back out with too many turnovers and offensive rebounds." Micah Hamrick and Frank Horne garnered 13 and 12 counters for the losers. In a 57–39 victory over Armuchee boys on Friday, January 9, the Dragons outshot, outrebounded, and out-defended the Indians to the point of never being in danger of losing. Hamrick led us on offense with 12 markers while Earle and Horne netted 9 each. The women's game was quite the opposite with Armuchee racing to a 10–1 first-stanza lead and increasing it to 28–9 at intermission in a 58–33 pasting; PHS senior Cindy Moore topped all scorers with 19 counters. January 13 was unlucky for the Dragonettes losing to a tough Cave Spring squad 64–42. The next morning's newspaper said, "The Cave Spring girls got off to a bit of a sluggish start, but easily forged ahead for a big win over Class 7-AAA Pepperell." The boys' contest ended with the CS Yellow Jackets on top 56–46; however, Coach Horne said afterward, "That wasn't a 10-point game; it was a one-point spread…We were only a point down and had the ball with 1:30 to go…If we had ever gotten in front, I think we could have won." JePail Barnett was the difference as he was the game's top scorer with 36 markers; more importantly, he netted 12 in the final frame when Lindale was making a run. Micah Hamrick had a great effort with 21 counters; Greg Shiflett added 10, but the good story was senior Keith Estes coming off the bench with 8 big counters in the final frame. In Russell Leonard Gym on Friday night, January 16, Chattooga pounded the Dragonettes 81–50 and followed that with a 67–63 win over Dragon men. There was much whistle blowing and marching up and down the floor in the girls' opener with the visitors attempting 55 free throws, making 27, while Pepperell put up 47, making 18 1-pointers. A dismayed coach Cynthia Kiser said later, "Chattooga can run and gun. They don't give you time to set up on defense and you can forget about a rebound…they are so quick." Cindy Moore scored well for the losers with 23 points. The nightcap started out as a visitor runaway with a 20–9 and 33–18 advantage at the first 2 breaks. Dragons fans who left at the half missed a fantastic rally by the home team; Horne's crew "exploded" for 29 fourth-period points before falling short at the end despite 2 starters fouling out early in the final frame. He said later, "We play everybody good…but just can't get over the hump." Mark Wheeler played well with 14 markers after the intermission; Micah Hamrick was next with 15 counters. The "snake-bit" syndrome continued in Lindale on Friday night, January 23, with Adairsville winning 63–59 in overtime. The local paper suggested Steve Horne was at local stores this morning looking for poison remedy. The score was knotted at 50–50 when the Tigers swished a basket with 12 seconds remaining in regulation; we came down the floor where Mark Wheeler shot and missed. However, the junior grabbed his own miscue and put back the tying points. The visitors won the extra period 11–7 courtesy of several PHS turnovers. The Dragons recorded rests at 3–11. Wheeler and Keith Estes came off the bench with 19 and 12 markers respectively; Bruce Banks added 11 counters. The girls' 64–52 loss was a contact sport as 50 personal fouls were called with Pepperell, connecting on 18 from the line; nevertheless, the Lady Tigers led all the way for their fifth win of the season. Cindy Moore netted 15 points for us while Lynn Osborne added 12 for the 1–13 Dragonettes. On January 27, Coosa girls continued their excellent basketball as they bolted to a 39–19 advantage and won going away 69–40 in Russell Leonard Memorial Gym; seniors Susan Morris and Cindy Moore led us with 15 and 13 markers. In the nightcap, Lindale led at all the stops but the last as the Eagles nipped us 42–41; late game cold shooting from the field, untimely turnovers, and a 46–30 deficit on the boards cost the hosts a victory. Actually with 9 seconds remaining, we made the first and missed the second try of a one-and-one at the charity stripe; Bruce Banks hit for 13 points in a losing effort. In Lindale on February 10, visiting Paulding County boys led 36–24 at the third-quarter break; however, the Dragons "opened" fast to cut the advantage to 6 early in quarter four. The Patriots then slowed the pace with a four-corner offense and moved to their region record to 6–1. Two Class 7-AAA South preliminary games took place in the Leonard on Tuesday, February 16, with the winners becoming eligible for the tourney. Our men romped over Coosa 53–33 to claim their spot while the Dragonettes were eliminated 43–42 by Rockmart. Horne's boys bolted to a 24–14 lead at intermission and then added a 29–19 advantage in the final stanza. The young coach was happy with his squad, saying, "We went out and got after them…our zone defense worked…they had trouble with perimeter shooting." Sophomore forward Frank Horne led the victory with 15 counters; Greg Shiflett was next with 10. In the women's contest, Rockmart held a 4-point lead entering final period but led by a single point with just seconds left; PHS senior guard Cindy Moore was fouled at the buzzer, and with no time remaining, she missed the first attempt of a one-on-one, and the game was over. In the first round of subregion in Lindale, the Cedartown quintet downed Pepperell 55–34; we led 17–15 at the intermission before the 'Dogs took a slim 32–31 in the third. However, the Polk County men outscored us by 9 in final frame to end our season. Senior center Bruce Banks was high man at 19 markers while Hamrick added a dozen.

1981–'82 Season

A struggling women's program turned to Steve Horne as head coach; he had assumed responsibility of both varsity teams for 1981–'82. In the season debut, West Rome came to Lindale on Tuesday, December 1, and won a doubleheader. The opening contest turned into perfect execution for the Lady Chieftains as they pounded PHS 70–30. Winning coach Ann Peery said afterward, "I wish we could have saved this effort for a sub-region tournament…I played all 13 of my players. It just seemed like the ball found a way to go in the hole." Junior Robin Williams led the losing squad with 11 markers. In the nightcap, the powerful men visitors could only manage an 18–15 advantage at intermission thanks to a slow methodical strategy by Pepperell; however, the victors outscored us by 10 in the third and pretty much coasted home to a convincing 58–38 victory. Mark Wheeler claimed point honors for the Dragons with 15. On the road in Calhoun on Friday night, December 4, PHS lost a second doubleheader; the girls ran into another squad playing extremely well. After the Lady Jackets established a 38–15 halftime lead, they exploded for 31 points in period three by hitting their first 8 shots; a full-court press converted 24 steals into easy baskets. In the 80–29 loss, Robin Williams again paced her 0–2 team with 17 counters. In the nightcap, hosts CHS took a 10–8, 26–2, and 44–26 at the first 3 breaks, yet they "almost blew it all in the final stanza." We came out hot after 24 minutes and cut the lead to 4, 52–48, before the winners regained their composure to win 61–48. In a Wednesday night, December 9, opener in Russell Leonard, West Rome again prevailed but not as much as the first meeting 8 days ago. The talented Lady Chieftains maintained their 40-point margin of victory by winning 46–16; they came out in a strong man-to-man defense which Steve Horne said, "We couldn't do much with it." Robin Williams managed 7 markers for the losers. In the closing game, 6-foot-6-inch Antwon Daniels was, according to Coach Horne, "the story of the game…he scored, rebounded, blocked shots and just controlled the middle." For the 0–4 Dragons, Mark Wheeler hung tough with 24 points. On Saturday night the twelfth, Pepperell gave Chattooga "all they could handle" before bowing 50–42; junior substitutes Tommy Swanson and David Hooper led us in scoring with 12 and 10 markers respectively. According to the local newspaper, the curtain-raiser girl's game "was no contest" as the Lady Indians won easily 73–23; Robin Williams again was high point with 11 counters for the 1–5 Lindaleans. Three nights later on the fifteenth, Coach Danny Singleton's Coosa boys went down 57–41 to the home-standing Dragons; the key to victory was Pepperell's ability to block out under the basket against the taller Eagles; this fundamental basketball reaped a 42–28 advantage in rebounding. After a 10–10 standoff at the first break, the shots began to fall for PHS as they fed off good defense and good free throw shooting with 21 of 36. Mark Wheeler scored 13 points and 13 rebounds; Greg Earle added 13 while David Hooper netted 10. Fifty-seven was the lucky number of the night in the Leonard but not for PHS girls who lost 57–26 to the Eaglettes. The visitors claimed a 40–26 edge in rebounding and shot 50 percent from the field; Robin Williams once again led us with 9 counters.

The twenty-eighth annual Holiday Festival basketball tournament began Friday afternoon at 4:00 p.m., December 19, with the finals scheduled for Wednesday, December 23. West Rome could possibly be the favorite in both men's and women's competitions. The first 23 years of the tourney was boys only; in 1977, the girls joined the event. Pepperell women played on Monday the twenty-first while the men opened earlier with Coosa on the eighteenth at 8:30 p.m. This game's final score resembled an oblong ball game as PHS boys "eked" out a 30–29 victory maybe because the losers did not have a time-out left. With 6 seconds remaining, PHS led 29–28 with Coosa shooting a one-and-one charity shot. The first was made to tie 29–29; the second was missed with Greg Earle claiming the miscue as he was fouled. At the other end of the floor, Earle hit the first, giving his team a 30–29 margin, but the backside of the one-and-one was missed with the Eagles getting the rebound; after racing down the floor with no time-outs left, a shot at the buzzer was off the mark, eliminating them from the tourney. Greg Earle hit 8 of our 14 free throws while Mark Wheeler added 10 points. Afterward, winning Coach Horne said, "Coosa really outplayed us." The opposite happened with our girls versus Rockmart, for they outplayed us 57–23, which was described as "no contest from the opening tip." The Lady Jackets ran up a 20–0 in the first-quarter mark and held us scoreless until 5:15 remained before intermission. Robin Williams had 7 counters; Jill Turner and Pam Ayers added 6 each. In the boys' semifinals on Tuesday night the twenty-second, West Rome would claim a 45–35 victory over PHS; although they led throughout, the Silver and Green could not put the Gold and White away. Coming off a big win over East Rome, Coach Hendricks's squad had a letdown against Pepperell in spite of warnings from the bench. He said later, "They are an improved team and played us tough." The Dragons cut the lead to four late, forcing the Chieftains to go four-corner stall to ice the game. David Hooper had 15 markers for Lindale with half coming in the final stanza; Greg Earle contributed 10 to the cause. In the finals, Chattooga women won by 20 over Cedartown while WR won by 5 in overtime against the Indians from Summerville. In the first counter games of Region 7-AAA, home-standing Cedartown copped a doubleheader from Pepperell; the Bulldog women won handily 43–19 by leading at all the breaks 10–3, 22–9, and 35–15. In the nightcap, neither squad showed much intensity; Lindale utilized a patient offense to take a 31–30 lead going into quarter four. However, several turnovers hurt us in closing minutes of the 52–39 loss. The Polk County 'Dogs had 9 players score while Greg Earle led the boys from South Floyd with 16 markers. On Friday night, January 8, Armuchee turned back "a determined" bunch of Dragonettes 48–29; although his girls were 1–9, Coach Horne said, "It might have been out best floor game of the season but we had trouble scoring especially late." Senior Kathy Cagle had her best night of the season with 14 points while sophomore Pam Ayers helped out with a dozen rebounds. Horne stayed on the same bench and directed Pepperell's 62–48 victory in the nightcap. His squad "stunned" Armuchee in the first stanza with a full-court press that produced an 18–9 lead at first break and led the rest of the way. The winners had good balanced scoring with Greg Earle, Mark Wheeler, and Tommy Swanson netting 16, 12, and 11 for the night; Wheeler claimed 14 rebounds for the improving 3–8 Dragons. A power outage forced a next-day playing time for Pepperell versus Rockmart. On Wednesday, January 20, the Jackets struggled to defeat the Dragons 41–39; a patient offense and a stingy defense kept Lindale in the game to the point of almost victory. With 30 seconds remaining, the Polk County Bees led 41–35, but 2 steals from our defense followed by 2 quick baskets, the last which came at the 2-second mark, almost turned defeat into victory. Horne said later, "The second period just killed us; we let them outscore us 14–4 and had to play catch up the rest of the way." Jeff Brannon had 11 markers, and Wheeler added 10 to the ledger of the 3–9 Dragons. When the Dragons faced off against the host Coosa Eagles on Tuesday night, January 26, the old saying "The third time is a charm" should have come into effect; however, it didn't for Coosa. Steve Horne's men won again 53–52 after previously defeating CHS 57–41 and 30–29. The contest was a seesaw battle that saw Danny Singleton's quintet lead by 5 markers late only to see turnovers lead to the 1-point loss. The winners Mark Wheeler scored 21 while Greg Earle helped with 14; free throw shooting was the difference as PHS made 21–30. The girls' game was, according to the *News-Tribune*, "an easy 67–32 rout." Coach Jody Puckett's lassies led 50–26 at quarter three break and coasted to victory; for the Dragonettes Robin Williams netted 10 counters.

When a basketball team makes 5 of 16 free throws, 16 of 66 from the floor, and turns the roundball over 22 times, victory is elusive; therefore, Carrollton defeated PHS men by "only" a dozen counters. Coach Horne said afterward that it should have been worse, for we missed 20 layups; Wheeler led the 5–11 Dragons with 13 markers and 10 rebounds. The women lost 43–26 to complete a Trojans sweep in which neither team "could buy a basket." Robin Williams was top scorer for the losers. The Friday morning, February 5, edition of the morning newspaper reported the game between Cave Spring and Lindale could go down as "one of the wildest finishes of all time." Larry Bing's men led at all stops and, with less than 2 minutes to play, held a semi-comfortable 8-point advantage. Although the Springers eventually won 35–34, the issue was in doubt, for Horne's Dragons solved their hosts' four-corner offense to cut the lead to a single marker 35–34; furthermore, Pepperell went to the foul line with 1 second showing and a chance at winning. Unfortunately, our first attempt at a one-and-one free throw was missed—game over. The girls' game was Lindale all the way, narrowly; the final score was 32–30 and marked our lassies' second victory of the season, both versus Cave Spring. Coach Horne thought his squad played with lots of confidence for 32 minutes. In the first round of 7-AAA South tournament play at Cassville on Wednesday, February 18, top-seeded Chattooga struggled early but soon pulled away from the Dragons to win 48–29; Randy Jackson was high point for the losers as the 1981–'82 basketball year ended for Gold and White. In the last week of February, a new sports editor for the *Rome News-Tribune* came on board; Kerry Yencer immediately began a "getting to know you" tour of the local high schools. One of the first was Pepperell and its venerable athletic director Coach Otis Gilbreath who treated the new man "like one of his own."

1982–'83 Season

Pepperell High School had produced many fine athletes, male and female; perhaps one stands above all others, for this athlete's performances were exemplary despite a handicap. Mark Wheeler was scheduled to begin his freshman year in the fall of 1979, but there was a problem; the school board believed the youngster should attend Georgia School for the Deaf because of a hearing impairment. In September 1964, the youngster was born deaf and remained so even after an unsuccessful acupuncture-type procedure in 1975. However, the foundation case of special education cited in Public Law 94-142 (codified on November 29, 1975, by the Ninety-Fourth Congress), which became effective in Mark's eighth-grade year, stated that "all handicapped children shall receive a free, appropriate public education, including to the maximum extent *appropriate, placement in a regular public school.*" Mark was happy in the Pepperell Middle environment and did not want to leave his childhood friends as they moved to ninth grade. Although GSD was an excellent system, the family felt there was not enough outside contact available for their friendly and outgoing son. In 1977, using the law's own script which states, "It is the responsibility of the school to screen for and identify potential special needs students and anticipate their needs accordingly," father Robert Wheeler filed suit against the board to mainstream his son and provide all necessaries. It was not his aim to challenge them but to reach a compromise, if possible, that would place his rising ninth grader in regular classes at Pepperell High. As a result, the county agreed to provide morning transportation to Cave Spring and noon transfer to Lindale. In addition, an in-class interpreter would be present for Mark. Notices went out in the Tuesday morning *RNT* that the twenty-ninth annual Holiday Festival basketball tournament would begin on Friday, December 17. First game up at 4:00 p.m. was West Rome girls versus Chattooga in Memorial Gymnasium; the event was sponsored by the *News-Tribune*, Rome/Floyd County Recreation Authority and Rome Coca-Cola Bottling Company. Pepperell would take on East Rome the following evening at 8:30 p.m. Coach Steve Horne welcomed back 6 players from last season's 7–17 squad; most prominent was 6-foot-3 senior forward Mark Wheeler who averaged 9 rebounds and scored 13 per contest. On the senior-ladened team, 5-foot-10-inch post Van Vaughn was a jumper who competed on defense; fellow twelfth grader Tommy Swanson was also 5 feet 10 and played the shooting wing position. The other average-sized veterans included Eric Stiles, Keith Austin, Lynn Cooper, Bryan Griffin, and Scott Edwards. Although the coach cited the lack of height a problem in Region 7-AAA, excellent team speed was a positive. Contributors from the underclass would be Morris, Curry, Abney, and Googe. First-year Dragonette coach Randy Hallmark could count on seniors Robin Williams and Jill Turner at the forward and guard positions; junior Pam Ayer was a returning 5-foot-10 center. Wendi Ozment, Patricia Smith, and Barbie Ewing would swing from guards to wings. Hallmark expressed concern with a lack of quickness. Armuchee came to Lindale on Tuesday, November 30, and gained a split decision; the visiting girls' quintet won a seesaw overtime battle 50–48. In second stanza, Pepperell's Robin Williams tied the game at 13–13; we inched ahead at intermission 21–18 before falling behind late in the third. Jill Turner hit a basket at the buzzer to put the home squad up 33–32 after 24 minutes of play. Hallmark's crew built a small advantage that dwindled to a lone bucket with 1 second on the clock; at this point, Denise Lowe let fly a shot that tied the game at 44–44 with no time left. Reporter Robert Howren described the scene later, "At this point pandemonium broke out with nearly everyone going wild with excitement or disbelief." In extra innings, Lowe hit 2 counters; Patricia Smith's 2 cut the visitors' lead to 50–48. Then we claimed an Armuchee miss but could not get a shot off before the horn sounded. The men's game was not as close but exciting nevertheless; we led narrowly in quarter one but pushed out to 27–19 at intermission. PHS cruised to 49–27 in the third before winning handily 64–44. Mark Wheeler scored 18 counters and collected 6 misses; Vaughn netted 16 with 6 rebounds also. At Coosa on Tuesday night, December 15, the Dragon men won 48–41 which evened their record at 2–2. Wheeler again led his squad with 16 markers. Tommy Swanson helped out with 10; the game swung on the charity stripe where PHS hit 16 of 25 while the Eagles were 1 of 5. CHS lassies took a quick 16–4 advantage in the first and were never headed in winning 72–33. Jill Turner was our leader with 10 points, but her team fell to 0–4. In the first round of Christmas Tourney play on December 17, Cedartown boys led 10–6 early in the second frame, but "the Dragons went on to miss their next 15 shots while the Bulldogs netted 24 consecutive points." Rodney Stallings and Scott Brown, measuring 6 feet 4 and 6 feet 6, accounted for 19 of the 2 dozen markers en route to a 52–33 victory. The winners went to a 1-3-1 offense that according to Coach Ragsdale "opened it up a little bit." PHS had no player in double figures. The following night, East Rome women knocked Pepperell out of the tourney 43–32; we were fortunate to trail only 25–14 at intermission, for the Lady Glads outrebounded us 13–4. The Dragonettes could get no closer than 7 points in the 2 final periods. Jill Turner scored 12 and Robin Williams scored 10 for the losers while Jennifer Mathis collected 10 missed shots. The new year brought good luck to the Dragons as Armuchee surrendered an 8-point lead in the final quarter by virtue of missing 9 of 27 charity shots; PHS countered with 12 of 19 free throws to take a 48–47 victory. Mark Wheeler netted 20 markers; Tommy Swanson added 10. Although the Lady Indians led at all the stops but one, we closed out the fourth stanza of the doubleheader 41–38; senior Robin Williams was the game's high point scorer with 16 markers to go with 10 rebounds; Jill Turner contributed a dozen markers to the win. *Rome News-Tribune* sportswriter Paul Martin began his article on Wednesday, January 12, with a remark from winning Cass coach Mick Pyle, "You want a quote?—They deserved to win the game!" Opposing mentor Steve Horne agreed, "I can't help but be happy with our players…they played their hearts out…we're getting better every night out." Pepperell used a full-court zone press which rattled the Colonels and twice erased 10-point leads. A pair of free throws by Tommy Swanson, Mark Wheeler's two buckets combined with Lynn Cooper's long jumper almost pulled it out for the Dragons. With 13 seconds remaining, our guys got a good shot that rimmed out as did the follow-up try. In the 44–43 loss, Wheeler was 6 of 9 from the field and 4 of 6 at the charity stripe to lead us. In the opener, Dragonette coach Randy Hallmark became so frustrated with his squad at the 4:40 mark of second stanza that he yanked all the starters; the others performed well enough but did not make a difference in the 48–24 loss. No one scored in double figures for PHS. At the end of week two in January 1983, Pepperell basketball team records were girls 1–10 and boys 5–6. On Saturday night, January 15, Adairsville fell to the Dragons 55–34; after a third-quarter surge, Mark Wheeler was on his way to scoring 21 points and "snaring" 11 rebounds; Van Vaughn followed closely with 18 markers and 9 caroms. In the women's game, Robin Williams had a career night with 43 points; Jill Turner contributed 16 counters and 9 assists. We came with an "eyelash" of surprising the Tigers before losing 74–71. Lindale traveled down US Highway 27 South to Carrollton on a school night, January 18, and lost a doubleheader but not before Mark Wheeler almost copied Robin Williams's outstanding performance of the previous week. The senior athlete hit 11 of 12 shots from the field, 3 of 3 from the charity stripe, and grabbed 8 rebounds in addition to 4 steals; however, the Trojans edged us 46–45. Carrollton's girls "clobbered" the Dragonettes 63–21 in the opener; Williams was high scorer with 9 points. Three nights later, West Rome girls defeated us 53–37; they led at all the stops 14–8, 22–17, and 36–25. The Green improved to 4–4 while the Gold and White fell to 1–12. The boys prevented a road sweep by winning 55–39; we reversed the girls' action by leading 9–6, 18–16, and 36–24 at the breaks; Wheeler was outstanding once more by scoring 33 points and grabbing 13 caroms; Van Vaughn added 11 to the cause. On Tuesday, January 25, the Dragons won their third victory in 4 games by beating host Chattooga 48–45; we led at the first 2 stops but fell behind at the end of the third, 37–36, before closing with the victory. Van Vaughn and Wheeler collected 10 rebounds each to go with 16 and 12 points; Swanson chipped in 12 counters. In the opening varsity game, the Lady Indians led all the way before finishing with a 65–25 win; Robin Williams was our only double figure scorer with 12 points. On Friday night, January 28, in Russell Leonard Gym, PHS edged Calhoun 36–33 before 250 fans. Mark Wheeler, who had been bedridden with the flu for the past 2 days, made it to the game and scored 18 points for his team's fourth straight victory. "That shows you how tough and how much of a competitor he is," said his coach Steve Horne. With 29 seconds left, Mark went to the line and hit 2 straight fouls to win the game by 3. We overcame dreadful shooting in the second quarter but compensated by playing really good defense. The Jackets ended the night with only 15 of 46 from the field. For the 7–8 Dragons, Wheeler netted 18; Swanson, 7; and Vaughn, 9. The Lindale lassies trailed by 4 at intermission but were outpaced 18–8 in stanza three; the Calhoun Ladies then coasted to a 65–46 victory. Williams led us in the score book with 14 followed by Casey and Ayer with 9 each. In Cedartown Friday night, February 4, Travis Ragsdale's men led 12–4 and 30–19 at the first 2 breaks, yet Horne's Dragons would not go away, keeping the score within 8 most of the second half before succumbing by 60–47. The Bulldogs were a difficult team to defeat that night, for they shot 54 percent from the floor and corralled 42 rebounds. Mark Wheeler continued his exemplary play with 21 points to lead all scorers; Erick Stiles added 10. The Pepperell girls lost 46–28; we kept the score fairly close until the last quarter when the home squad outscored us 10–2 down the home stretch. Robin Williams netted 18 for the visitors. Carrollton High School was welcomed as a guest to the Russell Leonard on Monday night, February 7; they responded by rudely sweeping a doubleheader. In the opener, PHS trailed all the way in losing 52–32 to the Lady Trojans; Robin Williams again led her team with 17 points and 14 rebounds. Dragonette record now sat at 1–16. The Carroll County boys were not as discourteous as their counterparts but nevertheless defeated us by a dozen—55–43; Wheeler hit for 18 points and claimed 11 caroms; Tommy Swanson helped with 10 counters to no avail as the Dragons fell to 7–11. In the final contests of the regular season, Adairsville claimed a home-standing 2-game sweep from Lindale. The visiting ladies were pounded 82–62 despite Robin Williams's 34 points and a dozen rebounds; her performance was offset by Tigerette Kim Howard's 42 markers. The boys' game was more competitive. Although we led at the first 2 stops, our hosts rallied late for a 43–35 win. Jason Busby led us with 12 points followed by Mark Wheeler's 10 counters. The 7-AAA South tournament opened Monday on Valentine's Day in Pepperell's Leonard Gym; the Lindale girls faced Coosa at 6:30 p.m. without starter Jill Turner who completed graduation requirements; an injured knee would have prevented further play for the senior. In the game, Coosa Ladies improved their record to 20–3 with a 64–39 victory over PHS, ending our season slate at 1–18. Tina Casey and Robin Williams scored their last 14 and 10 points for the Dragonettes. In men's action on Monday night, Chattooga downed Pepperell 68–55. However, overshadowing the athletic event was the birth of a baby girl for Indian headman Lamar Turner and his wife, Carter. "I have been in and out of Floyd Medical Center since 9:00 a.m. this morning," said the winning coach and new father. As game time neared, Carter told her husband, "Don't worry about me, just tell the kids to win." While improving its record to 15–7, the winners led at each break mainly because of a "sparkling" 28-of-32 performance at the foul line. The Dragons' scoring leaders, Wheeler and Vaughn, closed out their career with 22 and 14 points respectively.

1983–'84 Season

Pepperell Coach Steve Horne will start the new season versus Armuchee High School on Friday night, November 18. His visiting squad counted 4 lettermen but no returning starters; the holdovers from last year included Brad Morris, Mike Googe, Tom Curry, and Chuck Abney; Tim McBurnett and David Swanson would position in the front court while sophomores Mike Curry and Jeff Rickman would play out front. Horne thought quickness, good shooting, adequate size, and a scrappy mentality would produce a competitive quintet. Dragonette coach Randy Hallmark's women team was hoping to improve on last year's 1–19 mark; he was depending on seniors Tina Casey, Patricia Smith, and Pam Ayer in addition to junior Julie Ayer to perform as veterans. Melissa Goss, Angie and Pam Young, Lisa McGinty, and Christi White were juniors who should contribute to wins. Hallmark's assessment of talent spoke of a squad that would not outsize or outrun opponents but could be productive with "good fundamental" basketball. In the opener, Hallmark's strategy reaped a 56–53 win against Armuchee women; this matched last season's total. The contest was close from start to finish with the first break at 12–12; the home team led 41–40 at the intermission. We hit 13 of 19 attempts from the charity stripe to seal the victory. Tina Casey led us in points with 16 while Angie Young scored 15. In the men's finale, PHS fell in a close battle 42–38; the Indians led at all stops, controlled the backboards, sank 13 free throws, and narrowly outshot the visitors from the field. Mike Googe and Brad Morris tallied 8 counters each for the losing squad. On Saturday night, December 3, in Adairsville, the Pepperell girls improved their record to 2–1 with a 58–48 win over the Lady Tigers; Tina Casey led the victors in scoring with 17. Angie Young and Julie Ayer added 16 and 12 respectively. The boys did not fare as well, losing 69–53; the home team led 33–24 at the intermission. Pepperell closed to 48–42 going into the final 8 minutes, but the winners' 24 charity tosses as opposed to 13 for the visitors made a big difference. Tim McBurnett netted 18 markers while Tom Curry managed 11 for Lindale. On Wednesday night, December 14, at the Russell Leonard Gym, both Coosa quintets came out of the dressing room "all fired up." And it continued during the game as the Eaglettes prevailed 64–43; they did it by shooting 60 percent from the field, dominating the boards 55–25 and sinking 6 of 13 from the foul line. The game's leading scorer was Dragonette Tina Casey with 22 markers. In the nightcap, Coosa led 31–27 at the intermission but scored 14 consecutive points in the third to lead 53–37 entering the final quarter and winning 71–57. Dragon Tom Curry took game-scoring honors with 29 counters; after a slow start, he canned 9, 8, and 8 down the stretch which included several 25-foot "bombs." No other PHS player had more than 4 points. The visitors were "clutch" from the foul line sinking 31 of 36 (Pepperell did not shoot a free throw in the second half); the Eagles also claimed the board battle 35–14. On December 17, in a span of about 3.5 hours, our 2 basketball squads went down in the thirtieth annual Christmas Tourney. The Dragonettes started it at 7:00 p.m. with a 78–39 loss to Darlington; in the nightcap that started at 8:30 p.m., the boys went down to East Rome 70–46. Following a Tuesday night, January 4, visit to Chattooga, the Pepperell basketball team records were women, 2–4, and men, 0–6. The Lady Indians ran out to a 46–10 lead at the half thanks to a full/half-court press that caused 36 turnovers for the visitors; this strategy led to an 80–34 decision. In the nightcap, our boys led 16–8, 23–14, and 35–29 at the breaks; however, it was a 32-minute game. With 2:30 remaining, the home-standing Chattooga finally gained frontage and won 51–43. Coach Lamar Turner said afterward, "They got us into a halfcourt ballgame; we're not a good at that." CHS also had trouble stopping Mark Wheeler who tallied 24 points; Van Vaughn added 11. At the Leonard on Saturday night, January 8, the Dragons won a pair of close victories against Armuchee; the women triumphed 41–38 while the men nipped the Indians 48–47; Mark Wheeler netted 20 counters, and Tommy Swanson, 10. In the opener, our girls trailed at all the quarter breaks 14–10, 33–25, and 36–33, yet we closed with a 3-point victory thanks to Robin Williams's 16 points and 10 rebounds; Jill Turner added 12 markers to the cause. Friday the thirteenth proved unlucky for visiting PHS, for we lost a doubleheader on the Alabama Road. The opener was easy for the Lady Eagles as they won 84–46; they shot the ball exceptionally well on the way to leading at all the stops. The winning coach, Angela Garrett, said later, "We needed it bad…We had lost four straight." Pepperell was led by Tina Casey with

16 points, 14 rebounds, 1 assist, and 2 steals. In the finale, Coosa won 70–52 by virtue of 12 free throws, 28 field goals, 19 assists, and 36 rebounds; Tim McBurnett was the only Dragon in double figures with 22 points.

On Saturday night, January 21, things were looking up for the Lindale lassies; after trailing narrowly at all the breaks, we outscored West Rome 14–1 in the last quarter to win 50–41; 8 of our points were from the charity stripe. Tina Casey netted 25 big markers to go with 8 rebounds; Julie Ayer helped with 10. The second game was not as enjoyable for Lindale as the Chieftain men won handily 67–40; although Tom Curry tallied 9 counters, we had no player in double figures. In Summerville on Tuesday night, January 24, Pepperell lost by 30 and 37 points to the Indians. Our girls suffered a 73–43 setback to a team that had played well since Christmas, and according to the winning coach, they also had good chemistry. Julie Ayer and Melissa Goss tallied a dozen points each for the 5–11 Dragonettes. The men's game ended 67–30 in favor of Chattooga; they shot 27 of 55 from the field and 13 of 21 at the foul line. Pepperell managed 12 of 32 from the court and 6 of 12 at charity stripe. The first game in Calhoun on Friday night, January 27, was a "barn burner." With seconds remaining, the Lady Jackets hit 2 foul shots to lead 60–58; Tina Casey responded with 2 of her own, tying the game at 60–60 with 10 seconds to play. The home team inbounded to Patricia Christian who drove the right baseline and put up a 7-foot jumper as the buzzer sounded; final score Calhoun, 62; Pepperell, 60. The *News-Tribune* reported the game was won at the foul line where the winners sank 16 of 21. For PHS, Casey had 27 points; Goss, 18; and Julie Ayer, 13. In the boys' game, the Jackets led at all quarter breaks 13–4, 27–20, and 39–29 en route to a 63–39 victory; they hit 52 percent from the field and 68 percent at the free throw line. Mike Googe netted 9 points for Pepperell, yet no Dragon reached double figures in scoring. In Lindale on Friday, February 3, area scoring leader Rodney Stallings scored his usual 29 points in Cedartown's 65–49 victory over Pepperell. Tim McBurnett netted 20 points in a losing cause; Tony O'Neal added 8. In the girls game, the Lady Bulldogs nipped our women 55–51; the battle was tied 39 all going into the final 8 minutes; 2 starters for Cedartown combined for 34 rebounds, which was probably the difference. On February 7, Carrollton swept a doubleheader from PHS; the boys lost 51–31 while our girls fell 56–46. In the opening loss, Pepperell was paced by Tina Casey and Pam Ayer with 18 and 10 markers respectively; the Lady Trojans led at all stops en route to the 10-point defeat which left our record at 3–17. In the nightcap, Mike Googe, David Swanson, Tim McBurnett, and Tony O'Neal each netted 6 counters in our 20-point loss which matched our season record. The big news at the Leonard on Friday night, February 10, was Lady Dragons, 68; Adairsville, 59. "We put four quarters together…and out-rebounded them all night," said Coach Hallmark. His squad also shot almost 45% percent from the field and 72 percent at the charity stripe. Tina Casey had a career game with 31 counters and claimed 14 missed shots; Angie Young and Julie Ayer pitched in with 13 and 11 markers respectively. The long season for our boys continued as we lost by 11 points—60–49; the Tigers' free throw line decided the contest as they sank 24 of 36 or 66 percent freebies. Tom Curry and Tony O'Neal scored a dozen markers each for their team. On Monday, February 13, second-seeded Chattooga eliminated host PHS from the 7-AAA South tourney 67–45; Tom Curry tied the game 10–10 just before the first-quarter break with a "falling backwards" 45-footer; we would get no closer. The Indians led 45–31 entering the final stanza and steadily added to the winning margin. David Swanson and Tim McBurnett netted 14 and 12 markers in their final effort of the 1983–'84 season. The next evening, Carrollton ended the season for Pepperell girls 61–55; they led 47–26 beginning the final quarter and used reserves throughout. Melissa Goss and Tina Casey finished the season by scoring 16 and 12 points. On Sunday, February 19, the South all-tourney squads were recognized in the local newspaper. Tim McBurnett and Melissa Goss represented PHS on the second team.

1984–'85 Season

As Pepperell basketball prepared to get underway in late November, seventh-year coach Steve Horne had some seniors, and the height would be better. He suffered through last season with neither but told the local newspaper recently, "The attitude is good and that means a lot." On a rainy night in Georgia, the Dragons ended a long drought with a win by defeating Armuchee 62–42. Newcomer 6-foot-2 Calvin Harris made the difference with 20 points, 10 rebounds, and 5 steals. He excited the home crowd with our first slam dunk in 10 years. PHS scored the first 12 markers and was never threatened; Rob Dodson pulled down 13 misses. The girls' game was as close as the 49–47 victory; with 1:03 remaining, Julie Ayer's layup and Melissa Goss's free throw gave us the 2-point triumph. These two ladies netted 16 and 15 counters each. On Saturday night, December 8, host East Rome downed our boys 55–35; Calvin Harris was Pepperell and the game's leading scorer with 15. The girls lost 41–38 in overtime; the competitive contest was ultimately decided at the charity stripe where ER hit 5 straight in the final minute. Julie Ayer almost won for us as she "bombed home" 10 fourth-quarter shots to take game honors with 24. At Model on Tuesday night, December 12, our basketball squads rallied to win both contests. The boys edged their hosts 49–46 courtesy of a Mike Curry bounce pass to Rob Dodson who laid up with 5 seconds on the clock. Calvin Harris continued to lead Pepperell in scoring with 23 markers and 10 rebounds; a "variety of defenses" caused 23 Devil turnovers. The Dragonettes' victory was even more dramatic as we came from 9 points down in the last 1:35 to force overtime. A win turned to defeat, for the Lady Blue Devils failed to slow the game down in regulation, which ended at 50–50. In the extra period, Edwards, Young, and Ayer iced the 58–53 win with good play and foul shooting. In Lindale on Friday night, December 14, Armuchee's ladies surged from 8 points down in the second half to win 45–44; clutch fourth-quarter free throw shooting led AHS to victory in the Russell Leonard Gym—their first there in 2 years. For PHS, Julie Ayer had 18 markers; Katrina Edwards collected 9 rebounds while Goss made 3 steals. In the nightcap, the Pepperell men "bombarded" the visitors 54–28, but it was defense that impressed Steve Horne. "We played good. Anytime you hold a team to 28 points you're doing a good job," he said afterward. Calvin Harris played an all-around excellent game, scoring 17, collecting 10 rebounds, 5 steals, and 4 assists; Rob Dodson helped with 13 counters and 10 backboards while Norman Aycock came off the bench to gather 6 missed shots. The Dragons improved to a 3–3 record.

The thirty-first annual *Rome News-Tribune* Holiday Festival basketball tournament was scheduled to start on Tuesday, December 18, in West Third's Memorial Gym. Pepperell's girls would face Darlington the following day at 4:00 p.m. Our boys took the stage versus East

Rome in the following 5:30 game. Coach Randy Hallmark's lassies surprised defending tourney champs Darlington 41–40. With the Dragonettes up 1 point, the Lakeside girls missed 3 close-in shots with seconds left. Our excellent outside shooting was the game difference; Melissa Goss was the leader with 18 big markers. About the boys' contest that followed, *RNT* assistant sports editor Steve Sigafoose wrote on Thursday morning, "East Rome High School escaped with its basketball life Wednesday afternoon in turning back Pepperell 56–53." Winning coach Andy Akin told the press later, "I told you they have a good team…their press and quickness hurt us." To wit, the lead changed hands 5 times in addition to 6 ties. Our inability to inbound the ball at mid court with 38 seconds remaining and leading by 1 probably cost Lindale the game. The 5-second infraction gave East the ball which led to a missed shot, a putback, and a free throw. Junior Rob Dodson played well, logging 15 counters and 8 rebounds; Tim McBurnett added 13 to the scoreboard. On Friday, December 21, East Rome defeated our ladies in the semifinals 49–42. Coach Hallmark remarked afterward that "I think we were a little in awe of being one game from the championship contest." Other than that, he pinpointed the Lady Glads' superior rebounding as the difference, saying, "They at least doubled us in boards." Julie Ayer and Melissa Goss netted 10 markers each for PHS. Coosa High School won both consolation games on Saturday; for Lindale fans, the score that mattered was a 50–34 loss. The Lady Eagles scored the first 13 points and led at all the stops 18–4, 23–18, and 36–27. An effective full-court press reaped 17 steals in the 16-point win. Julie Ayer was Lindale's top scorer with 10. Melissa Goss was recognized as an all-tournament player.

Playing in our first game in 2 weeks, the Dragons lost a doubleheader versus Haralson County in Lindale on Friday, January 4. It took visitors a couple of adjustments to win the boys' game 46–42. Pepperell's Tim McBurnett gave his team an early lead by hitting several right-side baseline jumpers. Rebel coach Ralph Hilburn called time-out and switched to a box-and-one defense on Mac. After intermission, Calvin Harris began to score and almost pulled the game out for PHS before Hilburn again adjusted by fronting and sagging down on him. As a result, our inability to hit wide-open jumpers around the key cost us a victory. Harris and McBurnett led the Dragons in scoring with 19 and 12 points respectively. In the opener, the undefeated Rebelettes won 50–38. Period three saw Melissa Goss lead a 16–5 surge that caused some consternation on the HC bench, but the winners featured a rebounding front court that measured almost 6 feet; furthermore, the tall players lined up on the front of the zone press; they also can sink charity shots (14 of 24). On Friday the eleventh, we rebounded against Rockmart with double victories; the boys edged the visitors 36–34 while the Ladies won comfortably 51–23. Coach Horne remarked afterward that his team played badly but still won 36–34. The Jackets packed its defense inside, and our shooters couldn't take advantage. Although Tim McBurnett's driving "flip-shot" with 2 minutes remaining was the winning basket, the defense forced RHS into 5 missed shots and 2 bad passes as the clock dwindled. Harris and Googe gathered the misses while Dodson and McBurnett caught the bad throws. We had nobody score in double figures. The Polk Countians' record was 0–11; PHS was 4–6 overall. The Dragonettes were in charge the entire way against their opponent, leading 12–2, 30–12, and 40–16 at the breaks. We were clutch at the foul line hitting 1 of 15; Ayer and Young led us in scoring with 16 and 14. Pepperell's slate is 4–8. In Lindale on Tuesday night, January 15, the home-standing Dragonettes hit 9 of

10 free throws in quarter four to down Cartersville 42–37. This win avenged a 72–47 loss earlier in the season. Julie Ayer netted 18 counters for the winners; she led a third-quarter surge with 11 big points. Katrina Edwards's and Angie Young's steady foul shooting was the difference. In the boys' nightcap, Coach Bobby Carr, coach of sixth-ranked Class 7-AA Hurricanes, said, "Pepperell took us out of our game." The 12–1 Purple Hurricanes switched to a gambling defense in the second half which netted them a 47–37 victory. The change in tempo did not seem to bother Calvin Harris, for he had 18 points, 14 rebounds, and 4 assists in a losing cause. We took a road trip to Villa Rica on Friday, January 18, and came away happy with two victories. In the first contest, Randy Hallmark's crew won 63–53 behind Julie Ayer's 26 points; Melissa Goss and Katrina Edwards added 12 each to the tally while Angie Young contributed 8 markers and 7 assists. Although PHS led at the end of all quarters, clutch shooting (11 of 14) at the foul line was the difference. Coach Steve Horne was elated with his men's 59–57 road win; he was especially proud of Calvin Harris and Tim McBurnett who netted 21 and 20 points collectively. Jeff Rickman kept the defense honest with 11 markers. The Dragons trailed most of the game before Harris stole the ball off the wing and went the length of the floor for a slam dunk 31–30 lead. Horne said about the play, "From then on the momentum kind of switched to our side." He added, "When Tim can hit from the outside, it opens up Calvin underneath." In West Rome gym on Saturday night, January 26, the home team rallied to win both contests. The Chieftains came from behind in period three to post a 51–40 win while the home-standing girls scored a 65–52 victory thanks to freshman Vanita Thompson's 32 points and 22 rebounds. Dragonette Melissa Goss tried to match that with 22 points of her own; Angie Young pitched in 14 markers while Katrina Edwards corralled 8 boards. We traveled south on Georgia Route 101 on Tuesday night, January 29; once there, Pepperell squads took a doubleheader from Rockmart. In the nightcap, Calvin Harris "exploded" for 31 points to go with 17 rebounds in our 73–53 victory. The visitors changed to an up-tempo game offensively and man-to-man on the other end. Teams were sagging on Harris, so the Dragons were successful getting the ball to him before defenses could set up. In the open floor, it was junior Harris's slam dunk which "fired us up." Mike Googe had a nice game with 11 markers and 4 assists. Senior Tommy Atha was a "one-man show" for the Yellow Jackets with 26 counters. The Pepperell Ladies trailed at all the quarter breaks before finishing strong in the 42–35 triumph over home-standing Black and Gold. Julie Ayer sank 20 points, collected 8 rebounds, and 4 steals; Goss helped out with 10 markers and 8 caroms; Edwards pulled down 8 misses also. Coach Hallmark was not happy, saying, "We drug around...We don't have anywhere to practice since the water damage to our floor." We would be the "Road Dragons" for the rest of the year. Although we wore the home jerseys, PHS played at Model gym and defeated Shannon's boys 62–42. A balanced attack was the key to victory as Tim McBurnett scored 14, had 5 steals, and 3 assists. Mike Googe also added 14 counters. Calvin Harris netted 15, grabbed 13 rebounds, 6 steals, and had 3 assists. PHS was now 7–11 for the season. In the opener, our girls lost 56–33; the Lady Blue Devils shot well from the field (53 percent and 58.6 percent at the charity stripe in addition to collecting 35 rebounds. Julie Ayer was our only double-figure scorer with 10 markers. The regular season ended Friday night, February 8, on Alabama Road with a 51–40 loss to 16–5 Coosa boys. Coach Horne said afterward, "We would have liked to have played this one at home...practicing away and playing away has been diffi-

cult but the kids have been great." The Eagle boys took the lead for good in the second stanza, yet PHS refused to buckle and cut the advantage at 37–32 early in the last quarter before the winners shot back out to a 13-point lead. Calvin Harris was our only double-digit scorer with 16. The Pepperell girls broke out on top 8–0 before Coosa hit 13 of 16 shots in the second stanza for 26 points. Yet CHS led by only 5 at intermission. They outrebounded us 24–4 in the final 16 minutes which led to their 61–46 victory. Melissa Goss was our leading scorer with 17; Hallmark praised senior Kristi White for good defensive play in addition to claiming 6 rebounds. Ayer and Young chipped in with 11 and 10 markers respectively. In Tallapoosa on Thursday, February 14, for the Region 7-AA South tourney, senior Melissa Goss hit a last-second shot from the top of the key to give her team a 34–33 victory over Villa Rica; the basket moved Pepperell into the semifinals. In a game that changed hands 11 times in the final quarter and trailing 33–32, Goss inbounded the ball to Christi White at mid court with 7 seconds on the clock; White fed it back to her for the game winner. The duo were high scorers for PHS with 14 and 10 points. After the girls' victory, top-seeded Haralson County ended our boys' season 56–39. Winning coach Ralph Hilburn traditionally fielded a good shooting club, and this year's squad was no different. Dragon Calvin Harris finished an outstanding eleventh-grade year with 21 markers; senior Tim McBurnett was the next closest at 6. On Friday night, Rebelettes' size was again dominant versus Pepperell ladies 55–23. "We couldn't play with them. They are a bigger ballclub," said Coach Randy Hallmark. He praised his squad for great effort this year which ended with a record of 8–14. In the final contest of the year, Julie Ayer netted 8 points to lead us.

1985–'86 Season

On Christmas Day 1983, below-zero temperatures caused ruptured water pipes in Pepperell's Russell Leonard Memorial Gymnasium; this forced the remaining basketball games to be played on the road à la Dragon football. After repairs, another winter blast last winter resulted in the same problem of water, water everywhere. In preparations for roundball 1985–'86, an inch and a half of cement was poured across the playing surface; this was covered with five layers of a rubberlike polymer called Tartan. On Friday, November 29, the boys christened the new floor with a victory over unbeaten Coosa 44–41. Losing coach Larry Bing said afterward, "They were the ones who got the second shot and loose balls." We fell behind several times until a full-court press and good foul shooting put us up 42–41 with 30 seconds left; Jeff Rickman and Jamie McCord iced the contest at the free throw line; the latter led all scorers with 18 points. John Allen and Rob Dodson helped the win along with 7 rebounds each. The Dragonettes were not so fortunate, losing 49–36. A third-quarter rally died because of turnovers; Teresa Stone led us with 14 points while senior Debbie Chambers claimed 13 missed shots. At Armuchee on Tuesday, December 3, our men "bolted" to a 20–8 advantage at intermission and then "shot the ball terribly" (26 percent) but won anyway 35–30. Although Dodson scored 10 counters, it was John Allen who made a difference with 10 rebounds and 4 steals. The Lady Indians won by 34–24. Coach Randy Hallmark said about the 10-point loss, "We had 28 turnovers…We would pass up the good shots and take the bad." Debbie Chambers tallied 9 markers for PHS. On the tenth, we cleaned up our turnovers versus Trion and downed the visiting girls 71–20; with reserves playing much of the game, Carol McWhorter and Katrina Edwards netted 20 and 18 counters each. The Lindale boys moved to 4–0 by beating the Bulldogs 48–40 behind Jeff Rickman's 17 points and 8 assists; Allen added a dozen markers to go with 9 caroms; Dodson contributed 8 points and gathered 10 missed shots. Coach Horne noted afterward that "Rickman, McCord and Allen took charge in the fourth quarter with clutch buckets and free throws."

The thirty-second annual Christmas Tourney began Wednesday, December 18, with a 4:00 p.m. tip-off game between 1–5 Pepperell and 4–2 Coosa girls. Coach Hallmark thought limiting turnovers and improving outside shooting were the keys to winning. The now 1–6 Lindale women lost as Coosa exploded in the second half with a 36–9 run in a 56–15 victory. The lack of experience was "killing us," said Coach Hallmark. For $2 admission, fans could go to Floyd Junior College off US Highway 27 and watch the rubber match between Lindale and Shannon boys. For the Wednesday 8:30 p.m. nightcap, PHS coach Steve Horne thought, "Our offense could be crisper but overall the kids are having fun together." However, in the 53–47 loss to Blue, the Dragons committed 23 turnovers and did not shoot well; Jeff Rickman netted 21 while Calvin Clowers got 7 off the bench. Coming out of the Christmas break, the Dragon men jumped visiting Haralson County 14–2 in the first stanza; however, the Rebels countered in the second with 26 points to lead 28–21 at intermission, which eventually led to their 54–49 win. The difference was at the charity stripe as PHS hit 9 and HC countered with 18. McCord, Allen (14 rebounds), and Rickman were our top scorers with 20, 16, and 10 in order. Our girls lost handily 69–35, prompting their coach to remark, "It was close for the first five minutes and then we couldn't stop the little Levett girl." McWhorter led us in scoring with 13.

The number-one-ranked Class AA team Central of Carrollton Lions came to the Leonard on Tuesday, January 7, and "mauled" us 73–31; the Dragons "stumbled" to a 17–8 deficit in the first stanza and never recovered. We had no double-figure scorer in the contest. After winning our first 5 games, the record now sat at 5–5. PHS women fared no better, losing 67–23; Carol McWhorter netted 15 points on the home floor. In Bartow County on January 14, Cartersville gave our girls a "thrashing" 57–30, mostly because we turned the ball over 26 times. McWhorter again led us in points with 10. The Hurricanes pulled away from the Dragon men in the second stanza and breezed to a 74–48 victory. Jeff Rickman was the only visitor in double figures with 10 counters. Against visiting Villa Rica on January 17, the men won 49–48 in spite of themselves. During a time-out with 11 seconds to play and leading 49–46, Coach Horne told his squad, "Don't foul." However, we hacked the shooter on a 2-point basket underneath; fortunately, he missed a tying free throw. Other than that, we played pretty well, especially on offense where a healed Rob Dodson scored 14 markers; McCord added 11 to the winning cause. The Dragonettes fell 56–40 to a quicker, faster, and deeper Lady 'Cats squad. PHS actually outscored their opponents 23–22 in the last half but could not overcome a 16–3 first-quarter deficit. Katrina Edwards collected 17 markers and 7 rebounds for PHS. The visiting Pepperell girls took no prisoners Tuesday night in Trion, January 21, pounding the Lady Dogs 53–14. Thirteen different players scored for Coach Hallmark who said later, "It was a good game and a good break from getting beat." Senior Jill Willis led in the score book with 12 counters. The Trion boys were undermanned by illness but still took a surprising 62–45 victory over the Dragons. The winners slowed the pace, showed patience, and played good defense and got some easy buckets off our press. Although Jamie McCord led us with 16 points, we shot less than 30 percent from the field. On Friday night, January 24, both of our squads lost at Villa Rica with 61s—that is to say the ladies were beaten 71–61, and the men, 73–61. The boys could have gotten "home cooking," for 3 Lindale starters (Allen, Rickman, and McCord) fouled out which led to 27 of 39 free throws by the Wildcats. In the losing cause, Rickman canned 15 points while Brian Corntassel came off the bench to net 13. Our record fell to 7–9 for the season. Although the ladies' record dropped to 3–13, Coach Hallmark thought we played a "steady" game other than critical turnovers. Katrina Edwards and Teresa Stone topped our scorers with 23 and 11 respectively. At the Russell Leonard on Saturday night, January 25, East Rome was a little "flat" coming off a big victory over West (a seventh straight win); nevertheless, their inside game was too much for Pepperell 51–43. Coach Horne said his team "played their hearts out and didn't give in." The Lady Dragons lost 38–28 to an illness-depleted Gladiator quintet in the opener. Randy Hallmark's girls couldn't stop Tracy Creamer who netted 22 points in a slow-paced contest; Katrina Edwards led PHS with 12 counters. In Polk County on Thursday, January 30, the Dragonettes were suffering so much from illness to several players that the last few minutes of their 55–36 win over Rockmart was played with only 4 on the floor. Teresa Stone took charge for Pepperell in the last 90 seconds with clutch baskets; her 17 points and Tracy Smith's court execution against the Jacket press was critical in the victory. The Rockmart boys enjoyed their best overall game since Christmas in defeating PHS 55–36. Coach Horne thought the host's defense was a reason we did not play well in the nightcap, but John Allen did, leading the visitors with 18 points. On Tuesday night, February 4, the boys of Tallapoosa beat us 60–51. The contest was close at intermission, but the home-standing Rebels of Haralson County hit 19 points in the third to basically put the game away. John Allen again pounded the boards, getting 12 caroms while McCord was our only double-digit scorer with a dozen markers. The Rebelettes, who were ranked second in the state, used a superior running and pressing strategy to down the Dragonettes 66–36. "There's not much we could do about it," said Coach Hallmark afterward. McWhorter was the leader in a losing cause with 13 counters. Larry Bing's Coosa squad beat us pretty good just off Alabama Road on Friday, February 7. It was no fluke, for PHS shot 29 percent while the Eagles shot 52 percent; they also won the battle of the boards 41–32. "Coosa played good and we didn't. I have no other comments," said Coach Horne afterward. Jeff Rickman led the boys from Dragon Drive with 12 points. In the opening contest, the Dragonettes "dug their own grave" by making just 3 of 23 attempts in the first half. Mental mistakes, missed layups, and turnovers added to the deficit. The 16–5 Lady Eagles were good and played well the entire night. Katrina Edwards, who had been playing with an ailment, scored 10 markers; sophomore Karen Drew netted 7 points with 6 rebounds. In the 7-AA Subregion South tourney held in Haralson County gym on Thursday, February 13, both Pepperell squads were one and done. The boys dropped a 54–38 decision to Rockmart while the women fell to Cartersville 51–34. According to *RNT* sportswriter Bond Nickles, the Polk County Bees were lackluster; nevertheless, Lindale's patient offense and defense failed to extend its season. Explaining the loss, Coach Steve Horne lamented afterward, "We got the good shots but couldn't put them in." Meanwhile, the Jackets had 4 players in double figures; McCord had 13 and Rickman had 10 in the losing cause. The 1985–'86 Dragons ended their season at 7–15.

1986–'87 Season

The Dragon men opened their roundball season in the Russell Leonard Gym on Tuesday, December 2, with a 58–50 victory over Armuchee. John Allen carried the load, offensively scoring 20 points and claiming 17 rebounds despite missing much of the second half due to foul trouble. This allowed the visitors to cut a 20-point deficit down to 3; however, clutch free throw shooting by junior Scott Wilder who sank 16 total markers kept the home squad in front. Key baskets by Brian Corntassel and Jamie McCord also padded our lead late in the game. The Lindale girls were not so fortunate, losing 52–30. Midway of the third, Pepperell trailed 31–30 on Tierra Rush's 3-point play; however, the Lady Indians went on a 16–1 spurt that sealed the contest. Along the way, they used 5 players to tally 8 or more counters. On Saturday night the sixth, PHS split a doubleheader with rival Model. The boys won a tight 47–39 contest that was tied at intermission. Both squads came out "on fire" in the third with McCord and Blue Devil Bryant playing "dueling banjoes" in sinking baskets. Tempers and fouls flourished in the final stanza, prompting Milt Travis to say later, "When it came down to the tight ending, they executed and we didn't." Stacy Elliott tallied 10 points for Shannon while McCord netted 14 for Lindale. The Lady Dragons fell hard to the twin sister act of Daneene and Donna Barton, 67–36. Sportswriter John Barge noted the next morning in *RNT* that "the Blue Devils held the Dragons scoreless the entire first quarter and led at halftime 41–6." First-year girls' coach Ricky Naugher was playing mostly ninth and tenth graders. Naughter's crew continued to struggle on Tuesday night, December 9, at Darlington. Although Dragonette Carol McWhorter led all scorers with 17 markers, we lost at Lakeside 55–26. The Lindale boys gained some revenge in the nightcap, downing the Lakesiders 61–54 to improve to 4–0. Wilder and McCord led in points with 17 and 16 respectively; John Allen made it all possible by claiming 15 rebounds. A key to the battle was Jamie McCord's 12 of 14 free throws in the final quarter. Our men's first defeat of the season occurred in Bremen on the twelfth. It was a "stinging" loss, for we trailed by 7 with 2 minutes to play but tied it on a field goal by Allen at the 15-second mark. The home squad set up a last-second shot that "fell and so did the Dragons."

The thirty-third annual *Rome News-Tribune* Holiday Festival basketball tourney began for us versus Coosa on Tuesday, December 16, at Floyd Junior College. At the 3:30 mark just before half, we trailed 20–14; however, by 2:49 on the third-quarter clock, we had scored 17 unanswered points and led 31–22. Scott Wilder netted 15 points while John Allen and Jamie McCord contributed 10 each in the 48–30 victory. Coach Steve Horne said later, "John hit a couple of jumpers in the lane in the second quarter, and that seemed to open things up for us." The record stood at 6–1. In the first round of the girls' bracket, PHS was unfortunate to face Chattooga, winner of 5 titles in 6 years, and they romped to a 45–21 lead at intermission and were never threatened; Carol McWhorter connected on 26 points in a losing cause. The second-round boys' bracket featured Pepperell versus West Rome. We were "crushed" 60–36 by West's superior height inside and 4 players in double figures. Pepperell trailed by 14 early in second frame but narrowed the lead to 6 at intermission, mostly on short layups by John Allen. After the break, the winners boxed out Allen, forcing McCord and Wilder to perimeter shooting, but it was not enough. On the eleventh day of January, another last-second shot sent Pepperell down this time at Rockmart 52–51. A seesaw battle saw the score tied 6 times in the final 8 minutes. With the score knotted at 43–43, Marcellous Cook missed the front end of a one-and-one charity shot that would have awarded the victory to the Jackets; however, he missed, forcing overtime. Both teams were "ferocious" in the extra 3 minutes before Melvin Holt sank a 10-foot jumper at the 6-second mark to win. Allen had hit 2 clutch free throws prior to their winning bucket. He and McCord led Lindale with 11 and 14 markers respectively. The following week, Cartersville slammed us 75–51; however, the Dragons recovered in a visit to North Floyd where they completed the season sweep of Armuchee 60–52. Lindale built an early lead but only held a 5-point advantage late in the third when 2 technical fouls were assessed on AHS; we converted at the line and then scored a field goal to finish a 6-point trip downcourt. Losing coach Mike Durham told the local gazette, "We put as much pressure on them as we could." Brian Corntassel led the way for the winners with 17 counters and 10 rebounds; Wilder and Allen combined for 29 markers with John also claiming 12 boards, 8 steals, and 4 assists. McCord and Whichard paired up for 11 in the assists column. Coach Steve Horne said later, "We lost our last four games… we played this one for pride." Next, in the Russell Leonard Gym, our mid-December 2-point loss at Bremen was avenged 60–50; however, Cartersville swept the Pepperell regular season series with a 69–50 win. Darlington came to the Leonard on January 23 and departed with a 56–46 victory; 8 consecutive free throws in the final period was the deciding factor. For the 8–7 Dragons, John Allen netted 18 points and 13 boards; McCord chipped in with 13 markers. The Lady Tigers completed the doubleheader sweep with a 50–24 victory; Carol McWhorter led PHS with 11 counters. The talented Central of Carrollton Lions downed visiting Pepperell 82–49 to win the season home and home series, yet we rebounded with a nice victory over Haralson County 60–58. The Rebels came from behind and took a 43–42 in the third but could not contain John Allen who put up 26 points and claimed 13 missed shots. The win improved the club's overall record to 9–8. On Alabama Road, Friday, February 6, Lindale trailed by a point at intermission and by a field goal after 24 minutes. At this point, Coach Steve Horne ordered a switch to man-to-man defense, which limited the Coosa Eagles to a single bucket in the final frame. In the 51–43 victory, John Allen continued his exemplary play with 21 points and 13 boards; the Dragons improved their record to 10–8. Rockmart and Haralson County were left on the regular season schedule. In the first game, we avenged a last-second-shot loss earlier in the season to down the Polk County Jackets 55–48. In the second contest, PHS overcame a 30–29 deficit in the third quarter to win another close game over Haralson County 48–42. Senior John Allen continued excellent play with 24 points and 11 rebounds. When the Rock tried to take the ball inside, Allen made several key steals that helped us pull away. Coach Horne told the media, "He took over the game." Senior wingman Brian Corntassel was runner-up in scoring with 10 markers while Wilder chipped in with 8t; Pepperell's record was now 12–8 with the subregion tourney starting on Thursday, February 12, in Tallapoosa. In the first evening contest, the Lady Dragons fell to Cartersville 51–34; they ran out to a 17–3 lead in period one and were never headed. Carol McWhorter finished her career at PHS with 12 points. Coach Horne's quintet looked in control most of their game versus Rockmart, but in the end, "We got the good shots but we couldn't put them in," he said later.

On Sunday, March 15, *Rome News-Tribune* announced all-area squads. The Lady Dragons featured senior Carol McWhorter who led her teammates in practically every category including a 16-point average to go with 12 rebounds; the spiritual leader committed only 1 turnover per outing.

Senior John Allen "keyed the improved Pepperell attack" this year, scoring double figures in 20 of our 21 games; he shot 52 percent while averaging 16.2 counters and 12.4 rebounds per contest.

1987–'88 Season

The Pepperell boys would try to do better than last season's 10-year best 12–8 record. However, Coach Steve Horne thought it would be difficult because 7 graduated from that squad. The sole returning starter was 6-foot-3 Scott Wilder; he would pair up with another twelfth grader, 6-foot Calvin Clowers; 6-foot-1 backcourt freshman Scott Crabbe added size to the lineup. New Pepperell women's coach Gerald Payton had been impressed by his team's enthusiasm and love of the game; consequently, the group was 1–0 after downing host Armuchee 49–48 on Tuesday, December 1. We tied the game at 10–10 early in the first quarter before the home team raced ahead 30–19 early in the third quarter. Coach Payton ordered a trap to counter the opponent's slow-down offense. The strategy worked, for Karen Drew brought us even with a free throw at the 7:36 mark of quarter four. The Dragonettes then went on a run themselves to lead 47–42 with just over a minute to play. With 7 seconds left, the Lady Indians cut the advantage to 1 point, but time ran out. Ms. Drew played really well for PHS and led all scorers with 20 points in addition to several steals. The men opened with a 74–50 loss in North Floyd County. Indians' sharpshooter Joe Williams netted 24 points for the winners. In the opening game on Friday, December 4, PHS improved to 2–0 with a significant and convincing 54–36 win over visiting Coosa. This was half of our ladies' wins last season. Karen Drew and Pam Rush led us to 10 unanswered points in the first stanza—and we never looked back. Coach Payton said later, "We were bigger, taller and our press which yielded 16 first half turnovers really hurt them." PHS men evened their record at 1–1 by beating the Eagles 47–41 in overtime. We trailed 25–22 at the half before our guards began to drive to the basket and victory. One night later, Model girls raced to a 29–13 lead at the half and doubled us up 68–32 in the final. We had no answer to Lee-Anda Hutchens's 26 markers. However, the boys ran their record to 2–1 with a win over the Blue Devils. On Tuesday the eighth, Pepperell "sank like a stone" in period one versus Darlington; if not for Scott Wilder's 3-pointer at the buzzer, we would have been shut out in the first 8 minutes. However, the Dragons came charging back to eventually win 61–58 and improve to 3–1. When Brad Edwards converted 2 free throws at the 1:51 mark before half, the score stood 19–18—Pepperell. Late in the contest, Calvin Clowers got hot scoring with fadeaway jumpers; afterward, Wilder sank 2 charity shots with 10 seconds showing for the victory. Losing coach Jim Van Es said afterward, "We got outcoached and outplayed." The girls did not fare as well, for the Lakeside Ladies won 56–44; senior Karen Drew led us with 15 markers. Our season record was now 2–2. Since 1954, Christmas in Rome/Floyd County meant a high school basketball tournament. This year's games would be played at Floyd College on US 27 South beginning at 5:30 p.m., Tuesday, December 15, with the Dragonettes versus Coosa. Our boys would play the following day at 6:00 p.m. against Model. On the fifteenth, our girls bolted to an 18–4 lead in the first period and were never really challenged in the 56–41 victory; Karen Drew and sisters Pam and Tierra Rush led the team with 16, 15, and 11 points in order. Coach Payton explained that "we don't have a star like a lot of teams have." On Wednesday evening, Model avenged an earlier 3-point loss by eliminating our boys 51–34; it did not help that Lindale averaged 8 turnovers per quarter. "We got outplayed," said Coach Horne whose squad now sat at a respectable 4–2; Wilder led PHS with 23 markers, but no one else hit for more than 5 points. On Friday the eighteenth, Darlington removed our girls from tourney play 34–30 in a game that featured only 1 quarter of scoring in double figures. Yet the losing coach was not dejected, for although his girls performed poorly, they fought back from a 20–6 first-quarter deficit to pull within 31–30. In a strange game on Tuesday, January 5, 1988, in Lindale, Central of Carrollton defeated the Dragonettes 59–48. To start this contest, Pepperell received a gift of 10 free throws in the form of technical fouls because the Lady Lions' uniforms were in violation of GHSA rules. The *RNT* report did not elaborate on what constituted the infraction. Sophomore Pam Rush was tops in scoring for PHS with 16 counters. On Friday, January 15, Scott Wilder and Calvin Clowers combined for 33 points against visiting Armuchee. Unfortunately, 11 Indians made the score book in our 53–51 loss to AHS. Pepperell girls lost 54–41 to complete a roundball sweep for the Blueclads; Tierra Rush bucketed 19 markers while sister Pam added 11. The Dragonettes rebounded on the nineteenth with a good win versus visiting Cartersville 55–48. Sophomore Pam Rush scored 8 points in the second stanza while senior Tierra Rush contributed 6 that gave us a 27–19 advantage at intermission. Karen Drew returned from an injury to add 13; the team converted 17 of 26 from the charity line. On Friday night, January 22, Darlington boys avenged a previous 3-point loss to PHS with a hard-fought 54–48 victory. Although the contest was tied 21–21 at intermission, the Tigers inched ahead in the final quarter. Scott Wilder netted 21 points for PHS while Travis Cordell and Clowers each added 8 to the book. The Lakeside girls completed the doubleheader sweep 45–37. The Rush sisters contributed 14 markers apiece to lead their team.

On the last Friday night of January, Cedartown's Orr and Brown scored 40 points together; Pepperell's Scott Wilder almost matched them by hitting for 37. However, the 'Dogs prevailed 67–58, which left our squad with a 2–13 record. CHS bolted to a 32–21 advantage at the half and held on to win. Calvin Clowers helped Wilder by netting 13 counters. There was no score posted for the Dragonettes versus Lady Bulldogs; however, 1 night later, we beat Rockmart 46–45 to improve our record to 7–9. Pam Rush, Tierra Rush, and Karen Drew led us to victory with 18, 14, and 9 points. A 16-point second quarter was the difference. The PHS men held up their end of the doubleheader with 47–41 win over the Polk County Jackets; Wilder, Clowers, and Crabbe took scoring honors with 20, 17, and 8 markers. In a return match on Alabama Road on Friday, February 5, Coosa downed Lindale 65–45; they did it by holding high-scoring Scott Wilder to 11 points. Larry Bing's squad used an infrequently used defense called a diamond and one to limit the Dragon sharpshooter. A squad uses its best defender to play man-to-man on the target player while the other 4 help out their teammate with zone tactics. Another highlight of the evening was Coach Bing recording victory number 200 before the partisan crowd. Calvin Clowers was our leader in the score book with 14 counters. The 2–16 Lady Eagles upset the 8–11

Dragonettes 40–37 to complete the doubleheader sweep; Pam Rush tallied 14 markers, but no other teammate hit more than 5.

The 7-AA South playoffs began on Thursday, February 11, at 4:00 p.m. in Rockmart with Pepperell girls facing Cartersville. The Lady 'Canes were considered favorites, but Coach Payton remarked in pregame that "all I can say is we will have to scrap with them all the way." And scrap we did, for the final score ended PHS, 33; CHS, 30. Tierra Rush led us back from a halftime deficit with 13 points; Drew and P. Rush brought 7 and 6 counters respectively. The win moved our record to 10–12 or 3 times more victories than last season's 3-win team. Only thing was now we had to play a state-ranked Haralson County squad; Friday's game was not close as the Rebelettes won 82–38. Furthermore, the day before (Thursday), our boys lost to Cartersville 71–54, ending our season at 5–13.

1988–'89 Season

Coach Steve Horne prepared for his tenth season as headman of the Dragons without leading scorer Scott Wilder who averaged 18 points per game. Furthermore, his squad would depend on 7 sophomores for most of the playing time. A lack of size did not help either as our tallest was 6 feet 2. The Lady Pepperells won 11 victories last season, matching their highest wins in 15 winters. Second-year coach Gerald Payton listed his starters as guards Tracy Ridgeway and Kathleen Smallwood; forwards were Pam Rush paired with Robin Hight. The center position would be handled by Dana Joy Fisher. These players were instrumental in the Dragonettes' opening 46–42 win at Armuchee on Tuesday, November 29. The lead changed "early and often" until the final buzzer. We were down by 4 with 2:53 left before Hight sank 2 foul shots and Smallwood made a layup off a steal by Ridgeway to tie the game at 42–42. With 26 seconds showing, Kathleen put up an 18-footer that spun around the rim before falling in; Pam Rush added a close-in jumper for the last shot of the game and a final of 46–42. In the nightcap, our boys did not fare as well, losing 86–75; the winners were led by 5 players in double figures. PHS fell behind by 18 points before cutting it to single digits on Kelly Fourtain's 3-pointer and a driving layup by Robbie Dooley with 2 seconds left. On the second evening of December, the boys lost to host Coosa 68–53; the Fountain boys, Kelley and Kevin, netted 17 and 12 markers each. Our ladies were nipped by the Eaglettes 47–45; senior Dana Joy Fisher led us with 17 counters. In the Russell Leonard Gym on Tuesday night, December 11, rival Darlington eked out a win 48–43 in overtime. The home crowd thought we won it with 12 seconds left in regulation when Smallwood hit 2 clutch free throws to lead 41–39 especially after Tiger star Caroline Peek shot and missed; however, in the melee under the basket, she claimed and banked the ball in to tie 41–41 as the clock expired. Allie Weiner and Peek paired up to win the 5-point victory in OT. The visitors completed the clean sweep, overcoming our boys 58–44. They led 28–18 at intermission and 40–22 after 24 minutes. "I thought we got a little tired," said Steve Horne afterward. Kelley Fountain was high scorer for Lindale at 9 counters. As a preparation for the upcoming Christmas Tourney, the PHS women lost to Model 65–35; Dana Joy Fisher scored 13 in the loss. The men fell 67–59 under Johnny Boyd's and Lamar Spivey's 19- and 18-point barrage. Sophomore Kevin Fountain led Pepperell with 15 markers. At 4:00 p.m., Friday afternoon,

December 16, the first round of the thirty-fifth annual *Rome News-Tribune* Holiday Festival began at Floyd College gym. Twenty teams vied for the crown that according to *RNT* editor John Perry "has always been one of the highlights of the high-school basketball season." Chattooga girls and West Rome Chieftains would defend their championships. The games would end on Thursday, the twenty-second. The Dragons drew Darlington on Friday the sixteenth and were outscored/eliminated 78–43 by the Lakesiders; sophomore Ken Irvin was high point with 9 markers. Our ladies drew a first-round bye but were removed/lost to Darlington 40–24 on Monday the nineteenth. Dana Joy Fisher netted 13 points and claimed 10 rebounds in the loss; however, 22 turnovers and several easy misses under the basket spelled defeat. In the first game of the new year, East Rome Gladiators defeated winless Pepperell 81–52; in spite of that, Coach Horne believed his squad played their best outing of the year. The Dragons' 3-point shooting offense was led by Kelley Fountain with 19 while Irvin also added 15 to the score book. Winning Coach Dwight Henderson said of his opponent, "They played us hard the whole way and always hustle." In the opener at the Leonard on Tuesday, January 4, the Lady Glads nipped the 1–6 PHS squad 37–30. Junior Pam Rush was high scorer in the losing cause with 10 swishers. We followed that game with a close loss to Cartersville 55–48 on January 6; senior Dana Joy Fisher was game high with 17 counters. Kathleen Smallwood and Pam Rush each claimed 10 rebounds. The men suffered a 15-point loss (75–60) to the 3–7 Hurricanes. The Fountain brothers accounted for 32 of our 60 markers. Kevin Fountain logged all his 15 in the fourth quarter while Kelley was team high with 17 helped by Irvin's 13. Friday the thirteenth was unlucky for our men in a 77–61 defeat to Armuchee. Kelly Fountain again scored 17 points while brother Kevin hit 13 for 15 at the charity line. The Lady Dragons opened the evening with a 58–40 victory. The balanced scoring of 14, 13, and 12 counters from Pam Rush, Dana Joy Fisher, and Robin Hight were more than the Lady Indians could overcome. We led 37–29 going into the final stanza and outpaced AHS 21–11 in the last 8 minutes. On Tuesday, January 17, *Rome News-Tribune* sportswriter Thomas Monigan wrote that Steve Horne had experienced success and adversity as basketball coach in Lindale. There was a 0–22 season early on, but the 1986–'87 Gold and White went 13–8. Describing this year's 0–10 squad, he said, "We have just come upon a down cycle...Our lack of height has hurt...It's hard to win when all you can do is shoot the three-pointer." On the eighteenth, we led Cartersville by 3 going into the final quarter, but the 'Canes outscored us down the stretch 19–9 to win 55–48. Crabbe, Irvin, and Kelley Fountain led us with 14, 12, and 10 markers. Our women lost a thriller 41–40 in the opening game when we missed the front end of a one-and-one free throw. We overcame Cartersville's 11-point fourth-quarter lead to take a 40–39 advantage with 20 seconds left but couldn't get the critical foul shot to fall. On Friday night the twentieth, 1-loss Haralson County girls romped over PHS 65–30 to remain undefeated in region. Pam Rush led the visiting PHS ladies with 12 points. The second game of the evening was worse by 6 markers as the boys went down 82–41. We managed only 12 counters in the first half; Kevin Fountain led us with a dozen even. Tuesday, January 24, saw our Lady Dragons end their skid with a 51–44 victory over East Rome. Dana Joy Fisher and Tracy Ridgeway scored 14 each. In the nightcap, Lindale boys lost by 74–41 to the Gladiators; senior Robbie Dooley led us with 12 counters. Three nights later, PHS lost a doubleheader to the Polk County Bees; the girls lost 40–31 and the boys 58–39. Dana Joy Fisher and Scott Crabbe were the scoring leaders with 18 and 16 markers respectively versus the Rockmart Yellow Jackets. On the last Friday night of January, we traveled to Cedartown and were downed 82–36 by the 18–0 Bulldogs. A large crowd filled the parking lot and then watched the action. Athletic Director John Hill noted games had been sold out on several occasions this season. The Pepperell fans received some solace as our girls won the opener 40–38 thanks to Dana Joy Fisher's 16 points; Lindale eked out the win on the foul line, shooting 14 of 24 on the evening. Haralson County girls came visiting the Leonard on Tuesday, January 31, and departed with a 72–35 victory. Senior Candi Chester led us with 10 counters, 8 of which came in the final quarter. The Dragon men came close to upsetting the Rebels; sophomore Ken Irvin swished 16 while Kevin Fountain netted 11 markers. In the Russell Leonard Memorial Gym on Friday, February 3, PHS boys came close to breaking their losing streak. They had a 2-point lead late but could not convert free throws down the stretch in a 71–69 loss to Coosa. Coach Horne said later, "We played hard to even have a chance, but I guess it was not in the cards." Kelly Fountain and Rusty Day led our scorers with 25 and 18 markers. However, in the first game of the evening, the Lady Dragons downed the visitors 53–46 behind Pam Rush's 18 counters. On Tuesday, February 7, host Darlington won narrowly 38–33 over our ladies. Pam Rush again led us in points with 12; the girls' record was now 6–12 for the season. The men did not fare as well, losing 72–46; Ken Irvin hit a trio of 3-point goals to lead in the score book with 13 while Kelley Fountain added 9 markers. In the opening round of Region 7-AA South tourney held in Coosa's gym, Darlington High School received the Valentine's Day bouquet with an 81–64 victory over winless Pepperell boys. The word in the stands was PHS played full tilt the entire 32 minutes before falling to the Tigers. Although the Lindale men closed out their year on Tuesday, February 14, the following night, our Lady Dragons played Rockmart on Alabama Road, and if not for the Yellow Jackets' Deidre Jones, we would have continued tourney play. However, the junior center scored 28 points and all 6 of her team's markers in the 52–49 overtime win against Pepperell. Poor foul shooting in the final 17 seconds of regulation kept us from a victory and ended our season. Pam Rush led us in the score book with 23 big counters. Some all-area accolades were meted out by *News-Tribune* on Sunday, February 26, including honorable mention to Kelly Fountain and Ken Irvin. The girls' team listed two Lady Dragons for excellent play for 1988–'89, Dana Joy Fisher and Pam Rush.

1989–'90 Season

After a previous winless season, Pepperell men broke the losing streak on Tuesday, November 28, by downing Armuchee 62–59. Freshman Brandon Davis used his first varsity competition to score 22 points, collect 14 rebounds, block 3 shots, and hand out 4 assists. He had help from Kevin Fountain with 11; Ken Irvin and Scott Crabbe added 9 each. In the early game, our girls edged host AHS 44–41 behind Christy Peek's 19 points. The Lindale ladies almost won again on Friday against visiting Coosa before falling 57–50. Early in the final quarter, we trailed 51–26 before Coach Payton ordered a full-court press; Tracey Ridgeway and Christy Peek fed off the pressure to score a combined 19 markers. The Dragon boys were nipped 82–77 by the Eagles; however, ninth grader Brandon Davis hit for 29 points. Ken Irvin and Kelly Fountain added 15 and 12 markers respectively. At Darlington on Tuesday the fifth, the PHS men fell 62–54. The Tigers stymied Ken Irvin and Brandon Davis with a diamond-and-two defense that limited them to 25 points combined mostly in the first half. The latter had been averaging 20-plus counters per game. The visiting girls won the opener at Lakeside 34–29. Leading scorers Ridgeway and Peek were held to 11 markers total; however, other Dragons stepped up, including Cathe Chester with 5 counters and 9 rebounds. Junior Chrissy Roberson and sophomore Julie Smart contributed 6 points together in the score book. Cedartown boys and Chattooga girls would defend their Christmas Tourney crowns beginning on December 16 at Floyd College. Pepperell men would face Coosa at 7:00 p.m. on Monday the eighteenth after our girls' game at 5:30 p.m. versus Armuchee. A large crowd was expected for the tournament's thirty-sixth edition. Last year's semifinals between East Rome and Cedartown drew more than 2,000 spectators; this was a record for Floyd County basketball. Net distributed receipts for 1988 was $6,579. A week (December 8) before tip-off at Floyd College, our 4–1 Lady Dragons pounded visiting Red Bud 62–21. Christy Peek scored 14, Lisa Jennings added 12, and Roberson and Rush contributed 11 each with the latter claiming 8 rebounds. Down by 8 points early, the 3–2 Dragon men "resorted" to a full-court press which brought our boys back to win 64–53. Kelley Fountain, Irvin, Davis (15 rebounds), and Crabbe led us in scoring with 18, 15, 14, and 10 markers in order. On the twelfth of December, Model girls defeated us 48–30; a man-to-man defense contributed to their win. Ridgeway and Peek each hit 8 points for the 4–2 Lady Pepperells. In the nightcap, the host Blue Devils beat us pretty good 84–62; the Fountain boys combined for 29 counters while Irvin and Davis netted 27 together.

The Lady Dragons opened the Christmas Tourney with a 52–47 overtime win over Armuchee. As they played without starting point guard Christy Peek, Coach Gerald Payton urged senior Pammy Rush to pick up the slack, and she did, scoring a game-high 18 points with 10 in the first stanza. In the extra 3 minutes, PHS sank 4 of 6 free throws from Rush, Ridgeway, and Jennings to win by 5. Following that contest, Coosa's undefeated boys "controlled loose balls and burned the nets from the outside" to win 86–62 and remove us from the tourney. Once they busted our early full-court press, the Eagles leaped in front 39–26 at intermission. Brandon Davis scored 19 points; fellow freshman Ike Smith came off the bench for 10 markers. In Wednesday's semifinals, Chattooga "cruised" to an early lead and eliminated PHS girls 57–47. Pam Rush scored 14 points while Ridgeway and Jennings contributed 10 each. Former Pepperell star athlete Steve Turner coached the Lady Indians to a 10-point victory over his alma mater. In the ladies' consolation game on Thursday, December 21, Darlington retaliated from a home loss to Lindale and beat us by 49–34.

On the first Tuesday of 1990, home-standing East Rome ran their record to 8–0 with a 79–52 win over Pepperell boys. Despite playing the first 10 minutes without starters Saxton and Wood due to infraction of team rules, the Gladiators scored 23 points early en route to a 40–27 halftime lead. The visitors fought back midway of quarter three, cutting the advantage to 8, yet we could get no closer because the winners "played high enough around the basket rim to give the Dragons problems." B. Davis and Kelley Fountain led PHS in scoring with 12 each. In the opener, our girls were more successful, downing the home squad 65–26. The winners, now at 6–4 on the season, were led by Ridgeway, Chester, and Jennings with 14, 13, and 10 markers. Pepperell made its last trip to Red Bud on Friday, January 5, 1990. The school would soon consolidate with Fairmount to form Sonoraville High. In the opener, senior forward Tracey Ridgeway swished 10 counters to open the second half, and we proceeded to score 23 unanswered to win going away 52–22. Teammates Pam Rush and Christy Peek "chipped" in with 15 and 11 for the 7–4 Lady Dragons. In the nightcap, our men won 50–48 but not as handily as the women. It took a jumper from the baseline with 6 seconds left by Kelley Fountain to overcome the Cardinals by 2. Fountain's bucket was his 21 points of the game; Brandon Davis added 12 markers to the PHS cause. On Friday, January 12, Armuchee came visiting the Leonard with a substitute head coach. When illness sidelined Melinda Lewis, former AHS head coach Bill Thornton, who had stints (1976–'85) as girls' and boys' Armuchee coach, filled in. The *News-Tribune* reported on Sunday, "Sixty-nine personal fouls and 75 free throws later, the Lady Indians were 0–11 after a 58–51 defeat." The winners' Pammy Rush scored a game-high 16 points to go with Tracy Ridgeway's 7 of 10 free throws down the stretch that pushed their record to 8–5. In the second contest, PHS men won 62–50. Freshman Brandon Davis collected 15 markers and claimed 12 rebounds; Scott Crabbe netted 14 along with junior Rusty Mansell's and freshman Germaine Roberts's 10 and 8 counters. Visiting Haralson County eked out a 53–50 win over the Dragon men on Friday, January 19. We missed a shot to tie with 2 seconds remaining. Brandon Davis led Lindale again with 15 points and 14 rebounds; Kelley Fountain contributed 14 to the score book while Ken Irvin managed 11 with 6 assists. Our record evened out at 7–7. Traditionally, the Rebelettes from HC were tough to beat, and so was the case in the opening game on Friday as they downed the home squad 62–44. Pam Rush and Christy Peek were team high scorers with 13 and 12 markers. The state's number-one-ranked Class AA basketball team, winners of 30 straight games, came to Russell Leonard Gymnasium on Wednesday, January 23. They quickly fell behind the home squad 18–10 at the first break. The Pepperell boys then took a 30–19 advantage into the locker room at intermission. The *RNT* wrote morning next, "East Rome players narrowed their eyes as they left the floor" at the Leonard. The Gold and White retained a 6-point lead until center Scott Crabbe fouled out with 7:26 left. The Gladiators took advantage and caught us 43–43 at the 5:01 mark with Victor Saxton's jumper. The visitors' press, traps, and man-to-man defense finally wore our depleted roster down. In the 61–49 loss, Brandon Davis, who was a thorn in the side of the opponent all night, led his team with 15 points assisted by Kelley Fountain's 13. In the opener, Tracey Ridgeway and Pammy Rush tallied 14 markers each in leading us to a 44–27 win over the ER Ladies. Our girls pushed their record to 12–6 with a 59–53 conquest of Trion on Friday, January 26. Pam Rush and Christy Peek netted 14 points each while freshman Lisa Jennings hit for 12. The boys completed a doubleheader night by downing the Trion Bulldogs 72–62. Brandon Davis was high scorer for 8–8 Pepperell with 20 markers and 13 rebounds; the Fountain brothers combined for 29 counters. Ken Irvin handed off 11 assists in the 10-point win. On Tuesday the thirtieth versus Haralson County, Irvin topped that with a double-double 14 points, 10 assists; Brandon Davis swished 13 markers and claimed 10 Rebel-missed shots. The Dragon record now stood at 9–9. On the first Friday of February, Coosa girls outscored Pepperell 55–46. The third quarter was pivotable in the close game as the host Lady Eagles netted 17 markers to 9 for the Dragons. Ridgeway and Rush combined for 40 points but received little help from their teammates. The nightcap was also won by the home team 61–54, but it was a battle. With 4:34 left in the final quarter, Pepperell's Brandon Davis hit a 3-point play that cut Coosa's lead to 47–46; however, we would not get any closer, for the home team executed a backdoor play and was clutch (9 of 11) at the charity line. Davis and Crabbe finished with 18 and 13 counters. Coach Horne said of the winners, "They're a strong team...we played as hard as we could." The Eagles' record was 13–6 while PHS came in at 9–10. The 18–4 Darlington Ladies came to Lindale on Tuesday, February 6, as regular season 7-AA South champs and were bent upon revenge for an earlier 34–29 (December 5) loss to Pepperell. They scored 29 by the half and led 45–21 late in the third but "wound up having to scramble for a 59–50 victory." Christy Peek led PHS with 20 points while backcourt mate Tracey Ridgeway helped out with 12. The Region 7-AA tournament began for us on Tuesday, February 13, at host Coosa gym. It was an unlucky 13 for Pepperell boys, for they lost big 90–60 against a Darlington squad we defeated by 6 last week. Coach Horne said later, "Obviously, we weren't ready to play...the team had a good workout yesterday but were real flat-footed tonight." The Dragons' final record reached 10–13. The following night, Cartersville "blitzed" PHS women 65–31 with a "relentless transition offense." In her final game, senior Pammy Rush led Lindale with 14 markers; junior guard Christy Peek hit for 10. Yet our season record reached a very respectable 13–11. The Sunday, March 3, edition of *RNT* announced all-area squads. Freshman forward Brandon Davis was first team with honorable mention going to Ken Irvin and Kelley Fountain. The same HM went to 3 Lady Dragons Christy Peek, Tracey Ridgeway, and Pammy Rush. The men's Coach of the Year award went to Pepperell's Steve Horne. The Rogersville, Tennessee, native, known as a superior tactician, rebounded from last year's winless season to finish 1989–'90 at 10–13. He said, "I appreciate the honor but I can't be satisfied winning half of the games...We don't have real great basketball players at PHS every year, so we'll have some lean years."

1990–'91 Season

Because of our 1990 championship run to the 7-AA football crown, it was Christmas Tourney time before the local media wrote up Dragons basketball. Although we took a pretty good 55–19 whipping from last year's champion, Coosa Lady Eagles, in the first round of the tourney, Coach Gerald Payton still thought we would be competitive in the regular season. The champs' defense was solid, which led to our poor shooting. Christy Peek and Robin Bailiff led us with 7 points each. The Pepperell men faced 4–0 East Rome on Monday, December 17, at Floyd College. The question was which is worse, playing an athletic squad that has no track record or coaching a group of kids that have not had one practice? The Gladiators, who were in the former scenario, won 88–63. They raced out to a 31–10 first-quarter lead and were never headed. For PHS, Brandon Davis led all scorers with 17 markers followed by Ike Smith with 10. However, there was joy early in the morning of game day when Coach and Mrs. Steve Horne welcomed a new daughter, Emma Katheryne, into the world. The 1991 part of our season began with the boys visiting Coosa on Saturday night, January 5. It took 4 clutch free throws by the home team to eke out a 54–50 victory over Lindale. The winners improved to 7–3 while PHS was 0–2. Interim coach and Alabama native Neal Wester replaced Larry Bing who was serving a monthlong suspension due to an earlier altercation with officials. About his short-term squad,

Wester said, "They got it when we had to have it." For the losing squad, Brandon Davis led all point makers with 18. The Lady Eagles had little trouble with Pepperell girls, winning 50–34; senior Christy Peek led us with 13 points. On Tuesday the eighth in Russell Leonard Gym, visiting Cartersville forced 21 turnovers and won over winless PHS boys 49–27. We had no double-figure scorers. Friday night, January 11, saw Pepperell boys win their first game of 1991 in a 91–66 romp over host Trion; senior Kelley Fountain "burnt the cords" for 31 counters. On Saturday the twelfth, East Rome girls nipped our girls 46–42 in a game that saw all 5 PHS starters foul out. The culprit was a full-court press that worked up to a point. We led 23–18 at intermission but fell behind 33–27 going into the last 8 minutes. Seniors Crissy Roberson and Christy Peek led us with 20 and 12 markers. In Bartow County on Tuesday the fifteenth, there were 5 outstanding Dragon players in our 70–67 overtime victory over host Cartersville. Kelley Fountain swished a 3-pointer at the final buzzer for the win. Before that, Ken Irvin hit a trey to tie with 3 seconds left in regulation. Brandon Davis scored 23 markers and claimed 18 rebounds. Kevin Fountain had 12 points for the Dragons while Ike Smith contributed 10. Our record improved to 2–3. On Saturday the nineteenth, West Rome's NaNae Daniels dominated the game with 27 points in her team's 55–26 victory over Pepperell; Crissy Roberson scored 17 for the 1–6 Lindale ladies. Another exciting game happened in Haralson County on January 19 when Brandon Davis hit a free throw with 1 second left on the clock to win 70–69. He finished the contest with 22 markers; not far behind was Kelley Fountain with 20 points and brother Kevin's 12 counters. Although the Dragons had won 3 in a row counting Cartersville, Haralson, and West Rome, the 15–1 Gladiators of East Rome raced to a 21–7 lead at the end of the first stanza and never looked back en route to an 80–57 win. Coach Horne explained, "You just can't spot them by that many points and expect to win…they're too big, too strong." In the opener, Pepperell girls scored a 39–30 victory over ER ladies. For PHS, Peek, Roberson, and Chester scored 14, 10, and 9. Our 2 squads visited Rockmart on the last Friday of January 25. The Lady Jackets won their first region game with a narrow 59–58 squeaker. In the men's battle, we lost 68–56 despite Brandon Davis's 23 points; the abbreviated record now stood at 5–5. One night later (January 26, 1991), we improved to 6–5 with an easy 72–62 victory over visiting Trion; junior guard Kelley Fountain bucketed 18 points including 4 treys; Kevin Fountain netted 11 while Ken Irvin dished out 11 assists. In the opener, PHS girls won 48–27 over the Lady Bulldogs; Crissy Roberson hit for 12 points in the first half and finished with 17 to lead all scorers. On the last Tuesday of the month, visiting Haralson County revenged an earlier home loss to PHS by downing their hosts 59–54. Kelley Fountain led Lindale with 17 counters, 13 in the second half. Scott Crabbe added 10 to the cause. Coosa ladies came to the Leonard on February 1, and the results were exciting. With 14 seconds remaining in regulation and the score at 48–46 in favor of the visitors, Lady Eagles' Raylanda Johnson sank 2 free throws to give her team a four-point lead. This was significant, for Cathe Chester hit a 3-pointer as the horn sounded, giving Coosa a close victory 50–49. Peek and Roberson led PHS with 13 each. The nightcap contest was not as exciting but more fun for Lindale fans. Coosa's Tyree Clark was missing due to a sprained ankle; Ken Irvin was at Memphis University for an official football visit. Clark was averaging 20.5 points per game while Ken made 7.2 per outing. The math figured to give Pepperell a winning advantage, and it did. We "shot the eyes out" in a 96–60 victory. Kevin Fountain bucketed 11 counters in the first stanza to give

PHS a 20–14 lead; Kelley hit for 12 in the second for a 44–25 advantage at intermission. Winning coach Horne said afterward, "I thought all year that we've been getting better...I don't know if Clark could have made up the 36-point difference." Losing coach Larry Bing noted, "We just didn't do anything...give them credit." Rockmart High School visited on Saturday night, February 2, and went home with a split. Our girls won 56–40 in the opener as Crissy Roberson scored 19 points; Peek and Chester added 14 apiece to the victory. The 8-8 Jackets beat our boys pretty good in the nightcap 67–50; Brandon Davis had 15, and Kelley Fountain contributed 13 in the loss. The record now stood at 6–7 overall. We traveled 3 miles to Lakeside on Tuesday, February 5, and came away with a split. Darlington Girls (13–6) won by 19 as their Peek (Caroline) scored 21 points while our Peek (Christy) hit for 10 in the 57–38 loss. The Lindale boys (7–7) defeated the winless (0–15) Tigers 57–48.

Brandon Davis tallied 22 counters along with Kelley Fountain's 15. The Region 7-AA South tournament began on Wednesday night, February 13, at Floyd College gym. Pepperell girls upset third-seeded Cartersville 48–47. It was a bittersweet win for Coach Gerald Payton who days before suffered the loss of son Jerry Wayne to a long illness. Spectator coach Marie Lewis of Coosa, who would play PHS tomorrow, said later, "If anyone deserved to win a game like that, Gerald and his team did." Coach Payton said of the victory, "I just sat there and cheered them on." Afterward, he thanked the entire Lindale community for its support, saying, "Everyone has been very kind to us." About the game, Pepperell led most of the way; however, the Lady 'Canes closed to 46–45 with 1:09 to play. At this point, Christy Peek, who finished with 14 points, sank both ends of a one-on-one charity attempt to sew up the victory. Chrissy Roberson led in the score book with 17 counters. In the following boys' game, we had to fight off upset-minded Darlington for a 58–55 decision. The Tigers missed 3 chances to tie with a dwindling clock. Ken Irvin and Kelley Fountain iced free throws prior to the Purple and White misses. Balanced scoring from Brandon Davis, 13; Ike Smith, 12; Irvin, 11; and Kelley Fountain, 10, was the proved difference in winning. The Dragons were not as fortunate in Saturday night's February 16 semi-finals, losing to second-seed Rockmart 90–76. Losing coach Horne said later, "They got in their up-tempo style of play, and we just couldn't slow them down." Sophomore Brandon Davis bucketed 25 points for Pepperell while senior Kevin Fountain added 13. The Lady Dragons also ended their season on the same night. Coosa ran out to a 52–34 bulge in the third quarter and won easily 71–39; we got 13 and 10 points from seniors Christy Peek and Cathe Chester. The all-area first team was named on March 3 with Brandon Davis representing the PHS boys' quintet 2 years running. The squad's honorable mention players were Ken Irvin and Michael Tanner while Chrissy Roberson and Christy Peek were recognized for the Lady Dragons.

1991–'92 Season

Five days prior to suiting up for the annual Christmas Tourney on December 18, Pepperell junior Brandon Davis scored 20 points and corralled 11 rebounds in our 75–62 win over home-standing East Paulding. Senior David Drew pitched in with 14 markers and claimed 13 missed shots. Fellow twelfth graders Lee Morris and Royce Smith, who recorded 11 assists, contributed to the score book with 11 each. We have little history with the school, which was founded in 1991. It is located 50 miles south of Lindale on US Highway 278 in Dallas, Georgia. The following Saturday evening, we visited undefeated East Rome where the boys lost 77–54. The Glads took a 34–26 lead to the dressing room at intermission and extended it to 55–34 at the end of 24 minutes of action. Junior Brandon Davis hit for 19 counters while Smith added 8. In the first game, our girls lost 51–19; sophomore Karla Blythe shot the only 3-pointer of the contest in a losing cause while netting 8 points for the winless Lady Dragons. The girls played the 4:00 p.m. game in the Christmas Tourney at Floyd College on Wednesday, December 18, and lost for the third successive time to Model. Coach Andy Akin's crew powered their way to a 62–41 victory, prompting him to say later, "When you play someone three times, it helps." Opposing mentor Gerald Payton bemoaned the fact that "we didn't front the posts…you can't beat anybody playing behind them." Tenth grader Karla Blythe led PHS in scoring with 18 counters followed by senior Debbie Whaley's 10 buckets. Our men took the court in the late game and downed Chattooga 48–42. Winning coach Steve Horne explained, "We didn't give them any easy shots and we rebounded real well." Brandon Davis again led us in points with 14 against the Indians. We drew an early game on Friday, December 20, versus West Rome and won by 14 points by withstanding several runs by the Chieftains. Brandon Davis netted 16 markers while senior Darrell Clowers got 11 in the 53–39 victory. "They had us outsized at every position but our kids just played hard," said Coach Horne whose team was heading to the tourney finals against East Rome. At 8:30 p.m. on Saturday, we tipped it off at Floyd College. Playing in their last Christmas event as a high school (consolidation with WR took place next season) the undefeated Gladiators beat PHS 59–46 behind MVP Tony Woods's 25 big points. Brandon Davis and Lee Morris led the runners-up in scoring with 24 and 9 markers. The Dragons finished 1991 at 5–3 with 2 of those losses to ER. Pepperell men began the new year with a narrow 49–44 loss to host Cartersville on Tuesday, January 7. We led by 6 in the last quarter, but the 'Canes tied it with 1:30 left and won because we could not hit at the foul line. Brandon Davis scored 23 counters for PHS. On Friday night next, visiting Trion pushed Lindale men to the limit before falling 42–38. Freshman Darrell Clowers hit a basket with 20 seconds left, and Jason Wilder sank 2 charity shots to hold off the Bulldogs; senior Lee Morris led us with 11 points while fellow seniors David Drew and Mike Robinson claimed 10 rebounds each. On the following night, Pepperell Dragons won a doubleheader against visiting East Paulding. The ladies won a second straight contest by downing the Raiders 45–43. Karla Blythe and Robin Bailiff contributed 16 and 15 counters respectively. In the nightcap, Lindale boys got a 35-point effort from Brandon Davis in winning 92–78; Lee Morris helped out with 17 markers. On Tuesday, January 14, our ladies ran into a buzz saw from Bartow County and lost 64–20. The undefeated Carterville squad ran out to a 20–4 first-quarter lead and was never threatened. PHS coach Payton explained later that "we've got to get them motivated." Karla Blythe led us with 10 points. The boys fared much better as they blunted a last-minute rally by the visitors for a big win in the Leonard, 54–51. Lee Morris hit a layup with 10 seconds remaining that put us up by 3; a desperation trey by the 'Canes fell just short. Brandon Davis again led us in points with 22 followed by Morris with 13. Our record improved to 8–4 overall. On Friday night next in Haralson County, we downed the number-seven-ranked Class AA squad 59–55. It did not come easy as the Rebels raced to a quick 12–2 lead before we changed to a pressure defense which cut the advantage

22–21 at intermission. Brandon Davis had a game-high 20 points while Lee Morris contributed 13 markers. The top-ranked Class A squad East Rome came to Park Street on Tuesday night, January 21, and left with a 53–46 victory. Brandon Davis led a 21-point third-quarter surge that cut the 15–0 Glads' lead to 1. With 1:43 showing on the fourth-quarter game clock, we missed 2 foul shots that would have tied it. With 4 victories in a row over Trion, East Paulding, Cartersville, and state-ranked Haralson County driving us, Coach Horne thought Pepperell was probably at the top of their game. Brandon Davis was certainly sharp with 24 big counters. The Lady Gladiators downed PHS 51–25 by outscoring us 32–16 after intermission. On Friday, January 24, Lee Morris hit for 17 points while Brandon Davis added 15 as the Dragons beat host Trion 55–50. The win improved our record to 10–5. The following night, Rockmart came to the Russell Leonard and departed with a 2-point loss. Brandon Davis had 23 markers as the Dragons outlasted their Region 7-AA foe 60–58. Apparently, we had Haralson County's number. They came to Lindale ranked once more number ten and left with a 3-point defeat 50–47. The home team was behind 10 markers at intermission, but a 22-point fourth-quarter "outburst" provided impetus for the victory. Senior Lee Morris not only scored a team-high 14 counters but also claimed 12 rebounds. Freshman Darrell Clowers had 6 of his 8 points in the final stanza. Brandon Davis pitched in a dozen markers. Our record moved to 12–5 overall. The girls fell in the opener 57–28 with Jessica Lattimer leading the team with 12 markers. Haralson's slate was 13–3, a reverse of Pepperell's 2–13. On the last night in January, a very unselfish PHS squad led visiting Coosa by 17 points several times in the second half en route to a 69–59 victory. Winning coach Horne said, "We played the best we could for the first and third quarters." On the opposite bench, Larry Bing observed, "They just made us work harder for our shots than we made them work for theirs." Brandon Davis was game high with 21 points. At Darlington on Tuesday, February 4, Lindale outscored the Tigers 19–4 in a 3-minute, 52-second span of the third quarter on the way to a 52–47 victory. The Dragons, who were now 14–5 overall and in first place in the subregion with a 7–1 mark, used a rare full-court press to surprise the Lakesiders. Junior Brandon Davis's 26 points put him over 1,000 for a career that had 1 more year left. In the girls' game, Darlington took an early 13–1 lead and never looked back, winning 42–27. Tiffany Gladney led Pepperell with 9 markers. Coosa gained some revenge for last month's loss to PHS by winning 63–60 over the visiting Dragons. Despite hitting 5 3-pointers in the final quarter on Friday, February 7, Coach Horne's crew could not take the lead. Brandon Davis again led us with 26 counters. In the opener, *Rome News-Tribune* sports department wrote that Coosa girls led 29–6 at intermission and had little trouble downing the ladies from Lindale 55–16. A short trip south on Rockmart Road on February 11 was productive. The Dragon men won 62–49 behind Brandon Davis's 19 points and 15 rebounds; Lee Morris helped with 13 while David Drew and Jason Wilder scored 11 each. In our last regular season game, it was Pepperell, 55, and West Rome, 40. The Friday night contest saw Brandon Davis bucket 17 counters as his team took a 20–17 lead at the half and "never looked back." Our record stood at 16–7 entering the South Region tournament. Pepperell drew a first-round bye in the tourney held at Floyd College but faced Haralson County for a third time this season. PHS came away with a three-peat over the Rebels 51–50. However, the losers had a chance at the foul line with no time showing on the clock but missed the first of a one-plus-one shot. Thirty-two seconds before, freshman Darrell Clowers had put us ahead by 1 point on a putback of Royce Smith's missed free throw. The Gold and White led at all the breaks before HC inched ahead 48–42 in the final minutes, only to see their lead disappear at the end. Davis, Wilder, and Clowers were the offensive stars with 14, 12, and 11 markers. Basketball tournaments sometimes bring out the best of a team. This was the case in the Saturday night finals on February 22 at Floyd when Cartersville beat Pepperell 82–55. On this evening, the 18–4 Hurricanes roundball squad was uncommonly good at shooting 3-pointers (6), which enabled them to take control early and dominate. Winning coach Jesse Bonner said later, "We've never shot that well from the outside…It was the best game by far that we've played." In postseason accolades, Brandon Davis was named to the first-team all-area for 3 consecutive years; he would transfer in the summer. Honorable mention went to seniors Lee Morris and Royce Smith as well as Karla Blythe for the women's quintet.

1992–'93 Season

The Dragons improved to 2–1 on December 11 in a home game played at Floyd because of a "broken scoreboard" in the Russell Leonard Gym. We play well there normally, and Friday night was no exception as Coach Horne's crew won over Model 70–63 in overtime. The game seesawed back and forth most of the evening with the Devils leading 19–9 at first break; PHS countered to take a 31–29 advantage at intermission. The Blue forged back 45–39 at the end of 24 minutes. The visitors' Sedrick Askew put up a desperation buzzer-beater at the final horn to tie 61–61; the shot added 5 extra minutes to the game. Freshman Brian Smith scored 26 big points while brother Ike helped with 16; Germaine Roberts netted a dozen markers. The following Tuesday evening, December 15, home-standing Coosa downed the Gold and White 73–68. *News-Tribune* writer Jim Jaquish described the losers as "a bad cold that just wouldn't go away." Indeed, it took the Eagles hitting 17 of 23 charity shots to finally log the game in the win column. Brian Smith again led us in points with 22 while seniors Germaine Roberts and Jason Wilder contributed 14 and 10. In the first game, PHS Ladies led by 23–20 on a full-court pass and score by freshman Heather Jones as the half ended. However, the Lady Eagles went on a 12–3 run in the final stanza to win comfortably 54–41. Ninth graders Blythe and Jones scored a dozen points each for 0–4 Pepperell while another, Temeka Hayes, added 9. Coosa High coach Larry Bing played in his initial Christmas Tourney in 1965. He believed for the first time there was no great team or clear-cut favorite for the Gold Ball. The games began in 1954 and were known as Northwest Georgia Invitational Tournament. The 6 all-male squads began play at Rome's Memorial Gym on East Third where Lindale defeated Cave Spring 56–36 for the championship. Twenty-three years later in 1977, the ranks were opened to women with Model winning the championship. On December 18, Bing told the *News-Tribune,* "It's one of the best Christmas tournaments in the state I would think. We're very fortunate to be in it every year." In the men's first round on Saturday the nineteenth, eventual champion Rome held off the Dragons 55–47. Monday's second round saw Armuchee defeat Pepperell lassies 48–39. If we could have hit our foul shots, the score would have been reversed. We missed 14 of 17 in the first half, which included 12 of 13 in the second quarter. Junior Karla Blythe swished 12 markers while 2 freshmen, Heather Jones and Temeka Hayes, scored 12 and 11 points respectively. Brian

Smith ended 1992 by being named to the all-tournament team at Christmas. He picked up where he left off on Friday, January 8, in leading his squad to a 60–52 victory over host Trion. The big ninth grader "strutted his stuff" for 22 counters, claimed 17 missed shots, and blocked 5 shots for the 3–3 Dragons. On Tuesday night, January 12, Cartersville led our boys by 10 after 3 quarters of play. However, pressure defense and timely 3-pointers enabled the 'Canes to win going away 62–45. Brian Smith with 13 markers was our only double-figure scorer. Coach Horne said later, "I guess we're going to have nights like that." The Dragons would now face Haralson County on Friday evening, January 15 (a 61–38 loss), and Villa Rica (a 76–60 defeat) the next night. The Coosa Lady Eagles had not won since December 15 when they beat PHS by 13 markers. On Tuesday, January 19, they completed the sweep at Russell Leonard 46–38. Other than junior Karla Blythe's 20 points, the Gold and White struggled to score. No other Lindale player tallied more than 4 markers. Pepperell boys hosted number-five-ranked Coosa in the nightcap. The visitors went on an offensive explosion in the first half when they hit 20 of 31 shots. They used a half-court trap that made us play defensively when we had the ball. By period three, Larry Bing's Eagles led 61–28, yet we refused to quit and rallied to go on a 38–18 run down the stretch. Brian Smith netted 15 counters with sophomore Marcus Teems adding 11.

The boys next traveled to Polk County on January 29 where Rockmart pulled away in the last 2 minutes to defeat us 60–54. Senior Germaine Roberts and Brian Smith tallied 17 points each. The host Darlington girls edged us 39–36 on Tuesday, February 2. Actually both squads struggled to score the ball consistently; the final quarter saw 4–12 PHS net 4 points while the 7–8 Tigers could hit only 3. Blythe led Lindale with 16 markers; freshman Heather Jones was next with 9. The final 6:17 of the nightcap was kind to visiting Pepperell as they outscored Darlington 23–6 to win 68–56. We trailed most of the game until Roberts hit a bucket that started a 9-point surge; Brian Smith tallied 10 of his team-leading 20 counters during the run to victory. Clowers, Ike Smith, and McBurnett contributed 15, 13, and 10 markers respectively. In the Leonard Gym on February 9, Pepperell fell to Rockmart 71–64 in overtime. Although the Jackets won the game late at the foul line, Coach Horne said, "We were up 21–7, and they went on a 15–0 run on us. That was more important than the end." Brian Smith netted 30 points; he was supported by Clowers's 16 and Roberts with 11. The Lady Jackets outscored us 18–4 in the first stanza and won 56–36. Stacy Edwards and Renee Bailiff led PHS with 8 markers each. In a final regular season contest in Lindale, PHS girls downed Darlington 60–57 in overtime. The home team rallied for 19 points in the final 8 minutes to tie when Neely Snow connected on 2 free throws. In OT, Karla Blythe shot a 3-pointer with 5 seconds on the clock for the 3-point victory. The junior led our scoring with 14 markers followed by senior Amy Hale's 11. The boys completed the sweep with a 76–61 victory over the Tigers. Brian Smith swished the nets for 31, claimed 20 rebounds, and blocked 7 shots; his brother Ike finished with a dozen counters.

The Class 7-AA South tournament began at Floyd College on Tuesday, February 16. Villa Rica ended our year by converting Lady Dragon turnovers into layups for a 44–20 advantage at intermission en route to a convincing 70–44 win. Heather Jones and Temeka Hayes led us in the score book with 13 and 11 markers respectively. With the season over, senior Amy Hale reflected, "This year's team is one of the best that I have ever been on because even when we were behind no one gave up and everyone always played their best." In the 8:30 p.m. boys' game, "three times was the charm" for Pepperell. Twice we had lost to Rockmart, once last week in overtime. However, on this night, we held the serve 59–45. Coach Horne's crew limited RHS top scorer, Carlus Davis, to just 14 points while we moved ahead at the half 33–23. He thought, "We handled the ball against their pressure better this time around." It did not hurt that freshman Brian Smith tallied 31 points. On Thursday, February 18, Lindale lulled second-seeded 18-4 Cartersville to sleep in the first 16 minutes before "blowing them away" in the second half 57–50. The winning coach said later, "We came out and got our motor running a little after intermission." Indeed, PHS outscored them 18–4 in the third. In the waning moments of the final quarter, Brian Smith got a layup, and sophomore Chris McBurnett sank 2 free throws to ice the game. The Hurricanes boxed Smith in the first half, holding him to just 5 points; however, we beat them down the floor later, letting the big freshman explode for 24 total points. One night later, Haralson County lived up to their number nine state ranking by downing the upstart Dragons 69–50. They led at the end of one quarter 19–5 and just powered an inside game to victory. The winning coach Randy Patterson said later, "I thought it was the best overall game we have played in a while." Coach Horne thought, "They were huge compared to us." When the *RNT* all-area team was announced on April 11, Brian Smith was the only freshman. The paper called the 15-year-old a "phenom" averaging 21 points and hitting 50 percent of his shots from the post. Brian totaled 515 points and 389 rebounds during the season.

1993–'94 Season

The Dragons opened the new season in Russell Leonard Gym on Saturday night, December 4, with a nice 71–58 win over East Paulding High. Sophomore Brian Smith began where he left off last year by scoring 28 points and claiming 14 rebounds; teammate Micah Smith pitched in with 20 counters. Three nights later, we dispatched visiting Villa Rica 49–42. The opponent's game plan was to take away the post play of the Smith boys. However, the tenth grader Brian hit for 22 markers while the senior Mike added 12 to the score book; Darrell Clowers was also in double figures with 11 markers. Coach Horne said afterward, "We stood around a lot in the first half." He solved that by pressing the Wildcats into errors that led to 14 unanswered points in quarter four. Home-standing Calhoun had an easy time on Saturday, December 11, in downing previously unbeaten Pepperell 64–43. The Jackets men took an early lead in the first and never looked back. Brian Smith again led us in scoring with 12 buckets. In the opener, CHS girls took a 19–6 lead at the end of 8 minutes and never looked back in winning 49–42. Keisha Watkins led the Lady Dragons with 15 points. On Tuesday, Valentine's Day, Coosa won 64–58 by understanding Brian Smith would get his usual points (30 tonight) while the visiting Eagles concentrated on balanced scoring from their starting 5. It worked, for they had 3 players who tallied 15 points or more. Coach Horne thought, "The jury's still out on us...we don't do the little things it takes to win in our league." Both teams would play next week in the Holiday Festival. In Bartow County on Friday, December 10, junior Mardis Teems sank a 3-pointer at the buzzer in the second overtime to defeat host Cartersville 55–52. The home team led narrowly most of the game before Pepperell edged ahead by 3 with seconds left in regulation; however, Neon Winters nailed a trey as time expired to send the game into OT. It was a wasted 3 minutes, for neither squad scored, forcing another extra period. We traded baskets with them until Teems hit his game winner. Brian Smith tallied 17 markers with 10 rebounds; Darrell Clowers pitched in with 14 while Mardis added a dozen to the score book. The following Friday, our men began play in the opening nightcap of the Christmas Tourney, December 17. We won over Armuchee 65–52 when guard Mardis Teems "stepped up" with 27 big points. Opponents had packed the post to stop Brian Smith, which left our perimeter unguarded. Although both teams had suffered from lack of practice due to football playoffs, the Dragons shot better, and their press bothered the losers. One day later at 4:00 p.m., Steve Turner's Lady Indians eliminated Pepperell 56–33 using good outside shooting. Chattooga moved to a 32–18 halftime lead and maintained control. Heather Jones's led 1–5 PHS in scoring with 9 points. The boys played in their second game of the event at 5:00 p.m. on Monday, December 20, versus Cedartown. We led by 7 with 3:01 remaining in the third but got outscored by 12–2 in the next 6 minutes and lost by a single bucket 60–58. The 4–3 Dragons "had lots of chances in the final stanza but we fumbled the ball around," said Steve Horne afterward. In the new year, PHS boys claimed a 61–56 victory over Model by limiting their guards' point output to 25 markers. Meanwhile, Brian Smith collected 25 counters. *Rome News-Tribune* sportswriter Jay Stone witnessed the contest and described a fourth-quarter play by Pepperell's 6-foot-2, 230-pound 15-year-old phenom: "Brian steals, drives the right side of the lane. Two Model defenders slide step so as to cut off the right-handed drive. Smith, already in the air simply changes hands and softly drops in a running left-handed jumper." The big sophomore said later, "I've been working on that shot." He had become especially productive now that Jeff Hunnicutt and Mardis Teems had stepped up their outside shooting. Losing coach Milt Travis thought the winners "out-executed" them. In Haralson County on January 14, the Dragons won 55–48 behind Smith's 19 points and 13 rebounds. Jeff Hunnicutt netted 12 markers, all coming from long range. Saturday night in Gordon County was always an exciting time to play roundball; to wit, Brian Smith got his usual 22 points against 9–6 Calhoun, but it was Corey Rhodes who provided heroics. The sophomore hit a driving layup that rolled around the rim before falling home as time expired, giving 9–3 PHS a 56–54 over the Jackets. Another tenth grader, Jeff Hunnicutt, provided support for the other 2 with 12 points. In the opener, Pepperell ladies raced to an early 15–1 lead before withstanding a mid-game rally by the home squad. Sophomore guard Kisha Watkins scored a quick 8 markers of her 25 total and proved to be a problem for CHS. Her tenth-grade teammate Temeka Hayes hit for a dozen in support as we eventually closed out the contest with a 63–48 victory. On Friday, February 4, in the Leonard versus Cartersville, Kesha Watkins scored 17 points, and Leah Purcell pitched in 9, but it was not enough to offset Cartersville's offensive power. They averaged 20 markers per quarter in an 84–37 win over the home squad.

The boys' nightcap decided the top seed in Region 7-AA tournament. The Hurricanes won a nail-biter 46–43 when sophomore guard Neon Winters sank a 22-footer with 33 seconds left. We called time-out but could not get off a good shot. Previously at the end of the third, Winters's desperation half-court heave banked in to give them a 34–33 advantage. However, 1 official waved it off, but the other ruled differently. Coach Horne said the shot was decisive in the eventual outcome. Brian Smith netted 27 points but received little help from his teammates. The Dragons ended the night at 10–6 overall. In the opening round of the South tourney at

Floyd College played on Monday February 14, the Villa Rica ladies held off a late charge by Pepperell to win 50–41. Three long-range 3-pointers helped the Wildcats hold the lead and victory. Freshman point guard Kisha Watkins led us in the last game of the season with 21 points; senior Karla Blythe followed closely with 18. The boys' year ended also with a 49–44 semifinal loss to Haralson County on Wednesday, February 16. A tough box-and-one did not stop Brian Smith but limited his points to 16 counters. Senior and front-court teammate Mike Smith was missing due to a broken hand suffered in PE class hours before tip-off. A philosophical Steve Horne said later, "One guy getting hurt shouldn't make you lose." After the Rebels took a 38–27 lead into final stanza, we cut the margin to 5 with 2:11 remaining but could get no closer. On Sunday, March 20, the *Rome News-Tribune* named Brian Smith Area Player of the Year. Ninth grader Kisha Watkins was named to first team on the ladies' all-area squad.

1994–'95 Season

The *Rome News-Tribune* Holiday Festival tourney pairings were announced on Sunday, December 16. All games would again take place at Floyd College gym. The Lady Dragons would initiate play versus Model at 4:00 p.m. on Monday the nineteenth. The Pepperell boys would face Rome in the following contest. However, in regular season games on Friday, December 9, the Lady Dragons hosted Adairsville and won 58–49. Our 2–0 girls led 29–17 at intermission and extended that to 42–22 in the third. The Lady Tigers committed 27 turnovers which led to their downfall. Winning coach Beth Wade commended the defensive execution of sophomore guard Kisha Watkins who also scored 16 markers. In the nightcap at Russell Leonard Memorial Gymnasium, the men "thrashed" visiting Rome 62–39. Junior center Brian Smith collected 27 points, 15 rebounds, and blocked 6 shots. Steve Horne said later, "We probably have a lot of football in us but the intensity was there all the time." In the Leonard again on Tuesday the thirteenth, PHS battled 2-time region champ Coosa on even terms for the first 20 minutes before they turned the game into a full-court affair and out-quicked their host. A 13–0 run led to a 71–55 win. Brian Smith ended the contest with 27 points. In the opener, the Lady Dragons worked the inside/outside game with Hayes and Watkins to win 59–47. The former netted 17 markers while the latter hit long shots for 16. We closed the game out with 10 straight counters. Friday night December 16 was typical Pepperell versus Cartersville. The 'Canes surged ahead by as many as 8 points in the third quarter; then with 6:10 remaining, the turning point occurred. Sportswriter Scott Chancey described it, "Smith went inside, and missed and rebounded four consecutive shots on one possession and finally put in the fifth one being fouled in the process." He sank both charities plus a technical that were assessed to an opposing player. Cartersville never recovered. Coach Horne thought that sequence got his team's "motor" running. Outside shooting had kept us game close until Brian Smith went inside and scored the next 7 markers to take the lead at 34–32. The Lady 'Canes opened play earlier in the evening and scored a 55–45 victory over Lindale. They ran out to a 16–3 lead before we recovered somewhat. However, the 3–2 Pepperell squad who played without ailing point guard Kisha Watkins struggled to stop the opponent's outside 3-point shooting.

The opening round of the forty-second annual chase for the Gold Ball was not kind to PHS. Model knew Dragon point guard Kisha Watkins was not at full strength; therefore, they began the game in a full-court press. The result was a 21–0 lead in the first 7 minutes and a 62–32 victory. Coach Beth Wade said truthfully, "We just didn't play very well." The ensuing game against Rome men was not much better. The talented Wolves outmanned us 75–45. Brian Smith managed 17 points while Desmond Irvin bucketed 14 for Pepperell. The first game of the new year was a low-scoring affair won by Chattooga 37–30. The Indians slowed play down and executed team defense to raise their record to 3–6. Brian Smith scored his usual 20 markers, but the others did not hit their wide-open shots. In the opener, very good post play led to a 52–45 victory. Leah Purcell tallied 18 counters to go with a remarkable 20 rebounds. PHS guard Kisha Watkins helped out with 14 points. On Tuesday, January 11, Adairsville outscored the Dragons 16–3 in the second 8-minute period and limited the visitors to only 9 points in the first half. Brian Smith was held to single digits for the first time in his career; however, Kenneth Davenport and Joey Shiflett added 14 and 10 counters to our cause. But it was good news in the opener as the Lady Dragons moved above .500 in the win column at 5–4. We led 36–22 at intermission thanks to Kisha Watkins's 15 and Misty Allen's 10 markers. "We needed a win," Beth Wade said later. We did not get a win the next night out, for Model whipped us 77–47. Granted they were the number-three-state-ranked women's squad in Class A. The winners put 4 players in double figures; however, PHS guard Kisha Watkins led all scorers with 21 markers. At Coosa on Friday the thirteenth, PHS ladies won big 72–30, which improved their record to 6–4. We held the lead for 32 minutes with junior Meg Martin hitting for a team-high 12 markers; Leah Purcell added 10 points. Sports editor Jim O'Hara thought the winning coach (Bing) was upset and the losing mentor (Horne) was relaxed and talked about how hard his team had played. Although Larry Bing won 72–65, he said later, "If we keep making bad decisions and playing 'Hollywood' basketball, the future is not good." A botched pass off the backboard and technical foul for hanging on the rim brought about his ire. Steve Horne said his crew must play all out in order to win because "We've got some good athletes, but they aren't basketball players." Smith tallied 24 points, and Desmond Irvin, 21, and Jeff Hunnicutt canned 10 in the losing cause. On Tuesday night, January 17, the 12–4 Dade County boys handed us a 61–38 loss. We trailed 31–19 at intermission and "every now and then there were some bright moments." Brian Smith tallied 19 markers for Lindale. Chattooga men scored the winning basket with 30 seconds remaining to win 62–60 on Tuesday, January 24. We had a last shot to tie but missed. Kenneth Davenport led 3–11 Pepperell with 19 markers. In the first game, the Lady Indians overcame a 13-point lead entering the final 8 minutes to win 55–47; they did it by outscoring the Dragons 28–8 in quarter four. Kisha Watkins and Temeka Hayes led us with 13 and 10 points respectively. The women rebounded on Friday night the 27th, winning 67–54 at the Leonard versus Darlington. The Lakesiders fought back from a 54–28 deficit but could not overcome sophomore post Misty Allen's 21 points or Leah Purcell's 13. The winners were now 7–8 overall on the year and 4–3 in region. In the nightcap, a very good Tiger squad (12–5) led our boys 39–32 at intermission before Brian Smith led a 13-point surge that put us ahead 45–39. But the visitors regained control later and won 65–60. At Cartersville on the last day of January, the Lady Hurricanes bombed the nets for 10 treys and won easily 89–56. Pepperell was led in scoring by Leah Purcell's 17 markers. On Friday night, February 3, Model's ladies came to the Leonard and showed why they were considered one of the top squads in Georgia. They led 37–20 at the half and won 59–34. Coach Andy Akin was very pleased with his defense that caused 29 Dragon turnovers. The host team struggled to get the ball into the post and with good shot selection outside. Leah Purcell was top for PHS with 12 points followed by Kisha Watkins with 10. In the nightcap contest, the Blue Devils hit 7 treys in the first half and won 51–44. Kenneth Davenport and Brian Smith led us in the score book with 17 and 10 counters respectively. Both Pepperell squads visited Darlington on Tuesday, February 7. With 6:51 remaining in the opening game, Lindale trailed 54–42. After a Coach Beth Wade time-out, the visitors began to solve the opponent's pressing defense, which turned into some easy baskets. Pepperell sophomore Shauna Cox put her team up 57–56 at 2:01 mark with a short jumper. With 40 seconds left, Misty Allen took "a pass inside from Kisha Watkins and scored the go-ahead basket" for a very satisfying 62–60 victory. Cox led us in the score book with 19 markers followed by Allen's 10. Coach Wade's squad was now 8–10 but more importantly 5–4 in region. In the nightcap, our boys did not fare as well, losing 88–64. Opposing coach Jim Van Es thought the opponent had a good plan by sinking back into a tight zone and forcing outside shots. The Tigers took advantage by speeding up the game and scoring from the perimeter. Coach Horne said later, "They've got a good team…we helped them out a little bit." Freshman Joey Shiflett came off the bench to lead us in scoring with 17 markers, which included 3 treys. Sophomores Smith and Hunnicutt added 16 and 10 respectively.

Valentine's Day was not kind to Pepperell basketballers. In Region 7-AA play at Floyd gym on Tuesday, Darlington eliminated our ladies from competition 55–54. We led narrowly 21–17 at intermission before the Lady Tigers' Anna Huffman hit 7 of 9 shots in the second half to lead the victory. Dragon Leah Purcell led all scorers with 20 points. On the same night, Darlington ended our boys' season, 51–49, despite junior Jeff Hunnicutt's 18 points; his treys and foul shots kept us either ahead or close the entire contest. The seesaw battle culminated with Justin Allen's charity shot at the 26 mark that pulled us within 2 markers. Then Pepperell had the ball with a chance to tie or better but could not get a shot off. On Sunday, March 26, the *RNT* announced All-Area teams. For the women, 5-foot-10 junior Leah Purcell was first team; sophomore Kisha Watkins received Honorable Mention. Brian Smith was named first team with 17.2 points per game and 14.2 rebounds. The eleventh grader was already Pepperell's all-time leading scorer with 1,268 counters and has claimed 917 missed shots.

1995–'96 Season

On Tuesday, December 5, Pepperell boys hosted Trion in the Leonard's first high school game of the season. Unfortunately, the Bulldogs took a 10-point lead at the break and eventually won 51–40. Brian Smith scored over half of our points with 22 markers; PHS hit only 13 shots from the floor. Seven nights later, the Dragons downed Calhoun men 64–51 for our first win of the year. Smith and Fred Collins led us with 18 and 10 markers. The former also added 10 rebounds and 6 blocked shots. On Saturday evening the sixteenth, Coach Horne's crews won a big game against visiting Model 56–41. The first 2 quarters were close until the Gold and White outscored them 13–4 in the third stanza. Rebounding was the difference as

Smith collected 14 while Joey Shiflett claimed a dozen. In the opening game, the Blue Devil women took a 29–12 advantage at the end of 16 minutes and never looked back, winning 63–30. The 2–3 Lady Dragons were led by Kisha Watkins's 12 counters. At 5:30 p.m. on Monday, December 18, Pepperell opened the forty-second annual Christmas Tourney by downing outmanned Rockmart boys 69–53 in Floyd College gym. Brian Smith scored 23 points while Fred Collins and Joey Shiflett added 9 each. We have now evened our record at 3–3. The girls began Wednesday's play at 4:00 p.m. versus Rome High, a previous winner over Coosa. In a "sloppy, mistake-filled game" the Lady Wolves eked out a narrow 44–42 victory. Pepperell (2–3) fell behind 38–39 at the end of 3 quarters; however, we rallied to narrow the gap to 2 points and had a chance to win if Casey Bright's shot with 5 seconds had fallen through the hoop. In the final game of the evening, Chattooga fought back from a 19-point deficit in the third period to win 55–54 on a last-second shot in overtime. Pepperell led 30–14 at the break, but the Indians went on a 13–0 run late in the third. Coach Horne explained the loss, "We missed a lot of easy shots, free throws and layups." Brian Smith garnered 20 counters while Desmond Irvin contributed 14. For the fourth consecutive year, Brian was named to the all-tourney squad. In the first game of 1996, January 5, host Model defeated us 46–38. The Devils corralled 33 missed shots which contributed to the victory. The Dragons again did not shoot well either from the field (at one point, we went 11 minutes without a field goal) or the foul line. Brian tallied 15 markers while Irvin added 10. Despite his team defeating Pepperell 62–58 on January 12 in the Russell Leonard Memorial Gymnasium, Coosa coach Larry Bing thought, "We were trying not to lose, instead of trying to win." His undefeated squad led 52–39 going into the final stanza; however, in a comeback long remembered in Lindale, Jeff Hunnicutt drained a 3-pointer with 3:42 left to make the score 56–55. But a strong rebound and putback plus 2 foul shots gave the Eagles their fifteenth victory. Jeff netted 17 markers while Brian hit for 16. The Lady Dragons took the opener 59–54 over Coosa; we went on a 20–7 run in the third period to pull away for a Region 7-AA North victory. Senior CaSandra Shedd led us with 15 counters; Kisha Watkins and Meg Martin added 10 and 9 respectively. At Darlington on the nineteenth, Tommy Atha's 4–8 girls nipped Pepperell 51–48; PHS could not stop Anna Huffman who swished 27 markers. Leah Purcell led Lindale with 17 points. But Dragon men won the nightcap 62–56 using a 22–16 run in the second quarter; Brian Smith scored 15 counters while Fred Collins and Desmond Irvin pitched in with 11 each. Host Chattooga edged our girls 50–48 on Tuesday the twenty-third. The Lady Indians pulled away with an 8-point run in the final 8 minutes. Kisha Watkins and Leah Purcell were top scorers for PHS with 20 and 10 counters. Summerville won the boys' nightcap 75–58 by placing 4 players in double figures. Smith and Shiflett paced Lindale with 13 points each. In Cartersville on Friday night, January 26, Brian Smith brought his "A game." The big senior swished 24 points, which included 8 for 8 at the charity stripe in the final quarter, to upset the number-ten-ranked Purple Hurricanes 54–47; PHS sophomore Joey Shiflett contributed 11 markers. In the earlier girls' game, the host team overcame a three-point lead late to defeat the Lady Dragons 52–47. Leah Purcell led us in the score book with 14 counters. Darlington came visiting the Leonard on Friday, February 2, and left with a 57–42 victory. Host Pepperell came out with a flourish, but "sloppy" play and poor shooting spelled defeat. Yet it did not help that our two best players, Hunnicutt and Smith, played little in the second half because of foul trouble. Despite that, the two led us in scoring with 10 and 8 respectively. The Lady Dragons gained a bit of revenge by slamming the Lakesiders 54–27. Senior guard Kisha Watkins swished 9 of 12 charity shots to go with her 16-point total; twelfth graders Leah Purcell and Heather Jones added 13 and 10 to our cause. At Floyd College in the Region 7-AA North playoff on Monday, February 12, Brian Smith and Jeff Hunnicutt scored 20 and 18 points respectively to lead their team. Yet it was not enough to extend their PHS basketball careers, for Dade County won 73–61. Our girls defeated Chattooga 61–43 behind Meg Martin and Leah Purcell who scored 12 points each. The contest was tied 18–18 at the break; however, the Lady Dragons raced out to a comfortable lead and victory. Two nights later, we played the best team in Class AA; Dade County girls had little trouble with us in winning 74–45. They tallied the first 15 points and led 38–24 at intermission. Kisha Watkins finished her Pepperell career with a team leading 17 points. In late March, Brian Smith was recognized as all-area for the fourth consecutive year; joining him on the list was Lady Dragon Kisha Watkins.

1996–'97 Season

Pepperell boys opened the season with 2 consecutive losses, 1 of which was a 71–38 deficit to Calhoun. In the Leonard on Tuesday, December 10, CHS outscored us 20–5 in quarter two, and we never recovered; Desmond Irvin and Drew Talor had 8 points each. The evening's opening game saw Lady Jackets outscore us 16–6 in period three to "put the game away" 59–40. Pepperell's Summer Davis led all point makers with 14 counters. Before downing Region 6-AA Dade County 65–46 on Friday, December 13, we actually trailed by 1 point at intermission but "outnumbered" the Wolverines 38–18 in quarters three and four. Senior Matt Kerce led balanced scoring with 13 markers followed by Collins, Cochran, and Shiflett with 11, 9, and 7 counters. On Tuesday the seventeenth, winless Cedartown boys upset us 56–53 in the first round of the *Rome News-Tribune* Holiday Festival. With 3 minutes remaining, the Bulldogs led 56–44; at that point, PHS hit a trio of treys to cut the lead to 3 points; however, 3 beyond-the-line shots failed. Coach Horne said afterward, "We got some good looks at it, we just didn't make it." Kerce and Shiflett led Pepperell with 13 and 10 points respectively. The Lady Dragons fared much better versus Chattooga on Thursday the nineteenth as they "punched their ticket" to the final 4 with a 43–39 victory. Although we never trailed after a 10–2 run in the first period, the Lady Indians took advantage of a Kisha Watkins ankle injury with 4:33 remaining to narrow their deficit to only 1 bucket with under 1 minute left. But the free throw line was kind to us when sophomore Brandi Littlejohn sank a crucial shot with 7 seconds on the clock. In the third quarter, senior reserve Jessica Ayer scored all 5 of her points to "put her team ahead for good." But sometimes victory spells defeat.

Two-time women's defending Christmas Tourney champion Model "jumped" out to a 42–14 lead at intermission and never looked back in winning 70–34. On Saturday night, senior Shauna Cox netted 7 points for PHS. On Monday afternoon the twenty-third, Rome's Region 7-AAA Lady Wolves defeated Pepperell 46–32 in the tourney's consolation game. Kisha Watkins "burned" the Romans for 17 points despite a lame ankle. On January 7, 1997, the visiting Lady Bulldogs from north Chattooga County beat Lindale girls 62–32. It was a history-making ninth straight win for the squad from Trion mill village. The third stanza was not kind to our girls with just 3 points put in the score book. Allison Modlin was high point for the losers with 9 markers. In the men's game, Bulldog John David Gable scored 31 points, but Dragon Drew Taylor almost matched that with 27 as PHS won 67–58; Ernie Moses added 12 to the victory. On Friday, January 10, host Chattooga defeated our men 88–53. They jumped us 21–10 in the first and led by 20 points at intermission. Kerce and Shiflett netted 17 and 13 counters to lead their squad. Adairsville came into the Russell Leonard Gym on the second Saturday of January sporting a 7-game win streak and led Pepperell 49–41 at the end of 3 periods. However, Coach Horne's crew closed it out with a 22–12 run to upset the visiting Tigers 63–61. We did it at the charity stripe, hitting 12 of 15 in the last 8 minutes. Taylor and Shiflett led us in scoring with 18 and 16. The Cartersville basketball teams swept visiting Pepperell on Tuesday, January 14; the girls lost 61–35 mostly because we went 17 playing minutes with a field goal. Allison Medlin scored 9 markers. The men did not fare much better, losing in a blowout 90–37 in which Matt Kerce was high-point man with 7 counters. At the Leonard on Friday the seventeenth, Desmond Irvin sank 2 charity shots with 10 seconds left, and the Dragons won by 2, 58–56, over LaFayette's Ramblers. Ernie Moses was high-point man for us with 15 while Matt Kerce contributed 13; reserve Zach Battles claimed 10 big rebounds in the victory. The 5–8 Dragon men came back on the twenty-first and defeated Haralson County 63–52; Drew Taylor and Desmond Irvin led us with 12 and 11 points respectively. On the twenty-fourth in Dade County, Pepperell boys struggled in the first and third quarters but played great in the second stanza by blitzing the Wolverines 27–6; we took a 35–18 lead into intermission and won in a tough venue 56–48. Irvin and Moses led their team with 16 and 13 markers. The 17–1 Coosa High School boys completed a 2-game sweep of Pepperell boys on Tuesday, January 28, in Lindale with a 73–43 victory. They had downed us the previous Saturday night on Alabama Road. Coach Horne said of the Eagles, "They just played well in every phase of the game. They're a little better than us." Matt Kerce led PHS with 14 counters; Joey Shiflett contributed 11. On the same night (Saturday), Kisha Watkins buried 2 free throws with 4 seconds left to defeat the Lady Eagles. However, in the return match (Tuesday) in Lindale, Coosa girls got revenge 48–38. They did it by holding Watkins scoreless; in addition, none of her teammates broke double figures. But Kisha's off night motivated her to rebound with 20 points in Pepperell's 57–43 win over visiting Chattooga women on the last day of January. Her coach, Beth Wade, said of the senior who averaged 17 points per contest, "She does a lot of things for us…drives the ball well, passes well, shoots well." Truth was as Kisha went, so did the Pepperell girls team. There was help on the thirty-first as Allison Modlin and Carabeth Battles netted 14 and 12 markers in support. In the nightcap game, Drew Taylor and Joey Shiflett used inside play to tally 16 and 14 counters in the 75–49 victory over the Indians. The pair also claimed 24 boards between them. However, it was Matt Kerce who topped the scoreboard with 18 markers. The first time PHS boys played Cartersville, we scored only 37 points in a "lopsided" loss. In the return match on Tuesday, February 4, we netted 37 again but lost narrowly to the visitors 41–37. Coach Horne thought we played hard and executed superbly on defense, yet we were a little "tight" on offense. Joey Shiflett carried most of the shooting load with 16 counters. In the first game of the evening, our girls led 33–28 going into period four, but the Hurricanes went on a 9–0 run to win 47–44. Alison Modlin led us in scoring with 17 markers while Kisha added 13.

High school basketball (Region 6-AA tournament) arrived on the Oostanaula River in downtown Rome on Tuesday, February 11, 1997. The multipurpose forum arena was very kind to Chattooga, for they won a doubleheader versus Pepperell. First, in a competitive battle, the Lady Indians won in overtime 62–55. Kisha Watkins forced the extra period by sinking 2 foul shots with 6 seconds remaining in regulation. Unfortunately, CHS outscored us 11–4 in the 4 minutes of free basketball. Although Ms. Watkins fouled out right off in OT, she ended her career at Pepperell in style by hitting the nets for 31 big points. Coach Wade's crew ended their year at 8–14. In the second contest, Chattooga held us to 8 fourth-quarter points in winning 54–48. Coach Horne thought we played well enough on defense but could not get a "spurt" on the other end. Seniors Drew Taylor and Desmond Irvin finished their playing time for the Gold and White, netting 14 and 12 counters respectively. When the all-area team was announced on March 30, Kisha was again named first team. Honorable mention went to Allison Modlin for the Lady Dragons while Joey Shiflett represented the men.

1997–'98 Season

Not many freshmen girls can start on a high school varsity squad; Pepperell's Trina Bright was an exception. The youngster was also our leading scorer with 10 points in a 67–45 loss to host Calhoun on December 9. Former Dragon Tommy Swanson's Lady Jackets improved to 4–0 with the non-region win. The following week, local teams would vie for the forty-fourth Gold Ball presented to winners of the yearly Christmas Tourney. Coosa and Rome were considered favorites among the 10 contestants in the men's bracket; Armuchee or Model were the choices in women's play of this annual event sponsored by *Rome News-Tribune*. Our teams would play back-to-back games on Friday, December 19, at Floyd College gym with the girls beginning at 4:00 p.m. versus Coosa; the men followed against Adairsville. Coach Cindy Moore's 4–4 Eagles had little trouble with her alma mater, winning 57–25; our Lady Dragons did not make an outside shot the entire game due to a swarming defense. Although they were 0–5, 2 starters are out with injuries and sickness.

Basketball is a shooting sport, which makes it difficult for several of our athletes who had been in the state football playoffs; consequently, Pepperell managed 6 points in the first period while Adairsville netted 26 en route to a 72–45 victory. Coach Horne said later, "They looked like they were nervous and it showed on the scoreboard." Pedro Holiday, Greg Hunnicutt, and Eric Tant scored 8 points each. By Tuesday the twenty-third, all results were in, and the prognosticators were correct as "Rome, Model reign again." We found our touch from the field in Trenton on Tuesday, January 6; Lee Mitchell, Taft Cochran, and Joey Shiflett combined for 42 points in a 56–52 victory over Dade County. Our first win of the season was due to outscoring the Wolverines 18–12 in the final 8 minutes. The girls were not as fortunate in Northwest Georgia, for the home squad won easily 78–36. Carabeth Battles led us with 21 markers. Friday night, December 9, saw our home-standing girls win their first game 47–42. Chattooga tied the contest at 37–37 with 2 late foul shots to force overtime. In extra time, senior Mary Katherine Kuss hit a 3-pointer, and freshman Trina Bright sank 4 consecutive free throws to seal the victory. Not lost on the home crowd were Carabeth Battles's 17 markers. The next night (Saturday) in Trion, the host Bulldogs broke a 4-game losing streak with a 69–30 victory over Lindale; Carabeth Battles netted 11 counters for us. We kept the game close with visiting Cartersville boys on Tuesday, January 13, but faded in the final quarter before losing 45–30. Joey Shiflett led us with 10 markers. In the opening contest against the Lady 'Canes, sophomore Crystal Turner scored 11 points in a 55–49 region loss. In LaFayette on Friday, January 16, Carabeth Battles netted 17 points to lead Pepperell over the Lady Ramblers 52–44. Coach Brian Henderson described the "battle" as probably our best game of the year. In the nightcap, our men were not as fortunate, losing 61–51; Joey Shiflett scored 14 counters. Greg Hunnicutt was next at 11 while Taft Cochran and Lee Mitchell added 10 each. Haralson County girls came to Lindale on January 20 ranked tenth in Class AA with a 15–2 record while the Pepperell Lady Dragons were 2–10. Yet with 9 seconds left, PHS had the lead and possession until a turnover and a layup by a Lady Rebel gave them a 1-point lead and victory. A deflated Coach Henderson said afterward, "We were sick when it was over." Crystal Turner tallied 18 points while Carabeth Battle and Brandi Littlejohn contributed 12 and 10 respectively. The Rebels completed the road sweep by defeating our men 64–50; Cochran and Hunnicutt both scored a dozen markers. Three nights later, Dade visited Lindale and took control of the girls' game with a 17–3 surge in the second period en route to a 52–24 victory. Trina Bright and Carabeth Battles led the Lady Dragons with 7 points each. In the men's game, PHS trailed by 1 going into the final period, but Dade outscored us 21–14 down the stretch in winning 55–47. Taft Cochran and Lee Mitchell led us in the score book with 12 and 10 markers. On Tuesday the twenty-seventh, Coosa girls reached the 10-win plateau for the first time since 1993 with a 60–40 victory over visiting Pepperell. Carabeth Battles again led us in counters with 13. The men lost on Alabama Road also; the Eagles remained undefeated in region play by downing us 62–45. They did it with a 17–3 run in period one followed by a 22–12 surge to start the second half. Greg Hunnicutt was the only Dragon in double figures with 10 markers. On Friday night (January 30), our boys had a chance to tie on a last shot in Summerville but failed, and we lost 85–82. Due to illness in his family, Coach Horne missed the encounter; however, Bo McKenzie who substituted was proud of the effort and composure of the squad. Greg Hunnicutt had 21 big points and 9 rebounds; Joey Shiflett tacked on 16 more while T. J. Wilson netted 14 to go with 10 assists. One night later (Saturday) in Tallapoosa, Lindale boys won 59–54 over Haralson County. Eleventh grader Hunnicutt continued his scoring pace with 17 points; Wilson and Cochran added 12 points each while Shiflett also netted 12 markers to go with his 10 rebounds. Wilson provided support with 8 assists and 5 steals. But the Dragon girls lost 69–54 to the Rebelettes; Battles led us with 18 points while Turner contributed 15 counters for 3–14 Pepperell. On February 6, the lady Lindaleans closed out a 4–15 regular season with a 49–47 Friday night victory over LaFayette in Russell Leonard Memorial Gymnasium. Carabeth Battles and Trina Bright swished 15 and 10 points respectively. The men from Walker County were another matter for they brought an 18–4 record to the court and improved that by 1 with a 58–34 victory. Sophomore Patrick Collum and junior Greg Hunnicutt led us with 7 counters each. At Shorter College gym on Tuesday, February 10, both the boys and girls lost in Region 6-AA tournament. A small opening crowd watched the 4:00 p.m. opener between Pepperell and

Chattooga; our Lady Dragons managed a 20–18 advantage at the half; however, the Chattooga girls went on a 13–4 run in quarter three to win comfortably 50–38. Freshman Trina Bright netted 14 points while junior Carabeth added 11. After the final horn, Coach Henderson told his squad they should start preparing for next year. In the nightcap (8:30 p.m.), our men played tough against LaFayette until the 6-minute mark of the final period; from that point on, the Ramblers pulled away with a 9–0 run and won 55–36. Coach Horne said later, "We played good defense, we just couldn't score enough to stay in the game." Senior Taft Cochran finished his career by nailing a trio of 3-point shots. The *Rome News-Tribune* all-area squad was announced on March 29; Carabeth Battles was recognized first team for the ladies while Trina Bright and Greg Hunnicutt were named honorable mention respectively.

1998–'99 Season

When the brackets were posted for the forty-fifth annual Christmas Tourney, Pepperell girls were scheduled to play Cedartown in Floyd College gym on Friday, December 18, at 7:00 p.m. The boys followed in the nightcap at 8:30 p.m. versus Darlington. Because of football playoffs, the Dragons men practiced only 4 times before tip-off; the Tigers went one further as they were missing 7 players who were performing the next night in Lincoln County for the Class A title. Coach Horne said, "We're used to limited gym time before roundball begins; in 1990 (state championship) we beat Brown High on Saturday night and suited up on Monday in shorts and sneakers against East Rome." Although our bunch was a little rusty, we still downed Darlington 57–41. Junior Patrick Collum scored 7 quick points in the first period to give us a lead we would not relinquish; Lee Mitchell netted 14 while Corey Hutchins added 10. The roster was 2 short, for Greg Hunnicutt was recovering from a football injury and Pedro Holiday was ailing.

In the 7:00 p.m. contest, Alison Modlin had a 16-point night as Lindale defeated Cedartown girls 46–38. Although our first victory of the year was termed as sloppy, Brian Henderson's crew took an early lead and made it stand up. Carabeth Battles hit 2 treys and went 4 for 4 at the charity stripe to log 14 markers for the victors. We moved on to a 4:00 p.m. Monday (December 21) meeting against Armuchee. Previously on December 8, the Lady Indians had downed us in a pretournament game 77–49. The North Floyd girls defeated us again 66–52; they jumped ahead 32–10 at the half before South Floyd fought back behind Littlejohn and Modlin's 8 points each in the third. The former finished with 13 while the latter added 12 to the score book. Carabeth Battles outpaced them both with 16 counters. Coach Henderson thought, "They didn't give us anything. I think we played real well." After dispatching Darlington, our boys advanced to the semifinals by winning over Chattooga 58–47. Coach Horne was very pleased with his kids who took advantage of their height to move ahead 32–21 at intermission. Our leading scorer was Patrick Collum followed by C. W. Brock and Lee Mitchell with 13 and 11 respectively. Assistant sports editor Rick Woodall of the *RNT* announced on Wednesday the twenty-third that "there's an undefeated boys basketball team in the finals of the *Rome News-Tribune* Holiday Festival and it's not defending champion Rome." He was referring to the 3–0 Dragon men. Their coach was optimistic about his talent level which had some height and athleticism; however, he was a realist. PHS had won the Gold Ball only twice, the first tourney in 1954 and later 1969. Truth be known, Coach Steve Horne thought, "If Rome plays their best game, we probably can't beat them; yet, you never know." And the Wolves played well and won easily 62–33. Nevertheless, the losing coach was proud of his crew for competing in the finals. In a cold Russell Leonard Gymnasium on Monday, January 4, Haralson County boys warmed up the 3-point line by sinking 11 treys which totaled half of their field goals. Coach Horne was not happy with the 59–41 loss, saying, "They are a good shooting squad but when you stand around and watch." Lee Mitchell was the only Dragon in double figures with 10 markers. The Haralson girls bolted to a 38–21 lead at intermission en route to a 76–55 victory over the 1-7 Lady Dragons. Senior Brandy Littlejohn led Lindale with 15 counters followed by sophomore Trina Bright's 12. The girls' record improved by 1 the following night (Tuesday, January 4) when they downed visiting LaFayette 58–47 in a warmer Leonard gym. Trina Bright and Alison Modlin both netted 15 points; the winners led 30–23 at the half and 40–33 at the end of 24 minutes. The PHS boys did not fare as well, losing 49–28 to the Ramblers. A bad third quarter put us too far behind; Lee Mitchell led in the score book with 10 markers. On Friday night the eighth in Dade County, the Lady Wolverines won out 58–49 over Lindale; we did outscore them 34–29 in the second half behind Alison Modlin's 15 counters. There was no score posted for the men's game on the above date. On Saturday night, January 9, the Pepperell men downed Armuchee 66–46 with Greg Hunnicutt swishing 18 points. Unfortunately, our girls were hammered in the opener 71–47; Armuchee was 10–0 and ranked eleventh in Georgia. Trina Bright was high point for PHS with 11. On Tuesday the twelfth, our girls led host Chattooga 24–18 at the half and 34–26 with 1 quarter left to play; however, the Lady Indians outscored us by a dozen points in the final period resulting in a 55–51 loss. Alison Modlin tallied 20 markers; Trina Bright, 11; and Brandi Littlejohn, 10. The Dragon men reversed the first game by outscoring the home team 16–10 in the last stanza to win 49–43. Greg Hunnicutt netted 13; Lee Mitchell, 9; and Corey Hutchins, 8, for the 5–4 boys. On Friday the fifteenth, Cedartown put 4 players in double figures to defeat visiting PHS 64–55; C. W. Brock led us with 12 counters followed by Hunnicutt and Mitchell's 11 and 10. The Lady Bulldogs completed the 2-game sweep 72–59; Littlejohn, Battles, and Modlin finished with 17, 15, and 13 points respectively. At Trion on January 22, the Ladies eked by their hosts 57–56. Trina Bright tallied 13 markers for the winners. The Bulldog men fared better with a 62–56 victory over PHS; Lee Mitchell led 6–8 Pepperell with 19 counters. In Lindale on Tuesday, January 26, the Dragons jumped to a 27–10 advantage against Dade County and never looked back, winning 53–39; Patrick Collum netted 14 points while Hunnicutt and Hutchins each had 10. As the battle for region playoff slots continued, Pepperell downed visiting Chattooga 61–40; a third-quarter 16–6 surge made the difference. Although Coach Horne's squad was battling injuries and illness, Greg Hunnicutt and freshman Justin Bruce played strong along with sophomore C. W. Brock; the trio combined for 38 of our total points. In Lindale on Friday night, January 29, the Lady Dragons were "battling" for the last postseason slot; ultimately, the game came down to a 64–59 overtime victory versus Chattooga. On Sunday morning, sportswriter Scott Chancey wrote the headline, "BATTLES HELPS LIFT PEPPERELL PAST CHATTOOGA." Carabeth Battles claimed 17 rebounds and netted 15 points in the victory. Trina Bright helped a 19–11 advantage in the first period with 7 markers. Yet it was Battles who brought her team back in the final minutes with 7 markers to force a 53–53 tie at the end of regulation. Coach Henderson went to a 4-guard set, which opened up the inside game; Bright took advantage of this to score 6 of her 17 points in OT. On Tuesday, February 2, Cedartown girls made the playoffs for the first time since 1992 with a 68–53 victory over Pepperell. Battles and Littlejohn led us with 13 and 10 points respectively. In the nightcap, Polk County 'Dogs completed the sweep with a 59–49 victory; Corey Hutchins and C. W. Brock scored 13 and 10 markers. PHS sat at 8–10 for the season. The final 1999 home game, which was also senior night at Russell Leonard, had everything. "There were gutsy comebacks, thrilling last-second shots and great hustle from all." Only thing was Coosa girls won 59–55 in 2 overtimes. The Eagles led most of the way until Carabeth made a tying 3-pointer with less than 2 minutes to play. We almost won it at the end of the first OT; however, a last-second Coosa shot rolled around the rim and fell in to tie 48–48. The winners iced the game with 2 charity throws at the 22-second mark. Battles and Littlejohn tallied a dozen points each; Alison Modlin added 11. Before the boys' game, Coach Horne told his charges, "There's a huge crowd tonight to see you. If you can't play hard for them tonight, you never will." It was not close as we made a 15–2 run in the second period, played great defense, and rebounded strongly en route to a 59–30 win. Patrick Collum gave us 11 points off the bench, and C. W. Brock added 7. Senior Greg Hunnicutt finished with 13 markers. The victory earned a three seed in the region. Losing coach Bing said afterward, "It's not what we did or didn't do, they just outplayed us." In the Region 6-AA play-in game at Coosa on Monday, February 8, Chattooga girls came from behind to defeat Pepperell 50–47; PHS led by 7 going into the final quarter until the Lady Indians changed to man-to-man defense. With less than 2 minutes left, we missed a tying foul shot. On Tuesday, February 9, at Floyd gym, the Lindale boys needed a win over Central of Carroll to advance to state, but the Lions scored the first 8 points and were ahead 24–22 at intermission. Yet entering the final period, PHS led 37–35 before Central went on a 9–1 run to end our season with a 51–44 loss.

1999–'2000 Season

Coach Steve Horne began the new season against Cassville on Friday, December 3, with a roster that included 3 seniors, 5 juniors, 2 sophomores, and 2 freshmen. Although the Dragons were destined to finish as number two seed in Subregion 6-AA North, the 2–3 Cass Colonels defeated our boys 65–41. Coach Brian Henderson's rebuilding squad lost narrowly to the Lady Colonels 46–39. Kim Ball, Meredith Casey, and Crystal Turner were the only seniors. Other than a disappointing night at the foul line (11 of 28), Coach Horne was pleased with his varsity's 51–39 victory over host Armuchee on Tuesday, December 7. In the season's first win, PHS led 34–15 at intermission due to good passes into the post and lots of hands in the face of shooters. Corey Hutchins and Patrick Collum netted 20 and 12 points respectively. The home crowd in Russell Leonard Memorial Gymnasium got their money's worth on Friday night, December 10, as Trina Bright hit 2 foul shots with 1.5 seconds left to give the Lady Dragons a 36–35 victory over Cassville. The junior also led in scoring with 19 markers. In the nightcap after the crowd went outside for oxygen, a return trip was necessary because Pepperell's T. J. Wilson swished a 3-pointer at the buzzer, giving his team a dramatic 42–41 victory. Junior C. W. Brock led us with 14 points. The forty-fifth Christmas Tournament bracket was posted on the sixteenth by its sponsor *Rome News-Tribune*. There would be 20 high school coaches directing 215 players, competing for the Gold Ball. Our girls tipped off versus Coosa on Saturday the eighteenth at Floyd College and lost 51–39. Coach Henderson was pleased with the effort if not the outcome. Trina Bright and freshman Taryn Smith led us in points with 15 and 11. For the men playing on Tuesday the twenty-first, last year's all-tourney player Lee Mitchell tipped in a missed shot which keyed a 9–3 run in period three to put his team up 45–37 against a first-round-advancing Darlington squad. When the Tigers tried a comeback in the last quarter, Mitchell sank 8 straight foul shots to ice the game 56–50. Losing Coach Van Es cited Pepperell's 2-3 zone defense and his squad's lack of outside shooting for the loss. Two nights later in a game of runs, Coosa and PHS were tied at 41 with 6:18 left; unfortunately, the Eagles bucketed 11 markers in a row to eliminate us 61–46. Lee Mitchell continued his good play with 19 counters which included all 10 of his free throws; teammates Brock and Hutchins added 11 and 10 to the score book. Lindale did not play again until January 4 in LaFayette where the visiting boys won 58–48. In a good subregion victory, the Dragons outpaced Walker County's Ramblers 16–6 in quarter two; senior Lee Mitchell swished 21 markers followed by sophomore Justin Bruce's 13 and C. W. Brock's 10. In another region matchup at home on Friday the seventh, PHS won over Dade County boys 48–37. We went ahead in the second stanza with a 15–4 surge and controlled the contest thereafter. Senior Patrick Collum led us with 13 markers. In Summerville Tuesday night the eleventh, Brian Henderson's girls turned a single-point lead in period four into a 50–45 victory. Trina Bright topped our scorers with 17 points followed by Doran Mabry with a dozen. Although no final score was posted in *RNT*, we know the men lost their first subregion game to the Indians in the nightcap. Three nights later, Horne's Dragons rebounded big-time against visiting Cedartown; using an efficient inside and outside assault, we improved to 9–5 with the 62–36 victory. It was the Mitchell and Bruce show in the opening stanza which saw us bolt to a 22–6 lead; the former drilled treys while the latter scored 8 points while never straying more than 3 feet from the bucket. The Bulldogs helped out by hitting just 3 of 12 attempts in the first and never claimed an offensive rebound before intermission. The winners were led by Bruce with 15 counters; Mitchell and Hutchins added 13 and 12 to the cause. In a doubleheader played in Floyd College gym on Saturday night, January 15, the number-thirteen-ranked Calhoun girls defeated PHS 73–55. The 4–12 Lady Dragons put up a good fight until the visiting ladies outscored us 23–13 in quarter three; Trina Bright led us with 21 markers. Coach Ray Tucker's number-eleven-ranked men won easily 62–37 behind their best shooting accuracy of the year. Also they closed off our inside post game with deflected passes and untimely steals; however, insiders C. W. Brock and Collum totaled 28 points between them. On senior night, Friday, January 21, the Lady Dragons made a gutsy comeback against LaFayette before falling 52–51. We had a chance to tie only to miss a 3-pointer that was corralled and put back by Tara Alford as the horn sounded. Trina Bright netted 18 markers; Doran Mabry added 10. Appropriately, seniors T. J. Wilson, Lee Mitchell, and Patrick Collum scored 23 of our 28 markers in the second half to lead their team to a 53–40 victory over the visiting Ramblers. The win improved the total record at 10–7 to go with a 4–2 region mark. In Trenton on Tuesday, January 25, Horne's men outscored Dade 16–8 in the third stanza en route to a 50–43 victory. Other than poor foul shooting (7 of 23), our squad played well on the road; Patrick Collum and T. J. Wilson combined for 23 points to lead PHS. On Monday night the last day of January, leading scorer Trina Bright was in foul trouble; thankfully Doran Mabry stepped up with 17 big points to help her team win 49–35 over visiting Chattooga. Doran got help from Taryn Smith with 14 counters and sophomore Rebecca Alford's 15 rebounds. Coach Henderson's crew was now set for a subregion play-in game. Coach Horne's squad also won, but it took an overtime to settle the issue 67–61 in favor of the home team. We outscored Chattooga 10–4 in the extra period to improve to 12–7 on the year. C. W. Brock netted 24; Lee Mitchell added 18, and Patrick Collum swished 10. In the morning newspaper on Wednesday, February 2, PHS boys' coach Steve Horne commented after his team won 47–43, "It is always hard to beat Cedartown at home…We played better in the second half and had a little more than them tonight." Although we trailed by a single point going into the final stanza, our depth proved the difference as 4 Dragons scored in the last 8 minutes. C. W. Brock led us with 14 counters. The visiting girls suffered through a 57–28 loss to the Lady Bulldogs who had a dozen players score in 4 quarters; numerous turnovers led to our downfall. Senior night fans on the Alabama Road witnessed Coosa play "inspired" basketball, defeating Pepperell boys 68–49. The Friday night, February 4, win completed a 10–0 subregion sweep; PHS finished second with a 7–3 slate. The Eagles went ahead 15–5 in the first by playing an up-tempo game with crisp passes and effective shooting. The Dragons fought back in the third but the home squad answered with a 9–0 run to finish. The visiting crowd had one last cheer in the final minutes when 6-foot-2 junior Pedro Holiday "delivered a spectacular two-handed slam." In the earlier game, Cindy Moore's Coosa ladies rode a pair of "spurts" to a 58–47 victory that signaled her squad was reaching its peak at tournament time. On the opposite bench, Coach Brian Henderson's crew was led by Trina Bright's 19 points and Crystal Turner with 16; we would travel Monday night the seventh to LaFayette for subregion bracket play-in game. *Rome News-Tribune* reported on Tuesday morning that the game was a "play-out" contest for PHS as the Lady Ramblers defeated us 48–33. An "untimely offensive drought" in the third stanza turned a 17–17 halftime score into a 30–21 deficit, and we never recovered. The visitors finished the year with a 5–18 record; however, one highlight for the team was Trina Bright scoring her 300th career point. One day later at Floyd College, the Dragons were eliminated from subregion competition by Haralson County 47–35. Coach Horne had no qualms about how hard his squad fought; in the final quarter, PHS narrowed the lead to 38–35 before Haralson went on a 9–0 run to seal the win. But later he qualified the hustle evaluation with, "We just didn't make the shots from the outside." This was after the Rebels took star post player C. W. Brock out of the equation with a double team from start to finish which limited his points to 7 total. However, freshman Marcus Dixon did pick up some of the inside slack with 11 counters. Nevertheless, Pepperell ended the year with a respectable 13–9 record. When postseason accolades were announced by *RNT* on Sunday, February 2, Lee Mitchell, T. J. Wilson, and C. W. Brock were recognized as all-area honorable mention; the same honor went to Lady Dragons Trina Bright and Crystal Turner.

2000–'01 Season

New Lady Dragons head coach Jeff Rickman, who was a 1986 PHS letterman and graduate, worked on the women's game on Tuesday, November 14. In the Tiger Town Tip-Off Classic at Adairsville, Trion mentor Lamar Turner celebrated a forty-seventh birthday with an easy 76–40 victory over Lindale. They broke out to a 23–10 lead in the first and were never headed. Sophomore Taryn Smith led us with 12 points followed by Trina Bright's 10. At Gordon Central on Friday, December 1, the hosts used an 11-point run in the second half to defeat Pepperell 56–43. Taryn Smith again led us in markers with 14. Our boys shook off a bit of football-playoff syndrome but still lost 55–42 to the hometown Warriors. However, the winners had to overcome 21 points by C. W. Brock for the win. The next night (Saturday) in Walker County, Taryn Smith and junior Jesika Holloway scored 16 and 15 points in our 53–42 road win over the Lady Ramblers; we led comfortably at intermission 33–19. Pepperell boys did better than that with a 63–35 victory over host LaFayette. Senior Jarrett Gray netted 14 counters while Brock was close behind with 13; freshman Marcus Dixon had 11 for the 1–1 Dragons. In our home openers versus Forsyth Central, both contests went to overtime. Coach Rickman's crew came from 9 down in the fourth to send it into extra period before winning 70–63. Going into OT, Jeff told his crew, "We don't want to let this one get away." Taryn Smith and freshman Kasey Ramey teamed up for 10 of our 11 markers in OT. The former sank 20 points while the latter netted 19; Holloway added 10 to the score book, and junior Doran Mabry dished out 12 assists. The men tried to replicate their counterpart by coming back from a 10-point deficit to tie on a putback by Marcus Dixon with 2.1 seconds left; the freshman was fouled on the play, but the free throw rimmed out to force 5 extra minutes of play which led to a Forsyth 44–41 victory. Dixon, Josh Pilgrim, and Brock each scored 9 points.

On December 18, *Rome News-Tribune* printed brackets for the forty-seventh annual playing of the Christmas Tourney at Floyd College. Sixty-five-year-old Jack Pence was a Lindale Dragon in our first festival in 1954; this week he would referee several of the contests. He said there was a lot of prestige in being picked to officiate, and when not calling games he was an avid fan of the event. Some things had changed; more squads were involved now, and there were more spectators, but the enthusiasm remained the same. Back in the day, teams ran set plays, but now everything was so fast. Unfortunately, Pepperell boys were done in on the nineteenth when Darlington's Ryan Fox drained a trey at the buzzer. The opening-round loss sent us home for Christmas. At 4:00 p.m. on Wednesday the twentieth, Lindale girls upset the Lady Eagles 55–51 behind the "Holloway Festival" a.k.a. Jesika who scored 26 points, including all 15 of her team's counters in quarter three. With 5 minutes to play, we trailed 48–43 before Trina Bright rallied her team with short jumpers that closed out the game with a 6–0 run. Coach Rickman explained the significance of the action, saying, "This was the first time any of these girls have ever beaten Coosa." Cedartown High School moved to the finals of the tournament on Friday, December 22, by defeating the Lady Dragons 62–47. However, it was not easy for CHS as PHS cut a 13-point deficit in the third down to only a single basket. Alas, the Lady Bulldogs put the game away with a 10–0 run late. Nevertheless, Lindale lassies rebounded in the consolation game on Saturday the twenty-third with a convincing 76–53 victory over Adairsville. All-tournament player Holloway led the winners with 22 markers; Taryn Smith and Trina Bright added 16 and 14 respectively. The win was good enough for third place in the tourney. The Dragons began the 2001 new year with a nice 67–50 road win over Villa Rica on Friday the fifth; sophomore Josh Pilgrim and C. W. Brock swished 18 markers each in the Region 6-AAA affair. Marcus Dixon added 13 points. Our women hung with the Lady Wildcats until the second half when their hosts raced to a 42–27 lead. Trina Bright bucketed 17 counters while Holloway managed 13 in support. In the Russell Leonard Memorial Gym on Tuesday, December 9, Gold and White got 18 points from Jesika Holloway and 14 from Taryn Smith to defeat Black and Gold Carrollton 61–58. We followed that victory with a 54–48 loss to Cedartown because the winners outscored us 22–10 in the last quarter; Taryn Smith led 6–7 Lindale with 19 markers; Doran Mabry contributed 11. Visiting Hiram High School surprised the Lady Dragons 63–53 in the Leonard on January 16; they outscored the hosts 22–12 in the third to pull away. Holloway, Ramey, and Mabry swished 18, 16, and 11 points in the loss.

On Friday night, January 19, Rickman's crew almost upset Georgia's number-four-ranked Haralson County women; if not for a last shot that rolled off the Leonard Gymnasium rim, the game would have gone to extra innings. As it was, HC won 48–46. The Rebelettes led 6-AAA with a region slate of 6–0 and 13–2 total. The men's game was never in doubt after Pepperell bolted to a 16–7 lead in the first en route to a 60–47 victory. Josh Pilgrim was high point with 15 markers. Coach Steve Horne said later, "We were ready to play tonight…we are a good team when that happens, but if not, it's as bad as it gets." On Tuesday the twenty-third, it was host Pepperell, 62; Villa Rica, 54. Trina Bright, Kasey Ramsey, Jesika Holloway, and Taryn Smith combined for 54 counters; the ladies "exploded" for 20 fourth-quarter points for our seventh win. A nice road win in Carrollton occurred on Friday, January 26, when the Lady Dragons comfortably defeated Lady Trojans 58–44; Taryn Smith swished 20 points while Mabry and Holloway supported with 12 and 10 respectively. The South Floyd boys were starting to come together as we lifted our region slate to 5–4 with a 59–40 romp over visiting Cedartown. This coupled with our 65–61 overtime loss to number-ten-ranked Carrollton had raised team confidence. Coach Horne said the squad was shooting well, inside rebounding was better, and overall defense was improved. Against the Polk County Bulldogs on January 30, Josh Pilgrim followed his 14-point night against Carrollton with 11 markers; Justin Bruce netted the same number while Roderick Ware led a 12-point run for a 33–18 lead at intermission. On Tuesday, February 6, the Lindale Ladies traveled south on Highway 278 to Paulding County where they downed Hiram 71–59. Doran Mabry hit for 16 points while Holloway netted 11 in support; with the win, PHS improved to 9–12. A week later in the Region 6-AAA tourney on Hiram's court, Steve Horne's squad defeated Villa Rica, 56–53, to advance to the semis against Carrollton. Win or lose versus the Trojans, we were assured a state tournament berth. In the Villa game, we surged to a 33–19 advantage at intermission; C. W. Brock and Josh Pilgrim scored 14 and 9 points respectively. The Lady Dragons did not compete in the playoffs when it was discovered they used an ineligible player after Christmas.

There are two old roundball sayings that say, "It's not how you start but how you finish" and "Basketball is a tournament game." Adhering to those adages, Pepperell managed their biggest win of the year, downing number ten Carrollton 52–40 on February 15 in Hiram. PHS used an extended zone defense and accurate shooting to take a 1-point lead into quarter four; from there, we outscored the Black and Gold 19–10. Justin Bruce led the Dragons with 11 counters while Marcus Dixon pitched in 10. One night later on Friday the sixteenth, the Cinderella quintet from Floyd County was minutes away from a first-ever region championship before losing to

Central of Carrollton 45–42. The Lions led by 7 points entering the final period, and in order to protect that advantage, they spread the floor and slowed the pace to claim the 6-AAA tourney crown. For almost the entire season, Coach Horne's crew had not dressed all their starters at once because of injuries and football playoffs. That changed recently, resulting in victories over Villa Rica and Carrollton in addition to a narrow loss to Central in region finals. Number-three-seed Jackson County was next in line for our second-place squad. At 5:30 p.m. on Saturday, February 24, we tipped off in Jefferson, Georgia. The court is located northeast of Athens and 120 miles from Lindale. We trailed the Red, White, and Blue Panthers by a single point at intermission and 38–37 at the end of quarter three; until that time, C. W. Brock had kept us in contention with fine play. With 7:35 left in period four, Corey Hutchings scored on a follow-up; we never trailed again. When the hosts switched to man-to-man defense, we went inside to Justin Bruce, and the big center "gave us points each time." Seven clock minutes later, Josh Pilgrim sealed the win at the foul line with 2 free throws. C. W. Brock was team high with 11 counters followed by Bruce's 10; Pilgrim and Hutchins each added 8 to the score book. Twenty-three-year veteran Steve Horne said later, "By far we didn't play our best game, but we played hard all night long." In the North Sectionals "Sweet 16" inside Cobb Civic Center on Friday, March 2, perpetual state tournament team Gainesville employed a seldom-used outside game, pressure defense, intensity, and quick hands to stop Pepperell 72–41. The 24–6 Red Elephants led 34–18 at intermission and expanded it during the last 24 minutes. They allowed Brock and Bruce only 8 points between them by denying the ball inside. The 2000–'01 basketball squad started 1–4 and finished 10–13. When the all-area teams were announced on April 10, C. W. Brock was first team; Justin Bruce, Marcus Dixon, and Josh Pilgrim were tabbed for honorable mention. The PHS women honorees were Taryn Smith on second team; honorable mention accolades went to Trina Bright, Kasey Ramsey, and Doran Mabry. When the Mill closed on September 24, 2001, so did our story of PHS basketball.[174]

INTERSCHOLASTIC COMPETITION—BASEBALL

1952 Season

On Monday, April 9, 1951, the *News-Tribune* noted the inauguration of high school baseball in Lindale. Although the first full-fledged varsity baseball competition was a year away, Pepperell Junior High coaching staff was fast preparing in the spring of 1951. The squad, which was coached by James F. "Lefty" Murdock, was dealing with a freshman roster that initially listed 35 players, many of whom would become legendary at the new high school. On Monday, April 9, 1951, Lang Gammon featured in his "Lindale News" column that the staff would choose a starting lineup from the following prospects:

Catcher: Lloyd Allen, Beefy Teat, and Johnny Farr
Pitcher: Jimmy Green, Fireball Thompson, Bill Smith, Baltimore Smith
First base: Varnell Moore, Al Goss
Second base: Jack Carroll, Joe White
Shortstop: Ray Treglown
Third base: Baltimore Smith, J. W. Bennett
Outfield: Larry Lloyd, James Hopkins, Noonie Mathis, Bill Smith, Perry Farrer

On Tuesday, May 1, we downed visiting Aragon Junior High 15–2 behind the 2-hit pitching of Jerry Thompson. Teat batted 3 for 5 while Joe White went 2 for 2; Baltimore Smith and Lloyd

Allen "smacked homers for the Pepps." Model High School hosted and defeated our sophomores-to-be squad 12–3 on April 11. The schedule continued with a return match with the Blue Devils, a visit by McHenry varsity, in addition to Darlington and Rome JVs. The tradition and competitiveness of Lindale paid off when the Dragon 9 opened for business the following spring.

In their 8 years of existence, the 1969 New York Mets had never finished higher than ninth nor even had a winning season, yet they came on to win MLB's World Series over the Orioles. Two decades later, the 1990 Atlanta Braves finished last in the division but first in errors. One year later, they went from worst to first. Prior to the 1951–'52 school years, the Pepperell system operated as a junior high school only. Subsequently, students in grades 10 to 12 transferred to Rome High, McHenry, Cave Spring, or Darlington for graduation and to play varsity sports. In the spring of 1952, senior high baseball came to Lindale for the first time, and the squad delivered a State Class B championship to Park Street. With the passing of a half century, head coach and principal J. W. Sutton's first roster now reads like a Hall of Fame lineup: Baltimore Smith, Wallace Kelley, Jo Jo Stephens, Lloyd Allen, Bob Toole, Bud White, Ray Treglown, Varnell Moore, Perry Farrer, Clyde Boyd, Fireball Thompson, Jimmy Yarbrough, Melvin Mathis, Billy Teat, and Troy Coffia. Early on, Mr. Sutton prophesized his team, wearing gray with red caps, stockings, and lettering, "would cause someone plenty of trouble." From 32 preseason candidates, this group of 15 posted, according to the 1953 Dragon yearbook section on athletics, a regular season record of 24–7. This was followed by Georgia Class B competition, and then the squad qualified for all-class state championship series but lost to Richmond Academy; tournament play produced a 12–3 slate which brought our 1952 record to 36–10. Pitching mound aces Coffia (9–1) and White (8–2) led the way. Postseason accolades went to catcher Wallace Kelley who was chosen to play in the state all-star benefit game in Atlanta.

1952 Class B Georgia State Champions

First row—Jimmy Yarbrough, Jo Jo Stephens, Jerry Thompson, Lloyd Allen, and Clyde Boyd
Second row—Wallace Kelly, Varnell Moore, Beefy Teat, and Perry Farrer
Third row—Baltimore Smith, Bob Toole, Ray Treglown, Noonie Mathis, Bud White, and Troy Coffia

1953 Season

The decade of the Dragons continued in 1953. On Monday, March 16, two dozen prospects worked out for Coach J. W. Sutton. Ten steady veterans returned from last year's championship team including pitchers Troy Coffia, Bud White, and Jerry Thompson; infielders were Jo Jo Stephens, Baltimore Smith, and Varnell Moore. Beefy Teat, Perry Farrer, Bob Toole, and Jimmy Yarbrough would patrol the garden (outfield). Legion ball players would provide depth to the 12-man squad. It was almost May before the boys finally lost a contest, i.e., a Friday, April 24, 1-run loss to visiting Marietta Blue Devils; they ran out to a 20–2 record going into the Class B semifinals in Sylvania, Georgia. Fighting their way out of the losers' bracket, the Pepperell 9 downed Norcross, 3–1; Sylvania, 5–1, and doubled up on host Sylvania, 17–1, to win the Georgia Class B state crown going away. Outfielder Jim Yarbrough's batting average this year was .511 while third baseman Baltimore Smith followed closely with a .442 mark. This group won 25 of 30 games with each loss by a single run. The June 14, 1953, issue of *Rome News-Tribune* headlined, "SMITH, YARBROUGH SIGN WITH CINCINNATI REDS." The article explained that chief scout

Paul Florence inked the 2 power hitters yesterday afternoon. Both had been assigned to the Jacksonville Beach Seabirds of the Class D Florida State League.

James Walter Yarbrough was born on April 15, 1934, to John Columbus (J. C.) and Mary Dean Jenkins Yarbrough. His grandfather and namesake was a railroad man who decided that frequent moving was not good for raising a family; upon reaching Aragon, Georgia, after the turn of the century, he quit the railroad and went to work at the local cotton mill. They later moved 14 miles north to Pepperell Mill in Lindale where Jim was born at 411 Park Street. He attended Lindale school grades 1 and 2 and then McHenry grades 3 to 8 before returning to Pepperell for grade 9. As a 16-year-old sophomore, Jim moved to Rome High while working second shift in the number two weave room. In the summer of 1951, he made the Textile baseball team for the first time as a left fielder and in the fall enrolled back at Pepperell as a junior in time to suit up for the first ever football Dragons where he played end and wore jersey number 85. After the 1953 high school season, Jimmy and Baltimore reported to Jacksonville Beach and then north to Eufaula, Alabama, before finishing the 1953 season in Statesville, North Carolina, minus buddy Baltimore Smith who had returned to Lindale and wife, Barbara. The former Dragon was a 5-foot-10-inch infielder weighing in at 170 pounds with good speed and a strong arm. He remained in Lindale while working at General Electric and mentored youth for many years in village Twig League baseball. Donald Howard Smith was born on December 1, 1933, in South Lindale; he passed away at 69 in 2002. As to how he got the nickname Baltimore, legend has it family members would shout to opponents, "Get the ball-more-over-here!"

In the spring of 1955, Jim Yarbrough reported to Cincinnati's Army-like training center in Douglas, Georgia, located in Coffee County. They were housed in barracks with 800 other guys and spent each day working out in 2-hour increments. In the 1950s, all able-bodied men were required to serve 6 years' military service; consequently, Jim was drafted into the Army for 2 years' active duty—1956–1958. After honorable discharge, Cincinnati HOF pitcher Johnny Vandermeer, who was now managing the Reds' Topeka minor league team, asked for the veteran to be assigned to his team. Although Jimmy was an outfielder, plans changed when the starting catcher was injured; Vandermeer approached the Lindalean and said, "Jim, you've got to be my catcher." Unfortunately, while catching, a broken finger sidelined him. Surgery in Lincoln followed, but several weeks in an arm-length cast brought about retirement from professional baseball. On January 1, 1960, James Walker Yarbrough and Ruby Nell Freeman were united in marriage.

1954 Season

Winning has its benefits as the local American Legion Post announced at the end of last year's season the purchase of a $1,400 electric scoreboard; one month later, Superintendent Moulton notified the *News-Tribune* of new professional-type lighting system for the local baseball/football field. On April 2, 1954, Coach J. W. Sutton's 2-time defending Class B Pepperell began their schedule with a 7–0 road win over the Marietta Blue Devils. Our new lineup consisted of Spence Cantrell, pitcher; Lloyd Allen, catcher; Charles Williams, first; Jo Jo Stephens, second; Jerry Bolton, short; Ed Duke, third; and outfielders Harold Gresham, Beefy Teat, and

Jack Pence. By early May, they had raced to a 14–3 record over several North Georgia squads including Osborne, Acworth, Darlington, Rome, Buchanan, Model, and a May 5 shutout victory over Gordon Lee which gained them a state playoff berth. For the championship, the boys lost only once in downing West Point, Norcross, and Eastman to finish 20–5. Although the Dragons used 5 pitchers during the year, 1 was exemplary. For 3 years, Troy Coffia was the mainstay of the PHS staff; his credentials included state championships in 1952, '53, and '54. As a senior, he chalked up half of the team's wins (10) against only 2 losses. However, one need only read the *Rome News-Tribune* write-ups of high school baseball 1954 to appreciate the young athlete. Below is a potpourri of his accomplishments:

> Troy Coffia, on the mound for the Dragons, was well nigh invincible. He was robbed of a perfect game by a triple in the opening frame after two were out. He fanned 14 enemy batters and walked none.
>
> Troy Coffia worked three innings against Osborne in the 16–3 win.
>
> Troy Coffia limited the visitors to only four hits.
>
> Spence Cantrell started and was relieved by Troy Coffia.
>
> Troy Coffia let the visitors down with four hits and struck out nine.
>
> Troy Coffia struck out eight Rome batters while walking only two.
>
> Troy Coffia, who went the route for the Dragons, struck out 11 and issued only one base on balls.
>
> Coffia struck out 13 batters and gave up only two bases on balls.
>
> Coach Sutton has not named his starting hurler against the West Pointers, but it will likely be his ace, Troy Coffia.
>
> Troy Coffia hurled eight-hit ball for the winners and kept them well-scattered throughout.
>
> Troy Coffia went all the way for Pepperell to card his second win of the series.
>
> Coach J. W. Sutton has tabbed his ace hurler Troy Coffia to twirl the opener against Norcross.
>
> Troy Coffia on the hill for Pepperell gave up only three hits to the visitors.

Charles White, Pepperell's starting hurler, was a standout along with reliever Troy Coffia against runner-up Eastman H. S.

1955 Season

Coach J. W. Sutton's 1955 charges moved up a notch in classification, opening the season as a member of Region 3, Class A. Ten veterans returned including Ed Duke, third base; Harold Gresham; Billy Bohannon, Emory Moore, and Spence Cantrell in the outfield; Wesley Connell, first base; Jo Jo Stephens, second base; Jerry Bolton, shortstop; and Charles White and Harold Duke, pitchers. Others expected to contribute were Harold Jones, Billy Joe Scoggins, Bobby Roberson, Fred Mathis, Billiam Burkhalter, Weyland Burkhalter, Hillton Arnold, Jackie Padgett, Lowell Curry, Beanie Ozment, Willie Taff, and Butch Treglown. However, more and better athletes lurked in Class A. The 3-time Class B state champions played 21 games, losing 7. The *Rome News-Tribune* used descriptive phrases for many of Pepperell's games: "Dragons blanked Model's Blue Devils 1–0"; "Dragons slaughter Sprayberry nine"; "PHS wrapped up Canton"; "Dragons blank Newnan"; "Pepperell lops Tiger nine in 3–1 thriller"; "Lindale handed the LaFayette High nine a 9–4 defeat...were to play today in sub-region rubber game"; "Dragons drop southern 3-A crown, 4–1 to Newnan." Cougars' fastballing pitcher Ted Denney yielded 1 hit and struck out 9 Dragons en route to a 4–1 victory, giving his team the 3-A Southern Division championship.

Rome's local paper said it all on Sunday, May 8, 1955, on page 8: "The first man to face Denney, Lowell Curry in the initial frame, collected a single, and that was all the Dragons could do with him." Second baseman Jo Jo Stephens was selected to play for north all-star squad in Atlanta's Ponce de Leon Park on June 9. One consolation was Floyd County's Model High played for the finals in Class B.

Garland Howard "Jack" Smith (1909–1987)

Garland Howard "Jack" Smith was born in Fayette County, Alabama, on February 24, 1909, to Garland Spencer Smith and Adine Young Smith; he died in Floyd County, Georgia, on August 1, 1987. His hometown is located 40 miles north of Tuscaloosa and very near the Mississippi state line. It is assumed elementary and middle school grades were in the Vernon, Alabama, system as four different family pictures show sophomore class of 1923, junior class of 1924, and senior class of Vernon High 1925. In addition, there is a photo identified as the first football squad of that school dated 1924. One year later (1925), he graduated VHS at 16 years old. The diploma was signed by father, Garland Spenser Smith. Although research (by phone, newspapers, email, and online) in Fayette County proved fruitless, sometimes during the upper grades, young Garland learned to play baseball well, for he entered API (Auburn) in the fall and performed well enough to become a starter in the infield for Coach Slick Moulton's 1928 SEC conference champions. The slick-fielding clutch-hitting second baseman captained the Tigers his senior year of 1929. It was at this time he received the nickname "Jack Frost" because of shiny blond hair; in time, the "Frost" was left dangling somewhere, but "Jack" adhered (per Lindale, Georgia, historian Polly Gammon). After finishing at Auburn, the young man signed a professional baseball contract, eventually playing for Chattanooga in the Southern Association, the Georgia-Alabama League, and then he followed Mr. Moulton to Lindale where he played Class D, which transitioned into the popular textile league for Pepperell Mill. In 1929, Slick became athletic director for the company local school system as well as manager for the baseball team. At the same time, Jack was hired by Mr. Donald Harvey in a management position. When Mr. Harvey retired in 1955, the Alabama native became general manager of Pepperell Manufacturing in Lindale. After a very productive career in textiles, Garland H. Smith retired in 1970.

The Hugh R. Smith family migrated into Fayette County at the turn of the nineteenth century and became farmers and landowners. The great-great-grandfather of Jack Smith was George Washington Smith (1818–1864), and he was one of several children of pioneer Hugh R. Smith. This coincided with Larkin Barnett's arrival to settle the Lindale valley in Georgia's Floyd County. He married Elizabeth Ann Collins in the early 1840s and began raising a family near Mount Vernon. Records show farmer George Washington Smith joined the Fayette County Militia on June 15, 1864; he provided his own horse and was 47 years old; stood 5 feet, 8 inches; and had blue eyes, dark hair, and complexion. He was detached to South Alabama. A letter home dated September 19, 1864, at Demopolis, Alabama, G. W. stated that he was in tolerable health, but the war was "very gloomy at the present time." "We had been badly shipped at Atlanta...I don't see any signs of peace." He encouraged son Hiram Spenser to "mind your mother and learn all you can at school." Shortly after the letter was written, the soldier became ill and received a medicine furlough home to Mount Vernon; he did not survive the war, dying on November 12, 1864.

Our subject's grandparents were Hiram Spenser Smith (1857–1930) and Samantha Norris Smith. The couple had 12 children (6 boys and 6 girls), one of whom was Garland Spenser Smith (1887–1962), father of Jack. The father Smith married Adine Young on April 16, 1908, who gave birth to only child, Jack, in 1909. Garland Spenser entered Florence Normal College in 1910 as the first married male student. Returning to Lamar Company as teacher and coach, he eventually served as Lamar superintendent of schools beginning in 1917–1949. He was elected president of AEA in 1937. His brother T. W. was superintendent of Tuscaloosa County while another brother Alexander served 12 years as probate judge of Lamar County.

1956 Season

On April 7, 1956, Pepperell began its second baseball season in Class 3-A on Darlington campus. Coach Otis Gilbreath succeeded J. W. Sutton as headman for this year's edition. He welcomed back 6 players who contributed to the previous year including Connell, Bolton, Curry, Arnold, Duke, and Ozment, and they responded with a 13–9 victory at Lakeside, which was termed an exhibition. Early on, pitching was inconsistent as the staff gave up 39 runs in 5 contests; the defense was suspect also. However, by April 23, senior Jerry Bolton, junior Lowell Curry and sophomore Gary Henderson began to find their rhythm. On Friday night, May 11, Otis's group downed North Whitfield 4–2 for the Region 3-A championship. Next up was Southwest DeKalb in the state semifinals. Boosted by excellent pitching, the North Georgia trophy was theirs 4–1 and 3–1. On May 29, the home-standing Gray and Red eyed their fourth baseball title; it was not to be as Thomasville swept a day/night doubleheader 2–0 and 11–7. The second tilt was especially disappointing for the home squad as they blew a 7–0 lead late.

1957 Season

The championship year of 1957 was a season of playoffs. The schedule began on Thursday, April 11, at Darlington and seemingly jumped straight into the northern division elimination process. PHS won 4 consecutive games against Cassville and Ringgold to sweep the Region 1-A title and advance to the state semifinals against Southern champ McDonough in Henry County. We lost the first contest there 5–1 due to walks and miscues despite Gary Henderson giving the Warhawks only 2 hits. In game two played on Tuesday, May 21, in Lindale, we downed the Henry Countians 4–0. Junior Lowell Curry set a new Pepperell record by fanning 18 batters; in his last 2 wins (Ringgold and McDonough), the youngster sent 35 batters back to the dugout. At the plate, Jack Ozment tripled and singled while Curry's catcher Wilburn Bevels also tripled. On Thursday, May 23, pitcher Gary Henderson was the star in the deciding 7–2 semifinal victory at neutral site South Fulton Park in Atlanta as he threw a no-walk 3-hitter and also collected two bingles at the plate. Jerry Brumbelow "connected for a brace" of 3 singles to go with Lowell Curry's triple. North Habersham High of Clarkesville is located in extreme Northeast Georgia nestled against the South Carolina line; the school, which existed from 1951 to 1969, was set to host the first game of Class A state finals on Tuesday, May 28. The contest was set for a 4:00 p.m. first pitch at North Georgia Industrial Trade School in town. However, upon arrival, Coach Otis Gilbreath questioned the credentials of the umpires. When the officials were found lacking in state certification, Otis protested to Sam Burk, executive secretary of the High School Association. The *Rome News-Tribune* explained it this way on Wednesday, May 29, on page 6: "Since the umpires were not certified, the game could have been protested and probably upheld by the losing team; rules state that all umpires in play-offs must be certified." Mr. Burk decided the first game should be played in Lindale, not Clarkesville, with fully certified umpires. Lowell Curry responded with a five-hit effort in winning 3–0. He got into a couple of jams in the first and third innings but managed to escape. In the batter's box, Habersham was his own worst enemy in the firth frame when we loaded the bases; on a fielder's choice by Henderson, 1 run scored followed by Bevels bingle leaving the bases still loaded. When Beanie Ozment struck out, the Bobcat catcher dropped the baseball; in trying to get Curry coming in from third, he threw the ball away, giving us a 3–0 lead. In the last inning with 2 out and a runner on third, Curry proceeded to strike out Habersham cleanup batter Grady Heaton. In Clarkesville on Wednesday, May 29, Gary Henderson threw a 2-hit, 12-strike-out gem as Pepperell claimed the Class A state championship 1–0. Henderson was in trouble only once when the Bobcats loaded the bases in the fourth with no outs; however, he struck out the next 2 hitters and got the third out on a force play at home. In the fifth frame, Beanie Ozment singled and later scored the only run of the game on a passed ball.

On Thursday, July 11, the Rome/Floyd County Chamber of Commerce feted the Dragons and Class B champ Model in the General Forrest Hotel. Wright Bagby, vice president of civic affairs, acted as master of ceremonies as Principal J. W. Sutton praised the athletic performances of both schools. Coach Gilbreath presented 1957 letter jackets to Homer Mathis, Joe Abney, Jackie Brooks, Lowell Curry, Donald Ingle, Wilburn Bevels, Larry Highfield, Jack Ozment,

Roger Carney, Gary Henderson, and Jerry Brumbelow. Our District 7 claimed 3 state championships this season with Dade winning Class C.

1958 Season

The defending champs started their 1958 quest for a "two-peat" on Tuesday, April 8; Coach Gilbreath welcomed seven veterans and "several good players" up from the Pony League—enough to "make the vets step up to stay in the line-up." Pepperell High had lost nine days during the school year due to influenza last fall and extreme cold weather in February of this year (1958). Two sessions were made up during Easter and another on April 12. The system would hold classes this Saturday, May 3, which would leave five more makeup days.

After a few exhibition matches, the Dragons promptly won the Region 1-A South over Pickens County behind Gary Henderson's "two-hit mound job." The 4–0 win moved PHS into region finals on May 13 against North winner Lakeview. The victors of best two-of-three would then advance to state semifinals. It was no contest just off Park Street on Tuesday as Lowell Curry threw a no-hitter in the 5–1 win while Wilburn Bevels, Albert Burkhalter, and Billy Studdard supplied the offense. Two days later in game two held Thursday afternoon in Rossville, we completed the sweep 4–0; Gary Henderson was not to be outdone by Lowell as he also pitched a no-hitter; Bevels, Studdard, Burkhalter, and Roger Carney brought their bats. Behind its two ace mound men, the Dragons traveled to neutral site Thomaston on May 26 for the Georgia Class A state finals. Once there, Pepperell measured Madison (4–2) and Effingham (11–0) counties in double-elimination play. The *News-Tribune* headlined our wins on May 27, "HENDERSON HALTS MADISON; CURRY TOSSES 1-HITTER, FANS 17 TO BLANK EFFINGHAM." In the first game, Gary Henderson fanned 10 Red Raiders. This contest was tied 2–2 in the third before opposing pitcher Phil Butler issued walks to Billy Studdard, Ronnie Corntassel, Burkhalter, and Curry; another free pass next inning gave us the win 4–2.

In the nightcap, Curry whiffed 9 straight batters. At the plate, Albert Burkhalter almost hit for the cycle with a single, double, and triple. Despite all this, Madison County came out of the loser's bracket and surprised the Dragons 9–6 in the morning tilt of Wednesday, May 28, forcing an afternoon one-game winner take all. "It seemed extremely rocky for the Lindale Nine that day for the score stood 0–5 after one inning was played." This, of course, paraphrases Ernest Thayer's 1888 poem "Casey at the Bat." However, the *News-Tribune* printed on page 10 the next day that "Pepperell trimmed their deficit to two runs (5–3) in the top of the third when Albert Burkhalter connected with a three-base blow to score two teammates, then he followed them home on Curry's one-baser." When the Pepps loaded the bases in the sixth, Gary Henderson tripled Lindale to a 7–5 lead. Coach Gilbreath's crew wrapped up the state championship 10–5 with 3 more runs in the last frame. Curry took the win in the finale with 12 strikeouts, giving him a total of 29 for the tournament. The curveball artist finished his high school career with a 24–4 record, received his diploma on Friday, June 6, before reporting in a short week to Ponce de Leon Park for the annual all-star game.

Pepperell general manager and chairman of the school board of trustees G. Howard Smith presented handsome jackets to 17 members of the baseball squad in a fall ceremony before the entire student body. Coach Otis Gilbreath praised 7 Dragons who played on both the '57 and '58 championship squads: Curry, Henderson, Bevels, Ingle, Highfield, Brumbelow, and Carney.

1959 Season

Two weeks before the 1959 baseball workouts began on March 31, former Dragon catcher Wilburn Bevels of 108 F Street departed for the Dodgers' Vero Beach spring training camp. Wilburn was assigned to the Class C squad in Great Falls, Montana. In February of '59, another Pepperell player reported to professional baseball. Beanie Ozment had scored the winning run for our 1957 state championship; after playing out his eligibility that year, he signed with Detroit a year later and went to Lakeland, Florida, for spring training. However, a shoulder injury on his throwing arm side ended Jack's career. In 2007, he was inducted into the Rome/Floyd County Sports Hall of Fame. In Lindale, Coach Gilbreath welcomed 5 returning regulars from last year including Henderson, Green, Corntassel, Brumbelow, and Studdard. Kenneth Shiflett and Clayton Byars were expected to move into starting positions. Coach's squads had won 2 consecutive Class A titles (1957 and 1958) and were runners-up in 1956. The schedule started superbly on April 8 with Pepperell ace Gary Henderson throwing a no-hitter in the 3–0 win at Darlington. He fanned 12 Lakesiders along the way. The team followed that up with an 8–2 victory over East Rome. In the first region game, Henderson repeated his no-hit feat against Pickens County; four days later, he beat host Cartersville 6–2 while striking out 15 Hurricanes. Next, they blasted Cassville 16–3 with freshman right-hander Ross Blalock on the mound before traveling north to rip Pickens 20–2 and claim the Region 3-A South crown. Defending Class B champ Model moved up a class and promptly won the North title; they also downed the Pepps 5–1 in the first game playoff partly due to 5 errors by visiting Lindale. On Thursday, May 14, the Blue Devils won the North crown with an 8–3 win over the host Lindaleans. Hard-throwing Jackie Braden whiffed 13 batters with only 3 bases on balls. In Thomaston, the boys from Shannon beat Milton 6–2 and Winder-Barrow 2–1 for the diadem or state crown; the latter win happened when Bulldog pitcher Sonny Morris balked.

1960 Season

With high school baseball season on the horizon, *RNT* reported on page 3 in May 1 that former Pepperell catcher Wilburn Bevels signed his contract with the Dodgers and would soon move to Vero Beach for spring training. He would then fly to the West Coast for duty with the Triple-A Spokane Indians. The 19-year-old spent the winter working third shift in the Weave Department.

Floyd Countians woke up on Wednesday morning, March 2, to an ice storm that per the *News-Tribune*, "Ice Blanket Covers Rome Area; More of Same Due." All schools closed, traffic, utilities snarled. Pepperell Manufacturing Company suspended operations on Thursday, March 3, and remained so until Sunday's third shift. Approximately 1,500 students resumed studies on Thursday, March 10. Because of late football spring training, Lindale's diamond prospects began work on April 14. On the nineteenth, Coach Gilbreath gave his potential starting lineup to *RNT* which included Dan Bohannon at catcher; pitchers Blalock, Savage, and Peek; first base Corntassel; Vaughn at second; Holcomb at shortstop; Sewell at third; and outfielders would be McRay, Studdard, and Mathis. At home on April 22 versus Southern division foe Cartersville, Johnny Savage threw a 1-hitter, and our hitters rapped out 10 safeties in the 6–3 victory; 4 days later, we "coasted" to a 13–0 victory over Pickens County in which Johnny Savage starred again. The sophomore struck out a dozen batters and allowed only 3 singles in our second region win. We subdued visiting Cartersville again on Thursday, April 28; however, it took 2 extra innings to win 9–8. In the ninth, Dan Bohannon walked and stole second before Savage singled him home with the victory. Ross Blalock pitched into the sixth before Savage relieved him; the latter was credited with the save. In a night game off Park Street on Monday, May 3, PHS wrapped up the southern division of Region 3-A with a 4–2 triumph over Pickens County; Johnny Savage won his fourth straight outing. Trion High won the upper division while Pepperell took the lower. Host Lindale took the first game 4–3 in 10 innings in best-of-three series. A pair of juniors delivered the winning run when Sonny Mathis's slow grounder brought home "a scrambling" Larry Gresham from third base. We annexed the region crown 3–1 on Thursday May 12 in Trion behind Gresham's 3-hit ball in which he faced only 24 batters. Bob Sewell, Bohannon, Holcomb, Mathis, and McRay along with Gresham produced all our runs. Monday the twenty-third in the double-elimination state tournament at neutral site Thomaston saw us lose 7–0 to Winder-Barrow; however, PHS "roared" back that afternoon to eliminate Screven County 8–2. One day later, Pepperell knocked out Milton 10–5 with a hitting display; Johnny Savage pitched half of the way before being relieved by Gresham. Freshman catcher Dan Bohannon was injured and replaced by Thomas Jackson. On Tuesday, May 24, the Dragons were defeated in the finals by Winder 6–4; we rallied from a 0–4 deficit in the sixth with a Savage run scoring single and followed that with a pinch hit doubled by Dan "Yogi" Bohannon that cleared the bases. An extra inning (eighth) was necessary to break a 4–4 tie which Winder did by plating 2 runs to claim Georgia Class A baseball crown; in doing so, the Bulldogs removed the "A" championship from Floyd County for the first time in 4 years. Still, West Rome won the Class AA and Coosa the Class C titles.

1961 Season

With less than a week's practice, the Georgia state Class A runners-up were set to face West Rome on Saturday night, April 8, at 7:30 p.m. Coach Gilbreath was uncertain of his starting lineup; however, the 15 players suited up were Ross Blalock, Wallace Shiflett, Sonny Mathis, Larry Gresham, Jimmy Holcomb, Bill Studard, Steve McRay, Johnny Savage, Bob Sewell, Archie Vaughn, Jimmy Hinton, Dan Bohannon, Thomas Jackson, Gregg McGregor, and Jackie Shores. He did say Ross Blalock, Johnny Savage, Larry Gresham, and Jimmy Hinton would share mound duties. After bowing 4–3 to WR, the locals came from behind to defeat East Rome 7–5 on Tuesday, April 11. On April 19, the home squad came from behind twice to nip Carrollton's Trojans 8–7 in extra innings; with 2 out, Wallace Shiflett ran all the way to third on a ball misplayed by the outfield. He scored on an infield error to win. Two days later, they lost 3–2 at Darlington's lakeside diamond thanks to 6 infield errors. Sophomore Joe Knight and Junior Dan

Bohannon shared catching duties. By the second week in May, PHS ruled the South subregion with a 5–1 slate; Johnny Savage and Doyal Peek pitched 1-hitters against Rockmart and Pickens respectively while Gresham, Shiflett, Bohannon, and Vaughn supplied the batting. But disappointment awaited them in Shannon. On May 10, North champion Model scored 3 runs and held on to defeat PHS 3–1 in the best-of-three games to determine state playoff contention on the fourth week of May. The smooth pitching of Blue Devil Earl Barrett and Dragon Johnny Savage coupled with fine play afield assured our Class 3-A region a top-notch contender in Thomaston. On Friday, May 12, the second game belonged to Model 3–2; relief pitcher Joe House put down a Dragon rally in the seventh inning in addition to earlier doubling home 2 of his team's scores. However, the Blue Devils who won the Class B championship in 1959, ran into one of the top pitchers in the southeast, namely Loveard McMichael. The Americus High School star won his twelfth straight game on June 2 as well as hitting a 3-run homer; 2,000 home fans witnessed the 5-foot-10-inch, 165-pound "speedballer" throw a 2-hitter in the series sweep.

As the school year wound down, *News-Tribune* feature writer Langdon B. Gammon reported on April 21 that he received a 1961 PHS annual; in its dedicatory message to Ms. Sara Hightower, the senior class and staff wrote, "We dedicate the 1961 Dragon to one whose influence, help and encouragement make a lasting educational contribution to all Pepperell students; whose outstanding ability is recognized state-wide; whose proven loyalty to the students and school endears her to all...with love, appreciation and esteem proudly dedicate this volume to our librarian."

News from the high school baseball season ended with a Thursday, June 8, 1961, post in the *News-Tribune* reporting that former Pepperell catcher Wilburn Bevels was batting .304 for the Class C pioneer league. The Dodger minor leaguer was in his third year with the organization. His wife, the former Nancy Hatch, was in Great Falls, Montana, also. Wilburn was a 1958 grad whose parents, Mr. and Mrs. A. J. Bevels, lived at 106 F Street.

1962 Season

According to *News-Tribune* on April 8, Pepperell baseball started preseason practice on April 9 with 7 members of the defending Region 3-A South champions missing due to graduation. A few lettermen did return, including catcher Dan Bohannon, pitcher/infielder Johnny Savage, pitcher Ross Blalock, third baseman Wallace Shiflett, and outfielder David Erwin. Coach Gilbreath's crew would compete in the rugged South division of Region 3-A against Carrollton, Cartersville, Cass, and Rockmart. The coach told the *News-Tribune* on April 8, "We are going to lose some games this season but our building program should give us a lot to look forward to in the next year or two." First up was at the Lakeside where a wild and woolly battle ended with Darlington winning 10–8. Pepperell used 3 pitchers, Ricky Stephens, Jerry Henderson, and Johnny Savage; hitting was supplied by Wallace Shiflett who delivered a long 3-run blast in the third inning. Three days later, West Rome came from behind twice before winning 7–4. Johnny Savage was the losing hurler while Joe Knight led the hitters with a double and a single. An East Rome loss was followed by a 10–5 defeat in Carrollton, which left our boys with a 0–4 record as they traveled to Cassville on April 24. In extra innings, the Dragons won 5–4. Johnny Savage, who struck out 11 Colonels, pitched most of the game. In the top of the eighth, Joe Knight tripled home the winning run in the person of Jimmy Locklear who had singled. Lack of pitching staff depth had hampered the club so far. In Bartow County on the twenty-seventh, Pepperell committed 15 errors and still won mostly because young fireballer Ricky Stephens struck out 10 'Canes. The youngster also singled in the winning run. On May 3, it took 4 pitchers and 10 hits for the Dragons to revenge an earlier loss to Darlington 5–4. Six days later, the *News-Tribune* spoke eloquently about the Red and Gray's next contest, "The Carrollton High Trojans came to town Tuesday afternoon bubbling with an undefeated record on their hands, a couple of sure-fire professional baseballers and a chance to wrap up the Region 3-A South title, but had to make the long trek back home with nothing more than tired muscles." Left-hander Ricky Stephens recorded the 4–3 victory. The youngster had built a reputation for mound wildness; however, on this day, there was no better hurler in the county as he put a silencer on the Trojan bats with 11 strikeouts. In 9 innings, the visitors' "much sought-after" players Gerald Gross and Skeeter Robinson managed only 1 hit between them. Unfortunately, 3 games later, visiting Cartersville ended the Dragons' season with an 11–9 upset, eliminating them from the region championship.

1963 Season

With only 3 days' practice, Coach Otis Gilbreath's squad traveled to Darlington on April 4. Nine lettermen returned that finished second last year to subregion and eventual state 3-A champion Carrollton. At the Lakeside, Pepperell led 5–0 early until the Tigers tied it in the second inning. Jordan drew a walk. Sid Ransom and Billy Gordon followed with singles before Wright Bagby cleaned the bases with a 3-run triple. The fifth proved fatal to the visitors as they gave up 9 runs in the 14–8 loss. The highlight for the Dragons was catcher Dan Bohannon's long 2-run blast in the fourth. We evened our record the following day with a 3–1 victory over Johnson High. Prior to Pepperell's game with defending Class AA champions West Rome, Coach Nick Hyder expressed concern about Otis's team. He was quoted in the *News-Tribune* on Thursday, April 4, "Coach Gilbreath has some real fine boys from last year's team and they should be real strong." The sports page headlines of April 10 bore this out: "Dragon Baseballers Whip West Rome Chiefs, 12–5." Other than Gary Law's 2 home runs and a single, the game belonged to Lindale. For 5 innings, left-handed twirler Ricky Stephens was in complete control of the Green and White. The "speed-baller" then turned the game over to junior reliever Eddie Garrett. Our hitting department was led by Charles Henderson with 2 singles and a double while Tony Taylor collected 3 base knocks. Dan Bohannon also added a double and a single. Seven days later on April 17, the mighty Trojans visited Lindale. The *News-Tribune* summed it up with, "Stephens-Led Pepperell Slams Carrollton 15–4, Dragons Belt '62 Class A Champs." Young Ricky went the full 7 innings and scattered 4 hits while striking out an even dozen. He also had a perfect day at the plate with 4 singles and a double. His teammates collected 17 hits including Bohannon's single, double, and triple to go with David and Mike Erwin's pair of base knocks.

On April 19, the Berry High 9 went down 7–1 as our boys touched Falcon Jerry Chastain for 10 hits with Dan Bohannon, Larry Kinney, and Tony Taylor "contributing key blows" for the visitors. But all good things must come to an end as Dallas High slammed the Dragons 15–5 on May 3. And for good measure, they won the Region 3-A South championship. Consolation games are no fun; to wit, the East Rome Gladiators visited our home diamond and rallied for 6 runs in the last inning to down the Dragons 13–7. Ricky Stephens and Dan Bohannon both collected 3 hits for the losers. Pitcher Charles Henderson took the loss. The twelfth annual commencement exercises for PHS took place on Monday, June 3, in the campus auditorium. Assistant general manager of Pepperell Manufacturing Robert O. Simmons presented diplomas to 65 graduating seniors. Top academic honors went to Judy Betts, valedictorian, and Judy Sutton, salutatorian.

1964 Season

The 1964 Pepperell squad was scheduled to start drills on Saturday, April 4; however, inclement weather caused a sizable delay. It was April 20 before the diamond had dried enough to host the Dallas High Tigers. Coach Gilbreath said the biggest loss from last year's subregion runners-up came when "Dan Bohannon tucked his diploma under his arm and hung up his shin guards, breast protector and mask." But he was confident in replacement Joe Knight who was one of 11 returning lettermen. In the Dallas game, Charles Blalock threw a 5-hitter while Johnny Mathis and Steve Bennett went 3 for 3 and 2 for 2 at the plate. Lindale breezed to a 12–2 victory. Two days later, we beat Coosa 6–2 behind the 5-hit pitching of junior Eddie Garrett; the left-hander struck out a dozen Eagles in going the route. Steady hitting by Mathis, Bennett, and Boatner provided the runs. On May 1, visiting Darlington turned the tables on us 7–1. The Tigers rapped out 10 hits to only 3 for the Dragons. Coach Otis treated these early games as mere exhibitions; the veteran mentor knew how to ready his boys for the postseason. In the first round of a best-of-three series against Berry Academy, Pepperell overcame a 3-run deficit to win 8–5 in subregion competition. Eddie Garrett threw 5-hit ball with Joe Knight as his batterymate. The latter had a single and double while David Erwin and Garrett both collected triples. It helped that the Falcons committed 11 miscues. Two days later, our boys swept the Martha Berry series in Lindale 12–3; senior Charles Blalock gave up 9 hits while his teammates counted 13. Errors again plagued the visitors as they booted the baseball 8 times. For the championship of Region 3-A North, PHS hosted Gilmer County on Monday, May 11, and treated them rudely 15–0. Eddie Garrett pitched 4 innings, and Randy Scott finished; the duo only gave up 2 hits between them.

Two days later in Ellijay, it was "déjà vu all over again" as Joe Knight "came loaded with a big bat," rapping out 3 doubles. The winners plated "a trio of runs in the 3rd, two more in the 5th, three in the 6th and then unloaded on the hapless Bobcats in the 7th with seven big markers." In the second consecutive 15–0 drubbing, Charles Blalock hurled a neat four-hitter, struck out 4, and issued only 1 base on balls. The *News-Tribune* morning paper on May 14 headlined: "Dragons Best Gilmer For 3-A North Crown." The Dragons carried a 7–2 slate going into the Region 3-A championship series which was scheduled for Monday, May 18, in Lindale versus Cartersville; the second contest was set 2 days later in Bartow County. If a third was necessary, the coin flip would determine the site. Junior Eddie Garrett spaced out 7 hits in the 5–4 first game win; however, he trailed 4–2 in the sixth before Billy Mathis and Mike Erwin got on base in front of Jimmy Locklear who cleaned the sacks with a long double. Then Jimmy Mathis got the most important hit of the day, a single that scored Locklear with the eventual winning run. On Wednesday next, the Hurricanes eked out 3–2 victory to tie the series. With the game even at 2–2 in the seventh, Eddie Garrett relieved Blalock; then the "Hurricanes brewed up a storm" with a solo marker and the victory. Pepperell had only 5 hits and committed 3 errors. However, on Friday, May 29, the Red and Gray completed the trifecta of Berry, Gilmer, and Cartersville by unleashing its offensive power to slug the Bartow County contingent 17–12 for the Region 3-A crown. Local officials immediately made an effort to lure the state tournament to Rome but were outbid by Thomaston. The news was not good out of Upson County on May 26 as the *News-Tribune* reported, "Dragons Lose to Tucker, 4–1, then to Hughes, 5–2, in Thomaston Play." Although Eddie Garrett gave up only 3 safeties to Tucker High, his mates committed 3 miscues. Four hours later, Dudley Hughes High School of Macon came from behind with 5 runs to eliminate the boys from Floyd. As the curtain closed on school year 1964, Ms. Jeanne Sutton was honored as class valedictorian; she was a member of the Future Homemakers as well as Future Teachers Club, the Spanish Club, National Honor Society, varsity basketball, captain of the varsity football cheerleaders, Girls State, PHS chorus, and was a member of Silver Creek Presbyterian Church. The 17-year-old was the daughter of Mr. and Mrs. J. W. Sutton of 12 Central Avenue.

1965 Season

The defending Region 3-A champs prepared to open the new season at Darlington on Friday April 9. Although Coach Gilbreath had over 40 boys "seeking employment," the staff welcomed lettermen Toby Hamby, catcher; Charles Henderson and Eddie Garrett, pitchers and infielders; Steve Bennett, first base; Steve Johnston, second base; and Jimmy Treglown, Jimmy Brumbelow, Jimmy Mathis, and David Barton, outfielders. He told the press, "We're going to have a good team, but you can't lose boys like Joe Knight, David Ervin and Johnny Mathis and still be as strong." He believed defense and pitching would be strong again. In regard to the former freshman, Gary Wingo would probably man the shortstop position; he flitted up from the "chain" of Twig, Bronco, and Pony leagues. We would have veterans Henderson and Garrett on the mound. The season started well with a 14–7 win at Lakeside; this was followed by an extra inning 1–0 victory over former Dragon Beefy Teat's East Rome Gladiators. On April 14, Eddie Garrett went the distance in a 7–6 victory versus Rockmart; in a last-inning "outburst," the Dragons stayed undefeated by plating 3 runs behind hitters Hamby, Bennett, Mathis, and Henderson. Next on April 17, our boys recorded their second 1-run victory over East Rome 6–5. Charles Henderson pitched 7 rounds for the win; Larry Bing also went the distance but took the loss. Toby Hamby was the top batsman for us, going 3 for 4 with a triple. On the twenty-first at the Lindale diamond, "something's gotta give" as Model came in 7–0 to face 4–0 Pepperell; a big crowd was expected. They got their money's worth, for Charles Henderson came within 1 out of a no-hitter, and to boot, the Dragons' Joe Little scampered home from second base on a Blue Devil infield error to win 1–0. Four days later, Johnson High felt our wrath 12–1; Steve Bennett was the star hitter with a single, double, triple, and 5 RBIs. The Region 3-A playoffs were next; our opponent, Berry Academy, was unbeaten at the time. Two games later, they were not.

We trimmed the Falcons 8–2 in the first contest. Charles Henderson was the winning hurler with Toby Hamby catching. We collected several extra base hits by Wingo, Hamby, and Kinney (doubles); Bennett hammered a long triple. The following day, we routed Berry 13–5; Danny Morris collected 4 RBIs, and Henderson stroked 3 hits. Eddie Garrett was the winning pitcher for the 6–0 Red and Gray. All good things came to an end on April 30 in Lindale with a football score—Darlington, 20; Pepperell 15. Coach Gilbreath used 4 throwers Wingo, Scott, Farrer, and Steve Johnston as he rested the starters. The Tigers led in safeties 15 to 12. On May 3 in Lindale, our boys went 1 up in Region play downing Valley Point 5–2. A rested Charles Henderson was effective throughout as he threw a 3-hit ball for the win. Winning hitters were Hamby, Mathis, Wingo, and Kinney. Three days later in Dalton, we swept the series 11–7 behind Eddie Garrett's complete game. Actually we were down 0–3 before erupting for 4 runs in the fourth and 4 more in the sixth. The same familiar hitters led the way, i.e., Henderson, Wingo, Morris, Little, Hamby, and Bennett. We now await either Gilmer or Pickens in Lindale on Monday, May 10, to determine Region North champs. In a non-counter on May 7, Model won 5–2 over Pepperell. The Class B Blue Devils ran their record to 11–1 while the PHS was now 12–2 overall. The Dragons faced visiting Gilmer County on the tenth for the first of best-of-three contests in Region 3-A North; they came from 2 runs down to win 7–2 as Charles Henderson pitched a 5-hit complete game. At the plate, we stroked 1 triple and 5 singles, which were aided by 3 Bobcat errors. Three days later, PHS swept the series by blasting their host 19–2; we scored 3 in the first inning, 7 in the second, and 8 in the third. Barton, Kinney, and Hamby each collected 2 hits. The home squad misplayed 5 balls. Eddie Garrett threw a 4-hit ball for the win. We were scheduled to face Cartersville for the region crown on May 17 in Lindale then move to Bartow County for the second game with the third site being decided by coin toss. We played true to form in the first contest, winning by 8–5 but being outhit 10 to 11. Hamby and Wingo, sophomore and freshman, joined Garrett with 2 safeties each. Two days later, we carried a 3–2 lead into the bottom of the seventh and needed only 2 more outs to win region. However, the Purple Hurricanes batted last and scored the tying and winning marker on Bill Teague's bases-clearing single. After several rainouts, the finals took place in Lindale on Monday, May 24. The Dragons triumphed 4–2 behind Charles Henderson. *News-Tribune* staff writer Orbie Thaxton wrote, "Charles Henderson is a lad who eats your heart out if you're his coach, but he'll tear your heart out if you happen to be an opponent." The studious right-hander kept the Cartersville batters off-balance all day which resulted in easy grounders and pop-ups; a good defense behind him gave Lindale the region crown. The senior Henderson also ripped a single in the fifth inning, plating the winning run for the Region 3-A champs. Next, we faced Monroe High for the North title and a chance to compete against South Georgia for best in state. On June 1 in Lindale, the game was a "spine-tingler" with the Dragons going up by five in the first inning behind Wingo, Garrett, and Henderson's hitting; consequently, our crowd settled back anticipating a "cakewalk." However, with 2 out in their half of the seventh, the Purple Hurricanes rallied to cut Lindale's lead to 5–4. After Rowe lived on an error, Ward promptly doubled; then pinch hitter Sammy Kimsey bounced a single over second to put his team up 6–5. In the bottom of the seventh, we forced extra baseball when Kinney singled, was balked to second, and Henderson brought him home with a blooper. We won the game in the bottom of the eighth when Morris tripled and Hamby banged a single to end the game 7–6. Yet that was our last hurrah in '65, for in Monroe on Friday, June 4, we lost a doubleheader 14–13 and 5–0. The first slugfest didn't hurt as much as the final game loss because former Roman Jim Bolton, who grew up in our Little League system, tossed a no-hitter despite walking 7; it was Bolton's first appearance in the playoffs, prompting Coach Otis to say, "I don't know why they've been saving him...he pitched a fine game." On Monday, June 7, Pepperell plant manager Jack Smith presented 141 diplomas to the PHS fourteenth graduating class; Rose Marie McDonald gave the valedictory speech "Education, the American Ideal." Judith Evans followed with a salutatory address.

In the summertime, sports editor Don Biggers found himself defending Pepperell's domination of the Pony and Colt leagues; a parent from another community complained that Lindale had the choice of all boys in the area while others must go through a system of tryouts and bidding. Biggers noted that Lindale was a close-knit group who took baseball seriously. Danny Morris was a starter for Pepperell's Colt squad; he answered this criticism in the Sunday, August 1, issue of the *Rome News-Tribune*, saying, "Nobody has to play ball for Pepperell if they live in the area, they can participate elsewhere...Rome certainly has more population than Lindale so the opportunity is there...our players have grown up with baseball. They live it, they eat it. We are just a baseball town."

1966 Season

The season began Saturday afternoon, April 9, in Calhoun with a 9–4 loss. Gary Wright and Steve Johnston did mound work; Toby Hamby handled the catching and also hit a home run. Three days later, former Dragon Beefy Teat brought his East Rome 9 to Lindale and shut out his alma mater 5–0 behind the 4-hit pitching of Larry Bing. It did not help that we made 4 errors. Johnston started and took the loss with Barton relieving midway. Another Saturday afternoon clash brought our first victory versus visiting Darlington; the next week was busy with 4 games lined up, i.e., at Berry and Model with home battles with Coosa and Berry. We waxed the latter 14–2 behind Wright's 2-hitter and our 10 safeties which included Spence Millican's 2 for 3 and Steve Johnston's 2 for 4. On April 19, we won our third game, downing visiting Coosa 3–2. Coach Gilbreath said later, "It was a well played high school game." On the mound, young Sid Farrer battled the Eagles' Tim Broome down to the last inning tied at 2–2; first up Gary Wingo singled, and Steve Bennett tripled him home for the victory. Darlington defeated us 4–0 on April 26 in a rain-shortened game; we came back on May 3 to rip Model 10–2 courtesy of Kenneth Corntassel's 3-hitter and the slugging of Bennett, Kizziah, Hamby, and Wright. Although this group led a 7-run eruption in the second inning, our 9 errors were of concern. Two days later, we did it again—Dragons, 11; Blue Devils, 3. This time, Gary Wingo allowed 4 safeties with Toby Hamby catching. Coach Gilbreath's 9 hosted Pickens County on Monday, May 10, in a best-of-three series for the Subregion 3-A North crown; left-hander Gary Wright limited the visitors to 4 bingles in a 12–4 romp. At the same time, we pounded out 11 safeties; according to Lang Gammon, "Hamby got a double and a homer, Gary Wingo had a double and a single, Kent Millican and David Barton each had two singles, Steve Johnston hit a triple, Steve Bennett a two-bagger and Wright singled." Two days later, we closed them out, or as the local paper wrote, "Dragons Roar in Playoffs," on their playing field 10–6. Gary Wingo threw 5 good innings with David Barton taking over the last 2 frames. Bennett, Wright, Barton, and Mike Silvers led the way offensively. In a rain-plagued year, the region playoff was set for Monday, May 19, in Lindale with the Dragons versus North Cobb. The visitors won the first of a doubleheader 7–3 behind the "tight hurling" of David Giles; however, the Red and Gray roared back in the second game behind David Barton's pitching to tie the series 12–3. Alas, the defending 1964 and 1965 region champs were denied a trifecta when David Giles again stopped us "short in our tracks" 7–0 on Monday, May 23; only Hamby and Wingo managed to hit safely against host North Cobb's sharp-throwing mound man in 7 innings. Even worse, they built a 7–0 lead before Gary Wingo singled in the fifth; 4 errors led to our demise.

A few days before school turned out for the summer, *News-Tribune* reporter Langdon B. Gammon wrote on page 6 of the May 17, 1966, issue, "Moulton to Retire from Schools Here." The article documented Mr. Moulton's long and varied 37-year career as our superintendent of education. When the 29-year-old arrived in Lindale, he had already experienced a most interesting and exciting life which can be reviewed on pages 142–147 . Slick and wife, Cool would be moving to a beach house in Gulf Shores, Alabama, near Mobile. In a preretirement statement, he said, "I leave the schools of Lindale in good, capable and skillful hands; J. W. Sutton, who succeeds me as supervising principal, is one of the best school administrators in the state."

1967 Season

On Saturday, April 8, the 1967 edition of Pepperell baseball began behind the levee at Rome's Legion Field. Former Dragon Beefy Teat's East Rome squad edged us 8–6; it was a free-swinging affair with the winners leading in safeties 12 to 10; the losers committed 4 errors to go with 3 pitchers Kizziah, Wright, and Wingo. Our sluggers included Kizziah with 3 singles, Bennett and Hamby with 2 each, and Silver and Wingo with 1 bingle apiece. The only extra base knock was a double by Lynn Hunnicutt. By the time we defeated area rival Coosa 8–1 on April 18, the record stood at 3–2; victories over Pickens County and Model also were in 3-A while losses to East Rome and Calhoun were not Class 3-A. In the Eagles' game, Gary Wight threw a nifty 3-hitter while his mates collected 10 safeties off Ronnie Rose including Kizziah, Wingo, and Bennett with multiple singles; two extra base hits were a four-bagger by Toby Hamby and a double by Mike Silver. On Friday afternoon the twenty-first in Ellijay, Gary Wight pitched a 1-hitter, winning 3–0; opposing hurler Lee Sanford legged out a third-base grounder for Gilmer's only base knock. Steve Bennett and Hamby led the offense that collected 10 clouts. Next up the following Tuesday in Lindale, Berry Academy was downed 7–1; in a hero's role, Kenneth Corntassel struck out 8 in hurling a 1-hitter; we played error-free ball while garnering 7 safeties including Wingo and junior Mike Baird with 2 each. We lost 5–2 on a Friday road trip to Jasper; this put us in a tie with Coosa for the subregion lead. Gary Wingo started on the mound but received help in the fifth from Wright; sophomore Ronnie Hutchins led us at the plate going 2 for 4. Twenty-four hours later at the Lakeside, Darlington won a Saturday game 10–8. On Monday, May 1, the *News-Tribune* feature writer Lang Gammon posted, "Twig League Begins 10th Year of Play." With support of sponsors Lindale Methodist Church, Henderson-Frazier Funeral Home, McClain-

Sealock American Legion, and First Baptist Church, this youth baseball program for boys 9 through 12 was considered a "twig" on the larger tree of local recreation. Kenneth Corntassel followed his 1-hitter versus Berry with a 3-hit job against Model on Wednesday the third. The sophomore won 10–2 despite 9 errors by his mates; Kent Millican and Steve Bennett were the offensive stars. Five days later, Pepperell ran their subregion record to 7–1 with an 8–6 victory over Gilmer County; Charlie Gilbreath was the winning pitcher with some help from Gary Wright in the seventh. Wingo and Kizziah led the charge that scored all 8 runs in the first 3 innings. Gary Wright allowed 2 hits and received errorless play from his position players in an easy 6–0 victory over Coosa; the May 10 game sewed up the north subregion championship for Lindale. The usual cast of characters Bennett, Hamby, Wright, Dudley, and Hutchins supplied the winning runs. Rockmart finished first in the South and visited Lindale on May 17 for best-of-three series; a one-day rain delay must have helped both pitchers as our Gary Wright and their Wayne Evans allowed only 4 and 5 safeties respectively. However, it was an error that spelled defeat for the Polk County Bees. Ken Kizziah opened the fourth with a single, but the ball "scooted" past the left fielder, allowing the runner to reach third. Two outs later, right-handed swinger Toby Hamby hammered a single to the opposite field for the only score of the contest; it was the only time we threatened. Early on, Rockmart loaded the bases but failed a clutch hit. Neither hurler had trouble with walks. The next day, with the score tied 2–2, third baseman Andy Williams stroked a fifth-inning solo homer to "spark" his team over visiting PHS 4–2; Gary Wingo gave up only 3 hits but was in and out of trouble caused by wildness. Although we outslugged the home squad 6–3, the Dragons also made 6 errors. A coin toss sent us back to Polk County on May 19 for the final game of Region 3-A playoff. On Friday afternoon, pitcher Gary Wright was impeccable in setting down 18 straight Yellow Jacket batters; he gave up 3 measly hits but was never in danger of losing. On Sunday's sports page, the *News-Tribune* headlined, "Wright Sparks Pepperell Past Rockmart for Title." The Dragons claimed the championship by virtue of this sterling 3–0 triumph. We scored 2 runs in the third when Silver walked. Wingo lived on an error, and Kizziah singled to load the bases; Steve Bennett promptly stroked a base hit to put the Red and Gray up 2–0. Two innings later, it was Bennett again; this time, he laced a Wayne Evans pitch 325 feet over the left center field fence. The Class A North Georgia best-of-three series began in Lindale on Thursday, May 25; Westminster pounded 3 Pepperell pitchers for 15 hits in a 12–5 rout. They erupted for 5 runs in the third and 4 more an inning later, and "it was all over except for the shouting." On Friday, and with our backs to the wall, the Dragon 9 traveled to Buckhead's West Paces Ferry Road needing to win a doubleheader. Later, the local Rome newspaper posted news from the 180-acre campus, "Pepperell Loses Second Contest to Westminster." Wildcat mound man Paul Wisdom threw a 1-hitter at us in the 10–2 deciding game; his mates chipped in with 10 safeties.

1968 Season

On April 1, Coach Otis told the local paper he would rely on a veteran pitching staff and a "flip-flop" defense for the coming season in Region 7-AA. The former would come from Gary Wright, Kenneth Corntassel, Ken Kizziah, Charles Gilbreath, and Gary Wingo; youngsters

Phil Baker and Lamar Wright would join them. To knowledgeable Pepperell baseball fans, this group was practically a hall of fame roster. The abovementioned "switcheroo" defense would come from this pitching corps as they were all good athletes capable of playing multiple positions; the outfield had 2 returning starters in Ronnie Hutchins who was a top defensive center fielder last season and senior Richard Stager. However, there was one major problem—who could replace Toby Hamby behind the plate? The options were Jimmie Dudley, Ray Hines, and Wayne Chastain. The first boy had not played baseball in a while, the second choice manned the outfield last year, and the third alternative was a freshman up from the Pony League who had experience at catcher and should be around for 3 more seasons. Coach finished the interview with, "I'm hoping one of these boys will come through." Rain forced the postponement of 3 games before we finally met and defeated Coosa 1–0 at Legion Field on Friday, April 12; Gary Wright struck out 15 and walked only 1 while throwing a 4-hitter. Our batters managed a like number of hits but benefited from an Eagle wild pitch for the only score of the day. Five days later, Calhoun pounded out 12 safeties and performed flawlessly in the field to down us 12–6; Kenneth Corntassel took the mound loss. We responded 2 days later by thrashing East Rome 13–2; however, the Gladiators gained some revenge the following Wednesday, edging us 6–5. Pepperell outhit the squad from Turner McCall 7–5 but committed 3 errors. On an April 26 road trip to Jasper, Gary Wright fanned 10 batters while giving up only 4 bingles in a 5–0 victory over subregion foe Pickens County. The senior right-hander was in complete control throughout; the visitors from Floyd banged out 8 safeties including 3 each by Ronnie Hutchins and Gary Wingo. On the last day of May, Ken Kizziah threw a no-hitter at Coosa; it was the third such feat this season in Floyd County behind East Rome's Larry Bing and Model's Scott Howell. At Legion Field, the Dragons improved their record to 7–2 in the 13–1 victory; Wingo and Wright laced 3 base hits each. On May 6, Gary Wright and Phil Baker blasted home runs as we ran "roughshod" over host Berry Academy 23–2, but Baker's was a bases-loaded shot in the seventh inning. Corntassel went the distance on the mound with a spaced-out 6-hitter. On the eighth in Lindale, Darlington lost 7–1 to sophomore Lamar Wright's fine mound work. The difference in run production backfired on Tiger coach Reed Mottley who attempted to copy Otis Gilbreath's strategy of pitching youngsters in non-region contests; the host squad had 11 hits and 1 error. On May 10, we downed Model 5–0 in Lindale behind Ken Kizziah's masterful 1-hit gem. After the first man up rapped a single, he was virtually untouchable, utilizing lots of breaking stuff which had the Blue Devils off stride and bouncing balls to our infielders, especially short and third. We plated 2 runs in the first, 2 more in the fourth, and 1 in the fifth; Baker and Hutchins led us at the plate with 2 bingles each. Perhaps more importantly, the Dragons claimed the subregion crown and would travel to Kennesaw Park and face North Cobb High for the Region 3-A championship series on Monday, May 13. It took 8 innings for the good guys to win 4–3 behind Gary Wright's 6-hitter. With the contest tied 2–2 at the end of regulation, we plated 2 runs in the extra frame when Kizziah walked and went to third on Hutchins's third single of the game; then Jimmie Dudley drove both in with a single. For the return match in Lindale, it was rain, rain, go away. Four straight days of postponements passed before the 2 squads took the field at 4:30 p.m. on Monday, May 20. Ken Kizziah was set to pitch; Jimmy Dudley would be behind the plate. Charles Gilbreath would start at first, Phil Baker at second, Gary Wingo at shortstop, and

Gary Wright at third. This group was sitting on a 14–3 record. However, we could not solve the visiting Warriors' star Don McGarity who allowed only 3 safeties while striking out 10 Dragons; he also had 2 RBIs on 2 of the 5 hits surrendered by Kizziah. A day later on Polk County's neutral ground, pandemonium erupted in the Dragon dugout and bleachers when Ken Kizziah blasted a 3-run fourteenth-inning line shot over the center field fence for a 7–4 victory. We had "dodged a bullet" in the top of the frame when North Cobb loaded the bases and Otis sent Phil Baker to the mound. Although the Warriors had already "banged out" 15 safeties, the freshman responded by getting the side out without a run. As it happens in baseball, a great defender comes to the plate first up. Phil Baker was hit by a pitch, and Lamar Wright walked to set up the momentous home run by Kizziah. On Tuesday afternoon, May 28, it was back to West Paces Ferry Road to face Westminster School, the same team that eliminated us in North Georgia play last year. Coach Gilbreath noted they had a fine pitching staff; however, our aces Wright and Kizziah were rested and ready for duty. When the game got underway, the private school from Atlanta "jolted" the Dragons with a 5-run third inning en route to a 6–0 win; although starter Ken Kizziah only gave up 5 safeties, they came at the wrong time. Wildcat starter Tommy Wagner limited us to a pair of singles; Kenneth Corntassel allowed no runs in 2 innings of relief. On Friday, May 31, the 7-AA series moved to Floyd County, and it was déjà vu once more as we spotted the visitors a 5–0 lead and then spent the rest of the afternoon trying to catch up. The *News-Tribune* noted that "the Dragon Park crowd who turned out in large numbers to support their favorites was beginning to get a little discouraged." Suddenly the home team plated 3 runs and "hope sprung eternal within the human breast." We continued with an assembly of men on base, but the clutch hit would not come. After the 6–3 loss, Otis said, "We had the men we wanted coming to the plate and still couldn't do any damage."

1969 Season

On Tuesday afternoon, April 8, Ken Kizziah threw a 5-hitter versus visiting Cartersville; added to that were 12 strikeouts. However, it took 1 extra frame to put them away 9–2 with an eighth-inning uprising that produced 7 runs. Phil Baker and senior Steve Collins led at the plate with 2 bingles each. On Saturday 4 days later, we pounded Cass into submission 11–1 to go up 2–0 in the Class AA South division; Phil Baker threw a 3-hitter in a contest that lasted only 5 innings due to the 10-run mercy rule. Steve Collins, Kizziah, and Baker each collected 2 safeties. The Red and Gray blasted East Rome 7–2 on Saturday, April 19, as starter Phil Baker allowed only 1 hit late in the game. We collected 11 safeties in the "onslaught" with Baker, Ken Dudley, and Preston Cain collecting 2 each. Although the Pepperell's all-around record stood at 5–0, the buzz around Lindale was the upcoming battle with Cedartown on Tuesday the twenty-second; both squads were unbeaten in subregion play with the winner becoming a decided favorite for the crown. Afterward the *News-Tribune* wrote on Wednesday that it did not seem to matter whether Otis Gilbreath's teams competed in Class A or AA, they could still dominate; case in point was the Dragons' hard-fought 5–3 victory over Cedartown. Facing ace hurler Ross Murphy on the road, our boys put up 2 runs in the third and then added 3 more an inning later. Danny Hutchins, Ray Hines, and Ken Kizziah stroked 2 safeties each; the latter tossed a 6-hitter to go with his plate work. The 2 premier baseball squads in 7-AA met in Calhoun on Wednesday, April 23, anticipating a pitcher's duel. Hamp Alexander's North subregion 9 was once beaten by Westminster while Lindale was 6–0. It was no contest as the South boys romped 9–1 behind 4-hit pitching of Lamar Wright. The rampage began in the third when we erupted with 6 runs aided by the Jackets' 3 walks and 2 miscues; timely singles by Baker and Spence Millican put the game out of reach for the visiting 9. We improved our league standing on the twenty-ninth with another 9–1 road win compliments of Cassville High; Phil Baker slammed a four-bagger in addition to pitching a 1-hitter. Ken Kizziah collected 2 safeties while Preston Cain rapped a 2-run round-tripper. In a return match with powerful Calhoun, our boys proved the earlier win was not fluke. It took 10 innings on the last day of April to whip the Jackets 3–2 in a raggedly played game; Pepperell hurler Lamar Wright had 7 strikeouts but gave up 9 hits and 8 walks. For the losers, Vaughn Robbins whiffed 16 yet walked 8 and gave up 7 base hits. The tenth-frame-winning run happened when Chastain received a base on balls followed by Cain's hit by pitch and Johnny Sutton's free pass to load the bases. Then Phil Baker stroked a clutch single to win.

Continuing in the subregion play, we downed East Rome 5–2 on the sixth day of May behind Lamar Wright's 3-hitter; several batters contributed singles including Cain, Kizziah, Hutchins, and Baker; sophomore David O'Neil and Baker laced back-to-back doubles for our final marker. The 7-2 Cedartown Bulldogs would not go away, forcing the Dragons to travel to Polk County on Monday, May 12 for a rain-delayed game which would decide the championship of Region 7-AA South; in the 4:30 p.m. pitch-off, both 9s had 2 losses in league play. In the 13–12 Dragon victory, it was big bats and not big pitching as the teams combined for 27 safeties with a Ken Kizziah 3-run homer in the seventh deciding the outcome. A rested Calhoun squad waited on the fourteenth for the victorious Lindale 9. Two of the Jackets' 3 season losses were to Coach Gilbreath's squad. The Gordon County 9 of Hamp Alexander had revenge on their minds as they downed Lindale 8–2 in the first encounter with a strong plate attack and pitching of Vaughn Robbins. The next day, they swept the series with a 3–2 victory behind a 2-hit gem by Larry Gilbert; Kizziah and Collins registered our only safeties while the mound crew gave up 8 hits. Calhoun advanced to meet the Region 8-AA champion.

1970 Championship Baseball

Coach Gilbreath's squad had already recorded 2 shutouts (Coosa and West) when it defeated Berry Academy 5–0 on April 6. Ken Kizziah threw a sparkling 2-hitter, and a 4-run first inning gave us the margin we needed. Baker and Kizziah both walked before David O'Neal drove them home; then Gary Burkhalter walked, and Jimmy Farrer singled in 2 more markers. On the fourteenth, we improved to 7–0 after an extra-inning 2–1 victory over Cartersville; the win put us atop the South Region. Ken Kizziah went the distance and allowed the visitors only 2 safeties; on the way, he struck out 12 batters. With the game tied in the bottom of the eighth, O'Neal crossed the plate when Gary Burkhalter's grounder was muffed. Earlier in the fifth, Wayne Chastain doubled, and Johnny Sutton singled him home. The 7-AA Region title now appeared to be between Calhoun and Pepperell. In a best two-of-three subregion playoff series, the Dragons bombed Cass 19–0 on Tuesday, April 29, and came back the next day with a 10–2 verdict in which Phil Baker went 4 for 4 at the plate, including 2 round-trippers; Chastain almost matched his teammate with a homer and 2 bingles. In our twelfth victory without a loss, Kizziah was in complete control, allowing only 3 safeties. Cartersville finished off Cedartown in their playoffs and would visit Lindale on Tuesday, April 5, at 4:30 p.m. The winner would probably take on Calhoun for the Region 7-AA crown.

Well, we remained undefeated with a hard-fought eleventh-inning win over the Hurricanes on Tuesday Mat 5; Baker and Kizziah teamed up to limit the Purple-clads only 2 hits; Phil whiffed 9 batters while Ken cut down 6. But tomorrow was another day as visiting PHS went down 4–3; however, it took 13 innings before a single, a passed ball, and game-clinching base hit ended the marathon. We had 9 hits but committed 6 errors; Lamar Wright was the losing hurler. Behind the levee on Friday, May 8, we claimed the rubber game versus Cartersville 5–3 for the South division championship. However, it was not easy, for we were down 3–1 going into the last inning against an aroused Bartow County squad. The *News-Tribune* reported on Sunday, May 10, that the visitors' hard-throwing Darrell Teague was in complete control, so much so that "it was almost useless to have a seventh inning." But New York Yankee legend Yogi Berra had been quoted as saying, "It ain't over 'til it over." Consequently, Phil Baker singled with 1 out; Lamar Wright followed with a double, sending the runner home, cutting our deficit to 3–2. Kizziah was purposely walked, but with 2 outs, Wayne Chastain stroked a sharp single to plate Wright with the tying run; then Jimmy Farrer hit a line drive single, driving in Kizziah. Johnny Sutton was safe at first on a throwing error, enabling Chastain to put the score at 5–3 Pepperell. And that was how it ended, for Wright "cut the Hurricanes down in order" for the victory. On Monday the eleventh, unbeaten Calhoun came to Shannon's Claude Satterfield Park seeking the region crown against 1-loss Pepperell. Previously, Otis and Hamp Alexander met Saturday, May 9, "to map out plans" for the series; however, only one fact was sure—we would play on Monday. The 2 veterans could not settle on a site, or officials forcing Executive Director Sam Burke to direct chosen umpires showed up at Shannon's Claude Satterfield Park. The contest was about as expected, for Lamar Wright threw a 4-hitter while whiffing 9 Yellow Jackets in the 3–2 PHS victory. In his first loss of the season, Vaughn Robbins threw a 5-hitter with 8 strikeouts and 4 walks. Lindale scored single runs in the first, third, and bottom of the seventh to win. In the last frame, sophomore Don Jacobs walked; he was perfectly sacrificed to second by a Phil Baker bunt and came home when Lamar Wright won his own game with a base hit. Jacobs also started the third inning with a single and later scored to give us a 2–1 frontage. Two days later, we won 2–1 for the region championship as the *News-Tribune* headlined, "Pepperell Takes 7-AA Title...Baker Bests Fletcher in Mound Duel." The youngster gave up some hits but held the hard-hitting Gordon Countians down on the scoreboard. Opposing pitcher Johnny Fletcher gave up only 3 bingles, but the lefty issued 7 base on balls. We plated a sole run in the first inning when Baker walked, stole second, and came home on a misplayed grounder. The victory run came in the sixth frame when Preston Cain lived on a throwing error that allowed a move to second base; Jimmy Farrer promptly singled him home. Region 7-AA champ Pepperell at Region 8-AA powerhouse Elbert County in best-of-three series would be the opening round of state playoff. On Tuesday, May 19, we traveled 3 hours and 160 miles northeast to Elbert County, which is nestled against the South Carolina state line. The *News-Tribune* headlined the following day, "Wright Is Perfect as Pepperell Rolls Over Elbert, 10–0." After the victory, Coach Gilbreath said, "He was right and there wasn't much anyone could do." The coach was referring to senior left-hander Lamar Wright's perfect game in which he faced the minimum 21 batters. What was more amazing was only 1 ball got past the mound when the first batter grounded to second; later the catcher and pitcher each caught foul pop-ups, and then a soft grounder was handled by Wright. The perfectionist hurler got stronger as the game progressed, striking out the side in the sixth and seventh innings which totaled 17 for the afternoon; only 1 count went to 3–2. In the meantime, we pounded out as many hits as Elbert had strikeouts and plated runs in every frame except 2. This year's senior staff had recorded 3 no-hitters, Kizziah against Berry Academy and Baker versus East Rome. Wednesday was a travel day with 2 return games scheduled in Lindale. On Thursday, May 21, we ended the series by "upending" the visitors 4–2 behind Ken Kizziah's 4-hitter; along the way, he matched teammate Wright's 17 strikeouts 2 days before. We scored enough runs to never be in danger of losing; Jimmy Farrer led with 2 singles while Phil Baker stroked a booming triple. After dispatching the Elbert Blue Devils, we hosted East Atlanta on Friday and Saturday, June 5–6; due to pervasive wet grounds elsewhere, the Wildcats would overnight and play the entire series in Lindale. They were 15–0 and featured a strong pitching staff and balanced hitting. The visitors better be good, for our 3 starters, Kizziah, Wright, and Baker, boasted a 0.83 ERA to go with their .400 batting average. Overlooked during the season was an outstanding defense. Kizziah handled first base when he wasn't on the mound. Preston Cain was at third base; Jimmy Farrer usually filled in for Baker at shortstop when he toed the rubber while David O'Neil held down first base. Wright was normally in center field with Farrer in right if the latter was not playing infield; Ray Hines and Dana Burkhalter shared the left field chore while Wayne Chastain and O'Neil handled the catching.

On Friday, June 5, Lamar Wright tossed a 2-hitter in our 2–1 victory; the lefty completely stymied the unbeaten East Atlanta squad from Fulton County as he whiffed 10 batters in the opening round. Offensively, Phil Baker scored both of our runs following a first-inning walk and errors; then he hammered a triple in the sixth and scampered home on a wild pitch. Yet East Atlanta rebounded for a 4–1 win in Saturday's first game of a doubleheader; they used 2 singles and a walk to go ahead 3–0 and stayed in front all the way. Junior Phil Baker allowed only 3 hits but took the loss. After only 24 hours' rest, senior Lamar Wright showed "perfect exhibition on the mound" in the deciding game; he threw a no-hitter in the 2–0, win and if not for 2 walks, it would have been a perfect game. The first walker was cut down on a double play, and the second was picked off. We tallied a run early when Baker walked and eventually crossed the plate when Jimmy Farrer's grounder was bobbled; the final marker came in the third when Preston Cain lived on an error and advanced on 2 grounders. Don Jacobs then drilled a single for an insurance run which warranted this headline on page 1C of Sunday's *News-Tribune*, "Wright Hurls No-Hitter to Fire Dragons to North Georgia Title." Coach Gilbreath announced the state championship series with North Springs High School would start Tuesday, June 9, at 4:00 p.m. in Lindale. The NSHS campus was located at 7447 Roswell Road in Sandy Springs, Georgia. Our Dragons took the first step toward a state AA baseball downing the Spartans 6–3 behind Ken Kizziah's pitching and some clutch hitting. The opponent, who came into South Floyd County with a 17–6 slate, tallied 3 runs in the first 3 frames; however, we had already plated 5 to remain ahead 5–3. Home plate "kept jumping around" for the big strong-armed right-hander Kizziah before he settled down after the third and maintained complete shutout control for the last 4 innings. In the first, Baker, Wright, Farrer, Chastain, and Kizziah benefited from walks, hit batsmen and wild pitches to gain a 2–1 lead over mound opponent Jeff Robinson, but just when it appeared Robinson was out of trouble with 2 outs, dependable Don Jacobs drilled a 2–2 pitch into right center for a 2-run double, and they never recovered; later Gary Burkhalter singled and scored on an infield out. Our final marker came when Farrer and Chastain reached on base hits with the former crossing home on Johnny Sutton's key 2-out bingle to close out the 6–3 victory.

In Lindale on Wednesday, June 10, 1970, Pepperell became state champions with a 1–0 victory; the game took 10 innings to complete, and it was a classic. Although Lamar Wright fanned 7 and issued only 2 free passes, it was evident the lefty's curved and hopping fastball was not on par with other recent outings; however, even with some arm fatigue, he battled and was in general control throughout. Mound opponent Sammy Russell was wild, and we hit him with authority but straight at a fielder. With no score going into the bottom of the tenth, the dugout tension was palpable as first up Johnny Sutton worked Russell for a base on balls; freshman Gary Burkhalter lay down a perfect sacrifice bunt as the runner was off with the pitch. Everyone was safe when the first baseman threw high to second. After a long fly out to center field, pitcher Wright stepped into the box and hit a first pitch "screaming" liner base hit to left center; Sutton wasted no time in racing across the plate with the championship run. The *News-Tribune* expressed it eloquently, "With one swing of the bat, Pepperell's Lamar Wright enshrined himself in the minds and hearts of Dragon fans Wednesday afternoon in a thrilling 1–0 victory over North Springs." Above that quote was the headline, "Wright's Right—Dragons Wear State AA Crown as Pitcher Delivers Extra Inning Hit, Pepperell Takes a 1–0 Win." On Sunday, June 14, sports editor Don Biggers reflected on the stars and role players of the '70 squad. Without a doubt, Baker, Kizziah, and Wright were top-caliber performers on the mound, at bat, and in the field. Judging by the number of scouts and college coaches attending, this group would be offered scholarships or contracts soon. They led a fine team that wanted the state crown badly, yet there were others who played a sub role in the press that contributed greatly. Johnny Sutton, Preston Cain, Jimmy Farrer, Don Jacobs, Gary Burkhalter, Wayne Chastain, and David O'Neil all made their mark. North Springs pitcher and first baseman Jeff Robinson was a big good-natured fellow who sized in at 6 feet, 2 inches, 200 pounds; he was also one of the finest athletes around who quickly became a fan favorite with the "bleacher birds" in Lindale. Jeff noted undersized Gary Burkhalter "is really tough at the plate." Likewise, medium-sized Jimmy Farrer "attacks the ball like a lion…he doesn't back up for any pitcher." Mr. Biggers also mentioned the superstitious nature in the Pepperell dugout where scorekeeper Bob Baker, fan Pee-Wee Coffia, coaches Otis Gilbreath and Guy Hall homesteaded mandated seats on the bench.

1971 Season

When Coach Gilbreath met with the press as reported in Sunday's *RNT* March 21 issue, he was cautiously optimistic for the coming year. The newspaper posed this question, "When you are at the top where else is there to go?" Much of the pitching staff and some position players were off to college; however, starter Phil Baker and backup Preston Cain would provide some stability to the mound. Other returnees included outfielders Don Jacobs and Gary Burkhalter, infielders Johnny Knowles, Billy Fricks (also a backup pitcher), and catcher David O'Neal, who were capable; multi-position player Jimmy Farrer had started more games than not.

We opened the season on March 30 at Legion Field with Region 4-A Model and lost 5–3; the Dragons managed only 4 hits with Farrer getting half of those; Baker threw 6 innings, and Cain, 2 frames. We solved the hitting problem the next day against Berry Academy with a dozen safeties in the 12–3 win; Cain collected 3 bingles while O'Neal produced 4 RBIs; Billy Fricks and Billy Ingle threw a combined 3-hitter. By late Friday afternoon, April 9, the Dragons were 4–1 after a 6–4 victory over host Cedartown; Phil Baker whiffed 11 Bulldogs, almost matching mound opponent Mike Johnson's 13 strikeouts. We visited region foe Cass on Monday, April 12, where both squads were unbeaten in region play, yet when the dust had settled, the Colonels were in first place by virtue of a convincing 8–1 triumph. Jimmy Farrer collected 2 of our 3 hits. On April 14, West Rome felt the wrath of senior Phil Baker's 17 strikeouts in a 5–1 1-hitter decision. Three days later, we pounded out 26 safeties in a 20–1 win over Coosa to push our record to 7–2; Cain and Baker led us at the plate with 5 hits together. At this point in the season, Otis said there was nothing "flukish" about Cass especially when McPherson was "toeing the rubber." Our pitching depth worried the veteran mentor. The *News-Tribune* announced on Monday April 19 that "Baker Inks Georgia Scholarship." The signing took place at Holiday Inn on Sunday afternoon with his parents, Mr. and Mrs. Bob Baker of Summit Drive, Lindale, in addition to coaches Otis Gilbreath and Georgia's Jim Whatley. After 4 tremendous years, the youngster favored opportunities in baseball over football and basketball; he was a 4-year letterman in major sports at Pepperell High School. The local paper's Orbie Thaxton then noted Rome area had sent at least 1 athlete to college in 7 different sports recently with only wrestling left out at press time. Phil made the sports headlines again the following week with "BAKER STRIKES OUT 37, DRAGONS BEAT PAULDING." Not only was the number of batters retired by swings and misses extraordinary, but the game took 4 days to complete as darkness ended 12 scoreless frames of play in Dallas on Monday, April 19, and resumed on Thursday with 3 more turns at bat before Lindale won the fifteenth-inning marathon 4–1. East Rome's Phil Taylor pitched a 3–0 shutout gem against us on Saturday the twenty-third that muddled the subregion standings into a 3-way tie between PHS, Cass, and ER; however, the Colonels "bombed" the Gladiators 14–0 on Monday while we were downing Cedartown 3–2. Billy Ingle pitched into the sixth before Phil Baker relieved him in the 2–2 game; the deciding run happened in the fifth when the Bulldogs' Fincher balked home Ingle from third. The Rome newspaper noted on Thursday, April 29, that "the sweetest thing in athletics is revenge." It was referring to Pepperell's 3–1 victory over Cass the previous day, a game which saw Phil Baker throw a 3-hitter in Lindale. We scored in the third when Baker walked and was bunted to second by Farrer who scampered across the plate on Preston Cain's key single; we never trailed in the game as errors plagued the visitors which enabled the Dragons to take over first place in the subregion. In the first week of May, our squad needed wins over West Rome and Darlington to claim the championship. It did not come to that as the Chieftains eliminated Cassville 11–3 at the same time Pepperell's strong hitting and Phil Baker's clutch pitching were crushing the Lakesiders 8–0. Asked about his team's unexpected gift, Coach said, "We kinda came in the back door, but I'll take it." It had been a good season at 11–3 overall and a 9–2 league slate.

To determine the Region 7-AA championship, we drove 80 miles to face unbeaten Catoosa County's LFO on Monday night, May 10, at nearby East Lake Recreation Center in Chattanooga; in addition to a deep, talented pitching staff, Lakeview was a solid squad that didn't make a lot of mistakes, and we could not afford to get behind in the series. However, we lost the well-played first contest 1–0 despite Phil Baker's 2-hit 13 strikeout performance; even so, the Warriors' staff of Baty and Honeycutt allowed us only a first-inning single by Jimmy Farrer. The opposing 9 squelched 2 Dragon rallies with fine defensive plays. The return game in Lindale was rain postponed until Friday the fourteenth. We were down 4–0 in the sixth primarily because of an error and passed ball, but Pepperell hitters finally got a bead on future major leaguer Rick Honeycutt. Phil Baker walked, moved to second on a passed ball, and scored on Cain's double; Preston came home on O'Neal's single to make it 4–2. Lakeview's Fort Olglethorpe added a single run in the seventh before the Dragons started to rally in the last inning with Ingle's single; he stole second and went to third on a passed ball and was promptly bunted home by Lanny Ely which accounted for the 5–3 final. Preston Cain battled the Catoosa County crew, but 3 unearned runs determined the outcome.

An epilogue: As a high school junior and senior, Frederick Wayne "Ricky" Honeycutt excelled in 2 state championship squads (1971–'72), was named to all-American team at University of Tennessee, and drafted by the Pirates in 1976; he reached the majors a year later to begin a 21-year career. The Georgia native appeared in 797 games, was a 2-time all-star, and pitched in

3 consecutive World Series in 1988, 1989 (world champs), and 1990 before retiring in 1997. The Dodgers hired him as part of their coaching staff in 2006 to the present. On Sunday, May 30, the *News-Tribune* announced the city/county all-star squad; Pepperell's foursome included Phil Baker, Jimmy Farrer, Preston Cain and David O'Neil. Baker finished with a 9–2 pitching chart and batted .351; juniors Farrer and O'Neil hit .321 and .330; they would form the nucleus for 1972. Cain batted .360 as an infielder and pitcher.

Bob Baker's scrapbook is amazing as it documents son Phil's athletic career; post–high school, the young man received multiple offers to play baseball, football, or basketball in college. Most all the major universities wanted him for football including UGA, Georgia Tech, Wake Forrest, Clemson, Yale, VMI, Wofford, Appy State, North Carolina Charlotte, Furman, and Presbyterian. Coach Paul "Bear" Bryant called one day after he committed to Athens baseball. Maryland, Harvard, and Georgia Southern promoted him to basketball as did many; Middle Tennessee State, Georgia, Tech, and UT wanted him for baseball. Several of these universities offered a combination of two sports. After all was said and done, who could argue with his choice of Georgia baseball? Young Baker started as a freshman and had played the infield positions with occasional stints on the mound and in the garden; at times, he had led the team in hitting, was elected captain, and picked on the SEC all-academic squad for maintaining a 3.0 or better GPA. Phil culminated his college career as noted in this article on the Tuesday, June 24, issue of the *News-Tribune*: "PHIL BAKER TO SIGN BASEBALL PACT WITH KANSAS CITY CLUB."

1972 Season

"GILBREATH LOOKING FOR A FEW GOOD MEN." This paraphrased statement from a March 30 *News-Tribune* article on page 6A pretty much summed up Otis's concern about his 1972 baseball squad. Pitching was particularly troubling for 2 sophomores Billy Ingle and Fricks, plus a freshman David Burkhalter appeared to be atop the leaderboard; fortunately, all 3 had progressed through the Pepperell system. With only 3 position players returning, depth was also a problem; Jimmy Farrer at short, Gary Burkhalter in center, and catcher David O'Neal would have to lead the Red and Gray while the pitching staff would have to man the infield and garden when not throwing. Probably Tony Farrer would be at first base while Frankie Mathis and Mike Cabe handled second; Craig Smith would platoon at third. In the garden (outfield), candidates were David Bruce, Don Jacobs, and Keith Pitts. The Dragon mentor ended the interview with, "We have a lot of boys out but the biggest majority are unproven in high school, so it is a matter of wait and see." Lindale met East Rome this Saturday, April Fools' Day, and then Cass, Cedartown, Paulding, West Rome, and Darlington were lurking.

A rainout postponed East Rome, but on Monday, April 3, we went on a home run binge against Cass in winning 10–8 in extra innings; Jimmy Farrer and Ingle hit double round-trippers while our two Davids, Bruce and O'Neal, collected 1 four-bagger each; pitchers Ingle and Fricks gave up 9 hits in the tag team win. On April 10, we topped Paulding 7–2 behind the 2-hit pitching of Billy Ingle; although he also had a couple of singles in the game, it was David Bruce's 3-run slam that decided the contest. The Patriots' score box read 2 hits, 2 runs, and 2 errors. On April 11, the ground finally got dry enough to play 7 innings against visiting East Rome, and the Dragons responded with a 4–2 victory; we never trailed after Don Abercrombie started the third with a single to get things started on the way to plating a pair of runs; PHS capped that off with 2 more in the sixth. Billy Fricks and David O'Neal rapped 3 hits each while Ingle collected 2 safeties in the 10-hit affair. Fricks was the winning pitcher for Lindale, which needed only a victory over West to clinch first place in the region playoffs. On Thursday the thirteenth, *Rome News-Tribune* headlined on page 6A that "Dragons Upend Chiefs...Clinching the Regular Season Title in Region 7-AA." It was our fifth straight victory. In a contest described as "a tight, well-played game," West had a 1–0 advantage until the bottom of the sixth when Jimmy Farrer singled and Fricks reached on an error; catcher David O'Neal then laced a long triple to clean the bases and settle the final score at 2–1. Pepperell enjoyed beating Darlington and vice versa; in a last regular season game played on April 14, we downed our friends from the Lakeside 16–5. A big 7-run first inning was followed up with 3 more each in the second, fourth, and fifth frames. The home squad pounded out 15 hits with Gary Burkhalter getting 2 singles and a long triple; Billy Ingle pitched a complete game for the win. PHS hosted Paulding County on April 26 in the best-of-three region playoffs. We won the first encounter on Wednesday, but a day later, the Patriots' Elsberry served up a 2-hit masterpiece in winning 2–0; he was helped by 4 double plays and timely hitting by the visitors. It was the Dragons 'first loss of the year. Next, with revenge on our minds, Coach Gilbreath's crew combined 12 safeties with flawless fielding in a dominating 16–0 series win. The high score came about because of walks, errors, and clutch batting; Don Jacobs, David O'Neal, and Billy Ingle combined for 7 hits. On the mound, Ingle scattered 7 hits in winning.

On the first day of May, West Rome went 1 game up in best-of-three South Region playoffs, defeating host Pepperell 4–2 behind the pitching of junior right-hander Chris DiLorenzo and the hitting of Martin Rollinson. The former spaced 8 Dragon hits while the latter batted 3 for 4; Billy Fricks took the loss while Jacobs and Cabe collected 2 safeties each for the losers. The 2 squads planned to continue Wednesday on WR field. However, weather forced the second contest to Monday, May 8. The local pundits now thought "the odds are in the Chiefs favor." In addition to a 12–3 record, Coach Charles Tarpley believed his crew had "jelled" as a team. At game time, we were expecting DiLorenzo again on the mound; instead, Johnny Thompkins threw a "neat" 1-hitter in the 4–0 shutout sweep for the South championship. Unfortunately for the Chieftains, the winner of the North Region was the 1971 defending Class AA champion Lakeview who subsequently marched to their second consecutive state crown.

1973 Season

The Thursday, March 29, issue of Rome's newspaper highlighted, "Dragon Youth Movement Gets Off on Victory Note." It was referring to Pepperell's 8–3 win over Berry Academy the previous afternoon. Veteran junior pitcher Phil Langston was credited with the victory; however, in the late innings, Coach Gilbreath brought in freshman Jimmy Baker to give him some high school baseball experience in hopes he and sophomore David Burkhalter would help our club in the future; junior Billy Ingle also threw a short stint on the mound while junior Carl Crider was ready if needed. Ace left-hander Billy Fricks would pitch today against East Rome; all in all,

Otis thought we would be a youthful club with "pretty good pitching." A few lettermen returned from last year including catcher Tony Farrer, shortstop Frankie Mathis, and "the best outfielder around" Gary Burkhalter; senior Mike Cabe would have a role somewhere as would infielder Jim Jackson. A plethora of kids had flitted up from the summer leagues with Randy Green and Craig Smith leading the way; however, Jimmy Reagan, Tony Bradshaw, Joe Henderson, Doug Smith, Keith Pitts, and Sidney Sheffield would eventually make their mark. On Wednesday, April 4, we erupted for 3 runs at first bat to down Cedartown 4–2; PHS collected 5 hits, all singles, while our hurlers Langston, Crider, and Baker limited the Bulldogs to only 2 hits. Two days later, the Dragons encountered Coosa's "junk" pitcher Tommy Rhinehart who stymied them with a 2-hitter. The youngster kept batters off-balance all afternoon in winning 2–0. The loser's Billy Fricks threw well enough to win allowing only 5 singles; however, errors led to single runs in the third and fourth frames. During the second week of April, Pepperell schedule showed a home game with Cass and road trips to West Rome and Darlington. Our bats went silent versus WR in a 5–0 loss on April 11. The South subregion now shaped up with Cassville at number one followed by the Chieftains and Paulding County. After 5 innings at Lakeside on Friday, April 13, the game was a 4–4 standoff when all of a sudden "Pepperell took complete control of the situation." The result was a 12-run inning blasting of Darlington 17–7; strangely, the uprising occurred after the first 2 batters were retired. All told, we collected a dozen hits including 2 each by Burkhalter, Cabe, Ingle, and Sheffield; the Tigers were hurt by 4 errors. Billy Fricks allowed 7 hits and went the distance for the win.

After next Saturday's afternoon scores were posted, WR Green Machine "owed us one," for we surprised Cass 6–5, thereby gifting West Rome the South championship without them lifting a bat. By virtue of that victory, Lindale moved into third place. Versus the Colonels, our boys plated 3 runs each in the second and fourth innings helped along by errors and Gary Burkhalter's 2 safeties. Phil Langston and Billy Ingle shared the mound victory. On Monday, April 16, Paulding County used the long ball and 80 minutes to eke out a 3–2 victory over Lindale; the Patriots plated a solo run in the third and 2 more in the fifth—all on four-baggers. Our first marker came in the third when Sheffield walked followed by Jackson and Burkhalter's bingles; in a later inning, Mike Cabe and Ingle walked before Frankie Mathis drove in Cabe. One day later in Dallas, the home squad downed us for a second time; they pounded out 12 hits, mostly singles in the 9–2 pasting. Our first run came courtesy of a Sidney Sheffield single; in the last inning, Jimmy Reagan doubled, and Gary Burkhalter brought him home with a bingle. The 2 victories enabled Paulding County to compete in the South playoffs while we matched up and defeated Darlington 4–3 in a consolation game.

1974 Season

According to *News-Tribune* on March 31, veteran coach Otis Gilbreath's baseball in 1974 was "wait and see time." He wasn't sure of improvement over last year, for only Phil Langston returned to the pitching staff. The Dragons had plenty of throwers; however, how many were pitchers? Greg Jackson was up from the Pony League while a possibility was Alabama transfer Ronald Nance or letterman David Burkhalter; then there were Mark Gray, Tony Stansell, and

Jimmy Baker waiting for mound duty. In the infield, Phillip Ball was at first base with Baker at second and probably Sidney Sheffield at short; Greg Payne would back up Craig Smith at the "hot corner." In the garden, Doug Smith returned in left with Bobby Allen or Keith Pitts in right; Sheffield would patrol center field when not at shortstop. The schedule began Monday, April 1, at Cassville and after visiting Bartow County, it was "murders row" with games versus Cedartown, Coosa, Darlington, West Rome, Paulding, and East Rome. Cassville's Ronnie Arp pitched the top game of the day in a 5–1 subregion victory over PHS; he recorded 15 strikeouts and allowed only Sheffield to hit safely. Greg Jackson was the losing pitcher for Pepperell. In Lindale on Wednesday, April 3, Cedartown left no doubt their intentions to win as they plated 6 runs in the first frame en route to a 14–2 final. Bulldog pitcher Bobby Coile (sic) limited the Dragons to 3 safeties. At Darlington on April 24, the Lakesiders scored 3 in the fourth, 4 in the third, and 5 in the sixth to win going away 12–5. Starter Greg Jackson suffered the loss; Jimmy Reagan slugged 2 home runs for the losers. Two days later in Lindale, it was "déjà vu" as West Rome erupted for 3 runs in the first; 4 more in the third; 4 in the fifth, and then a half dozen in the sixth to blast the Dragons 16–5. On Monday, April 29, in Dallas, we couldn't stop Paulding County from scoring; they plated runs in every inning except the last to "lash" Pepperell 16–0; the visitors managed only 2 safeties in the game. It got worse on Tuesday, April 30, when East Rome's Ronnie Rowland threw a no-hitter against the Lindale 9; he struck out 8 batters and did not walk a man in the 10–0 shutout. Meanwhile, his offense hammered out 8 safeties off 2 unnamed PHS hurlers that produced 9 runs in the fourth inning. The Coosa Eagles defeated us on consecutive days in May; no score was posted for May 1. However, on the second, Alabama Road coach Sonny Mason's squad "whitewashed" the Red and Gray 5–0 behind Tommy Rhinehart's complete game 4-hitter. The losing battery were Greg Jackson and Jimmy Reagan. The winners ended their season at 5–8 while Pepperell finished at an astonishing 0–13. On May 7, as a footnote to the season, Calhoun Yellow Jackets edged West 7–6 in extra innings for the Region 7-AA championship. Closing out the school year, Pepperell High School graduated 176 seniors on Friday, May 31; valedictorian Davey Joe Roberson and salutatorian Sari Ann McCorkle spoke at the commencement.

1975 Season

Before the high school season began, word out of Athens was former Dragon Phil Baker would serve as team captain and starting second baseman for UGA. The first report on Pepperell baseball occurred on Tuesday, April 1, in the *News-Tribune*; the previous afternoon, West Rome won 2–1 by scoring 2 runs in the first and making it stand up. We avoided a shutout with a single marker in the sixth; the Red and Gray loaded the bases after Tim Hogan singled, but it took a bad pickoff throw to plate the run. For PHS, Steve Green started on the mound and took the loss although he was not around at the end. The following day, Pepperell won over Darlington 6–3; although the winners had only 4 hits, the Tigers helped out with 2 errors. Dennis Whatley led us with a double and single. On Friday, April 4, Tim Hogan and Barry Henderson stroked 2 hits each for Lindale in claiming a 13–10 victory over Shannon. It was pitching by committee as Greg Jackson, Todd Smith, and Hogan handled the mound work; both squads batted 9 safeties.

We picked up a second victory over Darlington on the eighth when Jimmy Reagan pounded a bases-loaded home run in the 14–7 win. At the time, the winners were down 5–3 to the Lakesiders; however, his blast "opened the dam" that led to 8 runs in the sixth inning; 3 more were added in the next frame. Reagan was 3 for 4 and teamed with Bradshaw and Pitts who collected 2 safeties each. Green was the starting pitcher but gave way to eventual winner Todd Smith in the fourth. On April 11, Chattanooga Valley came to Lindale and won a hard-fought Friday game 3–2. The home Dragons jumped to an early 2–0 advantage when Billy Bradshaw singled before Jimmy Riggins and Tim Hogan managed consecutive base on balls; then Doug Smith's sacrifice fly produced our first run. The second marker crossed home plate after a wild throw. Pepperell's record moved to 4–3 overall and 1–1 in the subregion. In a makeup game the next day, Coach Gilbreath's 9 ran roughshod over host and rival Model 19–5; the Blue Devils must have run out of pitching, for we trailed 5–2 as late as the fourth frame before starting on a tear. The Dragons plated 4 runs in the fourth, 4 in the fifth, 5 in the sixth, and 4 in the seventh; we doubled up the Blue in safeties 16–8. Tim Hogan increased his batting average with 4 base hits; Bradshaw and Jackson had 3 each. Greer collected the victory in relief. The subregion turned into a battle between Chattanooga Valley 5–0 and Pepperell 4–1.

The two leaders met on Tuesday, April 22, in the Valley, and as before, we lost to a close game 2–1; the winners scored solo runs in the second and fifth frames which bested our single tally in the fifth when Whatley and Jim Jackson walked followed by an RBI single by Greg Jackson. By virtue of the 2 victories over Pepperell, the Eagles won the crown. In a final game, the Red and Gray won a 1-run game versus visiting Model 3–2; these type of close contests had not been kind to the Dragons this year as we had lost 4 times by single digits. The squad finished 1975 with an 8–4 record thanks to "tight pitching" from Steve Green who allowed only 3 safeties in going the distance. Pepperell got a solo marker in the first when Hogan walked and advanced to second by Jim Reagan's bunt; Greg Jackson brought him home with a bingle. We knotted the game at 2–2 in the next inning with a Phil Ball walk and errors by the Devils; the game was won in our last at bat on a Barry Henderson single, a sacrifice to second by Gregg Payne and Tim Hogan's base hit to end the contest. The only thing left for the class of 1975 was graduation. The Rome City Auditorium seated 187 Pepperell High School seniors on Friday, May 30, where valedictorian Myrtle Yvonne Satcher and salutatorian Charles Frederick Palmer spoke to their classmates for a final time.

1976 Season

Coach Otis Gilbreath had always been available and honest with the press whether it was his team or opponents; this year was no different as the veteran mentor thought Region 4-A would be a "tough league" in 1976—one that could produce a champion. Chattanooga Valley had most of its squad back; Model expected to be improved, and Darlington could easily have a shot at the title. Although he did not say it, Pepperell should be a favorite with 9 returnees, 4 of whom were pitchers. Tim Hogan was a catcher/outfielder while Steve Green, Todd Smith, and Greg Jackson would be in the lineup somewhere. Other starters were catcher Barry Henderson; Chris Farrer, third; Billy Bradshaw, second base; and Sandy Lloyd and Michael Whatley in the garden. These last three were the only seniors. Young hurlers would come from Joel Little, Joe Marion, and Lee Hayes while backup outfielders were Gene Nelson, Steve Turner, Mark Fricks, and Greg Payne. True to form, the above performers played a large role in the Dragons' first game 16–3 victory over East Rome on Monday, March 29. We jumped the Gladiators' 7 runs in the first inning and never looked back; Green, Smith, Marion, and Little pitched some while Lloyd led us in hitting with April 4; Barry Henderson also contributed 2 safeties. We moved into the region on Friday, April 2, with a 6–3 win over Darlington; the game was close until the sixth when the winners "erupted" for 4 runs thanks to 4 walks, a wild pitch, and an error; Whatley led us with 2 bingles while Steve Green collected 7 strikeouts in going the distance. We went to Shannon on the sixth and hit for 11 safeties which plated 3 runs in the first, 1 in the second, 2 in the third, a singleton in the fourth, and 2 more the next inning. Although Green and Hogan each rapped 2 hits, the big blow was Michael Whatley's 3-run homer. Steve Green again pitched a complete game, striking out 10 Blue Devils in the 9–5 region victory. One day later, we welcomed East Rome to Lindale and treated them rudely again with a solid 16–8 win; although we trailed 7–4 going into the bottom of the fourth, a 12-hit 9-run inning spelled defeat for the visitors. In that frame, the Dragons had 5 extra base hits helped along by 2 walks and an error; Whatley slammed a four-bagger to straightaway center field; he and Greg Jackson each had three hits. Todd Smith was credited with the mound victory. In Lindale on Friday, April 9, Darlington surprised us 8–5; we led the Tigers 5–0 after 4 innings only to see the visitors' tally 1, 5, and 2 runs in the last 3 innings. Greg Jackson took the mound loss for PHS. Pepperell's record was now 5–2 and 1–1 in the region. The Red and Gray welcomed and lost to Chattanooga Valley on Monday, April 12; the visitors came away with a 7–5 verdict, leaving the Dragons at 5–3 overall and 1–2 in league play. The Eagles scored three in the first and then plated 4 more runs 3 frames later for the win; Steve Green was the losing hurler while Barry Henderson led at the bat with 2 safeties. However, Otis's boys rebounded on Thursday by shutting out Model 9–0; Tim Hogan fired a 2-hitter in striking out 11 and allowed only 1 walk. Steve Turner, Henderson, Jackson, and Bradshaw (triple) led a big 5-run uprising in the fourth inning. On Wednesday, April 21, the local paper wrote this about the Dragons' 9–1 victory over host Darlington, "Yesterday Pepperell's Steve Green turned in perhaps one of the best mound jobs of the season in leading Lindale past the Lakesiders. He went the distance, allowing only two hits, striking out nine, walking five and was in complete command throughout." We plated runs in the first, second, third, and sixth innings courtesy of opponent errors, hit batsmen, and multiple singles of which Green was top with 3 while Turner, Henderson, and Lloyd all had 2 each. In a Thursday, April 22, non-region slugfest against West Rome, we took the Legion Field game 13–10; Pepperell runs were caused by Steve Green and Steve Turner doubles and Barry Henderson, Tim Hogan, Greg Jackson, Bubba Bradshaw, and Sandy Lloyd singles; winning pitcher Keith Jackson contributed a 2-run homer late in the contest. The Dragons made a long trip to region leader Chattanooga Valley on the following day. The high school was located in Flintstone 12 miles from Tennessee; it consolidated after 1988 with Ridgeland. The Dragons were tied 6–6 until the bottom of the sixth frame when their host plated an 8-run "outburst" to win going away 14–6. The victory clinched 4-A North title for the Eagles. Hogan, Green, and freshman Joe Marion shared the mound duties; Henderson led all batter with 3 safeties while Jackson and Hogan rapped 2 bingles. The all-area team was announced on Sunday, May 2; the second 9 included Steve Green and Barry Henderson. The talk around the county was Coosa's first baseball playoff appearance; they downed George High School before being eliminated by Lakeview High.

1977 Season

Otis Gilbreath began the season with an interview with *News-Tribune* writer Darrell Black; in reflecting on Pepperell's six state championships, the veteran coach believes winning in high school baseball was different than other sports because most programs have to wait until spring football was over to get ready, and then there was seasonal disruptive weather. However, Lindale was a step ahead with their summer ball, which prepared good mound men and hitters early on. He said, "You can't win without good pitching." He put best athletes on the hill in the younger leagues and let them learn the craft. Tradition also helped the community produce good squads, for local kids expect to win while others were opposite in their outlook. Most Lindale champions had common traits; it helped to have a senior-laden 9 with a strong mental attitude. "I've had several teams that were better than some of our No. 1 state squads; the difference was self-discipline in that the champs refuse to get beat and would do whatever it takes to win." However, the "ball's got to also bounce just right for you." In addition, we were fortunate to line up in a competitive area. He finished by noting, "In 1970 the toughest baseball team we faced that year was Calhoun; the next year we were eliminated by state champion Lakeview who they told us later we were their top competition."

The Dragons opened 1977 on Thursday, March 24, versus Darlington in a non-counting region contest. Steve Green whiffed 15 Tigers while giving up 2 hits and 4 walks in the 7–3 decision. We plated 3 runs in the second, 2 more in the fourth, and 2 in the sixth; Buster Knowles, Steve Turner, Tim Hogan, and Green were the hitting stars. In the first week of April, we played in the Bulldog (Cedartown) tournament, and although it was billed as a pitching duel, we nipped Cass 8–7; Tim Hogan gave up 3 runs early but settled down and threw a 6-hitter. The Colonels jumped us a trio before Barry Henderson came home on Greg Jackson's double; the same players plated another marker in the third inning before we exploded for 5 unearned runs in the next frame courtesy of Cass errors, walks, and Jackson's third hit of the day. In the second week of April, we trounced East Rome in a 7-A contest 11–1; Steve Green recovered from recent illness, but the ace 6-foot-6 fireballer was good enough striking out 10 Gladiators while allowing only 2 hits. Otis said afterward, "He's not in full strength yet, but he looked pretty good today." Jackson, Fricks, Gentry, and Henderson all collected safeties as we scored in bunches. The local paper highlighted, "Dragons Roll" on page 1B of the Wednesday, April 13, issue. They were referring to Pepperell's 10–1 victory Tuesday over rival Darlington. Underneath, it stated that "a strong pitching performance and clutch hitting will spell victory every time." When this happened, "they're simply too stout for most high school teams." Senior Tim Hogan took the mound and went all the way striking out 7 while allowing the Tigers only 3 hits. Again, the Lindale boys scored in bunches with Turner, Gentry, Jackson, Green, and Fricks leading the batters. One day later, our squad won again by 10–1; this time, the Dragons avenged an earlier loss to Model. Although the season was young yet, the two teams were tied for subregion. Steve Green continued his dominance by striking out 11 batters and allowing only 3 hits. It was Darlington time again on Monday, April 18; we plated 10 markers in the third frame which shortened the 10–0 contest 2 innings later due to the mercy rule. Tim Hogan was the winning hurler allowing 3 Tiger safeties while his mates pounded the baseball. Mark Fricks had a grand slam; Steve Green slammed a 2-run homer. Barry Henderson garnered a pair of hits while Greg Jackson "continued his pace as a candidate for the area's top hitter going 4/4." April 20, we won 4–1 over Model and improved our record to 10–2; more importantly, the victory gave the Dragons a 2-game lead in the subregion chase. The game statistics indicated a tie because both squads managed just 3 safeties; each made 4 errors while both mound men struck out 6 and walked four. Pepperell's Steve Green threw 7 strong innings in the victory. Lindale plated 2 runs in the third on an error, 2 walks and a pass ball; the remaining makers happened on a single, a walk, a sacrifice, and Greg Payne's bingle that chased 2 runners home. Five days later, the Red and Gray moved one step closer to the North title with an 8–4 victory over Darlington; senior right-hander Tim Hogan hurled a complete game 4-hit outing while teammates were plating a solo run in the first, four markers in the second, and a trio in the sixth. Chris Shiflett collected 3 hits, and Steve Gentry, 2, that pushed Pepperell's overall record to 11–2 and 8–1 within the subregion. Back in early April, the Dragons trounced East Rome 11–1; on Tuesday the twenty-sixth, it was different, for the Rome squad was much improved. It took a stout pitching performance by Greg Jackson to subdue the Gladiators 2–1 which clinched the region crown for Lindale. He scattered 3 bingles behind a tight Dragon defense. Although ER's Robert Long threw well allowing only 5 safeties, the winners crossed home twice in the initial frame. Steve Turner singled, Steve Gentry doubled, and Steve Green brought both home with a bingle. Pepperell claimed the North Region with a 9–1 mark and 12–2 on the season so far. Three days later on Friday, April 29, it was East Rome again; once more, Coach Gilbreath's 9 came away a winner. Sophomore Buster Knowles got the start and responded with a 4-hit 4–1 victory; Gentry, Henderson, and Tim Hogan led a third-inning uprising that plated 3 runs. Carrollton High School had won the South Region 7-A; reports were that this team had fielding, hitting, and pitching, and were prime candidates for a championship. The Trojans hosted us on Tuesday, May 3, in the first of a best-of-three series. We struggled at the bat and lost 4–1; Otis said we had our chances with 6 hits to 5 for the Trojans, but 4 errors and untimely batting were our downfall. Steve Green threw well enough, but his teammates could manage only a solo home run by Jackson. Consequently, our boys needed to win a doubleheader in Lindale to advance farther, and we did. They defeated CHS 5–2 and 7–2 to take the Region crown. Steve Green hurled the first victory, limiting Black and Gold to a pair of singles while whiffing nine; his fastball was overwhelming. A 4-run fourth was all he needed to win the game; singles by Green himself, Shiflett, Turner, Gentry, and a 2-base hit by Hogan plated the markers. In the championship game later in the day, Tim Hogan allowed 6 hits in the 7–2 win but spaced them so the issue was never in doubt. The hitting stars were Turner, Fricks, Knowles, and Green. Coach Otis noted after the game that "we hit the ball pretty good, but more importantly we hit the ball at the right time." On Monday, May 9, we traveled to Ellenwood in South Dekalb County for a first game versus Cedar Grove and outslugged the home standers 10–5; Steve Green gave up only 5 hits, but 2 safeties in the third inning at the right time plated 3 markers for the opponent. We came back in the next frame to take a permanent lead 4–3; Shiflett, Knowles, Turner, Henderson, Jackson, and pitcher Green led the way at the plate. A big 2-run homer by Barry Henderson in the sixth "broke 'em up," said Coach Gilbreath. PHS did not waste any time the next day defeating the Saints 8–5 and being 1 of 4 teams left in Class A baseball playoffs. In the game, both Hogan and Story had similar stats, allowing 6 hits each, walking 8, and going 2 for 4 at the bat. But Hogan had a bases-clearing double and a 2-run triple in his favor; on the other hand, Story became only the second player in seven years to hit a ball out of Pepperell Park. Up next was a doubleheader with North Gwinett of Suwanee in the semifinals of state baseball. The squads were opposites, for the Bulldogs had a lineup stocked with good hitters, and Pepperell depended on excellent pitching. "They can really hit the ball," Coach Otis noted in his scouting report. The opposing coaches agreed to play the entire series in Lindale beginning on Wednesday, May 18. We lost the early game 4–2 before rallying in the late afternoon battle 6–5. In the opener, Lindale kept starter Tracy Floyd in hot water most of the game but left 13 runners stranded while waiting on a timely hit. Steve Green held a heavy hitting squad to only 6 safeties while Steve Turner, Henderson, and Jackson used singles to manufacture our 2 scores. In the second affair, it was necessary for the Dragons to come from behind late to defeat Gwinett by a run. After Pepperell plated 5 markers early on, the Bulldogs rallied to force an extra inning. The winning run came in the bottom of the eighth after Green singled. Hogan lived on a fielder's choice, moved to second when Fricks walked. Chris Shiflett then "laced his first pitch up the middle" as Hogan came across to win 6–5. In the third and deciding game, North Gwinett's first batter and starting pitcher Tracy Floyd swung late, hit a "sinking line drive over first that kicked right and rolled almost to the field house." He never stopped running on an inside-the-park home run and a 1–0 lead. But after that, Green threw perhaps his best game, allowing 2 safeties and whiffing 11 Bulldogs. The Dragons tied it in the fifth when Fricks singled. Shiflett was safe on a field's choice and sophomore Knowles "lofted" a long triple. PHS claimed the victory in the last inning when Fricks was on with an error. Shiflett was safe on a fielder's choice, and Turner was hit by pitch; with 2 on and 2 out, Gentry stroked a 2-2 pitch through the left side as Shiflett scampered home with the win. After a rain delay, the 20–5 Lindale 9 traveled 115 miles south on I-75 to Butts County where we faced Jackson High School. The Wednesday, May 25, doubleheader began the best-of-three series for state championship. Coach Gilbreath described the play as "beautiful baseball games." Red Devil hurler Andy Waldrop issued only a pair of bingles while whiffing 9 Dragons in the 2–1 victory; it was the most strikeouts for us all year. "He has a fine slider and we hadn't seen one of those this year," commented the losing coach. Our only score occurred in the fifth when our Jackson lived on an error, went to second on a wild throw, and came home on Chris Shiflett's single. Pepperell pitcher Steve Green threw well also, giving up only two hits also; however, these safeties came at the right time for the Devils. In the following clutch game, Tim Hogan pitched and won 4–1 while scattering 5 hits; the visitors put a run on the board in the second inning when Green walked, was sacrificed, and came home on a throwing miscue. In the sixth, "our bats came alive" as we plated a trio of markers to go up 4–0. Gentry, Henderson, and Green provided the sticks. At 2:00 p.m., Saturday, May 28, it was in Butts County again for the Class A championship game. Earlier, the *News-Tribune* mused that tradition was when the coach and athletic director had trouble remembering the number of the school's runners-up and state championships. "I think we've won about five times with about the same second places," Otis commented before the Jackson series began. The paper did its homework and determined 6 (the last in 1970) state crowns with 4 number-two finishes; the late May playoff with the Jackson Red Devils made 11 finals for Lindale.

Rome *News-Tribune* notified Northwest Georgia sports fans on Sunday morning, May 29, "Dragons Get Class A Title as 'Seven' Proves a Charm." Beneath that headline was "Green hurls five-hitter in finale." The lucky number was of course seven; 1970 was last number one. The seventh title came in 1977. Region 7-A winning pitcher walked 7 in the 7–2 win for the seventh school championship. The victory was not as close as the score would indicate, for Jackson plated 2 markers in the last inning; Green's "gutsy performance" allowed them only 5 hits and whiffed 9 batters. The Dragons' offense plated 4 runs in the third frame (the paper noted we could have closed shop at that time), a pair in the fifth, and a solo counter in, what else, the seventh. The host squad contributed 5 errors to the above rallies. Of our 7 safeties, Mark Fricks led with a single, double, and home run; Green helped his own cause with a single and double, hits that produced 3 RBIs. Afterward, a relaxed Otis Gilbreath told Darrell Black, "Back in March I thought we'd be pretty good and later felt that we were the best team I saw in Class A this season." He added, "A lot of the credit has to go to assistant coach Guy Hall. He's done an excellent, excellent job for us; I can't say enough good about the job he's done. He's worked these boys hard and it paid off. The most difficult part of a state crown is getting out of the region… Model was tough; Carrollton had a solid club; North Gwinnett had some sticks in their lineup." He noted Pepperell success on the diamond came from a strong summer program headed by Pony League manager Pee Wee Coffia. Postseason all-star accolades went to Steve Green, Greg Jackson, Barry Henderson, and Tim Hogan.

1978 Season

The big news in mid-February around Lindale concerned Coach Otis Gilbreath. The veteran mentor was nominated and inducted as a member of Rome/Floyd County Hall of Fame on Thursday night, February 9. This recognition only added to his credentials, which also included Georgia (six times), District 3, Southeastern, and National Coach of the Year. About all these accolades, Otis said, "Well, if you win the state or runner-up…you've got a chance because they've got to pick somebody."

In late March, there was good news from Athens where former Dragon and freshman Steve Green had a 2–0 record for the Bulldogs. On the local scene, the *News-Tribune* wondered, "Can Dragons repeat as 'A' champs?" They appeared as strong as last year except on the mound where all 3 primary hurlers graduated and signed scholarships. Catcher and infield were in excellent shape with Barry Henderson catching for a fourth year while Steve Gentry, Steve Turner, and Chris Shiflett were veterans in the infield. Senior Neal McChargue along with juniors Buster Knowles and Tim Hayes led a varied group of pitchers. The media practically conceded the region to Pepperell before a pitch had been made, but Coach Otis was not buying it, saying, "Model may have the best team overall…while East Rome and Darlington both made lots of progress in the summer programs." Rockmart came to Lindale on Tuesday, March

28; for unexplained reasons, the Jackets had not fielded a baseball team "in quite a while." In the game, Steve Turner stroked a 3-run double that broke a 3–3 tie in the sixth inning, giving us a 7–3 victory; McChargue and Lance Morris shared the mound duties, allowing 4 hits; the visitors committed a like amount of errors. Two days later, it was the Polk County Bees again, but this time, it took an extra inning to subdue host Rockmart 9–7; we exploded for 5 runs in the fourth frame to take a 6–2 lead thanks to errors, walks, and Henderson's bingle. The Jackets refused to yield as they knotted the game 7–7 in the sixth. In the top of the extra inning eighth, 2 walks preceded singles by Hayes and Morris, which ended the scoring. Benjie Shiflett and Buster Knowles pitched the win; the Dragons' record was now 3–1. On April 3, reality came to us versus East Rome; the visiting Dragons were leading 7–6 in the bottom of the ninth with 1 out to get for victory. But a base on balls was followed by Kevin McClinic's walk-off 2-run blast that gave the Glads an 8–7 win over Lindale. Coach Rick Walker said, "It's the first time we've beaten them in five years or more." Six of his players practiced only 2 days due to spring football. Henderson, Gentry, and Hayes each had 2 safeties for the losers whose record slipped to 5–2. Forty-eight hours later, we vented our frustration against Model by winning 18–6; the contest was close until the fourth when Pepperell sent 19 batters to the plate. Of those, 6 reached on errors, 6 reached on hits, and 3 were issued walks; junior Buster Knowles was excellent on the mound scattering 7 Blue Devils singles while striking out a dozen. Darlington was as good as predicted; first-year coach Sam Sprewell's crew fell behind the Lindale 9, 6–0, before falling 6–5 to the home Dragons as reported in the Sunday, April 8, local gazette. The first score and highlight of the battle was a mighty home run blast by senior catcher Barry Henderson. He "put a tag on it no doubt," said Otis, adding that it was the first four-bagger to clear the right field fence at Pepperell in 8 years. Lee Hayes hurled the first 6 innings with McChargue closing it in the seventh to improve our record at 7–2. The Dragons avenged an earlier loss to East Rome on April 10, claiming a 7–2 victory; the story of the game was Joe Marion's "fine showing" on the mound in limiting the opponent to just 2 hits through 6 innings; he was in control the entire contest. Steve Turner, Marion, Gentry, and Hayes led us at the plate to push our record to 8–2 overall and 3–1 in the subregion. On April 12, Model recovered from an earlier 18–6 fiasco versus Pepperell to win an upset 7–4; the Devils got good pitching from Ken Keith who scattered 7 hits and whiffed half a dozen Dragons. Neal McChargue provided a homer while Greg Shiflett and Everett added singles for the losers. The following Monday the seventeenth, it was "déjà vu all over again" as the Rome Gladiators won 6–5 again; as before, East was down to their last out trailing 5–4 with a lone runner on base. Freshman Eric Tutt chose this moment to hit a first career home run which cleared the center field fence for the victory. We led most of the game before Tutt's blast. On Thursday, April 20, visiting Model pitcher Ken Keith had a 5-hitter going into the sixth inning when control problems beset him. Pepperell turned 7 base on balls into 10 runs, and a close contest became a 14–5 win for Lindale. "It was a good game...but I think their pitcher got a little tired in the sixth inning." Although Joe Marion came on in late-inning relief, Neal McChargue picked up the mound win to move our record to 9–5. In the Sunday paper of April 23, Don Biggers wrote that it was only news when Pepperell lost; this article was followed by a description of Darlington's 9–1 victory in Lindale the day before. Senior right-hander Joey Abney checked the powerful Dragons "on but one hit" and was never in serious trouble to push the Tigers into a 1-game lead in the subregion. Meanwhile, his offense collected 9 safeties to go with several errors and walks by the home team. Losing pitchers Lee Hayes and Benjie Shiflett combined for 2 hits through the fourth before the abovementioned miscues took a toll. "They just came out and beat us. That's all there was to it," said Coach Otis. We rebounded on Monday the twenty-fourth versus East Rome with an 8–1 win; Joe Marion allowed 3 hits while facing only 4 batters over the minimum. Barry Henderson, Lee Hayes, Buster Knowles, Steve Gentry, and Tony Hyder plated runs in several innings to improve our record to 10–5. On April 27, PHS topped Model 8–6 for the third time this season; again, Steve Gentry, Buster Knowles, and Everett drove in markers for their squad, but the big blast was Barry Henderson's 2-run four-bagger in the fourth. That was the good news; however, first-place Darlington edged East Rome 8–6 to protect their 1-game advantage in the region. On Friday, April 28, PHS and DHS replayed a protested game at the Lakeside per GHSA ruling; if the hosts win, they were 7-A North champs and the Tigers rolled over Lindale 7–3 to claim the subregion championship; Lee Hayes took the mound loss for the visitors although Shiflett relieved him in the fourth. On page 6C of Sunday's paper, the sports headline featured, "DARLINGTON PICKS UP A 7–3 DECISION TO WIN SUB-REGION." The victors plated a 4-spot in the third inning and scored single runs in the fourth, fifth, and sixth to "put the game on ice." First-year Coach Sam Sprewell said, "I'm proud of my kids…Anytime you beat Pepperell you've got to feel happy." However, beginning on Tuesday, Haralson County won the region series by winning 2 of 3 games to advance. Postseason all-area accolades went to Dragon star catcher Barry Henderson and Cass pitcher Andy Arp; the two youngsters were returning members of the team. They were also chosen cocaptains.

1979 Season

The first noted documentation of PHS baseball 1979 occurred in Sunday's *News-Tribune* on April 1. The article described Coosa High's 10–9 "thriller" over the Dragons on Thursday, March 29, in which a combined 17 bases on balls were issued. The Eagles staged an 9-run fourth inning while Pepperell almost pulled it out with a 5-run seventh when Burkhalter, Stager, Burnett, Shiflett, and Henderson all had hits. On Friday the sixth, the Darlington coaching staff was upset though not necessarily because the Dragons administered a 9–1 licking to the Tigers, but "you just can't win when you walk 11 batters, get two hits and leave 10 runners stranded." Our pitchers Lance Morris and Jeff Brannon teamed up for the subregion victory; offensively, walks and opponent errors loaded the bases while Neal McChargue and Greg Shiflett drove them home. The latter had 3 safeties including a solo four-bagger as did Buster Knowles. On Tuesday the tenth, East Rome edged us 7–6 in extra innings; the game seesawed throughout before the home team tripled home the winning run in the ninth. Coach Otis Gilbreath blamed double plays for the defeat, saying, "They just kept taking us out of innings with them…they must have turned six of 'em." Brannon, Shiflett, Bennett, and Morris led us at the plate while Knowles and Lance Morris shared the mound duties. April 16 saw the Dragons outlast Model 12–9 thanks to 7 unearned markers; we collected 8 safeties with Shiflett and Knowles each going 2 of 4. The latter smashed a 3-run homer in the second inning. John Bennett and Jeff Burkhalter contributed a single and a double respectively to the cause. One day after downing Shannon, Lindale "walked" past rival Darlington 11–7; 10 free passes netted a half dozen scores. Marion, McChargue, Shiflett, Brannon, and Knowles all contributed RBIs in the second, third, fourth, and sixth innings. Knowles also hurled 5 frames with Morris finishing the last 2 to qualify for a save. In the "wild and wooly" subregion, PHS took over first place by downing East Rome 10–3 on Wednesday, April 18. We exploded for 8 runs in the bottom of the first and never looked back. Three errors, 3 walks, and 3 singles generated our scoring; Greg Gentry, Chris Shiflett, and John Bennett provided the only safeties. Sophomore Jeff Brannon gave up only 5 hits and 3 walks in going the distance for Pepperell; the region record now stood at 4–2. Two days later at Darlington, Sam Sprewell's crew upset the Dragons 9–4 behind the 5-hit pitching of Blake Ward; he also retired 11 batters in a row from the second through sixth innings. The Lakesiders took a 7–1 advantage in the third and won comfortably; Gentry, Morris, McChargue, and Shiflett were responsible for our 4 runs. At Shannon on the twenty-third, an error enabled us to squeak by the hosts 8–7 in 8 innings to improve our subregion record to 5–3. With the contest tied 7–7 in the top of the eighth, eventual winning pitcher Neal McChargue's foul pop fly was mishandled by the first baseman, giving him 1 more swing. The senior promptly tripled and then scored the go-ahead run on Greg Shiflett's sacrifice fly. Model coach Gary York was miserable over the loss. "I've had errors haunt me before, but never quite like this one," he said later. Although the 11–0 victory at Rockmart was Pepperell's first shutout of the season, Coach Otis had plenty of praise for his offense, saying, "We just really hit the ball today…We hit some long and we hit plenty hard." The *News-Tribune* report of the April 24 game bore him out; Shiflett solo homered in the second. Bennett, Knowles, and McChargue drove in 5 runs in the third; the latter player stroked a bases-empty four-bagger in the fifth. Joe Marion, Chris Mathis, and Buster Knowles then led a 2-score sixth-inning outburst to finish off the Yellow Jackets. In 1978, the Georgia High School Athletic Association outlawed the mercy rule. Previously, if a team trails by 10 or more runs and has gotten to bat in 5 innings, the umpires will end the game or a squad is ahead 15 points after 3 at bats. If a game stops before 5 innings, it's recorded as no contest. Unfortunately for the Dragons' opponents on Friday and Saturday, April 27 and 28, the rule no longer existed. Pepperell downed Darlington 39–4 while batting around 3 times in 6 innings, accumulating 20 hits; amazingly, they scored 8 in the second, 4 in the third, 10 in the fourth, and 14 more in the sixth. According to twenty-five-year veteran coach Otis Gilbreath, it was "the most runs ever scored by his Dragons and was also the greatest win margin…We've been hitting the ball real well lately and just managed to hit the ball in the gap or out of reach of the Tigers." He added, "These games happen to everybody sooner or later." Meanwhile, winning pitcher Lance Morris was limiting the Lakesiders to 3 safeties who earlier defeated PHS 4–2. The offensive surge continued the next day at East Rome with a 15–1 victory, which allowed us to move into first place in the subregion; much like the day before, we consistently plated runners starting with 4 in the first inning, 2 in the second, 5 in the fourth, and 4 in the seventh. However, the Dragon bats did this damage with only 6 hits courtesy of 14 base on balls from the Gladiator pitching staff. Our hurler, Neal McChargue, went the distance while scattering 5 hits, issuing 3 walks and striking out 6 batters. On Tuesday, May 1, the surging Lindale 9 improved their subregion record to 8–3 by virtue of a 13–8 defeat of visiting Model; the win assured them of a region playoff spot. The star of the game was Buster Knowles who picked up the mound victory with 3 innings of relief in addition to batting 3 for 4. The Blue Devils led or tied the game on 3 occasions; however, Brannon, Shiflett, Burkhalter, Marion, Bennett, Morris, and Knowles provided the necessary offense to win by 5 markers. Two days later in Lindale, the Dragons played a classic game of baseball in clinching first place in subregion. Coach Gilbreath said, "It was a good, quick game. There weren't a lot of walks or strike-outs. It took one hour and 35 minutes." The contest was tied going into the bottom of the seventh when 1 of the few errors occurred; an outfielder misplayed Buster Knowles's single, setting him up on third base; Neal McChargue then picked up his third RBI of the day with a game-ending bingle. He also claimed the mound victory with 4 innings in relief of Lance Morris. In the first round of region play on Thursday, May 10, both South squads dropped 1-run decisions to the North; East Rome lost 5–4 to Bowdon, and Pepperell was edged 4–3 by Haralson County. In Buchannan, we played "home run ball" in a losing cause as John Bennett blasted a solo in the third, and Lance Morris hit a 2-run shot to account for our scores; McChargue hurled the distance, allowing 7 hits. Coach Otis's crew returned to Lindale on Friday needing a doubleheader sweep to advance further. As it happens frequently in baseball, teams run out of pitching—Haralson County did, and the Dragons did not. Buster Knowles gave up 1 run in the first contest and was never in trouble; meanwhile, his mates plated 16 runs. In the nightcap, Lance Morris was almost as good throwing a 3-hitter that sparked his team to an 11–3 sweep. We started the 16–1 "hit parade" with 17 base hits and plated 10 markers before HC crossed home once; practically every member of the starting 9 recorded 1 or more safeties. The victory in the second game was a "breather" according to the local paper as we ran out to an 8-run lead and coasted home. PHS would now face East Rome on Tuesday, May 15, for the Region 7-AA championship; the Romans blasted Bowdon twice on Friday. Not only did the Gladiators stun the Dragons 8–1 in the first game, they took 2 of 3 to win Region. Although we came back on doubleheader day in Lindale to edge Coach Rick Walker's crew 7–6, they downed us in the deciding contest 7–1. Coach Gilbreath said afterward, "The errors just killed us. We might have been lucky to get out as well as we did. I guess it was just a bad day for us...our errors would put them on, then they's get the hits to bring them in." Both hurlers did well in the final with their Robert Long giving up 2 safeties and striking out 4; Jeff Brannon also pitched fine for us, allowing 8 bingles, but 5 walks in the first were a problem. Our bats went silent except in winning the second contest; Jeff Brannon, Joe Marion, and catcher Dave Stager led a second-inning rally that put us up 3–0. The latter also stroked a bingle in the third for a 4–0 advantage. However, it took clutch execution during the last at bat to win; with the score tied 6–6, Jeff Burkhalter walked, stole second, advanced to third on an error, and scored on Chris Shiflett's sacrifice fly. Yet at the end of the day, there was no "joy in Mudville" but elation in the other dugout, for it had been 12 years since ER competed for a region crown. Postseason recognition went to Buster Knowles as a *Rome News-Tribune* area all-star; the youngster was a solid slugger who hit for power and averaged as well as picking up several victories on the mound; he also saw action at first base and catcher. Later in the summer, he and Chris Shiflett signed scholarships with Shorter Hawks. Coach Hamp Alexander noted the latter was exactly what they looked for in a second baseman, and he believed Buster "might be the best all-around prospect in the region." Both athletes played on Lindale's 1977 state Class AA championship team.

East Rome swept a doubleheader from Cedar Grove and advanced to the finals against defending state champ Harlem; the South Georgia contingent outhit the locals in winning 10–4 and 10–1 games for the state crown.

1980 Season

The local gazette reported on Sunday, April 6, that the previous Friday was a day of big scores and big games; to wit, Cass beat Rockmart 8–6. Calhoun topped Model 9–3. Darlington clubbed West Rome 17–6, and Pepperell "exploded" past East Rome 30–5. One day before, Pepperell "ripped" host Darlington 10–1. Both squads were 2–1 with PHS losing to Cass early on. The next day, April 4, Coach Gilbreath's 9 bombed East Rome. Sunday's *News-Tribune* sports page featured, "Hamrick's Two Grand Slams Lead Dragons to 30–5 Win." The first baseman finished with 3 hits and 9 runs batted in; Morris, Brannon, and Benjie Shiflett also collected a trio of safeties. The Gladiators scored 3 markers in the top of the first which just made the Dragons mad, for they responded with a 16-hit barrage in which 8 starters contributed "base knocks." On Thursday, April 8, the morning newspaper noted PHS downed Darlington 6–2 to push their region mark to 3–0; the Tigers fell to 1–2, both losses coming at the hands of Lindale. The home squad led 2–1 until the fifth when the Dragons plated 4 markers. Actually, the contest provided one of the best 7-inning pitching battles of the year, for the winner Lance Morris and loser Jeff Bennett each gave up 4 safeties with 5 walks. On Wednesday, April 16, East Rome edged ahead 2–1 before hits by Benjie Shiflett, and Dave Stager plated 4 runs in the fifth frame; the singles combined with 4 walks and 2 errors were more than the Gladiators could overcome. Shiflett was the winning mound man. Two days later, we played through a steady rain to defeat Darlington 9–7 to improve our record at 10–1; the Tigers fell to 9–3 with all 3 losses coming against the Dragons. The Lakesiders led 1–0 early but never saw frontage again after PHS put 4 on the board in the second. In the fifth, Benjie Shiflett "blasted one out of the spacious field." Eventually Sam Sprewell's crew ran out of rallies due to walks and wild pitches; Jeff Brannon got the W on the mound. In Shannon on April 21, Model outhit us 12–10 but found themselves behind 13–4 going into the Devils' last at bat; the culprit was giving up 10 walks and several "untimely" errors. Granted, the home squad staged a 6-run rally in the bottom of the seventh, but it was too late as PHS won 13–10. We had several hitting stars including singles by Brannon, Hopkins, and Hamrick; Morris and Benjie Shiflett smacked doubles. Greg Gentry tripled; Jeff Brannon stroked a 2-run homer. Graciously, neither team's pitchers were mentioned in the morning sports write-up. This baseball season, Darlington surely hated to see the Red and Gray get off the team bus. The Lakesiders had a really good squad who were 12–4 overall; unfortunately, all losses were to North subregion rival and champion Pepperell, who carried a 14–1 slate. On Friday, April 25, the abovementioned Tigers took a 5–0 lead in the third inning only to see the visitors score 4 in the top of the sixth and add 4 more in the next at bat to win 8–6. Lance Morris pitched almost 5 innings in relief for the win. The usual cast of hitters, Greg and Benjie Shiflett, Morris, Hamrick, Brannon, Hooper, and Stager, rallied their team to victory. At East Rome on the last day of April, the Dragons continued their "one big inning approach." They plated 12 markers in the second frame to "zoom" past the Gladiators 18–2. Lindale scored

2 runs in the first and then exploded for a dozen; we put an exclamation mark on the final score with a pair of 2-run doubles by Mark Wheeler and Dave Stager. Kent Mathis went the distance on the mound, scattering 7 safeties. This contest ended the regular season with PHS finishing the schedule 15–1 and 12–0 in the subregion.

On Tuesday, May 6, Coach Otis's squad traveled 50 miles south on Highway 100 to Bowdon, Georgia, to face the South runner-up Red Devils. The Dragons won 9–5 by taking advantage of 3 errors and 4 walks. After the home team put 4 markers on the board in the second frame, winning pitcher Lance Morris launched a 3-run homer to cut the lead to 5–4. Then we plated 5 in the fifth to go up 8–4; errors, walks, a David Hooper sacrifice fly plus singles by Hamrick and Stager put the game out of reach. Morris allowed 8 hits in going the distance while walking only 1 and whiffing 5. On home turf the following day, PHS followed the same script of turning a fairly close contest into a 12–4 rout; we led 2–1 and 4–1 going into the sixth before the "roof caved in on Bowdon." In the marathon inning, 13 batters went to the plate courtesy of 4 walks, 2 wild pitches, several bingles, and 2 fielder's choices. Jeff Brannon picked up the victory, allowing only 7 safeties, 4 walks, and striking out 9. Tuesday, May 13, was unlucky for visiting PHS but not Darlington as the Lakesiders finally defeated their nemesis 4–0 to take a 1-game lead in subregion best-of-three series play. Winning left-hander Jeff Bennett went the distance while allowing 4 safeties, striking out 2, and walking 4; he kept the visitors off-balance which caused 8 pop-ups and 6 fly outs. Sam Sprewell also noted later, "We played come good defense behind him." Bennett also batted 2 for 2 while Benjie Shiflett and Dave Stager accounted for the loser's only hits. Although he did not win, Lance Morris was not bad in scattering 8 hits, 3 walks, and striking out 5. The next day in Lindale, things got back to normal as Pepperell triumphed 6–2 in the first contest and 4–3 in the Class 7-AA subregion championship game. On Friday morning, May 16, *Rome News-Tribune*'s sports page explained, "Dragons Double Dose of Shifletts Rips Tigers." The two young men (Ben and Greg) were cousins and winning pitchers for Otis Gilbreath's 19–2 warriors. Eleventh grader Benjie was first up on the mound versus Darlington; in 7 innings, he scattered 5 hits, 3 strikeouts, and 5 base on balls in the 6–2 victory. The winners ran up a 4–1 score in the second with some "sound" base running; Jeff Burkhalter walked, and then went to third on Stager's bingle; the latter took the next base on a throw to third. Both crossed the plate on Greg Shiflett's single. In the fourth frame, we increased the lead to 6–1 courtesy of walks to Greg Shiflett and Lance Morris, a sacrifice bunt, followed by a Tiger error. In the second and deciding contest, cousin Greg, who is also a junior, threw a complete game 4–3 victory; he walked 3, struck out 3, and spaced out 6 hits in 7 innings to win by 1. We trailed early 1–0, led 2–1, 3–1, and finally 4–1 on Dave Stager's third RBI of the day. The losing hurlers gave up just 4 hits, and to their credit, the Purple and White did not quit as they plated 2 more markers in the sixth but couldn't get a tying run past third in the seventh. The Lindale 9 prepared to meet East Hall in state competition on Tuesday, May 20, at home. Coach Otis Gilbreath would be seeking his eighth title with an unheard-of 4 solid pitchers; most high school teams had only 1, maybe 2 at the most and prayed for 3. Lance Morris, Jeff Brannon, and Benjie and Greg Shiflett would toe the rubber in succession; Micah Hamrick was his leading hitter as was catcher Dave Stager. The abovementioned hurlers were position players when not on the mound and had hit the ball well all year. Following region play, Pepperell and East Hall tried all week to start their best-of-three series in the first round of state competition; however, a rainy week in Georgia would not permit. Finally, the weather forecast in the local gazette for May 25 said, "A rainy week will give way to sunny skies." One day later on Monday, May 26, we boarded the yellow bird for Gainesville, which was 115 miles east of Lindale and 2 hours and 15 minutes by bus. The Dragons rallied for a 4–3 victory behind Jeff Brannon who threw 6 innings, whiffed 8, and gave up only 2 hits; Lance Morris pitched the seventh and struck out the side. We plated 2 runs in the second when Hamrick singled, moved around, and crossed home with the first run; Benjie Shiflett walked and later scored on Stager's sacrifice fly. It was "All Quiet on the Eastern Front" until the bottom of the fifth when the Vikings put 3 on the scoreboard courtesy of 2 walks, a hit by pitch, and their only 2 safeties which gave the Black and Gold a 3–2 advantage. The lead did not last long, for Hamrick opened the top of the sixth with a triple; Brannon brought him home with a single. With the contest tied at 3–3, an error and Dave Stager's bingle plated the winning run. Stager, Hamrick, and Brannon led us at the bat. One day later in the friendly confines of Dragon Field, we downed East Hall 5–1 to advance to the semifinals of state play. Senior right-hander Lance Morris threw a 3-hitter, struck out 5, and walked nobody in going the distance; he also stroked a pair of hits. We led 1–0, 2–0, and 5–0 before the visitors put 1 on the board on the last frame.

There is an old saying, "Win some, lose some and some are rained out." North Georgia Class AA baseball had added another curve to the old proverb, and that was "stopped by court order." All was set on Thursday, May 29, in Lindale for East Point's Headland High School to begin action versus the Dragons. The school located in south Fulton County was in existence from 1956 to 1982; their mascot is the Highlander with red and black school colors. The "rulers of the diamond" had claimed 3 Class AA state championships including 1964, 1965, and 1969. As the teams prepared to battle, a *News-Tribune* reporter noted, "The visitors had already taken batting practice and the Dragons were about to begin their round of infield warmup; the guests would be next. Umpires were standing in wait for the first pitch...but before play began the Rome-Floyd County Sheriff's Department notified PHS principal Gary Holmes by phone that Fulton County Judge William Daniel had signed a restraining order stopping the contest pending further court action." The directive was instigated by the North Fulton High School booster club. It seemed NF defeated Headland last week in a best-of-three playoff games; however, they did it with an ineligible head coach Gary Staab who was not a certified teacher. This was a direct rule violation, and GHSA executive secretary Bill Fordham responded by awarding the series to the losers (Headland). For the right to protest, North Fulton posted a $1,500 fee to the superior court, holding they did not receive a hearing; consequently, the complainant requested and received a restraining order to stop further play from Judge William Daniel. The Executive Committee of GHSA met for 3 hours on Wednesday, June 4, in Thomaston and upheld Fordham's ruling. The vote of 31–0 was given to appeals judge Issac Jenrette who could, according to Principal Holmes, "choose to carry this thing further." He added, "I know for sure we can't play until he says so."

On Friday afternoon, June 6, at 2:00 p.m., Jenrette emerged from his chamber and issued the verdict, "Play ball." Twenty minutes later, the first pitch was made to the plate in Lindale, and what took 8 days of mediation lasted less than 4 hours to decide on the Dragon Field diamond because Pepperell swept Headland 11–1 and 7–3. The 2 game outcomes were never in doubt as Benjie Shiflett and Jeff Brannon kept the Highlanders' bats in check; in doing so, the duo did not permit an earned run the entire afternoon. Benjie Shiflett closed out the initial contest with 5 strikeouts, 4 walks, and 3 scattered hits. We struck for 3 runs in each of the first 2 frames and plated 3 more in the sixth while the visitors could manage only 1 marker in their last at bat. Greg Shiflett, Morris, Hopkins, and Hamrick all connected for 2 safeties. The home Dragons started game two with a couple of runs in the second inning when Stager and Brannon singled; the former came home on a sacrifice fly by Ben Shiflett; the latter crossed home by virtue of an error. We increased our advantage to 4–0 in the top of the fourth when Greg Shiflett and Morris garnered 2-out singles each. However, the visitors closed the gap to 4–3 in their half of the fourth, but we retaliated in the next frame to end the scoring at 7–3. Pepperell tallied 21 safeties in the doubleheader and allowed only 7. On Tuesday, June 10, Pepperell High would take the field to try for their eighth state championship in 12 tries. A doubleheader against South champion Lee County was set for 1:00 p.m. The school is located in Leesburg, Georgia, just north of Albany; by ground transportation, it is 215 miles and 4 hours' travel time from South Floyd mostly on US 27S; the 1980 census showed 1,300 souls in the town. The Trojans of Coach Butch Watts were 19–5 and had won 4 of the last 6 Region 1-AA titles, yet this was their first trip to the state finals. It was no contest as Lindale rallied to win both games, 13–6 and 6–3. The morning *News-Tribune* noted, "Pepperell's bats came to life and the pitching and defense was steady." We jumped to a 4–0 lead in the initial contest only to see the visitors put 5 on the board in the fifth courtesy of 2 Dragon errors and some base on balls. Coach Gilbreath showed some concern as his squad left the bases loaded twice; not to worry, for the Red and Gray exploded for 9 markers in the bottom of the fifth. It started with a Hopkins single and a Burkhalter walk; Greg Shiflett moved them up with a bunt. The *RNT* reporter described what happened next, "In successive order, Morris doubled in two runs, Hamrick singled Morris home, Dave Stager doubled home Hamrick, Jeff Brannon and Benjie Shiflett singled, David Hooper doubled home Brannon, Hopkins walked and Burkhalter produce a three-run triple." By then, it was all over but the shoutin'. Lance Morris and Greg Shiflett shared in the pitching duties with both whiffing 3 opponents. In the 6–3 championship game, we fell behind 3–2 early caused by errors and walks before "a trio of Dragons crossed in the sixth to provide the winning tallies." Brannon and Benjie Shiflett started it with bingles; Hopkins singled one of them home before Burkhalter and Greg Shiflett drew bases-loaded walks, forcing in 2 more markers. In the top of the seventh, an insurance run gave us the final of 6–3; Stager walked, moved up on a single, and scored on Hooper's safety. Jeff Brannon pitched a complete game in the finale. He mixed 7 hits with 12 strikeouts while free-passing only 2 South Georgians. The squad finished with a 23–2 slate, losing only to Cass and Darlington both on the road. Otis believed the Tigers were the best team his crew faced all year. A happy winning coach told the media afterward, "This group worked awfully hard for this…they were a good bunch to work with…fortunately we got good pitching all season long from four hurlers…Lance Alworth Morris is the only senior." In recapping the Dragons on June 11, *News-Tribune* reporter Darrell Black noted slugging leader Morris stroked 6 for 7 on championship day including 4 doubles and a triple to go with 10 RBIs; junior first baseman Micah Hamrick led in season batting average while defensively "the leader was catcher Dave Stager." Postseason All-Area honors went to Morris, Hamrick, Stager, and

Brannon. In honor of the PHS 1980 State Baseball Championship squad, we reproduced musician John Fogerty's classic 1985 album title track "Centerfield" complete with lyrics:

> Well, a-beat the drum and hold the phone
> The sun came out today.
>
> We're born again, there's new grass on the field.
> A-roundin' third and headed for home
> It's a brown-eyed handsome man.
> Anyone can understand the way I feel.
>
> Oh, put me in coach, I'm ready to play today.
> Put me in coach, I'm ready to play today.
> Look at me, I can be centerfield.
>
> Well, I spent some time in the Mudville Nine
> Watching it from the bench.
> You know I took some lumps,
> When the mighty Case struck out.
> So say hey, Willie, Tyler Cobb
> And Joe Dimaggio.
> Don't say it ain't so, you know the time is now.
>
> Oh, put me in coach, I'm ready to play today.
> Put me in coach, I'm ready to play today.
> Look at me, I can be centerfield.
> Yeah, I got it, I got it.
> Got a beat-up glove, a home-made bat
> And a brand new pair of shoes.
>
> You know I think it's time to give this game a ride.
> Just to hit the ball, and touch 'em all.
> A moment in the sun
> It's a-gone and you can tell that one good-bye.
>
> Oh, put me in coach, I'm ready to play today
> Put me in coach, I'm ready to play today
> Look at me (yeah), I can be centerfield
>
> Oh, put me in coach, I'm ready to play today.
> Put me in coach, I'm ready to play today.
> Look at me, gotta be, centerfield.
> Yeah

1981 Season

Pepperell moved up to Class AAA with the beginning of a new season. Whether this would affect the defending AA champs or not remained to be played out. We started with a 9–2 victory over Darlington at Lakeside on Saturday, March 28, yet the score was misleading, for it took 14 innings or 2 full games to close them out. In regulation action, the Dragons tied the contest 2–2 in the top of the seventh; both squads had ample opportunities to win especially the hosts who had runners in scoring position in the tenth, eleventh, and thirteenth frames. The visitors won it in the fourteenth when they plated runners in "bunches" courtesy of 5 safeties (we totaled 13 for the day) and a costly Tiger error. To open, Stager and Benjie Shiflett singled, Mathis doubled, Hooper tripled, Wheeler singled. Greg Shiflett, Hamrick, Mathis, and Benjie Shiflett drew base on balls. We used several hurlers, but Brannon won by virtue of his work from the sixth to the fourteenth inning. Otis Gilbreath's Red and Gray had become a local version of the "Bronx Bombers" as most of their 4–0 record was attributed to home runs. He said, "We've been living off the homers…it's either that or a silent bat." On Thursday's April 2 victory in Rockmart, we managed but 5 hits; however, 2 were grand slams in the 8–0 victory. The next day versus Darlington again, the Lindale 9 got but 3 safeties but 1 was a 3-run blast by senior Bob Griffin in the 5–3 win. Otis noted good defense and pitching were also responsible for victories. He added, "We got a good game from Benjie Shiflett… he gave up only four hits in seven innings." In Dallas on April 8, Paulding County soundly defeated PHS 9–2 to take the lead in 7-AAA North. The "fine hitting" Patriots "just plain beat us," said Otis afterward. Pitchers Ben Shiflett and Mathis shared the loss, giving up 10 hits to the winners. In Carroll County on April 13, the Dragons had "trouble with the stick" in losing their third contest of the season to subregion foe Carrollton 3–2. Senior Greg Shiflett matched Trojan ace Tim Criswell as he allowed 7 hits, no walks while whiffing 9 hosts; the winners got solo markers in the second, fourth, and fifth frames while we managed 2 runs in our last at bat. Chattooga County came to Lindale on Wednesday, April 15, and defeated their hosts 6–3; the clutch hits known to Pepperell over the years were failing to come recently. After the contest was tied early, the Indians increased the lead to 4–2 in the fifth, 5–2 in the sixth, and 6–2 in the last at bat. Junior David Hooper collected 3 safeties for the losers while Brian Griffin pitched the final 5 frames and took the loss; our overall slate was now 5–4 but 3–4 in the North. From that point, the Dragons went on a tear and won 6 straight subregion games to improve to 9–4 in the counters. Calhoun provided the competition on May 1 and fell to Lindale 5–2; in the first inning, Micah Hamrick powered a 3-run homer; we added to the lead 2 frames later courtesy of 4 consecutive walks; Mark Wheeler drove in the final marker in the sixth. Ben Shiflett pitched 5 strong innings before turning it over to Jeff Brannon; together the duo allowed only 5 safeties. PHS seemed to be adjusting to Class AAA, for they welcomed and defeated Carrollton 7–1 on Monday, May 4. Greg Shiflett went the distance on the mound allowing only 3 hits, walking 2, and striking out 4; the Shiflett cousins Ben and Greg each had 2-run singles in the 5-run sixth frame. The Trojans came to town tied with Pepperell for second in the North and departed in the third slot. Unfortunately, we visited Summerville the next day and lost 4–3, putting us back into a tie for second place. However, the manner in which we lost was harder to stomach than the final; we outhit the Indians 7 to 1 and left 14 runners on base. The home squad gained their markers via 6 walks and 2 errors. All the scoring happened in the sixth inning when we opened with Wheeler's and Hooper's doubles followed by Hamrick's single and a defensive miscue. In the bottom half, walks and PHS errors gave the winners their 4 runs. Jeff Brannon threw 5 and 2/3 and struck out 10 batters. Lindale was now 12–5 with all losses to region foes. On Thursday, May 7, home-standing Coosa jumped us 4 runs in a game we had to win; thankfully, we answered them in the top of the second with 4 of our own only to see the Eagles gain the lead again 6–4 in their next at bat. After that, it was all Pepperell; with 2 outs in the fourth, Wheeler doubled, Hooper walked, Jeff Brannon doubled, and Micah Hamrick slammed a 3-run jack. Tommy Gentry put an exclamation mark to the game in the next frame with a solo home run that gave us a 10–6 victory. Ben Shiflett threw a complete game allowing only 3 hits, striking out 8, and free-passing 2. On Friday, May 8, Cedartown did us a favor by upsetting Carrollton 8–7, giving us second place in the subregion. On Monday the eleventh, the Dragons faced Ringgold at Tunnel Hill in first round of double elimination and lost 3–1. The Tuesday morning *News-Tribune* said it all, "Ringgold's Jones Fires No-Hitter at Pepperell." Our lone marker happened in the second inning when Greg Earle, Mark Wheeler, Dave Stager, and Ben Shiflett walked, forcing Earle across the plate. PHS hurler Jeff Brannon had a good afternoon giving up only 6 safeties. Back in Tunnel Hill on Tuesday, PHS rebounded with a 6–1 whipping of Northwest Whitfield Bruins. The relatively new school was formed in 1975 by consolidating North Whitfield and Westside high schools. Postgame comments by Assistant Coach Jimmy Farrer noted that "we've got a little confidence and can still win this thing...We are beginning to get our bats together." After they went ahead by 1 in the second, our cracking bats assisted by their "shaky defense" gave us 5 runners crossing home. Hamrick, Earle, Stager, Mathis, B. Shiflett, and David Hooper singled, walked, or reached on errors to fund the uprising. Greg Shiflett pitched a 4-hitter to go with 1 walk and 4 whiffs. "He had them under control," said Farrer.

With our backs to the wall, Lindale eliminated Paulding County (top-seed South) on Wednesday, the thirteenth. Brian Griffin was the star of the afternoon as he recorded the team's first shutout of the season; the sophomore scattered 5 hits and 4 walks for the 4–0 victory. David Hooper scored our first run in the first; entering the fourth frame, "Greg Earle came forth with a tremendous home run, then Dave Stager followed with another round-tripper." In the fifth, Jeff Brannon walked and eventually came home on Stager's fielder's choice for the final 4–0. On Thursday, May 14, Ringgold's ace pitcher Chad Jones did not pitch a no-hitter, but he smashed 2 round-trippers and accumulated 5 RBIs in eliminating us 9–3. They jumped us early on, and our bats went silent as Jones struck out a dozen Dragons while walking only 1. Afterward Assistant Coach Jimmy Farrer noted, "We didn't really swing the bats too well." Pepperell's Class AAA season record ended at 15–7.

1982 Season

Before high school baseball season got underway in Lindale, a former Dragon was breaking all-time NCAA and NAIA records. Last year, 1978 Pepperell graduate Steve Turner, who now played for Shorter, was "a demon on the base paths" in stealing 62 bases; the rising senior also set the bar high in runs scored for the college. Anytime schoolboy baseball is mentioned in Northwest Georgia, Pepperell will always be in the conversation. When interviewed by the local gazette, Coach Gilbreath noted, "We are in pretty good shape...We have good athletes and our pitching ought to be strong." With Otis, it always started with a good catcher a.k.a. 4-year letterman Dave Stager; infielders Mark Wheeler, David Hooper, and John Taylor would back up senior pitchers Jeff Brannon and Greg Earle in addition to junior Bryan Griffin. Twelfth grader Chris Mathis would patrol the garden once more; youngsters Steve Bennett, Tom Curry, and Mike Googe showed promise. Last year's squad went 16–6 and finished first in the South subregion. Projections were for Paulding County, Cass, and Carrollton to provide competition for PHS. Coach O then concluded his comments with, "Everybody is going to get kicked around some and I just hope we get kicked the least." His squad opened the season at home versus Cedartown on Monday, March 30, with an 11–9 victory; both teams scored 4 runs in big innings, but it was Pepperell's last at bat that proved fatal for the Polk County 9. With the contest knotted at 9, a new Bulldog pitcher walked the first 3 batters and then gave up a game-winning hit by PHS. Jeff Brannon was the winning hurler with 12 whiffs and 6 walks; hitters for the Dragons included Chris Mathis and Jeff Overby who blasted home runs. Wheeler and Brannon stroked doubles for the victors. On the last day of March, Rockmart took a 1–0 lead in the second inning; Pepperell countered the next frame with a 2-spot when sophomore Jeff Overby and Mark Wheeler singled and later advanced on a wild pitch. David Hooper brought both home thanks to an infield error for a 2–1 advantage. Pitcher Bryan Griffin was the winning pitcher with 4 strikeouts and 3 walks. Although in different classifications, Darlington playing Pepperell always provided good baseball; this held true on April 2 as a large crowd watched the area's 2 best teams go at it. A 3–0 victory surprised Tiger coach Sam Sprewell who never expected to shut out the Dragons; at one point, his pitcher Darrell Modlin struck out 10 straight PHS batters and allowed just 2 hits in the affair. A 2-run homer by Jim Talley in the first inning was all the Lakesiders needed to win on this day. Although Greg Earle went the distance and suffered the loss, he did not throw badly, allowing 7 safeties while striking out 5. Our 2 solo hits were by David Hooper and Kenneth Huckaby. Paulding County was considered a contender in 7-AAA; however, Lindale pitcher Jeff Brannon practically shut them down on Wednesday, April 7, hurling "a neat" 2-hitter while walking 2 and striking out 11 in the 2–1 victory. The winning run occurred in the fifth inning with the score tied at 1–1; Bryan Griffin singled, advanced on a wild pitch and a base hit by Curry. Mark Wheeler's sacrifice fly improved our region record to 3–0. In Calhoun on Friday, April 9, the Dragons were upset 5–2 by the home squad; the losing team had runners on base in every inning except 1 yet could not get a clutch hit. CHS left-hander Grant Walraven went the distance while scattering 4 PHS safeties; Bryan Griffin threw a 6-hitter in the losing effort but sat down 9 consecutive Jackets in the middle innings. On the following Monday, Mark Wheeler hit a sacrifice fly in the sixth frame, plating David Swanson from third in our 2–1 victory over visiting Carrollton; Jeff Brannon threw a 3-hitter while setting down 8 batters swinging. In Summerville on Thursday, April 22, PHS shut out Chattooga 6–0 behind Greg Earle's 2-hitter; we scored 2 markers early and then added solos in the third, fourth, fifth, and seventh innings. Two days later, Pepperell blasted Coosa 12–3 helped along by 18 base on balls; David Hooper had a pair of hits to lead the team. Although Bryan Griffin allowed 9 safeties, he also struck out 8 as the winning hurler. A pitching duel occurred in Dallas on Wednesday afternoon, April 28. Pepperell's Greg Earle and Paulding County's Johnny Cash battled evenly for 7 innings before the home team finally took the victory 3–2. Both hurlers gave up 4 hits and walked; Cash struck out a dozen Dragons while Earle whiffed 11 Patriots. The losing squad's runs came on a single and home run in the fifth. A 6-run uprising in the sixth inning netted PHS an 11–3 victory over visiting Cedartown on Thursday, April 29. The Bulldogs committed 7 errors in the loss and allowed the Dragons 9 hits. Bryan Griffin was the winning hurler, giving up 5 safeties. Jeff Overby led us at the plate with 2 base hits; Lindale improved their subregion record to 7–3. May got off to a good start for PHS; on the second, visiting Calhoun fell 11–2 behind a 7-run uprising in the opening frame. Brannon, Earle, Stager, and Curry all had hits to go with 3 walks. The home team added 4 more in the sixth courtesy of 3 more walks, a double by Stager combined with singles by Overby and Mathis. Jeff Brannon threw a complete game 5-hitter while striking out 8. A day later on Monday the third, PHS edged host Carrollton 5–4 to move into a tie with Cass in the subregion. We plated 3 runs in the fourth when Jeff Overby singled between base on balls to Curry and Hooper. Brannon then stroked a double; however, it was Bryan Griffin's 2-out single in the fifth that gave us the lead and winning marker. Winning pitcher Greg Earle threw the first 5 innings and got credit for the win; Brannon closed out the Trojans for a save. In a game apparently called 2 weeks ago in Rockmart because of darkness, the home team eked out a 5–4 victory in a 2 continuation extra-inning affair. The Tuesday, April 4, contest was won in the twelfth on a single, a sacrifice, and game-winning bingle by Michael Morgan. Jeff Brannon was the losing pitcher giving up 3 hits and 1 run. By defeating Chattooga 5–3 on Wednesday, April 5, PHS improved to 10–4 and regained a tie with Cass in the subregion; we scored 3 runs in the third, 1 each in the fourth and fifth frames. Dave Stager led the Dragons at the plate with 2 safeties. Bryan Griffin and Jeff Brannon teamed up for the mound victory. One day later, Pepperell downed Coosa 4–2 by scoring 1 run in the first, 2 in the second, and 1 in the sixth; our pitching was by committee with Greg Earle, Bryan Griffin, and Jeff Brannon all contributing to the victory. PHS won the subregion in Lindale on Friday, May 7, with a 5–0 shutout of Cassville; the falling rain failed to thin the large crowd who came to see who would be 1982 champs. The home squad plated 3 markers thanks to Wheeler's hit, Hooper's bunt, Brannon's walk, Stager's and Mathis's safe on errors, Curry's walk, and Overby's hit. The final 2 runs were courtesy of senior John Taylor's bingle that brought Mathis and Curry scampering home. Bryan Griffin was the winning pitcher in 7 innings; he gave the Colonels very little to hit and limited them to only 2 walks. In the double-elimination 7-AAA tourney at Cassville, PHS sent Fannin County into the loser's bracket with a 7–2 victory, Tuesday, May 11. Northwest Whitfield put home-standing Cass out with a 4–2 victory over the Colonels; Fannin and Whitfield would now battle to see who faced Pepperell on Thursday. In the Fannin game, the Dragons opened with a 5-run first inning; Hooper walked, Brannon doubled, Earle singled, Stager walked, Mathis doubled, and Curry singled. These early markers made it easy for starter Bryan Griffin who gave way to Brannon in the sixth; the two twirlers allowed only 3 hits on the afternoon. Win some, lose some. "Northwest Beats Dragons Twice in 7-AAA Finals." The *News-Tribune* printed this headline on Friday, May 14. The underneath article noted that the Pepperell Dragons "literally grabbed defeat from the jaws of victory." Needing only 1 win to advance to state, PHS lost a 4–0 and 4–3 doubleheader to Northwest Whitfield. "It's the first time I can remember us losing two," said Coach Gilbreath. He added later, "We had the opportunities but just didn't get the big hit...we stranded nine runners...The kids had a good season but just had a bad day today." Although we went with 8 right-handed hitters, southpaw pitcher Tony Bearden shut us down with 2 hits while striking out 6; Jeff Brannon did not throw that badly as he whiffed 7 and allowed 6 safeties. Bryan Griffin toed the rubber in the second contest; we took a 3–0 lead in the fifth and were cruising. Then the "charm began to wear off" the next inning when a single and home run cut the lead to 3–2. The drama began in the bottom of the seventh when Hargis walked, Pangle singled, and Bearden walked. A pitching change from Griffin to Brannon looked good as the latter fanned Fox on 3 "fast ones." With 2 outs and the bases full, Reed drilled a base hit to tie 3–3. Curry fielded Reed's ball and fired toward the relay man, trying to beat the runner rounding third; however, it was too late to stop Pangle who slid across plate with the victory.

1983 Season

In late March, Pepperell "cruised to a 22–4 triumph" over West Rome's inexperienced pitching staff; they issued 18 walks and hit 1 batter. Tom Curry and Steve Bennett were the batting stars. Losing coach George Carmeichal (sic) said later, "They just played better than we did." Six days later, Carrollton claimed a 5–3 victory to even our record at 1–1; we led 2–0 early, but the Trojans caught us in the middle innings. Bryan Griffin went the distance for PHS, giving up 10 safeties and 6 walks to go with 8 strikeouts. Rockmart "laced" Lindale 9–1 on Wednesday, March 30; the Jackets jumped us early and were never threatened. Chris Lansdale was the losing hurler but stroked 2 hits for his team. In Carroll County on Tuesday, April 19, we improved our record to 3–7 with a 2–1 victory over the Trojans; Tim McBurnett, Griffin, Kenneth Huckaby, and Jeff Lyon helped manufacture our 2-runs. Joey Gazero pitched a complete game, striking out 10 opponents. The following day, PHS edged visiting Chattooga County 5–4; Kenneth Huckaby went 3–3, a single, triple, and a home run, to lead us. Bryan Griffin scattered 9 hits for the win. Next on April 22, we "notched" a 7-AAA subregion home victory over Cassville 10–4; Bryan Griffin, Mike Irwin, Tony O'Neal, and Mark Wheeler combined to go 9–11 in the batter's box. Joey Gazero went the distance on the mound to improve to 3–2. We continued to get better on Tuesday, April 26, at home with a 6–4 win over Calhoun; winning hurler Brian Griffin struck out 7, walked 3 and allowed only 6 safeties. Huckaby, Bennett, and Wheeler were hitting stars. In Lindale on Thursday, April 28, West Rome struggled as they gave up 18 hits and 13 walks in losing 28–4; Bennett, Curry, O'Neal, and McBurnett led the hitting barrage. Lansdale came on early in relief and took the victory. It's always nice to beat Cedartown, and we did 9–7 on May 2 in Lindale; the usual suspects O'Neal, Wheeler, McBurnett, Curry, and Griffin produced RBIs. The latter also pitched a complete game as we improved to 7–5 in South division of 7-AAA. Although our bunch got much better as the season progressed, it was not good enough to qualify for postseason. In late May, Brian Griffin signed a letter of intent to play for Hamp Alexander's Shorter Hawks, marking the eighteenth Dragon player to do so in the past 11 years. The senior would graduate on June 2 along with 148 members of the class of 1983.

1984 Season

Unlike football, local newspapers seldom printed season schedules for high school baseball as game dates tended to fluctuate due to weather concerns. Fortunately, for historians, the *News-Tribune* gave us a look at Pepperell's 1984 slate: March 26—Model, March 27—at Carrollton, March 30—Chattooga, March 31—Darlington Tournament, April 2—Cass, April 4—Calhoun, April 5—at Darlington, April 6—at Coosa, April 9—Cedartown, April 11—at Paulding County, April 13—Carrollton, April 16—at Chattooga, April 18—at Cass, April 19—at West Rome (2), April 20—at Calhoun, April 23—at Coosa, and April 24—at Cedartown. We opened with a 14–0 victory at Model on Friday, March 23; Joey Gazero went the first 4 innings, and lefty Chris Lansdale finished up as they combined with a 3-hitter. Steve Bennett collected 4 safeties. Tim McBurnett knocked a homer and a single; Tom Curry, Clete Bonney, and Davis Swanson stroked 2 hits each. Four days later on Monday, the visiting Blue Devils scored a single run in the opening inning; they could "muster" no more markers against righties Doug Burnett, Mike Curry, and left-hander Glenn Atkins as PHS won 4–1 to improve to 2–0 (both wins over Shannon). At the plate for the winners, Tom Curry went 3 for 4 while Bennett was 2 for 3. Not only was Carrollton's John Driver an all-state tailback, but also he got Pepperell's vote the same as a baseball pitcher. On Tuesday, March 27, the senior limited the Red and Gray to 1 hit while striking out 11 in Trojans' 2–0 victory. Although Joey Gazero was the loser, he only surrendered 4 hits, gave up no walks, and struck out 8. Tony Lane collected our sole hit in the fourth inning. In a game reportedly played at Floyd Junior College on Friday, March 30, we won over Chattooga 2–1; both hurlers gave up 2 hits. The winning runs came when Steve Bennett doubled in the first frame and later Tom Curry delivered a RBI single in the third. Lansdale was "superb" on the hill, allowing 3 walks and the same strikeouts. In a round-robin tournament at Lakeside, PHS lost to the host 8–5; we rebounded with a 7–4 win over Cass. The Colonels visited Lindale twenty-four hours later and this time lost 14–3; Lansdale was masterful again pitching a 6-hitter with 3 walks and 6 whiffs; McBurnett, Lansdale, and Mike Curry had multiple hits for the 5–2 Dragons. Visiting Calhoun downed us 5–3 on Thursday, April 5, in a subregion contest; they plated 2 in the first, 2 in the second, and 1 in the seventh. Our 3 runs came after freshman Jamie McCord walked, then Tom Curry doubled him home; Lansdale and Tim McBurnett's singles brought home the other 2 markers. PHS record moved to 5–3 on the season. The slate dropped to 6–4 after host Paulding County whipped us 3–2 on Wednesday, April 11. Both squads had 4 safeties; however, the Dragons committed 3 errors. At FJC on Thursday, the twelfth, Tom Curry scored 4 runs on 1 single and 3 walks in our 8–3 triumph over Cedartown; Lansdale and Bennett provided a bulk of the hitting with 2 safeties each. Gazero went the route on the mound, allowing 7 hits while whiffing 8. On Monday, April 16, Tony O'Neal stroked a 3-run triple after Lansdale, McBurnett, and Bennett got on base; Joey Gazero scattered half dozen hits with only 1 walk while striking out 9; the victory gave us an 8–5 record. Chris Lansdale struck out 10 Bulldogs in Pepperell's 21–2 win over host Cedartown; Steve Bennett's 3-run second-inning home run ignited a 9-marker eruption. The April 25 contest moved the Dragons to 9–7 on the year, 6–5 in 7-AAA South subregion. On Thursday, April 26, at FJC, Coosa scored 5 runs or all the offense they would need in downing Lindale 5–4. We managed single runs in the fifth and seventh and

2 in the sixth. Tom Curry and Tony O'Neal had 2 safeties each for the Dragons. PHS's overall record was 9–7 with 6–6 in subregion. The last quote of the season in the *News-Tribune* was "Pepperell's regular season is finished." At Lakeside on Wednesday, May 30, sports editor Kerry Yencer reported Darlington's sweep of Hancock Central High School for the state Class AA championship. Pepperell High would face Hancock a year later in Sparta for the same crown.

"AN 'A' FOR EFFORT AT PEPPERELL." This was *RNT* staff writer Jeanne Ingram's lead headline on page 1 on Wednesday, April 17, 1985. Peering into the future, Ms. Ingram could have been reporting on what was to be a special 1985 Dragon baseball season; however, this was not the case. Her subject was an accreditation committee report from the Southern Association of Colleges and Schools (SACS) which occurred every ten years. Committee chairman Terry Callifer said students and faculty at PHS were "making the best of a bad situation...the conditions at the school itself are deplorable." In the last decade, South Floyd County residents missed their chances when they twice rejected referendums to build a new high school (the site proposed was controversial). Local superintendent Dr. Nevin Jones stated that current renovations at the present campus, which included a new athletic complex, would not alleviate long-term problems. He added, "These are second choices...we'd rather have a new school." Other SACS recommendations were goals to improve test taking; specialists in reading, math, and language were needed to expand the curriculum; the computer laboratory must be enlarged also; substance abuse courses should be offered; teachers should be paid a supplement for sponsoring extra-curricular activities; and the library should be updated with recent publications, replacing little used books. Principal Jim Laney agreed with the report, especially the criticism of existing facilities. Mr. Callifer and associates would return to Lindale in five years for a progress evaluation.

1985 Season

Head coach Jimmy Farrer welcomed 8 seniors to the 1985 roster. Some thought a region championship was possible; other players agreed that "our team could go pretty far because we've been playing together since freshman year." According to *News-Tribune* assistant sports editor Steve Sigafoose, one special four-year starter had given an arm and a leg to the Pepperell athletic program. In a prep profile on March 28, Tom Curry was featured as the all-area punter (leg) and leadoff hitter/center fielder (arm) for the Dragons. In between, he saw regular action in roundball. His coach said, "He's a real competitor and one of our leaders...he hits lead-off (.463 BA) and is good under pressure...the catalyst for us...can steal a base if needed." But defense in the middle of the garden was where he excelled. It is more than just catching the ball, for Tom got to make all the calls for fellow outfielders in addition to pop flies at the edge of the grass plus throwing to the right base. Beginning with the little leagues, this was his thirteenth year to play baseball. Other than sports, deep-sea fishing is a change of pace. "I have caught the most fish several times but not the big one (marlin/sailfish) yet," he said. The son of Nancy and Lowell Curry and brother of PHS junior pitcher Mike, he maintained a 3.4 GPA and planned to attend UGA.

On Saturday, March 30, Lindale beat Darlington at the Lakeside 7–4; the day before, the 2 squads tied 9–9 when darkness stopped play. Chris Lansdale scattered 7 hits in the win. A road trip down Highway 101 on Tuesday, April 2, proved fruitful with an 8–7 victory over Rockmart, yet we were down 7–2 in the sixth before McBurnett ignited the Dragons with an inside-the-park home run with 1 on. At the bat in the last inning, Tony Lane, Burnett, T. Curry, McBurnett, Bennett, and O'Neal gave the Red and Gray a single run lead; Glenn Atkins got the final 3 outs with 2 whiffs and a force out. McBurnett had 3 hits while McCord stroked 2 doubles. A trip down High 27 South on Thursday, April 4, was enjoyable, for we downed the Carrollton Trojans 11–3; Lansdale pitched a 3-hitter while Pepperell pounded out 16 safeties. Clete Bonney, M. Curry, Bennett, and O'Neal led us at the plate. We returned to our home at Floyd Junior College on Monday, April 8, in time to batter Haralson County 15–2 behind Mike Curry's 16 whiffs and 1 surrendered hit. The Red and Gray, who plated 11 runs in the first 3 innings, were led by McBurnett and T. Curry with 4 and 3 safeties each. Lindale returned to Six-Mile on the tenth and defeated subregion South foe Cartersville 6–3 behind Glenn Atkins's 6-hitter. Coach Farrer was now pleased with the pitch control of his staff. In the batter's box, 4 senior starters helped plate 5 runs by the third inning to improve the club's record at 4–0. In Villa Rica on Friday, April 12, the Wildcats got off to a quick 6-run lead in the bottom of the first; however, they would not score again until the seventh. Meanwhile, the visitors chipped away with scores in the first, second, and seventh to win 8–7; Tom Curry, Clete Bonney, Mike Curry, and Steve Bennett all batted 2 of 4; the latter stroked a home run in the first. Chris Lansdale came on early in relief and was the winning pitcher. On Wednesday the seventeenth, a big 7-run fourth inning swamped Central of Carrollton 11–4; Tony O'Neal had a 2-run single, which was followed by 2 walks and an M. Curry's RBI base hit. With the bases loaded, sophomore DH Jamie McCord "slammed" a homer over the left center field fence. Glenn Atkins went the distance scattering 7 hits to improve his record to 4–0. Winning on the road is good; a shutout is even better. To wit, in Tallapoosa, Georgia, Mike Curry allowed 3 hits and 1 walk while striking out 9 as we downed Haralson County 6–0. Brother Tom saved the shutout in the third when "he went up on the fence and snagged a long drive." McCord knocked in 2 runs while T. Curry, Bennett, and Burnett each had RBIs. PHS's record moved to 10–2–1 overall. On April 22, host Cassville dealt us a rare loss 15–8 by scoring early and often; the visitors' Jeff Shiflett collected 3 hits while Stansell, McCord, Earle, and Allen all rapped out 2 safeties each. The latter 2 players had RBI-producing doubles. In Cartersville's short field Dellinger Park, the Pepperell Dragons clinched the South 7-AA subregion crown with a 13–11 victory over the Hurricanes. In a venue where no lead is safe, Lindale built a 7–4 lead early and then saw it vanish with a Purple Hurricane 6-run in fourth. Catcher Tony O'Neal led us back in the next inning with a 2-run fence-clearing blast; he finished the day with 3 safeties. Tony Lane and Mike Curry won it in the seventh with RBI singles; the former collected 4 RBIs. Steve Bennett and McBurnett added 3 hits to our total of 18. Chris Lansdale was credited with the win in relief. Visiting Villa Rica didn't have a chance on Thursday, April 25, after Pepperell plated 5 runs in the second inning en route to a 10–2 victory. Glenn Atkins and Chris Lansdale combined for the mound win while offensively Bennett and Lane batted in 4 and 2 RBIs respectively. "The king is dead! Long live the king!" These words effectively translate to Pepperell High eliminating Georgia 1984 Class AA baseball champion Darlington with hopes to replace the Lakeside boys. Lindale swept to the South subregion title by blanking the host Tigers 6–0 on Friday, May 3, and then beating them 4–3 in 10 innings on Saturday at Floyd

Junior College. Kerry Yencer reported the first contest in simple terms, "PHS used the hitting of Tim McBurnett, the pitching of Mike Curry and the fielding of Clete Bonney" to win the game. On 2 occasions, Mac "unloaded" 2 run homers; Curry kept Darlington totally off stride while allowing only 3 safeties; Bonney speared a liner off the grass to start a rally killing double play and consistently turned in "sparkling" fielding gems. In Saturday's deciding battle, which was tied 3–3 in the bottom of the tenth frame, senior first baseman Steve Bennett stroked a no-out bases-loaded blast to the center field fence that brought in the winning run but just missed being a grand slam. Glenn Atkins pitched a complete game victory for the now 16–3–1 Dragons. After his team defeated Cartersville 11–5 in the first game of the Region 7-AA playoff in the short fences of Dellinger Park, Coach Jimmy Farrer declared, "I'd hate to make a living down here." But our 13-hit attack on May 7, which included 2 homers in the third to put us up 6–0 and 3 more in the seventh, worked to the Dragons' advantage. Tony O'Neal, Tony Lane, and Tom Curry all blasted round-trippers in the decisive last inning. Meanwhile, Chris Lansdale righted a streak of mid-game wildness compounded by some defensive lapses to take the win. The rains, which came on Thursday to Floyd College field, subsided long enough on Friday, May 10, for Pepperell to win the Class 7-AA Region crown 3–2 over Cartersville's Purple Hurricanes. The story of the game came on Sunday morning's sports headline: "Curry's 14 Strikeouts Lead Dragons to Title." As our bats were ailing somewhat, the junior right-hander pitched a superb 3-hitter for the victory. Following Billy Chubbs's 2-run single in the first, he recorded outs on 13 of the next 14 batters while striking out 5 in a row twice. The winning marker came in the bottom of the seventh after Clete Bonney doubled, took third on a missed bunt attempt, and came home when Jamie McCord lined out to right field. Coach Gary Wisener summed up the loss, saying, "They beat us four times. I guess they are better." It did not get any easier in the quarterfinals for the once-beaten (17–1) and 1983 state champion. Henry McNeal Turner High School of Atlanta came to Floyd College for round one. They brought the state's leading hitter, Lyndon Lewis, at .672 in addition to Dexter Higgins's .600 and .547 for Eric Rogers. Four of the senior-laden squad played on the '83 team. The Dragons were not without some "pop," for 6 regulars averaged .300 or better. On Tuesday, May 14, the Wolves were limited to 3 safeties by junior Glenn Atkins in Pepperell's 7–0 victory. The crafty left-hander moved his season record to 7–1 by whiffing a dozen while walking 3. By the second inning, Bennett, O'Neal, Bonney, and McBurnett had put the home squad up 4–0. In the fifth, Steve Bennett, Tony Lane, and Mike Curry added 3 more runs to the total. Losing pitcher Mario Brannon, who had given up only 18 safeties during the season, surrendered 8 hits to the Red and Gray; he struck out 2 Dragons, which was well below his average of 130 whiffs in 60 innings pitched. On Thursday, May 16, we traveled 60 miles to Benjamin E. Mays High School baseball complex in East Atlanta for game two. On a nice field but with no outfield fences, Pepperell eliminated Turner High 6–4 behind Chris Lansdale's 6 plus innings; Glenn Atkins came on to retire the last 4 Wolves' hitters. Offensively we scored 2 runs early behind Tony O'Neal and Tony Lane's hitting; in the third, O'Neal singled, Lane reached on an error, and the former came home on a balk. Then Mike Curry unleashed a deep triple in the left center field gap to give his team a 4–0 advantage; however, both skippers agreed that Clete Bonney's hit in the fifth was the difference in the game. Bennett and O'Neal had reached third and second via errors (only our initial run was earned) when Bonney laced a 2-run single to left, giving the visitors some insurance. On Tuesday, May 21, PHS traveled 115 miles toward Gainesville to face a veteran squad from East Hall High School. Coach Jim Lofton's 24–3 crew was a balanced and heavy-hitting team on which 8 starters had stroked home runs. His son Bob led the regulars with a .385 average; ace pitcher Phillip Cronic, who sported a 10–1 record, would oppose 6–0 Mike Curry. On the first day, PHS and EHHS traded victories in the North Georgia Class AA baseball championship series. Mike Curry went the distance in the opener, winning 4–2; the youngster retired the first batter in each inning in addition to striking out 5 and walking 3. Brother Tom prevented the Vikings from tying in the last inning by tracking down a long blast to center field. We plated runs in the second, third, fifth, and seventh courtesy of timely hitting by Burnett, McBurnett, Bennett, M. Curry, and O'Neal. In the second game of the doubleheader, Glenn Atkins struggled with control in the 10–3 loss. Coach Farrer said of the seven-run loss that "the hits weren't what really hurt. It was the walks in front of them." East Hall blasted a 3-run and a grand slam early in the game and played the rest of the way without any pressure at all. The championship North was decided the following day (Wednesday, May 22) on Vikings field. *Rome News-Tribune* sportswriter Phil Miller wrote on Thursday morning that "in athletic competition, in pressure situations, heroes emerge." For Pepperell, the first was bristly faced senior left-hander named Chris Lansdale, and the other was Jamie McCord, a quiet redheaded sophomore. One pitched while the other was hidden down in the lineup as a designated hitter. The results were a 5–0 beating of favored East Hall High. Lansdale spun a 5-hitter in 90 minutes while facing only 26 batters; he threw "junk" curves on the outside corners and then jammed them inside with fastballs. The losers, who finished at 25–5, were blanked for the first time this year. We moved to a 1–0 lead in the first when O'Neal drove in McBurnett. In the next inning, after Bonney walked, pitcher Jeff Cooper tipped off his curveball, and McCord blasted it over the left center field fence for a 3–0 advantage. At that point, the Dragons' number eight hitter in the batting order believed his team would win because "no one has come from behind on us all year." In the fifth, Clete Bonney singled in Tony Lane for a 4–0 lead; errors advanced him to third where McCord plated him with an RBI safety. A huge double play in the bottom of the same inning stymied the Black and Gold as did Bonney's scoop and throw to Bennett who snagged the low throw for the final out of the frame. South Georgia champion Hancock Central High School lies 165 east southeast of Lindale in Sparta, Georgia; their mascot is the Bulldog, and the squad had a 24–4 record. Coach James Bolden remarked to the media that "when we have to play defense, we play defense, and when we have to hit the ball, we hit it." Only 2 starters batted below .300. On Wednesday, May 29, the 2 squads split a doubleheader. In the first encounter, Tony O'Neal slammed a 3-run homer in the first inning; however, PHS failed to protect the quick 3–0 lead, and the Bulldogs came back to win 5–3. In the nightcap, the Dragons again jumped to a 3–0 advantage, but this time Glenn Atkins held the serve to win the second game 3–1. "Mostly I just threw knee high and lower junk the whole game." Opposing Coach Bolden said afterward, "We haven't faced many left-handers but we hit the ball—they just caught it." In our first at bat, Tony Lane scored Bennett with a single, and then Clete Bonney's RBI safety plated the only other run we would need to win. A third run happened when Doug Burnett walked to start the second; an infield hit moved him up, and the senior came home on a throwing error to lead 3–0. For Pepperell, after 28 games, it came down to 1 battle on Thursday, May 30. We thought they were out of pitching because senior Greg Warren threw 172 pitches in the first 2 contests and our left-hander Chris Lansdale was rested. However, the Friday morning issue of the *News-Tribune* spoke volumes, "SURPRISE HURLER WRECKS DRAGONS' DREAMS." Star pitcher Greg Warren and 2 others warmed up in the pre-game before infielder Kevin Hill took to the mound. Although he had not thrown in a game all year, Coach Bolden said, "I have been working with him off and on...if a good high school shortstop makes accurate throws to first, he can make the same to the plate." In the other dugout, Chris Lansdale could not overcome the Bulldogs' bats, speed (6 stolen bases) and, more importantly, 8 Pepperell errors (the earned runs were 5) to win going away 13–2. Atkins and Burnett relieved, but still the winners rapped out 17 hits. On offense, Jamie McCord accounted for both Dragon RBIs including a solo four-bagger in the last frame. There was disappointment but also a feeling of accomplishment in 1985. Coach Jimmy Farrer reflected in the Sunday paper that this group played hard the whole year, and "it came down to the last game and we got beat." Ninety-seven years earlier, Ernest Lawrence Thayer penned one of the best-known poems in American literature entitled "Casey at the Bat." The theme of his work featured in the June 3, 1888, *San Francisco Examiner* befitted the mood in Lindale.

> It seemed extremely rocky for the Mudville nine that day;
> The score stood four to six, with but an inning to play.
> And then when Cooney died at first, and Burrows did the same,
> A pallow wreathed the features of the patrons of the game.
>
> A straggling few got up to go leaving there the rest
> With all that hope which springs eternal within the human breast;
> For they thought, "If only Casey could get a whack at that—
> They'd put up even money with Casey at the bat."
>
> But Flynn preceeded Casey and likewise so did Blake.
> The former was a pudding and the latter was a fake.
> So on that stricken multitude a death-like silence sat,
> For there seemed little chance of Casey getting to the bat.
>
> But Flynn let drive a single to the wonderment of all,
> And the much despised Blakey torn the cover off the ball;
> And when the dust had settled and they saw what had occurred,
> There was Blakely safe on second and Flynn a-huggin' third.
>
> Then from five thousand throats and more there rose a lusty yell;
> It rumbled through the valley, it rattled in the dell;
> It pounded on the mountain and recoiled upon the flat.
> For Case, mighty Casey, was advancing to the bat.

RANDALL MCCORD

There was ease in Casey's manner as he stepped into his place;
There was pride in Casey's bearing and a smile lit Casey's face.
And when, responding to the cheers, he lightly doffed his hat,
No stranger in the crowed could doubt 'twas Casey at the bat.

Ten thousand eyes were on him as he rubbed his hands with dirt;
Five thousand tongues applauded when he wiped them on his shirt;
Then while the writhing pitcher ground the ball into his hip,
Defiance flashed in Casey's eye, a sneer curled Casey's lip.

And now the leather-covered sphere came hurtling through the air,
And Casey stood a-watching it in haughty grandeur there.
Close by the study batsman the ball unheeded sped—
"That ain't my style," said Casey. "Strike one!" the umpire said.

From the bleachers, black with people, there went up a muffled roar,
Like the beating of the storm-waves on a stern and distant shore;
"Kill him! Kill the umpire!" shouted someone in the stands;
And it's likely they'd have killed him had not Casey raised his hand.

With a smile of Christian charity great Casey's visage shone;
He stilled the rising tumult; he bade the game go on;
He signaled to the pitcher, and once more the dun sphere flew;
But Casey still ignored it and the umpire said, "Strike two!"

"Fraud!" cried the maddened thousands, and echo answered "Fraud!"
But one scornful look from Casey and the audience was awed.
They saw his face grow stern and cold, they sae his mscles strain;
And they knew that Casey wouldn't let that ball go by again.

The sneer is gone from Casey's lip, his teeth are clenched in hate,
He pounds with cruel violence his bat upon the plate.
And now the pitcher holds the ball, and now he lets it go,
And now the air is shattered by the force of Casey's blow.

Oh, somewhere in this favoured land the sun is shinning bright,
The band is playing somewhere, and womewhere hearts are light;
And somewhere men are laughing, and somewhere children shout,
But there is no joy in Mudville—mighty Casey has struck out.

    Eight seniors were among 162 graduates receiving diplomas on Sunday, June 2, in Rome City Auditorium, including Tom Curry, Steve Bennett, Tony Lane, Doug Burnett, Chris Lansdale,

Tim McBurnett, Larry Cook, and Mike Earle. A month later, Shorter College signed Steve Bennett and Chris Lansdale to baseball scholarships.

1986 Season

> "It was the best of times, it was the worst of times..." (Dickens, A Tale of Two Cities, Chapter 1.) "It was the winter (spring) of our discontent..." (Shakespeare, Richard III, Act I, Scene I.) Our bruised arms hung up for monuments...but there is no joy in Mudville...in 1986 the Dragons closed at 5–5 in 7-AA South sub-region play and 8–8 overall.

After an exemplary 1985 season that saw Coach Jimmy Farrer's squad go 22–5–1 with 1 of those losses being in the state championship game versus Hancock Central, we fell on hard times. Even the media paid little attention to the Dragons; the Rome newspaper reported a meager 7 write-ups about the team with the first coming on Sunday, March 23. Pepperell outscored host East Rome on Saturday the twenty-second; in the top of the first, Tony O'Neal homered us to a 2–0 lead before the Gladiators countered with 7 runs in the turn at bat. However, with 2 out in the first inning, junior Brian Corntassel came on in relief and shut out the home team for 6 and 2/3 innings. The right-hander claimed the victory by scattering 3 hits over the remaining course of the game. At the bat, the Dragons plated 7 of their own in the second and went on to score in each frame except the sixth. Sophomore Tony Cargle along with veterans Clete Bonney, O'Neal, and Keith Stansell supplied the RBIs with multiple safeties. The paper gave our record as 1–1. In a weekend baseball tourney held in Cartersville, we lost 7–6 to the 'Canes on Friday, March 28, but responded with Saturday wins over Cass, 15–10, and Adairsville, 22–7. Versus Cartersville, freshman right-hander Joey Wright threw 5 innings with senior Mike Curry finishing the job; they combined for 7 strikeouts and 6 walks. O'Neal rapped a four-bagger and single to lead the hitters. On Saturday against Cass High School, Brian Corntassel pitched into the fourth before sophomore Jason Ashley relieved; Curry came on for the final 2 frames. The official scorekeeper needed an extra page to record our at bats. Dusty Dowdy smacked 2 home runs. Jamie McCord singled twice and had 1 four-bagger. Tony Cargle collected 3 singles. Curry added a safety; then Jeff Shiflett slammed 4-base shots which added misery to the Cass Colonels. The nightcap was a 22–7 win over Adairsville, which was called after Jeff Shiflett slammed a bases-loaded home run, ending the game via the 15-run rule. We pounded Tiger pitchers with O'Neal, Bonney, Cargle, and Curry adding to the 16-hit barrage. Jason Ashley started on the mound and went 4 innings for his second win of the day; O'Neal and Corntassel also saw action from 60' 6 inches. Lindale evened its record at 3–3. At Floyd Junior College diamond on Tuesday, April Fools' Day, PHS downed Rockmart 4–3. The Jackets plated their 3 runs early before O'Neal, Bonney, and sophomore OF Chris Ashley moved us to within 1 run at 3–2. In the sixth, a walk and a single by Curry came before McCord doubled home both runners for a 4–3 advantage. Mike Curry went the distance on the mound, striking out a dozen while walking only 5. Next, the local gazette highlighted a "long afternoon" for PHS in Bartow County on Wednesday afternoon, April 9. We dropped a 20–3 5-inning game to Cartersville in shallow Dellinger Park. Tony Cargle's solo home run was lone positive for the Dragons who were now 1–3 in the subregion and 4–6 overall. Tony O'Neal took to the mound for Lindale in Rockmart on Monday, April 14, and he won a "squeaker" 7–6; the senior went 6 innings before giving way to Curry who worked the final frame. O'Neal benefited from an early 6-run lead courtesy of Cargle, Bonney, McCord, Shiflett, Atkins, and Matt Henderson who provided the hits as well as RBIs. At Six-Mile off Highway 27, PHS committed an uncharacteristic 6 errors in losing to Haralson County 8–5. We tried to rally from an 8–1 deficit with a 4-run fifth but could get no closer. Brian Corntassel pitched the final 5 innings in relief and did not allow an earned run for the Red and Gray. The loss left us at 4–4 in subregion and 7–7 for the season. The last write-up of the year for Lindale came on Friday, April 25; it described a 7–3 victory over home-standing Villa Rica. We plated single markers in the first and second frames before adding 5 in the last inning. Walks, errors, and Pepperell timely hitting were the Wildcats' downfall; the biggest miscue for Villa occurred in the crucial seventh with the bases loaded when Danny Robinson singled and an outfield error enabled all runners to score. Corntassel pitched a complete game, allowing 8 hits, 5 bases on ball, and striking out 3. The season ended in Villa with a 5–5 record in subregion and 8–8 total on the year. There is no joy in Mudville.

1987 Season

For the fourth consecutive season (1984–1987) the Dragons were basically playing all games on the road. The old baseball park was being rebuilt and reconfigured with the ongoing construction of a new athletic complex. Page 107 in the following year's annual described the season as "frustrating." There was solid pitching offset by costly errors on the diamond and few clutch base hits. The year ended with a 6–9 record which included victories over Armuchee (twice), Central of Carrollton, Cartersville, Darlington, and Haralson County. Seventeen players were shown in the team picture: C. Ashley, J. Ashley, C. Bishop, J. Wright, S. Presley, B. Woodard, M. Henderson, K. Stansell, M. Wright, K. Hutchins, J. Shiflett, J. McCord, B. Corntassel, M. Wade, T. Garrett, T. Cargle, and Robinson. The managers were D. Gunter and S. Lyles. Head coach Jimmy Farrer assisted by Steve Horne and Otis Gilbreath coached the 1987 squad which, according to all concerned, had the potential to win more than 6 victories.

On Thursday, April 2, at Floyd College field, we were sitting on a 2–3 record and hosting Central. Although the visitors were ahead when darkness fell, Region 7-AA South rules reverted back to the last completed inning, which ended with a 6–5 advantage Pepperell. As a consolation to the Lions, PHS was on the verge of winning outright with the contest tied 8–8 in the bottom of the seventh with the winning run on third. In the third frame, Tony Cargle and Mark Wade doubled in runs; Jamie McCord's second home run of the year put us up 3–0 early. Central came back with a 5-run fourth; we responded with one in the fifth and two in the sixth, thanks to Jeff Shiflett's RBI single and a couple of fielder's choices. The Dragons then went on a 1–5 losing streak before hosting Darlington at Floyd College field on Monday, April 20. Both teams used 3 pitchers in the 15–13 Red and Gray victory; the combined pitching staffs gave up a total of 28 runs and 22 hits; we won despite committing 5 errors. The home squad was down 13–9 late before Brian Corntassel singled in McCord. The *RNT* described what happened next under the heading of "McCord's Double Propels Pepperell": "Bobby Woodard singled in two runs, Ken Hitchins doubled in a run, Danny Robinson walked and Jamie McCord got his second hit of the inning—a two run double that broke a 13–13 tie and provided the winning edge." Pitcher Jason Ashley, 1–1, got the mound victory in relief. Tony Cargle led us in RBIs with 4. On a Tuesday, April 22, road trip to Cartersville's Dellinger Park, the Dragons were "pounded" by the home team 11–4. Truth be known, we were our own worst enemy in the narrow confines with 3 walks, 2 wild pitches, and 5 errors, which propelled the 'Canes to the region win. Pepperell closed out the season with a 5–4 victory over Haralson County. To do so, PHS had to come from behind on 3 occasions at Floyd College field. We were down 0–2 in the first before Danny Robinson doubled; Corntassel and McCord both singled to tie at 2–2. The visitors plated single runs in the second and seventh innings to lead 4–2, leaving the home team with 3 outs left. However, a 2-run winning rally ended the season on a high note, 5–4. Postseason honorable mention all-area accolades went to Tony Cargle and Jamie McCord.

1988 Season

According to the *Rome News-Tribune* on Tuesday, March 22, Pepperell High School baseball team played at home for the first time in 5 seasons. Field and stadium construction was completed recently. At the end of the day, Jimmy Farrer's squad defeated Coosa for the second time in this young season. Tuesday's 11–4 win was all but decided in the bottom of the second after we scored 7 times. The Eagles helped us with 4 walks, 2 wild pitches, and an error. With the bases loaded, Bobby Woodard and Joey Wright collected a triple and double. Sophomore right-hander Tim Garrett was credited with the win. The 225-plus-pound youngster threw mostly breaking pitches for strikes, prompting his coach to say later, "In high school, if you can get your kid to just throw strikes, you'll be in pretty good shape." We participated in a tournament in Cartersville's Dellinger Park on Saturday the twenty-sixth and came away with heavy-hitting victories over Calhoun, 20–6, and Adairsville, 20–14. Senior Mark Wade went 7 for 10 with a pair of four-baggers; senior Chris Ashley and sophomore third sacker Kevin Stansell each collected 5 safeties. The former rapped 2 home runs. Tim Garrett belted a grand slam while senior catcher Tony Cargle had 4 hits in 7 at bats. On April 4, the 7–1 Dragons won their sixth consecutive game in downing Darlington 7–4. The Tigers contributed to their demise on this "bright and breezy" afternoon by issuing 8 walks and hitting a batter in the first 3 innings. PHS served notice it would be a force in the subregion race. Haralson County came to Lindale on April 8 and won on a windy day 8–6. Although Joey Wright was the losing hurler, his coach thought, "He pitched better than eight runs." We committed 5 errors behind the senior. Our record now stood at 7–3 overall and 3–1 in region. On Wednesday the twentieth, we managed a 13–8 victory over Central of Carrolton in spite of leaving the bases loaded and committing 6 miscues. However, 2 home runs and a key sacrifice fly by junior shortstop Ken Hutchins pulled us through. Ace pitcher Joey Wright took the win by striking out 8 Lions and allowing only 2 earned runs. Mark Wade went 3 for 3, including his seventh four-bagger of the season. He drove in a total of 5 markers on this "warm, cloudless afternoon." Senior right fielder Bobby Woodard also contributed 2 hits and an RBI. The next 2 games with Haralson County and

Cartersville were critical in subregion play. Coach Farrer cannot afford to "save" star pitcher Joey Wright for later because absolutely we needed to defeat HC the next (Friday). Besides, freshman Eric Dowdy, senior Jason Ashley, and sophomore Kevin Stansell had been throwing well lately. The strategy worked, for PHS advanced into the region finals by downing visiting Cartersville 4–0. Joey Wright threw the shutout, striking out 5 with no walks; he retired 12 of the last 14 Hurricanes in order. Garrett, Michael Wright, and Hutchings were the offensive stars.

Playing outside the friendly confines of Dellinger Park's 300-foot fences, the losers were blanked for the first time this season. Sam Sprewell was amazed that 15 outs were made in the Darlington diamond garden where the power alleys were 375 feet and straightaway center was almost 400 feet. On the Lakeside field on Monday, April 25, we survived rain and a late-inning rally by Rockmart to "capture the flag" in the 7-AA South championship 8–6. The Dragons (12–4 and 8–3) won their fifth straight game by scoring 7 times in the first 4 frames. Senior catcher Tony Cargle provided the winning runs with a 2-run blast. Ultimately, the Jackets stranded 13 runners and gifted us 7 errors. Senior Jason Ashley who normally was the bullpen stopper almost went the distance, giving way to freshman Eric Dowdy for the last 2 outs.

The early twentieth-century comic strip entitled *Alphonse and Gaston* graphically describes our first game loss of a best-of-three series for the 7-AA Region crown. The two characters could never do anything because each insisted on the other preceding him. To wit, "Pepperell led 4–0 after two innings; Adairsville led 5–4 after three; Pepperell led 7–5 after five; Adairsville took a 10–7 lead into the seventh; Pepperell scored twice and loaded the bases in the top of the seventh; Adairsville slammed the door. 'They played well and we didn't,' explained Coach Jimmy Farrer, a serious man not given to displays of public emotions." Down 1–0 in the series, junior right-hander Joey Wright evened the playoffs by allowing only 1 earned run in a 9–1 victory. We had plated 7 markers by the fourth inning thanks to the hitting of Tony Cargle, Danny Robinson, Chris Ashley, and Kevin Stansell. The Tigers held their ace hurler Kerry Smith to the final game, and he delivered with a 4–1 win; Smith allowed 6 hits and forced PHS into 11 groundouts. Afterward, Farrer was philosophical, saying, "We had a good year. We'll come back next year."

1989 Season

In the season opener on Pepperell field on Tuesday, March 14, Cedartown claimed an 11–3 victory. Rain had impeded hitting and mound work for Lindale. The following day, West Rome debuted and won over home-standing PHS 6–5. We came up just short in a seventh-inning rally. The Dragons continued to struggle on the diamond and stumbled to a 1–5–1 start. This was somewhat unexpected, for most of last year's squad that competed for the region crown returned. However, by the third week in March, Coach Farrer remained upbeat, hoping a week's outside practice would be a cure to losing. On Monday the twenty-seventh, host Cartersville scored 6 times to down PHS 10–3. Senior Chad Bishop was our only highlight with a solo home run in the fourth frame. On March 29, we trailed visiting Rockmart 12–1 before rallying for 11 runs in the sixth to tie. Three frames later, freshman catcher Jody O'Neal walked with the bases loaded for a walk-off win 14–13. Darlington fell to Lindale 7–2 on April 11 when Kevin Stansell singled Michael Wright home in the fifth inning with the go-ahead and eventual winning run.

O'Neal batted 3 for 3 and contributed a trio of RBIs. Senior pitcher Joey Wright went the distance on the mound, whiffing 8 with only 1 base on balls. The locals had improved overall to 4–6–1, but the region record was 3–1. The undefeated (9–0 in South Region) Purple Hurricanes visited Lindale on April 12 and remained so with a 4–1 victory. It did not help that we left the bases loaded in the fourth. In Tallapoosa on Thursday, April 13, an unearned run in the sixth led to a 7–6 Pepperell victory over Haralson County. After Ken Hutchins reached on a miscue, Shane Knott's hit-and-run ground ball was also misplayed, allowing Hutchins to score from first. Sophomore Eric Dowdy picked up the win in 3 and 1/3 innings' relief. There was singing on the April 14 return bus from Polk County after Pepperell edged Rockmart 1–0 in a well-played baseball game. Ace Joey Wright threw a classic game using effective fastballs and curves; he struck out 5 and walked 2 in going the route. Senior left fielder Chad Bishop scored the only run on this cool and cloudy afternoon. In the third frame, Bishop drew a walk; Tim Garrett moved him to third with a single to right. Ken Hutchins brought him home with a grounder through the hole. We claimed second place in the subregion and improved the overall record to 6–7–1. Three days later, Coosa fell in Lindale 6–5 in 8 innings. PHS had a 5-run outburst in the first; however, the visitors fought back to tie in regulation before Michael Wright worked a bases-loaded walk to win. Junior right-hander Kevin Stansell went the distance while whiffing 12 Eagles. On Wednesday, April 19, host East Rome forced extra innings with a 3-run uprising in the seventh to tie at 9–9. In the top of the eighth with runners on first and third, Kevin Stansell drove a double to right center, clearing the bases in the 11–9 victory. Earlier senior second sacker Scottie Presley batted in 4 markers with 2 singles.

Going into Darlington on a warm afternoon on Thursday, April 20, PHS had finally reached .500 with an 8–8–1 slate. Although our pitching wildness gave up a dozen free passes, the Dragons held on to second place in region (8–3) with a 6–4 victory. Senior Joey Wright, who was known fondly by teammates as Einstein because of his ability to dissect opposing pitchers habits, hurled 5 2/3 frames before giving way to lanky Eric Dowdy who won in relief. At the plate, Hutchins doubled twice. Bishop had 2 safeties while Stansell and Dowdy each collected a pair of base knocks. In Coosa on April 24, we clinched the last spot in the Region 7-AA playoffs by downing the Eagles 4–2; it was the Dragons' ninth win in the past 11 contests. Shortstop Ken Hutchins was the hitting star. With the game tied at 2–2 late, the senior scored on 2 separate occasions after stroking doubles. Next up was region playoffs versus North opponent West Rome in Lindale on April 25. In the first of best-of-three games, Pepperell held off the Chieftains in a wild and woolly affair 11–10. But as Coach Farrer said, "We'll take it any way we can." Senior Michael Wright, sophomore Chris Wright, and senior Ken Hutchins were in the middle of our offensive outbursts. In a deciding doubleheader the following afternoon at West Rome, Pepperell lost the first game 4–3 but came back to win the elimination contest 16–12. With weary arms, both squads flayed away at each other in the hot sunshine, scoring a total of 35 runs. Lindale now moved on to face Cartersville for a state championship playoff slot. After a day of postponement because of rain, the Dragons fell to the Hurricanes 9–1 on Wednesday, May 3. Big, lanky sophomore Eric Dowdy pitched well enough, but 8 unearned runs were more than he could overcome. To advance to state, PHS must now win a doubleheader the next day. It did not happen. Although we hit 5 home runs with the "boom" of aluminum bats, the 'Canes swept us 13–8. At one point early in the year, we were 1–6–1 but rebounded to finish 12–11–1. Their coach said, "We could've folded several different times during the season but the kids kept at it." Eric Dowdy was named to the *RNT* all-area squad for 1990. To cap the season, Lindale honored its legend Otis Gilbreath on the first Sunday of May. Otis returned from World War II to his hometown and stayed. He coached all sports but was most proud of an amazing 551 baseball wins with only 117 losses.

1990 Season

In balmy weather, the Spring Classic hosted by Adairsville on Wednesday, March 14, got underway; however, the Cass Colonels "coasted" past us 10–2. For early season player protection, all tournament games ended at 90 minutes or 5 innings. The next day before a drizzle and dusk settled, PHS, 0–3, lost to Calhoun 7–2. Coach Farrer bemoaned our pitchers' issuing base on balls. When freshman right-hander Mike Robinson came on in relief throwing strikes, everything got better. Yet on Saturday, we joined the winner's circle, shutting out Model 8–0 primarily because Kevin Stansell walked 2, allowed 1 safety, and whiffed 10 Devils. Junior shortstop Shane Knott and senior Tim Garrett contributed at the plate with home runs. Amid falling temperatures on Monday the nineteenth, Pepperell inched closer to .500 by downing Armuchee 16–0. We plated 10 markers in the first frame behind Kevin Stansell's 2-run double and never looked back. Junior Eric Dowdy, back from winter hand surgery, recorded the win for 2–3 Lindale. Competing at home in Region South play on Tuesday the twentieth, Haralson County plated 7 runs in the top of the third on the way to an 8–3 win in Lindale. Again, walks "killed us," said Jimmy Farrer. He added, "You can't catch a base-on-balls." We were back in the round-robin Spring Classic on Saturday versus Adairsville where the host team swept us 3–1 to take the series crown undefeated at 5–0. Prior to that loss, Chattooga used heavy hitting to beat us 7–4. Playing our best game of the year in Lindale versus Cartersville, PHS won 2–1 behind Kevin Stansell's superb hurling. The senior allowed the 'Canes 4 hits, walked 2, and struck out 8. Meanwhile, the defense made several good plays in the field. In Polk County on Wednesday, March 28, ace Rockmart pitcher Bryan Culver struck out 12 Dragons (3–7, 1–2) in a 10–6 home victory. In the first frame, senior PHS third baseman Kevin Stansell smacked his third round-tripper of the year, a towering 2-run shot to left. At Darlington on Wednesday, April 4, a throwing error in the bottom of the seventh allowed the winning run to score from second, ending the game at 3–2 in favor of the Lakesiders. Pepperell benefited from 8 base-on-balls but also stranded 13 men on base. Two days later in Lindale versus Coosa, turnabout is fair play as Coosa's 2-out throwing error allowed the winning maker to score. We rallied for 5 runs in the last inning to improve our record to 5–8 overall and 3–3 in the region. Shane Knott, Jody O'Neal, and Kevin Stansell all drove in base runners. We traveled to Tallapoosa on Monday, April 9, for a region South contest and revenged an earlier loss to Haralson County 7–6. The Rebels rallied for 3 runs in the last inning to tie 5–5. However, we quickly went back up by 2 when Eddie Payne walked and Jody O'Neal reached on a miscue before Tim Garrett plated them both with a single. Coach Farrer praised his defense especially sophomores Scott Treglown and Bobby Simms. The former robbed HC of a homer in the seventh while the latter made a pair of "defensive gems" at shortstop late in the game.

The winners moved to 6–8 overall and 4–3 in region. Playing in the "cracker box" Dellinger Field on Friday, April 13, we jumped to a quick 4–0 on account of Scott Crabbe's 3-run double in the third. Host Cartersville retaliated with 4 home runs in winning 13–4, which dropped Pepperell to fourth place in 7-AA South. Coosa hosted the Dragons on Monday, April 16, still in the hunt for a playoff spot in the subregion while PHS was playing for pride. The Eagles helped their cause with a 3–0 victory. Coach Farrer said later, "We played pretty good but just didn't hit...we had hoped to carry something positive into next year." On Sunday, May 20, *Rome News-Tribune* sports department named "a quiet, extra-large" Tim Garrett to the all-area team as designated hitter. The senior hit .447 and drove in 12 RBIs on the year. Kevin Stansell was picked as honorable mention.

1991 Season

The 1992 Pepperell yearbook (1991 season) showed losses to Model and West Rome before a 14–11 victory over host Rockmart on Monday, March 18. Scott Crabbe's 2-run single in the first led to a 6-run uprising. Although the home squad came back to trail late 11–10, PHS continued to battle behind the complete game pitching of Eric Dowdy for a 14–11 win. And then the baseball seemed to shrink to "the size of a golf ball." On Tuesday the nineteenth, West Rome's Shane Pitts gave up 4 safeties while striking out 14 Dragons in a 6–5 win. The next day in Lindale, Darlington's sophomore Jason Dillon repeated Pitts's mound gem by whiffing 14 batters in winning 6–3. "I threw mostly fast balls...I was pitching in the right place at the right time," he said afterward. Because of wet ground, PHS had worked out in the Leonard Gymnasium with no live batting practice. We continued to struggle on March 25 when visiting Haralson County limited us to 3 hits in a 6–1 loss. "Right now we're in a slump," said Coach Jimmy Farrer. But all bad things come to an end. We carried the heavy lumber to Chattooga on Wednesday, March 27, and pounded out 21 hits in a 26–10 victory over the Indians. Scott Treglown, Mike Davis, and Shane Knott each collected 4 safeties. Chris Wright added another 2, 1 of which was a 2-run homer. The season was getting better on the Alabama Road on Monday, April 1, when Eric Dowdy struck out 11 in our 5–1 win over host Coosa. Eric's complete game improved our region record to 2–2. On Wednesday, *Rome News-Tribune* writer Michael Alpert wrote that "the drought is over." He was referring to Pepperell's struggle with lack of base hits in the early season. The next afternoon, we collected clutch singles by Robinson, Treglown, and Simms in defeat visiting Model 8–4. Walks and errors hurt us on Wednesday, April 3, when visiting Rockmart won 9–4. It was the Jackets' sixth straight victory. Dowdy, O'Neal, Knott, and Naugher picked up hits in the loss. It was always nice to beat rival Darlington, and we did 15–1 on Wednesday, April 17, at Lakeside. The win improved Lindale's subregion record to 5–4 and 7–8 overall. Chris Wright threw 5 full innings to pick up the victory; the junior allowed only 6 hits, 1 walk, and struck out 8 batters. But most of the damage was done at the plate where Shane Knott collected a triple, double, and a pair of singles; Eric Dowdy contributed a triple with 2 bingles (baseball slang in which the batter stops at first); Mike Robinson added 2 safeties. Bobby Simms also had a base hit. The Tigers' only run came in the third when future University of Alabama head baseball coach Brad Bohannon stroked a single and came home on a teammate's double. While playing on Adairsville's more rain-tolerant field, Coosa coach Eddie Brock tried 4 pitchers; however, it did not help as Pepperell won 20–0 in a game called after 5 innings due to the mercy rule. The Eagles, who were already eliminated from region play, appeared tired. On the other hand, PHS banged out 5 hits in the first and fourth frames and added 4 more in the third. Scott Treglown, Crabbe, and Simms were the offensive catalysts. In a game to decide the second seed in Region 7-AA South playoffs, Jimmy Farrer's squad defeated Haralson County 9–5; Chris Wright went the distance on the mound, spacing 10 hits in the victory. Chad Naugher, Mike Davis, Bobby Simms, Scott Crabbe, Mike Robinson, and Jody O'Neal were the stars at the plate. Jimmy Farrer said afterward, "It's a big accomplishment for our players." Number-one-seed Adairsville had the option of hosting the first contest or visiting. Coach Eddie Chastain chose the latter, knowing the last 2 games would be on his turf. It was a moot point, for they downed host PHS 7–2 on Thursday, April 25. Starting pitcher and cleanup hitter James Hufstetler executed a successful suicide squeeze and pitched a complete game 6-hitter. The following day in north Bartow County, Dennis Marsingale hit a sixth-inning 3-run homer over the right field fence that hit a blue van parked outside. The swat pretty much settled the outcome for the Tigers who completed the Region 7-AA sweep of Pepperell 6–2. "I wasn't trying for a home run…Coach said don't take any strikes," he said later. Dragon catcher Jody O'Neal stroked his sixth round-tripper of the season in the first inning, which proved to be our only safety. In all honesty, Pepperell senior Eric Dowdy pitched superbly, allowing only 3 hits and striking out 8. The Dragons closed out their year at 9–10 while the winners (23–2) moved on to face Rockmart for the region crown. On Sunday, May 26, Eric was named to the 1991 all-area team along with his catcher Jody O'Neal who led PHS in batting. Honorable mention recognition went to Shane Knott.

1992 Season

A paraphrase in the annual yearbook said, "As soon as warm spring breezes wafted across Pepperell High School campus, veterans and underclassmen began practicing their skills. It was made better by a new batting cage and a big truckload of the finest brick dust. This was used to smooth out the rough spots between the bases on Dragons Field." The season did not start well for the home team as they lost 6 of the first 9 games before rebounding to an 8–1 finish. The Lindale 9 closed out playoff squads Darlington and powerhouse Adairsville but lost in Region 7-AA finals to Rockmart. PHS traveled 3 miles to Darlington on Tuesday, March 25, and got hammered 10–2. The hosts hit in every inning but 1. However, as Tiger coach Gus Bell said later, "You can never be sure of anything against a quality team like Pepperell…They know how to play good baseball." Dragon senior Scott Treglown and Shawn Snow combined to take the pitching loss for their team. Several days later, we got revenge over DHS. Chris Wright struck out 12 batters and allowed only 4 hits in our 7–1 subregion win over the Lakesiders. The senior was now our best pitcher, for he had recently limited Cartersville, Rockmart, and Darlington to 4 safeties per team. The offense forged ahead by 5–0 with a big fifth inning. Wright, senior Shawn Snow, Cory Lively, Graham, Robinson, and Bobby Simms led the way at the plate; Simms's double to center field was a key hit. A good 13–2 Cedartown squad surprised us on Wednesday, April 8, by a score of 7–4. Chris Wright, Corey Lively, and Mike Robinson each produced RBIs in the loss. The *RNT* reported on April 12 that Pepperell defeated Haralson County on consecutive days 4–2 and 11–4 to improve our subregion slate to 5–3. In the latter contest, Graham, Wright, and Snow supplied the offense while Jody O'Neal moved his pitching record to 3–0; Jody and reliever Scott Treglown limited the Rebels to a pair of safeties. The Dragons continued to play good baseball in defeating Darlington 7–1. They visited the Alabama Road on April 16 and came away winning 12–7 over the Coosa Eagles. An 8-run third inning decided the game. Chris Wright had 4 hits and 3 RBIs while Clay Graham added 2 hits and 2 RBIs. On Friday, April 17, the *News-Tribune* reported, "Dragons Hold Off Tigers, 8–7." However, the story of the game was Pepperell senior pitcher Chris Wright. In eliminating Darlington from postseason contention, Wright went the distance on the mound although not without some tribulations. To wit, in the bottom of the seventh, Lakesiders Jason Dillon, Jamie Dunap, and Jason Payne hit consecutive home runs on fastballs. Normally the last few outs come from straight pitches, but Chris had learned his lesson as he and catcher O'Neal went to all curveballs. Leading 8–7 with 2 more outs to get, another four-bagger would have tied. But Wright induced a pop to second and a swinging strikeout for the win. The winner's hitting stars were Treglown, Wright, Simms, Davis, and O'Neal. The region playoffs on Tuesday afternoon, April 21, looked very familiar to Adairsville coach Eddie Chastain who said, "This will be the third time in four years we've played Pepperell." Coach Jimmy Farrer would pitch lanky 6-foot-2 senior Chris Wright in Lindale prompting Chastain to add, "I've heard when he on the mound, they're tough to beat." He was right, for the Dragons were "physically and mentally" ready to play and won easily 8–1 in the best-of-three series. Chris Wright threw a complete game 4-hitter. His teammates "exploded" for 6 runs in the fifth and never looked back. Hitting stars were many, but their coach noted, "O'Neal got some big hits with men on, as did Shawn Snow and Chris Wright." The Tigers won game two, but PHS defeated state runner-up Adairsville 11–1 in the third deciding game, thereby eliminating them from playoffs. Coach Farrer said, "I guess this is our miracle season." Losing coach Chastain said, "My hat goes off to Pepperell and their coach." For the region championship, heavy-hitting Rockmart came to Lindale on Tuesday, April 28, and won big 11–2. "We'd do well to forget this one completely," said Jimmy Farrer. On Thursday, the last day of April, in Polk County, the Jackets continued to pound the baseball, winning 7–4 and sweeping into the state AA playoffs. We stranded 6 runners in the first 3 innings and never recovered. Although our season ended, it was quite an accomplishment to begin the subregion at 0–3 and eventually compete for a region championship. Our 1992 season record was somewhat elusive; however, the *RNT* seems to be the most reliable in reporting a 13–10 overall slate. The all-area team was announced on Sunday, May 24, with batterymates Chris Wright and Jody O'Neal representing Pepperell.

1993 Season

The 1993 baseball season began with a weather report. The *Rome News-Tribune* wrote on page 1 of Friday's March 12 edition of "a bad moon rising." This quote reflects a belief that the moon exerts an influence on human affairs. The paper then headlined, "Winter Snowstorm on Way." It advised Floyd County residents to stay home. The blizzard of '93 knocked out power to 50,000 local citizens. When the 18 inches of snow melted, nature supplied an additional half a foot of rain in March. Teenage baseball players reported back to school on Monday, March 22, and practiced in the Leonard Gymnasium for days. On April 2, the local gazette reported that PHS defeated Haralson County 5–1. Jeff Baker went the distance on the mound, allowing the Rebels only 4 safeties. We scored 2 unearned runs in the fourth and then added 3 more in the last frame with 4 base hits. Pepperell's record was then posted as 2–4 overall and 1–3 in the subregion. For a sports researcher, this information was like coming in the middle of a movie. The only source available was the school yearbook which documented the start of the season as a win versus Calhoun, 13–6, and then a 9–8 loss at Model. In the latter game, Corey Lively gave us an early 2–0 lead with a four-bagger in the first inning; Jeff Baker followed in the next frame with a solo shot. Still we trailed 7–3 going into the fifth before plating 2 more markers which cut the Blue Devil lead to 7–5. PHS rallied to tie in the sixth when Wright Edge singled home Jeff Hunnicutt and Corey Lively. Senior Mike Robinson opened the seventh with a ringing double and scored the go-ahead 8–7 run on Jeff Baker's grounder. However, with 2 on and 1 out, the Blue Devils' number nine batter hit a bloop to right field, chasing home both runners for a 9–8 Shannon victory. Next, host Villa Rica pounded us pretty good in winning 20–5; this game was followed by a trip to Polk County where Rockmart claimed a 5–1 victory. On Monday, March 29, home-standing East Paulding scored 13 runs after Wright Edge had given us the lead with a 2-run homer in the first. The Raiders capitalized on 8 Dragon errors. Pepperell defeated visitors Haralson County 5–1 and then, according to the annual, lost to Cartersville, 12–4; Villa Rica, 6–2; and Rockmart, 3–1. The latter contest was written up in the *RNT* on Monday, April 12. Chris Hardy walked and later came home when Jeff Baker singled. The visiting Jackets tied and took a 2–1 lead for good in the sixth; they added another marker an inning later. Both late scores were the results of errors. Coach Jimmy Farrer said afterward, "Unearned runs have been the story of our season." Truth is youth had hampered his lineup all year, for it featured 2 juniors, 6 sophomores, and a freshman. At a time when practice was critical for newcomers, the blizzard delayed team development. After the Yellow Jackets' defeat, we were sitting on a 2–7 record; however, losses to Cartersville, 14–2, and 7–5 to Haralson dropped the slate to 2–9. A final game 10–5 victory over East Paulding in Lindale ended the year on a high note. Although Coach Farrer bemoaned the lack of seniors on his squad, it was junior Jeremy Guy who put everything in perspective on page 39 of the yearbook, commenting, "Each game was a lesson; some taught me how to play a better game, others taught me teamwork, and a few taught me how to win graciously."

1994 Season

On Friday, March 4, in Lindale, both Trion and Pepperell opened their baseball season. The host squad committed 6 miscues that led to a 4–2 Bulldog victory. Meanwhile, the winners played flawless in the field and held the Dragons hitless for the first 4 innings. Coach Jeff Bennett was very pleased with his squad; however, Jimmy Farrer said, "We will have to get better." And we did. The following afternoon, left-hander Josh Hopper pitched a 2-hitter for 5 innings to defeat visiting Calhoun 8–3. Outfielder Jeff Hunnicutt led us at the plate with safeties that drove in 2 runs; he also stole a pair of bases. Junior Jeff Baker teamed with senior Jeremy

Guy for RBI singles; the Jackets did not help themselves with 3 errors. On Monday afternoon, March 7, Model scored a 20–5 victory in Lindale. They reached starter Jeff Baker for 4 runs in the top of the first; we retaliated in our half of the inning with a trio of markers highlighted by senior catcher Clay Graham's double. The Blue Devils came right back with 6 runs in the next frame and were never headed. The losers committed 7 miscues, prompting Coach Farrer to say later, "We're giving up a lot of cheap runs." In Tallapoosa on Monday afternoon, March 14, we rolled to a 9–2 Region 7-AA South victory. The Dragons raced to a 5–0 advantage in the opening frame that featured Josh Hopper's 2-run single. We added a 3 spot in the fifth behind hitting stars Wright Edge, Jeff Baker, Jeff Hunnicutt, and Jeremy Guy; each contributed 2 safeties to our cause. On the seventeenth, Cartersville hit safely only twice in the game but benefited from 3 first-inning walks to take a narrow 4–2 victory over PHS. A day later on the eighteenth, a six-run second inning "sparked" Pepperell to a 9–4 win over visiting Coosa. Jeff Baker went the distance for the winners while striking out a half dozen and allowing the same amount of safeties. "Baker threw strikes and let the defense do the rest," said Assistant Coach Phil Williams who was substituting for an ailing Jimmy Farrer. A big second inning was keyed by Josh Hopper's double that knocked in Graham and Lively; Baker, Kris Hardy, and Eric Henry each had hits in the uprising. Later Jeremy Guy drove in Hardy and Hunnicutt to put the contest out of reach. Coosa coach Preston Cash said afterward, "Pepperell got hits when they needed them." We trekked north on March 30 and defeated Trion 8–3. The third inning proved decisive as we scored 7 runs in a 2-out rally. The big hit was a 2-run double by sophomore outfielder Jeff Hunnicutt; errors plagued the Bulldogs at critical times. The Rockmart Yellow Jackets were in the battle for postseason playoff. They needed a victory over home-standing Pepperell to stay tied with Cartersville for second place. On Monday afternoon, April 11, their pitcher Brandon Woods struck out 14 Dragons en route to a 6–1 victory. Coach Farrer said later, "I knew he had a bunch of strikeouts...I thought Corey Lively pitched well, too." A jubilant Coach Kent Mathis explained in the postgame, "This was a big game for us. If we had lost, it would have been over for us." PHS finished the season at Villa Rica on the thirteenth and East Paulding on Thursday, April 14. The season record for 1994 is difficult to determine. A post in the yearbook states a 6–12 slate; however, further research confirms a 6–7 win-loss year. We split with Trion, won over Calhoun, defeated Haralson twice and split with Coosa, lost to Cartersville and Villa Rica, lost to Rockmart, and split with East Paulding. Corey Lively came to the forefront with leadership. The senior led in home runs and batting average and was chosen with Jeremy Guy on the all-area honorable mention squad. Lefty Josh Hopper garnered the best earned run average on the team at 3.15.

1995 Season

On Friday, March 10, senior pitcher Wright Edge retired the first 9 Rockmart batters while the offense plated 5 runs in the second inning of a Pepperell High 8–5 victory. Freshmen Shiflett, Pate, and Huckaby contributed hits, walks, and RBIs while seniors Henry, Edge, and junior Hunnicutt provided sound baseball for season win number two. On Thursday the sixteenth in Lindale, senior left-hander Josh Hopper whiffed 8 visiting Dade County players and limited them to 3 hits plus 1 meager run in winning 4–1. Coach Jimmy Farrer said this about the southpaw, "In his three games, he's had 12, 10 and eight strikeouts." Josh fought through 2 rain delays but still retired 13 of the last 14 hitters. The 4-2 Dragon offensive stars were Greg Camp, Eric Henry, Joey Shiflett, Brian Huckaby, Wright Edge, Denver Pate, and Chris Youngblood. Strong pitching and great outfield play on the Alabama Road benefited Coosa's 3–2 win over Pepperell on Monday, March 20. Although our Brian Huckaby pitched well and hit 3 safeties as well on this windy day, his teammates left 9 runners on base for want of timely hitting. We took a 2–1 lead in the fifth when Hunnicutt singled, stole second (he had 3 on the day) and came home following a Pate single and sacrifice fly by Shiflett. However, the Eagles responded in their half with two go-ahead markers to win. On Friday, March 24, in Trion, the wheels fell off our pitching as the Bulldogs scored a 17–1 victory over the 45 Dragons from Lindale. Three different batters "notched" 3 safeties each for the winning squad. Their pitcher Jeremy Guinn whiffed 10 Dragons in revenging an earlier 8–5 loss to PHS. However, we recovered on Monday the 27th at the Lakeside with a satisfying 5–4 win over Darlington. Josh Hopper went the distance on the mound to improve his record to 4–1. The host squad had 4 more hits than the Dragons, but they "booted" the ball 9 times. Leading 3–2, we put the game away in the final inning when Pate and Hunnicutt scored courtesy of DHS errors. Our record stood at 5–5 overall and 2–3 in region. On the last Thursday in March, pitcher Brian Huckaby "stole the show" in Lindale; the big freshman carried a perfect game into the fourth inning after retiring the first 11 hitters. Later he recorded another streak of 7 consecutive outs in beating region foe Chattooga 6–1. His coach summed up the performance, "He threw his curveball for strikes, got ahead and didn't walk any." Former Dragon star and Indian coach Steve Turner said of Huckaby, "He had us off-stride all day." Shiflett and Hunnicutt had 2 hits each, and the winners added 6 stolen bases to the fray. The victory moved our record to 6–5 overall and 3–3 in 7-AA Region North. We visited Dade County on April 3 and pounded out 11 runs on 12 safeties; however, we could not stop the Wolverines from outscoring us 12–11. In our last at bat, PHS had the tying run on third but could not push it across. Offensive stars for the Dragons were freshmen Joey Shiflett who picked up 3 hits including a home run; Jeff Hunnicutt, Jeff Baker, and Eric Henry each hit safely twice. The victory gave Trenton sole possession of second place in region. Home team Model defeated the Dragons 9–5 on April 7 despite being outhit 11 to 9; however, we left 13 runners on base, and the Blue Devils took advantage. They were able to score 6 markers in the bottom of the sixth inning with only 2 safeties. Coach Farrer said, "We didn't execute on the field." Lindale took a 2–1 lead when Shiflett doubled in Johnny Ray Wheat; in the top of the fifth, Edge knocked in Pate. The former then scored on an error, giving us a 4–1 advantage. But Shannon exploded in the sixth to take a non-region win. PHS's record stood at 8–8 with 3–5 in region. The Wednesday, April 12, issue of *Rome News-Tribune* posted this sub-headline: "Dragons Get Win in Finale." Although we failed to qualify for the region playoffs, Josh Hopper pitched a complete game 7–5 victory over Darlington. In his last game as a Dragon, he threw 137 pitches to go with 5 strikeouts. We put up 5 runs in the fourth inning that the Lakesiders could not overcome. Offensively Henry, Edge, Baker, Youngblood, Huckaby, and Shiflett all had a hand in the batter's box. Coach Jimmy Farrer said afterward, "This gives the younger players something positive to look forward to for next year." The loss also eliminated the visitors from postseason play.

The 7–5 victory over Darlington on April 12, 1995, was Jimmy Farrer's farewell as Pepperell baseball coach. His career spanned parts of four decades beginning as a youngster behind the levee, starting in high school and Shorter College before finally assistant and head coaching the Dragons. He was the last link to play for and coach with Lindale legend Otis Gilbreath, who put this small village on the Georgia map and nation wise. In the student yearbook, sophomore Sarah A. Morgan recorded quotes from the 1995 squad. Tenth grader Denver Pate said, "He is someone that you like to be around." Sophomore Joey Shiflett thought, "I think he is a wonderful coach and a wonderful person to be around." James Curtis Farrer reflected, "There comes a time when you know it's time to move on or let someone else have a chance to be in charge."

1996 Season

In 1996, Phil Williams became just the fourth baseball coach in Pepperell Dragons' history. Mr. J. W. Sutton began the program in 1952; he was followed by legendary Otis Gilbreath and then former player Jimmy Farrer. By the first week in March, Lindale had suffered through rainy days to record a 5–0 record. Four of the victories occurred in the Georgia-Alabama Classic. In Summerville, sophomore Joey Shiflett was outstanding as he tallied 9 safeties, including 2 round-trippers, and 5 doubles. In the game versus Centre, Alabama freshman Matthew Middleton had the game-winning RBI while another ninth grader, Adam Stroupe, was the winning hurler. There was also a 4–3 win over Armuchee for the youthful Dragons who list only 4 seniors on the roster.

Sophomore Denver Pate, who went the distance against the Indians, was part of staff comprised of ninth and tenth graders. Williams said recently, "Considering how young we are, the season has been a surprise." In Lindale on Monday, March 11, Shiflett and Pate combined for a 3-hitter in downing Chattooga 5–4. We were trailing 4–1 early in the subregion game when senior Jeff Hunnicutt blasted a 2-run homer. Losing coach Steve Turner thought, "It was a good ballgame...back and forth." Another comeback happened on Thursday the fourteenth when PHS rallied from 4 runs down to defeat visiting Dade County 5–4. The decisive run-scoring hit to left was delivered by senior Corey Rhodes. With 2 out in the bottom of the seventh, junior Josh Adams doubled; freshman pinch-runner Shane Peveto replaced him and came home on Rhodes's bingle. Five of the 8 Dragons' victories have been come-from-behind affairs. In the Dade contest, pitcher Denver Pate rebounded from a tough start to shut down the Wolverines over the final 5 innings. Their head coach said later, "I would never, ever dreamed that we would be 8–0 right now." On Thursday, March 21, in Cartersville, the 'Canes jumped to a 4–0 lead and held on to nip Lindale 4–3. Although RBIs by Pate and Rhodes late in the game almost brought us back, the host squad administered our first loss in 10 tries. The next day, we got "back on track" against visiting Trion, winning 11–3. Denver Pate threw 6 strong innings while striking out 9 Bulldogs. Meanwhile, with Shiflett and Adams on base via walks, Corey Rhodes smacked a 3-run homer that put us ahead for good on a sunny and blustery spring day. We visited Chattooga on the twenty-ninth and won 4–3. It was not easy for the tying, and winning runs were on base with only 1 out when Joey Shiflett relieved Pate. However, the big sophomore retired 2 straight batters for the victory to improve our record to 11–2 overall. On the Alabama

Road on Thursday, April 4, Denver Pate put on a show by whiffing 11 batters while throwing a no-hitter in the 9–1 victory over Coosa. The right-hander hit one batsman and walked 2 in 7 innings. Right fielder Johnny Ray Wheat saved the pitching gem in the third by diving to his left to catch a ball stroked by Jeremiah Blanton. In the batter's box, Rhodes blasted a 3-run four-bagger; Pate had an RBI single, and Josh Adams suicide-squeezed Jeff Hunnicutt across the plate. The following day, it was "crunch-time" as number-one-ranked Cartersville came to Lindale for a big Class 7-AA North showdown. The Hurricanes scored 3 go-ahead runs in the fifth courtesy of PHS errors and went on to win 6–3. Rhodes, Shiflett, Hunnicutt, and Pate were responsible for our runs. The visitors gave us plenty of chances as they walked 11 Dragons; however, we could not get the big hit. Freshman Scott Peveto gave up 9 safeties in going the distance. On April 9 at Darlington, the 14-3 Dragons accomplished 2 things; we avenged one of the team's 3 losses and then locked in a region playoff berth for the first time in 6 years. The Tigers felt our wrath as we ran out to a 15–4 lead with 7 runs in the sixth frame en route to a 16–12 victory. Denver Pate was the winning pitcher. On Tuesday, April 16, PHS faced Villa Rica in Lindale where the South 7-AA Subregion champs won 5–0 despite Joey Shiflett striking out 13 Wildcats and allowing only 4 hits; 4 of the visitors' runs were unearned and scored with 2 outs. In the meantime, Pepperell had trouble getting the rawhide out of the infield as we managed only 3 safeties against ace right-hander Wes McClain. Coach Williams said later, "You shouldn't lose when you strike out 13." In the return game on the seventeenth, Lindale was cruising with a 7–1 lead over Villa in the sixth inning. Unfortunately, the Dragon defense collapsed in the bottom of the frame, and the home team ended our season at 14-5 with a come-from-behind 8–7 victory. Tough-luck loser Denver Pate pitched a complete game 6-hitter. Sophomore Joey Shiflett led us in the batter's box with a towering home run, a double, and 3 RBIs. In early June, the *Rome News-Tribune* all-area team was announced. Repeat selection outfielder Jeff Hunnicutt was recognized for his contribution with the glove, the bat, and on the base paths. Sophomore pitcher Joey Shiflett threw 6 complete games and recorded a 1.36 ERA; in addition, he batted .403 with 22 runs batted in. Honorable mention players were Denver Pate, Josh Adams, and Corey Rhodes.

1997 Season

To open the new season, host Cedartown handed the Dragons an 8–1 defeat in the first week of March. Joey Shiflett did not pitch badly; we just did not help him much in the field. However, PHS came back on Friday the seventh and beat the same Bulldogs 9–5 in Lindale. The home team plated 9 consecutive runs in just 2 innings while Shiflett and Lee Mitchell combined for the mound victory. In the first frame, Greg Camp and Bubba Owens started a 4-run rally with consecutive RBI bingles. We added 4 more counters in the next inning thanks to a solo home run by Mitchell, a walk, a hit batsman, and errors by the visitors. As the sun began to settle in Lindale, reliever Denver Pate came on to strike out the final 2 batters. On the twelfth, PHS downed Cherokee County, Alabama, 6–4 in the Chattooga Classic. Joey Shiflett went the distance whiffing 11 batters while walking 1. Lee Mitchell socked another four-bagger, and Brian Huckaby stroked a 2-run single as we improved to 2-1 on the young season. Joey continued to shine on Monday, March 17, in our first region contest on the road in Summerville; the junior threw a 7-hitter against the Indians including 9 strikeouts. Lee Mitchell broke the game open in the sixth with a 2-out grand slam. The inning started with Greg Camp's single and 3 straight base on balls; Lee then cleared the sacks with his blast. In the batter's box, Shiflett, Adams, Huckaby, and Camp each collected 2 safeties. On a trip south on Highway 101, we ran into Heath Morris not on the highway but on Rockmart's baseball diamond. The youngster homered 3 times in the Jackets' 13–6 win. Every time we fought back on the scoreboard, Morris came to bat and built back their cushion. Lee Mitchell took the mound loss. Once more, the Dragons had 4 players collecting 2 safeties apiece. On Thursday the twenty-seventh, Pepperell jumped on visiting LaFayette the same as Rockmart did us previously. Joey Shiflett was masterful as the eleventh grader struck out 8 and walked only 1 in our 10–2 win. While the Ramblers struggled to plate runners, we scored with "near impunity" courtesy of 7 hits, 8 walks, and 2 opponent errors. Lindale played a doubleheader in Trion on Tuesday, April Fools' Day, and combined for 49 runs and 51 hits (no fooling). The Dragons won the opener 21–11 with Shiflett and Pate having "monster" games. The former drove in 7 RBIs while the latter pushed 4 across the plate. Matt James and Lee Mitchell did their part with 4 hits each; the latter hit a 3-run jack. Sophomore Greg Hunnicutt collected 2 bingles and the same RBIs. On blue Monday, April 7, in Lindale, Chattooga's reliever Shane Woody came on with the bases loaded in the last of the seventh and proceeded to strike out the side to preserve his team's 6–4 region victory over PHS. Indian coach Steve Turner was proud of his hurlers and his batters who plated 4 runs in the third inning to take control. The 6–9 Dragons hurt themselves with 4 miscues in the field and the lack of clutch hitting. New coach Jeff Shiflett, who had succeeded Phil Williams, watched his squad squander several chances and said, "We just couldn't get the big hit." Four days later on Friday, April 11, we ran into another ace thrower. This time it was Cartersville's Brad Maddox who performed for the dominant team in Region North. On Friday, April 11, he struck our 14 Dragons including 8 in the final 3 innings to complete a season sweep of Lindale 9–3. The Hurricanes took advantage of 5 errors and 11 stolen bases in the victory. Coach Shiflett worried about his squad's inconsistency. With our backs to the wall in the subregion, the Red and Gray won at LaFayette 8–3. Once again, Mitchell and Shiflett led us with the latter pitching a complete game 5-hitter and adding 2 hits offensively; the former had 3 safeties including a pair of doubles. The win put us at 9–10 overall but 6–4 in subregion play. A cautionary warning of the 8–3 victory was that the LaFayette Ramblers must defeat Dade County the next day (April 18) for Pepperell to gain a berth in the playoffs. Coach Shiflett said, "We have a chance but I hate to depend on somebody else." As luck would have it, the Wolverines won, and the Dragons stayed at home. The *Rome News-Tribune* published all-area teams on June 1, 1997. Joey Shiflett was selected as Player of the Year because with a bat in his hand or standing on the pitching mound, he was the better player. He sported a .475 batting average with 30 RBIs. On the hill, he worked 59 innings, posted 56 strikeouts, walked just 7 batters, and finished with a 6–3 record. Teammates Lee Mitchell and Denver Pate were honorable mention.

1998 Season

In an early season tournament hosted in Summerville by Chattooga High School, Pepperell won its second game of the season 15–6 against Centre, Alabama. The Wednesday night crowd watched as former Dragon quarterback Denver Pate pitched a 5-hitter and hit a grand slam in the March 4 victory. Lee Mitchell and Bubba Owens matched his 3 safeties; Joey Shiflett wasn't far behind with 2 ringing doubles and 5 RBIs. On Tuesday the tenth in Lindale, the weather was more suited for ice hockey than baseball; nevertheless, we got a strong 9–0 shutout win from pitchers Joey Shiflett and Wayne Groves to go 3–0 on the season. In the batter's box, Denver Pate and Stewart Bratcher each had 2 hits and 3 RBIs. In Polk County on Wednesday, March 11, Denver Pate struck out 11 Yellow Jackets and allowed only 4 hits, but Rockmart's Jason Wheeler homered twice in his team's ominous 6–2 victory. Lee Mitchell led off the game with a solo blast, and later Josh Adams singled in a run to account for our scores. In a home game versus Cedartown on Tuesday the seventeenth, Denver Pate pitched, and Matt Middleton hit as the Dragons overwhelmed the Bulldogs 12–3. In a strange game on March 25 in Lindale, neither squad scored after the fifth inning; Joey Shiflett was 3 for 5 at the plate while Pate went 2 for 3 before darkness settled in to end it officially at 4–4. Last year's Player of the Year was on his game on Thursday the twenty-seventh in Lindale as he allowed the visiting Hurricanes 1 unearned run in a 5–1 Region North win. It was Cartersville's first league loss. In 19 innings of work this spring, Shiflett had not issued a base on balls for the 6-1-2 Dragons. Second-year coach Jeff Shiflett was proud of his crew especially in the field, saying, "We were diving around going for the ball." And then he added, "We hit the ball very well against a good pitcher (Justin McClain)." At Lafayette, twelfth grader Joey Shiflett went the distance in a 10–0 victory. When the Ramblers failed to score in the fifth, the 10-run rule applied to end the contest. Shiflett also blasted a 3-run homer on the last day of March. Lee Mitchell delivered a home run in the second and a double 3 innings later for 4 RBIs. On the first Thursday of April, sophomore Lee Mitchell gave up a mere 3 hits while striking out 4 in a 9–1 win over host Chattooga; he also doubled and singled in 3 runs to keep our subregion record perfect at 6–0. Senior Bubba Owens added 2 safeties for the Dragons. After Pepperell bolted to a 7-run lead in the first inning, home team Trion responded an inning later to tie the game at 7–7. Johnny Ray Wheat relieved and gave up only 1 safety the rest of the way while his mates (Mitchell, Adams, Shiflett, and Pate) pounded out 18 hits in the 17–7 victory, which was called after 5 frames. With 2 contests left in regular season, PHS was 7–1 in subregion; one more victory and the veteran squad was in the playoffs. And that win came on Wednesday, April 15, in Lindale. The Dragons subdued Dade County with only 4 hits in a 7–2 victory; unfortunately for the Wolverines, they made 8 errors. The triumvirate of Shiflett, Pate, and Mitchell provided most of the hits and RBIs. LaFayette visited South Floyd on Friday, April 17, and lost 11–9. Pepperell raced to a 9–0 lead at the end of the fourth frame before the Wolverines fought back with runs in the fifth, sixth, and seventh innings. The winning pitcher was Denver Pate who contributed 3 hits to his cause; teammates Adams, Shiflett, and Middleton also hit safely 3 times; the latter batted in 4 runs to lead in RBIs. Pepperell and Cartersville were now tied for first place in the Region North. On Monday, April 20, Cass High School provided a neutral site for the single game playoff which would determine first place and home field advantage. The Dragons exploded for 7 runs in the second inning and routed the Hurricanes 12–5. In a game that had a "softball mentality," starting pitcher Johnny Ray Wheat was in and out of trouble early but "bowed his neck" and eventually won the game. In the batter's box, Mitchell homered, and along with Adams, Middleton, Owens, and Wheat, all batted in runs with singles. Pepperell had 2 of the best hurlers in Region 7 going for them in a doubleheader against visiting Rockmart; furthermore, the duo had lost only 2 games combined. Yet the Polk County Bees came into Lindale on Tuesday, April 21, without being intimidated and won both contests. A 3-run first inning in the opener against Shiflett was portentous of things to come; the Jackets then registered 10 hits in the 7–3 victory. Meanwhile, their winning pitcher allowed only 3 safeties after the first frame. In the critical second battle, PHS jumped ahead 2–0 in first at bat, but Pate was unable to stop Coach Kent Mathis's "red hot" hitters who went ahead 3–2 in their half of the inning and never trailed afterward en route to a 7–5 triumph that clinched a berth in the Georgia AA state playoffs. The coach said later, "We hit the ball the best today we've hit it all year long." Although the Red and Gray fought back with RBIs by Shiflett, Owens, and Mitchell, it was not enough. Tuesday's playoff setback was the second disappointment in 3 years for Pepperell. When the *News-Tribune* 1998 all-area squad was announced on Sunday, May 31, Joey Shiflett and Denver Pate were recognized as first teamers. Honorable mention went to Lee Mitchell, Matt Middleton, Bubba Owens, Johnny Ray Wheat, and Josh Adams. At the end of the school year, standout Dragon Joey Shiflett fulfilled a dream by inking a scholarship with Division 1 Jacksonville State University. The youngster who started 4 years for Pepperell finished with a career batting average of .440 and 17–7 slate on the pitching mound.

1999 Season

The Dragons started the season with a bang on Monday, March 1, in Lindale as we rolled to a 13–3 over Rome. Sophomore Russ Atkins hit a grand slam in the first inning and later added a 2-run shot; Senior Stuart Bartcher and junior Jonathan Neighbors also homered. Sophomore Jason Ford went 5 frames on the mound for the victory. Coach Jeff Shiflett was pleased with his young squad's good start. Twenty-four hours later, Lindale visited Trion in a non-region contest. The host team jumped to a 9–0 lead before we awoke and scored 3 markers in the third and 11 more in the fifth. Coach Shiflett was happy with the way his crew battled back from a sizable hole to win 17–10. Senior Wayne Groves, who had recovered from a football injury, was the winning pitcher in relief. Home runs were again a factor in the win as Neighbors and Atkins both connected; senior Greg Hampton tripled while fellow twelfth graders Matt Middleton and Lee Mitchell rapped doubles, Sophomore Nick Hopper also hit a two-bagger. On Friday, March 5, in Lindale we won a nip and tuck affair against Darlington 5–3. In 3 contests, the Red and Gray had now experienced an early lead to win, overcome a large deficit to victory on the road, and advanced to 3–0 in a back-and-forth game. Jason Ford and reliever Adam Stroupe pitched well in the clutch while our offense benefited from dropped fly balls and failure to make routine plays by the visitors. Nick Hopper and Lee Mitchell led us at the plate going 2–4. Underdog, to say the least, Coosa came to South Floyd on Thursday, March 11; after back-to-back seasons without a win—1997 and 1998—and first 4 games this year, the

Alabama Road Eagles downed undefeated PHS 3–2. Winning coach Robert Cummings said afterward, "Beating a powerhouse like Pepperell on their home field is quite an accomplishment for a down program." The Dragons were up 2–1 late thanks to a 2 RBI single by senior Kevin Boatner; however, the visitors responded with three singles of their own to take the one-run lead and victory. Lindale suffered from lack of timely hitting. We remedied that on Tuesday, March 17, versus LaFayette with a 10–0 win that was called at the end of the fifth because of the mercy rule. Jason Ford pitched a complete game whiffing 5 Ramblers; Neighbors had 2 hits. Lee Mitchell walked on 3 occasions and hit an RBI double. The Dragons were now 5–1–1 on the year. Facing a 3–5 Armuchee team off Park Street on Saturday, March 20, the Red and Gray lost 9–8 primarily because we left the bases loaded twice. After the Indians took a 6–2 lead in the fifth, Russ Atkins and Luke Sheffield batted in runs to cut the lead to 6–4, but we couldn't keep them from scoring. Coach Shiflett said later, "It was a fun game…we just couldn't get the big hit." In a return match on Coosa's field, PHS revenged an earlier loss by blasting them 18–5. For Pepperell, it was the "day of the bat," for Russ Atkins hit a 3-run homer and finished with 4 RBIs; Matt Middleton had a trio of runs batted in with a pair of doubles. Lee Mitchell had 3 safeties and 2 RBIs; Jimmy Hillis knocked in 4 markers while Jonathan Neighbors collected a pair of doubles. The game was called after the fifth inning. Coach Shiflett's squad was now 7–3–1. We continued our hot hitting on a trip to Summerville where the Dragons downed Chattooga 15–9; Matt Middleton, Lee Mitchell, Nicholas Hopper, and Jonathan Neighbors were the hitting stars for the visitors who exploded for 9 runs in the fourth frame. At Dragon Field on Tuesday, March 30, we "clobbered" Cedartown 16–7. The *Rome News-Tribune* noted PHS was a "really hard squad to stop right now." Timely hitting by PHS combined with 8 walks and several errors by the Bulldogs contributed to the high score. Matt Middleton and Stuart Bratcher led us at the plate with 2 hits apiece; sophomore Josh Jenkins was the winning pitcher. On Thursday, April 8, host Rockmart got the hits when needed and came from behind to beat us 8–7 in extra innings. "We got lucky," said Jacket Coach Kent Mathis. Pepperell had a 7–4 lead with 2 out in the sixth inning when a base hit, a walk, and a 3-run homer tied the contest. The Yellow Jackets rallied again with 2 outs in the eighth with a single and 2 base on balls loaded the sacks; then a single to right field brought in the winner. At the plate for the visitors, Bratcher went 3 for 5 while Middleton hit 4 for 5. Coach Shiflett said afterward, "To be honest, we played better than we have lately." Pepperell hosted Chattooga following spring break on Tuesday April 13; we scored all our runs by the third inning to win comfortably 12–3. The Dragons played well defensively. Jason Ford threw strikes and walked only 1 batter. Offensively, Hopper, Mitchell, Neighbors, Luke Sheffield, and Hillis all had 2 hits. In a game to decide the top seed in Region North, host Cedartown defeated PHS 19–15. The Thursday, April 15, slugfest contained 29 hits, 19 walks, and 17 stolen bases. The Red and Gray took an early 7–0 first-inning lead when catcher Jimmy Hillis stroked a 2-out grand slam; next inning, Russ Atkins followed with a 2-run shot. However, Lindale could not keep them from scoring; all the while, CHS turned 2 fine double plays and made a diving outfield catch that probably cost us the game. In the best two-of-three playoff games versus top-seed number-ten-ranked Villa Rica, the Dragons were swept 4–0 and 12–0. In the first contest, good pitching by their ace Jessie Corn, who struck out 14 batters, behind no errors spelled doom for the visitors. The deciding and final game of the year was similar as we struck out a dozen times while the Wildcats plated multiple markers. The *News-Tribune* all-area team was announced on Sunday, May 30. First teamers for Pepperell were junior shortstop Lee Mitchell who had 32 hits in 72 chances; another junior was outfielder Matt Middleton who batted .411 for the season. Several Dragons were honorable mention including Jimmy Hillis, Stewart Bratcher, Nicholas Hopper, and Jonathan Neighbors.

2000 Season

On Tuesday, February 29 (leap year), the Region 6-AAA Pepperell High baseball honored its 1954 Class B 1-loss state championship squad. Unlike yesterday's slow-starting 18–5 victory over Trion, the Dragons celebrated by bolting to an early 10–0 lead over Rockmart; it began with Russ Mitchell's first swing in the bottom of the first which was a homer over the right field fence. Yet the Jackets fought back in the middle innings and cut the deficit to 10–6 before the game was called due to darkness. The 2 schools combined for 19 safeties which included 2 hits each by Russ Mitchell, Nick Hopper, Lee Mitchell, Russ Atkins, and Jonathan Neighbors. Junior Josh Jenkins surrendered 2 runs and struck out 4 while pitching almost 5 innings for the win. In Cassville on Wednesday, the first day of March, freshman Russ Mitchell won his first mound victory, 9–1, over the Colonels. The hitting stars of the day were Jonathan Neighbors, Paul McCoy, Jimmy Hillis, and young Mitchell, all of whom stroked 2 safeties each. The first 3 also plated 2 RBIs apiece. Playing in Murray County, Pepperell "exploded" for 11 runs in the first 2 innings en route to a convincing 13–6 win. Senior Jeffery Hillis claimed the victory pitching into the sixth; offensively, the Mitchell boys combined for 5 safeties and 4 RBIs. In Lindale on Thursday the tenth, Pepperell was clinging to a 4–1 lead late in the game when Rome High loaded the bases with 2 outs. At a meeting on the mound, Coach Jeff Shiflett spoke briefly, "Let's make a play somewhere, somehow." The next batter lined a 1–1 pitch toward shortstop Lee Mitchell who caught it and stepped on second base for the third out. Next inning, the same scenario occurred on the opposite mound with that man Mitchell at bat this time; following the pitcher/coach conference, Lee ripped an 0–1 pitch to left, driving in 2 runs which pretty much sealed the Dragons' 8–1 victory. Junior Luke Sheffield was instrumental in the win as he singled in a run, scored on a Wolves' error, and hit an RBI-scoring fielder's choice. On Tuesday, March 14, Lindale edged Chattooga 6–5 for a first win in subregion. The hard-luck Indians had lost 8 games this season by a single run. For the winners, Lee Mitchell and Nick Hopper picked up 2 safeties each; Jeffery Hillis pitched and won his third game of the year. One day later, Armuchee "invaded" Dragon Field and surprised us 8–3 in what was termed their biggest win of the year. The 7-3 Indians used a young pitcher out of the bullpen and multiple singles at the plate to record the victory. Strangely all 13 safeties in the game were of the one-base variety. The bad luck continued on the twenty-first when subregion foe Dade County came to South Floyd and won 7–5. Although we outhit and outplayed the Wolverines, Jeff Shiflett's boys could not get a timely hit. A first-inning injury to freshman Russ Mitchell seemed to dampen our spirits resulting in a 6–0 start for the visitors. By the time we recovered, it was too late. If not for Jonathan Neighbors' 2 great defensive plays, the deficit could have been larger than the 7–5 margin. In the third, an "over-the-shoulder one-handed stab of a long fly ball" saved 2 markers; in the fifth frame, Jonathan cut down a tagged-up runner at the plate with a perfect throw from center field. Two days later, the recurring script was, "And the hits just keep on coming." This time, it was a solo homer by visiting Murray County in the ninth inning that led to our 5–4 demise. For the Dragons, junior Luke Sheffield led us with 3 safeties; Atkins and Neighbors added 2 each. On the twenty-ninth in Walker County, we swapped leads with LaFayette throughout until they plated 2 markers in the sixth to take a 9–8 victory. For 10–5 Pepperell, junior Ben Woodall and freshman Russ Mitchell led us in the batter's box with 3 and 2 hits respectively. Twenty-four hours later, we traveled 9 miles north to Rome High and played to a 7–7 tie because of darkness. In the pre–daylight saving time seesaw battle, junior Mark Middleton blasted a 2-run homer, and Neighbors added 2 bingles. In a doubleheader on Saturday, April Fools' Day, home team Pepperell defeated subregion rival Cedartown but then lost for a second time this season to Armuchee. Coach Shiflett labeled the Bulldog game as our biggest win of the year. Using a flurry of RBI singles, we spaced all of our runs over 6 innings in the 10–0 victory that ended with the mercy rule. Neighbors collected 2 safeties and 3 RBIs while Woodall singled with the bases loaded. Josh Jenkins pitched his best career game in going the distance.

Although sophomore Noah Huckaby collected 2 safeties and the like amount of RBIs in the following Armuchee contest, the Red and Gray could not get a timely hit and lost 6–4; tenth grader Timmy Hooper toed the mound for Lindale. Cedartown's record for 2000 was 11–9 while Pepperell's was 12–6, but more importantly, the former was 5–1 (the only loss was to PHS) in the subregion as opposed to 4–3 for the latter. On Tuesday, April 4, the visiting Dragons were downed 6–4 by the league leaders who "hopped out" to an early lead and coasted into the win column. Nick Hopper had an RBI single, and Lee Mitchell blasted a 3-run homer to account for our markers. On Friday the seventh, Dade County welcomed our Dragons hoping to gain ground in the North Subregion race; however, a 12–4 victory by their visitors moved both teams into a tie for second place. Lee and Russ Mitchell led a strong offensive attack with 2 homers and 5 RBIs to go with Hopper, Sheffield, and Middleton's good hitting. Tuesday, April 11, saw the host Dragons win a critical game over Coosa 13–5; the win kept us in the picture for second place in subregion. We bolted in front 3–0 in the first frame, scored 2 more next inning, and put the game away with 5 markers in the bottom of the sixth. The offensive stars were Hopper, Sheffield, Middleton, and brothers Lee and Russ Mitchell. Two days later on the fourteenth, we defeated LaFayette, which set up a single elimination game with Dade County the following Monday at neutral site Ridgeland High School. It was no contest as freshman hurler Russ Mitchell threw 4 innings while giving up only 2 hits. Meanwhile, his mates scored plated 3 runs or more in every frame of the 13–0 victory; the mercy rule shortened the contest after 5 innings. "Bring on Rockmart" was the chant afterward. Although junior Josh Jenkins pitched valiantly in Polk County on Tuesday, the Jackets won game one by a 10–4 margin, yet we responded in the later battle with a decisive 15–5 triumph, which was called after the fifth. The losing coach remarked afterward, "Pepperell maintained their intensity but we seemed to lose ours." Lee Mitchell's performance backed that comment as he drilled a 3-run homer, a 2-run shot, and a solo blast; teammate Russ Atkins also hit a four-bagger. Twenty-four hours (Wednesday) later, fifth-ranked Rockmart carbon copied our romp over them into a 14–2 romp. They stroked 5 round-trippers including a grand slam that doomed us into the mercy rule. Needless to say, the Dragons ran out of pitching. The *Rome News-Tribune* all-area team recognized 2 Pepperell players—shortstop Lee Mitchell and utility specialist Russ Atkins. The former was a repeat selection who was signed to play baseball at UGA; the latter hit .471 with 5 homers, 9 doubles, a triple, and 30 RBIs. Honorable mention accolades went to Jonathan Neighbors, Nicholas Hopper (he would later sign to play baseball for Berry Vikings), Joshua Jenkins, Russ Mitchell, and Luke Sheffield.

2001 Season

Pepperell opened its season in Lindale on March 6 with an easy 11–1 victory over Model. The Blue Devils helped the Dragons' cause by walking 12 batters. Next, we downed host Armuchee 12–11 on March 9; the error-plagued game was played in chilly weather with frost-like fielding; however, our bats were warm. Three seniors and a junior led us in the batter's box with Nick Hopper, Ben Woodall, and Mark Middleton garnering 2 safeties each with like RBIs; eleventh grader Noah Huckaby contributed a 2-run homer to right field in the fifth. Pepperell's first-year coach Andy Henderson was not entirely disappointed in his team's pitching, citing senior Ryan Evans's "solid" relief in the middle innings, but added, "We need to work on our fielding." As it can happen in the early part of high school baseball, the Wednesday, March 14, return game between Armuchee and host Pepperell was called in the top of the seventh because of darkness; fortunately, the Dragons were ahead 13–9. Josh Jenkins ran his mound record to 2–0 and the team to 3–0. We fell behind early but rebounded with 7-, 4-, and 2-run innings; junior Britt Hubier and senior Woodall collected 3 hits each and plated the same RBIs; senior Luke Sheffield knocked in 2 runs with a double while fellow twelfth grader Brad Burnham scored 3 runs. In an interesting game on Friday, March 16, Model avenged an earlier 10-run loss to PHS with a 4–3 victory over the visiting Dragons. This time out, the Devils allowed only 3 walks as opposed to the 12 issued in the season's first outing. With the Red and Gray leading 3–2 in the sixth and Nick Hopper on first, Blue switched their pitcher to shortstop and brought in southpaw Brett White from the outfield to throw against Pepperell's next up left-handed batters. The strategy worked for the first man up drove a line drive to second base, doubling off Hopper. Model then scored 2 runs in the bottom of the sixth to take the 4–3 victory. Twenty-four hours later in a Saturday doubleheader, the host Dragons won the first contest 5–4 in 10 innings and lost the second 11–2 to Rome High. In the initial affair, a 4–4 tie game was ended when Chad Bullington's drag bunt was mishandled allowing the runner to score from third. Winning pitcher Michael Pruitt improved his record to 2–0. Nick Hopper stroked 3 safeties and stole the same amount of bases. The second battle was over quickly as the Wolves plated 5 runs early and used home runs to pad the lead in a 9-run win. We opened Region 6-AAA schedule with an 8–5 road win over Villa Rica; Josh Jenkins pitched well in winning his third game of the season; however, senior Ryan got the save by throwing only 3 pitches in the last inning, all of which resulted in outs. Britt Hubier and Mark Middleton each knocked in 3 runs. Rookie coach Andy Henderson had a philosophy: "Plan your work and work your plan." It must have worked, for his Lindale lads won their sixth straight game on Monday, April 2, with a 9–0 win against visiting Region 8-AAAA Newton County from Covington, Georgia. For the 10–2 Dragons, Ryan Evans threw 6 innings, allowing only 2 safeties; at the bat, Hopper, Hubier, and Bullington led the hitters; the latter blasted a "monster" home run to left center field as a wrap-up. We stole 6 bases and played without an error in the field. The Rams did not help their cause by committing 9 miscues. On Monday the ninth, PHS downed Haralson County 8–6 to stay undefeated in region play at 4–0. We plated all our runs early and then held the Rebels off for our 11th victory. Mark Middleton knocked in 2 runs with 3 hits; Pilgrim, Atkins, Sheffield, and Bullington each added RBIs. Visiting Cedartown was beaten 6–1 in Lindale on April 10; Josh Jenkins was the star of the day as he threw first-pitch strikes to 19 batters while whiffing a half dozen Bulldogs. The senior also limited them to a single earned run on 6 hits. Britt Hubier, Woodall, Hopper Pilgrim, Atkins, and Middleton were responsible for RBIs. Villa Rica left Lindale on Monday the sixteenth tied for the lead with PHS in 6-AAA after defeating them 11–10. Although the squads combined for 25 safeties, the hometown 9 committed 6 errors.

Junior Chad Bullington belted a 2-run jack and drove in 4 markers; Ben Woodall slapped 3 hits and a solo RBI. Hubier added 2 safeties and a pair of RBIs. Events transpired the next day (April 17) that bunched a trio of teams at the top. To wit, Pepperell defeated host Carrollton 3–0. Villa Rica was victorious over Cedartown, and Central of Carrollton was upset by Haralson County. In our road win at Carrollton, and his third straight complete game, Josh Jenkins did not allow a run while giving up just 4 hits and striking out 6 Trojans. Britt Hubier drove in the first 2 runs with a single while senior Russ Atkins batted in Ben Woodall with the last run; to make it easy, Ben had already stolen second and third bases. At Tallapoosa on Tuesday, April 24, Haralson County scored 2 runs in their last at bat to edge the Dragons 7–6. Nick Hopper had 2 hits to go with 2 RBIs and a pair of swiped bases; Woodall, Bullington, and Luke Sheffield also added safeties and RBIs. On Friday the twenty-seventh, Josh Jenkins moved his mound record to 7–0 with a 6–5 win over visiting Central of Carrollton; however, it took Michael Pruitt and Timmy Hooper relieving him in the seventh inning, needing 2 outs for a complete game victory. Each threw 1 pitch, and each got 1 out. With the bat, Atkins, Bullington, Hubier, and Hooper collected 2 bingles apiece while Luke Sheffield belted a round-tripper. Our 2001 regular season slate went to 14–5 and 7–3 in region.

On May Day in Lindale, PHS played like region champs for the first 4 innings as we hustled to a 6–1 advantage over Hiram High School. Brad Burnham, Luke Sheffield, and Mark Middleton, or the bottom trio of our batting order, led us out front. But down 10–5 in the last inning, Hiram fought back. They sent 9 men to the plate and trailed by only a single marker when reliever Michael Pruitt came to the mound. The senior retired the final 2 outs and saved the game with the tying run on third. Coach Henderson was not happy, saying, "If we play like that in region we'll be two-and-que (barbeque)." In Polk County on May 4, Cedartown pounded us pretty good in winning 13–6; the loss left PHS in a 3-way tie for first place in Region 6-AAA.

In the first round of state, Pepperell remained focused as they took on Chamblee High Bulldogs. Chamblee community is located 70 miles from Pepperell in northern DeKalb County; much like Lindale, it began as rural dairy farms and cropland. The school, which was established in 1917, had been moderately successful in athletics. Consequently, we proceeded to improve our record at 17–6 with a 5–2 and 7–6 doubleheader sweep of the Blue and Gold Bulldogs. Class AAA second round began for us versus number-one-ranked Gainesville High on Tuesday, May 15, at Ivey-Watson Field. In the pregame, *Rome News-Tribune* sportswriter Scott Chancey hinted the boys from South Floyd were overmatched against the 26–1 Red Elephants, for they featured 5 first-line pitchers who threw in the high 80s and low 90s. Their ace was John Carroll who had walked only 5 batters in 45 innings; he had whiffed 53 hitters and allowed just 12 runs all year. Their mound coach was former St. Louis Cardinal Cy Young winner Chris Carpenter. Timmy Hooper would start on the hill for PHS; Ben Woodall (.440 BA) and Chad Bullington, who was hero of game two against Chamblee, would be counted on for offense. Don't forget Nick Hopper who had stolen 17 straight bases. Our squad had not advanced this far in state since losing the championship game to Hancock Central in 1984. Ernest Lawrence Thayer penned in 1888 that "it seemed extremely rocky for the Mudville nine that day…When the dust had settled and they saw what had occurred." Gainesville had beaten us 10–0 and 14–1. Both contests were called after 5 innings because of the mercy rule. Coach Andy Henderson said afterward, "If they aren't the best team in the state, I'd hate to see who is." All-area players were recognized by *RNT* on Sunday, June 3. Josh Jenkins, Ben Woodall, and Nick Hopper were named starters on the mound, in the outfield, and utility. Honorable mention went to Chad Bullington. First was Jenkins who threw 4 complete games, recorded an ERA of 3.03, and ended with an 8–2 season slate. Secondly, outfielder Woodall was picked because of a .460 BA and 30 RBIs; he also stole 17 bases in 20 attempts. Finally, utility player Nickolas James Hopper was an all-around athlete and team captain for Pepperell; he hit .336 with 14 RBIs, swiped 19 bases without being caught, and even won 3 games (2.37 ERA) while toeing the rubber. Berry College was his next stop. With the closing of the mill in 2001, we also close the history of Lindale Leather.[175]

RICHARD WILLIAM WOLFE (1925–2008)

Richard Wolfe came to Lindale on July 1, 1977, as vice president of manufacturing and bought us twenty-plus more years of work. He began millwork in the summer of 1942 as a seventeen-year-old high school graduate sweeper at Dunson in LaGrange, Georgia; thirty-five years later, he became West Point Pepperell administrative manager of one of the largest textile companies in the world at Lanett, Alabama. His six plants were known locally as the mile-long mill. Yet in less than a year, the fifty-two-year-old executive quickly became restless without everyday contact with workers and machines. Word spread that another company had made an offer to the headman who was reportedly unhappy "managing managers." On a midsummer Friday afternoon in 1977, West Point Pepperell CEO Joe Lanier Jr. called him in and said, "Richard you've been bugging me now for months about a mill. I've got one for you—Lindale." The plant had worked over two thousand hands but was losing money. Lanier presented an option: rebuild the legacy and resources of the Floyd County site, making it generate revenue over expenses, or shut it down after eight decades of weaving. Lanier cautioned him about moving family, for it could be a short stay. Make no mistake about it—Richard William Wolfe gave Lindale twenty-four more years of life and productivity.[176] The World War II and textile veteran arrived on Park Street undaunted. Being a child of a LaGrange mill village, he understood the people; he was one of them. Now as overseer and vice president, the thought of putting people out of work was inconceivable. The plant had been innovative in the late 1950s developing Starbucks, the original wash-and-wear fabric. The next decade saw the mill develop a revolutionary new type of multifiber denim called Toughskin. When Wolfe arrived, most cloth production was greige, an unbleached, undyed state when taken from the loom. From day one, Wolfe was totally excited, enthused, and dedicated to the challenge. He began by using people skills developed years ago at Dunson. "Always be sensitive to the needs of people; be approachable; never aloof; never betray a trust and don't over-manage; delegate the work and leave it up to your people to get the job done." Charles Brock III, who was a supervisor, said later, "He demanded that you run your job at the highest level. If you gave only 90 percent, you were in trouble." The plan was to repurpose and save jobs. Tirelessly, Richard began by meeting with all the employees in "get acquainted" sessions. He presented them with a survival plan. First, build a solid foundation with better housekeeping. Secondly, improve physical facilities. Third, institute preventive maintenance, and finally upgrade the skills of the hands. The profit target now turned toward a growing all-cotton indigo denim market.[177] First, Mr. Wolfe addressed the problems he could solve. Defects which had to be cut out of the cloth were causing problems with customers. As much as 20 percent of the weave was downgraded, resulting in loss of 30 to 40 percent selling price. And then costly massive machinery rearrangements were necessary. Wolfe asked for help from corporate; at first, the response was small Band-Aids pertaining to already outmoded equipment. But two years later on Tuesday, November 6, 1979, Richard Wolfe somehow convinced the parent company to approve an historic investment for Lindale, which included fourteen major purchases of equipment.

Each of these purchases may be viewed in a newsletter dated December 1979. In early 1980, substantial projects began what was to become a serious modernization of the plant's equipment to meet the competitive standards of the time. After twenty-four months, the efforts to "build a new Lindale Mill" was in progress. Unfortunately, this occurred just in time for the recession of the early eighties. In a March 1982 newsletter to workers, the vice president bemoaned 9 percent unemployment nationwide, soft denim market, low housing starts, high energy costs combined with inflation, new car sales down, and prohibitive interest rates.[178]

There were two major significant upgrades to the plant. First, long-standing ring spinning was replaced by an open-end system. The former dated back decades (Arkwright's water frame) to the spinning wheel, which twisted small cotton fibers into yarn and then winded the resulting thread around a spindle (bobbin). An upgrade brought a twirling ring with an attached traveler which dispenses a single yarn thread evenly as it moves up and down the bobbin. The fully loaded bobbin is then fitted into a wooden shuttle for use on a floor loom. Since these machines are so well-known, they are easy to operate. They offer good strength and quality to the produce and can be used to spin most all textile fibers. Nevertheless, Mr. Wolfe's crew updated ring spinning with open-end spinning, which creates yarn without using a spindle. This system is much less labor-intensive and faster than ring spinning. The principle behind it, which was developed in the late 1960s, is similar to that of a clothes dryer spinning sheets. If you could open the door and pull out a sheet, it would spin together as you pulled it out. Sliver from the card goes into the rotor, is spun into yarn, and comes out wrapped up on a bobbin, all ready to go to the next step.

The second major development was the arrival of fifty-six Sulzer weaving machines from Switzerland. The Sulzer was a highly engineered machine that used a series of small steel projectiles propelled by a steel torsion rod system to deliver the strand of yarn through the weave at much higher speeds. They replaced the old fly shuttle, which was an extension of hand weaving technology. The old shuttles were made from a flat, narrow piece of wood with notches on the ends to hold the bobbin yarn. Most were sixteen inches in length and made of flowering dogwood because it is hard and resists splintering and can be polished to smooth finish. Many companies still use this system as they are easy to maintain. Even though Sulzer is an intricate process, the sophistication of the machine has fewer "loom stops" (when a loom is stopped to correct a weaving fault). In fact, one of these machines can produce approximately five times more fabric per hour than the fly shuttle loom it replaced. The amount of labor required per hour was greatly diminished, and the fabric was of far superior quality.[179]

By the middle eighties, the economy was rebounding. In May of 1985, Wolfe told the *Rome News-Tribune* that employment was very stable with approximately nine hundred people working and added that orders were plentiful although "it's hard to make a buck due to low prices." Nevertheless with new technology, soon the mill was making a million yards of denim a week. In a later newsletter, the headman noted that "if the cloth produced at Lindale Mill in one week were rolled out end to end, it would reach from Lindale to St. Louis, Missouri." In June of 1986, Greenwood Mills of South Carolina purchased the plant, which contained twenty-six acres of manufacturing floor space, for $10 million and planned to continue modernization into the 1990s per the denim market. Subsequently the plant entered the last decade of the millennium as a world-class operation. To wit, some profit-and-loss records have survived the Wolfe administration. In the first three years (1991–'93) of the decade, total sales were $328,500,000; profit for the same period was $31,900,000 which reads out to a 9.4 percent return on the investment.[180]

By the time Richard Wolfe retired in 1996, Lindale Mill had enjoyed twenty more years of life. Under his guidance, the company donated its auditorium to First Baptist Church and deeded land for a recreational area adjacent to the south side of the original redbrick walls. This ground is now a green space for all and known as the Richard Wolfe Park a.k.a. Twig League. Also, thirty-two and a half acres of land on the southeast corner was deeded in late 1983 to the Board of Education for a new football stadium and athletic buildings. Along the way, Silver Creek's Old Brick Mill was updated and successfully placed on the national historical register along with, unofficially, the sixty mascot ducks that paddled around in the stream's millrace water.[181]

Mrs. Marion Wolfe loved Rome and Lindale. During the war, she had been an accomplished clarinet and saxophone player for the local marching band that performed at various parades and military bases. She was a certified master gardener and a devoted member of First United

Methodist Church as well as the Coosa Country Club. Much like her husband, she was an excellent athlete, winning several tournaments and championships in golf.[182]

In August 18, 2003, Troup County archivist Mike Moncus conducted an oral interview with retired Richard W. Wolfe. The text is contained and paraphrased below.

His father, James Gartrue Wolfe, was an orphan boy born in east Alabama's Clay County very near middle Georgia state line. His mother was Lillie Bell Abney of Chambers County, Alabama, just south of Clay. When old enough, young James left the farm and moved to Fairfax in Chambers for millwork; it was there he met and married Ms. Abney who was from the area. Their union was performed in 1923 by a justice of the peace in West Point, Georgia; shortly afterward, the couple moved to Dunson Mill village in LaGrange for employment; it was here their first and only child was born at 13 Sirrene Street on March 7, 1925. The house, which was Richard's abode until age eighteen, still stands.

The Dunson Mill owned 330 structurally sound houses built to entice hands from farms and other mills; the dwellings were a bit more rustic than Lindale as there were kerosene lamps instead of electricity, no indoor plumbing, and only 1 fireplace with coal provided at 25¢ per week; a single communal water well serviced several families. The educational network was commonplace with elementary, junior, and lastly LaGrange senior high. The latter grades were happy days for the freshman who arose at 4:30 a.m. as parents prepared for work. Lessons were completed then, which always kept him among the top of the class academically. Because the fast afoot youngster weighed only 130 pounds, track and baseball became a sport of choice. In 1942, the LaGrange High graduate moved to enroll at nearby Alabama Polytechnic Institute at Auburn in hopes of becoming a chemical engineer; at the same time, he made the baseball team as a freshman. But as happens so many times, romance took precedent with weekend trips home courting Marion Howard. The Auburn coaches finally presented an ultimatum—the young lady or baseball.

In March of 1943, as the war was raging around the world, the newly turned eighteen-year-old enrolled in Navy flight school at Auburn; however, color blindness "called a halt to this endeavor." He soon received word from Troup County of an imminent high draft number resulting in a quick enlistment into the Army and basic training in Texas. High test scores soon brought the Georgian before a panel of officers who recommended Officer Candidate School (OCS). In the interview he told them, "No thanks. I want to be a paratrooper." The officers replied, "You don't weigh enough to even pull a chute down." Subsequently in a few days, he was on the way to El Paso's Fort Bliss for medical training and afterward shipped out to New Jersey for overseas duty in the ETO, which lasted for twenty-nine months. As a trained medic, he began combat in the Normandy landings of June 6, 1944, where only two of his outfit survived Omaha Beach; a Special Commendation for Meritorious Service was awarded for this valor. He was present at the furious Battle of the Bulge in Ardennes Forest with Bastogne as the focal point; the enemy temporarily encircled Wolfe's outfit at Malmedy, Belgium (referred to with American wit as being temporary POWs of the Germans). Eventually the troops crossed the Rhine River at Remagen Bridge before moving east where they assisted in liberating the concentration camp at Dachau. All told, the battles merited him five Bronze Stars and one Silver Star. These medals are awarded for gallantry in combat operations and/or meritorious service in same. Amazingly Richard survived these horrendous actions "without a scratch." Near the end of the Moncus interview, the veteran paused and said, "I am proud of my military service." And well he should be.

When the war ended, honorable discharge came on January 1, 1946, at Fort Gordon in Augusta. Ten days later, mother Lillie Bell passed away, and 8 days later, childhood sweethearts Marion Virginia Howard and Richard William Wolfe were married. With $300 mustering out pay, they honeymooned for 3 months, moving to Enterprise, Alabama, to be with Dad who had relocated. That summer, the World War II veteran played professional Class D baseball for Enterprise Boll Weevils. The team proposed a move up to the Southern League as a second baseman. At the same time, a lucrative offer came from Chicago to become a professional boxer (he had fought in the Golden Gloves arena before the war). Yet it was the third opportunity that spoke to his heart. Mr. Walter Morton, who was manager of Dunson Mill in LaGrange, sent word to "come home to your old job." Richard had been away from home for such a long time and thought it's time to return—and the rest, they say, is history. A quick progression to second hand, overseer, and head of carding department soon followed. With it came a right proper dwelling that had a phone and a bathtub; all these amenities were needed for the firstborn son birthed on May 1, 1948, named Richard C. Wolfe (Ricky). For the next 6 years, the couple tried unsuccessfully to have more children before finally seeking medical help. Family physician Dr. Willis Hendricks would update Richard on the process whenever they met, saying, "I'm still trying to get your wife pregnant." A smiling Wolfe told Mr. Moncus, "He was a witty guy anyway." Finally, the couple applied for adoption. Marion called one day all excited to tell him a baby was found for them. They took one look at infant Renee and immediately fell in love with her. Then, as often happens, Marion got pregnant with second son, Eric; less than 2 years later, another baby boy was birthed named Jeff. By 1968, the village kid had progressed from sweeper/oiler to plant manager of Dunson Mill. The family was happy at home and never thought of leaving. Yet in 1971, he accepted a promotion as manager of Lanett, Alabama, mill which employed 2,200 hands and was known as the mile-long mill. It took him 5 years to modernize the huge structured operation, which led to another major move upward to general manager of West Point Pepperell. But a year of administratively "managing the managers" of Lanett's half dozen mills left him unfulfilled. "I missed the people and the machinery." The Lindale assignment restored his energy.

When Mr. Wolfe came on board as VP of manufacturing in 1977, Sandra McCain had been secretary of the plant manager's office for four years. In 1979, she moved into human resources; one year later, the 1963 Pepperell graduate became personnel director. Therefore, she was able to see firsthand her boss's heartfelt concern for his mill and its people. Sandra has preserved and made available several papers showing a timeline of company management dating back to Captain Meikleham; in addition, there are documents that itemize the modernization program noted in the above paragraphs. Her records include a glossary of campaigns to unionize Lindale which first began in 1947 and came to pass twenty-two years later with a company/union contract. For half a century, the two entities sparred; a former plant manager reflected recently that perhaps employer/employees could have used more of their energy improving and managing the plants.

Ms. McCain remembers that Mr. Wolfe was fascinated with the Old Brick Mill. He directed the carpenter shop to repair and reset the waterwheel and then wholeheartedly supported

Polly Gammon's campaign to get it placed on the National Register of Historic Places. By this time, Polly had retired from the mill and took it upon herself to spearhead research and writing Lindale history. It took most of four years to complete the criteria and documentation required in the seventeen-step process to the National Register. Material was submitted on January 3, 1991 and the listing was received September 9, 1991. In an essay written later and noted in *Lindale Bulletin* number 35, Sandra quoted Mr. Wolfe, "I want Polly to get all the credit for getting the Old Brick Mill on the NHR. She spent countless hours, and had it not been for her, it would never have been listed. She was relentless in her pursuit of making this dream become a reality." The official plaque may be viewed on page 21.

Also with Mr. Wolfe's blessing, Sandra spearheaded continuing education for our mill workers in association with Coosa Valley Tech; this program was brought to the public attention with an article in *Rome News-Tribune* that featured interviews pointing out student basic skills. However, shortly afterward, the seed that really brought public attention appeared in Greater Rome Chamber of Commerce publication *New Horizons*, which highlighted Ms. McCain's article "Lindale Weaves Education into Its Success." As a result, the program received statewide recognition from Georgia Department of Technical and Adult Education for its innovative approach as well as the sheer number of associates that participated. Not to be overlooked in Wolfe's administration was the close cooperation between Lindale and the United Way project of which Ms. McCain acted as campaign chairperson in 1994. Under her leadership, the charity fund raised $1,212,849 or 101 percent of stated goals. Our mill also surpassed its goal by giving $85,820. In hiring, Richard Wolfe was an astute judge of character and ability; perhaps he saw what the yearbook staff at Pepperell High School already knew when they wrote under her senior picture. Sandra Lee Cox, "Now she enters the village street with book in hand and face demure." Editor's note: Ms. McCain's papers can be accessed and viewed from the author's files.

In 1990 at age sixty-five, Richard was thinking about retiring before Greenwood, which had bought the company in 1986, persuaded him to take up the building of a textile plant in Maracay, Venezuela. In the 2003 interview with Mr. Moncus, he said, "It was the most fun job I ever had." With Mr. Wolfe as group leader, five chosen industry veterans oversaw construction from the ground up including machinery; the joint venture with an established South American company was completed on time without complications excepting some language barrier. After the operation was alive and humming, the company hired chief as a technical assistant for two years.

Richard divided his time between home and "beautiful Venezuela." January 1, 1996, resounded with the last whistle blown on a fifty-four-year textile career. The following four years were difficult. Second son Eric succumbed to chronic diabetes, and childhood sweetheart Marion passed away in 2000. After Mom died, the children, Ricky, Rene, and Jeff, encouraged him to move back closer to his roots in LaGrange. Richard William Wolfe passed away on Tuesday, September 30, 2008, at age eighty-three in West Georgia Medical Center. Interment was in Shadowlawn Cemetery in Troup County. A notable distant relative of the family was early twentieth-century novelist Thomas Wolfe who wrote *Look Homeward, Angel* and *You Can Never Go Home Again*. Richard disagreed, saying, "I certainly favor to come home again; this is my home."[183]

THE DEMISE OF LINDALE MILL

I cannot but remember such things were,
That were most precious to me.

—*Macbeth* Act IV, Scene III

In the last months of World War II Russell Leonard closed out the annual company report with his customary foresight. He believed change would rule the postwar world in a way not seen before; it would be driven by the returning men and women who would be abler and better. Although he did not live to see a different world, it possibly began in Lindale on Sunday, September 11, 1960, when Pepperell general manager Garland Howard Smith served as host for Pepperell Mill's Quarter Century Club in a building named Russell Leonard Memorial Gymnasium. That afternoon, officers were installed for the 748-member (it would grow to over 800 in the mid-eighties) organization. After a fine meal, Mr. Smith thanked those present for making Lindale "such a fine community." He then recognized guest speaker Jim Teat of Charlotte, North Carolina, an associate of Southeastern Engineering of West Point, Georgia. In his remarks, Mr. Teat noted the local club was unmatched in total membership anywhere in textile communities; he also added that the prestigious Pepperell Dragon trademark is unequaled throughout America and around the world. However, in Manager Smith's opening remarks, there appeared a seventeen-word statement almost hidden among other casual dinner comments that should have posted an ominous warning to textiles: "The biggest problem facing us and the textile industry as a whole today is imports from abroad."[184]

For fifteen years at mid-century, Lindale still focused on Navy chambrays, Army twills, and denims. In March of 1965, the change predicted by Russell Leonard began to take shape when Pepperell merged with West Point Manufacturing. The former had markets in apparel fabrics and sheets and blankets; the latter's market was towels, industrial fabrics, carpet, and rugs. The merger provided complementary strength. In the early 1970s, Lindale, Sears, and DuPont developed a highly successful line of cloth that was very popular and remains active today. These textiles were named Toughskins and were designed for extreme durability, primarily in jeans wear. However, rather than being all cotton, they were a combination of engineered blends of cotton and polyester. The cotton in the filling gave the fabrics more of cotton-like feel while the synthetic nylon and polyester fibers provided remarkable durability. Although the dyeing process was labor-intensive, our mill was successful in producing Toughskins even on outmoded equipment. Sears reportedly had sales of the product that rivaled those of their Die-Hard batteries. As denim was fast becoming the dominant fashion, Lindale's indigo dye range could not meet the needs of both Toughskin and other denim. Consequently, WPP solved the problem by purchasing Mission Valley Mills in New Braunfels, Texas, which was equipped to supplement their dyeing capability. With that problem solved, another arose when the big three jeans producers, Levi's, Wrangler, and Lee, pressured manufacturers to make higher-quality fabrics with fewer defects at more competitive prices. Each of these companies had their own personality. Levi's was set on protecting their brand while Wrangler wanted to appeal to the multitudes of customers. Lee's goal was fit above all. Yet Park Street lacked modernization to meet this demand. The old equipment began to lose money.[185]

Jack Smith's statement on page 476 was made 33 years before the passage of the North American Free Trade Agreement (NAFTA). In his 1986 book *OLD SOUTH, NEW SOUTH*, Gavin Wright wrote, "The United States seemed for almost two centuries to be an economy unto itself, with its own markets, its own laws, its own technology, and its own business culture... and Southerners were a colonial economy because at every point had to deal with the large economic colossus to the North."[186] On page 275 of Gerald Andrews's 2019 publication *A Mill Village Story*, he penned this hindsight, "In the real economic world anything man-made can be done better and cheaper somewhere else, and it may not be in your hometown or even your nation." The 2 opposing camps of NAFTA were Democratic constituencies, labor unions, environmentalists, consumer advocates, and populist liberals. The other side featured Republicans who were generally lawyers who never lived in small towns or ever worked in the industry, business investors, and high-tech professionals.[187] Columnist Charley Reese may have explained it simply, "What it shows, of course, is that the financial elite in this country controls both major political parties."[188] However, Jerry Crawford of Rome Manufacturing stated in 1994 that "rightly or wrongly, textiles and apparels have been one of the most protected industries in American... like it or not the economy is becoming global." Yet 7 years before, the Congressional Office of Technology Assessment did not agree with Mr. Crawford, reporting, "The United States is one of the few nations that have left its markets largely open to foreign sales of textiles and apparel." Perhaps everyone has a different way of looking at the economic world.[189]

Six years after manager Smith's comment that September afternoon, Celanese Fibers of Rome announced a shutdown because of shrinking markets and decreasing prices; the company began making rayon in 1928 and once employed 1,700 hands.[190] Then in the summer of 1970, Aragon Mills announced its closing, idling 500 workers. This plant, located a few miles south of Rome in Polk County, began weaving in 1900. In 1974, Joe L. Lanier Jr. succeeded his father as CEO of West Point Pepperell; half a decade later, the company reached $2.2 billion in sales and employed 35,000 people in 15 states and 9 countries. Richard Wolfe came from WPP to South Floyd in 1977 just as the big company was dismantling its old operations in Lowell, Massachusetts. This shifted "a greater load of production to the Lindale mills."[191]

Ten years prior to his arrival, a revolutionary new type of multifiber blend denim fabric was developed locally. It consisted of a Dacron Type 59 polyester and Dupont 420 nylon and cotton; the tri-blend was called Toughskin. This innovative and profitable line exclusive to Sears was offered in a plethora of colors and received the Symbol of Excellence Award in 1974 and 1976.

Under the new superintendent Wolfe, 2 important related manufacturing improvements occurred in 1978 with the installation of 56 (soon to be 200) Sulzer shuttle-less weaving machines, which employed a projectile to produce 2 widths of cloth 130 inches wide with greater quality of cloth. Secondly, the adaptation of co-generated electricity; the heavy steam load that passes through on the way to dye and finish turned the turbine that produced 6,000 kilowatts or 40 percent of the power consumed at the plant. However, after modernization always come decline and adaptation. During the recession of the early 1980s, imports moved to claim 35 percent of the entire cloth market. Although Georgia lost 4,900 textile jobs, it still maintained 105,400. Those working logged 40.7 hours per week at $6.34 an hour. In a 12-month period of 1984–'85, *Rome News-Tribune* noted importers had cost Floyd workers $2.5 million in wages; it countered this by saying textiles provide 40 percent of jobs (5,270) in the county. At the same time, a Shannon mills vice president was quoted as saying, "Unless we restrict imports, our industry as we know it will be gone by 1995." He had a point, for the domestic market grew 2 percent last year (1984) while incoming products soared 34 percent.[192] In May of 1985 Vice President Anderson Huber of the Bank of America spoke to students and faculty in a special lecture at Berry College; the former member of the Army's 82nd Airborne Division in Korea pulled no punches in the following paraphrased comments: "The textile industry must stop feeling sorry for itself, stop bellyaching about imports and stop calling for protectionism. We must realize that its lifeblood depends on world trade. Somewhere along the way, America got fat and happy; we wanted to rest on our laurels. We believed ours was the only market worth having; actually China, with its huge population, is the only country that does not have to worry about economic alliances. At present 'other' nations are leading the world market. Huber believes our textile industry is literally dying."[193]

Rome businessman Martin Mitchell thought the United States was becoming a colony again; we are the world's major exporter of cotton; offshore countries take our fiber, finish it, and sell it back à la colonial Great Britain.[194] One bale of American cotton can make more than 200 pairs of jeans or 1,200 T-shirts.[195] As far back as 1549, English professor/ambassador Sir Thomas Smith wrote, "We must always take heed that we buy no more from strangers than we sell them, for so should we impoverish ourselves and enrich them."[196]

On June 1, 1986, Greenwood Mills entered the denim fabric business by purchasing the plant in Lindale from WPP for $10 million.[197] In late May 1987, a new term entered Northwest Georgia vernacular when a "hostile takeover" was used pertaining to buyout of Shannon's Burlington Industries which employed 1,250. Wikipedia describes a hostile takeover as an act that allows a bidder to take over a target company whose management is unwilling to agree to a merger or takeover. Conversely, a friendly takeover is an acquisition which is approved by the management of the target company. One year later, William Farley offered $48 a share for the West Point Pepperell Company. He used a simple strategy; spot an underachieving company whose stock price is undervalued with their assets and profit potential. He says it's no secret—everything is there on the computer screens for all to see. He leveraged the deal using other people's money.

William F. Farley was an American businessman, financier, and philanthropist born October 10, 1942, in Pawtucket, Rhode Island, to a working-class Irish Catholic family. He attended and graduated from Bowdoin College of Brunswick, Maine, in 1964 with a degree in government; the multisport athlete traveled to Mexico and California after completing school before settling in Los Angeles selling *Collier's Encyclopedia* door-to-door. He soon became the leading salesman. After attending law school at Boston College, he found lifework with NL Industries in New York City where he did analysis on potential acquisition targets. In October of 1976, he formed Farley Industries and raised enough funds including life savings of $25,000 to buy a small $1.9 million company. By 1985, he became chairman and CEO of the venerable (1851) Fruit of the Loom Company and operated it for fourteen years. In 1988, he closed on the family-owned West Point Pepperell for $3 billion by upping the per-share cost to $58 and then leveraging the remaining amount to bank debt and bonds. His offer was unanimously accepted and certainly not hostile. Nevertheless, the buyout began to destabilize mill village communities; as the "trust in others" disappeared. Pepperell was attractive because most of its labor force was nonunion and a recent $300 million capital spending program had brought its facilities up to state-of-the-art efficiency, yet the added debt incurred made the company vulnerable. Acquisition experts believed Farley paid more than he could afford for Pepperell, and he soon began to have trouble paying the buyout debt owed to several other dealers. Unfortunately, the company filed for bankruptcy four years later, and Farley resigned. Yet he retained his flagship Fruit of the Loom, serving as chairman and CEO from 1985 to 1999 that led to being named the White House's Presidential Award for Entrepreneurial Excellence in 1997.

Although Farley pushed to move the majority of Fruit of the Loom manufacturing offshore, he was maybe not a ruthless mogul from the north as many thought. Employee suggestions led to the disposal of unnecessary executive suites which added eight hundred hands in five of the plants; more than $80 million was spent on plant improvements and several millions on employee physical fitness, good nutrition, and smoking cessation at worksites within his realm. He installed baseball fields, tracks, and other fitness facilities at plants and factories. Along the way, he contributed millions to education, the arts, the American Heart Association, and the Boys and Girls Clubs of America.

North American Free Trade Agreement (NAFTA)

One year after Farley resigned from WPP, the US House of Representatives passed by a vote of 234–200 the epic agreement on November 17, 1993. The bill went through the Senate on November 20, 1993, with a vote of 61–38. President Clinton signed it into law on December 8, 1993. At the time, he said, "NAFTA means jobs; American jobs and good-paying wages." The treaty went into effect on January 1, 1994. It immediately eliminated tariffs in the free-trade zone of Canada, Mexico, and America. Britannia.com noted in 1992 that "the agreement was inspired by the success of the European Economic Community's eliminating tariffs to stimulate trade among its members. It was thought a free trade area in North America would bring prosperity through increased trade and production."[198]

A day after NAFTA was finalized in Washington, Lindale manager Richard Wolfe saw the bill as an opportunity to open new denim markets produced at his plant. The mill had recently added 153 positions to the already 1,100 who now produce 1 million yards of denim per week. Most of this cloth was used to make blue jeans, work shirts, and lightweight casual slacks. The South Floyd site was benefiting from a worldwide demand which has increased the local Floyd County workforce to about 5,000. A Greenwood Mills spokesman believed the treaty was good for US industry in the future. He said, "It comes down to a question of free trade versus protectionism." The *Rome News-Tribune* noted earlier on April 27, 1987, that the US textile and apparel markets have been open to foreign trade for years; however, we have neglected vital research that could counterbalance the flood of domestic imports.[199]

Still, a Lindale union spokesman said they were opposed to the treaty, adding, "The idea of whole industries moving to Mexico, where the manufacturing wage is just $2.35 an hour, will leave us out of work." US presidential candidate Ross Perot agreed, saying, "We have got to stop sending jobs overseas. It's pretty simple: If you're paying $12–14 an hour for factory workers and you can move your factory south of the border, pay a dollar an hour for labor,...have no health care, have no environmental controls, no pollution controls and nor retirement and you don't care about anything but making money, there will be a giant sucking sound going south." It was true that domestic textile jobs had already declined from 2.3 million in 1970 to 1.8 million in 1990. However, in a few short months, the agreement had quadrupled trade between the United States, Mexico, and Canada. Oil prices and inflation went lower because of less dependence on Iranian and Venezuelan imports. Automotive assembly now came from parts sourced from these three countries which give the seller an advantage over Japanese imports. Mexico now sells twice more cars to Americans than the Japanese. Also in a few short years, service exports increased by $81 billion. This is residents of one country selling services to citizens of another such as licenses, royalty fees, engineering as well as medical health information.[200]

A few years later, Peter Bondarenko of Britannica.com noted that "NAFTA produced mixed results...It turned out to be neither the magic bullet that its proponents had envisioned nor the devastating blow that its critics had predicted." The United States and Canada suffered from economic recessions; although Mexico increased its exports dramatically, its GDP grew at a lower rate than did other South American countries. Growth of income south of the border was insignificant. Infrastructure problems resulted in little investment by Canada and the Unites States; consequently, there was no significant job loss north of the border. Nevertheless, in the four years (1993–'97) US manufacturers did add more than eight hundred thousand jobs; eventually new jobs related to exports reached five million.[201]

However, in the last days of the twentieth century, workers at Lindale Manufacturing received word weaving would cease after 100 years. Twenty-six-year veteran and president of the mill workers' union Danny Wilson told the *Rome News-Tribune* on January 10, 1999, "We had an idea this might be coming for about a year. The tip off came last year when Greenwood's Liberty S. C. mill upgraded its weaving department with 104 new air-jet looms and Lindale got their old ones." The new system was three times faster than old style. The Park Street location would now spin and dye the denim yarn but would no longer make cloth; consequently, 450 jobs will be eliminated. It was the beginning of the end. After 105 years of manufacturing, the mill closed on September 24, 2001. It could not compete as textiles moved overseas. And Lindale became "a derelict factory with tall smokestacks, short ceiling heights, and creeping kudzu vines swallowing what was left of the buildings." And the proud village houses passed on to heirs who sold them or became absentee landlords for low-income renters.[202]

Southerner Rick Bragg expressed it eloquently in 2009: Across the industrial South, padlocks and logging chains bound the doors of silent textile mills...the mill had become almost a living thing here, rewarding the hard-working and careful with a means of survival... It was here before the automobile, before the flying machine, and its giant, coal-fired generators lit up the evening sky with the first electricity they ever saw. It roared across generations... In return, the mill let them live in stiff-necked dignity, right here, in the hills of their fathers. So, when death did come, to the red-dirt driveways, mobile homes and little mill village houses, no one had to ship their bodies home on a train. [202a]

THE LAST GENERATION

Thomas David Mathis

When Jack Maxwell Mathis passed away on November 2, 2015, his only son, David, placed part of his ashes in the ground under a newly family-planted ginkgo tree near Gilbreath Park in Lindale, Georgia. Underneath, a headstone read, "A Husband, Father, Grandfather and Friend to Everyone He Met." The monument company should have made two exact stones, for David is very much Jack walking around. The younger has navigated his way through life beginning as an elementary athlete, Dragon manager and trainer, which led him into sports management, and finally Athletic Director at Georgia Highlands College. By count, he has been recognized for leadership in fourteen different organizations, yet David's personality overshadows his accomplishments. He is a true baby boomer that benefited from ample opportunities in life courtesy of a more affluent and stable family life; this enabled him to spend more time with family and friends in Lindale. Growing up in the village imparted self-assurance and added a tremendous work ethic to his personality. Once of age (born August 18, 1957), he spent summers working in the Mill Spinning Room and Machine Shop before moving to permanent employment at Bekhaert Industry in 1978 two years after graduation. A year later, he and Kathy Rudolph were united in matrimony. Still, he missed the friendship and brotherhood of athletics from PHS days gone by with Otis. He had been adaptive in overcoming his own physical liabilities, realizing early on that playing point guard for the Knicks was not realistic. To this day, his former players affectionately call him Shorty. Legendary Dragon coach Otis Gilbreath saw something in the kid when he drafted him as an assistant in eighth grade. From then on, mom Gwendolyn remembers her son calling at the end of each school day, saying, "I'm going to help Otis." Little did David know this would be his life calling.[203]

In 1992, David was thirty-five years old; he and Kathy were established parents of three children, Brooks, Ryan, and Rachel. Two years earlier, Pepperell won its first state football championship, which seemed to kindle a burning desire to return to courtside, sideline, and dressing room. Yet a career change at this age is not easy on the individual or family. Nevertheless, a phone call from GHS employee and friend Linda Dyer came with a message, "The college is looking for a director of intramurals. Would you be interested?" It was manna from heaven for the Lindalean. Yet give the administration credit, for they knew he was right for the job. And "the rest is history."[204] He quickly administrated the intramurals and directed the GHSA region/state basketball tourneys. In 2011, the fifty-four-year-old was named assistant AD; one year later, the school entered men's and women's basketball, softball, and baseball community college competition. As a result, many young student athletes continued to pass on to major conferences across the country. However, he did not forget his roots. During the Lynn Hunnicutt era (1983–2006) at PHS, David used his vacation week from GHC to travel and work with the team during two-a-day football camps at West Georgia and later on the updated Dragon campus. For thirty-plus years, he faithfully supported all Dragon team activities with time, money, and leadership; by virtue, the school's athletics moved into the modern era beginning with a new on-campus stadium in 1983.[205]

Of the fourteen social organizations headed or supported by David, one stands above all—the National Youth Sports Program. This summer, GHC Foundation Camp, which is cosponsored by 100 Black Men of Rome, is designed to help at-risk males ten to sixteen achieve success through brotherhood with others and continuing education. The latter goal is not necessarily all academic studies. One of the foundation's activities teaches young men to become gentlemen in the real world, for example, how to tie a tie, how to change a tire, shake hands, make eye contact, and project a good first impression.[206] David Mathis's professional and social life is built upon being raised in a mill village. Lindale was a blue-collar churchgoing, loving community that favored family above all else. Lessons learned long ago from Otis had been passed to present-day disadvantaged youths; he does it with unpretentious camaraderie, and they trust him. On August 31, 2001, David and Kathy retired; although they will be missed in the everyday activities of Rome and Georgia Highlands, the couple begins anew in good health and being.

David Methvin Jones

Coach David Jones was born at Floyd Hospital on March 4, 1949, to Ralph Methvin and Mildred Louise Benson Jones. He attended Pepperell elementary school grades 1 to 4, moved to junior high for grades 5 to 7; upper classes were taken in the old high school building. The family has been in this area for a while. Great-grandfather William Henry Jones came from Wales as a miner and quickly settled in Lowndes County, South Carolina. Moving southward, he reached Taylorsville, Georgia (Bartow County), circa 1830 or about the time pioneer Larkin Barnett came to the Lindale valley. Much like Barnett, the grandfather accumulated land estimated at 4,500 acres during the Indian land rush/lottery period. Later the heirs gradually divided the land with Coach Jones's grandfather John Luther (January 31, 1879) receiving 500 acres "in the piney woods" along with a new wife, Maude Finley Nelson (February 28, 1886) from nearby Euharlee. Unfortunately, as World War I raged in Europe, the family lost the farm and relocated postwar 15 miles northwest to Floyd County where Luther found outside employment as dairy superintendent for Massachusetts Mills. A promotion inside to the Weaving Department improved the family's lot, and it was needed, for Luther and Maude were birthing 6 children—3 girls and 3 boys—with David's father, Ralph, being the youngest born on March 29, 1924. The patriarch Jones passed away in 1933, but wife Maude lived well into her eighties, dying in 1976.

Their youngest child attended Cave Spring where he played football and baseball for the Yellow Jackets. He worked in the Mill before and after graduation, but following Pearl Harbor, the eighteen-year-old enlisted in the Army. After 1942 recruit training and military police school at Fort Benning, he was assigned MP guard duty for German prisoners in Louisiana for most of 1943. With the buildup for D-Day beginning in early 1944, Ralph was transferred to the infantry;

he shipped out to England for training in a recon unit. Although he missed the invasion of France by two weeks, combat pay was earned during the Battle of the Bulge and ensuing Rhineland campaigns. When VE Day was declared on May 8, 1945, his unit boarded transports bound for the Pacific theater. Fortunately, VJ Day soon occurred, and the ships docked in Daytona, Florida.

Mildred Benson was the fourth child (May 18, 1921) of six siblings born to William David and Beatrice Maddux Benson of New Market, Alabama. Papa Benson was a kindhearted Middle Tennessee sharecropper most of his life who loved his dogs, foxhunting, and white whiskey. His daughter excelled as an athlete while playing on a volunteer state basketball championship squad. Upon reaching working age in 1937, the sixteen-year-old moved to Rome and boarded with sister Henrietta during the war years; subsequently, there was employment at Celanese Fibers, Lindale Mill, and as a surgical nurse for Dr. Lester Harbin. As the postwar generation began to socialize around Rome, Ralph met, wooed, and married Ms. Benson in December 1946. Previously he had returned to Lindale as a day hand (an employee who works whatever job is available) to ultimately superintendent of weaving. In 1978, the fifty-four-year old was offered and accepted the plant manager position at Clinton Mills in Geneva, Alabama, near the Florida state line. He died way too early at sixty-two years of age on June 5, 1986. Mildred remained primarily a homemaker until she died at eighty-seven in September of 2008.

Coach Jones followed his parents' love of sports although he claims not to be as good an athlete as either. There was never a time growing up without sporting events, for dad managed to take son to most all local games. Coach Gilbreath, who grew up with Ralph, told them, "Son is not a very good baseball player but football and golf could be his best sports." When the latter sport started up in sophomore year, David became a vital part of the squad that went to state in junior year, placing fourth overall. The football team excelled, also going to the playoffs in sophomore and junior years of 1965 and 1966 before losing to Carrollton twice by a total of eight points. Coach Jones remembers well future college players on the team, e.g., Gary Wingo, Bo Firestone, and Mike Abney. Late in senior season 1967, David had thoughts of a postgraduate football at prep school Darlington; however, an injured knee in the last minutes of the final game of the year against Rockmart ended his playing days.

The freshman attended Berry College from 1967 to winter of 1970. By his own admission, he was not a good student early on; after marriage to Wanda Kay Waters on June 25, 1969, he returned to the Mill's Carpenter Shop; in the fall of 1970, he moved to the pipe shop and stayed until 1972 when he joined the pipe fitter local in Rome to work for a plumbing company before returning to the mill in 1976. The same year, David entered textile management training and worked as shift supervisor until 1981; again, he left the Mill to work various contractor jobs as well as seeing after rental property upkeep for four years. During this period, the couple welcomed daughter, Shannon Nicole, on May 8, 1974.

In 1985, the thirty-six-year old returned to school at Floyd College before transferring back to Berry—this time as a much better dean's list student. Twelve months later, Coach Lynn Hunnicutt utilized him as intern scout coach on a squad that made the first state playoffs since 1967. The following year, Lynn helped establish a county middle school league for grades 6 to 8. The coach then hired David as the first Pepperell middle head football coach; after the fall season, he helped with basketball and baseball. In 1992 Lynn appointed him Dragon defensive coordinator; the following seasons were very successful thanks to Lynn and David being ahead of their time with organization and Xs and Os.

During football season of 2007, Wanda passed away; a year later, Mom became ill and succumbed also. In 2010, David stepped away from athletics, yet after a few years, he missed PHS; new head coach Jeff Shiflett gave him a chance to be a part of the program again, and the following years have been a blessing. He continued a role when Coach Rick Hurst was hired in 2015; Rick has continued the working class tradition of excellence in Lindale. The field house at Dragon Stadium has recently (2022) been named in honor of Coach David Methvin Jones.[207]

Timothy DeWayne Reynolds

On September 24, 2001, fourth-generation Tim Reynolds turned out the lights and locked the door of Lindale Mill. It was appropriate, for he was a 1998 Pepperell High School graduate who was born on December 21, 1978, in Floyd Hospital. His birthplace home was in the country on Reeseburg Road where he still resides. The youngster attended PHS K-12 and was president of the FFA senior year presiding over 150 members. In high school, he began working as a card room sweeper at age fifteen on second shift while attending classes in the mornings. Being mechanically inclined, he moved to the Mill shop after matriculating and stayed there for seventeen years. He met his future wife and Cedartown graduate, Jada Faye Pointer, when he was youth pastor of Polk County's Oak Grove Church; they were betrothed in the same sanctuary on June 16, 2007.

The Reynolds family story is similar to many of the start-up crew at Massachusetts Mills of Georgia; all were born in the nineteenth century and came to Lindale for steady work after hardscrabble farming in the Lyerly, Georgia, area. Great-grandfather Ruben Franklin Reynolds (July 8, 1886–September 6, 1950) was noticed by a cotton spotter for the upcoming mill when he was thirteen years old and encouraged him to come to Lindale. Along with a brother and a cousin, who had the same work ethic, the trio trekked to South Floyd and was immediately employed as first-generation mill hands. Ruben met and married Ethel Wilson (November 13, 1890–January 11, 1983) on July 20, 1912. They had known each other from times spent in nearby Alabama. Ethel remained a housewife off East First Street in the village for most of her life; she birthed 10 children, 4 girls and 6 boys, one of which was Tim's grandfather and second-generation mill worker, Thomas "Tom" Jefferson Reynolds (October 12, 1927– June 28, 1988). Tom married Billie Nelson on December 24, 1947, whom he had met at the mill. The couple worked in the card room, which was a family tradition for years. The third generation of Reynolds, Tom and Ms. Billie, had two sons, Thomas "Tommy," born in 1949, and Donald "Donnie" Arthur Reynolds in 1951. The latter was Tim's father who married Debra Teresa Quinn; together they birthed the fourth generation of Lindale Mill workers in sons Michael Jeffrey and Timothy DeWayne. The couple attended and graduated from Pepperell. They began work in the mill spinning room where Donnie was a fixer until the mill closed.[208] Former Mill superintendent Rip Johnston said this about Donnie on August 16, 2022, "He worked at Lindale for 28 years; he was a Card Room trooper who worked his way up into maintenance and then we made him a supervisor. Super fellow! He is the salt of the earth. Donnie told Rip recently, just prior to his death in September of 2022, that he personally opened the last bale of cotton on June 8th or 9th 2001. For a plant that consumed 300 plus a day (at 500 lbs each) that was the last of a lot of cotton. As an afterthought Rip wondered who in the world opened the first bale?"[209]

Not only has Tim's claim to fame turning out the last lights at the mill, Donnie's son has taken it upon himself to restore his hometown. In June of 2014, he incorporated Restore Lindale Inc. as nonprofit organization, making it eligible for various grants as well as gifts and donations from local businesses and individuals. It has worked diligently since then to clean up the duck pond with dedicated help from Berry College students, to continue hanging the Christmas star between the smokestacks, and to marshal the yule season parade down Park Street; in addition, he has taken over the beautiful hillside cemetery where many of the original hands are buried. "Historically this Mill built the community and it's up to us to keep these stories of Lindale alive for the future," said Reynolds recently. In summer of 2015, spokesperson Paula Blalock of the Rome Area Heritage Foundation addressed the project, "It is a rare find to discover a group of people in a community that has taken upon themselves to use their own funds and form an organization to preserve an area that they've grown up in…The area around the Mill is so important to their families and to their heritage." She then presented Tim with a special certificate of recognition honoring their efforts.[210] On Tuesday, June 9, 2020, *RNT* feature writer Doug Walker posted this headline: "Lindale Train Viewing Platform Opened." At the unveiling, Floyd County commissioner Wright Bagby noted the completely new structure will serve as the trailhead for recreational paths on abandoned Norfolk Southern lines that connect to Silver Creek and Kingfisher trails leading to downtown Rome. He also praised the private/public partnerships that made it happen. As train enthusiast, Holden Robinson cut the opening-day ribbon, he carried an RR scanner which broadcasts radio traffic between dispatchers and train crews on the Atlanta and Chattanooga route; Charles Brock, grandson of a longtime agent, donated the original train station sign atop the viewing platform; the present mill owner Joe Silva donated old red bricks from his site for the base foundation. Kevin Evans Construction provided the building work; the restoration club handled the landscaping. Local businessman Johnny Heuther supplied ornamental iron barriers around the platform. Floyd County Prison warden Mike Long and Public Works director Michael Skeen supplied inmate and county employees for the project. County manager and 1987 Pepperell graduate Jamie A. McCord supplied wholehearted support in words and deeds during the entire process.[211]

Reynolds said a movement is about to restore the old brick mill to operational standards. The building has dilapidated in many ways since the last update occurred in 1993 under the Richard Wolfe regime. Several qualified carpenters and engineers have surveyed the grist and reported the need for extensive and expensive professional repairs. The goal is to grind corn again on Silver Creek. The outgrowth of this dream project can only add to the central core of Lindale revitalization headed by Tim. But it will take the physical and monetary support of the last generation, many who grew up in the love of Park Street but now abide in other areas of Rome, Northwest Georgia, and beyond. The projected cost to grind corn once more is estimated at $200,000. We suspect these baby boomers will either bring the Mill up or let it fall into the creek. There is an old Southern colloquialism that states, "Don't forget your raising." It translates as the greater good is valued over personal gain. Popular *RNT* local columnist Severo

Avila unwittingly parodied several country songs on Tuesday, July 12, 2022. Among the amusing ditties was "My Booger Hollow Beauty"; "Lay Me Down on Myrtle Hill"; "The Battle of Brushy Branch"; "Cold, Cold Water (Ode to Cave Spring)"; "I Went to the Brewhouse and Now I'm In the Doghouse." However, at the top of the list was **"Leaving my heart in Lindale and living a Horseleg life." Amen.**[212]

Selah

NOTES

1. Rip Johnston multiple interviews.
2. Cooper Hall yearbook BAJEMP, 1939, 1940, and 1941 editions.
3. Margaret Johnston interview, February 11, 2022.
4. *Ibid.*
5. Bob Baker interview, May 17, 2022.
6. Scott Reese "Rip" Johnston Jr. interviews, September, 22, 2021.
7. Paraphrased introduction of David O. Selznick's 1939 film *Gone with the Wind*.
8. Polly Gammon, *A History of Lindale*, ed. Jim Gibbons (Georgia: Art Department of Rome, 1997).
   Bobby G. McElwee, *Images of America* (Charlestown, South Carolina: Floyd Co. Arcadia Publishing Co., 1998), 1.
   George Gillman Smith, *The Story of Georgia and the Georgia People 1732–1860* (Atlanta, Georgia: Franklin Printing and Publishing Co., 1900), 316, 431.
9. *Scottish Highlanders in Colonial Georgia*, www.UGAPress.org/index.php/books/scottish_highlanders
   www.jstor.org/stable
   w ww.gpb.org/georgiastories/scottish_highlanders
10. George Gillman Smith, *The Story of Georgia*, page 317.
    en.wikipedia.org/wiki/whig_party_U.S.
    George McGruder Battey, *A History of Rome and Floyd County* (Atlanta: Cherokee Publishing Company, 1922), 307.
11. National Register of Historic Places Continuation Sheet 1993.
    National Parks Service Section 8 reposted December 31, 2008, page 1
    Barry Wright, *John Paul Cooper: A Georgia Giant in the Revival of Cotton in the Early 1900s* (Centralia: Gorham Printing, March 2017), 86.
    deeprootsinthesouth.com/Cherokee_land_lotteries_north_ga.
12. Letter from Thomas Jefferson to Cherokee Nation, January 10, 1806, Founders.Archives.gov/documents.
    Gammon, *A History of Lindale*, 9.
13. Donald Gregory Jeane, "The Culture History of Grist Milling in Northwest Georgia," dissertation, Louisiana State University, August 1974, 47–50.
    Npgalley.nps.gov/get_asset
    Floor plan of Old Brick Mill by Polly Gammon, September 25, 1990.
14. Gammon, *A History of Lindale*, 30–31.
15. Floyd County deed recorded October 1, 1863. NPgallery.nps.gov. shows sale date as December 17, 1860.
16. National Register of Historic Places section 8, 1993, 8–10.
17. Gammon, *A History of Lindale*, 6.
18. Gammon, research papers, 8.
    Gammon, *A History of Lindale*, 26.
19. Gammon, *A History of Lindale*, 24.
20. Gotquestions.org/Primitivebaptist and georgiaencyclopedia.org/articles/primitivebaptists.
21. Silvercreekpcusa.org/about/history.
22. Real estate conveyance Barnett to Primitive Church, 1863.
23. M. L. Jackson, *History of Lindale*, third edition (January 1932), 19.
24. Silvercreekpcusa.org/about/history.
25. www.cotton.org/pubs/cottoncounts/storynational.
26. *Rome News-Tribune*, May 18, 1902, 1.
    en.wikipedia.org/wiki/cotton-factor.
27. Richard C. Wade, *Slavery in the Cities: The South, 1820–1860* (Oxford University Press: 1964), 8.
28. Mike Ragland, "How Cotton Built Rome," *Rome News-Tribune*, June 24, 2018, 1–4, 8.

29. Pepperell Fabric-Cator, *Cotton*, ed. Ish Williams (Lindale: December 1947), 3–4.
30. www.weavedesign.eu/weaving-history.
31. www.hamiton.edu/news/story/clothing-gandhi.
    News Publishing Company, August 2007, 6.
32. Pepperell Fabric-Cator, *The History of Cotton Textiles* (March 1949), 4–5.
33. en.wikipedia.org/wiki/Samuel_Slater.
34. www.investors.com/news/management/leaders-and-success/samuel-slater.
35. *Ibid*.
36. *Ibid*.
37. en.wikipedia.ors/wiki/eli_whitney.
38. *Ibid*.
39. www.biography.com/people/eli_whitney.
40. en.wikipedia.ors/wiki/eli-whitney.
41. Military.wikia.org/wiki/Eli_Whitney.
42. www.en.wikipedia.org/wiki/Henry_W_Grady.
43. George Magruder Battey Jr., *A History of Rome and Floyd County*, (Atlanta: Cherokee Publishing Company, 1922), 246–250.
44. en.wikipedia.org/wiki/Henry_W._Grady.
45. *Ibid*.
46. georgiainfo.galileo.usa.edu.
47. Porterbriggs.com/henry-grady-and-the-new-south.
48. *Rome News-Tribune*, July 7, 2019, C3.
49. brfencing.org/h202lectures/welcomefiles/newsouth.
50. en.wikipedia.org/wiki/Henry_W._Grady, 6.
51. Scott Wilson, "Past Times," *News Publishing Company*, August 2007, 98.
52. "Mill at Trion Started Operations Back in 1846," *News Publishing Company*, August 2008, 50.
53. Wright, *John Paul Cooper*, 3.
54. Wright, *John Paul Cooper*, preface.
55. Ragland, "How Cotton Built Rome," 5–6.
    Wright, *John Paul Cooper*, 85
    John Paul Cooper interview, August 21, 2019.
56. *Rome News-Tribune*, June 24, 2018, 2, 9.
57. Wright, *John Paul Cooper*, preface, 9–10.
58. Wright, *John Paul Cooper*, foreword, 27.
    en.wikipedia.org/wiki/cotton-factor.
59. Wright, *John Paul Cooper*, 65, 72.
60. Wright, *John Paul Cooper*, 80–81, 83, 91.
61. Wright, *John Paul Cooper*, 68–69.
    Letters to Charles Lovering, April 11, 1893, and April 26, 1893.
62. Wright, *John Paul Cooper*, 81.
63. Wright, *John Paul Cooper*, 68.
64. Wright, *John Paul Cooper*, 69.
65. Wright, *John Paul Cooper*, 72.
66. Wright, *John Paul Cooper*, 69, 72, 81.
67. Wright, *John Paul Cooper*, 72–73.
    Gammon, research papers, VI–VII, 5.
    Ronnie Kilgo interview, June 29, 2019.
68. Wright, John Paul Cooper, 83.
Atlanta Journal, April 27, 1895, 1.
69. *Rome News-Tribune*, December 10, 1895, 1.
    Rome News-Tribune, January 18, 1896.
    Glenn D. Hopkins, "Lindale: An Early History of the Town and Management Through the Meikleham Era 1894–1937," dissertation, Georgia Institute of Technology, November 28, 1983.
    Wright, *John Paul Cooper*, 76.
    Gammon, research papers, 1, 7, 11.

John Paul Cooper letter, April 20, 1895.
enwikipedia.org/wiki *The Man Who Shot Liberty Valance*.

[70] Gammon, *A History of Lindale*, 97.

[71] www.Findagrave.com/memorial/henry-parishmeikleham.
Hopkins, "Lindale: An Early History," 7.
Evelyn H. Knowlton, *Pepperell's Progress* (Harvard University Press, 1948), 313–314.
Gammon, research papers, 8, 14.
Lisa M. Russell, *Lost Mill Towns of North Georgia* (Charleston: History Press, 2020) 109.

[72] Beulah S. Moseley, *Rome News-Tribune*, December 14, 1902, page 10.
Gammon, research papers, 10, 11, 14.
Hattie McClung, *Eighty Years of Memories* (Sisson Company, 2002), 40.

[73] Gammon, research papers, 4, 13.
Earl and Herman Robinson interview, February 27, 2020.

[74] "Protection for Child Labor," *Rome News-Tribune*, September 8, 1904, page 12.
Gammon, research papers, 13.

[75] Charles Barzillai Spahr, *America's Working People* (New York: Longmans, Green and Company, 1900), 1–3.

[76] Gammon, research papers, 13.
"Big Barbecue..." *Rome News-Tribune*, July 4, 1901, page 1.

[77] *Rome News-Tribune*, January 24, 1902, 8.

[78] *Rome News-Tribune*, June 3, 1902, 1.
Gammon, research papers, 47.

[79] *Rome News-Tribune*, January 22, 1903, 4.
Charles Ogles, *Rome News-Tribune*, April 3, 1904.
Rome News-Tribune, May 3, 1902, 1
www.Romegeorgia.com/homeonthehill.
Rome News-Tribune, June 23, 1903, 3
Ragland, *Rome News-Tribune*, July 29, 2018, C4.

[80] *Rome News-Tribune*, June 17, 1902, 1.
Rome News-Tribune, October 28, 1902, 8.
Rome News-Tribune, September 23, 1902, 8.
Rome News-Tribune, December 2, 1902, 8.
Rome News-Tribune, November 1, 1902, 1.
Rome News-Tribune, November 25, 1903, 5.

[81] Gammon, *A History of Lindale*, 23.

[82] *Rome News-Tribune*, February 13, 1929, 8.

[83] Gammon, research papers, 12, 24–25.

[84] Clyde W. Jolley, *A Great Man In Lindale*, 2.

[85] Gammon, research papers, 24–25.

[86] en.wikipedia.org/wiki/panic_of_1893, 1870s & 80s US experience economic growth & expansion, 5.
Spahr, *America's Working People*, 1–5.
West Georgia University, *Textile Heritage Trail* (Arcadia Publishing, 2015), 8.

[87] *Rome News-Tribune*, February 27, 1930, 3.
Rome News-Tribune, December 26, 1929, 2.
Rome News-Tribune, November 14, 1929, 3.

[88] Ogles, "Lindale and Vicinity," *Rome News-Tribune*, 1929, 7.
Wright, *John Paul Cooper*, 77.

[89] McClung, *Eighty Years of Memories*, 27–29.

[90] Archives.ColumbusState.edu/oral_history/baker_vera.

[91] Nancy Smith Hunter interview, August 30, 2019.

[92] Northwest Georgia Historical & Genealogical Society, Inc., October 1978, 11.

[93] Gammon, research papers, 67.

[94] NWG Historical Society, 11.

[95] *Rome News-Tribune*, September 17, 1936, 9.
Rome News-Tribune, September 26, 1930, 3.
Rome News-Tribune, June 9, 1930, 8.

[96] Spahr, *America's Working People*, 1.
[97] Gammon, research papers, band.
[98] NWG Historical Society, 11.
[99] Gammon, research papers, band.
[100] Gammon, *A History of Lindale*, 15.
[101] *Rome News-Tribune*, March 28, 1929, 3.
Gammon, research papers, 68.
[102] *Rome News-Tribune*, April 22, 1929, 2.
Rome News-Tribune, May 29, 1929, 6.
Rome News-Tribune, May 10, 1929, 7.
Rome News-Tribune, May 12, 1929, 2.
Rome News-Tribune, June 4, 1929, 8.
[103] *Rome News-Tribune*, July 1, 1929, 7.
Rome News-Tribune, July 5, 1929, 3.
Rome News-Tribune, August 9, 1929, 3.
Rome News-Tribune, September 13, 1929, 2.
[104] *Rome News-Tribune*, March 27, 1903, 8.
[105] *Rome News-Tribune*, picture of 1912 team managed by Lillian Duke cited in Gammon's *A History of Lindale* (page 28).
[106] *Rome News-Tribune*, August 27, 1913, 4.
Rome News-Tribune, September 5, 1913, 6.
[107] *Rome News-Tribune*, July 7, 1963, 5.
Nancy Hunter's scrapbook, minutes of Distinguished Civic Service Award ceremony by Chamber of Commerce and Rome/Floyd County.
[108] *Rome News-Tribune*, March 3, 1944, 1.
Rome News-Tribune, March 5, 1944.
Patricia Harvey letter from Nancy Hunter's scrapbook.
[109] Mexican Revolution (1910–1920). April 21, 1914: American forces occupy Vera Cruz.
[110] *Rome News-Tribune*, July 28, 1937, 1.
[111] Gammon, *A History of Lindale*, 17.
Gammon, research papers, 104.
Rome News-Tribune, July 25, 1937, 3.
Rome News-Tribune, July 26, 1937, 2.
[112] *Rome News-Tribune*, July 26, 1937, 3.
Gammon, research papers, 107.
Rome News-Tribune, December 17, 1937, 5.
Gammon, *A History of Lindale*, 21.
Gammon, research papers, 106–115.
[113] "Past Times," *Rome News-Tribune*, August 2007, 86.
[114] Heather S. Shores, *Working to Play, Playing to Work* (2010), 1–3.
[115] Ken Burns, *Baseball: A Film by Ken Burns*, aired September 18, 1994, PBS. Pbs.org/KenBurns/baseball.
[116] Gammon, research papers, 15, 29.
Shores, *Working to Play, Playing to Work*, 3, 7.
[117] *Rome News-Tribune*, August 31, 1941, 2.
Rome News-Tribune, August 29, 1941, 1.
[118] *Rome News-Tribune*, August 31, 1941, 2.
Lang Gammon, "News of Lindale," *Rome News-Tribune*, September 3, 1941.
L. Gammon, "News of Lindale," *Rome News-Tribune*, September 5, 1941, 6.
L. Gammon, "News of Lindale," *Rome News-Tribune*, September 15, 1941.
[119] Tom Klenc, ed., *Research Guide* (McDonough: 2007), 177, 184.
L. Gammon, "News of Lindale," *Rome News-Tribune*, March 30, 1942, 5.
L. Gammon, "News of Lindale," *Rome News-Tribune*, May 2, 1942, 11.
L. Gammon, "News of Lindale," *Rome News-Tribune*, April 12, 1942, 8.
[120] Pepperell Manufacturing Company, *Home Front News*, September 1944, 5.

[121] *Rome News-Tribune*, April 15, 1943, 5.
Rome News-Tribune, June 14, 1942, 11.
[122] "Past Times," *Rome News-Tribune*, July 1996, 30.
[123] BobDylan.com/songs/times/they-are-changing.
En.wikipedia.org. "How Ya Gonna Keep 'em Down on the Farm?"
Klenc, *Research Guide*, 105–108.
[124] Suzanne Hall Allen interview, January 17, 2020.
Rome News-Tribune, February 7, 1993, 2A.
"Who's Who," Valley Head High School, 1931.
[125] Drdavidallen.com/general/a-bit-of-baseball-history.
[126] Drdavidallen.com/uncategorized/a-bit-of-baseball-history.
[127] Drdavidallen.com/uncategorized/a-bit-of-baseball-history.
[128] "Past Times," *News Publishing Company*, July 1996, 46.
[129] Dawn Nixon Brock email, December 20, 2019.
[130] *Lindale Bulletin Fabri-cator*, April 1946.
Bob Baker's scrapbook.
[131] "The 1947 Cardinal Classic," 20, 27, 53, 60.
[132] georgiaencyclopedia.org/articles/sports-out-door-recreation/willard-nixon-1928-2000.
[133] Dawn Nixon Brock email, December 11, 2019, 1–3.
[134] georgiaencyclopedia.org/articles/sports-out-door-recreation/willard-nixon-1928-2000.
[135] georgiaencyclopedia.org/articles/sports-out-door-recreation/willard-nixon-1928-2000.
[136] Richard Goldstein, *New York Times*, December 14, 2000, page 12.
[137] georgiaencyclopedia.org/articles/sports-out-door-recreation/willard-nixon-1928-2000.
[138] georgiaencyclopedia.org/articles/sports-out-door-recreation/willard-nixon-1928-2000.
Dawn Nixon Brock email February 3, 2020.
Sandra Cooper interview, September 14, 2020.
[139] Stewartthornley.net/millers_havana.
[140] Bill Nixon's scrapbook.
Time, December 25, 2000, 53.
[141] georgiaencyclopedia.org/articles/sports-out-door-recreation/willard-nixon-1928-2000.
[142] Pat Gaston email, March 12, 2020, and March 19, 2020.
Pat Gaston family letters, May 29, 1919–November 21, 1919.
[143] Bob Baker's scrapbook.
The Heritage of Floyd County, Georgia 1833–1999 (Mesa: FamilySearch Library), 235.
Lee Mowry, introductory speech, Rome/Floyd County Sports HOF, 1988.
Rome News-Tribune, February 25, 1942, 8.
L. Gammon, "News of Lindale."
[144] Bob Baker's scrapbook.
Army.mil/article/the_star_in_the_window.
[145] General Ira Eaker U. S. Air Force biography, Wikipedia.
Gary Bedingfield, *Baseball in Wartime*, 1–2.
Bedingfield, *The Boys of an English Summer*, 1–7.
Pat Gaston letter to Jack Gaston from his commanding general, October 9, 1943
Pat Gaston email, April 13, 2020.
[146] "Stewart Field U. S. Military Academy Prop Wash," spring and summer 1945.
Pat Gaston's scrapbook, February 22, 2020.
[147] Patsy Gaston emails, April 16, 19, and 21, 2020.
Mowry, introductory speech.
Pat Gaston's scrapbook, February 22, 2020.
[148] Sara Hightower, "A Brief History of the Schools of Lindale," May 6, 1945, 1-4.
P. Gammon, *A History of Lindale*, 36.
Rome News-Tribune, January 15, 1991, 2.
[149] *Rome News-Tribune*, November 11, 1962, 9.
[150] Archies – Colombusstate.edu/gah/1983.
P. Gammon, *A History of Lindale*, 36.

[151] *The Heritage of Floyd County 1833–1999,* 65.
Hightower, "A Brief History of the Schools of Lindale," 1.
[152] John Lewis Moulton, "The Meritorius Queen of Song, Annie Powers Moulton 1939," 1–23.
Clara Ellen "Cissy" Rogers's files.
Merchant marine documents, September 23, 1919.
Rogers's files.
[153] Cissy Rogers's interviews, May 30, 2019, and June 27, 2019.
"Football Issue," *Orange and Blue*, Auburn, Alabama, December 8, 1920, 1.
Clyde Bolton, *War Eagle, A Story of Auburn Football* (Huntsville: Strode Publishers), 129.
[154] Atlanta Historical Society, "Account Auburn-Army Game Saturday October 14, 1922," 84-94.
[155] www.ahsfhs.org/games by year, 1924 and 1925 Auburn High School.
Mississippi Football Historical Society, "Pascagoula Panthers All-Time records and scores for season of 1923."
[156] New England Mutual Life Insurance Company correspondence, February and March 1929.
[157] John W. Sutton Jr., "The Story of My Life," UGA Education 704, August 1946, 5.
[158] Johnny Sutton e-mails, February 22, 2020.
[159] Sutton Jr., "The Story of My Life," 2–5.
[160] *Lindale Bulletin*, March 1946.
[161] John Sutton's personal files, 1948–'49.
[162] Charlie Gilbreath files.
[163] *Rome News-Tribune*, May 29, 1942, and August 5, 1942.
[164] Charlie Gilbreath files.
[165] *Rome News-Tribune*, June 10, 2019, A3.
[166] Charlie Gilbreath files.
[167] Charlie Gilbreath files.
[168] Charles Brock email to Kevin Evans and Jamie McCord, September 27, 2020, 1–2.
[169] Pepperell High School Yearbook 1952, 1st ed. (Dallas: Taylor Company).
[170] Betty Burkhalter Shiflett interview, June 2020.
[171] Sandra Midkiff Cooper memoir, July 20, 2020.
[172] ghsfha.org/w/Special:SchoolHome.
[173] "PHS Football History," 146–299. Footnote documentation contained within text.
[174] "PHS Basketball History," 299–422. Footnote documentation contained within text.
[175] "PHS Baseball History," 422–510. Footnote documentation contained within text.
[176] Richard Wolfe interview, August 8, 2003.
Russell, *Lost Mill Towns of North Georgia*, 120.
[177] "Richard Wolfe: the Spirit of Lindale," Sandra McCain's files.
[178] West Point Pepperell, "Newsletter Message from the Vice President," December 1979, 1–3.
[179] "Richard Wolfe: the Spirit of Lindale," Sandra McCain's files.
[180] Lindale Mill sales/profit charts 1991–1993, 1–3.
[181] Bryant Steele, *Rome News-Tribune*, October 2, 2008, 1.
[182] Find a Grave.com/memorial, Marion Virginia Howard Wolfe 1928-2000.
[183] Richard Wolfe interview, August 8, 2003.
[184] *Rome News-Tribune*, September 12, 1960, 6.
Searsarchives.com Toughskins: 1971-present.
Rome News-Tribune, March 3, 1981, 3.
Gavin Wright, *Old South, New South* (Basic Books, Inc., 1986), preface, vii.
[185] Gerald B. Andrews, *A Mill Village Story* (Montgomery: New South Books, 2019), 266–267, 275, 280.
[186] Charlie Reese, *Rome News-Tribune*, November 26, 1993, 4.
[187] *Rome News-Tribune*, December 1, 1994, 1.
[188] *Rome News-Tribune*, October 11, 1966, 3.
[189] *Rome News-Tribune*, July 18, 2020, C3.7.
Rome News-Tribune, April 19, 1984, 11A.7.
[190] Anderson Huber, *Rome News-Tribune*, May 7, 1985, 1.
[191] *Rome News-Tribune*, December 9, 1985, 1.
[192] www.usda.gov. Economic Research Service.
Rome News-Tribune, August 5, 2001, 1D.

[193] *Rome News-Tribune*, November 15, 1988, 3.
Rome News-Tribune, December 20, 1988, 6A.
[194] Petr Behr, "An Empire Built on Borrowed Money," *Washington Post*, November 18, 1984, 1–2.
William F. Farley, Wikipedia.
Search.yahoo.com/williamfarley and fruit of the loom.
Rome News-Tribune, February 24, 1989, 6A.
[195] "Acquisition of Textile Giant Proves Troublesome for Bill Farley," *Associated Press News*, rereleased on March 7, 2022, 4–10.
[196] Adam S. Blinder, "Economists' Biggest Failure," August 2018, 1.
gceps.princeton.edu/wp.
[197] William F. Farley, Wikipedia.
[198] en.wikipedia.org/nafta.
Britannica.com/event/nafta.
[199] John M. Willis, *Rome News-Tribune*, November 18, 1993, 1.
Rome News-Tribune, April 27, 1987, 1.
[200] *CorporateFinanceInstitute*, "NAFTA—Overview," April 7, 2020, 3, 5, and 11.
[201] Britannica.com/event/nafta.
[202] David Brown, *Rome News-Tribune*, January 10, 1999, 1.
[203] David Mathis interview, August 4, 2022.
Gwen Mathis interview, October 11, 2022.
[204] David Mathis text message, November 1, 2022.
[205] David Mathis interview, August 2022.
[206] ghc.prestosports.com. Foundation Camp.
highlands.edu/foundation-camp.
highlands.edu. students-mentor-youth-foundation camp.
highlands.edu –combine – fun – science – character.
[207] David Methvin Jones interviews, June 27, 2022.
[208] Timothy DeWayne Reynolds interviews and emails, April 21, 2022.
[209] Rip Johnston email dated August 16, 2022.
[210] "Heritage Group Honors Restoration Lindale," northwestgeorgiannews.com.
[211] Doug Walker, *Rome News-Tribune*, June 9, 2020, A5.
[212] Severo Avila, *Rome News-Tribune*, "Leaving My Heart in Lindale and Living a Horseleg Life," July 12, 2022, 4.

ABOUT THE AUTHOR

Randall McCord is a 1957 graduate of Cherokee County High School in Centre, Alabama, where he was a three-sport letterman and captain of the football team. Although the youngster signed a grant-in-aid to play QB and LB for Chattanooga, he opted to meet military obligations with the US Navy Communications Security Group, which is serving tours on Oahu and the Philippine Islands. While in the fiftieth state, he enrolled at the University of Hawaii Manoa part-time and, upon honorable discharge in 1961, transferred to Jacksonville State College, receiving a Political Science BA degree in 1965. While there, he met and married Joyce Anne Pitts from Randolph County; after six years of teaching and coaching, the couple moved with their sons Scott and Jamie to Montevallo University for a master's in education. After ten years of coaching and teaching, the family changed professions as Randall entered the timber business with his biological father, C. L. McCord, in Rome, Georgia. Upon the death of the latter in 1980, he bought the company and has operated it successfully since. *Lindale, Lint, and Leather* is the third work by McCord, as he coauthored *The Cotton Picking Warriors* (2015) and wrote the semi-biographical *Tales of Trade Winds, Beaches, and Blue Waters* (2020).

Printed in the USA
CPSIA information can be obtained
at www.ICGtesting.com
LVHW060013220224
772188LV00004B/10